EP Literature and Composition II Reader

Lessons 1-90

This book belongs to:

____

EP Literature and Composition II Reader Lessons 1-90

This book, made by Tina Rutherford with permission from Easy Peasy All-in-One Homeschool, is based on the Reading portion of the Literature and Composition II component of Easy Peasy's curriculum. For EP's online curriculum visit allinonehighschool.com

This content was created in reference to the links used in the online Literature and Composition II course. The course page will contain any specific lesson source, as well as more practice in any concept that is difficult for the student to grasp. All written works contained in this book are either in the public domain or original to this author.

Cover design by Yuletide Media: www.yuletidemedia.com

Lovingly edited by Holly Dunn

ISBN: 9798491407422

First Edition: April, 2022

About this Book

This is an offline version of the reading selections for Lessons 1-90 of Easy Peasy All-in-One High School's Literature and Composition II course. We've modified and expanded upon the online activities and printable worksheets available at the Easy Peasy All-in-One High School website (allinonehighschool.com) so that you can work offline if desired. This book is ONLY the reading component of Literature and Composition II. It will not include any of the vocabulary, writing, or other language arts assignments and is not a complete English course on its own.

How to use this Book

This book is designed to be used in conjunction with the Literature and Composition II Language Arts and Vocabulary workbooks (for a full offline course) OR alongside the online Literature and Composition II course. As you proceed through this book, you will use the other Literature and Composition II workbooks or the online assignments to fill out the rest of the assignments.

This book follows the EP online Literature and Composition II course in sequential order, providing an offline version of the reading assignments. There will be slight differences from time to time, particularly where a reading assignment online was under copyright and a change needed to be made for the purposes of this book. But a student completing the assignments in this book along with the other Literature and Composition II workbooks or the other online assignments will complete one full high school English course.

Course Description: Reading Portion

This high school level course requires students to analyze a wide variety of literature including poetry, short stories, novels, and plays. Students will also read a variety of nonfiction. They will focus on poetic and literary devices such as metaphor, irony, theme, mood, and foreshadowing.

Course Reading List

Novels: *The Adventures of Tom Sawyer*, Twain; *Emma*, Austen; *Le Morte D'Arthur*, Malory

Plays: *Much Ado About Nothing*, Shakespeare

Short Stories: "Federigo's Falcon," Boccaccio; "The Story of an Hour," Chopin; "The Happy Prince," Wilde; "The Adventure of the Noble Bachelor," Doyle; "The Hunger Artist," Kafka

Nonfiction: speeches, news articles, excerpts from each of the following: *African Game Trails*, Roosevelt; *A Thousand Miles Up the Nile*, Edwards

Epic Poems: *The Odyssey*, Homer; *Idylls of the King* (partial), Tennyson

Poetry: Henry Longfellow, Robert Frost, Rudyard Kipling, Ralph Waldo Emerson, Edgar Allan Poe, and others

Table of Contents

Lesson 1

- Read the following poem. Explain to someone what he's feeling in the beginning of the poem and what he decides by the end. What mental shift does he make?

The Rainy Day
By Henry Wadsworth Longfellow (1807-1882)

The day is cold, and dark, and dreary;
It rains, and the wind is never weary;
The vine still clings to the mouldering wall,
But at every gust the dead leaves fall,
And the day is dark and dreary.

My life is cold, and dark, and dreary;
It rains, and the wind is never weary;
My thoughts still cling to the mouldering past,
But the hopes of youth fall thick in the blast,
And the days are dark and dreary.

Be still, sad heart, and cease repining;
Behind the clouds is the sun still shining;
Thy fate is the common fate of all,
Into each life some rain must fall,
Some days must be dark and dreary.

- Read this poem. What is he talking about? How do desire and hate play into this poem?

Fire and Ice
By Robert Frost (1874-1963)

Some say the world will end in fire,
Some say in ice.
From what I've tasted of desire
I hold with those who favor fire.
But if it had to perish twice,
I think I know enough of hate
To know that for destruction ice
Is also great
And would suffice.

(This is the end of Lesson 1 in your Reader. Be sure to check your Language Arts Workbook and your Vocabulary Workbook for the rest of your Lesson 1 assignments for the course.)

Lesson 2

- Read the following poem. It is the favorite poem of former president Bill Clinton. It was written to commemorate the completion of the Battle Monument to honor the fallen heroes of the battles of Lexington and Concord in the Revolutionary War.
- What lines from the poem show this purpose?

Concord Hymn
By Ralph Waldo Emerson
Sung at the completion of the Battle Monument, July 4, 1837

By the rude bridge that arched the flood,
Their flag to April's breeze unfurled,

Here once the embattled farmers stood
And fired the shot heard round the world.

The foe long since in silence slept;
Alike the conqueror silent sleeps;
And Time the ruined bridge has swept
Down the dark stream which seaward creeps.

On this green bank, by this soft stream,
We set to-day a votive stone;
That memory may their deed redeem,
When, like our sires, our sons are gone.

Spirit, that made those heroes dare
To die, and leave their children free,
Bid Time and Nature gently spare
The shaft we raise to them and thee.

- Read this poem. What does the line "Be not like dumb, driven cattle! Be a hero in the strife!" mean to you in your life?

A Psalm of Life
By Henry Wadsworth Longfellow

What The Heart Of The Young Man Said To The Psalmist.

Tell me not, in mournful numbers,
 Life is but an empty dream!
For the soul is dead that slumbers,
 And things are not what they seem.

Life is real! Life is earnest!
 And the grave is not its goal;
Dust thou art, to dust returnest,
 Was not spoken of the soul.

Not enjoyment, and not sorrow,
Is our destined end or way;
But to act, that each to-morrow
Find us farther than to-day.

Art is long, and Time is fleeting,
And our hearts, though stout and brave,
Still, like muffled drums, are beating
Funeral marches to the grave.

In the world's broad field of battle,
In the bivouac of Life,
Be not like dumb, driven cattle!
Be a hero in the strife!

Trust no Future, howe'er pleasant!
Let the dead Past bury its dead!
Act,— act in the living Present!
Heart within, and God o'erhead!

Lives of great men all remind us
We can make our lives sublime,
And, departing, leave behind us
Footprints on the sands of time;

Footprints, that perhaps another,
Sailing o'er life's solemn main,
A forlorn and shipwrecked brother,
Seeing, shall take heart again.

Let us, then, be up and doing,
With a heart for any fate;
Still achieving, still pursuing,
Learn to labor and to wait.

Lesson 3

- Read this poem. What book of the Bible does it remind you of? (Hint: one of Solomon's).

A Dream Within a Dream
By Edgar Allan Poe

Take this kiss upon the brow!
And, in parting from you now,
Thus much let me avow-
You are not wrong, who deem
That my days have been a dream;
Yet if hope has flown away
In a night, or in a day,
In a vision, or in none,
Is it therefore the less gone?
All that we see or seem
Is but a dream within a dream.

I stand amid the roar
Of a surf-tormented shore,
And I hold within my hand
Grains of the golden sand-
How few! yet how they creep
Through my fingers to the deep,
While I weep- while I weep!
O God! can I not grasp
Them with a tighter clasp?
O God! can I not save
One from the pitiless wave?
Is all that we see or seem
But a dream within a dream?

- This is a fun poem. What literary device is used in the last line? (Hint: it involves exaggeration.)

The Purple Cow
By Gelett Burgess (1866-1951)

I NEVER saw a Purple Cow,
I never hope to see one;
But I can tell you, anyhow,
I'd rather see than be one.

Some time later....

Ah, yes, I wrote the "Purple Cow"—
I'm Sorry, now, I wrote it;
But I can tell you Anyhow
I'll Kill you if you Quote it!

Lesson 4

- Read this poem.

I'm Nobody! Who are you?
By Emily Dickinson (1830-1886)

I'm Nobody! Who are you?
Are you – Nobody – too?
Then there's a pair of us!
Don't tell! they'd advertise – you know!

How dreary – to be – Somebody!
How public – like a Frog –
To tell one's name – the livelong June –
To an admiring Bog!

- This poem is advice/an inspirational pep talk for his son. Why are triumph and disaster "imposters"?

If
By Rudyard Kipling

If you can keep your head when all about you
 Are losing theirs and blaming it on you,
If you can trust yourself when all men doubt you,
 But make allowance for their doubting too;
If you can wait and not be tired by waiting,
 Or being lied about, don't deal in lies,
Or being hated, don't give way to hating,
 And yet don't look too good, nor talk too wise:

If you can dream—and not make dreams your master;
 If you can think—and not make thoughts your aim;
If you can meet with Triumph and Disaster
 And treat those two impostors just the same;
If you can bear to hear the truth you've spoken
 Twisted by knaves to make a trap for fools,
Or watch the things you gave your life to, broken,
 And stoop and build 'em up with worn-out tools:

If you can make one heap of all your winnings
 And risk it on one turn of pitch-and-toss,
And lose, and start again at your beginnings
 And never breathe a word about your loss;
If you can force your heart and nerve and sinew
 To serve your turn long after they are gone,
And so hold on when there is nothing in you

Except the Will which says to them: 'Hold on!'

If you can talk with crowds and keep your virtue,
Or walk with Kings—nor lose the common touch,
If neither foes nor loving friends can hurt you,
If all men count with you, but none too much;
If you can fill the unforgiving minute
With sixty seconds' worth of distance run,
Yours is the Earth and everything that's in it,
And—which is more—you'll be a Man, my son!

Lesson 5

- Read the following about your first novel of the year, *The Adventures of Tom Sawyer* by Mark Twain.

Summary: *The Adventures of Tom Sawyer* was written by Mark Twain and published in 1876. It is an adventure story depicting a young boy becoming a young man. It appeals to children who enjoy Tom's timeless adventures, as well as adults who read it and look back to their childhood years with fondness. This was the intent of the author, as he wrote in his preface to the first edition of Tom Sawyer. He wanted to appeal to both children and adults. As you read *The Adventures of Tom Sawyer,* you'll likely come across familiar scenes that you never knew originated with this book. You'll experience the spirit of childhood with all of its ups and downs, dreams and fears, excitement and terror.

Setting: The book is set in a small town north of St. Louis on the banks of the Mississippi River during the 1840s. The author, Mark Twain, grew up in Hannibal, Mississippi, and utilized his own town as the town his characters inhabited in the book (renamed St. Petersburg in his novel). Many of the places in the novel actually exist, such as the Jackson's Island, the cave that Injun Joe inhabited, and the houses of Widow Douglas and Aunt Polly.

Structure: *The Adventures of Tom Sawyer* is made up of various scenes or episodes that build into the story of Tom's life.

Satire: The author uses satire to criticize and commentate on human nature. After Tom manipulates others into painting a fence he is supposed to paint, Twain commentates that to make someone covet something, all you need to do is make it hard to attain. There are many examples of similar commentaries. Part of the overarching conflict of the novel is that Tom is growing into an adult, but Twain is constantly criticizing adult attitudes and behaviors.

- Read the book's Preface.

The Adventures of Tom Sawyer
By Mark Twain
Preface

MOST of the adventures recorded in this book really occurred; one or two were experiences of my own, the rest those of boys who were schoolmates of mine. Huck Finn is drawn from life; Tom Sawyer also, but not from an individual — he is a combination of the characteristics of three boys whom I knew, and therefore belongs to the composite order of architecture.

The odd superstitions touched upon were all prevalent among children and slaves in the West at the period of this story — that is to say, thirty or forty years ago.

Although my book is intended mainly for the entertainment of boys and girls, I hope it will not be shunned by men and women on that account, for part of my plan has been to try to pleasantly remind adults of what they once were themselves, and of how they felt and thought and talked, and what queer enterprises they sometimes engaged in.

The Author.
Hartford, 1876.

Lesson 6

- Read chapter 1 of *The Adventures of Tom Sawyer*.
- **Note:** This novel contains the occasional use of the words "negro" and "injun."

Chapter 1

"Tom!"

No answer.

"Tom!"

No answer.

"What's gone with that boy, I wonder? You TOM!"

No answer.

The old lady pulled her spectacles down and looked over them about the room; then she put them up and looked out under them. She seldom or never looked through them for so small a thing as a boy; they were her state pair, the pride of her heart, and were built for "style," not service — she could have seen through a pair of stove-lids just as well. She looked perplexed for a moment, and then said, not fiercely, but still loud enough for the furniture to hear:

"Well, I lay if I get hold of you I'll—"

She did not finish, for by this time she was bending down and punching under the bed with the broom, and so she needed breath to punctuate the punches with. She resurrected nothing but the cat.

"I never did see the beat of that boy!"

She went to the open door and stood in it and looked out among the tomato vines and "jimpson" weeds that constituted the garden. No Tom. So she lifted up her voice at an angle calculated for distance, and shouted:

"Y-o-u-u *Tom*!"

There was a slight noise behind her and she turned just in time to seize a small boy by the slack of his roundabout and arrest his flight.

"There! I might 'a' thought of that closet. What you been doing in there?"

"Nothing."

"Nothing! Look at your hands. And look at your mouth. What *is* that truck?"

"*I* don't know, aunt."

"Well, I know. It's jam — that's what it is. Forty times I've said if you didn't let that jam alone I'd skin you. Hand me that switch."

The switch hovered in the air — the peril was desperate —

"My! Look behind you, aunt!"

The old lady whirled round, and snatched her skirts out of danger. The lad fled, on the instant, scrambled up the high board fence, and disappeared over it.

His aunt Polly stood surprised a moment, and then broke into a gentle laugh.

"Hang the boy, can't I never learn anything? Ain't he played me tricks enough like that for me to be looking out for him by this time? But old fools is the biggest fools there is. Can't learn an old dog new tricks, as the saying is. But my goodness, he never plays them alike, two days, and how is a body to know what's coming? He 'pears to know just how long he can torment me before I get my dander up, and he knows if he can make out to put me off for a minute or make me laugh, it's all down again and I can't hit him a lick. I ain't doing my duty by that boy, and that's the

Lord's truth, goodness knows. Spare the rod and spile the child, as the Good Book says. I'm a-laying up sin and suffering for us both, *I* know. He's full of the Old Scratch, but laws-a-me! he's my own dead sister's boy, poor thing, and I ain't got the heart to lash him, somehow. Every time I let him off, my conscience does hurt me so, and every time I hit him my old heart most breaks. Well-a-well, man that is born of woman is of few days and full of trouble, as the Scripture says, and I reckon it's so. He'll play hookey this evening[1], and I'll just be obleeged to make him work, to-morrow, to punish him. It's mighty hard to make him work Saturdays, when all the boys is having holiday, but he hates work more than he hates anything else, and I've *got* to do some of my duty by him, or I'll be the ruination of the child."

Tom did play hookey, and he had a very good time. He got back home barely in season to help Jim, the small colored boy, saw next-day's wood and split the kindlings before supper — at least he was there in time to tell his adventures to Jim while Jim did three-fourths of the work. Tom's younger brother (or rather, half-brother), Sid, was already through with his part of the work (picking up chips), for he was a quiet boy, and had no adventurous, troublesome ways.

While Tom was eating his supper, and stealing sugar as opportunity offered, Aunt Polly asked him questions that were full of guile, and very deep — for she wanted to trap him into damaging revealments. Like many other simple-hearted souls, it was her pet vanity to believe she was endowed with a talent for dark and mysterious diplomacy, and she loved to contemplate her most transparent devices as marvels of low cunning, Said she:

"Tom, it was middling warm in school, warn't it?"

"Yes'm."

"Powerful warm, warn't it?"

"Yes'm."

"Didn't you want to go in a-swimming, Tom?"

---

[1] Southwestern for "afternoon."

A bit of a scare shot through Tom — a touch of uncomfortable suspicion. He searched Aunt Polly's face, but it told him nothing. So he said:

"No'm — well, not very much."

The old lady reached out her hand and felt Tom's shirt, and said:

"But you ain't too warm now, though." And it flattered her to reflect that she had discovered that the shirt was dry without anybody knowing that that was what she had in her mind. But in spite of her, Tom knew where the wind lay, now. So he forestalled what might be the next move:

"Some of us pumped on our heads — mine's damp yet. See?"

Aunt Polly was vexed to think she had overlooked that bit of circumstantial evidence, and missed a trick. Then she had a new inspiration:

"Tom, you didn't have to undo your shirt-collar where I sewed it, to pump on your head, did you? Unbutton your jacket!"

The trouble vanished out of Tom's face. He opened his jacket. His shirt-collar was securely sewed.

"Bother! Well, go 'long with you. I'd made sure you'd played hookey and been a-swimming. But I forgive ye, Tom. I reckon you're a kind of a singed cat, as the saying is — better'n you look. *This* time."

She was half sorry her sagacity had miscarried, and half glad that Tom had stumbled into obedient conduct for once.

But Sidney said:

"Well, now, if I didn't think you sewed his collar with white thread, but it's black."

"Why, I did sew it with white! Tom!"

But Tom did not wait for the rest. As he went out at the door he said:

"Siddy, I'll lick you for that."

In a safe place Tom examined two large needles which were thrust into the lapels of his jacket, and had thread bound about them — one needle carried white thread and the other black. He said.

"She'd never noticed if it hadn't been for Sid. Confound it! sometimes she sews it with white, and sometimes she sews it with black. I wish to geeminy she'd stick to one or t'other — *I* can't keep the run of 'em. But I bet you I'll lam Sid for that. I'll learn him!"

He was not the Model Boy of the village. He knew the model boy very well though — and loathed him.

Within two minutes, or even less, he had forgotten all his troubles. Not because his troubles were one whit less heavy and bitter to him than a man's are to a man, but because a new and powerful interest bore them down and drove them out of his mind for the time — just as men's misfortunes are forgotten in the excitement of new enterprises. This new interest was a valued novelty in whistling, which he had just acquired from a negro, and he was suffering to practise it undisturbed. It consisted in a peculiar birdlike turn, a sort of liquid warble, produced by touching the tongue to the roof of the mouth at short intervals in the midst of the music — the reader probably remembers how to do it, if he has ever been a boy. Diligence and attention soon gave him the knack of it, and he strode down the street with his mouth full of harmony and his soul full of gratitude. He felt much as an astronomer feels who has discovered a new planet — no doubt, as far as strong, deep, unalloyed pleasure is concerned, the advantage was with the boy, not the astronomer.

The summer evenings were long. It was not dark, yet. Presently Tom checked his whistle. A stranger was before him — a boy a shade larger than himself. A new-comer of any age or either sex was an impressive curiosity in the poor little shabby village of St. Petersburg. This boy was well dressed, too — well dressed on a week-day. This was simply astounding. His cap was a dainty thing, his close-buttoned blue cloth roundabout was new and natty, and so were his pantaloons. He had shoes on — and it was only Friday. He even wore a necktie, a bright bit of ribbon. He had a citified air about him that ate into Tom's vitals. The more Tom stared at the splendid marvel, the higher he turned up his nose at his finery and the shabbier and shabbier his own outfit seemed to him to grow. Neither boy spoke. If one moved, the other moved — but only sidewise, in a circle; they kept face to face and eye to eye all the time. Finally Tom said:

"I can lick you!"

"I'd like to see you try it."

"Well, I can do it."

"No you can't, either."

"Yes I can."

"No you can't."

"I can."

"You can't."

"Can!"

"Can't!"

An uncomfortable pause. Then Tom said:

"What's your name?"

"Tisn't any of your business, maybe."

"Well I 'low I'll *make* it my business."

"Well why don't you?"

"If you say much, I will."

"Much — much — *much*. There now."

"Oh, you think you're mighty smart, *don't* you? I could lick you with one hand tied behind me, if I wanted to."

"Well why don't you *do* it? You *say* you can do it."

"Well I *will*, if you fool with me."

"Oh yes — I've seen whole families in the same fix."

"Smarty! You think you're *some*, now, *don't* you? Oh, what a hat!"

"You can lump that hat if you don't like it. I dare you to knock it off— and anybody that'll take a dare will suck eggs."

"You're a liar!"

"You're another."

"You're a fighting liar and dasn't take it up."

"Aw—take a walk!"

"Say — if you give me much more of your sass I'll take and bounce a rock off'n your head."

"Oh, of *course* you will."

"Well I *will*."

"Well why don't you *do* it then? What do you keep *saying* you will for? Why don't you *do* it? It's because you're afraid."

"I *ain't* afraid."

"You are."

"I ain't."

"You are."

Another pause, and more eying and sidling around each other. Presently they were shoulder to shoulder. Tom said:

"Get away from here!"

"Go away yourself!"

"I won't."

"*I* won't either."

So they stood, each with a foot placed at an angle as a brace, and both shoving with might and main, and glowering at each other with hate. But neither could get an advantage. After struggling till both were hot and flushed, each relaxed his strain with watchful caution, and Tom said:

"You're a coward and a pup. I'll tell my big brother on you, and he can thrash you with his little finger, and I'll make him do it, too."

"What do I care for your big brother? I've got a brother that's bigger than he is — and what's more, he can throw him over that fence, too." [Both brothers were imaginary.]

"That's a lie."

"*Your* saying so don't make it so."

Tom drew a line in the dust with his big toe, and said:

"I dare you to step over that, and I'll lick you till you can't stand up. Anybody that'll take a dare will steal sheep,"

The new boy stepped over promptly, and said:

"Now you said you'd do it, now let's see you do it."

"Don't you crowd me now; you better look out."

"Well, you *said* you'd do it — why don't you do it?"

"By jingo! for two cents I *will* do it."

The new boy took two broad coppers out of his pocket and held them out with derision. Tom struck them to the ground. In an instant both boys were rolling and tumbling in the dirt, gripped together like cats; and for the space of a minute they tugged and tore at each other's hair and clothes, punched and scratched each other's noses, and covered themselves with dust and glory. Presently the confusion took form and through the fog of battle Tom appeared, seated astride the new boy, and pounding him with his fists.

"Holler 'nuff!" said he.

The boy only struggled to free himself. He was crying — mainly from rage,

"Holler 'nuff!" — and the pounding went on.

At last the stranger got out a smothered "'Nuff!" and Tom let him up and said:

"Now that'll learn you. Better look out who you're fooling with next time."

The new boy went off brushing the dust from his clothes, sobbing, snuffling, and occasionally looking back and shaking his head and threatening what he would do to Tom the "next time he caught him out." To which Tom responded with jeers, and started off in high feather, and as soon as his back was turned the new boy snatched up a stone, threw it and hit him between the shoulders and then turned tail and ran like an antelope. Tom chased the traitor home, and thus found out where he lived He then held a position at the gate for some time, daring the enemy to come outside, but the enemy only made faces at him through the window and declined. At last the enemy's mother appeared, and called Tom a bad, vicious, vulgar child, and ordered him away. So he went away, but he said he ""lowed" to "lay" for that boy.

He got home pretty late, that night, and when he climbed cautiously in at the window, he uncovered an ambuscade, in the person of his aunt; and when she saw the state his clothes were in her resolution to turn his Saturday holiday into captivity at hard labor became adamantine in its firmness.

- Describe Tom.
- He starts out the novel very immature. He thinks the world should revolve around him. He's very selfish He doesn't think of others and doesn't care about what others are feeling. He's obviously not one to admire or emulate, as you don't want to be immature. He'll do some growing up before the novel is done.
- Look up Proverbs 12:1 and Proverbs 10:17 in a Bible. What do these verses say about Tom?

Lesson 7

- Read chapters 2 and 3 of *The Adventures of Tom Sawyer.*

Chapter 2
The Glorious Whitewasher

Saturday morning was come, and all the summer world was bright and fresh, and brimming with life. There was a song in every heart; and if the heart was young the music issued at the lips. There was cheer in every face and a spring in every step. The locust trees were in bloom and the fragrance of the blossoms filled the air. Cardiff Hill, beyond the village and above it, was green with vegetation, and it lay just far enough away to seem a Delectable Land, dreamy, reposeful, and inviting.

Tom appeared on the sidewalk with a bucket of whitewash and a long-handled brush. He surveyed the fence, and all gladness left him and a deep melancholy settled down upon his spirit. Thirty yards of board fence nine feet high. Life to him seemed hollow, and existence but a burden. Sighing he dipped his brush and passed it along the topmost plank; repeated the operation; did it again; compared the insignificant whitewashed streak with the far-reaching continent of unwhitewashed fence, and sat down on a tree-box discouraged. Jim came skipping out at the gate with a tin pail, and singing "Buffalo Gals." Bringing water from the town pump had always been hateful work in Tom's eyes, before, but now it did not strike him so. He remembered that there was company at the pump. White, mulatto, and negro boys and girls were always there waiting their turns, resting, trading playthings, quarreling, fighting, skylarking. And he remembered that although the pump was only a hundred and fifty yards off, Jim never got back with a bucket of water under an hour — and even then somebody generally had to go after him. Tom said:

"Say, Jim, I'll fetch the water if you'll whitewash some."

Jim shook his head and said:

"Can't, Mars Tom. Ole missis, she tole me I got to go an' git dis water an' not stop foolin' roun' wid anybody. She say she spec' Mars Tom gwine to ax me to whitewash, an' so she tole me go 'long an' 'tend to my own business — she 'lowed she'd 'tend to de whitewashin'."

"Oh, never you mind what she said, Jim. That's the way she always talks. Gimme the bucket — I won't be gone only a minute. She won't ever know."

"Oh, I dasn't, Mars Tom. Ole missis she'd take an' tar de head off'n me. 'Deed she would."

"*She*! She never licks anybody — whacks 'em over the head with her thimble — and who cares for that, I'd like to know. She talks awful, but talk don't hurt — anyways it don't if she don't cry, Jim, I'll give you a marvel. I'll give you a white alley!"

Jim began to waver.

"White alley, Jim! And it's a bully taw."

"My! Dat's a mighty gay marvel, I tell you! But Mars Tom I's powerful 'fraid ole missis —"

"And besides, if you will I'll show you my sore toe."

Jim was only human — this attraction was too much for him. He put down his pail, took the white alley, and bent over the toe with absorbing interest while the bandage was being unwound. In another moment he was flying down the street with his pail and a tingling rear, Tom was whitewashing with vigor, and Aunt Polly was retiring from the field with a slipper in her hand and triumph in her eye.

But Tom's energy did not last. He began to think of the fun he had planned for this day, and his sorrows multiplied. Soon the free boys would come tripping along on all sorts of delicious expeditions, and they would make a world of fun of him for having to work — the very thought of it burnt him like fire. He got out his worldly wealth and examined it — bits of toys, marbles, and trash; enough to buy an exchange of work, maybe, but not half enough to buy so much as half an hour of pure freedom. So he returned his straitened means to his pocket, and gave up the idea of trying to buy the boys. At this dark and hopeless moment an inspiration burst upon him! Nothing less than a great, magnificent inspiration.

He took up his brush and went tranquilly to work. Ben Rogers hove in sight presently — the very boy, of all boys, whose ridicule he had been dreading. Ben's gait was the hop-skip-and-jump — proof enough that his heart was light and his anticipations high. He was eating an apple, and giving a long, melodious whoop, at intervals, followed by a deep-toned ding-dong-dong, ding-dong-dong, for he was personating a steamboat. As he drew near, he slackened speed, took the middle of the street, leaned far over to starboard and rounded to ponderously and with laborious pomp and circumstance — for he was personating the *Big Missouri*, and considered himself to be drawing nine feet of water. He was boat and captain and engine-bells combined, so he had to imagine himself standing on his own hurricane-deck giving the orders and executing them:

"Stop her, sir! Ting-a-ling-ling!" The headway ran almost out and he drew up slowly toward the sidewalk.

"Ship up to back! Ting-a-ling-ling!" His arms straightened and stiffened down his sides.

"Set her back on the stabboard! Ting-a-ling-ling! Chow! ch-chow-wow! Chow!" His right hand, meantime, describing stately circles — for it was representing a forty-foot wheel.

"Let her go back on the labboard! Ting-a-ling-ling Chow-ch-chow-chow!" The left hand began to describe circles.

"Stop the stabboard! Ting-a-ling-ling! Stop the labboard! Come ahead on the stabboard! Stop her! Let your outside turn over slow! Ting-a-ling-ling! Chow-ow-ow! Get out that head-line? *Lively* now! Come — out with your spring-line — what're you about there! Take a turn round that stump with the bight of it! Stand by that stage, now — let her go! Done with the engines, sir! Ting-a-ling-ling! *Sh't! s'h't! sh't!*" (trying the gaugecocks).

Tom went on whitewashing — paid no attention to the steamboat. Ben stared a moment and then said:

"Hi-*yi*! You're up a stump, ain't you!"

No answer. Tom surveyed his last touch with the eye of an artist, then he gave his brush another gentle sweep and surveyed the result, as before. Ben ranged up alongside of him. Tom's mouth watered for the apple, but he stuck to his work. Ben said:

"Hello, old chap, you got to work, hey?"

Tom wheeled suddenly and said:

"Why, it's you, Ben! I warn't noticing."

"Say — *I*'m going in a-swimming, *I* am. Don't you wish you could? But of course you'd druther *work* — wouldn't you? Course you would!"

Tom contemplated the boy a bit, and said:

"What do you call work?"

"Why, ain't *that* work?"

Tom resumed his whitewashing, and answered carelessly:

"Well, maybe it is, and maybe it ain't. All I know, is, it suits Tom Sawyer."

"Oh come, now, you don't mean to let on that you *like* it?"

The brush continued to move.

"Like it? Well, I don't see why I oughtn't to *like* it. Does a boy get a chance to whitewash a fence every day?"

That put the thing in a new light. Ben stopped nibbling his apple. Tom swept his brush daintily back and forth — stepped back to note the effect — added a touch here and there — criticized the effect again — Ben watching every move and getting more and more interested, more and more absorbed. Presently he said:

"Say, Tom, let *me* whitewash a little."

Tom considered, was about to consent; but he altered his mind:

"No — no — I reckon it wouldn't hardly do, Ben. You see, Aunt Polly's awful particular about this fence — right here on the street, you know — but if it was the back fence I wouldn't mind and she wouldn't. Yes, she's awful particular about this fence; it's got to he done very careful; I reckon there ain't one boy in a thousand, maybe two thousand, that can do it the way it's got to be done."

"No — is that so? Oh come, now — lemme just try. Only just a little — I'd let *you*, if you was me, Tom."

"Ben, I'd like to, honest injun; but Aunt Polly — well, Jim wanted to do it, but she wouldn't let him; Sid wanted to do it, and she wouldn't let Sid. Now don't you see how I'm fixed? If you was to tackle this fence and anything was to happen to it—"

"Oh, shucks, I'll be just as careful. Now lemme try. Say — I'll give you the core of my apple."

"Well, here— No, Ben, now don't. I'm afeard—"

"I'll give you *all* of it!"

Tom gave up the brush with reluctance in his face, but alacrity in his heart. And while the late steamer *Big Missouri* worked and sweated in the sun, the retired artist sat on a barrel in the shade close by, dangled his legs, munched his apple, and planned the slaughter of more innocents. There was no lack of material; boys happened along every little while; they came to jeer, but remained to whitewash. By the time Ben was fagged out, Tom had traded the next chance to Billy Fisher for a kite, in good repair; and when *he* played out, Johnny Miller bought in for a dead rat and a string to swing it with — and so on, and so on, hour after hour. And when the middle of the afternoon came, from being a poor poverty-stricken boy in the morning, Tom was literally rolling in wealth. He had beside the things before mentioned, twelve marbles, part of a jews'-harp, a piece of blue bottle-glass to look through, a spool cannon, a key that wouldn't unlock anything, a fragment of chalk, a glass stopper of a decanter, a tin soldier, a couple of tadpoles, six firecrackers, a kitten with only one eye, a brass door-knob, a dog-collar — but no dog — the handle of a knife, four pieces of orange-peel, and a dilapidated old window-sash.

He had had a nice, good, idle time all the while — plenty of company — and the fence had three coats of whitewash on it! If he hadn't run out of whitewash, he would have bankrupted every boy in the village.

Tom said to himself that it was not such a hollow world, after all. He had discovered a great law of human action, without knowing it — namely, that in order to make a man or a boy covet a thing, it is only necessary to make the thing difficult to attain. If he had been a great and wise philosopher, like the writer of this book, he would now have comprehended that Work consists of whatever a body is obliged to do, and that Play consists of whatever a body is not obliged to do. And this would help him to understand why constructing artificial flowers or performing on a treadmill is work, while rolling tenpins or climbing Mont Blanc is only amusement. There are wealthy gentlemen in England who drive four-horse passenger-coaches twenty or thirty miles on a daily line, in the summer, because the privilege costs them considerable money; but if they were offered wages for the service, that would turn it into work and then they would resign.

The boy mused awhile over the substantial change which had taken place in his worldly circumstances, and then wended toward headquarters to report.

Chapter 3
Busy at War and Love

Tom presented himself before Aunt Polly, who was sitting by an open window in a pleasant rearward apartment, which was bedroom, breakfast-room, dining-room, and library, combined. The balmy summer air, the restful quiet, the odor of the flowers, and the drowsing murmur of the bees had had their effect, and she was nodding over her knitting — for she had no company but the cat, and it was asleep in her lap. Her spectacles were propped up on her gray head for safety. She had thought that of course Tom had deserted long ago, and she wondered at seeing him place himself in her power again in this intrepid way. He said: “Mayn’t I go and play now, aunt?”

“What, a’ ready? How much have you done?”

“It’s all done, aunt.”

“Tom, don’t lie to me — I can’t bear it.”

“I ain’t, aunt; it *is* all done.”

Aunt Polly placed small trust in such evidence. She went out to see for herself; and she would have been content to find twenty per cent, of Tom’s statement true. When she found the entire fence white-washed, and not only whitewashed but elaborately coated and recoated, and even a streak added to the ground, her astonishment was almost unspeakable. She said:

"Well, I never! There's no getting round it, you can work when you're a mind to, Tom." And then she diluted the compliment by adding, "But it's powerful seldom you're a mind to, I'm bound to say. Well, go 'long and play; but mind you get back some time in a week, or I'll tan you."

She was so overcome by the splendor of his achievement that she took him into the closet and selected a choice apple and delivered it to him, along with an improving lecture upon the added value and flavor a treat took to itself when it came without sin through virtuous effort. And while she closed with a happy Scriptural flourish, he "hooked" a doughnut.

Then he skipped out, and saw Sid just starting up the outside stairway that led to the back rooms on the second floor. Clods were handy and the air was full of them in a twinkling. They raged around Sid like a hail-storm; and before Aunt Polly could collect her surprised faculties and sally to the rescue, six or seven clods had taken personal effect, and Tom was over the fence and gone. There was a gate, but as a general thing he was too crowded for time to make use of it. His soul was at peace, now that he had settled with Sid for calling attention to his black thread and getting him into trouble.

Tom skirted the block, and came round into a muddy alley that led by the back of his aunt's cow- stable. He presently got safely beyond the reach of capture and punishment, and hastened toward the public square of the village, where two "military" companies of boys had met for conflict, according to previous appointment. Tom was General of one of these armies, Joe Harper (a bosom friend) General of the other. These two great commanders did not condescend to fight in person — that being better suited to the still smaller fry — but sat together on an eminence and conducted the field operations by orders delivered through aides-de-camp. Tom's army won a great victory, after a long and hard-fought battle. Then the dead were counted, prisoners exchanged, the terms of the next disagreement agreed upon, and the day for the necessary battle appointed; after which the armies fell into line and marched away, and Tom turned homeward alone.

As he was passing by the house where Jeff Thatcher lived, he saw a new girl in the garden — a lovely little blue-eyed creature with yellow hair plaited into two long tails, white summer frock and embroidered pantalettes. The fresh-crowned hero fell without firing a shot. A certain Amy Lawrence vanished out of his heart and left not even a memory of herself behind. He had thought he loved her to distraction, he had regarded his passion as adoration; and behold it was only a poor little evanescent partiality. He had been months winning her; she had confessed hardly a week ago; he had been the happiest and the proudest boy in the world only seven short days, and here in one instant of time she had gone out of his heart like a casual stranger whose visit is done.

He worshiped this new angel with furtive eye, till he saw that she had discovered him; then he pretended he did not know she was present, and began to "show off" in all sorts of absurd boyish ways, in order to win her admiration. He kept up this grotesque foolishness for some time; but by and by, while he was in the midst of some dangerous gymnastic performances, he glanced aside and saw that the little girl was wending her way toward the house. Tom came up to the fence and leaned on it, grieving, and hoping she would tarry yet awhile longer. She halted a moment on the steps and then moved toward the door. Tom heaved a great sigh as she put her foot on the threshold. But his face lit up, right away, for she tossed a pansy over the fence a moment before she disappeared.

The boy ran around and stopped within a foot or two of the flower, and then shaded his eyes with his hand and began to look down street as if he had discovered something of interest going on in that direction. Presently he picked up a straw and began trying to balance it on his nose, with his head tilted far back; and as he moved from side to side, in his efforts, he edged nearer and nearer toward the pansy; finally his bare foot rested upon it, his pliant toes closed upon it, and he hopped away with the treasure and disappeared round the corner. But only for a minute — only while he could button the flower inside his jacket, next his heart — or next his stomach, possibly, for he was not much posted in anatomy, and not hypercritical, anyway.

He returned, now, and hung about the fence till nightfall, "showing off," as before; but the girl never exhibited herself again, though Tom comforted himself a little with the hope that she had been near some window, meantime, and been aware of his attentions. Finally he rode home reluctantly, with his poor head full of visions.

All through supper his spirits were so high that his aunt wondered "what had got into the child." He took a good scolding about clodding Sid, and did not seem to mind it in the least. He tried to steal sugar under his aunt's very nose, and got his knuckles rapped for it. He said:

"Aunt, you don't whack Sid when he takes it."

"Well, Sid don't torment a body the way you do. You'd be always into that sugar if I warn't watching you."

Presently she stepped into the kitchen, and Sid, happy in his immunity, reached for the sugar-bowl — a sort of glorying over Tom which was well-nigh unbearable. But Sid's fingers slipped and the bowl dropped and broke. Tom was in ecstasies. In such ecstasies that he even controlled his tongue and was silent. He said to himself that he would not speak a word, even when his aunt came in, but would sit perfectly still till she asked who did the mischief; and then he would tell, and there would be nothing so good in the world as to see that pet model "catch it." He was so brim full of exultation that he could hardly hold himself when the old lady came back and stood above the wreck discharging lightnings of wrath from over her spectacles. He said to himself, "Now it's coming!" And the next instant he was sprawling on the floor! The potent palm was uplifted to strike again when Tom cried out:

''Hold on, now, what 'er you belting *me* for? — Sid broke it!"

Aunt Polly paused, perplexed, and Tom looked for healing pity. But when she got her tongue again, she only said:

"Umf! Well, you didn't get a lick amiss, I reckon. You been into some other audacious mischief when I wasn't around, like enough."

Then her conscience reproached her, and she yearned to say something kind and loving; but she judged that this would be construed into a confession that she had been in the wrong, and discipline forbade that. So she kept silence, and went about her affairs with a troubled heart. Tom sulked in a corner and exalted his woes. He knew that in her heart his aunt was on her knees to him, and he was morosely gratified by the consciousness of it. He would hang out no signals, he would take notice of none. He knew that a yearning glance fell upon him, now and then, through a film of tears, but he refused recognition of it. He pictured himself lying sick unto death and his aunt bending over him beseeching one little forgiving word, but he would turn his face to the wall, and die with that word unsaid. Ah, how would she feel then? And he pictured himself brought home from the river, dead, with his curls all wet, and his sore heart at rest. How she would throw herself upon him, and how her tears would fall like rain, and her lips pray God to give her back her boy and she would never, never abuse him any more! But he would lie there cold and white and make no sign — a poor little sufferer, whose griefs were at an end. He so worked upon his feelings with the pathos of these dreams, that he had to keep swallowing, he was so like to choke; and his eyes swam in a blur of water, which overflowed when he winked, and ran down and trickled from the end of his nose. And such a luxury to him was this petting of his sorrows, that he could not bear to have any worldly cheeriness or any grating delight intrude upon it; it was too sacred for such contact; and so, presently, when his cousin Mary danced in, all alive with the joy of seeing home again after an age-long visit of one week to the country, he got up and moved in clouds and darkness out at one door as she brought song and sunshine in at the other.

He wandered far from the accustomed haunts of boys, and sought desolate places that were in harmony with his spirit. A log raft in the river invited him, and he seated himself on its outer edge and contemplated the dreary vastness of the stream, wishing, the while, that he could only be drowned, all at once and unconsciously, without undergoing the uncomfortable routine devised by nature. Then he thought of his flower. He got it out, rumpled and wilted, and it mightily increased his dismal felicity. He wondered if she would pity him if she knew? Would she cry, and wish that she had a right to put her arms around his neck and comfort him? Or would she turn coldly away like all the hollow world? This picture brought such an agony of pleasurable suffering that he worked it over and over again in his mind and set it up in new and varied lights, till he wore it threadbare. At last he rose up sighing and departed in the darkness.

About half past nine or ten o'clock he came along the deserted street to where the Adored Unknown lived; he paused a moment; no sound fell upon his listening ear; a candle was casting a dull glow upon the curtain of a second-story window. Was the sacred presence there? He climbed the fence, threaded his stealthy way through the plants, till he stood under that window; he looked up at it long, and with emotion; then he laid him down on the ground under it, disposing himself upon his back, with his hands clasped upon his breast and holding his poor wilted flower.

And thus he would die — out in the cold world, with no shelter over his homeless head, no friendly hand to wipe the death-damps from his brow, no loving face to bend pityingly over him when the great agony came. And thus *she* would see him when she looked out upon the glad morning, and oh! would she drop one little tear upon his poor, lifeless form, would she heave one little sigh to see a bright young life so rudely blighted, so untimely cut down?

The window went up, a maid-servant's discordant voice profaned the holy calm, and a deluge of water drenched the prone martyr's remains!

The strangling hero sprang up with a relieving snort. There was a whiz as of a missile in the air, mingled with the murmur of a curse, a sound as of shivering glass followed, and a small, vague form went over the fence and shot away in the gloom.

Not along after, as Tom, all undressed for bed, was surveying his drenched garments by the light of a tallow dip, Sid woke up; but if he had any dim idea of making any "references to allusions," he thought better of it and held his peace, for there was danger in Tom's eye.

Tom turned in without the added vexation of prayers, and Sid made mental note of the omission.

- Here's an example of irony. Aunt Polly thinks he did a great job but threatens him anyway. Tom tells his Aunt Polly that he completed his chores. She is so surprised by how great a job was done that she says, "Well, go 'long and play; but mind you get back some time in a week, or I'll tan you." (Special thanks to Rebecca Wire for reading *Tom Sawyer* and making comments for us to share with the students.)

Lesson 8

- Read chapter 4 of *The Adventures of Tom Sawyer.*

Chapter 4
Showing Off in Sunday-School

The sun rose upon a tranquil world, and beamed down upon the peaceful village like a benediction. Breakfast over, Aunt Polly had family worship: it began with a prayer built from the ground up of solid courses of Scriptural quotations, welded together with a thin mortar of originality; and from the summit of this she delivered a grim chapter of the Mosaic Law, as from Sinai.

Then Tom girded up his loins, so to speak, and went to work to "get his verses." Sid had learned his lesson days before. Tom bent all his energies to the memorizing of five verses, and he chose part of the Sermon on the Mount, because he could find no verses that were shorter. At the end of half an hour Tom had a vague general idea of his lesson, but no more, for his mind was traversing the whole field of human thought, and his hands were busy with distracting recreations. Mary took his book to hear him recite, and he tried to find his way through the fog:

"'Blessed are the — a — a —"

"Poor — "

"Yes — poor; blessed are the poor — a — a —"

"In spirit —"

"In spirit; blessed are the poor in spirit, for they — they —"

"*Theirs* —"

"For *theirs*. Blessed are the poor in spirit, for *theirs* is the kingdom of heaven. Blessed are they that mourn, for they — they —"

"Sh —"

"For they — a —"

"S, H, A —"

"For they S, H — Oh, I don't know what it is!"

"*Shall*!"

"Oh, *shall*! for they shall — for they shall — a — a — shall mourn — a — a — blessed are they that shall — they that — a — they that shall mourn, for they shall — a — shall *what*? Why don't you tell me, Mary? — what do you want to be so mean for?"

"Oh, Tom, you poor thick-headed thing, I'm not teasing you. I wouldn't do that. You must go and learn it again. Don't you be discouraged, Tom, you'll manage it — and if you do, I'll give you something ever so nice. There, now, that's a good boy."

"All right! What is it, Mary? tell me what it is."

"Never you mind, Tom. You know if I say it's nice, it is nice."

"You bet you that's so, Mary. All right, I'll tackle it again."

And he did "tackle it again" — and under the double pressure of curiosity and prospective gain, he did it with such spirit that he accomplished a shining success. Mary gave him a brand-new "Barlow" knife worth twelve and a half cents; and the convulsion of delight that swept his system shook him to his foundations, True, the knife would not cut anything, but it was a "sure-enough" Barlow, and there was inconceivable grandeur in that — though where the Western boys ever got the idea that such a weapon could possibly be counterfeited to its injury, is an imposing mystery and will always remain so, perhaps. Tom contrived to scarify the cupboard with it, and was arranging to begin on the bureau, when he was called off to dress for Sunday-school.

Mary gave him a tin basin of water and a piece of soap, and he went outside the door and set the basin on a little bench there; then he dipped the soap in the water and laid it down; turned up his sleeves; poured out the water on the ground, gently, and then entered the kitchen and began to wipe his face diligently on the towel behind the door. But Mary removed the towel and said:

"Now ain't you ashamed, Tom! You mustn't be so bad. Water won't hurt you."

Tom was a trifle disconcerted. The basin was refilled, and this time he stood over it a little while, gathering resolution; took in a big breath and began. When he entered the kitchen presently, with both eyes shut and groping for the towel with his hands, an honorable testimony of suds and water was dripping from his face. But when he emerged from the towel, he was not yet satisfactory, for the clean territory stopped short at his chin and his jaws, like a mask; below and beyond this line there was a dark expanse of unirrigated soil that spread downward in front and backward around his neck. Mary took him in hand, and when she was done with him he was a man and a brother, without distinction of color, and his saturated hair was neatly brushed, and its short curls wrought into a dainty and symmetrical general effect. [He privately smoothed out the curls, with labor and difficulty, and plastered his hair close down to his head; for he held curls to be effeminate, and his own filled his life with bitterness.] Then Mary got out a suit of his clothing that had been used only on Sundays during two years — they were simply called his "other clothes" — and so by that we know the size of his wardrobe. The girl "put him to rights" after he had dressed himself; she buttoned his neat roundabout up to his chin, turned his vast shirt-collar down over his shoulders, brushed him off and crowned him with his speckled straw hat. He now looked exceedingly improved and uncomfortable. He was fully as uncomfortable as he looked; for there was a restraint about whole clothes and cleanliness that galled him. He hoped that Mary would forget his shoes, but the hope was blighted; she coated them thoroughly with tallow, as was the custom, and brought them out. He lost his temper and said he was always being made to do everything he didn't want to do. But Mary said, persuasively:

"Please, Tom — that's a good boy."

So he got into the shoes snarling. Mary was soon ready, and the three children set out for Sunday-school — a place that Tom hated with his whole heart; but Sid and Mary were fond of it.

Sabbath-school hours were from nine to half past ten; and then church service. Two of the children always remained for the sermon voluntarily, and the other always remained too — for stronger reasons. The church's high-backed, uncushioned pews would seat about three hundred persons; the edifice was but a small, plain affair, with a sort of pine board tree-box on top of it for a steeple. At the door Tom dropped back a step and accosted a Sunday-dressed comrade:

"Say, Billy, got a yaller ticket?"

"Yes."

"What'll you take for her?"

"What'll you give?"

"Piece of lickrish and a fish-hook."

"Less see 'em."

Tom exhibited. They were satisfactory, and the property changed hands. Then Tom traded a couple of white alleys for three red tickets, and some small trifle or other for a couple of blue ones. He waylaid other boys as they came, and went on buying tickets of various colors ten or fifteen minutes longer. He entered the church, now, with a swarm of clean and noisy boys and girls, proceeded to his seat and started a quarrel with the first boy that came handy. The teacher, a grave, elderly man, interfered; then turned his back a moment and Tom pulled a boy's hair in the next bench, and was absorbed in his book when the boy turned around; stuck a pin in another boy, presently, in order to hear him say "Ouch!" and got a new reprimand from his teacher. Tom's whole class were of a pattern — restless, noisy, and troublesome. When they came to recite their lessons, not one of them knew his verses perfectly, but had to be prompted all along. However, they worried through, and each got his reward — in small blue tickets, each with a passage of Scripture on it; each blue ticket was pay for two verses of the recitation. Ten blue tickets equaled a red one, and could be exchanged for it; ten red tickets equaled a yellow one; for ten yellow tickets the superintendent gave a very plainly bound Bible (worth forty cents in those easy times) to the pupil. How many of my readers would have the industry and application to memorize two thousand verses, even for a Doré

Bible? And yet Mary had acquired two Bibles in this way — it was the patient work of two years — and a boy of German parentage had won four or five. He once recited three thousand verses without stopping; but the strain upon his mental faculties was too great, and he was little better than an idiot from that day forth — a grievous misfortune for the school, for on great occasions, before company, the superintendent (as Tom expressed it) had always made this boy come out and "spread himself." Only the older pupils managed to keep their tickets and stick to their tedious work long enough to get a Bible, and so the delivery of one of these prizes was a rare and noteworthy circumstance; the successful pupil was so great and conspicuous for that day that on the spot every scholar's heart was fired with a fresh ambition that often lasted a couple of weeks. It is possible that Tom's mental stomach had never really hungered for one of those prizes, but unquestionably his entire being had for many a day longed for the glory and the éclat that came with it.

In due course the superintendent stood up in front of the pulpit, with a closed hymn-book in his hand and his forefinger inserted between its leaves, and commanded attention. When a Sunday-school superintendent makes his customary little speech, a hymn-book in the hand is as necessary as is the inevitable sheet of music in the hand of a singer who stands forward on the platform and sings a solo at a concert — though why, is a mystery: for neither the hymn-book nor the sheet of music is ever referred to by the sufferer. This superintendent was a slim creature of thirty-five, with a sandy goatee and short sandy hair; he wore a stiff standing-collar whose upper edge almost reached his ears and whose sharp points curved forward abreast the corners of his mouth — a fence that compelled a straight lookout ahead, and a turning of the whole body when a side view was required; his chin was propped on a spreading cravat which was as broad and as long as a bank-note, and had fringed ends; his boot-toes were turned sharply up, in the fashion of the day, like sleigh-runners — an effect patiently and laboriously produced by the young men by sitting with their toes pressed against a wall for hours together. Mr. Walters was very earnest of mien, and very sincere and honest at heart; and he held sacred things and places in such reverence, and so separated them from worldly matters, that unconsciously to himself his Sunday-school voice had acquired a peculiar intonation which was wholly absent on week-days. He began after this fashion:

"Now, children, I want you all to sit up just as straight and pretty as you can and give me all your attention for a minute or two. There — that is it. That is the way good little boys and girls should do. I see one little girl who is looking out of the window — I am afraid she thinks I am out there somewhere — perhaps up in one of the trees making a speech to the little birds. [Applausive titter.] I want to tell you how good it makes me feel to see so many bright, clean little faces assembled in a place like this, learning to do right and be good." And so forth and so on. It is not necessary to set down the rest of the oration. It was of a pattern which does not vary, and so it is familiar to us all. The latter third of the speech was marred by the resumption of fights and other recreations among certain of the bad boys, and by fidgetings and whisperings that extended far and wide, washing even to the bases of isolated and incorruptible rocks like Sid and Mary. But now every sound ceased suddenly, with the subsidence of Mr. Walters's voice, and the conclusion of the speech was received with a burst of silent gratitude.

A good part of the whispering had been occasioned by an event which was more or less rare — the entrance of visitors: lawyer Thatcher, accompanied by a very feeble and aged man; a fine, portly, middle-aged gentleman with iron-gray hair; and a dignified lady who was doubtless the latter's wife. The lady was leading a child. Tom had been restless and full of chafings and repinings; conscience-smitten, too — he could not meet Amy Lawrence's eye, he could not brook her loving gaze. But when he saw this small new-comer his soul was all ablaze with bliss in a moment. The next moment he was "showing off" with all his might — cuffing boys, pulling hair, making faces — in a word, using every art that seemed likely to fascinate a girl and win her applause. His exaltation had but one alloy — the memory of his humiliation in this angel's garden — and that record in sand was fast washing out, under the waves of happiness that were sweeping over it now.

The visitors were given the highest seat of honor, and as soon as Mr. Walters's speech was finished, he introduced them to the school. The middle-aged man turned out to be a prodigious personage — no less a one than the county judge — altogether the most august creation these children had ever looked upon — and they wondered what kind of material he was made of — and they half wanted to hear him roar, and were half afraid he might, too. He was from Constantinople, twelve miles away — so he had traveled, and seen the world — these very eyes had looked upon the county courthouse — which was said to have a tin roof. The awe which these reflections inspired was attested by the impressive silence and the ranks of staring eyes. This was the great Judge Thatcher, brother of their own lawyer. Jeff

Thatcher immediately went forward, to be familiar with the great man and be envied by the school. It would have been music to his soul to hear the whisperings:

"Look at him, Jim! He's a-going up there. Say — look! he's a-going to shake hands with him — he *is* shaking hands with him! By jings, don't you wish you was Jeff?"

Mr. Walters fell to "showing off," with all sorts of official bustlings and activities, giving orders, delivering judgments, discharging directions here, there, everywhere that he could find a target. The librarian "showed off." — running hither and thither with his arms full of books and making a deal of the splutter and fuss that insect authority delights in. The young lady teachers "showed off" — bending sweetly over pupils that were lately being boxed, lifting pretty warning fingers at bad little boys and patting good ones lovingly. The young gentlemen teachers "showed off" with small scoldings and other little displays of authority and fine attention to discipline — and most of the teachers, of both sexes, found business up at the library, by the pulpit; and it was business that frequently had to be done over again two or three times (with much seeming vexation). The little girls "showed off" in various ways, and the little boys "showed off" with such diligence that the air was thick with paper wads and the murmur of scuffiings. And above it all the great man sat and beamed a majestic judicial smile upon all the house, and warmed himself in the sun of his own grandeur — for he was "showing off," too.

There was only one thing wanting, to make Mr. Walters's ecstasy complete, and that was a chance to deliver a Bible prize and exhibit a prodigy. Several pupils had a few yellow tickets, but none had enough — he had been around among the star pupils inquiring. He would have given worlds, now, to have that German lad back again with a sound mind.

And now at this moment, when hope was dead, Tom Sawyer came forward with nine yellow tickets, nine red tickets, and ten blue ones, and demanded a Bible. This was a thunderbolt out of a clear sky. Walters was not expecting an application from this source for the next ten years. But there was no getting around it — here were the certified checks, and they were good for their face. Tom was therefore elevated to a place with the Judge and the other elect, and the great news was announced from headquarters. It was the most stunning surprise of the decade, and so profound was the sensation that it lifted the new hero up to the judicial one's altitude, and the school had two marvels to gaze upon in place of one. The boys were all eaten up with envy — but those that suffered the bitterest pangs were those who perceived too late that they themselves had contributed to this hated splendor by trading tickets to Tom for the wealth he had amassed in selling whitewashing privileges. These despised themselves, as being the dupes of a wily fraud, a guileful snake in the grass.

The prize was delivered to Tom with as much effusion as the superintendent could pump up under the circumstances; but it lacked somewhat of the true gush, for the poor fellow's instinct taught him that there was a mystery here that could not well bear the light, perhaps; it was simply preposterous that this boy had warehoused two thousand sheaves of Scriptural wisdom on his premises — a dozen would strain his capacity, without a doubt.

Amy Lawrence was proud and glad, and she tried to make Tom see it in her face — but he wouldn't look. She wondered; then she was just a grain troubled; next a dim suspicion came and went — came again; she watched; a furtive glance told her worlds — and then her heart broke, and she was jealous, and angry, and the tears came and she hated everybody. Tom most of all (she thought).

Tom was introduced to the Judge; but his tongue was tied, his breath would hardly come, his heart quaked — partly because of the awful greatness of the man, but mainly because he was her parent. He would have liked to fall down and worship him, if it were in the dark. The Judge put his hand on Tom's head and called him a fine little man, and asked him what his name was. The boy stammered, gasped, and got it out:

"Tom."

"Oh, no, not Tom— it is—"

"Thomas."

"Ah, that's it. I thought there was more to it, maybe. That's very well. But you've another one I dare say, and you'll tell it to me, won't you?"

"Tell the gentleman your other name, Thomas," said Walters, "and say sir. You mustn't forget your manners."

“Thomas Sawyer — sir.”

“That’s it! That’s a good boy. Fine boy. Fine, manly little fellow. Two thousand verses is a great many — very, very great many. And you never can be sorry for the trouble you took to learn them; for knowledge is worth more than anything there is in the world; it’s what makes great men and good men; you’ll be a great man and a good man yourself, some day, Thomas, and then you’ll look back and say, It’s all owing to the precious Sunday-school privileges of my boyhood — it’s all owing to my dear teachers that taught me to learn — it’s all owing to the good superintendent, who encouraged me, and watched over me, and gave me a beautiful Bible — a splendid elegant Bible — to keep and have it all for my own, always — it’s all owing to right bringing up! That is what you will say, Thomas — and you wouldn’t take any money for those two thousand verses — no indeed you wouldn’t. And now you wouldn’t mind telling me and this lady some of the things you’ve learned — no, I know you wouldn’t — for we are proud of little boys that learn. Now, no doubt you know the names of all the twelve disciples. Won’t you tell us the names of the first two that were appointed?”

Tom was tugging at a button-hole and looking sheepish. He blushed, now, and his eyes fell. Mr. Walters’s heart sank within him. He said to himself, it is not possible that the boy can answer the simplest question — why did the Judge ask him? Yet he felt obliged to speak up and say:

“Answer the gentleman, Thomas — don’t be afraid.”

Tom still hung fire.

“Now I know you’ll tell me” said the lady. “The names of the first two disciples were —”

“DAVID AND GOLIATH!”

Let us draw the curtain of charity over the rest of the scene.

Lesson 9

- Read chapter 5 of *The Adventures of Tom Sawyer.*

Chapter 5
The Pinch-Bug and his Prey

About half past ten the cracked bell of the small church began to ring, and presently the people began to gather for the morning sermon. The Sunday-school children distributed themselves about the house and occupied pews with their parents, so as to be under supervision. Aunt Polly came, and Tom and Sid and Mary sat with her — Tom being placed next the aisle, in order that he might be as far away from the open window and the seductive outside summer scenes as possible. The crowd filed up the aisles: the aged and needy postmaster, who had seen better days; the mayor and his wife — for they had a mayor there, among other unnecessaries; the justice of the peace; the widow Douglas, fair, smart, and forty, a generous, good-hearted soul and well-to-do, her hill mansion the only palace in the town, and the most hospitable and much the most lavish in the matter of festivities that St. Petersburg could boast; the bent and venerable Major and Mrs. Ward; lawyer Riverson, the new notable from a distance; next the belle of the village, followed by a troop of lawn-clad and ribbon-decked young heart-breakers; then all the young clerks in town in a body — for they had stood in the vestibule sucking their cane-heads, a circling wall of oiled and simpering admirers, till the last girl had run their gantlet; and last of all came the Model Boy, Willie Mufferson, taking as heedful care of his mother as if she were cut glass. He always brought his mother to church, and was the pride of all the matrons. The boys all hated him, he was so good. And besides, he had been "thrown up to them" so much. His white handkerchief was hanging out of his pocket behind, as usual on Sundays — accidentally. Tom had no handkerchief, and he looked upon boys who had, as snobs.

The congregation being fully assembled, now, the bell rang once more, to warn laggards and stragglers, and then a solemn hush fell upon the church which was only broken by the tittering and whispering of the choir in the gallery. The choir always tittered and whispered all through service. There was once a church choir that was not ill-bred, but I have forgotten where it was, now. It was a great many years ago, and I can scarcely remember anything about it, but I think it was in some foreign country.

The minister gave out the hymn, and read it through with a relish, in a peculiar style which was much admired in that part of the country. His voice began on a medium key and climbed steadily up till it reached a certain point, where it bore with strong emphasis upon the topmost word and then plunged down as if from a spring-board:

> Shall I be car-ri-ed toe the skies, on flow'ry *beds*
> of ease,
>
> Whilst others fight to win the prize, and sail thro' *blood-*
> y seas?

He was regarded as a wonderful reader. At church "sociable" he was always called upon to read poetry; and when he was through, the ladies would lift up their hands and let them fall helplessly in their laps, and "wall" their eyes, and shake their heads, as much as to say, "Words cannot express it; it is *too* beautiful, too beautiful for this mortal earth."

After the hymn had been sung, the Rev. Mr. Sprague turned himself into a bulletin-board, and read off "notices" of meetings and societies and things till it seemed that the list would stretch out to the crack of doom — a queer custom which is still kept up in America, even in cities, away here in this age of abundant newspapers. Often, the less there is to justify a traditional custom, the harder it is to get rid of it.

And now the minister prayed. A good, generous prayer it was, and went into details: it pleaded for the church, and the little children of the church; for the other churches of the village; for the village itself; for the county; for the state; for the state officers; for the United States; for the churches of the United States; for Congress; for the President; for the officers of the government; for poor sailors, tossed by stormy seas; for the oppressed millions groaning under the heel of European monarchies and Oriental despotisms; for such as have the light and the good tidings, and yet have not eyes to see nor ears to hear withal; for the heathen in the far islands of the sea; and closed with a supplication that the words he was about to speak might find grace and favor, and be as seed sown in fertile ground, yielding in time a grateful harvest of good. Amen.

There was a rustling of dresses, and the standing congregation sat down. The boy whose history this book relates did not enjoy the prayer, he only endured it — if he even did that much. He was restive all through it; he kept tally of the details of the prayer, unconsciously — for he was not listening, but he knew the ground of old, and the clergyman's regular route over it — and when a little trifle of new matter was interlarded, his ear detected it and his whole nature resented it; he considered additions unfair, and scoundrelly. In the midst of the prayer a fly had lit on the back of the pew in front of him and tortured his spirit by calmly rubbing its hands together, embracing its head with its arms, and polishing it so vigorously that it seemed to almost part company with the body, and the slender thread of a neck was exposed to view; scraping its wings with its hind legs and smoothing them to its body as if they had been coat-tails; going through its whole toilet as tranquilly as if it knew it was perfectly safe. As indeed it was; for as sorely as Tom's hands itched to grab for it they did not dare — he believed his soul would be instantly destroyed if he did such a thing while the prayer was going on. But with the closing sentence his hand began to curve and steal forward; and the instant the "Amen" was out the fly was a prisoner of war. His aunt detected the act and made him let it go.

The minister gave out his text and droned along monotonously through an argument that was so prosy that many a head by and by began to nod — and yet it was an argument that dealt in limitless fire and brimstone and thinned the predestined elect down to a company so small as to be hardly worth the saving. Tom counted the pages of the sermon; after church he always knew how many pages there had been, but he seldom knew anything else about the discourse. However, this time he was really interested for a little while. The minister made a grand and moving picture of the assembling together of the world's hosts at the millennium when the lion and the lamb should lie down together and a little child should lead them. But the pathos, the lesson, the moral of the great spectacle were lost upon the boy; he only thought of the conspicuousness of the principal character before the onlooking nations; his face lit with the thought, and he said to himself that he wished he could be that child, if it was a tame lion.

Now he lapsed into suffering again, as the dry argument was resumed. Presently he bethought him of a treasure he had and got it out. It was a large black beetle with formidable jaws — a "pinchbug," he called it. It was in a percussion-cap box. The first thing the beetle did was to take him by the finger. A natural fillip followed, the beetle went floundering into the aisle and lit on its back, and the hurt finger went into the boy's mouth. The beetle lay there working its helpless legs, unable to turn over. Tom eyed it, and longed for it; but it was safe out of his reach. Other people uninterested in the sermon, found relief in the beetle, and they eyed it too. Presently a vagrant poodle-dog came idling along, sad at heart, lazy with the summer softness and the quiet, weary of captivity, sighing for change. He spied the beetle; the drooping tail lifted and wagged. He surveyed the prize; walked around it; smelt at it from a safe distance; walked around it again; grew bolder, and took a closer smell; then lifted his lip and made a gingerly snatch at it, just missing it; made another, and another; began to enjoy the diversion; subsided to his stomach with the beetle between his paws, and continued his experiments; grew weary at last, and then indifferent and absent-minded. His head nodded, and little by little his chin descended and touched the enemy, who seized it. There was a sharp yelp, a flirt of the poodle's head, and the beetle fell a couple of yards away, and lit on its back once more. The neighboring spectators shook with a gentle inward joy, several faces went behind fans and handkerchiefs, and Tom was entirely happy. The dog looked foolish, and probably felt so; but there was resentment in his heart, too, and a craving for revenge. So he went to the beetle and began a wary attack on it again; jumping at it from every point of a circle, lighting with his fore paws within an inch of the creature, making even closer snatches at it with his teeth, and jerking his head till his ears flapped again. But he grew tired once more, after a while; tried to amuse himself with a fly but found no relief; followed an ant around, with his nose close to the floor, and quickly wearied of that; yawned, sighed, forgot the beetle entirely, and sat down on it. Then there was a wild yelp of agony and the poodle went sailing up the aisle; the yelps continued, and so did the dog; he crossed the house in front of the altar; he flew down the other aisle; he crossed before the doors; he clamored up the home-stretch; his anguish grew with his progress, till presently he was but a woolly comet moving in its orbit with the gleam and the speed of light. At last the frantic sufferer sheered from its course, and sprang into its master's lap; he flung it out of the window, and the voice of distress quickly thinned away and died in the distance.

By this time the whole church was red-faced and suffocating with suppressed laughter, and the sermon had come to a dead standstill. The discourse was resumed presently, but it went lame and halting, all possibility of impressiveness being at an end; for even the gravest sentiments were constantly being received with a smothered burst of unholy mirth, under cover of some remote pew-back, as if the poor parson had said a rarely facetious thing. It was a genuine relief to the whole congregation when the ordeal was over and the benediction pronounced.

Tom Sawyer went home quite cheerful, thinking to himself that there was some satisfaction about divine service when there was a bit of variety in it. He had but one marring thought; he was willing that the dog should play with his pinchbug, but he did not think it was upright in him to carry it off.

- What do you know so far about the protagonist/antagonist?
- What main plot points have passed?

Lesson 10

- Read chapter 6 of *The Adventures of Tom Sawyer*.

Chapter 6
Tom Meets Becky

Monday morning found Tom Sawyer miserable. Monday morning always found him so — because it began another week's slow suffering in school. He generally began that day with wishing he had had no intervening holiday, it made the going into captivity and fetters again so much more odious. Tom lay thinking. Presently it occurred to him that he wished he was sick; then he could stay home from school. Here was a vague possibility. He canvassed his system. No ailment was found, and he investigated again. This time he thought he could detect colicky symptoms, and he began to encourage them with considerable hope. But they soon grew feeble, and presently died wholly away. He reflected further. Suddenly he discovered something. One of his upper front teeth was loose. This was lucky; he was about to begin to groan, as a "starter," as he called it, when it occurred to him that if he came into court with that argument, his aunt would pull it out, and that would hurt. So he thought he would hold the tooth in reserve for the present, and seek further. Nothing offered for some little time, and then he remembered hearing the doctor tell about a certain thing that laid up a patient for two or three weeks and threatened to make him lose a finger. So the boy eagerly drew his sore toe from under the sheet and held it up for inspection. But now he did not know the necessary symptoms. However, it seemed well worth while to chance it, so he fell to groaning with considerable spirit.

But Sid slept on unconscious.

Tom groaned louder, and fancied that he began to feel pain in the toe.

No result from Sid.

Tom was panting with his exertions by this time. He took a rest and then swelled himself up and fetched a succession of admirable groans.

Sid snored on.

Tom was aggravated. He said, “Sid, Sid!” and shook him. This course worked well, and Tom began to groan again. Sid yawned, stretched, then brought himself up on his elbow with a snort, and began to stare at Tom. Tom went on groaning. Sid said:

“Tom! Say, Tom!” [No response.] “Here, Tom! *Tom*! What is the matter, Tom?” And he shook him and looked in his face anxiously.

Tom moaned out:

“Oh, don’t, Sid. Don’t joggle me.”

“Why, what’s the matter, Tom? I must call auntie.”

“No — never mind. It’ll be over by and by, maybe. Don’t call anybody.”

“But I must! *Don’t* groan so, Tom, it’s awful. How long you been this way?”

“Hours. Ouch! Oh, don’t stir so, Sid, you’ll kill me.”

"Tom, why didn't you wake me sooner? Oh, Tom, *don't*! It makes my flesh crawl to hear you. Tom, what is the matter?"

"I forgive you everything, Sid. [Groan.] Everything you've ever done to me. When I'm gone —"

"Oh, Tom, you ain't dying, are you? Don't, Tom — oh, don't. Maybe —"

"I forgive everybody, Sid. [Groan.] Tell 'em so, Sid. And Sid, you give my window-sash and my cat with one eye to that new girl that's come to town, and tell her —"

But Sid had snatched his clothes and gone. Tom was suffering in reality, now, so handsomely was his imagination working, and so his groans had gathered quite a genuine tone.

Sid flew down-stairs and said:

"Oh, Aunt Polly, come! Tom's dying!"

"Dying!"

"Yes'm. Don't wait — come quick!"

"Rubbage! I don't believe it!"

But she fled up-stairs, nevertheless, with Sid and Mary at her heels. And her face grew white, too, and her lip trembled. When she reached the bedside she gasped out:

"You, Tom! Tom, what's the matter with you?"

"Oh, auntie, I'm—"

"What's the matter with you — what *is* the matter with you, child?"

"Oh, auntie, my sore toe's mortified!"

The old lady sank down into a chair and laughed a little, then cried a little, then did both together. This restored her and she said:

"Tom, what a turn you did give me. Now you shut up that nonsense and climb out of this."

The groans ceased and the pain vanished from the toe. The boy felt a little foolish, and he said:

"Aunt Polly, it seemed mortified, and it hurt so I never minded my tooth at all."

"Your tooth, indeed! What's the matter with your tooth?"

"One of them's loose, and it aches perfectly awful."

"There, there, now, don't begin that groaning again. Open your mouth. Well — your tooth is loose, but you're not going to die about that. Mary, get me a silk thread, and a chunk of fire out of the kitchen."

Tom said:

"Oh, please auntie, don't pull it out. It don't hurt any more. I wish I may never stir if it does. Please don't, auntie. *I* don't want to stay home from school."

"Oh, you don't, don't you? So all this row was because you thought you'd get to stay home from school and go a-fishing? Tom, Tom, I love you so, and you seem to try every way you can to break my old heart with your outrageousness." By this time the dental instruments were ready. The old lady made one end of the silk thread fast to Tom's tooth with a loop and tied the other to the bedpost. Then she seized the chunk of fire and suddenly thrust it almost into the boy's face. The tooth hung dangling by the bedpost, now.

But all trials bring their compensations. As Tom wended to school after breakfast, he was the envy of every boy he met because the gap in his upper row of teeth enabled him to expectorate in a new and admirable way. He gathered quite a following of lads interested in the exhibition; and one that had cut his finger and had been a center of fascination and homage up to this time, now found himself suddenly without an adherent, and shorn of his glory. His heart was heavy, and he said with a disdain which he did not feel, that it wasn't anything to spit like Tom Sawyer; but another boy said "Sour grapes!" and he wandered away a dismantled hero.

Shortly Tom came upon the juvenile pariah of the village, Huckleberry Finn, son of the town drunkard. Huckleberry was cordially hated and dreaded by all the mothers of the town, because he was idle and lawless and vulgar and bad — and because all their children admired him so, and delighted in his forbidden society, and wished they dared to be like him. Tom was like the rest of the respectable boys, in that he envied Huckleberry his gaudy outcast condition, and was under strict orders not to play with him. So he played with him every time he got a chance. Huckleberry was always dressed in the cast-off clothes of full-grown men, and they were in perennial bloom and fluttering with rags. His hat was a vast ruin with a wide crescent lopped out of its brim; his coat, when he wore one, hung nearly to his heels and had the rearward buttons far down the back; but one suspender supported his trousers; the seat of the trousers bagged low and contained nothing; the fringed legs dragged in the dirt when not rolled up.

Huckleberry came and went, at his own free will. He slept on doorsteps in fine weather and in empty hogsheads in wet; he did not have to go to school or to church, or call any being master or obey anybody; he could go fishing or swimming when and where he chose, and stay as long as it suited him; nobody forbade him to fight; he could sit up as late as he pleased; he was always the first boy that went barefoot in the spring and the last to resume leather in the fall; he never had to wash, nor put on clean clothes; he could swear wonderfully. In a word, everything that goes to make life precious, that boy had. So thought every harassed, hampered, respectable boy in St. Petersburg.

Tom hailed the romantic outcast:

"Hello, Huckleberry!"

"Hello yourself, and see how you like it."

"What's that you got?"

"Dead cat."

"Lemme see him, Huck. My, he's pretty stiff. Where'd you get him?"

"Bought him off'n a boy."

"What did you give?"

"I give a blue ticket and a bladder that I got at the slaughter-house."

"Where'd you get the blue ticket?"

"Bought it off'n Ben Rogers two weeks ago for a hoop-stick."

"Say — what is dead cats good for, Huck?"

"Good for? Cure warts with."

"No! Is that so? I know something that's better."

"I bet you don't. What is it?"

"Why, spunk-water."

"Spunk- water! I wouldn't give a dern for spunk-water."

"You wouldn't, wouldn't you? D'you ever try it?"

"No, I hain't. But Bob Tanner did."

"Who told you so?"

"Why, he told Jeff Thatcher, and Jeff told Johnny Baker, and Johnny told Jim Hollis, and Jim told Ben Rogers, and Ben told a negro, and the negro told me. There now!"

"Well, what of it? They'll all he. Leastways all but the negro. I don't know *him*. But I never see a negro that *wouldn't* lie. Shucks! Now you tell me how Bob Tanner done it, Huck."

"Why, he took and dipped his hand in a rotten stump where the rain-water was."

"In the daytime?"

"Certainly."

"With his face to the stump?"

"Yes. Least I reckon so."

"Did he say anything?"

"I don't reckon he did. I don't know."

"Aha! Talk about trying to cure warts with spunk-water such a blame-fool way as that! Why, that ain't a-going to do any good. You got to go all by yourself, to the middle of the woods, where you know there's a spunk-water stump, and just as it's midnight you back up against the stump and jam your hand in and say:

> 'Barley-corn, Barley-corn, injun-meal shorts,
> Spunk-water, spunk-water, swaller these warts,'

and then walk away quick, eleven steps, with your eyes shut, and then turn around three times and walk home without speaking to anybody. Because if you speak the charm's busted."

"Well, that sounds like a good way; but that ain't the way Bob Tanner done."

"No, sir, you can bet he didn't, becuz he's the wartiest boy in this town; and he wouldn't have a wart on him if he'd knowed how to work spunk-water. I've took off thousands of warts off of my hands that way, Huck. I play with frogs so much that I've always got considerable many warts. Sometimes I take 'em off with a bean."

"Yes, bean's good. I've done that."

"Have you? What's your way?"

"You take and split the bean, and cut the wart so as to get some blood, and then you put the blood on one piece of the bean and take and dig a hole and bury it 'bout midnight at the crossroads in the dark of the moon, and then you burn up the rest of the bean. You see that piece that's got the blood on it will keep drawing and drawing, trying to fetch the other piece to it, and so that helps the blood to draw the wart, and pretty soon off she comes."

"Yes, that's it, Huck — that's it; though when you're burying it if you say 'Down bean; off wart: come no more to bother me!' it's better. That's the way Joe Harper does, and he's been nearly to Coonville and most everywheres. But say — how do you cure 'em with dead cats?"

"Why, you take your cat and go and get in the graveyard 'long about midnight when somebody that was wicked has been buried; and when it's midnight a devil will come, or maybe two or three, but you can't see 'em, you can only hear something like the wind, or maybe hear 'em talk; and when they're taking that feller away, you heave your cat after 'em and say, 'Devil follow corpse, cat follow devil, warts follow cat, *I'm* done with ye!' That'll fetch *any* wart."

"Sounds right. D'you ever try it, Huck?"

"No, but old Mother Hopkins told me."

"Well, I reckon it's so, then. Becuz they say she's a witch."

"Say! Why, Tom, I *know* she is. She witched pap. Pap says so his own self. He come along one day, and he see she was a-witching him, so he took up a rock, and if she hadn't dodged, he'd 'a' got her. Well, that very night he rolled off'n a shed wher' he was a-layin' drunk, and broke his arm."

"Why, that's awful. How did he know she was a-witching him?"

"Lord, pap can tell, easy. Pap says when they keep looking at you right stiddy, they're a-witching you. Specially if they mumble. Becuz when they mumble they're saying the Lord's Prayer backards."

"Say, Hucky, when you going to try the cat?"

"To-night. I reckon they'll come after old Hoss Williams to-night."

"But they buried him Saturday. Didn't they get him Saturday night?"

"Why, how you talk! How could their charms work till midnight? — and *then* it's Sunday. Devils don't slosh around much of a Sunday, I don't reckon."

"I never thought of that. That's so. Lemme go with you?"

"Of course — if you ain't afeard."

"Afeard! 'Tain't likely. Will you meow?"

"Yes — and you meow back, if you get a chance. Last time, you kep' me a-meowing around till old Hays went to throwing rocks at me and says 'Dern that cat!' and so I hove a brick through his window — but don't you tell."

"I won't. I couldn't meow that night, becuz auntie was watching me, but I'll meow this time. Say— what's that?"

"Nothing but a tick."

"Where'd you get him?"

"Out in the woods."

"What'll you take for him?"

"I don't know. I don't want to sell him."

"All right. It's a mighty small tick, anyway."

“Oh, anybody can run a tick down that don’t belong to them. I’m satisfied with it. It’s a good enough tick for me.”

“Sho, there’s ticks a-plenty. I could have a thousand of ‘em if I wanted to.”

“Well, why don’t you? Becuz you know mighty well you can’t. This is a pretty early tick, I reckon. It’s the first one I’ve seen this year.”

“Say, Huck — I’ll give you my tooth for him.”

“Less see it.”

Tom got out a bit of paper and carefully unrolled it. Huckleberry viewed it wistfully. The temptation was very strong. At last he said:

“Is it genuwyne?”

Tom lifted his lip and showed the vacancy.

“Well, all right,” said Huckleberry, “it’s a trade.”

Tom inclosed the tick in the percussion-cap box that had lately been the pinchbug’s prison, and the boys separated, each feeling wealthier than before.

When Tom reached the little isolated frame schoolhouse, he strode in briskly, with the manner of one who had come with all honest speed. He hung his hat on a peg and flung himself into his seat with businesslike alacrity. The master, throned on high in his great splint-bottom arm-chair, was dozing, lulled by the drowsy hum of study. The interruption roused him.

“Thomas Sawyer!”

Tom knew that when his name was pronounced in full, it meant trouble.

“Sir!”

"Come up here. Now, sir, why are you late again, as usual?"

Tom was about to take refuge in a lie, when he saw two long tails of yellow hair hanging down a back that he recognized by the electric sympathy of love; and by that form was the only vacant place on the girls' side of the schoolhouse. He instantly said:

"I STOPPED TO TALK WITH HUCKLEBERRY FINN!"

The master's pulse stood still, and he stared helplessly. The buzz of study ceased. The pupils wondered if this foolhardy boy had lost his mind. The master said:

"You— you did what?"

"Stopped to talk with Huckleberry Finn."

There was no mistaking the words.

"Thomas Sawyer, this is the most astounding confession I have ever listened to. No mere ferule will answer for this offense. Take off your jacket."

The master's arm performed until it was tired and the stock of switches notably diminished. Then the order followed:

"Now, sir, go and sit with the *girls*! And let this be a warning to you."

The titter that rippled around the room appeared to abash the boy, but in reality that result was caused father more by his worshipful awe of his unknown idol and the dread pleasure that lay in his high good fortune. He sat down upon the end of the pine bench and the girl hitched herself away from him with a toss of her head. Nudges and winks and whispers traversed the room, but Tom sat still, with his arms upon the long, low desk before him, and seemed to study his book.

By and by attention ceased from him, and the accustomed school murmur rose upon the dull air once more. Presently the boy began to steal furtive glances at the girl. She observed it, "made a mouth" at him and gave him the back of her head for the space of a minute. When she cautiously faced around again, a peach lay before her.

She thrust it away. Tom gently put it back. She thrust it away again, but with less animosity. Tom patiently returned it to its place. Then she let it remain. Tom scrawled on his slate, "Please take it — I got more." The girl glanced at the words, but made no sign. Now the boy began to draw something on the slate, hiding his work with his left hand. For a time the girl refused to notice; but her human curiosity presently began to manifest itself by hardly perceptible signs. The boy worked on, apparently unconscious. The girl made a sort of non-committal attempt to see it, but the boy did not betray that he was aware of it. At last she gave in and hesitatingly whispered:

"Let me see it."

Tom partly uncovered a dismal caricature of a house with two gable ends to it and a corkscrew of smoke issuing from the chimney. Then the girl's interest began to fasten itself upon the work and she forgot everything else. When it was finished, she gazed a moment, then whispered:

"It's nice — make a man."

The artist erected a man in the front yard, that resembled a derrick. He could have stepped over the house; but the girl was not hypercritical; she was satisfied with the monster, and whispered:

"It's a beautiful man — now make me coming along."

Tom drew an hour-glass with a full moon and straw limbs to it and armed the spreading fingers with a portentous fan. The girl said:

"It's ever so nice — I wish I could draw."

"It's easy," whispered Tom, "I'll learn you."

"Oh, will you? When?"

"At noon. Do you go home to dinner?"

"I'll stay if you will."

"Good — that's a whack. What's your name?"

"Becky Thatcher. What's yours? Oh, I know. It's Thomas Sawyer."

"That's the name they lick me by. I'm Tom when I'm good. You call me Tom, will you?"

"Yes."

Now Tom began to scrawl something on the slate, hiding the words from the girl. But she was not backward this time. She begged to see. Tom said:

"Oh, it ain't anything."

"Yes it is."

"No it ain't. You don't want to see."

"Yes I do, indeed I do. Please let me."

"You'll tell."

"No I won't — deed and deed and double deed I won't."

"You won't tell anybody at all? Ever, as long as you live?"

"No, I won't ever tell *any*body. Now let me."

"Oh, *you* don't want to see!"

"Now that you treat me so, I will see." And she put her small hand upon his and a little scuffle ensued, Tom pretending to resist in earnest but letting his hand slip by degrees till these words were revealed: "*I love you.*"

"Oh, you bad thing!" And she hit his hand a smart rap, but reddened and looked pleased, nevertheless.

Just at this juncture the boy felt a slow, fateful grip closing on his ear, and a steady lifting impulse. In that vise he was borne across the house and deposited in his own seat, under a peppering fire of giggles from the whole school. Then the master stood over him during a few awful moments, and finally moved away to his throne without saying a word. But although Tom's ear tingled, his heart was jubilant.

As the school quieted down Tom made an honest effort to study, but the turmoil within him was too great. In turn he took his place in the reading class and made a botch of it; then in the geography class and turned lakes into mountains, mountains into rivers, and rivers into continents, till chaos was come again; then in the spelling class, and got "turned down," by a succession of mere baby words, till he brought up at the foot and yielded up the pewter medal which he had worn with ostentation for months.

- There is a character in the book named Injun Joe. He's a Native American. They consider him bad because he's an "Injun," an Indian. In chapter 9 he even describes himself this way, "The Injun blood ain't in me for nothing," as if his blood, his ethnicity, caused him to act in such a bad way. He's bought into the stereotype and is fulfilling it.
- Are you aware of how you stereotype others? When do you do it? Are there stereotypes that you fall into just because it's expected of you?

Lesson 11

- Huckleberry Finn is "cordially hated and dreaded by all the mothers of the town," but he is seen as a hero by the children. What is that an example of?
- What do you know about Huck and his dad? People see Huck as a bad kid, but remember that there is always a back story. Everybody has a story.
- Read chapter 7 of *The Adventures of Tom Sawyer*.

Chapter 7
Tick-Running and a Heartbreak

The harder Tom tried to fasten his mind on his book, the more his ideas wandered. So at last, with a sigh and a yawn, he gave it up. It seemed to him that the noon recess would never come. The air was utterly dead. There was not a breath stirring. It was the sleepiest of sleepy days. The drowsing murmur of the five and twenty studying scholars soothed the soul like the spell that is in the murmur of bees. Away off in the flaming sunshine, Cardiff Hill lifted its soft green sides through a shimmering veil of heat, tinted with the purple of distance; a few birds floated on lazy wing high in the air; no other living thing was visible but some cows, and they were asleep. Tom's heart ached to be free, or else to have something of interest to do to pass the dreary time. His hand wandered into his pocket and his face lit up with a glow of gratitude that was prayer, though he did not know it. Then furtively the percussion-cap box came out. He released the tick and put him on the long flat desk. The creature probably glowed with a gratitude that amounted to prayer, too, at this moment, but it was premature: for when he started thankfully to travel off, Tom turned him aside with a pin and made him take a new direction.

Tom's bosom friend sat next him, suffering just as Tom had been, and now he was deeply and gratefully interested in this entertainment in an instant. This bosom friend was Joe Harper. The two boys were sworn friends all the week, and embattled enemies on Saturdays. Joe took a pin out of his lapel and began to assist in exercising the prisoner. The sport grew in interest momently. Soon Tom said that they were interfering with each other, and neither getting the fullest benefit of the tick. So he put Joe's slate on the desk and drew a line down the middle of it from top to bottom.

"Now," said he, "as long as he is on your side you can stir him up and I'll let him alone; but if you let him get away and get on my side, you're to leave him alone as long as I can keep him from crossing over."

"All right, go ahead; start him up."

The tick escaped from Tom, presently, and crossed the equator. Joe harassed him awhile, and then he got away and crossed back again. This change of base occurred often. While one boy was worrying the tick with absorbing interest, the other would look on with interest as strong, the two heads bowed together over the slate, and the two souls dead to all things else. At last luck seemed to settle and abide with Joe. The tick tried this, that, and the other course, and got as excited and as anxious as the boys themselves, but time and again just as he would have victory in his very grasp, so to speak, and Tom's fingers would be twitching to begin, Joe's pin would deftly head him off, and keep possession. At last Tom could stand it no longer. The temptation was too strong. So he reached out and lent a hand with his pin. Joe was angry in a moment. Said he:

"Tom, you let him alone."

"I only just want to stir him up a little, Joe."

"No, sir, it ain't fair; you just let him alone."

"Blame it, I ain't going to stir him much."

"Let him alone, I tell you."

"I won't!"

"You shall — he's on my side of the line."

"Look here, Joe Harper, whose is that tick?"

"*I* don't care whose tick he is — he's on my side of the line, and you sha'n't touch him."

"Well, I'll just bet I will, though. He's my tick and I'll do what I blame please with him, or die!"

A tremendous whack came down on Tom's shoulders, and its duplicate on Joe's; and for the space of two minutes the dust continued to fly from the two jackets and the whole school to enjoy it. The boys had been too absorbed to notice the hush that had stolen upon the school awhile before when the master came tiptoeing down the room and stood over them. He had contemplated a good part of the performance before he contributed his bit of variety to it.

When school broke up at noon, Tom flew to Becky Thatcher, and whispered in her ear:

"Put on your bonnet and let on you're going home; and when you get to the corner, give the rest of 'em the slip, and turn down through the lane and come back. I'll go the other way and come it over 'em the same way."

So the one went off with one group of scholars, and the other with another. In a little while the two met at the bottom of the lane, and when they reached the school they had it all to themselves. Then they sat together, with a slate before them, and Tom gave Becky the pencil and held her hand in his, guiding it, and so created another surprising house. When the interest in art began to wane, the two fell to talking. Tom was swimming in bliss. He said:

"Do you love rats?"

"No! I hate them!"

"Well, I do, too — *live* ones. But I mean dead ones, to swing round your head with a string."

"No, I don't care for rats much, anyway. What *I* like is chewing-gum."

"Oh, I should say so. I wish I had some now."

"Do you? I've got some. I'll let you chew it awhile, but you must give it back to me."

That was agreeable, so they chewed it turn about, and dangled their legs against the bench in excess of contentment.

"Was you ever at a circus?" said Tom.

"Yes, and my pa's going to take me again some time, if I'm good."

"I been to the circus three or four times — lots of times. Church ain't shucks to a circus. There's things going on at a circus all the time. I'm going to be a clown in a circus when I grow up."

"Oh, are you! That will be nice. They're so lovely, all spotted up."

"Yes, that's so. And they get slathers of money — most a dollar a day, Ben Rogers says. Say, Becky, was you ever engaged?"

"What's that?"

"Why, engaged to be married."

"No."

"Would you like to?"

"I reckon so. I don't know. What is it like?"

"Like? Why it ain't like anything. You only just tell a boy you won't ever have anybody but him, ever ever ever, and then you kiss and that's all. Anybody can do it."

"Kiss? What do you kiss for?"

"Why, that, you know, is to — well, they always do that."

"Everybody?"

"Why, yes, everybody that's in love with each other. Do you remember what I wrote on the slate?"

"Ye— yes."

"What was it?"

"I sha'n't tell you."

"Shall I tell *you*?"

"Ye — yes — but some other time."

"No, now."

"No, not now — to-morrow."

"Oh, no, *now*. Please, Becky — I'll whisper it, I'll whisper it ever so easy."

Becky hesitating, Tom took silence for consent, and passed his arm about her waist and whispered the tale ever so softly, with his mouth close to her ear. And then he added:

"Now you whisper it to me — just the same."

She resisted, for a while, and then said:

"You turn your face away so you can't see, and then I will. But you mustn't ever tell anybody —will you, Tom? Now you won't, will you?"

"No, indeed, indeed I won't. Now, Becky."

He turned his face away. She bent timidly around till her breath stirred his curls and whispered, "I — love — you!"

Then she sprang away and ran around and around the desks and benches, with Tom after her, and took refuge in a corner at last, with her little white apron to her face. Tom clasped her about her neck and pleaded:

"Now, Becky, it's all done — all over but the kiss. Don't you be afraid of that — it ain't anything at all. Please, Becky." And he tugged at her apron and the hands.

By and by she gave up, and let her hands drop; her face, all glowing with the struggle, came up and submitted. Tom kissed the red lips and said:

"Now it's all done, Becky. And always after this, you know, you ain't ever to love anybody but me, and you ain't ever to marry anybody but me, never never and forever. Will you?"

"No, I'll never love anybody but you, Tom, and I'll never marry anybody but you — and you ain't to ever marry anybody but me, either."

"Certainly. Of course. That's *part* of it. And always coming to school or when we're going home, you're to walk with me, when there ain't anybody looking — and you choose me and I choose you at parties, because that's the way you do when you're engaged."

"It's so nice. I never heard of it before."

"Oh, it's ever so gay! Why, me and Amy Lawrence —"

The big eyes told Tom his blunder and he stopped, confused.

"Oh, Tom! Then I ain't the first you've ever been engaged to!"

The child began to cry. Tom said:

"Oh, don't cry, Becky, I don't care for her any more."

"Yes, you do, Tom — you know you do."

Tom tried to put his arm about her neck, but she pushed him away and turned her face to the wall, and went on crying. Tom tried again, with soothing words in his mouth, and was repulsed again. Then his pride was up, and he strode away and went outside. He stood about, restless and uneasy, for a while, glancing at the door, every now and then, hoping she would repent and come to find him. But she did not. Then he began to feel badly and fear that he was in the wrong. It was a hard struggle with him to make new advances, now, but he nerved himself to it and entered. She was still standing back there in the corner, sobbing, with her face to the wall. Tom's heart smote him. He went to her and stood a moment, not knowing exactly how to proceed. Then he said hesitatingly:

"Becky, I — I don't care for anybody but you."

No reply — but sobs.

"Becky," — pleadingly. "Becky, won't you say something?"

More sobs.

Tom got out his chiefest jewel, a brass knob from the top of an andiron, and passed it around her so that she could see it, and said:

"Please, Becky, won't you take it?"

She struck it to the floor. Then Tom marched out of the house and over the hills and far away, to return to school no more that day. Presently Becky began to suspect. She ran to the door; he was not in sight; she flew around to the play-yard; he was not there. Then she called:

"Tom! Come back, Tom!"

She listened intently, but there was no answer. She had no companions but silence and loneliness. So she sat down to cry again and upbraid herself; and by this time the scholars began to gather again, and she had to hide her griefs and still her broken heart and take up the cross of a long, dreary, aching afternoon, with none among the strangers about her to exchange sorrows with.

Lesson 12

- Read chapter 8 of *The Adventures of Tom Sawyer*.

Chapter 8
A Pirate Bold to Be

Tom dodged hither and thither through lanes until he was well out of the track of returning scholars, and then fell into a moody jog. He crossed a small "branch" two or three times, because of a prevailing juvenile superstition that to cross water baffled pursuit. Half an hour later he was disappearing behind the Douglas mansion on the summit of Cardiff Hill, and the schoolhouse was hardly distinguishable away off in the valley behind him. He entered a dense wood, picked his pathless way to the center of it, and sat down on a mossy spot under a spreading oak. There was not even a zephyr stirring; the dead noonday heat had even stilled the songs of the birds; nature lay in a trance that was broken by no sound but the occasional far-off hammering of a woodpecker, and this seemed to render the pervading silence and sense of loneliness the more profound. The boy's soul was steeped in melancholy; his feelings were in happy accord with his surroundings. He sat long with his elbows on his knees and his chin in his hands, meditating. It seemed to him that life was but a trouble, at best, and he more than half envied Jimmy Hodges, so lately released; it must be very peaceful, he thought, to lie and slumber and dream forever and ever, with the wind whispering through the trees and caressing the grass and the flowers over the grave, and nothing to bother and grieve about, ever any more. If he only had a clean Sunday-school record he could be willing to go, and be done with it all. Now as to this girl. What had he done? Nothing. He had meant the best in the world, and been treated like a dog — like a very dog. She would be sorry some day — maybe when it was too late. Ah, if he could only die *temporarily*!

But the elastic heart of youth cannot be compressed into one constrained shape long at a time. Tom presently began to drift insensibly back into the concerns of this life again. What if he turned his back, now, and disappeared mysteriously? What if he went away — ever so far away, into unknown countries beyond the seas — and never came back any more! How would she feel then! The idea of being a clown recurred to him now, only to fill him with disgust. For frivolity and jokes and spotted tights were an offense, when they intruded themselves upon a spirit that was exalted into the vague august realm of the romantic. No, he would be a soldier, and return after long years, all war-worn and illustrious. No — better still, he would join the Indians, and hunt buffaloes and go on the warpath in the mountain ranges and the trackless great plains of the Far West, and away in the future come back a great chief, bristling with feathers, hideous with paint, and prance into Sunday-school, some drowsy summer morning, with a blood-curdling war-whoop, and sear the eyeballs of all his companions with unappeasable envy. But no, there was something gaudier even than this. He would be a pirate! That was it! *Now* his future lay plain before him, and glowing with unimaginable splendor. How his name would fill the world, and make people shudder! How gloriously he would go plowing the dancing seas, in his long, low, black-hulled racer, the *Spirit of the Storm*, with his grisly flag flying at the fore! And at the zenith of his fame, how he would suddenly appear at the old village and stalk into church, brown and weather-beaten, in his black velvet doublet and trunks, his great jack-boots, his crimson sash, his belt bristling with horse-pistols, his crime-rusted cutlass at his side, his slouch hat with waving plumes, his black flag unfurled, with the skull and cross-bones on it, and hear with swelling ecstasy the whisperings, "It's Tom Sawyer the Pirate! — the Black Avenger of the Spanish Main!"

Yes, it was settled; his career was determined. He would run away from home and enter upon it. He would start the very next morning. Therefore he must now begin to get ready. He would collect his resources together. He went to a rotten log near at hand and began to dig under one end of it with his Barlow knife. He soon struck wood that sounded hollow. He put his hand there and uttered this incantation impressively:

"What hasn't come here, *come*! What's here, stay here!"

Then he scraped away the dirt, and exposed a pine shingle He took it up and disclosed a shapely little treasure-house whose bottom and sides were of shingles. In it lay a marble. Tom's astonishment was boundless! He scratched his head with a perplexed air, and said:

"Well, that beats anything!"

Then he tossed the marble away pettishly, and stood cogitating. The truth was, that a superstition of his had failed, here, which he and all his comrades had always looked upon as infallible. If you buried a marble with certain necessary incantations, and left it alone a fortnight, and then opened the place with the incantation he had just used, you would find that all the marbles you had ever lost had gathered themselves together there, meantime, no matter how widely they had been separated. But, now this thing had actually and unquestionably failed. Tom's whole structure of faith was shaken to its foundations. He had many a time heard of this thing succeeding, but never of its failing before. It did not occur to him that he had tried it several times before, himself, but could never find the hiding-places afterward. He puzzled over the matter some time, and finally decided that some witch had interfered and broken the charm. He thought he would satisfy himself on that point; so he searched around till he found a small sandy spot with a little funnel-shaped depression in it. He laid himself down and put his mouth close to this depression and called:

"Doodle-bug, doodle-bug, tell me what I want to know! Doodle-bug, doodle-bug, tell me what I want to know!"

The sand began to work, and presently a small black bug appeared for a second and then darted under again in a fright.

"He dasn't tell! So it *was* a witch that done it. I just knowed it."

He well knew the futility of trying to contend against witches, so he gave up discouraged. But it occurred to him that he might as well have the marble he had just thrown away, and therefore he went and made a patient search for it. But he could not find it. Now he went back to his treasure-house and carefully placed himself just as he had been standing when he tossed the marble away; then he took another marble from his pocket and tossed it in the same way, saying:

"Brother, go find your brother!"

He watched where it stopped, and went there and looked. But it must have fallen short or gone too far, so he tried twice more. The last repetition was successful. The two marbles lay within a foot of each other.

Just here the blast of a toy tin trumpet came faintly down the green aisles of the forest. Tom flung off his jacket and trousers, turned a suspender into a belt, raked away some brush behind the rotten log, disclosing a rude bow and arrow, a lath sword and a tin trumpet, and in a moment had seized these things and bounded away, barelegged, with fluttering shirt. He presently halted under a great elm, blew an answering blast, and then began to tiptoe and look warily out, this way and that. He said cautiously — to an imaginary company:

"Hold, my merry men! Keep hid till I blow."

Now appeared Joe Harper, as airily clad and elaborately armed as Tom. Tom called:

"Hold! Who comes here into Sherwood Forest without my pass?"

"Guy of Guisborne wants no man's pass. Who art thou that — that —"

"Dares to hold such language," said Tom, prompting — for they talked "by the book," from memory.

"Who art thou that dares to hold such language?"

"I, indeed! I am Robin Hood, as thy caitiff carcass soon shall know."

"Then art thou indeed that famous outlaw? Right gladly will I dispute with thee the passes of the merry wood. Have at thee!"

They took their lath swords, dumped their other traps on the ground, struck a fencing attitude, foot to foot, and began a grave, careful combat, "two up and two down." Presently Tom said:

"Now, if you've got the hang, go it lively!"

So they "went it lively," panting and perspiring with the work. By and by Tom shouted:

"Pall! fall! Why don't you fall?"

"I sha'n't! Why don't you fall yourself? You're getting the worst of it."

"Why, that ain't anything. *I* can't fall; that ain't the way it is in the book. The book says, 'Then with one back-handed stroke he slew poor Guy of Guisborne.' You're to turn around and let me hit you in the back."

There was no getting around the authorities, so Joe turned, received the whack and fell.

"Now," said Joe, getting up, "you got to let me kill *you*. That's fair."

"Why, I can't do that, it ain't in the book."

"Well, it's blamed mean— that's all."

"Well, say, Joe, you can be Friar Tuck or Much the miller's son, and lam me with a quarter-staff; or I'll be the Sheriff of Nottingham and you be Robin Hood a little while and kill me."

This was satisfactory, and so these adventures were carried out. Then Tom became Robin Hood again, and was allowed by the treacherous nun to bleed his strength away through his neglected wound. And at last Joe, representing a whole tribe of weeping outlaws, dragged him sadly forth, gave his bow into his feeble hands, and Tom said, "Where this arrow falls, there bury poor Robin Hood under the greenwood tree." Then he shot the arrow and fell back and would have died, but he lit on a nettle and sprang up too gaily for a corpse.

The boys dressed themselves, hid their accoutrements, and went off grieving that there were no outlaws any more, and wondering what modern civilization could claim to have done to compensate for their loss. They said they would rather be outlaws a year in Sherwood Forest than President of the United States forever.

- In this chapter we read some foreshadowing. Tom thinks about wanting to become a pirate after he fights with Becky. This is foreshadowing his later travels to Jackson's Island.

Lesson 13

- Read chapter 9 of *The Adventures of Tom Sawyer*.

Chapter 9
Tragedy in the Graveyard

At half past nine, that night, Tom and Sid were sent to bed, as usual. They said their prayers, and Sid was soon asleep. Tom lay awake and waited, in restless impatience. When it seemed to him that it must be nearly daylight, he heard the clock strike ten! This was despair. He would have tossed and fidgeted, as his nerves demanded, but he was afraid he might wake Sid. So he lay still, and stared up into the dark. Everything was dismally still. By and by, out of the stillness, little, scarcely perceptible noises began to emphasize themselves. The ticking of the clock began to bring itself into notice. Old beams began to crack mysteriously. The stairs creaked faintly. Evidently spirits were abroad. A measured, muffled snore issued from Aunt Polly's chamber. And now the tiresome chirping of a cricket that no human ingenuity could locate, began. Next the ghastly ticking of a death-watch in the wall at the bed's head made Tom shudder — it meant that somebody's days were numbered. Then the howl of a far-off dog rose on the night air, and was answered by a fainter howl from a remoter distance. Tom was in an agony. At last he was satisfied that time had ceased and eternity begun; he began to doze, in spite of himself; the clock chimed eleven, but he did not hear it. And then there came, mingling with his half-formed dreams, a most melancholy caterwauling. The raising of a neighboring window disturbed him. A cry of "Scat! you devil!" and the crash of an empty bottle against the back of his aunt's woodshed brought him wide awake, and a single minute later he was dressed and out of the window and creeping along the roof of the "ell" on all fours. He "meow'd" with caution once or twice, as he went; then jumped to the roof of the woodshed and thence to the ground. Huckleberry Finn was there, with his dead cat. The boys moved off and disappeared in the gloom. At the end of half an hour they were wading through the tall grass of the graveyard.

It was a graveyard of the old-fashioned Western kind. It was on a hill, about a mile and a half from the village. It had a crazy board fence around it, which leaned inward in places, and outward the rest of the time, but stood upright nowhere. Grass and weeds grew rank over the whole cemetery. All the old graves were sunken in, there was not a tombstone on the place; round-topped, worm-eaten boards staggered over the graves, leaning for support and finding none. "Sacred to the memory of" So-and-So had been painted on them once, but it could no longer have been read, on the most of them, now, even if there had been light.

A faint wind moaned through the trees, and Tom feared it might be the spirits of the dead, complaining of being disturbed. The boys talked little, and only under their breath, for the time and the place and the pervading solemnity and silence oppressed their spirits. They found the sharp new heap they were seeking, and ensconced themselves within the protection of three great elms that grew in a bunch within a few feet of the grave.

Then they waited in silence for what seemed a long time. The hooting of a distant owl was all the sound that troubled the dead stillness. Tom's reflections grew oppressive. He must force some talk. So he said in a whisper:

"Hucky, do you believe the dead people like it for us to be here?"

Huckleberry whispered:

"I wisht I knowed. It's awful solemn like, *ain't* it?"

"I bet it is."

There was a considerable pause, while the boys canvassed this matter inwardly. Then Tom whispered:

"Say, Hucky — do you reckon Hoss Williams hears us talking?"

"O' course he does. Least his sperrit does."

Tom, after a pause:

"I wish I'd said *Mister* Williams. But I never meant any harm. Everybody calls him Hoss."

"A body can't be too partic'lar how they talk 'bout these yer dead people, Tom."

This was a damper, and conversation died again.

Presently Tom seized his comrade's arm and said:

"'Sh!"

"What is it, Tom?" And the two clung together with beating hearts.

"'Sh! There 'tis again! Didn't you hear it?"

"There! Now you hear it."

"Lord, Tom, they're coming! They're coming, sure. What'll we do?"

"I dono. Think they'll see us?"

"Oh, Tom, they can see in the dark, same as cats. I wisht I hadn't come."

"Oh, don't be afeard. *I* don't believe they'll bother us. We ain't doing any harm. If we keep perfectly still, maybe they won't notice us at all."

"I'll try to, Tom, but Lord, I'm all of a shiver."

"Listen!"

The boys bent their heads together and scarcely breathed. A muffled sound of voices floated up from the far end of the graveyard.

"Look! See there!" whispered Tom. "What is it?"

"It's devil-fire. Oh, Tom, this is awful."

Some vague figures approached through the gloom, swinging an old-fashioned tin lantern that freckled the ground with innumerable little spangles of light. Presently Huckleberry whispered with a shudder:

“It’s the devils, sure enough. Three of ‘em! Lordy, Tom, we’re goners! Can you pray?”

“I’ll try, but don’t you be afeard. They ain’t going to hurt us. Now I lay me down to sleep, I—”

“’Sh!”

“What is it, Huck?”

“They’re *humans*! One of ‘em is, anyway. One of ‘em’s old Muff Potter’s voice.”

“No — tain’t so, is it?”

“I bet I know it. Don’t you stir nor budge. *He* ain’t sharp enough to notice us. Drunk, the same as usual, likely — blamed old rip!”

“All right, I’ll keep still. Now they’re stuck. Can’t find it. Here they come again. Now they’re hot. Cold again. Hot again. Red hot! They’re p’inted right, this time. Say, Huck, I know another o’ them voices; it’s Injun Joe.”

“That’s so — that murderin’ half-breed! I’d druther they was devils a dern sight. What kin they be up to?”

The whisper died wholly out, now, for the three men had reached the grave and stood within a few feet of the boys’ hiding-place.

“Here it is,” said the third voice; and the owner of it held the lantern up and revealed the face of young Dr. Robinson.

Potter and Injun Joe were carrying a handbarrow with a rope and a couple of shovels on it. They cast down their load and began to open the grave. The doctor put the lantern at the head of the grave and came and sat down with his back against one of the elm trees. He was so close the boys could have touched him.

"Hurry, men!" he said in a low voice; "the moon might come out at any moment.

They growled a response and went on digging. For some time there was no noise but the grating sound of the spades discharging their freight of mold and gravel. It was very monotonous. Finally a spade struck upon the coffin with a dull woody accent, and within another minute or two the men had hoisted it out on the ground. They pried off the lid with their shovels, got out the body and dumped it rudely on the ground. The moon drifted from behind the clouds and exposed the pallid face. The barrow was got ready and the corpse placed on it, covered with a blanket, and bound to its place with the rope. Potter took out a large spring-knife and cut off the dangling end of the rope and then said:

"Now the cussed thing's ready, Sawbones, and you'll just out with another five, or here she stays."

"That's the talk!" said Injun Joe.

"Look here, what does this mean?" said the doctor. "You required your pay in advance, and I've paid you."

"Yes, and you done more than that," said Injun Joe, approaching the doctor, who was now standing. "Five years ago you drove me away from your father's kitchen one night, when I come to ask for something to eat, and you said I warn't there for any good; and when I swore I'd get even with you if it took a hundred years, your father had me jailed for a vagrant. Did you think I'd forget? The Injun blood ain't in me for nothing. And now I've got you, and you got to *settle*, you know!"

He was threatening the doctor, with his fist in his face, by this time. The doctor struck out suddenly and stretched the ruffian on the ground. Potter dropped his knife, and exclaimed:

"Here, now, don't you hit my pard!" and the next moment he had grappled with the doctor and the two were struggling with might and main, trampling the grass and tearing the ground with their heels. Injun Joe sprang to his feet, his eyes flaming with passion, snatched up Potter's knife, and went creeping, catlike and stooping, round and round about the combatants, seeking an opportunity. All at once the doctor flung himself free, seized the heavy head-board of Williams' grave and felled Potter to the earth with it — and in the same instant the half-breed saw his chance and drove the knife to the hilt in the young man's breast. He reeled and fell partly upon Potter, flooding him with his blood, and in the same moment the clouds blotted out the dreadful spectacle and the two frightened boys went speeding away in the dark.

Presently, when the moon emerged again, Injun Joe was standing over the two forms, contemplating them. The doctor murmured inarticulately, gave a long gasp or two and was still. The half-breed muttered:

"*That* score is settled — damn you."

Then he robbed the body. After which he put the fatal knife in Potter's open right hand, and sat down on the dismantled coffin. Three — four — five minutes passed, and then Potter began to stir and moan. His hand closed upon the knife; he raised it, glanced at it, and let it fall, with a shudder. Then he sat up, pushing the body from him, and gazed at it, and then around him, confusedly. His eyes met Joe's.

"Lord, how is this, Joe?" he said.

"It's a dirty business," said Joe, without moving. "What did you do it for?"

"I! I never done it!"

"Look here! That kind of talk won't wash."

Potter trembled and grew white.

"I thought I'd got sober. I'd no business to drink to-night. But it's in my head yet — worse'n when we started here. I'm all in a muddle; can't recollect anything of it, hardly. Tell me, Joe — honest, now, old feller — did I do it? Joe, I never meant to — 'pon my soul and honor, I never meant to, Joe. Tell me how it was, Joe. Oh, it's awful — and him so young and promising."

"Why, you two was scuffling, and he fetched you one with the headboard and you fell flat; and then up you come, all reeling and staggering, like, and snatched the knife and jammed it into him, just as he fetched you another awful clip — and here you've laid, as dead as a wedge till now."

"Oh, I didn't know what I was a-doing. I wish I may die this minute if I did. It was all on account of the whisky; and the excitement, I reckon. I never used a weepon in my life before, Joe. I've fought, but never with weepons. They'll all say that. Joe, don't tell! Say you won't tell, Joe — that's a good feller. I always liked you, Joe, and stood up for you, too. Don't you remember? You *won't* tell, *will* you, Joe?" And the poor creature dropped on his knees before the stolid murderer, and clasped his appealing hands.

"No, you've always been fair and square with me, Muff Potter, and I won't go back on you. There, now, that's as fair as a man can say."

"Oh, Joe, you're an angel. I'll bless you for this the longest day I live." And Potter began to cry.

"Come, now, that's enough of that. This ain't any time for blubbering. You be off yonder way and I'll go this. Move, now, and don't leave any tracks behind you."

Potter started on a trot that quickly increased to a run. The half-breed stood looking after him. He muttered:

"If he's as much stunned with the lick and fuddled with the rum as he had the look of being, he won't think of the knife till he's gone so far he'll be afraid to come back after it to such a place by himself — chicken-heart!"

Two or three minutes later the murdered man, the blanketed corpse, the lidless coffin, and the open grave were under no inspection but the moon's. The stillness was complete again, too.

- Here are some more notes from the book. Before Huck and Tom go to the graveyard, Tom hears a ticking clock. It is described as a "deathwatch" and it terrifies him. Then Mr. Robinson dies, so the foreshadowing was for the murder in the graveyard.

- How does suspense build in this chapter?

Lesson 14

- Read chapter 10 of *The Adventures of Tom Sawyer*.

Chapter 10
Dire Prophecy of the Howling Dog

The two boys flew on and on, toward the village, speechless with horror. They glanced backward over their shoulders from time to time, apprehensively, as if they feared they might be followed. Every stump that started up in their path seemed a man and an enemy, and made them catch their breath; and as they sped by some outlying cottages that lay near the village, the barking of the aroused watch-dogs seemed to give wings to their feet.

“If we can only get to the old tannery before we break down!” whispered Tom, in short catches between breaths, “I can’t stand it much longer.”

Huckleberry’s hard pantings were his only reply, and the boys fixed their eyes on the goal of their hopes and bent to their work to win it. They gained steadily on it, and at last, breast to breast, they burst through the open door and fell grateful and exhausted in the sheltering shadows beyond. By and by their pulses slowed down, and Tom whispered:

“Huckleberry, what do you reckon’ll come of this?”

“If Dr. Robinson dies, I reckon hanging’ll come of it.”

“Do you though?”

"Why, I *know* it, Tom."

Tom thought awhile, then he said:

"Who'll tell? We?"

"What are you talking about? S'pose something happened and Injun Joe *didn't* hang? Why he'd kill us some time or other, just as dead sure as we're a-laying here."

"That's just what I was thinking to myself, Huck."

"If anybody tells, let Muff Potter do it, if he's fool enough. He's generally drunk enough."

Tom said nothing — went on thinking. Presently he whispered:

"Huck, Muff Potter don't know it. How can he tell?"

"What's the reason he don't know it?"

"Because he'd just got that whack when Injun Joe done it. D' you reckon he could see anything? D' you reckon he knowed anything?"

"By hokey, that's so, Tom!"

"And besides, look-a-here — maybe that whack done for *him*!"

"No, tain't likely, Tom. He had liquor in him; I could see that; and besides, he always has. Well, when pap's full, you might take and belt him over the head with a church and you couldn't phase him. He says so, his own self. So it's the same with Muff Potter, of course. But if a man was dead sober, I reckon maybe that whack might fetch him; I dono."

After another reflective silence, Tom said:

"Hucky, you sure you can keep mum?"

"Tom, we *got* to keep mum. *You* know that. That Injun devil wouldn't make any more of drownding us than a couple of cats, if we was to squeak 'bout this and they didn't hang him. Now, look-a-here, Tom, less take and swear to one another — that's what we got to do — swear to keep mum."

"I'm agreed. It's the best thing. Would you just hold hands and swear that we —"

"Oh, no, that wouldn't do for this. That's good enough for little rubbishy common things — specially with gals, cuz *they* go back on you anyway, and blab if they get in a huff — but there orter be writing 'bout a big thing like this. And blood."

Tom's whole being applauded this idea. It was deep, and dark, and awful; the hour, the circumstances, the surroundings, were in keeping with it. He picked up a clean pine shingle that lay in the moonlight, took a little fragment of "red keel" out of his pocket, got the moon on his work, and painfully scrawled these lines, emphasizing each slow down-stroke by clamping his tongue between his teeth, and letting up the pressure on the up-strokes.

Huckleberry was filled with admiration of Tom's facility in writing, and the sublimity of his language. He at once took a pin from his lapel and was going to prick his flesh, but Tom said:

"Hold on! Don't do that. A pin's brass. It might have verdigrease on it."

"What's verdigrease?"

"It's p'ison. That's what it is. You just swaller some of it once — you'll see."

So Tom unwound the thread from one of his needles, and each boy pricked the ball of his thumb and squeezed out a drop of blood. In time, after many squeezes, Tom managed to sign his initials, using the ball of his little finger for a pen. Then he showed Huckleberry how to make an H and an F, and the oath was complete. They buried the shingle close to the wall, with some dismal ceremonies and incantations, and the fetters that bound their tongues were considered to be locked and the key thrown away.

> *"Huck Finn and Tom Sawyer swears they will keep mum about this and they wish they may drop down dead in their tracks if they ever tell and rot."*

A figure crept stealthily through a break in the other end of the ruined building, now, but they did not notice it.

"Tom," whispered Huckleberry, "does this keep us from *ever* telling — *always*?"

"Of course it does. It don't make any difference *what* happens, we got to keep mum. We'd drop down dead — don't *you* know that?"

"Yes, I reckon that's so."

They continued to whisper for some little time. Presently a dog set up a long, lugubrious howl just outside — within ten feet of them. The boys clasped each other suddenly, in an agony of fright.

"Which of us does he mean?" gasped Huckleberry.

"I dono — peep through the crack. Quick!"

"No, *you*, Tom!"

"I can't— I can't *do* it, Huck!"

"Please, Tom. There 'tis again!"

"Oh, lordy, I'm thankful!" whispered Tom. "I know his voice. It's Bull Harbison."[2]

"Oh, that's good — I tell you, Tom, I was most scared to death; I'd 'a' bet anything it was a *stray* dog."

The dog howled again. The boys' hearts sank once more.

"Oh, my! that ain't no Bull Harbison!" whispered Huckleberry. "*Do*, Tom!"

Tom, quaking with fear, yielded, and put his eye to the crack. His whisper was hardly audible when he said:

"Oh, Huck, IT'S A STRAY DOG!"

"Quick, Tom, quick! Who does he mean?"

"Huck, he must mean us both — we're right together."

"Oh, Tom, I reckon we're goners. I reckon there ain't no mistake 'bout where *I'll* go to. I been so wicked."

"Dad fetch it! This comes of playing hookey and doing everything a feller's told not to do. I might 'a' been good, like Sid, if I'd 'a' tried — but no, I wouldn't, of course. But if ever I get off this time, I lay I'll just *waller* in Sunday-schools!" And Tom began to snuffle a little.

---

[2] If Mr. Harbison had owned a slave named Bull, Tom would have spoken of him as "Harbison's Bull," but a son or a dog of that name was "Bull Harbison."

"*You* bad!" and Huckleberry began to snuffle too. "Consound it, Tom Sawyer, you're just old pie, 'longside o' what I am. Oh, *lordy*, lordy, lordy, I wisht I only had half your chance."

Tom choked off and whispered:

"Look, Hucky, look! He's got his *back* to us!"

Hucky looked, with joy in his heart.

"Well, he has, by jingoes! Did he before?"

"Yes, he did. But I, like a fool, never thought. Oh, this is bully, you know. *Now* who can he mean?"

The howling stopped. Tom pricked up his ears.

"'Sh! What's that?" he whispered.

"Sounds like — like hogs grunting. No — it's somebody snoring, Tom."

"That is it! Where'bouts is it, Huck?"

"I bleeve it's down at 'tother end. Sounds so, anyway. Pap used to sleep there, sometimes, 'long with the hogs, but laws bless you, he just lifts things when he snores. Besides, I reckon he ain't ever coming back to this town any more."

The spirit of adventure rose in the boys' souls once more.

"Hucky, do you das't to go if I lead?"

"I don't like to, much. Tom, s'pose it's Injun Joe!"

Tom quailed. But presently the temptation rose up strong again and the boys agreed to try, with the understanding that they would take to their heels if the snoring stopped. So they went tiptoeing stealthily down, the one behind the other. When they had got to within five steps of the snorer, Tom stepped on a stick, and it broke with a sharp snap. The man moaned, writhed a little, and his face came into the moonlight. It was Muff Potter. The boys' hearts had stood still, and their hopes too, when the man moved, but their fears passed away now. They tiptoed out, through the broken weather-boarding, and stopped at a little distance to exchange a parting word. That long, lugubrious howl rose on the night air again! They turned and saw the strange dog standing within a few feet of where Potter was lying, and *facing* Potter, with his nose pointing heavenward.

"Oh, geeminy, it's him!" exclaimed both boys, in a breath.

"Say, Tom — they say a stray dog come howling around Johnny Miller's house, 'bout midnight, as much as two weeks ago; and a whippoorwill come in and lit on the banisters and sung, the very same evening; and there ain't anybody dead there yet."

"Well, I know that. And suppose there ain't. Didn't Grade Miller fall in the kitchen fire and burn herself terrible the very next Saturday?"

"Yes, but she ain't *dead*. And what's more, she's getting better, too."

"All right, you wait and see. She's a goner, just as dead sure as Muff Potter's a goner. That's what the negros say, and they know all about these kind of things, Huck."

Then they separated, cogitating. When Tom crept in at his bedroom window the night was almost spent. He undressed with excessive caution, and fell asleep congratulating himself that nobody knew of his escapade. He was not aware that the gently snoring Sid was awake, and had been so for an hour.

When Tom awoke, Sid was dressed and gone. There was a late look in the light, a late sense in the atmosphere. He was startled. Why had he not been called — persecuted till he was up, as usual? The thought filled him with bodings. Within five minutes he was dressed and down-stairs, feeling sore and drowsy. The family were still at table, but they had finished breakfast. There was no voice of rebuke; but there were averted eyes; there was a silence and an air of solemnity that struck a chill to the culprit's heart. He sat down and tried to seem gay, but it was up-hill work; it roused no smile, no response, and he lapsed into silence and let his heart sink down to the depths.

After breakfast his aunt took him aside, and Tom almost brightened in the hope that he was going to be flogged; but it was not so. His aunt wept over him and asked him how he could go and break her old heart so; and finally told him to go on, and ruin himself and bring her gray hairs with sorrow to the grave, for it was no use for her to try any more. This was worse than a thousand whippings, and Tom's heart was sorer now than his body. He cried, he pleaded for forgiveness, promised to reform over and over again, and then received his dismissal, feeling that he had won but an imperfect forgiveness and established but a feeble confidence.

He left the presence too miserable to even feel revengeful toward Sid; and so the latter's prompt retreat through the back gate was unnecessary. He moped to school gloomy and sad, and took his flogging, along with Joe Harper, for playing hookey the day before, with the air of one whose heart was busy with heavier woes and wholly dead to trifles. Then he betook himself to his seat, rested his elbows on his desk and his jaws in his hands, and stared at the wall with the stony stare of suffering that has reached the limit and can no further go. His elbow was pressing against some hard substance. After a long time he slowly and sadly changed his position, and took up this object with a sigh. It was in a paper. He unrolled it. A long, lingering, colossal sigh followed, and his heart broke. It was his brass andiron knob!

This final feather broke the camel's back.

- We see superstition again in this chapter. What does 1 Timothy 4:7 have to say about it?

Lesson 15

- Read chapters 11 and 12 of *The Adventures of Tom Sawyer*.

Chapter 11
Conscience Racks Tom

Close upon the hour of noon the whole village was suddenly electrified with the ghastly news. No need of the as yet undreamed-of telegraph; the tale flew from man to man, from group to group, from house to house, with little less than telegraphic speed. Of course the schoolmaster gave holiday for that afternoon; the town would have thought strangely of him if he had not.

A gory knife had been found close to the murdered man, and it had been recognized by somebody as belonging to Muff Potter — so the story ran. And it was said that a belated citizen had come upon Potter washing himself in the "branch" about one or two o'clock in the morning, and that Potter had at once sneaked off — suspicious circumstances, especially the washing, which was not a habit with Potter. It was also said that the town had been ransacked for this "murderer" (the public are not slow in the matter of sifting evidence and arriving at a verdict), but that he could not be found. Horsemen had departed down all the roads in every direction, and the Sheriff "was confident" that he would be captured before night.

All the town was drifting toward the graveyard. Tom's heartbreak vanished and he joined the procession, not because he would not a thousand times rather go anywhere else, but because an awful, unaccountable fascination drew him on. Arrived at the dreadful place, he wormed his small body through the crowd and saw the dismal spectacle. It seemed to him an age since he was there before. Somebody pinched his arm. He turned, and his eyes met Huckleberry's. Then both looked elsewhere at once, and wondered if anybody had noticed anything in their mutual glance. But everybody was talking, and intent upon the grisly spectacle before them.

"Poor fellow!" "Poor young fellow!" "This ought to be a lesson to grave-robbers!" "Muff Potter'll hang for this if they catch him!" This was the drift of remark; and the minister said, "It was a judgment; His hand is here."

Now Tom shivered from head to heel; for his eye fell upon the stolid face of Injun Joe. At this moment the crowd began to sway and struggle, and voices shouted, "It's him! it's him! he's coming himself!"

"Who? Who?" from twenty voices.

"Muff Potter!"

"Hallo, he's stopped! — Look out, he's turning! Don't let him get away!"

People in the branches of the trees over Tom's head said he wasn't trying to get away — he only looked doubtful and perplexed.

"Infernal impudence!" said a bystander; "wanted to come and take a quiet look at his work, I reckon — didn't expect any company."

The crowd fell apart, now, and the Sheriff came through, ostentatiously leading Potter by the arm. The poor fellow's face was haggard, and his eyes showed the fear that was upon him. When he stood before the murdered man, he shook as with a palsy, and he put his face in his hands and burst into tears.

"I didn't do it, friends," he sobbed; "'pon my word and honor I never done it."

"Who's accused you?" shouted a voice.

This shot seemed to carry home. Potter lifted his face and looked around him with a pathetic hopelessness in his eyes. He saw Injun Joe, and exclaimed:

"Oh, Injun Joe, you promised me you'd never —"

"Is that your knife?" and it was thrust before him by the Sheriff.

Potter would have fallen if they had not caught him and eased him to the ground. Then he said:

"Something told me 't if I didn't come back and get —" He shuddered; then waved his nerveless hand with a vanquished gesture and said, "Tell 'em, Joe, tell 'em — it ain't any use any more."

Then Huckleberry and Tom stood dumb and staring, and heard the stony-hearted liar reel off his serene statement, they expecting every moment that the clear sky would deliver God's lightnings upon his head, and wondering to see how long the stroke was delayed. And when he had finished and still stood alive and whole, their wavering impulse to break their oath and save the poor betrayed prisoner's life faded and vanished away, for plainly this miscreant had sold himself to Satan and it would be fatal to meddle with the property of such a power as that.

"Why didn't you leave? What did you want to come here for?" somebody said.

"I couldn't help it— I couldn't help it," Potter moaned. "I wanted to run away, but I couldn't seem to come anywhere but here." And he fell to sobbing again.

Injun Joe repeated his statement, just as calmly, a few minutes afterward on the inquest, under oath; and the boys, seeing that the lightnings were still withheld, were confirmed in their belief that Joe had sold himself to the devil. He was now become, to them, the most balefully interesting object they had ever looked upon, and they could not take their fascinated eyes from his face.

They inwardly resolved to watch him, nights, when opportunity should offer, in the hope of getting a glimpse of his dread master.

Injun Joe helped to raise the body of the murdered man and put it in a wagon for removal; and it was whispered through the shuddering crowd that the wound bled a little! The boys thought that this happy circumstance would turn suspicion in the right direction; but they were disappointed, for more than one villager remarked:

"It was within three feet of Muff Potter when it done it."

Tom's fearful secret and gnawing conscience disturbed his sleep for as much as a week after this; and at breakfast one morning Sid said:

"Tom, you pitch around and talk in your sleep so much that you keep me awake half the time."

Tom blanched and dropped his eyes.

"It's a bad sign," said Aunt Polly, gravely. "What you got on your mind, Tom?"

"Nothing. Nothing 't I know of." But the boy's hand shook so that he spilled his coffee.

"And you do talk such stuff," Sid said. "Last night you said 'it's blood, it's blood, that's what it is!' You said that over and over. And you said, 'Don't torment me so— I'll tell!' Tell *what*? What is it you'll tell?"

Everything was swimming before Tom. There is no telling what might have happened, now, but luckily the concern passed out of Aunt Polly's face and she came to Tom's relief without knowing it. She said:

"Sho! It's that dreadful murder. I dream about it most every night myself. Sometimes I dream it's me that done it."

Mary said she had been affected much the same way. Sid seemed satisfied. Tom got out of the presence as quick as he plausibly could, and after that he complained of toothache for a week, and tied up his jaws every night. He never knew that Sid lay nightly watching, and frequently slipped the bandage free and then leaned on his elbow listening a good while at a time, and afterward slipped the bandage back to its place again. Tom's distress of mind wore off gradually and the toothache grew irk- some and was discarded. If Sid really managed to make anything out of Tom's disjointed mutterings, he kept it to himself.

It seemed to Tom that his schoolmates never would get done holding inquests on dead cats, and thus keeping his trouble present to his mind. Sid noticed that Tom never was coroner at one of these inquiries, though it had been his habit to take the lead in all new enterprises; he noticed, too, that Tom never acted as a witness — and that was strange; and Sid did not overlook the fact that Tom even showed a marked aversion to these inquests, and always avoided them when he could. Sid marveled, but said nothing. However, even inquests went out of vogue at last, and ceased to torture Tom's conscience.

Every day or two, during this time of sorrow, Tom watched his opportunity and went to the little grated jail-window and smuggled such small comforts through to the "murderer" as he could get hold of. The jail was a trifling little brick den that stood in a marsh at the edge of the village, and no guards were afforded for it; indeed it was seldom occupied. These offerings greatly helped to ease Tom's conscience.

The villagers had a strong desire to tar and feather Injun Joe and ride him on a rail, for body-snatching, but so formidable was his character that nobody could be found who was willing to take the lead in the matter, so it was dropped. He had been careful to begin both of his inquest statements with the fight, without confessing the grave-robbery that preceded it; therefore it was deemed wisest not to try the case in the courts at present.

Chapter 12
The Cat amd the Pain-Killer

One of the reasons why Tom's mind had drifted away from its secret troubles was, that it had found a new and weighty matter to interest itself about. Becky Thatcher had stopped coming to school. Tom had struggled with his pride a few days, and tried to "whistle her down the wind," but failed. He began to find himself hanging around her father's house, nights, and feeling very miserable. She was ill. What if she should die! There was distraction in the thought. He no longer took an interest in war, nor even in piracy. The charm of life was gone; there was nothing but dreariness left. He put his hoop away, and his bat; there was no joy in them any more. His aunt was concerned. She began to try all manner of remedies on him. She was one of those people who are infatuated with patent medicines and all new-fangled methods of producing health or mending it. She was an inveterate experimenter in these things. When something fresh in this line came out she was in a fever, right away, to try it; not on herself, for she was never ailing, but on anybody else that came handy. She was a subscriber for all the "Health" periodicals and phrenological frauds; and the solemn ignorance they were inflated with was breath to her nostrils. All the "rot" they contained about ventilation, and how to go to bed, and how to get up, and what to eat, and what to drink, and how much exercise to take, and what frame of mind to keep one's self in, and what sort of clothing to wear, was all gospel to her, and she never observed that her health-journals of the current month customarily upset everything they had recommended the month before. She was as simple-hearted and honest as the day was long, and so she was an easy victim. She gathered together her quack periodicals and her quack medicines, and thus armed with death, went about on her pale horse, metaphorically speaking, with "hell following after." But she never suspected that she was not an angel of healing and the balm of Gilead in disguise, to the suffering neighbors.

The water treatment was new, now, and Tom's low condition was a windfall to her. She had him out at daylight every morning, stood him up in the woodshed and drowned him with a deluge of cold water; then she scrubbed him down with a towel like a file, and so brought him to; then she rolled him up in a wet sheet and put him away under blankets till she sweated his soul clean and "the yellow stains of it came through his pores" — as Tom said.

Yet notwithstanding all this, the boy grew more and more melancholy and pale and dejected. She added hot baths, sitz baths, shower baths, and plunges. The boy remained as dismal as a hearse. She began to assist the water with a slim oatmeal diet and blister-plasters. She calculated his capacity as she would a jug's, and filled him up every day with quack cure-alls.

Tom had become indifferent to persecution by this time. This phase filled the old lady's heart with consternation. This indifference must be broken up at any cost. Now she heard of Pain-killer for the first time. She ordered a lot at once. She tasted it and was filled with gratitude. It was simply fire in a liquid form. She dropped the water treatment and everything else, and pinned her faith to Pain-killer. She gave Tom a teaspoonful and watched with the deepest anxiety for the result. Her troubles were instantly at rest, her soul at peace again; for the "indifference" was broken up. The boy could not have shown a wilder, heartier interest if she had built a fire under him.

Tom felt that it was time to wake up; this sort of life might be romantic enough, in his blighted condition, but it was getting to have too little sentiment and too much distracting variety about it. So he thought over various plans for relief, and finally hit upon that of professing to be fond of Pain-killer. He asked for it so often that he became a nuisance, and his aunt ended by telling him to help himself and quit bothering her. If it had been Sid, she would have had no misgivings to alloy her delight; but since it was Tom, she watched the bottle clandestinely. She found that the medicine did really diminish, but it did not occur to her that the boy was mending the health of a crack in the sitting-room floor with it.

One day Tom was in the act of dosing the crack when his aunt's yellow cat came along, purring, eying the teaspoon avariciously, and begging for a taste. Tom said:

Don't ask for it unless you want it, Peter."

But Peter signified that he did want it.

"You better make sure."

Peter was sure.

"Now you've asked for it, and I'll give it to you, because there ain't anything mean about me; but if you find you don't like it, you mustn't blame anybody but your own self."

Peter was agreeable. So Tom pried his mouth open and poured down the Pain-killer. Peter sprang a couple of yards in the air, and then delivered a war-whoop and set off round and round the room, banging against furniture, upsetting flower-pots, and making general havoc. Next he rose on his hind feet and pranced around, in a frenzy of enjoyment, with his head over his shoulder and his voice proclaiming his unappeasable happiness. Then he went tearing around the house again spreading chaos and destruction in his path. Aunt Polly entered in time to see him throw a few double somersets, deliver a final mighty hurrah, and sail through the open window, carrying the rest of the flower-pots with him. The old lady stood petrified with astonishment, peering over herglasses; Tom lay on the floor expiring with laughter.

"Tom, what on earth ails that cat?"

"*I* don't know, aunt," gasped the boy.

"Why, I never see anything like it. What *did* make him act so?"

"'Deed I don't know, Aunt Polly; cats always act so when they're having a good time."

"They do, do they?" There was something in the tone that made Tom apprehensive.

"Yes'm. That is, I believe they do."

"You *do*?"

"Yes'm."

The old lady was bending down, Tom watching, with interest emphasized by anxiety. Too late he divined her "drift." The handle of the telltale teaspoon was visible tinder the bed-valance. Aunt Polly took it, held it up. Tom winced, and dropped his eyes. Aunt Polly raised him by the usual handle — his ear — and cracked his head soundly with her thimble.

"Now, sir, what did you want to treat that poor dumb beast so for?"

"I done it out of pity for him — because he hadn't any aunt."

"Hadn't any aunt! — you numskull. What has that got to do with it?"

"Heaps. Because if he'd 'a' had one she'd 'a' burnt him out herself! She'd 'a' roasted his bowels out of him 'thout any more feeling than if he was a human!"

Aunt Polly felt a sudden pang of remorse. This was putting the thing in a new light; what was cruelty to a cat *might* be cruelty to a boy, too. She began to soften; she felt sorry. Her eyes watered a little, and she put her hand on Tom's head and said gently:

"I was meaning for the best, Tom. And, Tom, it *did* do you good."

Tom looked up in her face with just a perceptible twinkle peeping through his gravity:

"I know you was meaning for the best, auntie, and so was I with Peter. It done *him* good, too. I never see him get around so since —"

"Oh, go 'long with you, Tom, before you aggravate me again. And you try and see if you can't be a good boy, for once, and you needn't take any more medicine."

Tom reached school ahead of time. It was noticed that this strange thing had been occurring every day latterly. And now, as usual of late, he hung about the gate of the schoolyard instead of playing with his comrades. He was sick, he said, and he looked it. He tried to seem to be looking everywhere but whither he really was looking — down the road. Presently Jeff Thatcher hove in sight, and Tom's face lighted; he gazed a moment, and then turned sorrowfully away. When Jeff arrived, Tom accosted him, and "led up" warily to opportunities for remark about Becky, but the giddy lad never could see the bait. Tom watched and watched, hoping whenever a frisking frock came in sight, and hating the owner of it as soon as he saw she was not the right one. At last frocks ceased to appear, and he dropped hopelessly into the dumps; he entered the empty school-house and sat down to suffer. Then one more frock passed in at the gate, and Tom's heart gave a great bound. The next instant he was out, and "going on" like an Indian; yelling, laughing, chasing boys, jumping over the fence at risk, of life and limb, throwing hand-springs, standing on his head — doing all the heroic things he could conceive of, and keeping a furtive eye out, all the while, to see if Becky Thatcher was noticing. But she seemed to be unconscious of it all; she never looked. Could it be possible that she was not aware that he was there? He carried his exploits to her immediate vicinity; came war- whooping around, snatched a boy's cap, hurled it to the roof of the school-house, broke through a group of boys, tumbling them in every direction, and fell sprawling, himself, under Becky's nose, almost upsetting her — and she turned, with her nose in the air, and he heard her say: "Mf! some people think they're mighty smart — always showing off!"

Tom's cheeks burned. He gathered himself up and sneaked off, crushed and crestfallen.

Lesson 16

- Read chapter 13 of *The Adventures of Tom Sawyer*.

Chapter 13
The Pirate Crew Set Sail

Tom's mind was made up now. He was gloomy and desperate. He was a forsaken, friendless boy, he said; nobody loved him; when they found out what they had driven him to, perhaps they would be sorry; he had tried to do right and get along, but they would not let him; since nothing would do them but to be rid of him, let it be so; and let them blame him for the consequences — why shouldn't they? What right had the friendless to complain? Yes, they had forced him to it at last: he would lead a life of crime. There was no choice.

By this time he was far down Meadow Lane, and the bell for school to "take up" tinkled faintly upon his ear. He sobbed, now, to think he should never, never hear that old familiar sound any more — it was very hard, but it was forced on him; since he was driven out into the cold world, he must submit — but he forgave them. Then the sobs came thick and fast.

Just at this point he met his soul's sworn comrade, Joe Harper — hard-eyed, and with evidently a great and dismal purpose in his heart. Plainly here were "two souls with but a single thought." Tom, wiping his eyes with his sleeve, began to blubber out something about a resolution to escape from hard usage and lack of sympathy at home by roaming abroad into the great world never to return; and ended by hoping that Joe would not forget him.

But it transpired that this was a request which Joe had just been going to make of Tom, and had come to hunt him up for that purpose. His mother had whipped him for drinking some cream which he had never tasted and knew nothing about; it was plain that she was tired of him and wished him to go; if she felt that way, there was nothing for him to do but succumb; he hoped she would be happy, and never regret having driven her poor boy out into the unfeeling world to suffer and die.

As the two boys walked sorrowing along, they made a new compact to stand by each other and be brothers and never separate till death relieved them of their troubles. Then they began to lay their plans. Joe was for being a hermit, and living on crusts in a remote cave, and dying, some time, of cold and want and grief; but after listening to Tom, he conceded that there were some conspicuous advantages about a life of crime, and so he consented to be a pirate.

Three miles below St. Petersburg, at a point where the Mississippi River was a trifle over a mile wide, there was a long, narrow, wooded island, with a shallow bar at the head of it, and this offered well as a rendezvous. It was not inhabited; it lay far over toward the further shore, abreast a dense and almost wholly unpeopled forest. So Jackson's Island was chosen. Who were to be the subjects of their piracies, was a matter that did not occur to them. Then they hunted up Huckleberry Finn, and he joined them promptly, for all careers were one to him; he was indifferent. They presently separated to meet at a lonely spot on the river-bank two miles above the village at the favorite hour — which was midnight. There was a small log raft there which they meant to capture. Each would bring hooks and lines, and such provision as he could steal in the most dark and mysterious way — as became outlaws. And before the afternoon was done, they had all managed to enjoy the sweet glory of spreading the fact that pretty soon the town would "hear something." All who got this vague hint were cautioned to "be mum and wait."

About midnight Tom arrived with a boiled ham and a few trifles, and stopped in a dense undergrowth on a small bluff overlooking the meeting-place. It was starlight, and very still. The mighty river lay like an ocean at rest. Tom listened a moment, but no sound disturbed the quiet. Then he gave a low, distinct whistle. It was answered from under the bluff. Tom whistled twice more; these signals were answered in the same way. Then a guarded voice said:

"Who goes there?"

"Tom Sawyer, the Black Avenger of the Spanish Main. Name your names."

"Huck Finn the Red-Handed, and Joe Harper the Terror of the Seas." Tom had furnished these titles, from his favorite literature.

"'Tis well. Give the countersign."

Two hoarse whispers delivered the same awful word simultaneously to the brooding night:

"BLOOD!"

Then Tom tumbled his ham over the bluff and let himself down after it, tearing both skin and clothes to some extent in the effort. There was an easy, comfortable path along the shore under the bluff, but it lacked the advantages of difficulty and danger so valued by a pirate.

The Terror of the Seas had brought a side of bacon, and had about worn himself out with getting it there. Finn the Red-Handed had stolen a skillet and a quantity of half-cured leaf tobacco, and had also brought a few corn-cobs to make pipes with. But none of the pirates smoked or “chewed” but himself. The Black Avenger of the Spanish Main said it would never do to start without some fire. That was a wise thought; matches were hardly known there in that day. They saw a fire smoldering upon a great raft a hundred yards above, and they went stealthily thither and helped themselves to a chunk. They made an imposing adventure of it, saying, “Hist!” every now and then, and suddenly halting with finger on lip; moving with hands on imaginary dagger-hilts; and giving orders in dismal whispers that if “the foe” stirred, to “let him have it to the hilt,” because “dead men tell no tales.” They knew well enough that the raftsmen were all down at the village laying in stores or having a spree, but still that was no excuse for their conducting this thing in an unpiratical way.

They shoved off, presently, Tom in command, Huck at the after oar and Joe at the forward. Tom stood amidships, gloomy-browed, and with folded arms, and gave his orders in a low, stern whisper:

“Luff, and bring her to the wind!”

“Aye-aye, sir!”

“Steady, steady-y-y-y!”

“Steady it is, sir!”

“Let her go off a point!”

“Point it is, sir!”

As the boys steadily and monotonously drove the raft toward midstream it was no doubt understood that these orders were given only for "style," and were not intended to mean anything in particular.

"What sail's she carrying?"

"Courses, tops'ls, and flying-jib, sir."

"Send the r'yals up! Lay out aloft, there, half a dozen of ye — foretopmaststuns'l! Lively, now!"

"Aye-aye, sir!"

"Shake out that maintogalans'l! Sheets and braces! *Now*, my hearties!"

"Aye-aye, sir!"

"Hellum-a-lee — hard a port! Stand by to meet her when she comes! Port, port! *Now*, men! With a will! Stead-y-y-y!"

"Steady it is, sir!"

The raft drew beyond the middle of the river; the boys pointed her head right, and then lay on their oars. The river was not high, so there was not more than a two or three mile current. Hardly a word was said during the next three-quarters of an hour, Now the raft was passing before the distant town. Two or three glimmering lights showed where it lay, peacefully sleeping, beyond the vague vast sweep of star-gemmed water, unconscious of the tremendous event that was happening. The Black Avenger stood still with folded arms, "looking his last" upon the scene of his former joys and his later sufferings, and wishing "she" could see him now, abroad on the wild sea, facing peril and death with dauntless heart, going to his doom with a grim smile on his lips. It was but a small strain on his imagination to remove Jackson's Island beyond eye-shot of the village, and so he "looked his last" with a broken and satisfied heart. The other pirates were looking their last, too; and they all looked so long that they came near letting the current drift them out of the range of the island. But they discovered the danger in time, and made shift to avert it. About two o'clock in the morning the raft grounded on the bar two hundred yards above the head of the island, and they waded back and forth until they had landed their freight. Part of the little raft's belongings consisted of an old sail, and this they spread over a nook in the bushes for a tent to shelter their provisions; but they themselves would sleep in the open air in good weather, as became outlaws.

They built a fire against the side of a great log twenty or thirty steps within the somber depths of the forest, and then cooked some bacon in the frying-pan for supper, and used up half of the corn "pone" stock they had brought. It seemed glorious sport to be feasting in that wild free way in the virgin forest of an unexplored and uninhabited island, far from the haunts of men, and they said they never would return to civilization. The climbing fire lit up their faces and threw its ruddy glare upon the pillared tree-trunks of their forest temple, and upon the varnished foliage and festooning vines.

When the last crisp slice of bacon was gone, and the last allowance of corn pone devoured, the boys stretched themselves out on the grass, filled with contentment. They could have found a cooler place, but they would not deny themselves such a romantic feature as the roasting camp-fire.

"*Ain't* gay?" said Joe.

"It's *nuts*!" said Tom. "What would the boys say if they could see us?"

"Say? Well, they'd just die to be here — hey, Hucky!"

"I reckon so," said Huckleberry; "anyways, *I'm* suited. I don't want nothing better'n this. I don't ever get enough to eat, gen'ally — and here they can't come and pick at a feller and bullyrag him so."

"It's just the life for me," said Tom. "You don't have to get up, mornings, and you don't have to go to school, and wash, and all that blame foolishness. You see a pirate don't have to do *anything*, Joe, when he's ashore, but a hermit he has to be praying considerable, and then he don't have any fun, anyway, all by himself that way."

"Oh, yes, that's so," said Joe, "but I hadn't thought much about it, you know. I'd a good deal rather be a pirate, now that I've tried it."

"You see," said Tom, "people don't go much on hermits, nowadays, like they used to in old times but a pirate's always respected. And a hermit's got to sleep on the hardest place he can find, and put sackcloth and ashes on his head, and stand out in the rain, and —"

"What does he put sackcloth and ashes on his head for?" inquired Huck.

"*I* dono. But they've *got* to do it. Hermits always do. You'd have to do that if you was a hermit."

"Dern'd if I would," said Huck.

"Well, what would you do?"

"I dunno. But I wouldn't do that."

"Why, Huck, you'd *have* to. How'd you get around it?"

"Why, I just wouldn't stand it. I'd run away."

"Run away! Well, you *would* be a nice old slouch of a hermit. You'd be a disgrace."

The Red-Handed made no response, being better employed. He had finished gouging out a cob, and now he fitted a weed stem to it, loaded it with tobacco, and was pressing a coal to the charge and blowing a cloud of fragrant smoke — he was in the full bloom of luxurious contentment. The other pirates envied him this majestic vice, and secretly resolved to acquire it shortly. Presently Huck said:

"What does pirates have to do?"

Tom said:

"Oh, they have just a bully time — take ships and burn them, and get the money and bury it in awful places in their island where there's ghosts and things to watch it, and kill everybody in the ships — make 'em walk a plank."

"And they carry the women to the island," said Joe; "they don't kill the women."

"No," assented Tom, "they don't kill the women — they're too noble. And the women's always beautiful, too."

"And don't they wear the bulliest clothes! Oh, no! All gold and silver and di'monds," said Joe, with enthusiasm.

"Who?" said Huck.

"Why, the pirates."

Huck scanned his own clothing forlornly.

"I reckon I ain't dressed fitten for a pirate," said he, with a regretful pathos in his voice; "but I ain't got none but these."

But the other boys told him the fine clothes would come fast enough, after they should have begun their adventures. They made him understand that his poor rags would do to begin with, though it was customary for wealthy pirates to start with a proper wardrobe.

Gradually their talk died out and drowsiness began to steal upon the eyelids of the little waifs. The pipe dropped from the fingers of the Red-Handed, and he slept the sleep of the conscience-free and the weary. The Terror of the Seas and the Black Avenger of the Spanish Main had more difficulty in getting to sleep. They said their prayers inwardly, and lying down, since there was nobody there with authority to make them kneel and recite aloud; in truth, they had a mind not to say them at all, but they were afraid to proceed to such lengths at that, lest they might call down a sudden and special thunderbolt from Heaven. Then at once they reached and hovered upon the imminent verge of sleep — but an intruder came, now, that would not "down." It was conscience. They began to feel a vague fear that they had been doing wrong to run away; and next they thought of the stolen meat, and then the real torture came. They tried to argue it away by reminding conscience that they had purloined sweetmeats and apples scores of times; but conscience was not to be appeased by such thin plausibilities; it seemed to them, in the end, that there was no getting around the stubborn fact that taking sweetmeats was only "hooking," while taking bacon and hams and such valuables was plain simple *stealing* — and there was a command against that in the Bible. So they inwardly resolved that so long as they remained in the business, their piracies should not again be sullied with the crime of stealing. Then conscience granted a truce, and these curiously inconsistent pirates fell peacefully to sleep.

Lesson 17

- Read chapters 14 and 15 of *The Adventures of Tom Sawyer.*

Chapter 14
Happy Camp of the Freebooters

When Tom awoke in the morning, he wondered where he was. He sat up and rubbed his eyes and looked around. Then he comprehended. It was the cool gray dawn, and there was a delicious sense of repose and peace in the deep pervading calm and silence of the woods. Not a leaf stirred; not a sound obtruded upon great Nature's meditation. Beaded dewdrops stood upon the leaves and grasses. A white layer of ashes covered the fire, and a thin blue breath of smoke rose straight into the air. Joe and Huck still slept.

Now, far away in the woods a bird called; another answered; presently the hammering of a woodpecker was heard. Gradually the cool dim gray of the morning whitened, and as gradually sounds multiplied and life manifested itself. The marvel of Nature shaking off sleep and going to work unfolded itself to the musing boy. A little green worm came crawling over a dewy leaf, lifting two-thirds of his body into the air from time to time and "sniffing around," then proceeding again — for he was measuring, Tom said; and when the worm approached him, of its own accord, he sat as still as a stone, with his hopes rising and falling, by turns, as the creature still came toward him or seemed inclined to go elsewhere; and when at last it considered a painful moment with its curved body in the air and then came decisively down upon Tom's leg and began a journey over him, his whole heart was glad — for that meant that he was going to have a new suit of clothes — without the shadow of a doubt a gaudy piratical uniform. Now a procession of ants appeared, from nowhere in particular, and went about their labors; one struggled manfully by with a dead spider five times as big as itself in its arms, and lugged it straight up a tree-trunk. A brown spotted lady-bug climbed the dizzy height of a grass-blade, and Tom bent down close to it and said, "Lady-bug, lady-bug, fly away home, your house is on fire, your children's alone," and she took wing and went off to see about it — which did not surprise the boy, for he knew of old that this insect was credulous about conflagrations, and he had practised upon its simplicity more than once. A tumblebug came next, heaving sturdily at its ball, and Tom touched the creature, to set it shut its legs against its body and pretend to be dead. The birds were fairly rioting by this time. A catbird, the Northern mocker, lit in a tree over Tom's head, and trilled out her imitations of her neighbors in a rapture of enjoyment; then a shrill jay swept down, a flash of blue flame, and stopped on a twig almost within the boy's reach, cocked his head to one side and eyed the strangers with a consuming curiosity; a gray squirrel and a big fellow of the "fox" kind came scurrying along, sitting up at intervals to inspect and chatter at the boys, for the wild things had probably never seen a human being before and scarcely knew whether to be afraid or not. All Nature was wide awake and stirring, now; long lances of sunlight pierced down through the dense foliage far and near, and a few butterflies came fluttering upon the scene.

Tom stirred up the other pirates and they all clattered away with a shout, and in a minute or two were stripped and chasing after and tumbling over each other in the shallow limpid water of the white sand-bar. They felt no longing for the little village sleeping in the distance beyond the majestic waste of water. A vagrant current or a slight rise in the river had carried off their raft, but this only gratified them, since its going was something like burning the bridge between them and civilization.

They came back to camp wonderfully refreshed, glad-hearted, and ravenous; and they soon had the camp-fire blazing up again. Huck found a spring of clear cold water close by, and the boys made cups of broad oak or hickory leaves, and felt that water, sweetened with such a wildwood charm as that, would be a good enough substitute for coffee. While Joe was slicing bacon for breakfast, Tom and Huck asked him to hold on a minute; they stepped to a promising nook in the river-bank and threw in their lines; almost immediately they had reward. Joe had not had time to get impatient before they were back again with some handsome bass, a couple of sun-perch, and a small catfish — provisions enough for quite a family. They fried the fish with the bacon, and were astonished; for no fish had ever seemed so delicious before. They did not know that the quicker a fresh- water fish is on the fire after he is caught the better he is; and they reflected little upon what a sauce open-air sleeping, open-air exercise, bathing, and a large ingredient of hunger makes, too.

They lay around in the shade, after breakfast, while Huck had a smoke, and then went off through the woods on an exploring expedition. They tramped gaily along, over decaying logs, through tangled underbrush, among solemn monarchs of the forest, hung from their crowns to the ground with a drooping regalia of grapevines. Now and then they came upon snug nooks carpeted with grass and jeweled with flowers.

They found plenty of things to be delighted with, but nothing to be astonished at. They discovered that the island was about three miles long and a quarter of a mile wide, and that the shore it lay closest to was only separated from it by a narrow channel hardly two hundred yards wide. They took a swim about every hour, so it was close upon the middle of the afternoon when they got back to camp. They were too hungry to stop to fish, but they fared sumptuously upon cold ham, and then threw themselves down in the shade to talk. But the talk soon began to drag, and then died. The stillness, the solemnity that brooded in the woods, and the sense of loneliness, began to tell upon the spirits of the boys. They fell to thinking. A sort of undefined longing crept upon them. This took dim shape, presently — it was budding homesickness. Even Finn the Red-Handed was dreaming of his doorsteps and empty hogsheads. But they were all ashamed of their weakness, and none was brave enough to speak his thought.

For some time, now, the boys had been dully conscious of a peculiar sound in the distance, just as one sometimes is of the ticking of a clock which he takes no distinct note of. But now this mysterious sound became more pronounced, and forced a recognition. The boys started, glanced at each other, and then each assumed a listening attitude. There was a long silence, profound and unbroken; then a deep, sullen boom came floating down out of the distance.

"What is it!" exclaimed Joe, under his breath.

"I wonder," said Tom in a whisper.

"'Tain't thunder," said Huckleberry, in an awed tone, "becuz thunder —"

"Hark!" said Tom. "Listen— don't talk."

They waited a time that seemed an age, and then the same muffled boom troubled the solemn hush.

"Let's go and see."

They sprang to their feet and hurried to the shore toward the town. They parted the bushes on the bank and peered out over the water. The little steam ferryboat was about a mile below the village, drifting with the current. Her broad deck seemed crowded with people. There were a great many skiffs rowing about or floating with the stream in the neighborhood of the ferryboat, but the boys could not determine what the men in them were doing. Presently a great jet of white smoke burst from the ferryboat's side, and as it expanded and rose in a lazy cloud, that same dull throb of sound was borne to the listeners again.

"I know now!" exclaimed Tom; "somebody's drownded!"

"That's it!" said Huck; "they done that last summer, when Bill Turner got drownded; they shoot a cannon over the water, and that makes him come up to the top. Yes, and they take loaves of bread and put quicksilver in 'em and set 'em afloat, and wherever there's anybody that's drownded, they'll float right there and stop."

"Yes, I've heard about that," said Joe. "I wonder what makes the bread do that."

"Oh, it ain't the bread, so much," said Tom; "I reckon it's mostly what they *say* over it before they start it out."

"But they don't say anything over it," said Huck. "I've seen 'em and they don't."

"Well, that's funny," said Tom. "But maybe they say it to themselves. Of *course* they do. Anybody might know that."

The other boys agreed that there was reason in what Tom said, because an ignorant lump of bread, uninstructed by an incantation, could not be expected to act very intelligently when sent upon an errand of such gravity.

“By jings, I wish I was over there, now,” said Joe.

“I do too,” said Huck. “I’d give heaps to know who it is.”

The boys still listened and watched. Presently a revealing thought flashed through Tom’s mind, and he exclaimed:

“Boys, I know who’s drownded— it’s us!”

They felt like heroes in an instant. Here was a gorgeous triumph; they were missed; they were mourned; hearts were breaking on their account; tears were being shed; accusing memories of unkindnesses to these poor lost lads were rising up, and unavailing regrets and remorse were being indulged: and best of all, the departed were the talk of the whole town, and the envy of all the boys, as far as this dazzling notoriety was concerned. This was fine. It was worth while to be a pirate, after all. As twilight drew on, the ferryboat went back to her accustomed business and the skiffs disappeared. The pirates returned to camp. They were jubilant with vanity over their new grandeur and the illustrious trouble they were making. They caught fish, cooked supper and ate it, and then fell to guessing at what the village was thinking and saying about them; and the pictures they drew of the public distress on their account were gratifying to look upon — from their point of view. But when the shadows of night closed them in, they gradually ceased to talk, and sat gazing into the fire, with their minds evidently wandering elsewhere. The excitement was gone, now, and Tom and Joe could not keep back thoughts of certain persons at home who were not enjoying this fine frolic as much as they were. Misgivings came; they grew troubled and unhappy; a sigh or two escaped, unawares. By and by Joe timidly ventured upon a roundabout “feeler” as to how the others might look upon a return to civilization — not right now, but —

Tom withered him with derision! Huck, being uncommitted as yet, joined in with Tom, and the waverer quickly “explained,” and was glad to get out of the scrape with as little taint of chicken-hearted homesickness clinging to his garments as he could. Mutiny was effectually laid to rest for the moment.

As the night deepened, Huck began to nod, and presently to snore. Joe followed next. Tom lay upon his elbow motionless, for some time, watching the two intently. At last he got up cautiously, on his knees, and went searching among the grass and the flickering reflections flung by the camp-fire. He picked up and inspected several large semicylinders of the thin white bark of a sycamore, and finally chose two which seemed to suit him. Then he knelt by the fire and painfully wrote something upon each of these with his "red keel"; one he rolled up and put in his jacket pocket, and the other he put in Joe's hat and removed it to a little distance from the owner. And he also put into the hat certain school-boy treasures of almost inestimable value — among them a lump of chalk, an India-rubber ball, three fishhooks, and one of that kind of marbles known as a "sure'nough crystal." Then he tiptoed his way cautiously among the trees till he felt that he was out of hearing, and straightway broke into a keen run in the direction of the sand-bar.

Chapter 15
Tom's Stealthy Visit Home

A few minutes later Tom was in the shoal water of the bar, wading toward the Illinois shore. Before the depth reached his middle he was halfway over; the current would permit no more wading, now, so he struck out confidently to swim the remaining hundred yards. He swam quartering upstream, but still was swept downward rather faster than he had expected. However, he reached the shore finally, and drifted along till he found a low place and drew himself out. He put his hand on his jacket pocket, found his piece of bark safe, and then struck through the woods, following the shore, with streaming garments. Shortly before ten o'clock he came out into an open place opposite the village, and saw the ferryboat lying in the shadow of the trees and the high bank. Everything was quiet under the blinking stars. He crept down the bank, watching with all his eyes, slipped into the water, swam three or four strokes, and climbed into the skiff that did "yawl" duty at the boat's stern. He laid himself down under the thwarts and waited, panting.

Presently the cracked bell tapped and a voice gave the order to "cast off." A minute or two later the skiff's head was standing high up, against the boat's swell, and the voyage was begun. Tom felt happy in his success, for he knew it was the boat's last trip for the night. At the end of a long twelve or fifteen minutes the wheels stopped, and Tom slipped overboard and swam ashore in the dusk, landing fifty yards down-stream, out of danger of possible stragglers.

He flew along unfrequented alleys, and shortly found himself at his aunt's back fence. He climbed over, approached the "ell," and looked in at the sitting-room window, for a light was burning there. There sat Aunt Polly, Sid, Mary, and Joe Harper's mother, grouped together, talking. They were by the bed, and the bed was between them and the door. Tom went to the door and began to softly lift the latch; then he pressed gently, and the door yielded a crack; he continued pushing cautiously, and quaking every time it creaked, till he judged he might squeeze through on his knees; so he put his head through and began, warily.

"What makes the candle blow so?" said Aunt Polly. Tom hurried up. "Why that door's open, I believe. Why of course it is. No end of strange things now. Go 'long and shut it, Sid."

Tom disappeared under the bed just in time. He lay and "breathed" himself for a time, and then crept to where he could almost touch his aunt's foot.

"But as I was saying," said Aunt Polly, "he warn't *bad*, so to say — only misch*ee*vous. Only just giddy, and harum-scarum, you know. He warn't any more responsible than a colt. *He* never meant ny harm, and he was the best-hearted boy that ever was" — and she began to cry.

"It was just so with my Joe — always full of his devilment, and up to every kind of mischief, but he was just as unselfish and kind as he could be — and laws bless me, to think I went and whipped him for taking that cream, never once recollecting that I throwed it out myself because it was sour, and I never to see him again in this world, never, never, never, poor abused boy!" And Mrs. Harper sobbed as if her heart would break.

"I hope Tom's better off where he is," said Sid, "but if he'd been better in some ways —"

"*Sid!*" Tom felt the glare of the old lady's eye, though he could not see it. "Not a word against my Tom, now that he's gone! God'll take care of *him* — never you trouble *your*self, sir! Oh, Mrs. Harper, I don't know how to give him up! I don't know how to give him up! He was such a comfort to me, although he tormented my old heart out of me, 'most."

"The Lord giveth and the Lord hath taken away, — blessed be the name of the Lord! But it's so hard — oh, it's so hard! Only last Saturday my Joe busted a firecracker right under my nose and I knocked him sprawling. Little did I know then how soon — Oh, if it was to do over again I'd hug him and bless him for it."

"Yes, yes, yes, I know just how you feel, Mrs. Harper, I know just exactly how you feel. No longer ago than yesterday noon, my Tom took and filled the cat full of Pain-killer, and I did think the cretur would tear the house down. And God forgive me, I cracked Tom's head with my thimble, poor boy, poor dead boy. But he's out of all his troubles now. And the last words I ever heard him say was to reproach—"

But this memory was too much for the old lady, and she broke entirely down. Tom was snuffling, now, himself — and more in pity of himself than anybody else. He could hear Mary crying, and putting in a kindly word for him from time to time. He began to have a nobler opinion of himself than ever before. Still, he was sufficiently touched by his aunt's grief to long to rush out from under the bed and overwhelm her with joy — and the theatrical gorgeousness of the thing appealed strongly to his nature, too, but he resisted and lay still.

He went on listening, and gathered by odds and ends that it was conjectured at first that the boys had got drowned while taking a swim; then the small raft had been missed; next, certain boys said the missing lads had promised that the village should "hear something" soon; the wise-heads had "put this and that together" and decided that the lads had gone off on that raft and would turn up at the next town below, presently; but toward noon the raft had been found, lodged against the Missouri shore some five or six miles below the village — and then hope perished; they must be drowned, else hunger would have driven them home by nightfall if not sooner. It was believed that the search for the bodies had been a fruitless effort merely because the drowning must have occurred in mid-channel, since the boys, being good swimmers, would otherwise have escaped to shore. This was Wednesday night. If the bodies continued missing until Sunday, all hope would be given over, and the funerals would be preached on that morning. Tom shuddered.

Mrs. Harper gave a sobbing good night and turned to go. Then with a mutual impulse the two bereaved women flung themselves into each other's arms and had a good, consoling cry, and then parted. Aunt Polly was tender far beyond her wont, in her good night to Sid and Mary. Sid snuffled a bit and Mary went off crying with all her heart.

Aunt Polly knelt down and prayed for Tom so touchingly, so appealingly, and with such measureless love in her words and her old trembling voice, that he was weltering in tears again long before she was through.

He had to keep still long after she went to bed, for she kept making broken-hearted ejaculations from time to time, tossing unrestfully, and turning over. But at last she was still, only moaning a little in her sleep. Now the boy stole out, rose gradually by the bedside, shaded the candlelight with his hand, and stood regarding her. His heart was full of pity for her. He took out his sycamore scroll and placed it by the candle. But something occurred to him, and he lingered considering. His face lighted with a happy solution of his thought; he put the bark hastily in his pocket. Then he bent over and kissed the faded lips, and straightway made his stealthy exit, latching the door behind him.

He threaded his way back to the ferry landing, found nobody at large there, and walked boldly on board the boat, for he knew she was tenantless except that there was a watchman, who always turned in and slept like a graven image. He untied the skiff at the stern, slipped into it, and was soon rowing cautiously up-stream. When he had pulled a mile above the village, he started quartering across and bent himself stoutly to his work. He hit the landing on the other side neatly, for this was a familiar bit of work to him. He was moved to capture the skiff, arguing that it might be considered a ship and therefore legitimate prey for a pirate, but he knew a thorough search would be made for it and that might end in revelations. So he stepped ashore and entered the wood.

He sat down and took a long rest, torturing himself meantime to keep awake, and then started warily down the home-stretch. The night was far spent. It was broad daylight before he found himself fairly abreast the island bar. He rested again until the sun was well up and gilding the great river with its splendor, and then he plunged into the stream. A little later he paused, dripping, upon the threshold of the camp, and heard Joe say:

"No, Tom's true-blue, Huck, and he'll come back. He won't desert. He knows that would be a disgrace to a pirate, and Tom's too proud for that sort of thing. He's up to something or other. Now I wonder what?"

"Well, the things is ours, anyway, ain't they?"

"Pretty near, but not yet, Huck. The writing says they are if he ain't back here to breakfast."

"Which he is!" exclaimed Tom, with fine dramatic effect, stepping grandly into camp.

A sumptuous breakfast of bacon and fish was shortly provided, and as the boys set to work upon it, Tom recounted (and adorned) his adventures. They were a vain and boastful company of heroes when the tale was done. Then Tom hid himself away in a shady nook to sleep till noon, and the other pirates got ready to fish and explore.

Lesson 18

- Read chapters 16 and 17 of *The Adventures of Tom Sawyer*.

Chapter 16
First Pipes — "I've Lost My Knife"

After dinner all the gang turned out to hunt for turtle eggs on the bar. They went about poking sticks into the sand, and when they found a soft place they went down on their knees and dug with their hands. Sometimes they would take fifty or sixty eggs out of one hole. They were perfectly round white things a trifle smaller than an English walnut. They had a famous fried-egg feast that night, and another on Friday morning.

After breakfast they went whooping and prancing out on the bar, and chased each other round and round, shedding clothes as they went, until they were naked, and then continued the frolic far away up the shoal water of the bar, against the stiff current, which latter tripped their legs from under them from time to time and greatly increased the fun. And now and then they stooped in a group and splashed water in each other's faces with their palms, gradually approaching each other, with averted faces to avoid the strangling sprays, and finally gripping and struggling till the best man ducked his neighbor, and then they all went under in a tangle of white legs and arms, and came up blowing, sputtering, laughing, and gasping for breath at one and the same time.

When they were well exhausted, they would run out and sprawl on the dry, hot sand, and lie there and cover themselves up with it, and by and by break for the water again and go through the original performance once more. Finally it occurred to them that their naked skin represented flesh-colored "tights" very fairly; so they drew a ring in the sand and had a circus — with three clowns in it, for none would yield this proudest post to his neighbor.

Next they got their marbles and played "knucks" and "ring-taw" and "keeps" till that amusement grew stale. Then Joe and Huck had another swim, but Tom would not venture, because he found that in kicking off his trousers he had kicked his string of rattlesnake rattles off his ankle, and he wondered how he had escaped cramp so long without the protection of this mysterious charm. He did not venture again until he had found it, and by that time the other boys were tired and ready to rest. They gradually wandered apart, dropped into the "dumps," and fell to gazing longingly across the wide river to where the village lay drowsing in the sun. Tom found himself writing "BECKY" in the sand with his big toe; he scratched it out, and was angry with himself for his weakness. But he wrote it again, nevertheless; he could not help it. He erased it once more and then took himself out of temptation by driving the other boys together and joining them.

But Joe's spirits had gone down almost beyond resurrection. He was so homesick that he could hardly endure the misery of it. The tears lay very near the surface. Huck was melancholy, too. Tom was downhearted, but tried hard not to show it. He had a secret which he was not ready to tell, yet, but if this mutinous depression was not broken up soon, he would have to bring it out. He said, with a great show of cheerfulness:

"I bet there's been pirates on this island before, boys. We'll explore it again. They've hid treasures here somewhere. How'd you feel to light on a rotten chest full of gold and silver — hey?"

But it roused only a faint enthusiasm, which faded out, with no reply. Tom tried one or two other seductions; but they failed, too. It was discouraging work. Joe sat poking up the sand with a stick and looking very gloomy. Finally he said:

"Oh, boys, let's give it up. I want to go home. It's so lonesome."

"Oh, no, Joe, you'll feel better by and by," said Tom. "Just think of the fishing that's here."

"I don't care for fishing. I want to go home."

"But, Joe, there ain't such another swimming-place anywhere."

"Swimming's no good. I don't seem to care for it, somehow, when there ain't anybody to say I sha'n't go in. I mean to go home."

"Oh, shucks! Baby! You want to see your mother, I reckon."

"Yes, I do want to see my mother — and you would, too, if you had one. I ain't any more baby than you are." And Joe snuffled a little.

"Well, we'll let the cry-baby go home to his mother, won't we Huck? Poor thing — does it want to see its mother? And so it shall. You like it here, *don't* you, Huck? We'll stay, won't we?"

Huck said "Y-e-s" — without any heart in it.

"I'll never speak to you again as long as I live," said Joe, rising. "There now!" And he moved moodily away and began to dress himself.

"Who cares!" said Tom. "Nobody wants you to. Go 'long home and get laughed at. Oh, you're a nice pirate. Huck and me ain't cry-babies. We'll stay, won't we, Huck? Let him go if he wants to. I reckon we can get along without him, per'aps."

But Tom was uneasy, nevertheless, and was alarmed to see Joe go sullenly on with his dressing. And then it was discomforting to see Huck eying Joe's preparations so wistfully, and keeping up such an ominous silence. Presently, without a parting word, Joe began to wade off toward the Illinois shore. Tom's heart began to sink. He glanced at Huck. Huck could not bear the look, and dropped his eyes. Then he said:

"I want to go, too, Tom. It was getting so lonesome anyway, and now it'll be worse. Let's us go, too, Tom."

"I won't! You can all go, if you want to. I mean to stay."

"Tom, I better go."

"Well, go 'long — who's hendering you?"

Huck began to pick up his scattered clothes. He said:

"Tom, I wisht you'd come, too. Now you think it over. We'll wait for you when we get to shore."

"Well, you'll wait a blame long time, that's all."

Huck started sorrowfully away, and Tom stood looking after him, with a strong desire tugging at his heart to yield his pride and go along too. He hoped the boys would stop, but they still waded slowly on. It suddenly dawned on Tom that it was become very lonely and still. He made one final struggle with his pride, and then darted after his comrades, yelling:

"Wait! Wait! I want to tell you something!"

They presently stopped and turned around. When he got to where they were, he began unfolding his secret, and they listened moodily till at last they saw the "point" he was driving at, and then they set up a war-whoop of applause and said it was "splendid!" and said if he had told them at first, they wouldn't have started away. He made a plausible excuse; but his real reason had been the fear that not even the secret would keep them with him any very great length of time, and so he had meant to hold it in reserve as a last seduction.

The lads came gaily back and went at their sports again with a will, chattering all the time about Tom's stupendous plan and admiring the genius of it. After a dainty egg and fish dinner, Tom said he wanted to learn to smoke, now. Joe caught at the idea and said he would like to try, too. So Huck made pipes and filled them. These novices had never smoked anything before but cigars made of grapevine, and they "bit" the tongue, and were not considered manly anyway.

Now they stretched themselves out on their elbows and began to puff, charily, and with slender confidence. The smoke had an unpleasant taste, and they gagged a little, but Tom said:

"Why, it's just as easy! If I'd 'a' knowed *this* was all, I'd 'a' learnt long ago."

"So would I," said Joe. "It's just nothing."

"Why, many a time I've looked at people smoking, and thought well I wish I could do that; but I never thought I could," said Tom.

"That's just the way with me, hain't it, Huck? You've heard me talk just that way— haven't you, Huck? I'll leave it to Huck if I haven't."

"Yes — heaps of times," said Huck.

"Well, I have too," said Tom; "oh, hundreds of times. Once down by the slaughter-house. Don't you remember, Huck? Bob Tanner was there, and Johnny Miller, and Jeff Thatcher, when I said it. Don't you remember, Huck, 'bout me saying that?"

"Yes, that's so," said Huck. "That was the day after I lost a white alley. No, 'twas the day before."

"There— I told you so," said Tom. "Huck recollects it."

"I bleeve I could smoke this pipe all day," said Joe. "*I* don't feel sick."

"Neither do I," said Tom. "*I* could smoke it all day. But I bet you Jeff Thatcher couldn't."

"Jeff Thatcher! Why, he'd keel over just with two draws. Just let him try it once. *He'd* see!"

"I bet he would. And Johnny Miller — I wish I could see Johnny Miller tackle it once."

"Oh, don't *I,*" said Joe. "Why, I bet you Johnny Miller couldn't any more do this than nothing. Just one little snifter would fetch *him.*"

"'Deed it would, Joe. Say — I wish the boys could see us now."

"So do I."

"Say — boys, don't say anything about it, and some time when they're around, I'll come up to you and say, 'Joe, got a pipe? I want a smoke.' And you'll say, kind of careless like, as if it warn't anything, you'll say, 'Yes, I got my *old* pipe, and another one, but my tobacker ain't very good.' And I'll say, 'Oh, that's all right, if it's *strong* enough.' And then you'll out with the pipes, and we'll light up just as ca'm, and then just see 'em look!"

"By jings, that'll be gay, Tom! I wish it was *now*!"

"So do I! And when we tell 'em we learned when we was off pirating, won't they wish they'd been along?"

"Oh, I reckon not! I'll just *bet* they will!"

So the talk ran on. But presently it began to flag a trifle, and grow disjointed. The silences widened; the expectoration marvelously increased. Every pore inside the boys' cheeks became a spouting fountain; they could scarcely bail out the cellars under their tongues fast enough to prevent an inundation; little overflowings down their throats occurred in spite of all they could do, and sudden retchings followed every time. Both boys were looking very pale and miserable, now. Joe's pipe dropped from his nerveless fingers. Tom's followed.

Both fountains were going furiously and both pumps bailing with might and main. Joe said feebly:

"I've lost my knife. I reckon I better go and find it."

Tom said, with quivering lips and halting utterance:

"I'll help you. You go over that way and I'll hunt around by the spring. No, you needn't come, Huck — we can find it."

So Huck sat down again, and waited an hour. Then he found it lonesome, and went to find his comrades. They were wide apart in the woods, both very pale, both fast asleep. But something informed him that if they had had any trouble they had got rid of it.

They were not talkative at supper that night. They had a humble look, and when Huck prepared his pipe after the meal and was going to prepare theirs, they said no, they were not feeling very well — something they ate at dinner had disagreed with them.

About midnight Joe awoke, and called the boys. There was a brooding oppressiveness in the air that seemed to bode something. The boys huddled themselves together and sought the friendly companionship of the fire, though the dull dead heat of the breathless atmosphere was stifling. They sat still, intent and waiting. The solemn hush continued. Beyond the light of the fire everything was swallowed up in the blackness of darkness. Presently there came a quivering glow that vaguely revealed the foliage for a moment and then vanished. By and by another came, a little stronger. Then another. Then a faint moan came sighing through the branches of the forest and the boys felt a fleeting breath upon their cheeks, and shuddered with the fancy that the Spirit of the Night had gone by. There was a pause. Now a weird flash turned night into day and showed every little grass-blade, separate and distinct, that grew about their feet. And it showed three white, startled faces, too. A deep peal of thunder went rolling and tumbling down the heavens and lost itself in sullen rumblings in the distance. A sweep of chilly air passed by, rustling all the leaves and snowing the flaky ashes broadcast about the fire. Another fierce glare lit up the forest, and an instant crash followed that seemed to rend the treetops right over the boys' heads. They clung together in terror, in the thick gloom that followed. A few big raindrops fell pattering upon the leaves.

"Quick, boys! go for the tent!" exclaimed Tom.

They sprang away, stumbling over roots and among vines in the dark, no two plunging in the same direction. A furious blast roared through the trees, making everything sing as it went. One blinding flash after another came, and peal on peal of deafening thunder. And now a drenching rain poured down and the rising hurricane drove it in sheets along the ground. The boys cried out to each other, but the roaring wind and the booming thunderblasts drowned their voices utterly. However, one by one they straggled in at last and took shelter under the tent, cold, scared, and streaming with water; but to have company in misery seemed something to be grateful for. They could not talk, the old sail flapped so furiously, even if the other noises would have allowed them. The tempest rose higher and higher, and presently the sail tore loose from its fastenings and went winging away on the blast. The boys seized each other's hands and fled, with many tumblings and bruises, to the shelter of a great oak that stood upon the river-bank. Now the battle was at its highest. Under the ceaseless conflagration of lightning that flamed in the skies, everything below stood out in clean-cut and shadowless distinctness: the bending trees, the billowy river, white with foam, the driving spray of spume-flakes, the dim outlines of the high bluffs on the other side, glimpsed through the drifting cloud-rack and the slanting veil of rain. Every little while some giant tree yielded the fight and fell crashing through the younger growth; and the unflagging thunder-peals came now in ear-splitting explosive bursts, keen and sharp, and unspeakably appalling. The storm culminated in one matchless effort that seemed likely to tear the island to pieces, burn it up, drown it to the treetops, blow it away, and deafen every creature in it, all at one and the same moment. It was a wild night for homeless young heads to be out in.

But at last the battle was done, and the forces retired with weaker and weaker threatenings and grumblings, and peace resumed her sway. The boys went back to camp, a good deal awed; but they found there was still something to be thankful for, because the great sycamore, the shelter of their beds, was a ruin now, blasted by the lightnings, and they were not under it when the catastrophe happened.

Everything in camp was drenched, the camp-fire as well; for they were but heedless lads, like their generation, and had made no provision against rain. Here was matter for dismay, for they were soaked through and chilled. They were eloquent in their distress; but they presently discovered that the fire had eaten so far up under the great log it had been built against (where it curved upward and separated itself from the ground), that a handbreadth or so of it had escaped wetting; so they patiently wrought until, with shreds and bark gathered from the under sides of sheltered logs, they coaxed the fire to burn again. Then they piled on great dead boughs till they had a roaring furnace, and were glad-hearted once more. They dried their boiled ham and had a feast, and after that they sat by the fire and expanded and glorified their midnight adventure until morning, for there was not a dry spot to sleep on, anywhere around.

As the sun began to steal in upon the boys, drowsiness came over them and they went out on the sand-bar and lay down to sleep. They got scorched out by and by, and drearily set about getting breakfast. After the meal they felt rusty, and stiff - jointed, and a little homesick once more. Tom saw the signs, and fell to cheering up the pirates as well as he could. But they cared nothing for marbles, or circus, or swimming, or anything. He reminded them of the imposing secret, and raised a ray of cheer. While it lasted, he got them interested in a new device. This was to knock off being pirates, for a while, and be Indians for a change. They were attracted by this idea; so it was not long before they were stripped, and striped from head to heel with black mud, like so many zebras — all of them chiefs, of course — and then they went tearing through the woods to attack an English settlement.

By and by they separated into three hostile tribes, and darted upon each other from ambush with dreadful war-whoops, and killed and scalped each other by thousands. It was a gory day. Consequently it was an extremely satisfactory one.

They assembled in camp toward supper-time, hungry and happy; but now a difficulty arose— hostile Indians could not break the bread of hospitality together without first making peace, and this was a simple impossibility without smoking a pipe of peace. There was no other process that ever they had heard of. Two of the savages almost wished they had remained pirates. However, there was no other way; so with such show of cheerfulness as they could muster they called for the pipe and took their whiff as it passed, in due form.

And behold, they were glad they had gone into savagery, for they had gained something; they found that they could now smoke a little without having to go and hunt for a lost knife; they did not get sick enough to be seriously uncomfortable. They were not likely to fool away this high promise for lack of effort. No, they practised cautiously, after supper, with right fair success, and so they spent a jubilant evening. They were prouder and happier in their new acquirement than they would have been in the scalping and skinning of the Six Nations. We will leave them to smoke and chatter and brag, since we have no further use for them at present.

- Tom and his friends smoke tobacco. We know even more today the health dangers of doing so.

Chapter 17
Pirates At Their Own Funeral

But there was no hilarity in the little town that same tranquil Saturday afternoon. The Harpers, and Aunt Polly's family, were being put into mourning, with great grief and many tears. An unusual quiet possessed the village, although it was ordinarily quiet enough, in all conscience. The villagers conducted their concerns with an absent air, and talked little; but they sighed often. The Saturday holiday seemed a burden to the children. They had no heart in their sports, and gradually gave them up.

In the afternoon Becky Thatcher found herself moping about the deserted school-house yard, and feeling very melancholy. But she found nothing there to comfort her. She soliloquized:

"Oh, if I only had a brass andiron-knob again! But I haven't got anything now to remember him by." And she choked back a little sob.

Presently she stopped, and said to herself:

"It was right here. Oh, if it was to do over again, I wouldn't say that — I wouldn't say it for the whole world. But he's gone now; I'll never never never see him any more."

This thought broke her down and she wandered away, with the tears rolling down her cheeks. Then quite a group of boys and girls — playmates of Tom's and Joe's — came by, and stood looking over the paling fence and talking in reverent tones of how Tom did so-and-so, the last time they saw him, and how Joe said this and that small trifle (pregnant with awful prophecy, as they could easily see now!) — and each speaker pointed out the exact spot where the lost lads stood at the time, and then added something like "and I was a-standing just so — just as I am now, and as if you was him — I was as close as that — and he smiled, just this way — and then something seemed to go all over me, like — awful, you know — and I never thought what it meant, of course, but I can see now!"

Then there was a dispute about who saw the dead boys last in life, and many claimed that dismal distinction, and offered evidences, more or less tampered with by the witness; and when it was ultimately decided who did see the departed last, and exchanged the last words with them, the lucky parties took upon themselves a sort of sacred importance, and were gaped at and envied by all the rest. One poor chap, who had no other grandeur to offer, said with tolerably manifest pride in the remembrance:

"Well, Tom Sawyer he licked me once."

But that bid for glory was a failure. Most of the boys could say that, and so that cheapened the distinction too much. The group loitered away, still recalling memories of the lost heroes, in awed voices.

When the Sunday-school hour was finished, the next morning, the bell began to toll, instead of ringing in the usual way. It was a very still Sabbath, and the mournful sound seemed in keeping with the musing hush that lay upon nature. The villagers began to gather, loitering a moment in the vestibule to converse in whispers about the sad event. But there was no whispering in the house; only the funereal rustling of dresses as the women gathered to their seats disturbed the silence there. None could remember when the little church had been so full before. There was finally a waiting pause, an expectant dumbness, and then Aunt Polly entered, followed by Sid and Mary, and they by the Harper family, all in deep black, and the whole congregation, the old minister as well, rose reverently and stood, until the mourners were seated in the front pew. There was another communing silence, broken at intervals by muffled sobs, and then the minister spread his hands abroad and prayed. A moving hymn was sung, and the text followed: "I am the Resurrection and the Life."

As the service proceeded, the clergyman drew such pictures of the graces, the winning ways, and the rare promise of the lost lads, that every soul there, thinking he recognized these pictures, felt a pang in remembering that he had persistently blinded himself to them always before, and had as persistently seen only faults and flaws in the poor boys. The minister related many a touching incident in the lives of the departed, too, which illustrated their sweet, generous natures, and the people could easily see, now, how noble and beautiful those episodes were, and remembered with grief that at the time they occurred they had seemed rank rascalities, well deserving of the cowhide. The congregation became more and more moved, as the pathetic tale went on, till at last the whole company broke down and joined the weeping mourners in a chorus of anguished sobs, the preacher himself giving way to his feelings, and crying in the pulpit.

There was a rustle in the gallery, which nobody noticed; a moment later the church door creaked; the minister raised his streaming eyes above his handkerchief, and stood transfixed! First one and then another pair of eyes followed the minister's, and then almost with one impulse the congregation rose and stared while the three dead boys came marching up the aisle, Tom in the lead, Joe next, and Huck, a ruin of drooping rags, sneaking sheepishly in the rear! They had been hid in the unused gallery listening to their own funeral sermon!

Aunt Polly, Mary, and the Harpers threw themselves upon their restored ones, smothered them with kisses and poured out thanksgivings, while poor Huck stood abashed and uncomfortable, not knowing exactly what to do or where to hide from so many unwelcoming eyes. He wavered, and started to slink away, but Tom seized him and said:

"Aunt Polly, it ain't fair. Somebody's got to be glad to see Huck."

"And so they shall. *I*'m glad to see him, poor motherless thing!" And the loving attentions Aunt Polly lavished upon him were the one thing capable of making him more uncomfortable than he was before.

Suddenly the minister shouted at the top of his voice: "Praise God from whom all blessings flow — SING! — and put your hearts in it!"

And they did. Old Hundred swelled up with a triumphant burst, and while it shook the rafters Tom Sawyer the Pirate looked around upon the envying juveniles about him and confessed in his heart that this was the proudest moment of his life.

As the "sold" congregation trooped out they said they would almost be willing to be made ridiculous again to hear Old Hundred sung like that once more.

Tom got more cuffs and kisses that day — according to Aunt Polly's varying moods — than he had earned before in a year; and he hardly knew which expressed the most gratefulness to God and affection for himself.

Lesson 19

- Read chapter 18 of *The Adventures of Tom Sawyer*.

Chapter 18
Tom Reveals His Dream Secret

That was Tom's great secret — the scheme to return home with his brother pirates and attend their own funerals. They had paddled over to the Missouri shore on a log, at dusk on Saturday, landing five or six miles below the village; they had slept in the woods at the edge of the town till nearly daylight, and had then crept through back lanes and alleys and finished their sleep in the gallery of the church among a chaos g£ invalided benches.

At breakfast, Monday morning, Aunt Polly and Mary were very loving to Tom, and very attentive to his wants. There was an unusual amount of talk. In the course of it Aunt Polly said:

“Well, I don’t say it wasn’t a fine joke, Tom, to keep everybody suffering ‘most a week so you boys had a good time, but it is a pity you could be so hard-hearted as to let me suffer so. If you could come over on a log to go to your funeral, you could have come over and give me a hint some way that you warn’t dead, but only run off.”

“Yes, you could have done that, Tom,” said Mary; “and I believe you would if you had thought of it.”

“Would you, Tom?” said Aunt Polly, her face lighting wistfully. “Say, now, would you, if you’d thought of it?”

“I — well, I don’t know. ‘Twould ‘a’ spoiled everything.”

“Tom, I hoped you loved me that much,” said Aunt Polly, with a grieved tone that discomforted the boy. “It would have been something if you’d cared enough to think of it, even if you didn’t do it.”

“Now, auntie, that ain’t any harm,” pleaded Mary; “it’s only Tom’s giddy way — he is always in such a rush that he never thinks of anything.”

“More’s the pity. Sid would have thought. And Sid would have come and done it, too. Tom, you’ll look back, some day, when it’s too late, and wish you’d cared a little more for me when it would have cost you so little.”

“Now, auntie, you know I do care for you,” said Tom.

“I’d know it better if you acted more like it.”

“I wish now I’d thought,” said Tom, with a repentant tone; “but I dreamed about you, anyway. That’s something, ain’t it?”

"It ain't much — a cat does that much — but it's better than nothing. What did you dream?"

"Why, Wednesday night I dreamt that you was sitting over there by the bed, and Sid was sitting by the woodbox, and Mary next to him."

"Well, so we did. So we always do. I'm glad your dreams could take even that much trouble about us."

"And I dreamt that Joe Harper's mother was here."

"Why, she was here! Did you dream any more?"

"Oh, lots. But it's so dim, now."

"Well, try to recollect — can't you?"

"Somehow it seems to me that the wind — the wind blowed the — the —"

"Try harder, Tom! The wind did blow something. Come!"

Tom pressed his fingers on his forehead an anxious minute, and then said:

"I've got it now! I've got it now! It blowed the candle!"

"Mercy on us! Go on, Tom — go on!"

"And it seems to me that you said, 'Why, I believe that that door —'"

"Go on, Tom!"

"Just let me study a moment — just a moment. Oh, yes — you said you believed the door was open."

"As I'm sitting here, I did! Didn't I, Mary! Go on!"

"And then — and then — well I won't be certain, but it seems like as if you made Sid go and — and —"

"Well? Well? What did I make him do, Tom? What did I make him do?"

"You made him — you — Oh, you made him shut it."

"Well, for the land's sake! I never heard the beat of that in all my days! Don't tell me there ain't anything in dreams, any more. Sereny Harper shall know of this before I'm an hour older. I'd like to see her get around this with her rubbage 'bout superstition. Go on, Tom!"

"Oh, it's all getting just as bright as day, now. Next you said I warn't bad, only mischeevous and harum-scarum, and not any more responsible than — than — I think it was a colt, or something."

"And so it was! Well, goodness gracious! Go on, Tom!"

"And then you began to cry."

"So I did. So I did. Not the first time, neither. And then—"

"Then Mrs. Harper she began to cry, and said Joe was just the same, and she wished she hadn't whipped him for taking cream when she'd throwed it out her own self —"

"Tom! The sperrit was upon you! You was a-prophesying — that's what you was doing! Land alive, go on, Tom!"

"Then Sid he said — he said —"

"I don't think I said anything," said Sid.

"Yes you did, Sid," said Mary.

"Shut your heads and let Tom go on I What did he say, Tom?"

"He said — I think he said he hoped I was better off where I was gone to, but if I'd been better sometimes —"

"There, d'you hear that! It was his very words!"

"And you shut him up sharp."

"I lay I did! There must 'a' been an angel there. There was an angel there, somewheres!"

"And Mrs. Harper told about Joe scaring her with a firecracker, and you told about Peter and the Pain-killer—"

"Just as true as I live!"

"And then there was a whole lot of talk 'bout dragging the river for us, and 'bout having the funeral Sunday, and then you and old Miss Harper hugged and cried, and she went."

"It happened just so! It happened just so, as sure as I'm a-sitting in these very tracks. Tom, you couldn't told it more like, if you'd 'a' seen it! And then what? Go on, Tom!"

"Then I thought you prayed for me — and I could see you and hear every word you said. And you went to bed, and I was so sorry, that I took and wrote on a piece of sycamore bark, 'We ain't dead — we are only of being pirates,' and put it on the table by the candle; and then you looked so good, laying there asleep, that I thought I went and leaned over and kissed you on the lips."

"Did you, Tom, did you! I just forgive you everything for that!" And she seized the boy in a crushing embrace that made him feel like the guiltiest of villains.

"It was very kind, even though it was only a — dream," Sid soliloquized just audibly.

"Shut up, Sid! A body does just the same in a dream as he'd do if he was awake. Here's a big Milum apple I've been saving for you, Tom, if you was ever found again — now go 'long to school. I'm thankful to the good God and Father of us all I've got you back, that's long-suffering and merciful to them that believe on Him and keep His word, though goodness knows I'm unworthy of it, but if only the worthy ones got His blessings and had His hand to help them over the rough places, there's few enough would smile here or ever enter into His rest when the long night comes. Go 'long, Sid, Mary, Tom — take yourselves off — you've hendered me long enough."

The children left for school, and the old lady to call on Mrs. Harper and vanquish her realism with Tom's marvelous dream. Sid had better judgment than to utter the thought that was in his mind as he left the house. It was this: "Pretty thin — as long a dream as that, without any mistakes in it!"

What a hero Tom was become, now! He did not go skipping and prancing, but moved with a dignified swagger as became a pirate who felt that the public eye was on him. And indeed it was; he tried not to seem to see the looks or hear the remarks as he passed along, but they were food and drink to him. Smaller boys than himself flocked at his heels, as proud to be seen with him, and tolerated by him, as if he had been the drummer at the head of a procession or the elephant leading a menagerie into town. Boys of his own size pretended not to know he had been away at all; but they were consuming with envy, nevertheless. They would have given anything to have that swarthy, sun-tanned skin of his, and his glittering notoriety; and Tom would not have parted with either for a circus.

At school the children made so much of him and of Joe, and delivered such eloquent admiration from their eyes, that the two heroes were not long in becoming insufferably "stuck up." They began to tell their adventures to hungry listeners — but they only began; it was not a thing likely to have an end, with imaginations like theirs to furnish material. And finally, when they got out their pipes and went serenely puffing around, the very summit of glory was reached.

Tom decided that he could be independent of Becky Thatcher now. Glory was sufficient. He would live for glory. Now that he was distinguished, maybe she would be wanting to "make up." Well let her — she should see that he could be as indifferent as some other people. Presently she arrived, Tom pretended not to see her. He moved away and joined a group of boys and girls and began to talk. Soon he observed that she was tripping gaily back and forth with flushed face and dancing eyes, pretending to be busy chasing schoolmates, and screaming with laughter when she made a capture; but he noticed that she always made her captures in his vicinity, and that she seemed to cast a conscious eye in his direction at such times, too. It gratified all the vicious vanity that was in him; and so, instead of winning him, it only "set him up" the more and made him the more diligent to avoid betraying that he knew she was about. Presently she gave over skylarking, and moved irresolutely about, sighing once or twice and glancing furtively and wistfully toward Tom. Then she observed that now Tom was talking more particularly to Amy Lawrence than to any one else. She felt a sharp pang and grew disturbed and uneasy at once. She tried to go away, but her feet were treacherous, and carried her to the group instead. She said to a girl almost at Tom's elbow — with sham vivacity:

"Why, Mary Austin! you bad girl, why didn't you come to Sunday-school?"

"I did come— didn't you see me?"

"Why, no! Did you? Where did you sit?"

"I was in Miss Peters's class, where I always go. I saw you.''

"Did you? Why, it's funny I didn't see you. I wanted to tell you about the picnic."

"Oh, that's jolly. Who's going to give it?"

"My ma's going to let me have one."

"Oh, goody; I hope she'll let me come."

"Well, she will. The picnic's for me. She'll let anybody come that I want, and I want you."

"That's ever so nice. When is it going to be?"

"By and by. Maybe about vacation."

"Oh, won't it be fun! You going to have all the girls and boys?"

"Yes, every one that's friends to me — or wants to be"; and she glanced ever so furtively at Tom, but he talked right along to Amy Lawrence about the terrible storm on the island, and how the lightning tore the great sycamore tree "all to flinders" while he was "standing within three feet of it."

"Oh, may I come?" said Gracie Miller.

"Yes."

"And me?" said Sally Rogers.

"Yes."

"And me, too?" said Susy Harper. "And Joe?"

"Yes."

And so on, with clapping of joyful hands till all the group had begged for invitations but Tom and Amy. Then Tom turned coolly away, still talking, and took Amy with him. Becky's lips trembled and the tears came to her eyes; she hid these signs with a forced gaiety and went on chattering, but the life had gone out of the picnic, now, and out of everything else; she got away as soon as she could and hid herself and had what her sex call "a good cry." Then she sat moody, with wounded pride, till the bell rang. She roused up, now, with a vindictive cast in her eye, and gave her plaited tails a shake and said she knew what she'd do.

At recess Tom continued his flirtation with Amy with jubilant self-satisfaction. And he kept drifting about to find Becky and lacerate her with the performance. At last he spied her, but there was a sudden falling of his mercury. She was sitting cozily on a little bench behind the school-house looking at a picture-book with Alfred Temple — and so absorbed were they, and their heads so close together over the book, that they did not seem to be conscious of anything in the world besides. Jealousy ran red-hot through Tom's veins. He began to hate himself for throwing away the chance Becky had offered for a reconciliation. He called himself a fool, and all the hard names he could think of. He wanted to cry with vexation. Amy chatted happily along, as they walked, for her heart was singing, but Tom's tongue had lost its function. He did not hear what Amy was saying, and whenever she paused expectantly he could only stammer an awkward assent, which was as often misplaced as otherwise. He kept drifting to the rear of the school-house, again and again, to sear his eyeballs with the hateful spectacle there. He could not help it. And it maddened him to see, as he thought he saw, that Becky Thatcher never once suspected that he was even in the land of the living. But she did see, nevertheless; and she knew she was winning her fight, too, and was glad to see him suffer as she had suffered.

Amy's happy prattle became intolerable. Tom hinted at things he had to attend to; things that must be done; and time was fleeting. But in vain — the girl chirped on. Tom thought, "Oh, hang her, ain't I ever going to get rid of her?" At last he must be attending to those things — and she said artlessly that she would be "around" when school let out. And he hastened away, hating her for it.

"Any other boy!" Tom thought, grating his teeth. "Any boy in the whole town but that Saint Louis smarty that thinks he dresses so fine and is aristocracy! Oh, all right, I licked you the first day you ever saw this town, mister, and I'll lick you again! You just wait till I catch you out! I'll just take and —"

And he went through the motions of thrashing an imaginary boy — pummeling the air, and kicking and gouging. "Oh, you do, do you? You holler 'nough, do you? Now, then, let that learn you!" And so the imaginary flogging was finished to his satisfaction.

Tom fled home at noon. His conscience could not endure any more of Amy's grateful happiness, and his jealousy could bear no more of the other distress. Becky resumed her picture inspections with Alfred, but as the minutes dragged along and no Tom came to suffer, her triumph began to cloud and she lost interest; gravity and absent-mindedness followed, and then melancholy; two or three times she pricked up her ear at a footstep, but it was a false hope; no Tom came. At last she grew entirely miserable and wished she hadn't carried it so far. When poor Alfred, seeing that he was losing her, he did not know how, kept exclaiming: "Oh, here's a jolly one! look at this!" she lost patience at last, and said, "Oh, don't bother me! I don't care for them!" and burst into tears, and got up and walked away.

Alfred dropped alongside and was going to try to comfort her, but she said:

"Go away and leave me alone, can't you! I hate you!"

So the boy halted, wondering what he could have done — for she had said she would look at pictures all through the nooning — and she walked on, crying. Then Alfred went musing into the deserted schoolhouse. He was humiliated and angry. He easily guessed his way to the truth — the girl had simply made a convenience of him to vent her spite upon Tom Sawyer. He was far from hating Tom the less when this thought occurred to him. He wished there was some way to get that boy into trouble without much risk to himself. Tom's spelling-book fell under his eye. Here was his opportunity. He gratefully opened to the lesson for the afternoon and poured ink upon the page.

Becky, glancing in at a window behind him at the moment, saw the act, and moved on, without discovering herself. She started homeward, now, intending to find Tom and tell him; Tom would be thankful and their troubles would be healed. Before she was half-way home, however, she had changed her mind. The thought of Tom's treatment of her when she was talking about her picnic came scorching back and filled her with shame. She resolved to let him get whipped on the damaged spelling-book's account, and to hate him forever, into the bargain.

Lesson 20

- Read chapters 19 and 20 of *The Adventures of Tom Sawyer.*

Chapter 19
The Cruelty of "I Didn't Think"

Tom arrived at home in a dreary mood, and the first thing his aunt said to him showed him that he had brought his sorrows to an unpromising market:

"Tom, I've a notion to skin you alive!"

"Auntie, what have I done?"

"Well, you've done enough. Here I go over to Sereny Harper, like an old softy, expecting I'm going to make her believe all that rubbage about that dream, when lo and behold you she'd found out from Joe that you was over here and heard all the talk we had that night. Tom, I don't know what is to become of a boy that will act like that. It makes me feel so bad to think you could let me go to Sereny Harper and make such a fool of myself and never say a word."

This was a new aspect of the thing. His smartness of the morning had seemed to Tom a good joke before, and very ingenious. It merely looked mean and shabby now. He hung his head and could not think of anything to say for a moment. Then he said:

"Auntie, I wish I hadn't done it — but I didn't think."

"Oh, child, you never think. You never think of anything but your own selfishness. You could think to come all the way over here from Jackson's Island in the night to laugh at our troubles, and you could think to fool me with a lie about a dream; but you couldn't ever think to pity us and save us from sorrow."

"Auntie, I know now it was mean, but I didn't mean to be mean. I didn't, honest. And besides, I didn't come over here to laugh at you that night."

"What did you come for, then?"

"It was to tell you not to be uneasy about us, because we hadn't got drownded."

"Tom, Tom, I would be the thankfulest soul in this world if I could believe you ever had as good a thought as that, but you know you never did — and *I* know it, Tom."

"Indeed and 'deed I did, auntie — I wish I may never stir if I didn't."

"Oh, Tom, don't lie — don't do it. It only makes things a hundred times worse."

"It ain't a lie, auntie, it's the truth. I wanted to keep you from grieving — that was all that made me come."

"I'd give the whole world to believe that — it would cover up a power of sins, Tom. I'd 'most be glad you'd run off and acted so bad. But it ain't reasonable; because, why didn't you tell me, child?"

"Why, you see, when you got to talking about the funeral, I just got all full of the idea of our coming and hiding in the church, and I couldn't somehow bear to spoil it. So I just put the bark back in my pocket and kept mum."

"What bark?"

"The bark I had wrote on to tell you we'd gone pirating. I wish, now, you'd waked up when I kissed you — I do, honest."

The hard lines in his aunt's face relaxed and a sudden tenderness dawned in her eyes.

"*Did* you kiss me, Tom?"

"Why, yes, I did."

"Are you sure you did, Tom?"

"Why, yes, I did, auntie — certain sure."

"What did you kiss me for, Tom?"

"Because I loved you so, and you laid there moaning and I was so sorry."

The words sounded like truth. The old lady could not hide a tremor in her voice when she said:

"Kiss me again, Tom! — and be off with you to school, now, and don't bother me any more."

The moment he was gone, she tan to a closet and got out the ruin of a jacket which Tom had gone pirating in. Then she stopped, with it in her hand, and said to herself:

"No, I don't dare. Poor boy, I reckon he's lied about it — but it's a blessed, blessed lie, there's such a comfort come from it. I hope the Lord — I *know* the Lord will forgive him, because it was such goodheartedness in him to tell it. But I don't want to find out it's a lie. I won't look."

She put the jacket away, and stood by musing a minute. Twice she put out her hand to take the garment again, and twice she refrained. Once more she ventured, and this time she fortified herself with the thought: "It's a good lie — it's a good lie — I won't let it grieve me." So she sought the jacket pocket. A moment later she was reading Tom's piece of bark through flowing tears and saying: "I could forgive the boy, now, if he'd committed a million sins!"

Chapter 20
Tom Takes Becky's Punishment

There was something about Aunt Polly's manner, when she kissed Tom, that swept away his low spirits and made him light-hearted and happy again. He started to school and had the luck of coming upon Becky Thatcher at the head of Meadow Lane. His mood always determined his manner. Without a moment's hesitation he ran to her and said:

"I acted mighty mean to-day, Becky, and I'm so sorry. I won't ever, ever do that way again, as long as ever I live — please make up, won't you?"

The girl stopped and looked him scornfully in the face:

"I'll thank you to keep yourself *to* yourself, Mr. Thomas Sawyer. I'll never speak to you again."

She tossed her head and passed on. Tom was so stunned that he had not even presence of mind enough to say "Who cares, Miss Smarty?" until the right time to say it had gone by. So he said nothing. But he was in a fine rage, nevertheless. He moped into the schoolyard wishing she were a boy, and imagining how he would trounce her if she were. He presently encountered her and delivered a stinging remark as he passed. She hurled one in return, and the angry breach was complete.

It seemed to Becky, in her hot resentment, that she could hardly wait for school to "take in," she was so impatient to see Tom flogged for the injured spelling-book. If she had had any lingering notion of exposing Alfred Temple, Tom's offensive fling had driven it entirely away.

Poor girl, she did not know how fast she was nearing trouble herself. The master, Mr. Dobbins, had reached middle age with an unsatisfied ambition. The darling of his desires was to be a doctor, but poverty had decreed that he should be nothing higher than a village schoolmaster. Every day he took a mysterious book out of his desk and absorbed himself in it at times when no classes were reciting. He kept that book under lock and key. There was not an urchin in school but was perishing to have a glimpse of it, but the chance never came. Every boy and girl had a theory about the nature of that book; but no two theories were alike, and there was no way of getting at the facts in the case. Now, as Becky was passing by the desk, which stood near the door, she noticed that the key was in the lock! It was a precious moment. She glanced around; found herself alone, and the next instant she had the book in her hands. The title-page — Professor Somebody's *Anatomy* — carried no information to her mind; so she began to turn the leaves. She came at once upon a handsomely engraved and colored frontispiece — a human figure, stark naked. At that moment a shadow fell on the page and Tom Sawyer stepped in at the door, and caught a glimpse of the picture. Becky snatched at the book to close it, and had the hard luck to tear the pictured plate half down the middle. She thrust the volume into the desk, turned the key, and burst out crying with shame and vexation.

"Tom Sawyer, you are just as mean as you can be, to sneak up on a person and look at what they're looking at."

"How could *I* know you was looking at anything?"

"You ought to be ashamed of yourself, Tom Sawyer; you know you're going to tell on me, and oh, what shall I do, what shall I do! I'll be whipped, and I never was whipped in school."

Then she stamped her little foot and said:

"*Be* so mean if you want to! I know something that's going to happen. You just wait and you'll see! Hateful, hateful, hateful!" — and she flung out of the house with a new explosion of crying?

Tom stood still, rather flustered by this onslaught. Presently he said to himself:

"What a curious kind of a fool a girl is. Never been licked in school! Shucks. What's a licking! That's just like a girl — they're so thin-skinned and chicken-hearted. Well, of course *I* ain't going to tell old Dobbins on this little fool, because there's other ways of getting even on her that ain't so mean; but what of it? Old Dobbins will ask who it was tore his book. Nobody'll answer. Then he'll do just the way he always does — ask first one and then t'other, and when he comes to the right girl he'll know it, without any telling. Girls' faces always tell on them. They ain't got any backbone. She'll get licked. Well, it's a kind of a tight place for Becky Thatcher, because there ain't any way out of it." Tom conned the thing a moment longer and then added: "All right, though; she'd like to see me in just such a fix — let her sweat it out!"

Tom joined the mob of skylarking scholars outside. In a few moments the master arrived and school "took in." Tom did not feel a strong interest in his studies. Every time he stole a glance at the girls' side of the room Becky's face troubled him. Considering all things, he did not want to pity her, and yet it was all he could do to help it. He could get up no exultation that was really worthy the name. Presently the spelling-book discovery was made, and Tom's mind was entirely full of his own matters for a while after that. Becky roused up from her lethargy of distress and showed good interest in the proceedings. She did not expect that Tom could get out of his trouble by denying that he spilt the ink on the book himself; and she was right. The denial only seemed to make the thing worse for Tom. Becky supposed she would be glad of that, and she tried to believe she was glad of it, but she found she was not certain. When the worst came to the worst, she had an impulse to get up and tell on Alfred Temple, but she made an effort and forced herself to keep still — because, said she to herself, "he'll tell about me tearing the picture sure. I wouldn't say a word, not to save his life!"

Tom took his whipping and went back to his seat not at all broken-hearted, for he thought it was possible that he had unknowingly upset the ink on the spelling-book himself, in some skylarking bout — he had denied it for form's sake and because it was custom, and had stuck to the denial from principle.

A whole hour drifted by, the master sat nodding in his throne, the air was drowsy with the hum of study. By and by, Mr. Dobbins straightened himself up, yawned, then unlocked his desk, and reached for his book, but seemed undecided whether to take it out or leave it. Most of the pupils glanced up languidly, but there were two among them that watched his movements with intent eyes. Mr. Dobbins fingered his book absently for a while, then took it out and settled himself in his chair to read! Tom shot a glance at Becky. He had seen a hunted and helpless rabbit look as she did, with a gun leveled at its head. Instantly he forgot his quarrel with her. Quick — something must be done! done in a flash, too! But the very imminence of the emergency paralyzed his invention. Good! — he had an inspiration! He would run and snatch the book, spring through the door and fly. But his resolution shook for one little instant, and the chance was lost — the master opened the volume. If Tom only had the wasted opportunity back again! Too late. There was no help for Becky now, he said. The next moment the master faced the school. Every eye sank under his gaze. There was that in it which smote even the innocent with fear. There was silence while one might count ten, the master was gathering his wrath. Then he spoke:

"Who tore this book?"

There was not a sound. One could have heard a pin drop. The stillness continued; the master searched face after face for signs of guilt.

"Benjamin Rogers, did you tear this book?"

A denial. Another pause.

"Joseph Harper, did you?"

Another denial. Tom's uneasiness grew more and more intense under the slow torture of these proceedings. The master scanned the ranks of boys — considered awhile, then turned to the girls:

"Amy Lawrence?"

A shake of the head.

"Grade Miller?"

The same sign.

"Susan Harper, did you do this?"

Another negative. The next girl was Becky Thatcher. Tom was trembling from head to foot with excitement and a sense of the hopelessness of the situation.

"Rebecca Thatcher" [Tom glanced at her face — it was white with terror] — "did you tear — no, look me in the face" [her hands rose in appeal] — "did you tear this book?"

A thought shot like lightning through Tom's brain. He sprang to his feet and shouted — "*I* done it!"

The school stared in perplexity at this incredible folly. Tom stood a moment, to gather his dismembered faculties; and when he stepped forward to go to his punishment the surprise, the gratitude, the adoration that shone upon him out of poor Becky's eyes seemed pay enough for a hundred floggings.

Inspired by the splendor of his own act, he took without an outcry the most merciless flaying that even Mr. Dobbins had ever administered; and also received with indifference the added cruelty of a command to remain two hours after school should be dismissed — for he knew who would wait for him outside till his captivity was done, and not count the tedious time as loss, either.

Tom went to bed that night planning vengeance against Alfred Temple; for with shame and repentance Becky had told him all, not forgetting her own treachery; but even the longing for vengeance had to give way, soon, to pleasanter musings, and he fell asleep at last, with Becky's latest words lingering dreamily in his ear —

"Tom, how could you be so noble!"

- In this chapter Tom takes Becky's punishment. What does that say about Tom? (Think about how he used to react to punishment from Aunt Polly.)
- Has he matured at all?

Lesson 21

- Read chapter 21 of *The Adventures of Tom Sawyer.*

Chapter 21
Eloquence and the Master's Gilded Dome

Vacation was approaching. The schoolmaster, always severe, grew severer and more exacting than ever, for he wanted the school to make a good showing on "Examination" day. His rod and his ferule were seldom idle now — at least among the smaller pupils. Only the biggest boys, and young ladies of eighteen and twenty, escaped lashing. Mr. Dobbins's lashings were very vigorous ones, too; for although he carried, under his wig, a perfectly bald and shiny head, he had only reached middle age and there was no sign of feebleness in his muscle. As the great day approached, all the tyranny that was in him came to the surface; he seemed to take a vindictive pleasure in punishing the least shortcomings. The consequence was, that the smaller boys spent their days in terror and suffering and their nights in plotting revenge. They threw away no opportunity to do the master a mischief. But he kept ahead all the time. The retribution that followed every vengeful success was so sweeping and majestic that the boys always retired from the field badly worsted. At last they conspired together and hit upon a plan that promised a dazzling victory. They swore in the sign-painter's boy, told him the scheme, and asked his help. He had his own reasons for being delighted, for the master boarded in his father's family and had given the boy ample cause to hate him. The master's wife would go on a visit to the country in a few days, and there would be nothing to interfere with the plan; the master always prepared himself for great occasions by getting pretty well fuddled, and the sign-painter's boy said that when the dominie had reached the proper condition on Examination Evening he would "manage the thing" while he napped in his chair; then he would have him awakened at the right time and hurried away to school.

In the fullness of time the interesting occasion arrived. At eight in the evening the school-house was brilliantly lighted, and adorned with wreaths and festoons of foliage and flowers. The master sat throned in his great chair upon a raised platform, with his blackboard behind him. He was looking tolerably mellow. Three rows of benches on each side and six rows in front of him were occupied by the dignitaries of the town and by the parents of the pupils. To his left, back of the rows of citizens, was a spacious temporary platform upon which were seated the scholars who were to take part in the exercises of the evening; rows of small boys, washed and dressed to an intolerable state of discomfort; rows of gawky big boys; snowbanks of girls and young ladies clad in lawn and muslin and conspicuously conscious of their bare arms, their grandmothers' ancient trinkets, their bits of pink and blue ribbon and the flowers in their hair. All the rest of the house was filled with non-participating scholars.

The exercises began. A very little boy stood up and sheepishly recited, "You'd scarce expect one of my age to speak in public on the stage," etc. — accompanying himself with the painfully exact and spasmodic gestures which a machine might have used — supposing the machine to be a trifle out of order. But he got through safely, though cruelly scared, and got a fine round of applause when he made his manufactured bow and retired.

A little shamefaced girl lisped "Mary had a little lamb," etc., performed a compassion-inspiring curtsy, got her meed of applause, and sat down flushed and happy.

Tom Sawyer stepped forward with conceited confidence and soared into the unquenchable and indestructible "Give me liberty or give me death" speech, with fine fury and frantic gesticulation, and broke down in the middle of it. A ghastly stagefright seized him. his legs quaked under him and he was like to choke. True, he had the manifest sympathy of the house — but he had the house's silence, too, which was even worse than its sympathy. The master frowned, and this completed the disaster. Tom struggled awhile and then retired, utterly defeated. There was a weak attempt at applause, but it died early.

"The Boy Stood on the Burning Deck" followed; also "The Assyrian Came Down," and other declamatory gems. Then there were reading exercises and a spelling-fight. The meager Latin class recited with honor. The prime feature of the evening was in order now — original "compositions" by the young ladies. Each in her turn stepped forward to the edge of the platform, cleared her throat, held up her manuscript (tied with dainty ribbon), and proceeded to read, with labored attention to "expression" and punctuation. The themes were the same that had been illuminated upon similar occasions by their mothers before them, their grandmothers, and doubtless all their ancestors in the female line clear back to the Crusades. "Friendship" was one; "Memories of Other Days"; "Religion in History"; "Dream Land"; "The Advantages of Culture"; "Forms of Political Government Compared and Contrasted"; "Melancholy"; "Filial Love"; " Heart Longings," etc., etc.

A prevalent feature in these compositions was a nursed and petted melancholy; another was a wasteful and opulent gush of "fine language"; another was a tendency to lug in by the ears particularly prized words and phrases until they were worn entirely out; and a peculiarity that conspicuously marked and marred them was the inveterate and intolerable sermon that wagged its crippled tail at the end of each and every one of them. No matter what the subject might be, a brain-racking effort was made to squirm it into some aspect or other that the moral and religious mind could contemplate with edification. The glaring insincerity of these sermons was not sufficient to compass the banishment of the fashion from the schools, and it is not sufficient to-day; it never will be sufficient while the world stands, perhaps. There is no school in all our land where the young ladies do not feel obliged to close their compositions with a sermon; and you will find that the sermon of the most frivolous and the least religious girl in the school is always the longest and the most relentlessly pious. But enough of this. Homely truth is unpalatable.

Let us return to the "Examination." The first composition that was read was one entitled "Is this, then, Life?" Perhaps the reader can endure an extract from it:

> In the common walks of life, with what delightful emotions does the youthful mind look forward to some anticipated scene of festivity! Imagination is busy sketching rose-tinted pictures of joy. In fancy, the voluptuous votary of fashion sees herself amid the festive throng, "the observed of all observers." Her graceful form, arrayed in snowy robes, is

> whirling through the mazes of the joyous dance; her eye is brightest, her step is lightest in the gay assembly.
>
> In such delicious fancies time quickly glides by, and the welcome hour arrives for her entrance into the elysian world, of which she has had such bright dreams. How fairylike does everything appear to her enchanted vision! Each new scene is more charming than the last. But after a while she finds that beneath this goodly exterior, all is vanity: the flattery which once charmed her soul now grates harshly upon her ear; the ballroom has lost its charms; and with wasted health and embittered heart she turns away with the conviction that earthly pleasures cannot satisfy the longings of the soul!

And so forth and so on. There was a buzz of gratification from time to time during the reading, accompanied by whispered ejaculations of "How sweet!" "How eloquent!" "So true!" etc., and after the thing had closed with a peculiarly afflicting sermon the applause was enthusiastic.

Then arose a slim, melancholy girl, whose face had the "interesting" paleness that comes of pills and indigestion, and read a "poem," Two stanzas of it will do:

A MISSOURI MAIDEN'S FAREWELL TO ALABAMA

Alabama, good-by! I love thee well!
But yet for a while do I leave thee now!
Sad, yes, sad thoughts of thee my heart doth swell,
And burning recollections throng my brow!
For I have wandered through thy flowery woods:
Have roamed and read near Tallapoosa's stream;
Have listened to Tallassee's warring floods,
And wooed on Coosa's side Aurora's beam.

Yet shame I not to bear an o'er-full heart,
Nor blush to turn behind my tearful eyes;
'Tis from no stranger land I now must part,
'Tis to no strangers left I yield these sighs.
Welcome and home were mine within this State,
Whose vales I leave — whose spires fade fast from me;

And cold must be mine eyes, and heart, and tête,
When, dear Alabama! they turn cold on thee!

There were very few there who knew what "*tête*" meant, but the poem was very satisfactory, nevertheless.

Next appeared a dark-complexioned, black-eyed, black-haired young lady, who paused an impressive moment, assumed a tragic expression, and began to read in a measured, solemn tone.

A VISION

> Dark and tempestuous was night. Around the throne on high not a single star quivered; but the deep intonations of the heavy thunder constantly vibrated upon the ear; whilst the terrific lightning reveled in angry mood through the cloudy chambers of heaven, seeming to scorn the power exerted over its terror by the illustrious Franklin! Even the boisterous winds unanimously came forth from their mystic homes, and blustered about as if to enhance by their aid the wildness of the scene.
>
> At such a time, so dark, so dreary, for human sympathy my very spirit sighed; but instead thereof,
>
> "My dearest friend, my counselor, my comforter and guide —
> My joy in grief, my second bliss in joy," came to my side.
>
> She moved like one of those bright beings pictured in the sunny walks of fancy's Eden by the romantic and young, a queen of beauty unadorned save by her own transcendent loveliness. So soft was her step, it failed to make even a sound, and but for the magical thrill imparted by her genial touch, as other unobtrusive beauties, she would have glided away unperceived — unsought. A strange sadness rested upon her features, like icy tears upon the robe of December, as she pointed to the contending elements without, and bade me contemplate the two beings presented.

This nightmare occupied some ten pages of manuscript and wound up with a sermon so destructive of all hope to non-Presbyterians that it took the first prize.

This composition was considered to be the very finest effort of the evening. The mayor of the village, in delivering the prize to the author of it, made a warm speech in which he said that it was by far the most "eloquent" thing he had ever listened to, and that Daniel Webster himself might well be proud of it.

It may be remarked, in passing, that the number of compositions in which the word "beauteous" was over-fondled, and human experience referred to as "life's page," was up to the usual average.

Now the master, mellow almost to the verge of geniality, put his chair aside, turned his back to the audience, and began to draw a map of America on the blackboard, to exercise the geography class upon. But he made a sad business of it with his unsteady hand, and a smothered titter rippled over the house. He knew what the matter was and set himself to right it. He sponged out lines and remade them; but he only distorted them more than ever, and the tittering was more pronounced. He threw his entire attention upon his work, now, as if determined not to be put down by the mirth. He felt that all eyes were fastened upon him; he imagined he was succeeding, and yet the tittering continued; it even manifestly increased. And well it might. There was a garret above, pierced with a scuttle over his head; and down through this scuttle came a cat, suspended around the haunches by a string; she had a rag tied about her head and jaws to keep her from mewing; as she slowly descended she curved upward and clawed at the string, she swung downward and clawed at the intangible air. The tittering rose higher and higher — the cat was within six inches of the absorbed teacher's head — down, down, a little lower, and she grabbed his wig with her desperate claws, clung to it, and was snatched up into the garret in an instant with her trophy still in her possession! And how the light did blaze abroad from the master's bald pate — for the sign-painter's boy had gilded it!

That broke up the meeting. The boys were avenged. Vacation had come.

NOTE. — The pretended "compositions" quoted in this chapter are taken without alteration from a volume entitled "Prose and Poetry, by a Western Lady" — but they are exactly and precisely after the school-girl pattern, and hence are much happier than any mere imitations could be

Lesson 22

- Read chapter 22 of *The Adventures of Tom Sawyer.*

Chapter 22
Huck Finn Quotes Scriptures

Tom joined the new order of Cadets of Temperance, being attracted by the showy character of their "regalia" He promised to abstain from smoking, chewing, and profanity as long as he remained a member. Now he found out a new thing — namely, that to promise not to do a thing is the surest way in the world to make a body want to go and do that very thing. Tom soon found himself tormented with a desire to drink and swear; the desire grew to be so intense that nothing but the hope of a chance to display himself in his red sash kept him from withdrawing from the order. Fourth of July was coming; but he soon gave that up — gave it up before he had worn his shackles over forty-eight hours — and fixed his hopes upon old Judge Frazer, justice of the peace, who was apparently on his deathbed and would have a big public funeral, since he was so high an official. During three days Tom was deeply concerned about the Judge's condition and hungry for news of it. Sometimes his hopes ran high — so high that he would venture to get out his regalia and practise before the looking-glass. But the Judge had a most discouraging way of fluctuating. At last he was pronounced upon the mend — and then convalescent. Tom was disgusted; and felt a sense of injury, too. He handed in his resignation at once — and that night the Judge suffered a relapse and died. Tom resolved that he would never trust a man like that again.

The funeral was a fine thing. The Cadets paraded in a style calculated to kill the late member with envy. Tom was a free boy again, however — there was something in that. He could drink and swear, now — but found to his surprise that he did not want to. The simple fact that he could took the desire away, and the charm of it.

Tom presently wondered to find that his coveted vacation was beginning to hang a little heavily on his hands.

He attempted a diary — but nothing happened during three days, and so he abandoned it.

The first of all the negro minstrel shows came to town, and made a sensation. Tom and Joe Harper got up a band of performers and were happy for two days.

Even the Glorious Fourth was in some sense a failure, for it rained hard, there was no procession in consequence, and the greatest man in the world (as Tom supposed), Mr. Benton, an actual United States Senator, proved an overwhelming disappointment — for he was not twenty-five feet high, nor even anywhere in the neighborhood of it.

A circus came. The boys played circus for three days afterward in tents made of rag carpeting — admission, three pins for boys, two for girls — and then circusing was abandoned.

A phrenologist and a mesmerizer came — and went again and left the village duller and drearier than ever.

There were some boys-and-girls' parties, but they were so few and so delightful that they only made the aching voids between ache the harder.

Becky Thatcher was gone to her Constantinople home to stay with her parents during vacation — so there was no bright side to life anywhere.

The dreadful secret of the murder was a chronic misery. It was a very cancer for permanency and pain.

Then came the measles.

During two long weeks Tom lay a prisoner, dead to the world and its happenings. He was very ill, he was interested in nothing. When he got upon his feet at last and moved feebly down-town, a melancholy change had come over everything and every creature. There had been a "revival," and everybody had "got religion" not only the adults, but even the boys and girls. Tom went about, hoping against hope for the sight of one blessed sinful face, but disappointment crossed him everywhere. He found Joe Harper studying a Testament, and turned sadly away from the depressing spectacle. He sought Ben Rogers, and found him visiting the poor with a basket of tracts. He hunted up Jim Hollis, who called his attention to the precious blessing of his late measles as a warning. Every boy he encountered added another ton to his depression; and when, in desperation, he flew for refuge at last to the bosom of Huckleberry Finn and was received with a Scriptural quotation, his heart broke and he crept home and to bed realizing that he alone of all the town was lost, forever and forever.

And that night there came on a terrific storm, with driving rain, awful claps of thunder and blinding sheets of lighting. He covered his head with the bedclothes and waited in a horror of suspense for his doom; for he had not the shadow of a doubt that all this hubbub was about him. He believed he had taxed the forbearance of the powers above to the extremity of endurance and that this was the result. It might have seemed to him a waste of pomp and ammunition to kill a bug with a battery of artillery, but there seemed nothing incongruous about the getting up such an expensive thunderstorm as this to knock the turf from under an insect like himself.

By and by the tempest spent itself and died without accomplishing its object. The boy's first impulse was to be grateful, and reform. His second was to wait — for there might not be any more storms.

The next day the doctors were back; Tom had relapsed. The three weeks he spent on his back this time seemed an entire age. When he got abroad at last he was hardly grateful that he had been spared, remembering how lonely was his estate, how companionless and forlorn he was. He drifted listlessly down the street and found Jim Hollis acting as judge in a juvenile court that was trying a cat for murder, in the presence of her victim, a bird. He found Joe Harper and Huck Finn up an alley eating a stolen melon. Poor lads! they — like Tom — had suffered a relapse.

Lesson 23

- Read chapters 23 and 24 of *The Adventures of Tom Sawyer*.

Chapter 23
The Salvation of Muff Potter

At last the sleepy atmosphere was stirred — and vigorously: the murder trial came on in the court. It became the absorbing topic of village talk immediately. Tom could not get away from it. Every reference to the murder sent a shudder to his heart, for his troubled conscience and fears almost persuaded him that these remarks were put forth in his hearing as "feelers"; he did not see how he could be suspected of knowing anything about the murder, but still he could not be comfortable in the midst of this gossip. It kept him in a cold shiver all the time. He took Huck to a lonely place to have a talk with him. It would be some relief to unseal his tongue for a little while; to divide his burden of distress with another sufferer. Moreover, he wanted to assure himself that Huck had remained discreet.

"Huck, have you ever told anybody about — that?"

"'Bout what?"

"You know what."

"Oh— 'course I haven't."

"Never a word?"

"Never a solitary word, so help me. What makes you ask?"

"Well, I was afeard."

"Why, Tom Sawyer, we wouldn't be alive two days if that got found out. You know that."

Tom felt more comfortable. After a pause:

"Huck, they couldn't anybody get you to tell, could they?"

"Get me to tell? Why, if I wanted that half-breed devil to drownd me they could get me to tell. They ain't no different way."

"Well, that's all right, then. I reckon we're safe as long as we keep mum. But let's swear again, anyway. It's more surer."

"I'm agreed."

So they swore again with dread solemnities.

"What is the talk around, Huck? I've heard a power of it."

"Talk? Well, it's just Muff Potter, Muff Potter, Muff Potter all the time. It keeps me in a sweat, constant, so's I want to hide som'ers."

"That's just the same way they go on round me. I reckon he's a goner. Don't you feel sorry for him, sometimes?"

"Most always — most always. He ain't no account; but then he hain't ever done anything to hurt anybody. Just fishes a little, to get money to get drunk on — and loafs around considerable; but lord, we all do that — leastways most of us — preachers and such like. But he's kind of good — he give me half a fish, once, when there warn't enough for two; and lots of times he's kind of stood by me when I was out of luck."

"Well, he's mended kites for me, Huck, and knitted hooks on to my line. I wish we could get him out of there."

"My! we couldn't get him out, Tom. And besides, 'twouldn't do any good; they'd ketch him again."

"'Yes — so they would. But I hate to hear 'em abuse him so like the dickens when he never done —that."

"I do too, Tom. Lord, I hear 'em say he's the bloodiest-looking villain in this country, and they wonder he wasn't ever hung before."

"Yes, they talk like that, all the time. I've heard 'em say that if he was to get free they'd lynch him."

"And they'd do it, too."

The boys had a long talk, but it brought them little comfort. As the twilight drew on, they found themselves hanging about the neighborhood of the little isolated jail, perhaps with an undefined hope that something would happen that might clear away their difficulties. But nothing happened; there seemed to be no angels or fairies interested in this luckless captive.

The boys did as they had often done before — went to the cell grating and gave Potter some tobacco and matches. He was on the ground floor and there were no guards.

His gratitude for their gifts had always smote their consciences before — it cut deeper than ever, this time. They felt cowardly and treacherous to the last degree when Potter said:

"You've been mighty good to me, boys — better'n anybody else in this town. And I don't forget it, I don't. Often I says to myself, says I, 'I used to mend all the boys' kites and things, and show 'em where the good fishin'- places was, and befriend 'em what I could, and now they've all forgot old Muff when he's in trouble; but Tom don't, and Huck don't — *they* don't forget him,' says I, 'and I don't forget them.' Well, boys, I done an awful thing — drunk and crazy at the time — that's the only way I account for it — and now I got to swing for it, and it's right. Right, and *best*, too, I reckon — hope so, anyway. Well, we won't talk about that. I don't want to make *you* feel bad; you've befriended me. But what I want to say, is, don't you ever get drunk — then you won't ever get here. Stand a litter furder west — so — that's it; it's a prime comfort to see faces that's friendly when a body's in such a muck of trouble, and there don't none come here but yourn. Good friendly faces — good friendly faces. Git up on one another's backs and let me touch 'em. That's it. Shake hands — yourn'll come through the bars, but mine's too big. Little hands, and weak — but they've helped Muff Potter a power, and they'd help him more if they could."

Tom went home miserable, and his dreams that night were full of horrors. The next day and the day after, he hung about the courtroom, drawn by an almost irresistible impulse to go in, but forcing himself to stay out. Huck was having the same experience. They studiously avoided each other. Each wandered away, from time to time, but the same dismal fascination always brought them back presently. Tom kept his ears open when idlers sauntered out of the courtroom, but invariably heard distressing news — the toils were closing more and more relentlessly around poor Potter. At the end of the second day the village talk was to the effect that Injun Joe's evidence stood firm and unshaken, and that there was not the slightest question as to what the jury's verdict would be.

Tom was out late that night, and came to bed through the window. He was in a tremendous state of excitement. It was hours before he got to sleep. All the village flocked to the courthouse the next morning, for this was to be the great day. Both sexes were about equally represented in the packed audience. After a long wait the jury filed in and took their places; shortly afterward, Potter, pale and haggard, timid and hopeless, was brought in, with chains upon him, and seated where all the curious eyes could stare at him; no less conspicuous was Injun Joe, stolid as ever. There was another pause, and then the judge arrived and the sheriff proclaimed the opening of the court. The usual whisperings among the lawyers and gathering together of papers followed. These details and accompanying delays worked up an atmosphere of preparation that was as impressive as it was fascinating.

Now a witness was called who testified that he found Muff Potter washing in the brook, at an early hour of the morning that the murder was discovered, and that he immediately sneaked away. After some further questioning, counsel for the prosecution said:

"Take the witness."

The prisoner raised his eyes for a moment, but dropped them again when his own counsel said:

"I have no questions to ask him."

The next witness proved the finding of the knife near the corpse. Counsel for the prosecution said:

"Take the witness."

"I have no questions to ask him," Potter's lawyer replied.

A third witness swore he had often seen the knife in Potter's possession.

"Take the witness."

Counsel for Potter declined to question him. The faces of the audience began to betray annoyance.

Did this attorney mean to throw away his client's life without an effort?

Several witnesses deposed concerning Potter's guilty behavior when brought to the scene of the murder. They were allowed to leave the stand without being cross-questioned.

Every detail of the damaging circumstances that occurred in the graveyard upon that morning which all present remembered so well was brought out by credible witnesses, but none of them were cross-examined by Potter's lawyer. The perplexity and dissatisfaction of the house expressed itself in murmurs and provoked a reproof from the bench. Counsel for the prosecution now said:

"By the oaths of citizens whose simple word is above suspicion, we have fastened this awful crime, beyond all possibility of question, upon the unhappy prisoner at the bar. We rest our case here."

A groan escaped from poor Potter, and he put his face in his hands and rocked his body softly to and fro, while a painful silence reigned in the courtroom. Many men were moved, and many women's compassion testified itself in tears. Counsel for the defense rose and said:

"Your honor, in our remarks at the opening of this trial, we foreshadowed our purpose to prove that our client did this fearful deed while under the influence of a blind and irresponsible delirium produced by drink. We have changed our mind. We shall not offer that plea." [Then to the clerk:] "Call Thomas Sawyer!"

A puzzled amazement awoke in every face in the house, not even excepting Potter's. Every eye fastened itself with wondering interest upon Tom as he rose and took his place upon the stand. The boy looked wild enough, for he was badly scared. The oath was administered.

"Thomas Sawyer, where were you on the seventeenth of June, about the hour of midnight?"

Tom glanced at Injun Joe's iron face and his tongue failed him. The audience listened breathless, but the words refused to come. After a few moments, however, the boy got a little of his strength back, and managed to put enough of it into his voice to make part of the house hear:

"In the graveyard!"

"A little bit louder, please. Don't be afraid. You were —"

"In the graveyard."

A contemptuous smile flitted across Injun Joe's f ace.

"Were you anywhere near Horse Williams's grave?"

"Yes, sir."

"Speak up — just a trifle louder. How near were you?"

"Near as I am to you."

"Were you hidden, or not?"

"I was hid."

"Where?"

"Behind the elms that's on the edge of the grave."

Injun Joe gave a barely perceptible start.

"Any one with you?"

"Yes, sir. I went there with —"

"Wait — wait a moment. Never mind mentioning your companion's name. We will produce him at the proper time. Did you carry anything there with you."

Tom hesitated and looked confused.

"Speak out, my boy — don't be diffident. The truth is always respectable. What did you take there?"

"Only a — a — dead cat."

There was a ripple of mirth, which the court checked.

"We will produce the skeleton of that cat. Now, my boy, tell us everything that occurred — tell it in your own way — don't skip anything, and don't be afraid."

Tom began — hesitatingly at first, but as he warmed to his subject his words flowed more and more easily; in a little while every sound ceased but his own voice; every eye fixed itself upon him; with parted lips and bated breath the audience hung upon his words, taking no note of time, rapt in the ghastly fascinations of the tale. The strain upon pent emotion reached its climax when the boy said:

"— and as the doctor fetched the board around and Muff Potter fell, Injun Joe jumped with the
knife and —"

Crash! Quick as lightning the half-breed sprang for a window, tore his way through all opposers, and was gone!

- In *Tom Sawyer*, what foreshadowing, suspense, and irony have you noticed?

Chapter 24
Splendid Days and Fearsome Nights

Tom was a glittering hero once more — the pet of the old, the envy of the young. His name even went into immortal print, for the village paper magnified him. There were some that believed he would be President, yet, if he escaped hanging.

As usual, the fickle, unreasoning world took Muff Potter to its bosom and fondled him as lavishly as it had abused him before. But that sort of conduct is to the world's credit; therefore it is not well to find fault with it.

Tom's days were days of splendor and exultation to him, but his nights were seasons of horror. Injun Joe infested all his dreams, and always with doom in his eye. Hardly any temptation could persuade the boy to stir abroad after nightfall. Poor Huck was in the same state of wretchedness and terror, for Tom had told the whole story to the lawyer the night before the great day of the trial, and Huck was sore afraid that his share in the business might leak out, yet, notwithstanding Injun Joe's flight had saved him the suffering of testifying in court. The poor fellow had got the attorney to promise secrecy, but what of that? Since Tom's harassed conscience had managed to drive him to the lawyer's house by night and wring a dread tale from lips that had been sealed with the dismalest and most formidable of oaths, Huck's confidence in the human race was well-nigh obliterated.

Daily Muff Potter's gratitude made Tom glad he had spoken; but nightly he wished he had sealed up his tongue.

Half the time Tom was afraid Injun Joe would never be captured; the other half he was afraid he would be. He felt sure he never could draw a safe breath again until that man was dead and he had seen the corpse.

Rewards had been offered, the country had been scoured, but no Injun Joe was found. One of those omniscient and awe-inspiring marvels, a detective, came up from St. Louis, moused around, shook his head looked wise, and made that sort of astounding success which members of that craft usually achieve. That is to say, he "found a clew." But you can't hang a "clew" for murder, and so after that detective had got through and gone home, Tom felt just as insecure as he was before.

The slow days drifted on, and each left behind it a slightly lightened weight of apprehension.

- How does suspense build in this chapter?

Lesson 24

- Read chapter 25 of *The Adventures of Tom Sawyer*.

Chapter 25
Seeking the Buried Treasure

There comes a time in every rightly constructed boy's life when he has a raging desire to go somewhere and dig for hidden treasure. This desire suddenly came upon Tom one day. He sallied out to find Joe Harper, but failed of success. Next he sought Ben Rogers; he had gone fishing. Presently he stumbled upon Huck Finn the Red-Handed. Huck would answer. Tom took him to a private place and opened the matter to him confidentially. Huck was willing. Huck was always willing to take a hand in any enterprise that offered entertainment and required no capital, for he had a troublesome superabundance of that sort of time which is *not* money.

"Where'll we dig?" said Huck.

"Oh, most anywhere."

"Why, is it hid all around?"

“No indeed it ain’t. It’s hid in mighty particular places, Huck — sometimes on islands, sometimes in rotten chests under the end of a limb of an old dead tree, just where the shadow falls at midnight; but mostly under the floor in ha’nted houses.”

“Who hides it?”

“Why, robbers, of course — who’d you reckon? Sunday-school sup’rintendents?”

“I don’t know. If ‘twas mine I wouldn’t hide it; I’d spend it and have a good time.”

“So would I. But robbers don’t do that way. They always hide it and leave it there.”

“Don’t they come after it any more?”

“No, they think they will, but they generally forget the marks, or else they die. Anyway, it lays there a long time and gets rusty; and by and by somebody finds an old yellow paper that tells how to find the marks — a paper that’s got to be ciphered over about a week because it’s mostly signs and hy’roglyphics.”

“Hyro— which?”

“Hy’roglyphics — pictures and things, you know, that don’t seem to mean anything.”

“Have you got one of them papers, Tom?”

“No.”

“Well then, how you going to find the marks?”

“I don’t want any marks. They always bury it under a ha’nted house or on an island, or under a dead tree that’s got one limb sticking out. Well, we’ve tried Jackson’s Island a little, and we can try it again some time; and there’s the old ha’nted house up the Still-House branch, and there’s lots of dead-limb trees — dead loads of ‘em.”

“Is it under all of them?”

"How you talk! No!"

"Then how you going to know which one to go for?"

"Go for all of 'em!"

"Why, Tom, it'll take all summer."

"Well, what of that? Suppose you find a brass pot with a hundred dollars in it, all rusty and gay, or a rotten chest full of di'monds. How's that?"

Huck's eyes glowed.

"That's bully. Plenty bully enough for me. Just you gimme the hundred dollars and I don't want no di'monds."

"All right. But I bet you *I* ain't going to throw off on di'monds. Some of 'em's worth twenty dollars apiece — there ain't any, hardly, but's worth six bits or a dollar."

"No! Is that so?"

"Cert'nly — anybody'll tell you so. Hain't you ever seen one, Huck?"

"Not as I remember."

"Oh, kings have slathers of them."

"Well, I don't know no kings, Tom."

"I reckon you don't. But if you was to go to Europe you'd see a raft of 'em hopping around."

"Do they hop?"

"Hop? — your granny! No!"

“Well, what did you say they did, for?”

“Shucks, I only meant you’d *see* ‘em — not hopping, of course — what do they want to hop for? — but I mean you’d just see ‘em — scattered around, you know, in a kind of a general way. Like that old humpbacked Richard.”

“Richard? What’s his other name?”

“He didn’t have any other name. Kings don’t have any but a given name.”

“No?”

“But they don’t.”

“Well, if they like it, Tom, all right; but I don’t want to be a king and have only just a given name, like a negro. But say — where you going to dig first?”

“Well, I don’t know. S’pose we tackle that old dead-limb tree on the hill t’other side of Still-House branch?”

“I’m agreed.”

So they got a crippled pick and a shovel, and set out on their three-mile tramp. They arrived hot and panting, and threw themselves down in the shade of a neighboring elm to rest and have a smoke.

“I like this,” said Tom.

“So do I.”

“Say, Huck, if we find a treasure here, what you going to do with your share?”

“Well, I’ll have pie and a glass of soda every day, and I’ll go to every circus that comes along. I bet I’ll have a gay time.”

“Well, ain’t you going to save any of it?”

"Save it? What for?"

"Why, so as to have something to live on, by and by."

"Oh, that ain't any use. Pap would come back to thish yer town some day and get his claws on it if I didn't hurry up, and I tell you he'd clean it out pretty quick. What you going to do with yourn, Tom?"

"I'm going to buy a new drum, and a sure-'nough sword, and a red necktie and a bull pup, and get married."

"Married!"

"That's it."

"Tom, you — why, you ain't in your right mind."

"Wait— you'll see."

"Well, that's the foolishest thing you could do. Look at pap and my mother. Fight! Why, they used to fight all the time. I remember, mighty well."

"That ain't anything. The girl I'm going to marry won't fight."

"Tom, I reckon they're all alike. They'll all comb a body. Now you better think 'bout this awhile. I tell you you better. What's the name of the gal?"

"It ain't a gal at all — it's a girl."

"It's all the same, I reckon; some says gal, some says girl — both's right, like enough. Anyway, what's her name, Tom?"

"I'll tell you some time — not now."

"All right — that'll do. Only if you get married I'll be more lonesomer than ever."

"No you won't. You'll come and live with me. Now stir out of this and we'll go to digging."

They worked and sweated for half an hour. No result. They toiled another half - hour. Still no result. Huck said:

"Do they always bury it as deep as this?"

"Sometimes — not always. Not generally. I reckon we haven't got the right place."

So they chose a new spot and began again. The labor dragged a little, but still they made progress. They pegged away in silence for some time. Finally Huck leaned on his shovel, swabbed the beaded drops from his brow with his sleeve, and said:

"Where you going to dig next, after we get this one?"

"I reckon maybe we'll tackle the old tree that's over yonder on Cardiff Hill back of the widow's."

"I reckon that'll be a good one. But won't the widow take it away from us, Tom? It's on her land."

"She take it away! Maybe she'd like to try it once. Whoever finds one of these hid treasures, it belongs to him. It don't make any difference whose land it's on."

That was satisfactory. The work went on. By and by Huck said:

"Blame it, we must be in the wrong place again. What do you think?"

"It *is* mighty curious, Huck. I don't understand it. Sometimes witches interfere. I reckon maybe that's what's the trouble now."

"Shucks, witches ain't got no power in the day- time."

"Well, that's so. I didn't think of that. Oh, *I* know what the matter is! What a blamed lot of fools we are! You got to find out where the shadow of the limb falls at midnight, and that's where you dig!"

"Then consound it, we've fooled away all this work for nothing. Now hang it all, we got to come back in the night. It's an awful long way. Can you get out?"

"I bet I will. We've got to do it to-night, too, because if somebody sees these holes they'll know in a minute what's here and they'll go for it."

"Well, I'll come around and maow to-night."

"All right. Let's hide the tools in the bushes."

The boys were there that night, about the appointed time. They sat in the shadow waiting. It was a lonely place, and an hour made solemn by old traditions. Spirits whispered in the rustling leaves, ghosts lurked in the murky nooks, the deep baying of a hound floated up out of the distance, an owl answered with his sepulchral note. The boys were subdued by these solemnities, and talked little. By and by they judged that twelve had come; they marked where the shadow fell, and began to dig. Their hopes commenced to rise. Their interest grew stronger, and their industry kept pace with it. The hole deepened and still deepened, but every time their hearts jumped to hear the pick strike upon something, they only suffered a new disappointment. It was only a stone or a chunk. At last Tom said;

"It ain't any use, Huck, we're wrong again "

"Well, but we *can't* be wrong. We spotted the shadder to a dot."

"I know it, but then there's another thing."

"What's that?"

"Why, we only guessed at the time. Like enough it was too late or too early."

Huck dropped his shovel.

"That's it," said he. "That's the very trouble. We got to give this one up. We can't ever tell the right time, and besides this kind of thing's too awful, here this time of night with witches and ghosts a-fluttering around so. I feel as if something's behind me all the time; and I'm afeard to turn around, becuz maybe there's others in front a-waiting for a chance. I been creeping all over, ever since I got here."

"Well, I've been pretty much so, too, Huck. They most always put in a dead man when they bury a treasure under a tree, to look out for it."

"Lordy!"

"Yes, they do. I've always heard that."

"Tom, I don't like to fool around much where there's dead people. A body's bound to get into trouble with 'em, sure."

"I don't like to stir 'em up, either. S'pose this one here was to stick his skull out and say something!"

"Don't, Tom! It's awful."

"Well, it just is. Huck, I don't feel comfortable a bit."

"Say, Tom, let's give this place up, and try somewheres else."

"All right, I reckon we better."

"What'll it be?"

Tom considered awhile, and then said:

"The ha'nted house. That's it!"

"Blame it, I don't like ha'nted houses, Tom. Why, they're a dern sight worse'n dead people. Dead people might talk, maybe, but they don't come sliding around in a shroud, when you ain't noticing, and peep over your shoulder all of a sudden and grit their teeth, the way a ghost does. I couldn't stand such a thing as that, Tom — nobody could."

"Yes, but, Huck, ghosts don't travel around only at night. They won't bender us from digging there in the daytime."

"Well, that's so. But you know mighty well people don't go about that ha'nted house in the day nor the night."

"Well, that's mostly because they don't like to go where a man's been murdered, anyway — but nothing's ever been seen around that house except in the night — just some blue lights slipping by the windows — no regular ghosts."

"Well, where you see one of them blue lights flickering around, Tom, you can bet there's a ghost mighty close behind it. It stands to reason. Becuz *you* know that they don't anybody but ghosts use 'em."

'Yes, that's so. But anyway they don't come around in the daytime, so what's the use of our being afeard?'

"Well, all right. We'll tackle the ha'nted house if you say so — but I reckon it's taking chances."

They had started down the hill by this time. There in the middle of the moonlit valley below them stood the "ha'nted" house, utterly isolated, its fences gone long ago, rank weeds smothering the very doorsteps, the chimney crumbled to ruin, the window-sashes vacant, a corner of the roof caved in. The boys gazed awhile, half expecting to see a blue light flit past a window; then talking in a low tone, as befitted the time and the circumstances, they struck far off to the right, to give the haunted house a wide berth, and took their way homeward through the woods that adorned the rearward side of Cardiff Hill.

Lesson 25

- Read chapter 26 of *The Adventures of Tom Sawyer*.

Chapter 26
Real Robbers Seize the Box of Gold

About noon the next day the boys arrived at the dead tree; they had come for their tools. Tom was impatient to go to the haunted house; Huck was measurably so, also — but suddenly said:

"Lookyhere, Tom, do you know what day it is?"

Tom mentally ran over the days of the week, and then quickly lifted his eyes with a startled look in them —

"My! I never once thought of it, Huck!"

"Well, I didn't neither, but all at once it popped onto me that it was Friday."

"Blame it, a body can't be too careful, Huck. We might 'a' got into an awful scrape, tackling such a thing on a Friday."

"*Might*! Better say we *would*! There's some lucky days, maybe, but Friday ain't."

"Any fool knows that. I don't reckon *you* was the first that found it out, Huck."

"Well, I never said I was, did I? And Friday ain't all, neither. I had a rotten bad dream last night — dreampt about rats."

"No! Sure sign of trouble. Did they fight?"

"No."

"Well, that's good, Huck. When they don't fight it's only a sign that there's trouble around, you know. All we got to do is to look mighty sharp and keep out of it. We'll drop this thing for to-day, and play. Do you know Robin Hood, Huck?"

"No. Who's Robin Hood?"

"Why, he was one of the greatest men that was ever in England — and the best. He was a robber."

"Cracky, I wisht I was. Who did he rob?"

"Only sheriffs and bishops and rich people and kings, and such like. But he never bothered the poor. He loved 'em. He always divided up with 'em perfectly square."

"Well, he must 'a' been a brick."

"I bet you he was, Huck. Oh, he was the noblest man that ever was. They ain't any such men now, I can tell you. He could lick any man in England, with one hand tied behind him; and he could take his yew bow and plug a ten-cent piece every time, a mile and a half."

"What's a *yew* bow?"

"*I* don't know. It's some kind of a bow, of course. And if he hit that dime only on the edge he would set down and cry — and curse, But we'll play Robin Hood — it's nobby fun. I'll learn you."

"I'm agreed."

So they played Robin Hood all the afternoon, now and then casting a yearning eye down upon the haunted house and passing a remark about the morrow's prospects and possibilities there. As the sun began to sink into the west they took their way homeward athwart the long shadows of the trees and soon were buried from sight in the forests of Cardiff Hill.

On Saturday, shortly after noon, the boys were at the dead tree again. They had a smoke and a chat in the shade, and then dug a little in their last hole, not with great hope, but merely because Tom said there were so many cases where people had given up a treasure after getting down within six inches of it, and then somebody else had come along and turned it up with a single thrust of a shovel. The thing failed this time, however, so the boys shouldered their tools and went away feeling that they had not trifled with fortune, but had fulfilled all the requirements that belong to the business of treasure-hunting.

When they reached the haunted house there was something so weird and grisly about the dead silence that reigned there under the baking sun, and something so depressing about the loneliness and desolation of the place, that they were afraid, for a moment, to venture in. Then they crept to the door and took a trembling peep. They saw a weed-grown, floorless room, unplastered, an ancient fireplace, vacant windows, a ruinous staircase; and here, there, and everywhere hung ragged and abandoned cobwebs. They presently entered, softly, with quickened pulses, talking in whispers, ears alert to catch the slightest sound, and muscles tense and ready for instant retreat.

In a little while familiarity modified their fears and they gave the place a critical and interested examination, rather admiring their own boldness, and wondering at it, too. Next they wanted to look up-stairs. This was something like cutting off retreat, but they got to daring each other, and of course there could be but one result — they threw their tools into a corner and made the ascent. Up there were the same signs of decay. In one corner they found a closet that promised mystery, but the promise was a fraud — there was nothing in it. Their courage was up now and well in hand. They were about to go down and begin work when —

"'Sh!" said Tom.

"What is it?" whispered Huck, blanching with fright.

"'Sh! . . . There! . . . Hear it?"

"Yes! . . . Oh, my! Let's run!"

"Keep still! Don't you budge! They're coming right toward the door."

The boys stretched themselves upon the floor with their eyes to knot-holes in the planking, and lay waiting, in a misery of fear.

"They've stopped. . . . No — coming. . . . Here they are. Don't whisper another word, Huck. My goodness, I wish I was out of this!"

Two men entered. Each boy said to himself: "There's the old deaf and dumb Spaniard that's been about town once or twice lately — never saw t'other man before."

"T'other" was a ragged, unkempt creature, with nothing very pleasant in his face. The Spaniard was wrapped in a *serape*; he had bushy white whiskers; long white hair flowed from under his sombrero, and he wore green goggles. When they came in, "t'other" was talking in a low voice; they sat down on the ground, facing the door, with their backs to the wall, and the speaker continued his remarks. His manner became less guarded and his words more distinct as he proceeded:

"No," said he, "I've thought it all over, and I don't like it. It's dangerous."

"Dangerous!" grunted the "deaf and dumb" Spaniard — to the vast surprise of the boys. "Milksop!"

This voice made the boys gasp and quake. It was Injun Joe's! There was silence for some time. Then Joe said:

"What's any more dangerous than that job up yonder — but nothing's come of it."

"That's different. Away up the river so, and not another house about. 'Twon't ever be known that we tried, anyway, long as we didn't succeed."

"Well, what's more dangerous than coming here in the daytime! — anybody would suspicion us that saw us."

"*I* know that. But there warn't any other place as handy after that fool of a job. I want to quit this shanty. I wanted to yesterday, only it warn't any use trying to stir out of here with those infernal boys playing over there on the hill right in full view."

"Those infernal boys" quaked again under the .inspiration of this remark, and thought how lucky it was that they had remembered it was Friday and concluded to wait a day. They wished in their hearts they had waited a year.

The two men got out some food and made a luncheon. After a long and thoughtful silence, Injun Joe said:

"Look here, lad — you go back up the river where you belong. Wait there till you hear from me. I'll take the chances on dropping into this town just once more, for a look. We'll do that 'dangerous' job after I've spied around a little and think things look well for it. Then for Texas! We'll leg it together!"

This was satisfactory. Both men presently fell to yawning, and Injun Joe said:

"I'm dead for sleep! It's your turn to watch."

He curled down in the weeds and soon began to snore. His comrade stirred him once or twice and he became quiet. Presently the watcher began to nod; his head drooped lower and lower, both men began to snore now.

The boys drew a long, grateful breath. Tom whispered:

"Now's our chance — come!"

Huck said:

"I can't — I'd die if they was to wake."

Tom urged — Huck held back. At last Tom rose slowly and softly, and started alone. But the first step he made wrung such a hideous creak from the crazy floor that he sank down almost dead with fright. He never made a second attempt. The boys lay there counting the dragging moments till it seemed to them that time must be done and eternity growing gray; and then they were grateful to note that at last the sun was setting.

Now one snore ceased. Injun Joe sat up, stared around — smiled grimly upon his comrade, whose head was drooping upon his knees — stirred him up with his foot and said:

"Here! *You're* a watchman, ain't you! All right, though — nothing's happened."

"My! have I been asleep?"

"Oh, partly, partly. Nearly time for us to be moving, pard. What'll we do with what little swag we've got left?"

"I don't know — leave it here as we've always done, I reckon. No use to take it away till we start south. Six hundred and fifty in silver's something to carry."

"Well — all right — it won't matter to come here once more."

"No — but I'd say come in the night as we used to do — it's better."

"Yes: but look here; it may be a good while before I get the right chance at that job; accidents might happen; 'tain't in such a very good place; we'll just regularly bury it — and bury it deep."

"Good idea," said the comrade, who walked across the room, knelt down, raised one of the rearward hearthstones and took out a bag that jingled pleasantly. He subtracted from it twenty or thirty dollars for himself and as much for Injun Joe and passed the bag to the latter, who was on his knees in the corner, now, digging with his bowie-knife.

The boys forgot all their fears, all their miseries in an instant. With gloating eyes they watched every movement. Luck! — the splendor of it was beyond all imagination! Six hundred dollars was money enough to make half a dozen boys rich! Here was treasure-hunting under the happiest auspices — there would not be any bothersome uncertainty as to where to dig. They nudged each other every moment — eloquent nudges and easily understood, for they simply meant — "Oh, but ain't you glad now we're here!"

Joe's knife struck upon something.

"Hello!" said he.

"What is it?" said his comrade.

"Half -rotten plank — no, it's a box, I believe. Here — bear a hand and we'll see what it's here for. Never mind, I've broke a hole."

He reached his hand in and drew it out —

"Man, it's money!"

The two men examined the handful of coins. They were gold. The boys above were as excited as themselves, and as delighted.

Joe's comrade said:

"We'll make quick work of this. There's an old rusty pick over amongst the weeds in the corner the other side of the fireplace — I saw it a minute ago."

He ran and brought the boys' pick and shovel. Injun Joe took the pick, looked it over critically, shook his head, muttered something to himself, and then began to use it. The box was soon unearthed. It was not very large; it was iron-bound and had been very strong before the slow years had injured it. The men contemplated the treasure awhile in blissful silence.

"Pard, there's thousands of dollars here," said Injun Joe.

"'Twas always said that Murrel's gang used to be around here one summer," the stranger observed.

"I know it," said Injun Joe; "and this looks like it, I should say."

"*Now* you won't need to do that job."

The half-breed frowned. Said he:

"You don't know me. Least you don't know all about that thing. 'Tain't robbery altogether — it's *revenge*!" and a wicked light flamed in his eyes. "I'll need your help in it. When it's finished — then Texas. Go home to your Nance and your kids, and stand by till you hear from me."

"Well — if you say so. What'll we do with this — bury it again?"

"Yes. [Ravishing delight overhead.] *No*! by the great Sachem, no! [Profound distress overhead.] I'd nearly forgot. That pick had fresh earth on it! [The boys were sick with terror in a moment.] What business has a pick and a shovel here? What business with fresh earth on them? Who brought them here — and where are they gone? Have you heard anybody? — seen anybody? What! bury it again and leave them to come and see the ground disturbed? Not exactly — not exactly. We'll take it to my den."

"Why, of course! Might have thought of that before. You mean Number One?"

"No — Number Two — under the cross. The other place is bad — too common."

"All right. It's nearly dark enough to start."

Injun Joe got up and went about from window to window cautiously peeping out. Presently he said:

"Who could have brought those tools here? Do you reckon they can be up-stairs?"

The boys' breath forsook them. Injun Joe put his hand on his knife, halted a moment, undecided, and then turned toward the stairway. The boys thought of the closet, but their strength was gone. The steps came creaking up the stairs — the intolerable distress of the situation woke the stricken resolution of the lads — they were about to spring for the closet, when there was a crash of rotten timbers and Injun Joe landed on the ground amid the debris of the ruined stairway. He gathered himself up cursing, and his comrade said:

"Now what's the use of all that? If it's anybody, and they're up there, let them *stay* there — who cares? If they want to jump down, now, and get into trouble, who objects? It will be dark in fifteen minutes — and then let them follow us if they want to. I'm willing. In my opinion, whoever hove those things in here caught a sight of us and took us for ghosts or devils or something. I'll bet they're running yet."

Joe grumbled awhile; then he agreed with his friend that what daylight was left ought to be economized in getting things ready for leaving. Shortly afterward they slipped out of the house in the deepening twilight, and moved toward the river with their precious box.

Tom and Huck rose up, weak but vastly relieved, and stared after them through the chinks between the logs of the house. Follow? Not they. They were content to reach ground again without broken necks, and take the townward track over the hill. They did not talk much. They were too much absorbed in hating themselves — hating the ill luck that made them take the spade and the pick there. But for that, Injun Joe never would have suspected. He would have hidden the silver with the gold to wait there till his "revenge" was satisfied, and then he would have had the misfortune to find that money turn up missing. Bitter, bitter luck that the tools were ever brought there!

They resolved to keep a lookout for that Spaniard when he should come to town spying out for chances to do his revengeful job, and follow him to "Number Two," wherever that might be. Then a ghastly thought occurred to Tom:

"Revenge? What if he means us, Huck!"

"Oh, don't!" said Huck, nearly fainting.

They talked it all over, and as they entered town they agreed to believe that he might possibly mean somebody else — at least that he might at least mean nobody but Tom, since only Tom had testified.

Very, very small comfort it was to Tom to be alone in danger! Company would be a palpable improvement, he thought.

Lesson 26

- Read chapter 27 of *The Adventures of Tom Sawyer*.

Chapter 27

Trembling on the Trail

The adventure of the day mightily tormented Tom's dreams that night. Four times he had his hands on that rich treasure and four times it wasted to nothingness in his fingers as sleep forsook him and wakefulness brought back the hard reality of his misfortune. As he lay in the early morning recalling the incidents of his great adventure, he noticed that they seemed curiously subdued and far away — somewhat as if they had happened in another world, or in a time long gone by. Then it occurred to him that the great adventure itself must be a dream! There was one very strong argument in favor of this idea — namely, that the quantity of coin he had seen was too vast to be real. He had never seen as much as fifty dollars in one mass before, and he was like all boys of his age and station in life, in that he imagined that all references to "hundreds" and "thousands" were mere fanciful forms of speech, and that no such sums really existed in the world. He never had supposed for a moment that so large a sum as a hundred dollars was to be found in actual money in any one's possession. If his notions of hidden treasure had been analyzed, they would have been found to consist of a handful of real dimes and a bushel of vague, splendid, ungraspable dollars.

But the incidents of his adventure grew sensibly sharper and clearer under the attrition of thinking them over, and so he presently found himself leaning to the impression that the thing might not have been a dream, after all. This uncertainty must be swept away. He would snatch a hurried breakfast and go and find Huck.

Huck was sitting on the gunwale of a flatboat, listlessly dangling his feet in the water and looking very melancholy. Tom concluded to let Huck lead up to the subject. If he did not do it, then the adventure would be proved to have been only a dream.

"Hello, Huck!"

"Hello, yourself."

Silence for a minute.

"Tom, if we'd 'a' left the blame tools at the dead tree, we'd 'a' got the money. Oh, ain't it awful!"

"'Tain't a dream, then, 'tain't a dream! Somehow I most wish it was. Dog'd if I don't, Huck."

"What ain't a dream?"

"Oh, that thing yesterday. I been half thinking it was."

"Dream! If them stairs hadn't broke down you'd 'a' seen how much dream it was! I've had dreams enough all night — with that patch-eyed Spanish devil going for me all through 'em— rot him!"

"No, not rot him. *Find* him! Track the money!"

"Tom, we'll never find him. A feller don't have only one chance for such a pile — and that one's lost. I'd feel mighty shaky if I was to see him, anyway."

"Well, so'd I; but I'd like to see him, anyway — and track him out — to his Number Two."

"Number Two — yes, that's it. I ben thinking 'bout that. But I can't make nothing out of it. What do you reckon it is?"

"I dono. It's too deep. Say, Huck — maybe it's the number of a house!"

"Goody! . . . No, Tom, that ain't it. If it is, it ain't in this one-horse town. They ain't no numbers here."

"Well, that's so. Lemme think a minute. Here — it's the number of a room — in a tavern, you know!"

"Oh, that's the trick! They ain't only two taverns. We can find out quick."

"You stay here, Huck, till I come."

Tom was off at once. He did not care to have Huck's company in public places. He was gone half an hour. He found that in the best tavern, No. 2 had long been occupied by a young lawyer, and was still so occupied. In the less ostentatious house No. 2 was a mystery. The tavern-keeper's young son said it was kept locked all the time, and he never saw anybody go into it or come out of it except at night; he did not know any particular reason for this state of things; had had some little curiosity, but it was rather feeble; had made the most of the mystery by entertaining himself with the idea that that room was "ha'nted"; had noticed that here was a light in there the night before.

"That's what I've found out, Huck. I reckon that's the very No. 2 we're after."

"I reckon it is, Tom. Now what you going to do?"

"Lemme think."

Tom thought a long time. Then he said:

"I'll tell you. The back door of that No. 2 is the door that comes out into that little close alley between the tavern and the old rattletrap of a brick store. Now you get hold of all the doorkeys you can find, and I'll nip all of auntie's, and the first dark night we'll go there and try 'em. And mind you, keep a lookout for Injun Joe, because he said he was going to drop into town and spy around once more for a chance to get his revenge. If you see him, you just follow him; and if he don't go to that No. 2, that ain't the place."

"Lordy, I don't want to foller him by myself!"

"Why, it'll be night, sure. He mightn't ever see you — and if he did, maybe he'd never think anything."

"Well, if it's pretty dark I reckon I'll track him. I dono— I dono. I'll try."

"You bet *I*'ll follow him, if it's dark, Huck. Why, he might 'a' found out he couldn't get his revenge, and be going right after that money."

"It's so, Tom, it's so. I'll foller him; I will, by jingoes!"

"Now you're *talking*! Don't you ever weaken, Huck, and I won't."

Lesson 27

- Read chapters 28 and 29 of *The Adventures of Tom Sawyer.*

Chapter 28
In the Lair of Injun Joe

That night Tom and Huck were ready for their adventure. They hung about the neighborhood of the tavern until after nine, one watching the alley at a distance and the other the tavern door. Nobody entered the alley or left it; nobody resembling the Spaniard entered or left the tavern door. The night promised to be a fair one; so Tom went home with the understanding that if a considerable degree of darkness came on, Huck was to come and "maow," whereupon he would slip out and try the keys. But the night remained clear, and Huck closed his watch and retired to bed in an empty sugar hogshead about twelve.

Tuesday the boys had the same ill luck. Also Wednesday. But Thursday night promised better. Tom slipped out in good season with his aunt's old tin lantern, and a large towel to blindfold it with. He hid the lantern in Huck's sugar hogshead and the watch began. An hour before midnight the tavern closed up and its lights (the only ones thereabouts) were put out. No Spaniard had been seen. Nobody had entered or left the alley. Everything was auspicious. The blackness of darkness reigned, the perfect stillness was interrupted only by occasional mutterings of distant thunder.

Tom got his lantern, lit it in the hogshead, wrapped it closely in the towel, and the two adventurers crept in the gloom toward the tavern. Huck stood sentry and Tom felt his way into the alley. Then there was a season of waiting anxiety that weighed upon Huck's spirits like a mountain. He began to wish he could see a flash from the lantern — it would frighten him, but it would at least tell him that Tom was alive yet. It seemed hours since Tom had disappeared. Surely he must have fainted; maybe he was dead; maybe his heart had burst under terror and excitement. In his uneasiness Huck found himself drawing closer and closer to the alley; fearing all sorts of dreadful things, and momentarily expecting some catastrophe to happen that would take away his breath. There was not much to take away, for he seemed only able to inhale it by thimblefuls, and his heart would soon wear itself out, the way it was beating. Suddenly there was a flash of light and Tom came tearing by him:

“Run!” said he; “run for your life!”

He needn’t have repeated it; once was enough; Huck was making thirty or forty miles an hour before the repetition was uttered. The boys never stopped till they reached the shed of a deserted slaughter-house at the lower end of the village. Just as they got within its shelter the storm burst and the rain poured down. As soon as Tom got his breath he said:

“Huck, it was awful! I tried two of the keys, just as soft as I could; but they seemed to make such a power of racket that I couldn’t hardly get my breath I was so scared. They wouldn’t turn in the lock, either. Well, without noticing what I was doing, I took hold of the knob, and open comes the door! It warn’t locked! I hopped in, and shook off the towel, and, *great Caesar’s ghost*!”

“What — what’d you see, Tom?”

“Huck, I most stepped onto Injun Joe’s hand!”

“No!”

“Yes! He was laying there, sound asleep on the floor, with his old patch on his eye and his arms spread out.”

“Lordy, what did you do? Did he wake up?”

“No, never budged. Drunk, I reckon. I just grabbed that towel and started!”

“I’d never ‘a’ thought of the towel, I bet!”

“Well, *I* would. My aunt would make me mighty sick if I lost it.”

"Say, Tom, did you see that box?"

"Huck, I didn't wait to look around. I didn't see the box, I didn't see the cross. I didn't see anything but a bottle and a tin cup on the floor by Injun Joe; yes, and I saw two barrels and lots more bottles in the room. Don't you see, now, what's the matter with that ha'nted room?"

"How?"

"Why, it's ha'nted with whisky! Maybe *all* the Temperance Taverns have got a ha'nted room, hey, Huck?"

"Well, I reckon maybe that's so. Who'd 'a' thought such a thing? But say, Tom, now's a mighty good time to get that box, if Injun Joe's drunk."

"It is that! You try it!"

Huck shuddered.

"Well, no— I reckon not."

"And I reckon not, Huck. Only one bottle alongside of Injun Joe ain't enough. If there'd been three, he'd be drunk enough and I'd do it."

There was a long pause for reflection, and then Tom said:

"Lookyhere, Huck, le's not try that thing any more till we know Injun Joe's not in there. It's too scary. Now, if we watch every night, we'll be dead sure to see him go out, some time or other, and then we'll snatch that box quicker'n lightning."

"Well, I'm agreed. I'll watch the whole night long, and I'll do it every night, too, if you'll do the other part of the job."

"All right, I will. All you got to do is to trot up Hooper Street a block and maow — and if I'm asleep, you throw some gravel at the window and that'll fetch me."

"Agreed, and good as wheat!"

"Now, Huck, the storm's over, and I'll go home. It'll begin to be daylight in a couple of hours. You go back and watch that long, will you?"

"I said I would, Tom, and I will. I'll ha'nt that tavern every night for a year! I'll sleep all day and I'll stand watch all night."

"That's all right. Now, where you going to sleep?"

"In Ben Rogers's hayloft. He lets me, and so does his pap's negro man, Uncle Jake. I tote water for Uncle Jake whenever he wants me to, and any time I ask him he gives me a little something to eat if he can spare it. That's a mighty good negro, Tom. He likes me, becuz I don't ever act as if I was above him. Sometimes I've set right down and eat with him. But you needn't tell that. A body's got to do things when he's awful hungry he wouldn't want to do as a steady thing."

"Well, if I don't want you in the daytime, I'll let you sleep. I won't come bothering around. Any time you see something's up, in the night, just skip right around and maow."

Chapter 29
Huck Saves the Widow

The first thing Tom heard on Friday morning was a glad piece of news — Judge Thatcher's family had come back to town the night before. Both Injun Joe and the treasure sank into secondary importance for a moment, and Becky took the chief place in the boy's interest. He saw her, and they had an exhausting good time playing "hi-spy" and "gully-keeper" with a crowd of their schoolmates. The day was completed and crowned in a peculiarly satisfactory way: Becky teased her mother to appoint the next day for the long-promised and long-delayed picnic, and she consented. The child's delight was boundless; and Tom's not more moderate. The invitations were sent out before sunset, and straightway the young folks of the village were thrown into a fever of preparation and pleasurable anticipation. Tom's excitement enabled him to keep awake until a pretty late hour, and he had good hopes of hearing Huck's "maow," and of having his treasure to astonish Becky and the picnickers with, next day; but he was disappointed. No signal came that night.

Morning came, eventually, and by ten or eleven o'clock a giddy and rollicking company were gathered at Judge Thatcher's, and everything was ready for a start. It was not the custom for elderly people to mar picnics with their presence. The children were considered safe enough under the wings of a few young ladies of eighteen and a few young gentlemen of twenty-three or thereabouts. The old steam-ferryboat was chartered for the occasion; presently the gay throng filed up the main street laden with provision-baskets. Sid was sick and had to miss the fun; Mary remained at home to entertain him. The last thing Mrs. Thatcher said to Becky was:

"You'll not get back till late. Perhaps you'd better stay all night with some of the girls that live near the ferry landing, child."

"Then I'll stay with Susy Harper, mamma."

"Very well. And mind and behave yourself and don't be any trouble."

Presently, as they tripped along, Tom said to Becky:

"Say — I'll tell you what we'll do. 'Stead of going to Joe Harper's we'll climb right up the hill and stop at the Widow Douglas's. She'll have ice-cream! She has it most every day — dead loads of it. And she'll be awful glad to have us."

"Oh, that will be fun!"

Then Becky reflected a moment and said:

"But what will mamma say?"

"How'll she ever know?"

The girl turned the idea over in her mind, and said reluctantly:

"I reckon it's wrong — but —"

"But shucks! Your mother won't know, and so what's the harm? All she wants is that you'll be safe; and I bet you she'd 'a' said go there if she'd 'a' thought of it. I know she would!"

The Widow Douglas's splendid hospitality was a tempting bait. It and Tom's persuasions presently carried the day. So it was decided to say nothing to anybody about the night's program. Presently it occurred to Tom that maybe Huck might come this very night and give the signal. The thought took a deal of the spirit out of his anticipations. Still he could not bear to give up the fun at Widow Douglas's. And why should he give it up, he reasoned — the signal did not come the night before, so why should it be any more likely to come to-night? The sure fun of the evening outweighed the uncertain treasure; and boy like, he determined to yield to the stronger inclination and not allow himself to think of the box of money another time that day.

Three miles below town the ferryboat stopped at the mouth of a woody hollow and tied up. The crowd swarmed ashore and soon the forest distances and craggy heights echoed far and near with shoutings and laughter. All the different ways of getting hot and tired were gone through with, and by and by the rovers straggled back to camp fortified with responsible appetites, and then the destruction of the good things began. After the feast there was a refreshing season of rest and chat in the shade of spreading oaks. By and by somebody shouted:

"Who's ready for the cave?"

Everybody was. Bundles of candles were procured, and straightway there was a general scamper up the hill. The mouth of the cave was up the hillside — an opening shaped like a letter A. Its massive oaken door stood unbarred. Within was a small chamber, chilly as an icehouse, and walled by Nature with solid limestone that was dewy with a cold sweat. It was romantic and mysterious to stand here in the deep gloom and look out upon the green valley shining in the sun. But the impressiveness of the situation quickly wore off, and the romping began again. The moment a candle was lighted there was a general rush upon the owner of it; a struggle and a gallant defense followed, but the candle was soon knocked down or blown out, and then there was a glad clamor of laughter and a new chase. But all things have an end. By and by the procession went filing down the steep descent of the main avenue, the flickering rank of lights dimly revealing the lofty walls of rock almost to their point of junction sixty feet overhead. This main avenue was not more than eight or ten feet wide. Every few steps other lofty and still narrower crevices branched from it on either hand — for McDougal's cave was but a vast labyrinth of crooked aisles that ran into each other and out again and led nowhere. It was said that one might wander days and nights together through its intricate tangle of rifts and chasms, and never find the end of the cave; and that he might go down and down, and still down, into the earth, and it was just the same — labyrinth underneath labyrinth, and no end to any of them. No man "knew" the cave. That was an impossible thing. Most of the young men knew a portion of it, and it was not customary to venture much beyond this known portion. Tom Sawyer knew as much of the cave as any one.

The procession moved along the main avenue some three-quarters of a mile, and then groups and couples began to slip aside into branch avenues, fly along the dismal corridors, and take each other by surprise at points where the corridors joined again. Parties were able to elude each other for the space of half an hour without going beyond the "known" ground.

By and by, one group after another came straggling back to the mouth of the cave, panting, hilarious, smeared from head to foot with tallow drippings, daubed with clay, and entirely delighted with the success of the day. Then they were astonished to find that they had been taking no note of time and that night was about at hand. The clanging bell had been calling for half an hour. However, this sort of close to the day's adventures was romantic and therefore satisfactory. When the ferryboat with her wild freight pushed into the stream, nobody cared sixpence for the wasted time but the captain of the craft.

Huck was already upon his watch when the ferryboat's lights went glinting past the wharf. He heard no noise on board, for the young people were as subdued and still as people usually are who are nearly tired to death. He wondered what boat it was, and why she did not stop at the wharf — and then he dropped her out of his mind and put his attention upon his business. The night was growing cloudy and dark. Ten o'clock came, and the noise of vehicles ceased, scattered lights began to wink out, all straggling foot-passengers disappeared, the village betook itself to its slumbers and left the small watcher alone with the silence and the ghosts. Eleven o'clock came, and the tavern lights were put out; darkness everywhere, now. Huck waited what seemed a weary long time, but nothing happened. His faith was weakening. Was there any use? Was there really any use? Why not give it up and turn in?

A noise fell upon his ear. He was all attention in an instant. The alley door closed softly. He sprang to the corner of the brick store. The next moment two men brushed by him, and one seemed to have something under his arm. It must be that box! So they were going to remove the treasure. Why call Tom now? It would be absurd — the men would get away with the box and never be found again. No, he would stick to their wake and follow them; he would trust to the darkness for security from discovery. So communing with himself, Huck stepped out and glided along behind the men, catlike, with bare feet, allowing them to keep just far enough ahead not to be invisible.

They moved up the river street three blocks, then turned to the left up a cross-street. They went straight ahead, then, until they came to the path that led up Cardiff Hill; this they took. They passed by the old Welshman's house, half-way up the hill, without hesitating, and still climbed upward. Good, thought Huck; they will bury it in the old quarry. But they never stopped at the quarry. They passed on, up the summit. They plunged into the narrow path between the tall sumach bushes, and were at once hidden in the gloom. Huck closed up and shortened his distance, now, for they would never be able to see him. He trotted along awhile; then slackened his pace, fearing he was gaining too fast; moved on a piece, then stopped altogether; listened; no sound; none, save that he seemed to hear the beating of his own heart. The hooting of an owl came from over the hill — ominous sound! But no footsteps. Heavens, was everything lost! He was about to spring with winged feet, when a man cleared his throat not four feet from him! Huck's heart shot into his throat, but he swallowed it again; and then he stood there shaking as if a dozen agues had taken charge of him at once, and so weak that he thought he must surely fall to the ground. He knew where he was. He knew he was within five steps of the stile leading into Widow Douglas's grounds. Very well, he thought, let them bury it there; it won't be hard to find.

Now there was a voice — a very low voice — Injun Joe's:

"Damn her, maybe she's got company — there's lights, late as it is."

"I can't see any."

This was that stranger's voice — the stranger of the haunted house. A deadly chill went to Huck's heart — this, then, was the "revenge" job! His thought was, to fly. Then he remembered that the Widow Douglas had been kind to him more than once, and maybe these men were going to murder her. He wished he dared venture to warn her; but he knew he didn't dare — they might come and catch him. He thought all this and more in the moment that elapsed between the stranger's remark and Injun Joe's next — which was —

"Because the bush is in your way. Now — this way — now you see, don't you?"

"Yes. Well, there *is* company there, I reckon. Better give it up."

"Give it up, and I just leaving this country forever! Give it up and maybe never have another chance. I tell you again, as I've told you before, I don't care for her swag — you may have it. But her husband was rough on me — many times he was rough on me — and mainly he was the justice of the peace that jugged me for a vagrant. And that ain't all. It ain't a millionth part of it! He had me *horsewhipped*! — horsewhipped in front of the jail, like a negro! — with all the town looking on! Horsewhipped! — do you understand? He took advantage of me and died. But I'll take it out of *her*."

"Oh, don't kill her! Don't do that!"

"Kill? Who said anything about killing? I would kill him if he was here; but not her. When you want to get revenge on a woman you don't kill her — bosh! you go for her looks. You slit her nostrils — you notch her ears like a sow!"

"By God, that's—"

"Keep your opinion to yourself! It will be safest for you. I'll tie her to the bed. If she bleeds to death, is that my fault? I'll not cry, if she does. My friend, you'll help in this thing — for my sake — that's why you're here — I mightn't be able alone. If you flinch, I'll kill you. Do you understand that? And if I have to kill you, I'll kill her — and then I reckon nobody'll ever know much about who done this business."

"Well, if it's got to be done, let's get at it. The quicker the better — I'm all in a shiver."

"Do it *now*? And company there? Look here — I'll get suspicious of you, first thing you know. No — we'll wait till the lights are out — there's no hurry."

Huck felt that a silence was going to ensue — a thing still more awful than any amount of murderous talk; so he held his breath and stepped gingerly back; planted his foot carefully and firmly, after balancing, one-legged, in a precarious way and almost toppling over, first on one side and then on the other. He took another step back, with the same elaboration and the same risks; then another and another, and — a twig snapped under his foot! His breath stopped and he listened. There was no sound — the stillness was perfect. His gratitude was measureless. Now he turned in his tracks, between the walls of sumach bushes — turned himself as carefully as if he were a ship — and then stepped quickly but cautiously along. When he emerged at the quarry he felt secure, and so he picked up his nimble heels and flew. Down, down he sped, till he reached the Welshman's. He banged at the door, and presently the heads of the old man and his two stalwart sons were thrust from windows.

"What's the row there? Who's banging? What do you want?"

"Let me in — quick! I'll tell everything."

"Why, who are you?"

"Huckleberry Finn — quick, let me in!"

"Huckleberry Finn, indeed! It ain't a name to open many doors, I judge! But let him in, lads, and let's see what's the trouble."

"Please don't ever tell *I* told you," were Huck's first words when he got in. "Please don't — I'd be killed, sure — but the widow's been good friends to me sometimes, and I want to tell — I will tell if you'll promise you won't ever say it was me."

"By George, he *has* got something to tell, or he wouldn't act so!" exclaimed the old man; "out with it and nobody here'll ever tell, lad."

Three minutes later the old man and his sons, well armed, were up the hill, and just entering the sumach path on tiptoe, their weapons in their hands. Huck accompanied them no farther. He hid behind a great boulder and fell to listening. There was a lagging, anxious silence, and then all of a sudden there was an explosion of firearms and a cry.

Huck waited for no particulars. He sprang away and sped down the hill as fast as his legs could carry him.

Lesson 28

- Read chapter 30 of *The Adventures of Tom Sawyer.*

Chapter 30
Tom and Becky in the Cave

As the earliest suspicion of dawn appeared on Sunday morning, Huck came groping up the hill and rapped gently at the old Welshman's door. The inmates were asleep, but it was a sleep that was set on a hair-trigger, on account of the exciting episode of the night. A call came from a window:

"Who's there!"

Huck's scared voice answered in a low tone:

"Please let me in! It's only Huck Finn!"

"It's a name that can open this door night or day, lad! — and welcome!"

These were strange words to the vagabond boy's ears, and the pleasantest he had ever heard. He could not recollect that the closing word had ever been applied in his case before. The door was quickly unlocked, and he entered. Huck was given a seat and the old man and his brace of tall sons speedily dressed themselves.

“Now, my boy, I hope you’re good and hungry, because breakfast will be ready as soon as the sun’s up, and we’ll have a piping hot one, too — make yourself easy about that! I and the boys hoped you’d turn up and stop here last night.”

“I was awful scared,” said Huck, “and I run. I took out when the pistols went off, and I didn’t stop for three mile. I’ve come now becuz I wanted to know about it, you know; and I come before daylight becuz I didn’t want to run acrost thern devils, even if they was dead.”

“Well, poor chap, you do look as if you’d had a hard night of it — but there’s a bed here for you when you’ve had your breakfast. No, they ain’t dead, lad — we are sorry enough for that. You see we knew right where to put our hands on them, by your description; so we crept along on tiptoe till we got within fifteen feet of them — dark as a cellar that sumach path was — and just then I found I was going to sneeze. It was the meanest kind of luck! I tried to keep it back, but no use — ‘twas bound to come, and it did come! I was in the lead with my pistol raised, and when the sneeze started those scoundrels a-rustling to get out of the path, I sung out, ‘Fire, boys!’ and blazed away at the place where the rustling was. So did the boys. But they were off in a jiffy, those villains, and we after them, down through the woods. I judge we never touched them. They fired a shot apiece as they started, but their bullets whizzed by and didn’t do us any harm. As soon as we lost the sound of their feet we quit chasing, and went down and stirred up the constables. They got a posse together, and went off to guard the river-bank, and as soon as it is light the sheriff and a gang are going to beat up the woods. My boys will be with them presently. I wish we had some sort of description of those rascals — ‘twould help a good deal. But you couldn’t see what they were like, in the dark, lad, I suppose?”

“Oh, yes, I saw them down -town and follered them.”

“Splendid! Describe them — describe them, my boy!”

“One’s the old deaf and dumb Spaniard that’s ben around here once or twice, and t’other’s a mean-looking, ragged —”

"That's enough, lad, we know the men! Happened on them in the woods back of the widow's one day, and they slunk away. Off with you, boys, and tell the sheriff — get your breakfast to-morrow morning!"

The Welshman's sons departed at once. As they were leaving the room Huck sprang up and exclaimed:

"Oh, please don't tell *anybody* it was me that blowed on them! Oh, please!"

"All right if you say it, Huck, but you ought to have the credit of what you did."

"Oh, no, no! Please don't tell!"

When the young men were gone, the old Welshman said:

"They won't tell — and I won't. But why don't you want it known?"

Huck would not explain, further than to say that he already knew too much about one of those men and would not have the man know that he knew anything against him for the whole world — he would be killed for knowing it, sure.

The old man promised secrecy once more, and said:

"How did you come to follow these fellows, lad? Were they looking suspicious?"

Huck was silent while he framed a duly cautious reply. Then he said:

"Well, you see, I'm a kind of a hard lot — least everybody says so, and I don't see nothing agin it — and sometimes I can't sleep much on accounts of thinking about it and sort of trying to strike out a new way of doing. That was the way of it last night. I couldn't sleep, and so I come along up street 'bout midnight, a-turning it all over, and when I got to that old shackly brick store by the Temperance Tavern, I backed up agin the wall to have another think. Well, just then along comes these two chaps slipping along close by me, with something under their arm and I reckoned they'd stole it. One was a-smoking, and t'other one wanted a light; so they stopped right before me and the cigars lit up their faces and I see that the big one was the deaf and dumb Spaniard, by his white whiskers and the patch on his eye, and t'other one was a rusty, ragged-looking devil."

"Could you see the rags by the light of the cigars?"

This staggered Huck for a moment. Then he said:

"Well, I don't know — but somehow it seems as if I did."

"Then they went on, and you —"

"Follered 'em — yes. That was it. I wanted to see what was up — they sneaked along so. I dogged 'em to the widder's stile, and stood in the dark and heard the ragged one beg for the widder, and the Spaniard swear he'd spile her looks just as I told you and your two —"

"What! The *deaf and dumb* man said all that!"

Huck had made another terrible mistake! He was trying his best to keep the old man from getting the faintest hint of who the Spaniard might be, and yet his tongue seemed determined to get him into trouble in spite of all he could do. He made several efforts to creep out of his scrape, but the old man's eye was upon him and he made blunder after blunder. Presently the Welshman said:

"My boy, don't be afraid of me. I wouldn't hurt a hair of your head for all the world. No — I'd protect you — I'd protect you. This Spaniard is not deaf and dumb; you've let that slip without intending it; you can't cover that up now. You know something about that Spaniard that you want to keep dark. Now trust me — tell me what it is, and trust me — I won't betray you."

Huck looked into the old man's honest eyes a moment, then bent over and whispered in his ear:

"'Tain't a Spaniard— it's Injun Joe!"

The Welshman almost jumped out of his chair. In a moment he said:

"It's all plain enough, now. When you talked about notching ears and slitting noses I judged that that was your own embellishment, because white men don't take that sort of revenge. But an Injun! That's a different matter altogether."

During breakfast the talk went on, and in the course of it the old man said that the last thing which he and his sons had done, before going to bed, was to get a lantern and examine the stile and its vicinity for marks of blood. They found none, but captured a bulky bundle of —

"Of WHAT?"

If the words had been lightning they could not have leaped with a more stunning suddenness from Huck's blanched lips. His eyes were staring wide, now, and his breath suspended — waiting for the answer. The Welshman started — stared in return — three seconds — five seconds — ten — then replied:

"Of burglar's tools. Why, what's the matter with you?"

Huck sank back, panting gently, but deeply, unutterably grateful. The Welshman eyed him gravely, curiously — and presently said:

"Yes, burglar's tools. That appears to relieve you a good deal. But what did give you that turn? What were you expecting we'd found?"

Huck was in a close place — the inquiring eye was upon him — he would have given anything for material for a plausible answer — nothing suggested itself — the inquiring eye was boring deeper and deeper — a senseless reply offered — there was no time to weigh it, so at a venture he uttered it — feebly:

"Sunday-school books, maybe."

Poor Huck was too distressed to smile, but the old man laughed loud and joyously, shook up the details of his anatomy from head to foot, and ended by saying that such a laugh was money in a man's pocket, because it cut down the doctor's bills like everything. Then he added:

"Poor old chap, you're white and jaded — you ain't well a bit — no wonder you're a little flighty and off your balance. But you'll come out of it. Rest and sleep will fetch you out all right, I hope."

Huck was irritated to think he had been such a goose and betrayed such a suspicious excitement, for he had dropped the idea that the parcel brought from the tavern was the treasure, as soon as he had heard the talk at the widow's stile. He had only *thought* it was not the treasure, however — he had not known that it wasn't — and so the suggestion of a captured bundle was too much for his self-possession. But on the whole he felt glad the little episode had happened, for now he knew beyond all question that that bundle was not *the* bundle, and so his mind was at rest and exceedingly comfortable. In fact, everything seemed to be drifting just in the right direction, now; the treasure must be still in No. 2, the men would be captured and jailed that day, and he and Tom could seize the gold that night without any trouble or any fear of interruption.

Just as breakfast was completed there was a knock at the door. Huck jumped for a hiding-place, for he had no mind to be connected even remotely with the late event. The Welshman admitted several ladies and gentlemen, among them the Widow Douglas, and noticed that groups of citizens were climbing up the hill — to stare at the stile. So the news had spread.

The Welshman had to tell the story of the night to the visitors. The widow's gratitude for her preservation was outspoken.

"Don't say a word about it, madam. There's another that you're more beholden to than you are to me and my boys, maybe, but he don't allow me to tell his name. We wouldn't have been there but for him."

Of course this excited a curiosity so vast that it almost belittled the main matter — but the Welshman allowed it to eat into the vitals of his visitors, and through them be transmitted to the whole town, for he refused to part with his secret. When all else had been learned, the widow said:

"I went to sleep reading in bed and slept straight through all that noise. Why didn't you come and wake me?"

"We judged it warn't worth while. Those fellows warn't likely to come again — they hadn't any tools left to work with, and what was the use of waking you up and scaring you to death? My three negro men stood guard at your house all the rest of the night. They've just come back."

More visitors came, and the story had to be told and retold for a couple of hours more.

There was no Sabbath-school during day-school vacation, but everybody was early at church. The stirring event was well canvassed. News came that not a sign of the two villains had been yet discovered. When the sermon was finished, Judge Thatcher's wife dropped alongside of Mrs. Harper as she moved down the aisle with the crowd and said:

"Is my Becky going to sleep all day? I just expected she would be tired to death."

"Your Becky?"

"Yes," with a startled look — "didn't she stay with you last night?"

"Why, no."

Mrs. Thatcher turned pale, and sank into a pew, just as Aunt Polly, talking briskly with a friend, passed by. Aunt Polly said:

"Good morning, Mrs. Thatcher. Good morning, Mrs. Harper. I've got a boy that's turned up missing. I reckon my Tom stayed at your house last night — one of you. And now he's afraid to come to church. I've got to settle with him."

Mrs. Thatcher shook her head feebly and turned paler than ever.

"He didn't stay with us," said Mrs. Harper, beginning to look uneasy. A marked anxiety came into Aunt Polly's face.

"Joe Harper, have you seen my Tom this morning?"

"No'm."

"When did you see him last?"

Joe tried to remember, but was not sure he could say. The people had stopped moving out of church. Whispers passed along, and a boding uneasiness took possession of every countenance. Children were anxiously questioned, and young teachers. They all said they had not noticed whether Tom and Becky were on board the ferryboat on the homeward trip; it was dark; no one thought of inquiring if any one was missing. One young man finally blurted out his fear that they were still in the cave! Mrs. Thatcher swooned away. Aunt Polly fell to crying and wringing her hands.

The alarm swept from lip to lip, from group to group, from street to street, and within five minutes the bells were wildly clanging and the whole town was up! The Cardiff Hill episode sank into instant insignificance, the burglars were forgotten, horses were saddled, skiffs were manned, the ferryboat ordered out, and before the horror was half an hour old two hundred men were pouring down highroad and river toward the cave.

All the long afternoon the village seemed empty and dead. Many women visited Aunt Polly and Mrs. Thatcher and tried to comfort them. They cried with them, too, and that was still better than words. All the tedious night the town waited for news; but when the morning dawned at last, all the Word that came was, "Send more candles — and send food." Mrs. Thatcher was almost crazed; and Aunt Polly, also. Judge Thatcher sent messages of hope and encouragement from the cave, but they conveyed no real cheer.

The old Welshman came home toward daylight, spattered with candle-grease, smeared with clay, and almost worn out. He found Huck still in the bed that had been provided for him, and delirious with fever. The physicians were all at the cave, so the Widow Douglas came and took charge of the patient. She said she would do her best by him, because, whether he was good, bad, or indifferent, he was the Lord's, and nothing that was the Lord's was a thing to be neglected. The Welshman said Huck had good spots in him, and the widow said:

"You can depend on it. That's the Lord's mark. He don't leave it off. He never does. Puts it somewhere on every creature that comes from His hands."

Early in the forenoon parties of jaded men began to straggle into the village, but the strongest of the citizens continued searching. All the news that could be gained was that remotenesses of the cavern were being ransacked that had never been visited before; that every corner and crevice was going to be thoroughly searched; that wherever one wandered through the maze of passages, lights were to be seen flitting hither and thither in the distance, and shoutings and pistol-shots sent their hollow reverberations to the ear down the somber aisles. In one place, far from the section usually traversed by tourists, the names "BECKY & TOM" had been found traced upon the rocky wall with candle-smoke, and near at hand a grease-soiled bit of ribbon. Mrs. Thatcher recognized the ribbon and cried over it. She said it was the last relic she should ever have of her child; and that no other memorial of her could ever be so precious, because this one parted latest from the living body before the awful death came. Some said that now and then, in the cave, a far-away speck of light would glimmer, and then a glorious shout would burst forth and a score of men go trooping down the echoing aisle — and then a sickening disappointment always followed; the children were not there; it was only a searcher's light. Three dreadful days and nights dragged their tedious hours along, and the village sank into a hopeless stupor. No one had heart for anything. The accidental discovery, just made, that the proprietor of the Temperance Tavern kept liquor on his premises, scarcely fluttered the public pulse, tremendous as the fact was. In a lucid interval, Huck feebly led up to the subject of taverns, and finally asked — dimly dreading the worst — if anything had been discovered at the Temperance Tavern since he had been ill.

"Yes," said the widow.

Huck started up in bed, wild-eyed:

"What! What was it?"

"Liquor! — and the place has been shut up. Lie down, child — what a turn you did give me!"

"Only tell me just one thing — only just one — please! Was it Tom Sawyer that found it?"

The widow burst into tears. “Hush, hush, child, hush! I’ve told you before, you must not talk. You are very, very sick!”

Then nothing but liquor had been found; there would have been a great powwow if it had been the gold. So the treasure was gone forever — gone forever! But what could she be crying about? Curious that she should cry.

These thoughts worked their dim way through Huck’s mind, and under the weariness they gave him he fell asleep. The widow said to herself:

“There — he’s asleep, poor wreck. Tom Sawyer find it! Pity but somebody could find Tom Sawyer! Ah, there ain’t many left, now, that’s got hope enough, or strength enough, either, to go on searching.”

Lesson 29

- Read chapters 31 and 32 of *The Adventures of Tom Sawyer*.

Chapter 31
Found and Lost Again

Now to return to Tom and Becky’s share in the picnic. They tripped along the murky aisles with the rest of the company, visiting the familiar wonders of the cave — wonders dubbed with rather over-descriptive names, such as “The Drawing Room,” “The Cathedral,” “Aladdin’s Palace,” and so on. Presently the hide-and-seek frolicking began, and Tom and Becky engaged in it with zeal until the exertion began to grow a trifle wearisome; then they wandered down a sinuous avenue holding their candles aloft and reading the tangled web-work of names, dates, post-office addresses, and mottoes with which the rocky walls had been frescoed (in candle-smoke). Still drifting along and talking, they scarcely noticed that they were now in a part of the cave whose walls were not frescoed. They smoked their own names under an overhanging shelf and moved on. Presently they came to a place where a little stream of water, trickling over a ledge and carrying a limestone sediment with it, had, in the slow-dragging ages, formed a laced and ruffled Niagara in gleaming and imperishable stone. Tom squeezed his small body behind it in order to illuminate it for Becky's gratification. He found that it curtained a sort of steep natural stairway which was inclosed between narrow walls, and at once the ambition to be a discoverer seized him. Becky responded to his call, and they made a smoke-mark for future guidance, and started upon their quest. They wound this way and that, far down into the secret depths of the cave, made another mark, and branched off in search of novelties to tell the upper world about. In one place they found a spacious cavern, from whose ceiling depended a multitude of shining stalactites of the length and circumference of a man's leg; they walked all about it, wondering and admiring, and presently left it by one of the numerous passages that opened into it. This shortly brought them to a bewitching spring, whose basin was incrusted with a frostwork of glittering crystals; it was in the midst of a cavern whose walls were supported by many fantastic pillars which had been formed by the joining of great stalactites and stalagmites together, the result of the ceaseless water-drip of centuries. Under the roof vast knots of bats had packed themselves together, thousands in a bunch; the lights disturbed the creatures, and they came flocking down by hundreds, squeaking and darting furiously at the candles. Tom knew their ways and the danger of this sort of conduct. He seized Becky's hand and hurried her into the first corridor that offered; and none too soon, for a bat struck Becky's light out with its wing while she was passing out of the cavern. The bats chased the children a good distance; but the fugitives plunged into every new passage that offered, and at last got rid of the perilous things. Tom found a subterranean lake, shortly, which stretched its dim length away until its shape was lost in the shadows. He wanted to explore its borders, but concluded that it would be best to sit down and rest awhile, first. Now, for the first time, the deep stillness of the place laid a clammy hand upon the spirits of the children. Becky said:

"Why, I didn't notice, but it seems ever so long since I heard of any of the others."

"Come to think, Becky, we are away down below them — and I don't know how far away north, or south, or east, or whichever it is. We couldn't hear them here."

Becky grew apprehensive.

"I wonder how long we've been down here, Tom. We better start back."

"Yes, I reckon we better. P'raps we better."

"Can you find the way, Tom? It's all a mixed-up crookedness to me."

"I reckon I could find it — but then the bats. If they put both our candles out it will be an awful fix. Let's try some other way, so as not to go through there."

"Well. But I hope we won't get lost. It would be so awful!" and the girl shuddered at the thought of the dreadful possibilities.

They started through a corridor, and traversed it in silence a long way, glancing at each new opening to see if there was anything familiar about the look of it; but they were all strange. Every time Tom made an examination, Becky would watch his face for an encouraging sign, and he would say cheerily:

"Oh, it's all right. This ain't the one, but we'll come to it right away!"

But he felt less and less hopeful with each failure, and presently began to turn off into diverging avenues at sheer random, in desperate hope of finding the one that was wanted. He still said it was "all right," but there was such a leaden dread at his heart that the words had lost their ring and sounded just as if he had said, "All is lost!" Becky clung to his side in an anguish of fear, and tried hard to keep back the tears, but they would come. At last she said:

"Oh, Tom, never mind the bats, let's go back that way! We seem to get worse and worse off all the time."

Tom stopped.

"Listen!" said he.

Profound silence; silence so deep that even their breathings were conspicuous in the hush. Tom shouted. The call went echoing down the empty aisles and died out in the distance in a faint sound that resembled a ripple of mocking laughter.

"Oh, don't do it again, Tom, it is too horrid," said Becky.

"It is horrid, but I better, Becky; they *might* hear us, you know," and he shouted again.

The "might" was even a chillier horror than the ghostly laughter, it so confessed a perishing hope. The children stood still and listened; but there was no result. Tom turned upon the back track at once, and hurried his steps. It was but a little while before a certain indecision in his manner revealed another fearful fact to Becky — he could not find his way back!

"Oh, Tom, you didn't make any marks!"

"Becky, I was such a fool! Such a fool! I never thought we might want to come back! No— I can't find the way. It's all mixed up."

"Tom, Tom, we're lost! we're lost! We never can get out of this awful place! Oh, why *did* we ever leave the others!"

She sank to the ground and burst into such a frenzy of crying that Tom was appalled with the idea that she might die, or lose her reason. He sat down by her and put his arms around her; she buried her face in his bosom, she clung to him, she poured out her terrors, her unavailing regrets, and the far echoes turned them all to jeering laughter. Tom begged her to pluck up hope again, and she said she could not. He fell to blaming and abusing himself for getting her into this miserable situation; this had a better effect. She said she would try to hope again, she would get up and follow wherever he might lead if only he would not talk like that any more. For he was no more to blame than she, she said.

So they moved on again — aimlessly — simply at random — all they could do was to move, keep moving. For a little while, hope made a show of reviving — not with any reason to back it, but only because it is its nature to revive when the spring has not been taken out of it by age and familiarity with failure.

By and by Tom took Becky's candle and blew it out. This economy meant so much, words were not needed. Becky understood, and her hope died again. She knew that Tom had a whole candle and three or four pieces in his pockets — yet he must economize.

By and by, fatigue began to assert its claims; the children tried to pay no attention, for it was dreadful to think of sitting down when time was grown to be so precious; moving, in some direction, in any direction, was at least progress and might bear fruit; but to sit down was to invite death and shorten its pursuit.

At last Becky's frail limbs refused to carry her farther. She sat down. Tom rested with her, and they talked of home, and the friends there, and the comfortable beds and, above all, the light! Becky cried, and Tom tried to think of some way of comforting her, but all his encouragements were grown threadbare with use, and sounded like sarcasms. Fatigue bore so heavily upon Becky that she drowsed off to sleep. Tom was grateful. He sat looking into her drawn face and saw it grow smooth and natural under the influence of pleasant dreams; and by and by a smile dawned and rested there. The peaceful face reflected somewhat of peace and healing into his own spirit, and his thoughts wandered away to bygone times and dreamy memories. While he was deep in his musings, Becky woke up with a breezy little laugh — but it was stricken dead upon her lips, and a groan followed it.

"Oh, how *could* I sleep! I wish I never, never had waked! No! No, I don't, Tom! Don't look so! I won't say it again."

"I'm glad you've slept, Becky; you'll feel rested, now, and we'll find the way out."

"We can try, Tom; but I've seen such a beautiful country in my dream. I reckon we are going there."

"Maybe not, maybe not. Cheer up, Becky, and let's go on trying."

They rose up and wandered along, hand in hand and hopeless. They tried to estimate how long they had been in the cave, but all they knew was that it seemed days and weeks, and yet it was plain that this could not be, for their candles were not gone yet. A long time after this — they could not tell how long — Tom said they must go softly and listen for dripping water — they must find a spring. They found one presently, and Tom said it was time to rest again. Both were cruelly tired, yet Becky said she thought she could go on a little farther. She was surprised to hear Tom dissent. She could not understand it. They sat down, and Tom fastened his candle to the wall in front of them with some clay. Thought was soon busy; nothing was said for some time. Then Becky broke the silence:

"Tom, I am so hungry!"

Tom took something out of his pocket.

"Do you remember this?" said he.

Becky almost smiled.

"It's our wedding-cake, Tom."

"Yes — I wish it was as big as a barrel, for it's all we've got."

"I saved it from the picnic for us to dream on, Tom, the way grown-up people do with wedding-cake — but it'll be our —"

She dropped the sentence where it was, Tom divided the cake and Becky ate with good appetite, while Tom nibbled at his moiety. There was abundance of cold water to finish the feast with.

By and by Becky suggested that they move on again. Tom was silent a moment. Then he said:

"Becky, can you bear it if I tell you something?"

Becky's face paled, but she thought she could.

"Well, then, Becky, we must stay here, where there's water to drink. That little piece is our last candle!"

Becky gave loose to tears and wailings. Tom did what he could to comfort her, but with little effect.

At length Becky said:

"Tom!"

"Well, Becky?"

"They'll miss us and hunt for us!"

"Yes, they will! Certainly they will!"

"Maybe they're hunting for us now, Tom."

"Why, I reckon maybe they are. I hope they are."

"When would they miss us, Tom?"

"When they get back to the boat, I reckon."

"Tom, it might be dark then — would they notice we hadn't come?"

"I don't know. But anyway, your mother would miss you as soon as they got home."

A frightened look in Becky's face brought Tom to his senses and he saw that he had made a blunder. Becky was not to have gone home that night! The children became silent and thoughtful. In a moment a new burst of grief from Becky showed Tom that the thing in his mind had struck hers also — that the Sabbath morning might be half spent before Mrs. Thatcher discovered that Becky was not at Mrs, Harper's.

The children fastened their eyes upon their bit of candle and watched it melt slowly and pitilessly away; saw the half-inch of wick stand alone at last; saw the feeble flame rise and fall, climb the thin column of smoke, linger at its top a moment, and then — the horror of utter darkness reigned!

How long afterward it was that Becky came to a slow consciousness that she was crying in Tom's arms, neither could tell. All that they knew was, that after what seemed a mighty stretch of time, both awoke out of a dead stupor of sleep and resumed their miseries once more. Tom said it might be Sunday, now — maybe Monday. He tried to get Becky to talk, but her sorrows were too oppressive, all her hopes were gone. Tom said that they must have been missed long ago, and no doubt the search was going on. He would shout and maybe some one would come. He tried it; but in the darkness the distant echoes sounded so hideously that he tried it no more.

The hours wasted away, and hunger came to torment the captives again. A portion of Tom's half of the cake was left; they divided and ate it. But they seemed hungrier than before. The poor morsel of food only whetted desire.

By and by Tom said:

"'*Sh!* Did you hear that?"

Both held their breath and listened. There was a sound like the faintest, far-off shout. Instantly Tom answered it, and, leading Becky by the hand, started groping down the corridor in its direction. Presently he listened again; again the sound was heard, and apparently a little nearer.

"It's them!" said Tom; "they're coming! Come along, Becky — we're all right now!"

The joy of the prisoners was almost overwhelming. Their speed was slow, however, because pitfalls were somewhat common, and had to be guarded against. They shortly came to one and had to stop. It might be three feet deep, it might be a hundred — there was no passing it, at any rate. Tom got down on his breast and reached as far down as he could. No bottom. They must stay there and wait until the searchers came. They listened; evidently the distant shoutings were growing more distant! a moment or two more and they had gone altogether. The heart-sinking misery of it! Tom whooped until he was hoarse, but it was of no use. He talked hopefully to Becky; but an age of anxious waiting passed and no sounds came again.

The children groped their way back to the spring. The weary time dragged on; they slept again, and awoke famished and woe-stricken. Tom believed it must be Tuesday by this time.

Now an idea struck him. There were some side passages near at hand. It would be better to explore some of these than bear the weight of the heavy time in idleness. He took a kite-line from his pocket, tied it to a projection, and he and Becky started,

Tom in the lead, unwinding the line as he groped along. At the end of twenty steps the corridor ended in a "jumping-off place." Tom got down on his knees and felt below, and then as far around the corner as he could reach with his hands conveniently; he made an effort to stretch yet a little farther to the right, and at that moment, not twenty yards away, a human hand, holding a candle, appeared from behind a rock! Tom lifted up a glorious shout, and instantly that hand was followed by the body it belonged to — Injun Joe's! Tom was paralyzed; he could not move. He was vastly gratified the next moment to see the "Spaniard" take to his heels and get himself out of sight. Tom wondered that Joe had not recognized his voice and come over and killed him for testifying in court. But the echoes must have disguised the voice. Without doubt, that was it, he reasoned. Tom's fright weakened every muscle in his body. He said to himself that if he had strength enough to get back to the spring he would stay there, and nothing should tempt him to run the risk of meeting Injun Joe again. He was careful to keep from Becky what it was he had seen. He told her he had only shouted "for luck."

But hunger and wretchedness rise superior to fears in the long run. Another tedious wait at the spring and another long sleep brought changes. The children awoke tortured with a raging hunger. Tom believed that it must be Wednesday or Thursday or even Friday or Saturday, now, and that the search had been given over. He proposed to explore anther passage. He felt willing to risk Injun Joe and all other terrors. But Becky was very weak. She had sunk into a dreary apathy and would not be roused. She said she would wait, now, where she was, and die — it would not be long. She told Tom to go with the kite-line and explore if he chose; but she implored him to come back every little while and speak to her; and she made him promise that when the awful time came, he would stay by her and hold her hand until all was over.

Tom kissed her, with a choking sensation in his throat, and made a show of being confident of finding the searchers or an escape from the cave; then he took the kite-line in his hand and went groping down one of the passages on his hands and knees, distressed with hunger and sick with bodings of coming doom.

Chapter 32
"Turn Out! They're Found!"

Tuesday afternoon came, and waned to the twilight. The village of St. Petersburg still mourned. The lost children had not been found. Public prayers had been offered up for them, and many and many a private prayer that had the petitioner's whole heart in it; but still no good news came from the cave. The majority of the searchers had given up the quest and gone back to their daily vocations, saying that it was plain the children could never be found. Mrs. Thatcher was very ill, and a great part of the time delirious. People said it was heartbreaking to hear her call her child, and raise her head and listen a whole minute at a time, then lay it wearily down again with a moan. Aunt Polly had drooped into a settled melancholy, and her gray hair had grown almost white. The village went to its rest on Tuesday night, sad and forlorn.

Away in the middle of the night a wild peal burst from the village bells, and in a moment the streets were swarming with frantic half-clad people, who shouted, "Turn out! turn out! they're found! they're found!" Tin pans and horns were added to the din, the population massed itself and moved toward the river, met the children coming in an open carriage drawn by shouting citizens, thronged around it, joined its homeward march, and swept magnificently up the main street roaring huzzah after huzzah!

The village was illuminated; nobody went to bed again; it was the greatest night the little town had ever seen. During the first half-hour a procession of villagers filed through Judge Thatcher's house, seized the saved ones and kissed them, squeezed Mrs. Thatcher's hand, tried to speak but couldn't — and drifted out raining tears all over the place.

Aunt Polly's happiness was complete, and Mrs. Thatcher's nearly so. It would be complete, however, as soon as the messenger despatched with the great news to the cave should get the word to her husband. Tom lay upon a sofa with an eager auditory about him and told the history of the wonderful adventure, putting in many striking additions to adorn it withal; and closed with a description of how he left Becky and went on an exploring expedition; how he followed two avenues as far as his kite-line would reach; how he followed a third to the fullest stretch of the kite-line, and was about to turn back when he glimpsed a far-off speck that looked like daylight; dropped the line and groped toward it, pushed his head and shoulders through a small hole and saw the broad Mississippi rolling by! And if it had only happened to be night he would not have seen that speck of daylight and would not have explored that passage any more! He told how he went back for Becky and broke the good news and she told him not to fret her with such stuff, for she was tired, and knew she was going to die, and wanted to. He described how he labored with her and convinced her; and how she almost died for joy when she had groped to where she actually saw the blue speck of daylight; how he pushed his way out at the hole and then helped her out; how they sat there and cried for gladness; how some men came along in a skiff and Tom hailed them and told them their situation and their famished condition; how the men didn't believe the wild tale at first, "because," said they, "you are five miles down the river below the valley the cave is in" — then took them aboard, rowed to a house, gave them supper, made them rest till two or three hours after dark, and then brought them home.

Before day-dawn, Judge Thatcher and the handful of searchers with him were tracked out, in the cave, by the twine clews they had strung behind them, and informed of the great news.

Three days and nights of toil and hunger in the cave were not to be shaken off at once, as Tom and Becky soon discovered. They were bedridden all of Wednesday and Thursday, and seemed to grow more and more tired and worn all the time. Tom got about a little on Thursday, was down-town Friday, and nearly as whole as ever Saturday; but Becky did not leave her room until Sunday, and then she looked as if she had passed through a wasting illness.

Tom learned of Huck's sickness and went to see him on Friday, but could not be admitted to the bedroom; neither could he on Saturday or Sunday. He was admitted daily after that, but was warned to keep still about his adventure and introduce no exciting topic. The Widow Douglas stayed by to see that he obeyed. At home Tom learned of the Cardiff Hill event; also that the "ragged man's" body had eventually been found in the river near the ferry landing; he had been drowned while trying to escape, perhaps.

About a fortnight after Tom's rescue from the cave, he started off to visit Huck, who had grown plenty strong enough, now, to hear exciting talk, and Tom had some that would interest him, he thought. Judge Thatcher's house was on Tom's way, and he stopped to see Becky. The Judge and some friends set Tom to talking, and some one asked him ironically if he wouldn't like to go to the cave again. Tom said he thought he wouldn't mind it. The Judge said:

"Well, there are others just like you, Tom, I've not the least doubt. But we have taken care of that. Nobody will get lost in that cave any more."

"Why?"

"Because I had its big door sheathed with boiler iron two weeks ago, and triple-locked — and I've got the keys."

Tom turned as white as a sheet.

"What's the matter, boy! Here, run, somebody! Fetch a glass of water!"

The water was brought and thrown into Tom's face.

"Ah, now you're all right. What was the matter with you, Tom?"

"Oh, Judge, Injun Joe's in the cave!"

Lesson 30

- Read chapter 33 of *The Adventures of Tom Sawyer*.

Chapter 33
The Fate of Injun Joe

Within a few minutes the news had spread, and a dozen skiff-loads of men were on their way to McDougal's cave, and the ferryboat, well filled with passengers, soon followed. Tom Sawyer was in the skiff that bore Judge Thatcher.

When the cave door was unlocked, a sorrowful sight presented itself in the dim twilight of the place. Injun Joe lay stretched upon the ground, dead, with his face close to the crack of the door, as if his longing eyes had been fixed, to the latest moment, upon the light and the cheer of the free world outside. Tom was touched, for he knew by his own experience how this wretch had suffered. His pity was moved, but nevertheless he felt an abounding sense of relief and security, now, which revealed to him in a degree which he had not fully appreciated before how vast a weight of dread had been lying upon him since the day he lifted his voice against this bloody-minded outcast.

Injun Joe's bowie-knife lay close by, its blade broken in two. The great foundation-beam of the door had been chipped and hacked through, with tedious labor; useless labor, too, it was, for the native rock formed a sill outside it, and upon that stubborn material the knife had wrought no effect; the only damage done was to the knife itself. But if there had been no stony obstruction there the labor would have been useless still, for if the beam had been wholly cut away Injun Joe could not have squeezed his body under the door, and he knew it. So he had only hacked that place in order to be doing something — in order to pass the weary time — in order to employ his tortured faculties. Ordinarily one could find half a dozen bits of candle stuck around in the crevices of this vestibule, left there by tourists; but there were none now. The prisoner had searched them out and eaten them. He had also contrived to catch a few bats, and these, also, he had eaten, leaving only their claws. The poor unfortunate had starved to death. In one place near at hand, a stalagmite had been slowly growing up from the ground for ages, builded by the water-drip from a stalactite overhead. The captive had broken off the stalagmite, and upon the stump had placed a stone, wherein he had scooped a shallow hollow to catch the precious drop that fell once in every three minutes with the dreary regularity of a clock-tick — a dessert-spoonful once in four-and-twenty hours. That drop was falling when the Pyramids were new; when Troy fell; when the foundations of Rome were laid; when Christ was crucified; when the Conqueror created the British empire; when Columbus sailed; when the massacre at Lexington was "news." It is falling now; it will still be falling when all these things shall have sunk down the afternoon of history and the twilight of tradition and been swallowed up in the thick night of oblivior. Has everything a purpose and a mission? Did this drop fall patiently during five thousand years to be ready for this flitting human insect's need? and has it another important object to accomplish ten thousand years to come? No matter. It is many and many a year since the hapless half-breed scooped out the stone to catch the priceless drops, but to this day the tourist stares longest at that pathetic stone and that slow-dropping water when he comes to see the wonders of McDougal's Cave. Injun Joe's cup stands first in the list of the cavern's marvels; even "Aladdin's Palace" cannot rival it.

Injun Joe was buried near the mouth of the cave; and people flocked there in boats and wagons from the towns and from all the farms and hamlets for seven miles around; they brought their children, and all sorts of provisions, and confessed that they had had almost as satisfactory a time at the funeral as they could have had at the hanging.

This funeral stopped the further growth of one thing — the petition to the Governor for Injun Joe's pardon. The petition had been largely signed; many tearful and eloquent meetings had been held, and a committee of sappy women been appointed to go in deep mourning and wail around the Governor, and implore him to be a merciful ass and trample his duty under foot. Injun Joe was believed to have killed five citizens of the village, but what of that? If he had been Satan himself there would have been plenty of weaklings ready to scribble their names to a pardon petition, and drip a tear on it from their permanently impaired and leaky water-works.

The morning after the funeral Tom took Huck to a private place to have an important talk. Huck had learned all about Tom's adventure from the Welshman and the Widow Douglas, by this time, but Tom said he reckoned there was one thing they had not told him; that thing was what he wanted to talk about now. Huck's face saddened. He said:

"I know what it is. You got into No. 2 and never found anything but whisky. Nobody told me it was you; but I just knowed it must 'a' ben you, soon as I heard 'bout that whisky business; and I knowed you hadn't got the money becuz you'd 'a' got at me some way or other and told me even if you was mum to everybody else. Tom, something's always told me we'd never get holt of that swag."

"Why, Huck, *I* never told on that tavern-keeper. *You* know his tavern was all right the Saturday I went to the picnic. Don't you remember you was to watch there that night?"

"Oh, yes! Why, it seems 'bout a year ago. It was that very night that I follered Injun Joe to the widder's."

"*You* followed him?"

"Yes — but you keep mum. I reckon Injun Joe's left friends behind him, and I don't want 'em souring on me and doing me mean tricks. If it hadn't ben for me he'd be down in Texas now, all right."

Then Huck told his entire adventure in confidence to Tom, who had only heard of the Welshmen's part of it before.

"Well," said Huck, presently, coming back to the main question, "whoever nipped the whisky in No. 2 nipped the money, too, I reckon — anyways it's a goner for us, Tom."

"Huck, that money wasn't ever in No. 2!"

"What!" Huck searched his comrade's face keenly. "Tom, have you got on the track of that money again?"

"Huck, it's in the cave!"

Huck's eyes blazed.

"Say it again, Tom."

"The money's in the cave!"

"Tom — honest injun, now — is it fun or earnest?"

"Earnest, Huck — just as earnest as ever I was in my life. Will you go in there with me and help get it out?"

"I bet I will! I will if it's where we can blaze our way to it and not get lost."

"Huck, we can do that without the least little bit of trouble in the world."

"Good as wheat! What makes you think the money's —"

"Huck, you just wait till we get in there. If we don't find it I'll agree to give you my drum and everything I've got in the world. I will, by jings."

"All right — it's a whiz. When do you say?"

"Right now, if you say it. Are you strong enough?"

"Is it far in the cave? I ben on my pins a little, three or four days, now, but I can't walk more'n a mile, Tom — least I don't think I could."

"It's about five mile into there the way anybody but me would go, Huck, but there's a mighty short cut that they don't anybody but me know about. Huck, I'll take you right to it in a skiff. I'll float the skiff down there, and I'll pull it back again all by myself. You needn't ever turn your hand over."

"Less start right off, Tom."

"All right. We want some bread and meat, and our pipes, and a little bag or two, and two or three kite-strings, and some of these new-fangled things they call lucifer matches. I tell you, many's the time I wished I had some when I was in there before."

A trifle after noon the boys borrowed a small skiff from a citizen who was absent, and got under way at once. When they were several miles below "Cave Hollow," Tom said:

"Now you see this bluff here looks all alike all the way down from the cave hollow — no houses, no woodyards, bushes all alike. But do you see that white place up yonder where there's been a landslide? Well, that's one of my marks. We'll get ashore, now."

They landed.

"Now, Huck, where we're a-standing you could touch that hole I got out of with a fishing-pole. See if you can find it."

Huck searched all the place about, and found nothing. Tom proudly marched into a thick clump of sumach bushes and said:

"Here you are! Look at it, Huck; it's the snuggest hole in this country. You just keep mum about it. All along I've been wanting to be a robber, but I knew I'd got to have a thing like this, and where to run across it was the bother. We've got it now, and we'll keep it quiet, only we'll let Joe Harper and Ben Rogers in — because of course there's got to be a Gang, or else there wouldn't be any style about it. Tom Sawyer's Gang — it sounds splendid, don't it, Huck?"

"Well, it just does, Tom. And who'll we rob?"

"Oh, most anybody. Waylay people — that's mostly the way."

"And kill them?"

"No, not always. Hive them in the cave till they raise a ransom."

"What's a ransom?"

"Money. You make them raise all they can, off'n their friends; and after you've kept them a year, if it ain't raised then you kill them. That's the general way. Only you don't kill the women. You shut up the women, but you don't kill them. They're always beautiful and rich, and awfully scared. You take their watches and things, but you always take your hat off and talk polite. They ain't anybody as polite as robbers — you'll see that in any book. Well, the women get to loving you, and after they've been in the cave a week or two weeks they stop crying and after that you couldn't get them to leave. If you drove them out they'd turn right around and come back. It's so in all the books."

"Why, it's real bully, Tom. I b'lieve it's better'n to be a pirate."

"Yes, it's better in some ways, because it's close to home and circuses and all that."

By this time everything was ready and the boys entered the hole, Tom in the lead. They toiled their way to the farther end of the tunnel, then made their spliced kite-strings fast and moved on. A few steps brought them to the spring, and Tom felt a shudder quiver all through him. He showed Huck the fragment of candle-wick perched on a lump of clay against the wall, and described how he and Becky had watched the flame struggle and expire.

The boys began to quiet down to whispers, now, for the stillness and gloom of the place oppressed their spirits. They went on, and presently entered and followed Tom's other corridor until they reached the "jumping-off place." The candles revealed the fact that it was not really a precipice, but only a steep clay hill twenty or thirty feet high. Tom whispered:

"Now I'll show you something, Huck."

He held his candle aloft and said:

"Look as far around the corner as you can. Do you see that? There — on the big rock over yonder — done with candle-smoke."

"Tom, it's a *cross*!"

"*Now* where's your Number Two? '*Under the cross*' hey? Right yonder's where I saw Injun Joe poke up his candle, Huck!"

Huck stared at the mystic sign awhile, and then said with a shaky voice:

"Tom, le's git out of here!"

"What! and leave the treasure?"

"Yes — leave it. Injun Joe's ghost is round about there, certain."

"No it ain't, Huck, no it ain't. It would ha'nt the place where he died — away out at the mouth of the cave — five mile from here."

"No, Tom, it wouldn't. It would hang round the money. I know the ways of ghosts, and so do you."

Tom began to fear that Huck was right. Misgivings gathered in his mind. But presently an idea occurred to him —

"Looky here, Huck, what fools we're making of ourselves! Injun Joe's ghost ain't a-going to come around where there's a cross!"

The point was well taken. It had its effect.

"Tom, I didn't think of that. But that's so. It's luck for us, that cross is. I reckon we'll climb down there and have a hunt for that box."

Tom went first, cutting rude steps in the clay hill as he descended. Huck followed. Four avenues opened out of the small cavern which the great rock stood in. The boys examined three of them with no result. They found a small recess in the one nearest the base of the rock, with a pallet of blankets spread down in it; also an old suspender, some bacon rind, and the well-gnawed bones of two or three fowls. But there was no money-box. The lads searched and re-searched this place, but in vain. Tom said:

"He said *under* the cross. Well, this comes nearest to being under the cross. It can't be under the rock itself, because that sets solid on the ground."

They searched everywhere once more, and then sat down discouraged. Huck could suggest nothing. By and by Tom said:

"Looky here, Huck, there's footprints and some candle-grease on the clay about one side of this rock, but not on the other sides. Now, what's that or? I bet you the money *is* under the rock. I'm going to dig in the clay."

"That ain't no bad notion, Tom!" said Huck with animation.

Tom's "real Barlow" was out at once, and he had not dug four inches before he struck wood.

"Hey, Huck! — you hear that?"

Huck began to dig and scratch now. Some boards were soon uncovered and removed. They had concealed a natural chasm which led under the rock. Tom got into this and held his candle as far under the rock as he could, but said he could not see to the end of the rift. He proposed to explore. He stooped and passed under; the narrow way descended gradually. He followed its winding course, first to the right, then to the left, Huck at his heels. Tom turned a short curve, by and by, and exclaimed:

"My goodness, Huck, looky here!"

It was the treasure-box, sure enough, occupying a snug little cavern, along with an empty powder-keg, a couple of guns in leather cases, two or three pairs of old moccasins, a leather belt, and some other rubbish well soaked with the water-drip.

"Got it at last!" said Huck, plowing among the tarnished coins with his hand. "My, but we're rich, Tom!"

"Huck, I always reckoned we'd get it. It's just too good to believe, but we *have* got it, sure! Say — let's not fool around here. Let's snake it out. Lemme see if I can lift the box."

It weighed about fifty pounds. Tom could lift it, after an awkward fashion, but could not carry it conveniently.

"I thought so," he said; "*they* carried it like it was heavy, that day at the ha'nted house. I noticed that. I reckon I was right to think of fetching the little bags along."

The money was soon in the bags and the boys took it up to the cross rock.

"Now le's fetch the guns and things," said Huck.

"No, Huck — leave them there. They're just the tricks to have when we go to robbing. We'll keep them there all the time, and we'll hold our orgies there, too. It's an awful snug place for orgies."

"What's orgies?"

"*I* dono. But robbers always have orgies, and of course we've got to have them, too. Come along, Huck; we've been in here a long time. It's getting late, I reckon. I'm hungry, too. We'll eat and smoke when we get to the skiff."

They presently emerged into the clump of sumach bushes, looked warily out, found the coast clear, and were soon lunching and smoking in the skiff. As the sun dipped toward the horizon they pushed out and got under way. Tom skimmed up the shore through the long twilight, chatting cheerily with Huck, and landed shortly after dark.

"Now, Huck," said Tom, "we'll hide the money in the loft of the widow's woodshed, and I'll come up in the morning and we'll count it and divide, and then we'll hunt up a place out in the woods for it where it will be safe. Just you lay quiet here and watch the stuff till I run and hook Benny Taylor's little wagon; I won't be gone a minute."

He disappeared, and presently returned with the wagon, put the two small sacks into it, threw some old rags on top of them, and started off, dragging his cargo behind him. When the boys reached the Welshman's house, they stopped to rest. Just as they were about to move on, the Welshman stepped out and said:

"Hello, who's that?"

"Huck and Tom Sawyer."

"Good! Come along with me, boys; you are keeping everybody waiting. Here — hurry up, trot ahead — I'll haul the wagon for you. Why, it's not as light as it might be. Got bricks in it? — or old metal?"

"Old metal," said Tom.

"I judged so; the boys in this town will take more trouble and fool away more time hunting up six bits' worth of old iron to sell to the foundry than they would to make twice the money at regular work. But that's human nature — hurry along, hurry along!"

The boys wanted to know what the hurry was about.

"Never mind; you'll see when we get to the Widow Douglas's."

Huck said with some apprehension — for he was long used to being falsely accused:

"Mr. Jones, we haven't been doing nothing."

The Welshman laughed.

"Well, I don't know, Huck, my boy. I don't know about that. Ain't you and the widow good friends?"

"Yes. Well, she's ben good friends to me, anyways."

"All right, then. What do you want to be afraid for?"

This question was not entirely answered in Huck's slow mind before he found himself pushed, along with Tom, into Mrs. Douglas's drawing-room. Mr. Jones left the wagon near the door and followed.

The place was grandly lighted, and everybody that was of any consequence in the village was there. The Thatchers were there, the Harpers, the Rogerses, Aunt Polly, Sid, Mary, the minister, the editor, and a great many more, and all dressed in their best. The widow received the boys as heartily as any one could well receive two such looking beings. They were covered with clay and candle-grease. Aunt Polly blushed crimson with humiliation, and frowned and shook her head at Tom. Nobody suffered half as much as the two boys did, however. Mr. Jones said:

"Tom wasn't at home, yet, so I gave him up; but I stumbled on him and Huck right at my door, and so I just brought them along in a hurry."

"And you did just right," said the widow. "Come with me, boys."

She took them to a bedchamber and said:

"Now wash and dress yourselves. Here are two new suits of clothes — shirts, socks, everything complete. They're Huck's — no, no thanks, Huck — Mr. Jones bought one and I the other. But they'll fit both of you. Get into them. We'll wait — come down when you are slicked up enough."

Then she left.

Lesson 31

- Read chapters 34 and 35 of *The Adventures of Tom Sawyer*.

Chapter 34
Floods of Gold

Huck said: "Tom, we can slope, if we can find a rope. The window ain't high from the ground."

"Shucks, what do you want to slope for?"

"Well, I ain't used to that kind of a crowd. I can't stand it. I ain't going down there, Tom."

"Oh, bother! It ain't anything. I don't mind it a bit. I'll take care of you."

Sid appeared.

"Tom," said he, "auntie has been waiting for you all the afternoon. Mary got your Sunday clothes ready, and everybody's been fretting about you. Say — ain't this grease and clay, on your clothes?"

"Now, Mr. Siddy, you jist 'tend to your own business. What's all this blow-out about, anyway?"

"It's one of the widow's parties that she's always having. This time it's for the Welshman and his sons, on account of that scrape they helped her out of the other night. And say — I can tell you something, if you want to know."

"Well, what?"

"Why, old Mr. Jones is going to try to spring something on the people here to-night, but I overheard him tell auntie to-day about it, as a secret, but I reckon it's not much of a secret now. Everybody knows — the widow, too, for all she tries to let on she don't. Mr. Jones was bound Huck should be here — couldn't get along with his grand secret without Huck, you know!"

"Secret about what, Sid?"

"About Huck tracking the robbers to the widow's. I reckon Mr. Jones was going to make a grand time over his surprise, but I bet you it will drop pretty flat."

Sid chuckled in a very contented and satisfied way.

"Sid, was it you that told?"

"Oh, never mind who it was. *Somebody* told — that's enough."

"Sid, there's only one person in this town mean enough to do that, and that's you. If you had been in Huck's place you'd 'a' sneaked down the hill and never told anybody on the robbers. You can't do any but mean things, and you can't bear to see anybody praised for doing good ones. There — no thanks, as the widow says" — and Tom cuffed Sid's ears and helped him to the door with several kicks. "Now go and tell auntie if you dare — and tomorrow you'll catch it!"

Some minutes later the widow's guests were at the supper-table, and a dozen children were propped up at little side-tables in the same room, after the fashion of that country and that day. At the proper time Mr. Jones made his little speech, in which he thanked the widow for the honor she was doing himself and his sons, but said that there was another person whose modesty —

And so forth and so on. He sprung his secret about Huck's share in the adventure in the finest dramatic manner he was master of, but the surprise it occasioned was largely counterfeit and not as clamorous and effusive as it might have been under happier circumstances. However, the widow made a pretty fair show of astonishment, and heaped so many compliments and so much gratitude upon Huck that he almost forgot the nearly intolerable discomfort of his new clothes in the entirely intolerable discomfort of being set up as a target for everybody's gaze and everybody's laudations.

The widow said she meant to give Huck a home under her roof and have him educated; and that when she could spare the money she would start him in business in a modest way. Tom's chance was come. He said:

"Huck don't need it. Huck's rich."

Nothing but a heavy strain upon the good manners of the company kept back the due and proper complimentary laugh at this pleasant joke. But the silence was a little awkward. Tom broke it:

"Huck's got money. Maybe you don't believe it, but he's got lots of it. Oh, you needn't smile — I reckon I can show you. You just wait a minute."

Tom ran out of doors. The company looked at each other with a perplexed interest — and inquiringly at Huck, who was tongue-tied.

"Sid, what ails Tom?" said Aunt Polly. "He — well, there ain't ever any making of that boy out. I never —"

Tom entered, struggling with the weight of his sacks, and Aunt Polly did not finish her sentence. Tom poured the mass of yellow coin upon the table and said:

"There— what did I tell you? Half of it's Huck's and half of it's mine!"

The spectacle took the general breath away. All gazed, nobody spoke for a moment. Then there was a unanimous call for an explanation. Tom said he could furnish it, and he did. The tale was long, but brimful of interest. There was scarcely an interruption from any one to break the charm of its flow. When he had finished, Mr. Jones said:

"I thought I had fixed up a little surprise for this occasion, but it don't amount to anything now. This one makes it sing mighty small, I'm willing to allow."

The money was counted. The sum amounted to a little over twelve thousand dollars. It was more than any one present had ever seen at one time before, though several persons were there who were worth considerably more than that in property.

Chapter 35
Respectable Huck Joins the Gang

The reader may rest satisfied that Tom's and Huck's windfall made a mighty stir in the poor little village of St. Petersburg. So vast a sum, all in actual cash, seemed next to incredible. It was talked about, gloated over, glorified, until the reason of many of the citizens tottered under the strain of the unhealthy excitement. Every "haunted" house in St. Petersburg and the neighboring villages was dissected, plank by plank, and its foundations dug up and ransacked for hidden treasure — and not by boys, but men — pretty grave, unromantic men, too, some of them. Wherever Tom and Huck appeared they were courted, admired, stared at. The boys were not able to remember that their remarks had possessed weight before; but now their sayings were treasured and repeated; everything they did seemed somehow to be regarded as remarkable; they had evidently lost the power of doing and saying commonplace things; moreover, their past history was raked up and discovered to bear marks of conspicuous originality. The village paper published biographical sketches of the boys.

The Widow Douglas put Huck's money out at six per cent., and Judge Thatcher did the same with Tom's at Aunt Polly's request. Each lad had an income, now, that was simply prodigious — a dollar for every week-day in the year and half of the Sundays. It was just what the minister got — no, it was what he was promised — he generally couldn't collect it. A dollar and a quarter a week would board, lodge, and school a boy in those old simple days — and clothe him and wash him, too, for that matter.

Judge Thatcher had conceived a great opinion of Tom. He said that no commonplace boy would ever have got his daughter out of the cave. When Becky told her father, in strict confidence, how Tom had taken her whipping at school, the Judge was visibly moved; and when she pleaded grace for the mighty lie which Tom had told in order to shift that whipping from her shoulders to his own, the Judge said with a fine outburst that it was a noble, a generous, a magnanimous lie — a lie that was worthy to hold up its head and march down through history breast to breast with George Washington's lauded Truth about the hatchet! Becky thought her father had never looked so tall and so superb as when he walked the floor and stamped his foot and said that. She went straight off and told Tom about it.

Judge Thatcher hoped to see Tom a great lawyer or a great soldier some day. He said he meant to look to it that Tom should be admitted to the National Military Academy and afterward trained in the best law school in the country, in order that he might be ready for either career or both.

Huck Finn's wealth and the fact that he was now under the Widow Douglas's protection introduced him into society — no, dragged him into it, hurled him into it — and his sufferings were almost more than he could bear. The widow's servants kept him clean and neat, combed and brushed, and they bedded him nightly in unsympathetic sheets that had not one little spot or stain which he could press to his heart and know for a friend. He had to eat with knife and fork; he had to use napkin, cup, and plate; he had to learn his book, he had to go to church; he had to talk so properly that speech was become insipid in his mouth; whithersoever he turned, the bars and shackles of civilization shut him in and bound him hand and foot.

He bravely bore his miseries three weeks, and then one day turned up missing. For forty-eight hours the widow hunted for him everywhere in great distress. The public were profoundly concerned; they searched high and low, they dragged the river for his body. Early the third morning Tom Sawyer wisely went poking among some old empty hogsheads down behind the abandoned slaughter-house, and in one of them he found the refugee. Huck had slept there; he had just breakfasted upon some stolen odds and ends of food, and was lying off, now, in comfort, with his pipe. He was unkempt, uncombed, and clad in the same old ruin of rags that had made him picturesque in the days when he was free and happy. Tom routed him out, told him the trouble he had been causing, and urged him to go home. Huck's face lost its tranquil content, and took a melancholy cast. He said:

‘‘Don't talk about it, Tom. I've tried it, and it don't work; it don't work, Tom. It ain't for me; I ain't used to it. The widder's good to me, and friendly; but I can't stand them ways. She makes me git up just at the same time every morning; she makes me wash, they comb me all to thunder; she won't let me sleep in the woodshed; I got to wear them blamed clothes that just smothers me, Tom; they don't seem to let any air git through ‘em, somehow; and they're so rotten nice that I can't set down, nor lay down, nor roll around anywher's; I hain't slid on a cellar-door for — well, it ‘pears to be years; I got to go to church and sweat and sweat — I hate them ornery sermons! I can't ketch a fly in there, I can't chaw. I got to wear shoes all Sunday. The widder eats by a bell; she goes to bed by a bell; she gits up by a bell — everything's so awful reg'lar a body can't stand it."

"Well, everybody does that way, Huck."

"Tom, it don't make no difference. I ain't everybody, and I can't *stand* it. It's awful to be tied up so. And grub comes too easy — I don't take no interest in vittles, that way. I got to ask to go a-fishing; I got to ask to go in a-swimming — dern'd if I hain't got to ask to do everything. Well, I'd got to talk so nice it wasn't no comfort — I'd got to go up in the attic and rip out awhile, every day, to git a taste in my mouth, or I'd ‘a' died, Tom. The widder wouldn't let me smoke; she wouldn't let me yell, she wouldn't let me gape, nor stretch, nor scratch, before folks —" [Then with a spasm of special irritation and injury] — "And dad fetch it, she prayed all the time! I never *see* such a woman! I *had* to shove, Tom — I just had to. And besides, that school's going to open, and I'd ‘a' had to go to it — well, I wouldn't stand *that*, Tom. Looky here, Tom, being rich ain't what it's cracked up to be. It's just worry and worry, and sweat and sweat, and a-wishing you was dead all the time. Now these clothes suits me, and this bar'l suits me, and I ain't ever going to shake ‘em any more. Tom, I wouldn't ever got into all this trouble if it hadn't ‘a' been for that money; now you just take my sheer of it along with your'n, and gimme a ten-center sometimes — not many times, becuz I don't give a dern for a thing ‘thout it's tollable hard to git — and you go and beg off for me with the widder."

"Oh, Huck, you know I can't do that. ‘Tain't fair; and, besides, if you'll try this thing just awhile longer you'll come to like it."

"Like it! Yes — the way I'd like a hot stove if I was to set on it long enough. No, Tom, I won't be rich, and I won't live in them cussed smothery houses. I like the woods, and the river, and hogs-heads, and I'll stick to 'em, too. Blame it all! just as we'd got guns, and a cave, and all just fixed to rob, here this dern foolishness has got to come up and spile it all!"

Tom saw his opportunity —

"Looky here, Huck, being rich ain't going to keep me back from turning robber."

"No! Oh, good-licks, are you in real deadwood earnest, Tom?"

"Just as dead earnest as I'm a-sitting here. But, Huck, we can't let you into the gang if you ain't respectable, you know."

Huck's joy was quenched.

"Can't let me in, Tom? Didn't you let me go for a pirate?"

"Yes, but that's different. A robber is more high-toned than what a pirate is — as a general thing. In most countries they're awful high up in the nobility — dukes and such."

"Now, Tom, hain't you always ben friendly to me? You wouldn't shet me out, would you, Tom? You wouldn't do that, now, would you, Tom?"

"Huck, I wouldn't want to, and I *don't* want to — but what would people say? Why, they'd say, 'Mph! Tom Sawyer's Gang! pretty low characters in it!' They'd mean you, Huck. You wouldn't like that, and I wouldn't."

Huck was silent for some time, engaged in a mental struggle. Finally he said:

"Well, I'll go back to the widder for a month and tackle it and see if I can come to stand it, if you'll let me b'long to the gang, Tom."

"All right, Huck, it's a whiz! Come along, old chap, and I'll ask the widow to let up on you a little, Huck."

"Will you, Tom — now will you? That's good. If she'll let up on some of the roughest things, I'll smoke private and cuss private, and crowd through or bust. When you going to start the gang and turn robbers?"

"Oh, right off. We'll get the boys together and have the initiation to-night, maybe."

"Have the which?"

"Have the initiation."

"What's that?"

"It's to swear to stand by one another, and never tell the gang's secrets, even if you're chopped all to flinders, and kill anybody and all his family that hurts one of the gang."

"That's gay — that's mighty gay, Tom, I tell you."

"Well, I bet it is. And all that swearing's got to be done at midnight, in the lonesomest, awfulest place you can find — a ha'nted house is the best, but they're all ripped up now."

"Well, midnight's good, anyway, Tom."

"Yes, so it is. And you've got to swear on a coffin, and sign it with blood."

"Now, that's something *like*! Why, it's a million times bullier than pirating. I'll stick to the widder till I rot, Tom; and if I git to be a reg'lar ripper of a robber, and everybody talking 'bout it, I reckon she'll be proud she snaked me in out of the wet."

Conclusion

So endeth this chronicle. It being strictly a history of a *boy*, it must stop here; the story could not go much further without becoming the history of a *man*. When one writes a novel about grown people, he knows exactly where to stop — that is, with a marriage; but when he writes of juveniles, he must stop where he best can.

Most of the characters that perform in this book still live, and are prosperous and happy. Some day it may seem worth while to take up the story of the younger ones again and see what sort of men and women they turned out to be; therefore it will be wisest not to reveal any of that part of their lives at present.

THE END

Lesson 32

- Read the short story, "Federico's Falcon." You have some charts to fill in in your Language Arts workbook as you read.

"Federigo's Falcon"
by Giovanni Boccaccio
Originally published in 1353
Translation by Mark Musa and Peter Bondanella

There was once in Florence a young man named Federigo, the son of Messer Filippo Alberighi, renowned above all other men in Tuscany for his prowess in arms and for his courtliness. As often happens to most gentlemen, he fell in love with a lady named Monna Giovanna, in her day considered to be one of the most beautiful and one of the most charming women that ever there was in Florence; and in order to win her love, he participated in jousts and tournaments, organized and gave feasts, and spent his money without restraint; but she, no less virtuous than beautiful, cared little for these things done on her behalf, nor did she care for him who did them. Now, as Federigo was spending far beyond his means and was taking nothing in, as easily happens he lost his wealth and became poor, with nothing but his little farm to his name (from whose revenues he lived very meagerly) and one falcon which was among the best in the world.

More in love than ever, but knowing that he would never be able to live the way he wished to in the city, he went to live at Campi, where his farm was. There he passed his time hawking whenever he could, asked nothing of anyone, and endured his poverty patiently. Now, during the time that Federigo was reduced to dire need, it happened that the husband of Monna Giovanna fell ill, and realizing death was near, he made his last will. He was very rich, and he made his son, who was growing up, his heir, and, since he had loved Monna Giovanna very much, he made her his heir should his son die without a legitimate heir; and then he died.

Monna Giovanna was now a widow, and as is the custom among our women, she went to the country with her son to spend a year on one of her possessions very close by to Federigo's farm, and it happened that this young boy became friends with Federigo and began to enjoy birds and hunting dogs; and after he had seen Federigo's falcon fly many times, it pleased him so much that he very much wished it were his own, but he did not dare to ask for it, for he could see how dear it was to Federigo. And during this time, it happened that the young boy took ill, and his mother was much grieved, for he was her only child and she loved him enormously. She would spend the entire day by his side, never ceasing to comfort him, and often asking him if there was anything he desired, begging him to tell her what it might be, for if it were possible to obtain it, she would certainly do everything possible to get it. After the young boy had heard her make this offer many times, he said:

"Mother, if you can arrange for me to have Federigo's falcon, I think I would be well very soon."

When the lady heard this, she was taken aback for a moment, and she began to think what she should do. She knew that Federigo had loved her for a long while, in spite of the fact that he never received a single glance from her, and so, she said to herself:

"How can I send or go and ask for this falcon of his which is, as I have heard tell, the best that ever flew, and besides this, his only means of support? And how can I be so insensitive as to wish to take away from this gentleman the only pleasure which is left to him?"

And involved in these thoughts, knowing that she was certain to have the bird if she asked for it, but not knowing what to say to her son, she stood there without answering him. Finally the love she bore her son persuaded her that she should make him happy, and no matter what the consequences might be, she would not send for the bird, but rather go herself for it and bring it back to him; so she answered her son:

"My son, take comfort and think only of getting well, for I promise you that the first thing I shall do tomorrow morning is to go for it and bring it back to you."

The child was so happy that he showed some improvement that very day. The following morning, the lady, accompanied by another woman, as if going for a stroll, went to Federigo's modest house and asked for him. Since it was not the season for it, Federigo had not been hawking for some days and was in his orchard, attending to certain tasks. When he heard that Monna Giovanna was asking for him at the door, he was very surprised and happy to run there. As she saw him coming, she greeted him with feminine charm, and once Federigo had welcomed her courteously, she said:

"Greetings, Federigo!" Then she continued: "I have come to compensate you for the harm you have suffered on my account by loving me more than you needed to; and the compensation is this: I, along with this companion of mine, intend to dine with you—a simple meal—this very day."

To this Federigo humbly replied: "Madonna, I never remember having suffered any harm because of you. On the contrary, so much good have I received from you that if ever I have been worth anything, it has been because of your merit and the love I bore for you; and your generous visit is certainly so dear to me that I would spend all over again that which I spent in the past; but you have come to a poor host."

And having said this, he received her into his home humbly, and from there he led her into his garden, and since he had no one there to keep her company, he said:

"My lady, since there is no one else, this good woman here, the wife of this workman, will keep you company while I go to set the table."

Though he was very poor, Federigo, until now, had never before realized to what extent he had wasted his wealth; but this morning, the fact that he found nothing with which he could honor the lady for the love of whom he had once entertained countless men in the past gave him cause to reflect. In great anguish, he cursed himself and his fortune and, like a man beside himself, he started running here and there, but could find neither money nor a pawnable object. The hour was late and his desire to honor the gracious lady was great, but not wishing to turn for help to others (not even to his own workman), he set his eyes upon his good falcon, perched in a small room; and since he had nowhere else to turn, he took the bird, and finding it plump, he decided that it would be a worthy food for such a lady. So, without further thought, he wrung its neck and quickly gave it to his servant girl to pluck, prepare, and place on a spit to be roasted with care; and when he had set the table with the whitest of tablecloths (a few of which he still had left), he returned, with a cheerful face, to the lady in his garden, saying that the meal he was able to prepare for her was ready.

The lady and her companion rose, went to the table together with Federigo, who waited upon them with the greatest devotion, and they ate the good falcon without knowing what it was they were eating. And having left the table and spent some time in pleasant conversation, the lady thought it time now to say what she had come to say, and so she spoke these kind words to Federigo:

"Federigo, if you recall your past life and my virtue, which you perhaps mistook for harshness and cruelty, I do not doubt at all that you will be amazed by my presumption when you hear what my main reason for coming here is; but if you had children, through whom you might have experienced the power of parental love, it seems certain to me that you would, at least in part, forgive me. But, just as you have no child, I do have one, and I cannot escape the common laws of other mothers; the force of such laws compels me to follow them, against my own will and against good manners and duty, and to ask of you a gift which I know is most precious to you; and it is naturally so, since your extreme condition has left you no other delight, no other pleasure, no other consolation; and this gift is your falcon, which my son is so taken by that if I do not bring it to him, I fear his sickness will grow so much worse that I may lose him. And therefore I beg you, not because of the love that you bear for me, which does not oblige you in the least, but because of your own nobility, which you have shown to be greater than that of all others in practicing courtliness, that you be pleased to give it to me, so that I may say that I have saved the life of my son by means of this gift, and because of it I have placed him in your debt forever."

When he heard what the lady requested and knew that he could not oblige her since he had given her the falcon to eat, Federigo began to weep in her presence, for he could not utter a word in reply. The lady, at first, thought his tears were caused more by the sorrow of having to part with the good falcon than by anything else, and she was on the verge of telling him she no longer wished it, but she held back and waited for Federigo's reply after he stopped weeping. And he said:

"My lady, ever since it pleased God for me to place my love in you, I have felt that Fortune has been hostile to me in many things, and I have complained of her, but all this is nothing compared to what she has just done to me, and I must never be at peace with her again, thinking about how you have come here to my poor home where, while it was rich, you never deigned to come, and you requested a small gift, and Fortune worked to make it impossible for me to give it to you; and why this is so I shall tell you briefly. When I heard that you, out of your kindness, wished to dine with me, I considered it fitting and right, taking into account your excellence and your worthiness, that I should honor you, according to my possibilities, with a more precious food than that which I usually serve to other people; therefore, remembering the falcon that you requested and its value, I judged it a food worthy of you, and this very day you had it roasted and served to you as best I could; but seeing now that you desired it in another way, my sorrow in not being able to serve you is so great that I shall never be able to console myself again."

And after he had said this, he laid the feathers, the feet, and the beak of the bird before her as proof. When the lady heard and saw this, she first reproached him for having killed such a falcon to serve as a meal to a woman; but then to herself she commended the greatness of his spirit, which no poverty was able or would be able to diminish; then, having lost all hope of getting the falcon and, perhaps because of this, of improving the health of her son as well, she thanked Federigo both for the honor paid to her and for his good will, and she left in grief, and returned to her son. To his mother's extreme sorrow, either because of his disappointment that he could not have the falcon, or because his illness must have necessarily led to it, the boy passed from this life only a few days later.

After the period of her mourning and bitterness had passed, the lady was repeatedly urged by her brothers to remarry, since she was very rich and was still young; and although she did not wish to do so, they became so insistent that she remembered the merits of Federigo and his last act of generosity—that is, to have killed such a falcon to do her honor—and she said to her brothers:

"I would prefer to remain a widow, if that would please you; but if you wish me to take a husband, you may rest assured that I shall take no man but Federigo degli Alberighi."

In answer to this, making fun of her, her brothers replied:

"You foolish woman, what are you saying? How can you want him; he hasn't a penny to his name?"

To this she replied: "My brothers, I am well aware of what you say, but I would rather have a man who needs money than money that needs a man."

Her brothers, seeing that she was determined and knowing Federigo to be of noble birth, no matter how poor he was, accepted her wishes and gave her in marriage to him with all her riches. When he found himself the husband of such a great lady, whom he had loved so much and who was so wealthy besides, he managed his financial affairs with more prudence than in the past and lived with her happily the rest of his days.

Lesson 33

- Read "The Story of an Hour" by Kate Chopin.
- Continue to fill in your irony and foreshadowing charts as you read.

"The Story of An Hour"
By Kate Chopin (1894)

Knowing that Mrs. Mallard was afflicted with a heart trouble, great care was taken to break to her as gently as possible the news of her husband's death.

It was her sister Josephine who told her, in broken sentences; veiled hints that revealed in half concealing. Her husband's friend Richards was there, too, near her. It was he who had been in the newspaper office when intelligence of the railroad disaster was received, with Brently Mallard's name leading the list of "killed." He had only taken the time to assure himself of its truth by a second telegram, and had hastened to forestall any less careful, less tender friend in bearing the sad message.

She did not hear the story as many women have heard the same, with a paralyzed inability to accept its significance. She wept at once, with sudden, wild abandonment, in her sister's arms. When the storm of grief had spent itself she went away to her room alone. She would have no one follow her.

There stood, facing the open window, a comfortable, roomy armchair. Into this she sank, pressed down by a physical exhaustion that haunted her body and seemed to reach into her soul.

She could see in the open square before her house the tops of trees that were all aquiver with the new spring life. The delicious breath of rain was in the air. In the street below a peddler was crying his wares. The notes of a distant song which some one was singing reached her faintly, and countless sparrows were twittering in the eaves.

There were patches of blue sky showing here and there through the clouds that had met and piled one above the other in the west facing her window.

She sat with her head thrown back upon the cushion of the chair, quite motionless, except when a sob came up into her throat and shook her, as a child who has cried itself to sleep continues to sob in its dreams.

She was young, with a fair, calm face, whose lines bespoke repression and even a certain strength. But now there was a dull stare in her eyes, whose gaze was fixed away off yonder on one of those patches of blue sky. It was not a glance of reflection, but rather indicated a suspension of intelligent thought.

There was something coming to her and she was waiting for it, fearfully. What was it? She did not know; it was too subtle and elusive to name. But she felt it, creeping out of the sky, reaching toward her through the sounds, the scents, the color that filled the air.

Now her bosom rose and fell tumultuously. She was beginning to recognize this thing that was approaching to possess her, and she was striving to beat it back with her will--as powerless as her two white slender hands would have been. When she abandoned herself a little whispered word escaped her slightly parted lips. She said it over and over under her breath: "free, free, free!" The vacant stare and the look of terror that had followed it went from her eyes. They stayed keen and bright. Her pulses beat fast, and the coursing blood warmed and relaxed every inch of her body.

She did not stop to ask if it were or were not a monstrous joy that held her. A clear and exalted perception enabled her to dismiss the suggestion as trivial. She knew that she would weep again when she saw the kind, tender hands folded in death; the face that had never looked save with love upon her, fixed and gray and dead. But she saw beyond that bitter moment a long procession of years to come that would belong to her absolutely. And she opened and spread her arms out to them in welcome.

There would be no one to live for during those coming years; she would live for herself. There would be no powerful will bending hers in that blind persistence with which men and women believe they have a right to impose a private will upon a fellow-creature. A kind intention or a cruel intention made the act seem no less a crime as she looked upon it in that brief moment of illumination.

And yet she had loved him--sometimes. Often she had not. What did it matter! What could love, the unsolved mystery, count for in the face of this possession of self-assertion which she suddenly recognized as the strongest impulse of her being!

"Free! Body and soul free!" she kept whispering.

Josephine was kneeling before the closed door with her lips to the keyhold, imploring for admission. "Louise, open the door! I beg; open the door--you will make yourself ill. What are you doing, Louise? For heaven's sake open the door."

"Go away. I am not making myself ill." No; she was drinking in a very elixir of life through that open window. Her fancy was running riot along those days ahead of her. Spring days, and summer days, and all sorts of days that would be her own. She breathed a quick prayer that life might be long. It was only yesterday she had thought with a shudder that life might be long.

She arose at length and opened the door to her sister's importunities. There was a feverish triumph in her eyes, and she carried herself unwittingly like a goddess of Victory. She clasped her sister's waist, and together they descended the stairs. Richards stood waiting for them at the bottom.

Some one was opening the front door with a latchkey. It was Brently Mallard who entered, a little travel-stained, composedly carrying his grip-sack and umbrella. He had been far from the scene of the accident, and did not even know there had been one. He stood amazed at Josephine's piercing cry; at Richards' quick motion to screen him from the view of his wife.

When the doctors came they said she had died of heart disease--of the joy that kills.

- What would you say is the theme of this story?

- Read this analysis of "The Story of An Hour" written by Jennifer Appel.

Story of an Hour Literary Critique

The Story of an Hour written by Kate Chopin starts with the death of the husband. We don't learn his name until later, but his name isn't what is significant. The significance is in the way Mrs. Mallard feels about the death in juxtaposition to how her sister and husband's friend thought she would feel. Her heart condition is what troubled them the most, as they were certain she wasn't stable enough for such delicate news. Is our author giving us a deeper meaning here with her heart being the organ afflicted?

Mrs. Mallard does indeed break down in tears when first given the news of her husband's untimely passing - a railroad accident. But once she is alone, her feelings give way to something much different. The tone of the writing changes. Instead of dreary imaging, we see lively and hopeful imagery scattered before us to lead along in her life. We are taken on a short journey into her mind and heart. Her heart cries change to freedom. She actually allows the words to escape her lips, "Free, free, free." Why do you suppose she felt freedom from a marriage that otherwise seems solid? She doesn't describe him as a harsh or abusive husband. In fact, kind is the word that comes up when she pictures him in the casket. And yet freedom is the feeling that pervades rather than mourning in that first hour after hearing of his untimely death. Could it be she was ready for a different life? Did she regret her past choices that made her feel tied down to the life she now led? She did have a heart condition as was mentioned at the beginning. Was she thinking she had minimal time left and wanted to spend that without having to consult someone else in what they wanted or how they wanted to spend their time? The freedom that comes with only being accountable to yourself can be a heady one.

She allowed her mind to take on the fancy of thinking of all sorts of solo adventures in that short space of time, so much so that her sister became concerned for her being alone for such a long period of time. One has to wonder what her sister could overhear from the hall. Did she hear her cries of freedom?

Eventually she is talked out of her room, and in doing so it's said that she leaves "a goddess of Victory." She had won the battle over death as she had been the one sick and yet her husband had passed before her, leaving her to live her life.

The story culminates in a splendor of irony as she descends the stairs to find someone opening the front door. The shock of the person at the door activates her heart condition in the worst way possible. An hour before, they had been consoling Mrs. Mallard at the death of her husband. Now, they are to console Mr. Mallard at the death of his wife.

- Here are some examples of literary devices used in "The Story of An Hour." Did you see others?
    - Metaphor: breath of rain; storm of grief
    - Simile: she carried herself unwittingly like a goddess of Victory

- Paradox: revealed in half-concealing; joy that kills
- Personification: physical exhaustion that haunted her body
- Oxymoron: monstrous joy
- Alliteration: **s**ong which **s**omeone was **s**inging
- Foreshadowing: the opening line about Mrs. Mallard's heart condition foreshadows the ending where she dies of a heart issue.
- Irony: doctors think she dies of joy at seeing her husband, whereas the reader knows the opposite is true.

Lesson 34

- Read the short story, "The Happy Prince."

"The Happy Prince"
By Oscar Wilde

High above the city, on a tall column, stood the statue of the Happy Prince. He was gilded all over with thin leaves of fine gold, for eyes he had two bright sapphires, and a large red ruby glowed on his sword-hilt.

He was very much admired indeed. "He is as beautiful as a weathercock," remarked one of the Town Councillors who wished to gain a reputation for having artistic tastes; "only not quite so useful," he added, fearing lest people should think him unpractical, which he really was not.

"Why can't you be like the Happy Prince?" asked a sensible mother of her little boy who was crying for the moon. "The Happy Prince never dreams of crying for anything."

"I am glad there is some one in the world who is quite happy," muttered a disappointed man as he gazed at the wonderful statue.

"He looks just like an angel," said the Charity Children as they came out of the cathedral in their bright scarlet cloaks and their clean white pinafores.

"How do you know?" said the Mathematical Master, "you have never seen one."

"Ah! but we have, in our dreams," answered the children; and the Mathematical Master frowned and looked very severe, for he did not approve of children dreaming.

One night there flew over the city a little Swallow. His friends had gone away to Egypt six weeks before, but he had stayed behind, for he was in love with the most beautiful Reed. He had met her early in the spring as he was flying down the river after a big yellow moth, and had been so attracted by her slender waist that he had stopped to talk to her.

"Shall I love you?" said the Swallow, who liked to come to the point at once, and the Reed made him a low bow. So he flew round and round her, touching the water with his wings, and making silver ripples. This was his courtship, and it lasted all through the summer.

"It is a ridiculous attachment," twittered the other Swallows; "she has no money, and far too many relations"; and indeed the river was quite full of Reeds. Then, when the autumn came they all flew away.

After they had gone he felt lonely, and began to tire of his lady-love. "She has no conversation," he said, "and I am afraid that she is a coquette, for she is always flirting with the wind." And certainly, whenever the wind blew, the Reed made the most graceful curtseys. "I admit that she is domestic," he continued, "but I love travelling, and my wife, consequently, should love travelling also."

"Will you come away with me?" he said finally to her; but the Reed shook her head, she was so attached to her home.

"You have been trifling with me," he cried. "I am off to the Pyramids. Good-bye!" and he flew away.

All day long he flew, and at night-time he arrived at the city. "Where shall I put up?" he said; "I hope the town has made preparations."

Then he saw the statue on the tall column.

"I will put up there," he cried; "it is a fine position, with plenty of fresh air." So he alighted just between the feet of the Happy Prince.

"I have a golden bedroom," he said softly to himself as he looked round, and he prepared to go to sleep; but just as he was putting his head under his wing a large drop of water fell on him. "What a curious thing!" he cried; "there is not a single cloud in the sky, the stars are quite clear and bright, and yet it is raining. The climate in the north of Europe is really dreadful.

The Reed used to like the rain, but that was merely her selfishness."

Then another drop fell.

"What is the use of a statue if it cannot keep the rain off?" he said; "I must look for a good chimney-pot," and he determined to fly away.

But before he had opened his wings, a third drop fell, and he looked up, and saw—Ah! what did he see?

The eyes of the Happy Prince were filled with tears, and tears were running down his golden cheeks. His face was so beautiful in the moonlight that the little Swallow was filled with pity.

"Who are you?" he said.

"I am the Happy Prince."

"Why are you weeping then?" asked the Swallow; "you have quite drenched me."

"When I was alive and had a human heart," answered the statue, "I did not know what tears were, for I lived in the Palace of Sans-Souci, where sorrow is not allowed to enter. In the daytime I played with my companions in the garden, and in the evening I led the dance in the Great Hall. Round the garden ran a very lofty wall, but I never cared to ask what lay beyond it, everything about me was so beautiful. My courtiers called me the Happy Prince, and happy indeed I was, if pleasure be happiness. So I lived, and so I died. And now that I am dead they have set me up here so high that I can see all the ugliness and all the misery of my city, and though my heart is made of lead yet I cannot chose but weep."

"What! is he not solid gold?" said the Swallow to himself. He was too polite to make any personal remarks out loud.

"Far away," continued the statue in a low musical voice, "far away in a little street there is a poor house. One of the windows is open, and through it I can see a woman seated at a table. Her face is thin and worn, and she has coarse, red hands, all pricked by the needle, for she is a seamstress. She is embroidering passion-flowers on a satin gown for the loveliest of the Queen's maids-of-honour to wear at the next Court-ball. In a bed in the corner of the room her little boy is lying ill. He has a fever, and is asking for oranges. His mother has nothing to give him but river water, so he is crying. Swallow, Swallow, little Swallow, will you not bring her the ruby out of my sword-hilt? My feet are fastened to this pedestal and I cannot move."

"I am waited for in Egypt," said the Swallow. "My friends are flying up and down the Nile, and talking to the large lotus-flowers. Soon they will go to sleep in the tomb of the great King. The King is there himself in his painted coffin. He is wrapped in yellow linen, and embalmed with spices. Round his neck is a chain of pale green jade, and his hands are like withered leaves."

"Swallow, Swallow, little Swallow," said the Prince, "will you not stay with me for one night, and be my messenger? The boy is so thirsty, and the mother so sad."

"I don't think I like boys," answered the Swallow. "Last summer, when I was staying on the river, there were two rude boys, the miller's sons, who were always throwing stones at me. They never hit me, of course; we swallows fly far too well for that, and besides, I come of a family famous for its agility; but still, it was a mark of disrespect."

But the Happy Prince looked so sad that the little Swallow was sorry. "It is very cold here," he said; "but I will stay with you for one night, and be your messenger."

"Thank you, little Swallow," said the Prince.

So the Swallow picked out the great ruby from the Prince's sword, and flew away with it in his beak over the roofs of the town.

He passed by the cathedral tower, where the white marble angels were sculptured. He passed by the palace and heard the sound of dancing. A beautiful girl came out on the balcony with her lover. "How wonderful the stars are," he said to her, "and how wonderful is the power of love!"

"I hope my dress will be ready in time for the State-ball," she answered; "I have ordered passion-flowers to be embroidered on it; but the seamstresses are so lazy."

He passed over the river, and saw the lanterns hanging to the masts of the ships. He passed over the Ghetto, and saw the old Jews bargaining with each other, and weighing out money in copper scales. At last he came to the poor house and looked in. The boy was tossing feverishly on his bed, and the mother had fallen asleep, she was so tired. In he hopped, and laid the great ruby on the table beside the woman's thimble. Then he flew gently round the bed, fanning the boy's forehead with his wings. "How cool I feel," said the boy, "I must be getting better"; and he sank into a delicious slumber.

Then the Swallow flew back to the Happy Prince, and told him what he had done. "It is curious," he remarked, "but I feel quite warm now, although it is so cold."

"That is because you have done a good action," said the Prince. And the little Swallow began to think, and then he fell asleep. Thinking always made him sleepy.

When day broke he flew down to the river and had a bath. "What a remarkable phenomenon," said the Professor of Ornithology as he was passing over the bridge. "A swallow in winter!" And he wrote a long letter about it to the local newspaper. Every one quoted it, it was full of so many words that they could not understand.

"To-night I go to Egypt," said the Swallow, and he was in high spirits at the prospect. He visited all the public monuments, and sat a long time on top of the church steeple. Wherever he went the Sparrows chirruped, and said to each other, "What a distinguished stranger!" so he enjoyed himself very much.

When the moon rose he flew back to the Happy Prince. "Have you any commissions for Egypt?" he cried; "I am just starting."

"Swallow, Swallow, little Swallow," said the Prince, "will you not stay with me one night longer?"

"I am waited for in Egypt," answered the Swallow. "To-morrow my friends will fly up to the Second Cataract. The river-horse couches there among the bulrushes, and on a great granite throne sits the God Memnon. All night long he watches the stars, and when the morning star shines he utters one cry of joy, and then he is silent. At noon the yellow lions come down to the water's edge to drink. They have eyes like green beryls, and their roar is louder than the roar of the cataract.

"Swallow, Swallow, little Swallow," said the Prince, "far away across the city I see a young man in a garret. He is leaning over a desk covered with papers, and in a tumbler by his side there is a bunch of withered violets. His hair is brown and crisp, and his lips are red as a pomegranate, and he has large and dreamy eyes. He is trying to finish a play for the Director of the Theatre, but he is too cold to write any more. There is no fire in the grate, and hunger has made him faint.

"I will wait with you one night longer," said the Swallow, who really had a good heart. "Shall I take him another ruby?"

"Alas! I have no ruby now," said the Prince; "my eyes are all that I have left. They are made of rare sapphires, which were brought out of India a thousand years ago. Pluck out one of them and take it to him. He will sell it to the jeweller, and buy food and firewood, and finish his play."

"Dear Prince," said the Swallow, "I cannot do that"; and he began to weep.

"Swallow, Swallow, little Swallow," said the Prince, "do as I command you."

So the Swallow plucked out the Prince's eye, and flew away to the student's garret. It was easy enough to get in, as there was a hole in the roof. Through this he darted, and came into the room. The young man had his head buried in his hands, so he did not hear the flutter of the bird's wings, and when he looked up he found the beautiful sapphire lying on the withered violets.

"I am beginning to be appreciated," he cried; "this is from some great admirer. Now I can finish my play," and he looked quite happy.

The next day the Swallow flew down to the harbour. He sat on the mast of a large vessel and watched the sailors hauling big chests out of the hold with ropes. "Heave a-hoy!" they shouted as each chest came up. "I am going to Egypt"! cried the Swallow, but nobody minded, and when the moon rose he flew back to the Happy Prince.

"I am come to bid you good-bye," he cried.

"Swallow, Swallow, little Swallow," said the Prince, "will you not stay with me one night longer?"

"It is winter," answered the Swallow, "and the chill snow will soon be here. In Egypt the sun is warm on the green palm-trees, and the crocodiles lie in the mud and look lazily about them. My companions are building a nest in the Temple of Baalbec, and the pink and white doves are watching them, and cooing to each other. Dear Prince, I must leave you, but I will never forget you, and next spring I will bring you back two beautiful jewels in place of those you have given away. The ruby shall be redder than a red rose, and the sapphire shall be as blue as the great sea."

"In the square below," said the Happy Prince, "there stands a little match-girl. She has let her matches fall in the gutter, and they are all spoiled. Her father will beat her if she does not bring home some money, and she is crying. She has no shoes or stockings, and her little head is bare. Pluck out my other eye, and give it to her, and her father will not beat her."

"I will stay with you one night longer," said the Swallow, "but I cannot pluck out your eye. You would be quite blind then."

"Swallow, Swallow, little Swallow," said the Prince, "do as I command you."

So he plucked out the Prince's other eye, and darted down with it. He swooped past the match-girl, and slipped the jewel into the palm of her hand. "What a lovely bit of glass," cried the little girl; and she ran home, laughing.

Then the Swallow came back to the Prince. "You are blind now," he said, "so I will stay with you always."

"No, little Swallow," said the poor Prince, "you must go away to Egypt."

"I will stay with you always," said the Swallow, and he slept at the Prince's feet.

All the next day he sat on the Prince's shoulder, and told him stories of what he had seen in strange lands.

He told him of the red ibises, who stand in long rows on the banks of the Nile, and catch gold-fish in their beaks; of the Sphinx, who is as old as the world itself, and lives in the desert, and knows everything; of the merchants, who walk slowly by the side of their camels, and carry amber beads in their hands; of the King of the Mountains of the Moon, who is as black as ebony, and worships a large crystal; of the great green snake that sleeps in a palm-tree, and has twenty priests to feed it with honey-cakes; and of the pygmies who sail over a big lake on large flat leaves, and are always at war with the butterflies.

"Dear little Swallow," said the Prince, "you tell me of marvellous things, but more marvellous than anything is the suffering of men and of women. There is no Mystery so great as Misery. Fly over my city, little Swallow, and tell me what you see there."

So the Swallow flew over the great city, and saw the rich making merry in their beautiful houses, while the beggars were sitting at the gates. He flew into dark lanes, and saw the white faces of starving children looking out listlessly at the black streets. Under the archway of a bridge two little boys were lying in one another's arms to try and keep themselves warm. "How hungry we are!" they said. "You must not lie here," shouted the Watchman, and they wandered out into the rain.

Then he flew back and told the Prince what he had seen.

"I am covered with fine gold," said the Prince, "you must take it off, leaf by leaf, and give it to my poor; the living always think that gold can make them happy."

Leaf after leaf of the fine gold the Swallow picked off, till the Happy Prince looked quite dull and grey. Leaf after leaf of the fine gold he brought to the poor, and the children's faces grew rosier, and they laughed and played games in the street. "We have bread now!" they cried.

Then the snow came, and after the snow came the frost. The streets looked as if they were made of silver, they were so bright and glistening; long icicles like crystal daggers hung down from the eaves of the houses, everybody went about in furs, and the little boys wore scarlet caps and skated on the ice.

The poor little Swallow grew colder and colder, but he would not leave the Prince, he loved him too well. He picked up crumbs outside the baker's door when the baker was not looking and tried to keep himself warm by flapping his wings.

But at last he knew that he was going to die. He had just strength to fly up to the Prince's shoulder once more. "Good-bye, dear Prince!" he murmured, "will you let me kiss your hand?"

"I am glad that you are going to Egypt at last, little Swallow," said the Prince, "you have stayed too long here; but you must kiss me on the lips, for I love you."

"It is not to Egypt that I am going," said the Swallow. "I am going to the House of Death. Death is the brother of Sleep, is he not?"

And he kissed the Happy Prince on the lips, and fell down dead at his feet.

At that moment a curious crack sounded inside the statue, as if something had broken. The fact is that the leaden heart had snapped right in two. It certainly was a dreadfully hard frost.

Early the next morning the Mayor was walking in the square below in company with the Town Councillors. As they passed the column he looked up at the statue: "Dear me! how shabby the Happy Prince looks!" he said.

"How shabby indeed!" cried the Town Councillors, who always agreed with the Mayor; and they went up to look at it.

"The ruby has fallen out of his sword, his eyes are gone, and he is golden no longer," said the Mayor in fact, "he is little better than a beggar!"

"Little better than a beggar," said the Town Councillors.

"And here is actually a dead bird at his feet!" continued the Mayor. "We must really issue a proclamation that birds are not to be allowed to die here." And the Town Clerk made a note of the suggestion.

So they pulled down the statue of the Happy Prince. "As he is no longer beautiful he is no longer useful," said the Art Professor at the University.

Then they melted the statue in a furnace, and the Mayor held a meeting of the Corporation to decide what was to be done with the metal. "We must have another statue, of course," he said, "and it shall be a statue of myself."

"Of myself," said each of the Town Councillors, and they quarrelled. When I last heard of them they were quarrelling still.

"What a strange thing!" said the overseer of the workmen at the foundry. "This broken lead heart will not melt in the furnace. We must throw it away." So they threw it on a dust-heap where the dead Swallow was also lying.

"Bring me the two most precious things in the city," said God to one of His Angels; and the Angel brought Him the leaden heart and the dead bird.

"You have rightly chosen," said God, "for in my garden of Paradise this little bird shall sing for evermore, and in my city of gold the Happy Prince shall praise me.

Lesson 38 (no reading for Lessons 35-37)

- Read about epic heroes.

An epic is a poem that spells out the adventures of heroic or legendary figures. It typically centers around an epic hero, generally a man, though not always a "good guy" as epic heroes can be evil as well. This hero is usually of some elevated status such as a king or someone related to the divine.

Some examples of epic heroes include King Arthur from British Literature, fighting for the good of his kingdom and battling with the supernatural to complete his quest. Darth Vader from Star Wars shows how not all epic heroes are the good guys. Vader is a man but has elevated status, and has to harness the supernatural "Force" and try to bring balance to it. Aragorn from The Lord of the Rings is a king on a quest to help Frodo get the ring to Mordor for destruction.

In The Odyssey, the epic hero is Odysseus. He faces many challenges that test his skill, bravery, and stamina on his ten-year journey home. As is the case with most epic heroes, Odysseus seems to be on the verge of being conquered time and time again, but he continually gets out of situations by the skin of his teeth and ultimately prevails.

But Odysseus was a different kind of Greek hero. He tended to use his intelligence and logic instead of strength and force to get out of situations. He had fully human parents, whereas most Greek heroes were related to divinity in some way. He chooses to live a long life rather than taking the gift of immortality that is presented to him, or dying a "hero's death" in battle.

- Read about the Trojan War.

The Legend of the Trojan War

This summary, which has been prepared by Ian Johnston of Malaspina University-College, Nanaimo, BC (now Vancouver Island University), for students in Classics 101 and Liberal Studies, is a brief account of a number of different old stories about the Trojan war, arranged in more or less chronological sequence. There are several different, even contradictory, versions of events. There is no one authoritative narrative of the whole war. Many of these stories were obviously current before Homer, and the story continued to be embellished by the Romans, Medieval, and Renaissance writers.

1. The gods Apollo and Poseidon, during a time when they were being punished by having to work among men, built the city of Troy for Priam's father, Laomedon. They invited the mortal man Aeacus (the son of Zeus and Aegina and grandfather of Achilles) to help them, since destiny had decreed that Troy would one day be captured in a place built by human hands (so a human being had to help them).

2. When newly constructed, Troy was attacked and captured by Hercules, Telamon, and Peleus (son of Aeacus), as a punishment for the fact that Laomedon had not given Hercules a promised reward of immortal horses for rescuing Laomedon's daughter Hesione. Telamon killed Laomedon and took Hesione as a concubine.

3. Priam, king of Troy and son of Laomedon, had a son from his wife Hecuba, who dreamed that she had given birth to a flaming torch. Cassandra, the prophetic daughter of Priam, foretold that the new-born son, Paris (also called Alexandros or Alexander), should be killed at birth or else he would destroy the city. Paris was taken out to be killed, but he was rescued by shepherds and grew up away from the city in the farms by Mount Ida. As a young man he returned to Troy to compete in the athletic games, was recognized, and returned to the royal family.

4. Peleus fell in love with the sea nymph Thetis, whom Zeus, the most powerful of the gods, also had designs upon. But Zeus learned of an ancient prophecy that Thetis would give birth to a son greater than his father, so he gave his divine blessing to the marriage of Peleus, a mortal king, and Thetis (a minor divine being). All the immortal gods were invited to the celebration, except, by a deliberate oversight, Eris, the goddess of strife. She came anyway and brought a golden apple, upon which was written "For the fairest." Hera (Zeus's wife and sister), Aphrodite (Zeus's daughter), and Athena (Zeus's daughter) all made a claim for the apple, and

they appealed to Zeus for judgment. He refused to adjudicate a beauty contest between his wife and two of his daughters, and the task of choosing a winner fell to Paris (while he was still a herdsman on Mount Ida, outside Troy). The goddesses each promised Paris a wonderful prize if he would pick her: Hera offered power, Athena offered military glory and wisdom, and Aphrodite offered him the most beautiful woman in the world as his wife. In the famous Judgement of Paris, Paris gave the apple to Aphrodite.

5. Helen, daughter of Tyndareus and Leda, was also the daughter of Zeus, who had made love to Leda in the shape of a swan (she is the only female child of Zeus and a mortal). Her beauty was famous throughout the world. Her father Tyndareus, king of Sparta, would not agree to any man's marrying her, until all the Greek warrior leaders made a promise that they would collectively avenge any insult to her. When the leaders made such an oath, Helen then married Menelaus. Her twin (non-divine) sister Clytaemnestra, born at the same time as Helen but not a daughter of Zeus, married Agamemnon, king of Argos, and brother of Menelaus. Agamemnon was the most powerful leader in Hellas (Greece).

6. Paris, back in the royal family at Troy, made a journey to Sparta as a Trojan ambassador, at a time when Menelaus was away. Paris and Helen fell in love and left Sparta together, taking with them a vast amount of the city's treasure and returning to Troy via Cranae, an island off Attica, Sidon, and Egypt, among other places. The Spartans set off in pursuit but could not catch the lovers. When the Spartans learned that Helen and Paris were back in Troy, they sent a delegation (Odysseus, king of Ithaca, and Menelaus, the injured husband) to Troy demanding the return of Helen and the treasure. When the Trojans refused, the Spartans appealed to the oath which Tyndareus had forced them all to take (see 5 above), and the Greeks assembled an army to invade Troy, asking all the allies to meet in preparation for embarkation at Aulis. Some stories claimed that the real Helen never went to Troy, for she was carried off to Egypt by the god Hermes, and Paris took her double to Troy.

7. Achilles, the son of Peleus and Thetis, was educated as a young man by Chiron, the centaur (half man and half horse). One of the conditions of Achilles's parents' marriage (the union of a mortal with a divine sea nymph) was that the son born to them would die in war and bring great sadness to his mother. To protect him from death in battle his mother bathed the infant in the waters of the river Styx, which

conferred invulnerability to any weapon. And when the Greeks began to assemble an army, Achilles's parents hid him at Scyros disguised as a girl. While there he met Deidameia, and they had a son Neoptolemos (also called Pyrrhus). Calchas, the prophet with the Greek army, told Agamemnon and the other leaders that they could not conquer Troy without Achilles. Odysseus found Achilles by tricking him; Odysseus placed a weapon out in front of the girls of Scyros, and Achilles reached for it, thus revealing his identity. Menoitios, a royal counsellor, sent his son Patroclus to accompany Achilles on the expedition as his friend and advisor.

8. The Greek fleet of one thousand ships assembled at Aulis. Agamemnon, who led the largest contingent, was the commander-in-chief. The army was delayed for a long time by contrary winds, and the future of the expedition was threatened as the forces lay idle. Agamemnon had offended the goddess Artemis by an impious boast, and Artemis had sent the winds. Finally, in desperation to appease the goddess, Agamemnon sacrificed his daughter Iphigeneia. Her father lured her to Aulis on the pretext that she was to be married to Achilles (whose earlier marriage was not known), but then he sacrificed her on the high altar. One version of her story claims that Artemis saved her at the last minute and carried her off to Tauris where she became a priestess of Artemis in charge of human sacrifices. In any case, after the sacrifice Artemis changed the winds, and the fleet sailed for Troy.

9. On the way to Troy, Philoctetes, the son of Poeas and leader of the seven ships from Methone, suffered a snake bite when the Greeks landed at Tenedos to make a sacrifice. His pain was so great and his wound so unpleasant (especially the smell) that the Greek army abandoned him against his will on the island.

10. The Greek army landed on the beaches before Troy. The first man ashore, Protesilaus, was killed by Hector, son of Priam and leader of the Trojan army. The Greeks sent another embassy to Troy, seeking to recover Helen and the treasure. When the Trojans denied them, the Greek army settled down into a siege which lasted many years.

11. In the tenth year of the war (where the narrative of the *Iliad* begins), Agamemnon insulted Apollo by taking as a slave-hostage the girl Chryseis, the daughter of Chryses, a prophet of Apollo, and refusing to return her when her father offered compensation. In revenge, Apollo sent nine days of plague down upon the Greek army. Achilles called an assembly to determine what the Greeks should do.

In that assembly, he and Agamemnon quarrelled bitterly, Agamemnon confiscated from Achilles his slave girl Briseis, and Achilles, in a rage, withdrew himself and his forces (the Myrmidons) from any further participation in the war. He asked his mother, Thetis, the divine sea nymph, to intercede on his behalf with Zeus to give the Trojans help in battle, so that the Greek forces would recognize how foolish Agamemnon had been to offend the best warrior under his command. Thetis made the request of Zeus, reminding him of a favour she had once done for him, and he agreed.

12. During the course of the war, numerous incidents took place, and many died on both sides. Paris and Menelaus fought a duel, and Aphrodite saved Paris just as Menelaus was about to kill him. Achilles, the greatest of the Greek warriors, slew Cycnus, Troilus, and many others. He also, according to various stories, was a lover of Patroclus, Troilus, Polyxena, daughter of Priam, Helen, and Medea. Odysseus and Diomedes slaughtered thirteen Thracians (Trojan allies) and stole the horses of King Rhesus in a night raid. Telamonian Ajax (the Greater Ajax) and Hector fought a duel with no decisive result. A common soldier, Thersites, challenged the authority of Agamemnon and demanded that the soldiers abandon the expedition. Odysseus beat Thersites into obedience. In the absence of Achilles and following Zeus's promise to Thetis (see 11), Hector enjoyed great success against the Greeks, breaking through their defensive ramparts on the beach and setting the ships on fire.

13. While Hector was enjoying his successes against the Greeks, the latter sent an embassy to Achilles, requesting him to return to battle. Agamemnon offered many rewards in compensation for his initial insult (see 11). Achilles refused the offer but did say that he would reconsider if Hector ever reached the Greek ships. When Hector did so, Achilles's friend Patroclus (see 7) begged to be allowed to return to the fight. Achilles gave him permission, advising Patroclus not to attack the city of Troy itself. He also gave Patroclus his own suit of armour, so that the Trojans might think that Achilles had returned to the war. Patroclus resumed the fight, enjoyed some dazzling success (killing one of the leaders of the Trojan allies, Sarpedon from Lycia), but he was finally killed by Hector, with the help of Apollo.

14. In his grief over the death of his friend Patroclus, Achilles decided to return to the battle. Since he had no armour (Hector had stripped the body of Patroclus and had put on the armour of Achilles), Thetis asked the divine artisan Hephaestus, the crippled god of the forge, to prepare some divine armour for her son. Hephaestus

did so, Thetis gave the armour to Achilles, and he returned to the war. After slaughtering many Trojans, Achilles finally cornered Hector alone outside the walls of Troy. Hector chose to stand and fight rather than to retreat into the city, and he was killed by Achilles, who then mutilated the corpse, tied it to his chariot, and dragged it away. Achilles built a huge funeral pyre for Patroclus, killed Trojan soldiers as sacrifices, and organized the funeral games in honour of his dead comrade. Priam travelled to the Greek camp to plead for the return of Hector's body, and Achilles relented and returned it to Priam in exchange for a ransom.

15. In the tenth year of the war the Amazons, led by Queen Penthesilea, joined the Trojan forces. She was killed in battle by Achilles, as was King Memnon of Ethiopa, who had also recently reinforced the Trojans. Achilles's career as the greatest warrior came to an end when Paris, with the help of Apollo, killed him with an arrow which pierced him in the heel, the one vulnerable spot, which the waters of the river Styx had not touched because his mother had held him by the foot (see 7) when she had dipped the infant Achilles in the river. Telamonian Ajax, the second greatest Greek warrior after Achilles, fought valiantly in defense of Achilles's corpse. At the funeral of Achilles, the Greeks sacrificed Polyxena, the daughter of Hecuba, wife of Priam. After the death of Achilles, Odysseus and Telamonian Ajax fought over who should get the divine armour of the dead hero. When Ajax lost the contest, he went mad and committed suicide. In some versions, the Greek leaders themselves vote and decide to award the armour to Odysseus.

16. The Greeks captured Helenus, a son of Priam, and one of the chief prophets in Troy. Helenus revealed to the Greeks that they could not capture Troy without the help of Philoctetes, who owned the bow and arrows of Hercules and whom the Greeks had abandoned on Tenedos (see 9 above). Odysseus and Neoptolemus (the son of Achilles) set out to persuade Philoctetes, who was angry at the Greeks for leaving him alone on the island, to return to the war, and by trickery they succeeded. Philoctetes killed Paris with an arrow shot from the bow of Hercules.

17. Odysseus and Diomedes ventured into Troy at night, in disguise, and stole the Palladium, the sacred statue of Athena, which was supposed to give the Trojans the strength to continue the war. The city, however, did not fall. Finally the Greeks devised the strategy of the wooden horse filled with armed soldiers. It was built by Epeius and left in front of Troy. The Greek army then withdrew to Tenedos (an island off the coast), as if abandoning the war. Odysseus went into Troy disguised,

and Helen recognized him. But he was sent away by Hecuba, the wife of Priam, after Helen told her. The Greek soldier Sinon stayed behind when the army withdrew and pretended to the Trojans that he had deserted from the Greek army because he had information about a murder Odysseus had committed. He told the Trojans that the horse was an offering to Athena and that the Greeks had built it to be so large that the Trojans could not bring it into their city. The Trojan Laocoon warned the Trojans not to believe Sinon ("I fear the Greeks even when they bear gifts"); in the midst of his warnings a huge sea monster came from the surf and killed Laocoon and his sons.

18. The Trojans determined to get the Trojan Horse into their city. They tore down a part of the wall, dragged the horse inside, and celebrated their apparent victory. At night, when the Trojans had fallen asleep, the Greek soldiers hidden in the horse came out, opened the gates, and gave the signal to the main army which had been hiding behind Tenedos. The city was totally destroyed. King Priam was slaughtered at the altar by Achilles's son Neoptolemos. Hector's infant son, Astyanax, was thrown off the battlements. The women were taken prisoner: Hecuba (wife of Priam), Cassandra (daughter of Priam), and Andromache (wife of Hector). Helen was returned to Menelaus.

19. The gods regarded the sacking of Troy and especially the treatment of the temples as a sacrilege, and they punished many of the Greek leaders. The fleet was almost destroyed by a storm on the journey back. Menelaus's ships sailed all over the sea for seven years—to Egypt (where, in some versions, he recovered his real wife in the court of King Proteus—see 6 above). Agamemnon returned to Argos, where he was murdered by his wife Clytaemnestra and her lover, Aegisthus. Cassandra, whom Agamemnon had claimed as a concubine after the destruction of Troy, was also killed by Clytaemnestra. Aegisthus was seeking revenge for what the father of Agamemnon (Atreus) had done to his brother (Aegisthus's father) Thyestes. Atreus had given a feast for Thyestes in which he fed to him the cooked flesh of his own children (see the family tree of the House of Atreus given below). Clytaemnestra claimed that she was seeking revenge for the sacrifice of her daughter Iphigeneia (see 8 above).

20. Odysseus (called by the Romans Ulysses) wandered over the sea for many years before reaching home. He started with a number of ships, but in a series of misfortunes, lasting ten years because of the enmity of Poseidon, the god of the sea,

he lost all his men before returning to Ithaca alone. His adventures took him from Troy to Ismareos (land of the Cicones); to the land of the Lotos Eaters, the island of the cyclops (Poseidon, the god of the sea, became Odysseus's enemy when Odysseus put out the eye of Polyphemus, the cannibal cyclops, who was a son of Poseidon); to the cave of Aeolos (god of the winds), to the land of the Laestrygonians, to the islands of Circe and Calypso, to the underworld (where he talked to the ghost of Achilles); to the land of the Sirens, past the monster Scylla and the whirlpool Charybdis, to the pastures of the cattle of Helios, the sun god, to Phaiacia. Back in Ithaca in disguise, with the help of his son Telemachus and some loyal servants, he killed the young princes who had been trying to persuade his wife, Penelope, to marry one of them and who had been wasting the treasure of the palace and trying to kill Telemachus. Odysseus proved who he was by being able to string the famous bow of Odysseus, a feat which no other man could manage, and by describing for Penelope the secret of their marriage bed, that Odysseus had built it around an old olive tree.

21. After the murder of Agamemnon by his wife Clytaemnestra (see 19 above), his son Orestes returned with a friend Pylades to avenge his father. With the help of his sister Electra (who had been very badly treated by her mother, left either unmarried or married to a poor farmer so that she would have no royal children, Orestes killed his mother and Aegisthus. Then he was pursued by the Furies, the goddesses of blood revenge. Suffering fits of madness, Orestes fled to Delphi, then to Tauri, where, in some versions, he met his long-lost sister, Iphigeneia. She had been rescued from Agamemnon's sacrifice by the gods and made a priestess of Diana in Tauri. Orestes escaped with Iphigeneia to Athens. There he was put on trial for the matricide. Apollo testified in his defense. The jury vote was even; Athena cast the deciding vote in Orestes's favour. The outraged Furies were placated by being given a permanent place in Athens and a certain authority in the judicial process. They were then renamed the Eumenides (The Kindly Ones). Orestes was later tried for the same matricide in Argos, at the insistence of Tyndareus, Clytaemnestra's father. Orestes and Electra were both sentenced to death by stoning. Orestes escaped by capturing Helen and using her as a hostage.

22. Neoptolemus, the only son of Achilles, married Hermione, the only daughter of Helen and Menelaus. Neoptolemus also took as a wife the widow of Hector, Andromache. There was considerable jealously between the two women. Orestes had wished to marry Hermione; by a strategy he arranged it so that the people of

Delphi killed Neoptolemus. Then he carried off Hermione and married her. Menelaus tried to kill the son of Neoptolemus, Molossus, and Andromache, but Peleus, Achilles's father, rescued them. Andromache later married Helenus. Orestes's friend Pylades married Electra, Orestes sister.

23. Aeneas, the son of Anchises and the goddess Aphrodite and one of the important Trojan leaders in the Trojan War, fled from the city while the Greeks were destroying it, carrying his father, Anchises, his son Ascanius, and his ancestral family gods with him. Aeneas wandered all over the Mediterranean. On his journey to Carthage, he had an affair with Dido, Queen of Carthage. He abandoned her without warning, in accordance with his mission to found another city. Dido committed suicide in grief. Aeneas reached Italy and there fought a war against Turnus, the leader of the local Rutulian people. He did not found Rome but Lavinium, the main centre of the Latin league, from which the people of Rome sprang. Aeneas thus links the royal house of Troy with the Roman republic.

The Cultural Influence of the Legend of the Trojan War

No story in our culture, with the possible exception of the Old Testament and the story of Jesus Christ, has inspired writers and painters over the centuries more than the Trojan War. It was the fundamental narrative in Greek education (especially in the version passed down by Homer, which covers only a small part of the total narrative), and all the tragedians whose works survive wrote plays upon various aspects of it, and these treatments, in turn, helped to add variations to the traditional story. No one authoritative work defines all the details of the story outlined above.

Unlike the Old Testament narratives, which over time became codified in a single authoritative version, the story of the Trojan War exists as a large collection of different versions of the same events (or parts of them). The war has been interpreted as a heroic tragedy, as a fanciful romance, as a satire against warfare, as a love story, as a passionately anti-war tale, and so on. Just as there is no single version which defines the "correct" sequence of events, so there is no single interpretative slant on how one should understand the war. Homer's poems enjoyed a unique authority, but they tell only a small part of the total story.

The following notes indicate only a few of the plays, novels, and poems which have drawn on and helped to shape this ancient story.

1. The most famous Greek literary stories of the war are Homer's *Iliad* and *Odyssey*, our first two epic poems, composed for oral recitation probably in the eighth century before Christ. The theme of the *Iliad* is the wrath of Achilles at the action of Agamemnon, and the epic follows the story of Achilles's withdrawal from the war and his subsequent return (see paragraphs 11, 12, 13, and 14 above). The *Odyssey* tells the story of the return of Odysseus from the war (see 20 above). A major reason for the extraordinary popularity and fecundity of the story of the Trojan War is the unquestioned quality and authority of these two great poems, even though they tell only a small part of the total narrative and were for a long time unavailable in Western Europe (after they were lost to the West, they did not appear until the fifteenth century). The *Iliad* was the inspiration for the archaeological work of Schliemann in the nineteenth century, a search which resulted in the discovery of the site of Troy at Hissarlik, in modern Turkey.

2. The Greek tragedians, we know from the extant plays and many fragments, found in the story of the Trojan War their favorite material, focusing especially on the events after the fall of the city. Aeschylus's famous trilogy, the *Oresteia* (*Agamemnon*, *Choephoroi* [*Libation Bearers*], and *Eumenides* [*The Kindly Ones*]), tells of the murder of Agamemnon and Cassandra by Clytaemnestra and Aegisthus, the revenge of Orestes, and the trial for the matricide. Both Sophocles and Euripides wrote plays about Electra, and Euripides also wrote a number of plays based on parts the larger story: the *Trojan Women*, the *Phoenissae*, *Orestes*, *Helen*, and *Iphigeneia in Tauris* (see 21 and 22 above). Sophocles also wrote *Philoctetes* (see 16) and *Ajax* (see 15) on events in the Trojan War.

3. Greek philosophers and historians used the Trojan War as a common example to demonstrate their own understanding of human conduct. So Herodotus and Thucydides, in defining their approach to the historical past, both offer an analysis of the origins of the war. Plato's *Republic* uses many parts of Homer's epics to establish important points about political wisdom (often citing Homer as a negative example). Alexander the Great carried a copy of the *Iliad* around with him in a special royal casket which he had captured from Darius, king of the Persians.

4. The Romans also adopted the story. Their most famous epic, Virgil's *Aeneid*, tells the story of Aeneas (see 23). And in the middle ages, the Renaissance, and right up to the present day, writers have retold parts of the ancient story. These

adaptations often make significant changes in the presentation of particular characters, notably Achilles, who in many versions becomes a knightly lover, and Odysseus/Ulysses, who is often a major villain. Ulysses and Diomedes appear in Dante's Inferno. Of particular note are Chaucer's and Shakespeare's treatments of the story of Troilus and Cressida.

5. Modern writers who have drawn on the literary tradition of this ancient cycle of stories include Sartre (*The Flies*), O'Neill (*Mourning Becomes Electra*), Giradoux (*Tiger at the Gates*), Joyce (*Ulysses*), Eliot, Auden, and many others. In addition, the story has formed the basis for operas and ballets, and the story of Odysseus has been made into a mini-series for television. This tradition is a complicated one, however, because many writers, especially in Medieval times, had no direct knowledge of the Greek sources and re-interpreted the details in very non-Greek ways (e.g., Dante, Chaucer, and Shakespeare). Homer's text, for example, was generally unknown in Western Europe until the late fifteenth century.

6. For the past two hundred years there has been a steady increase in the popularity of Homer's poems (and other works dealing with parts of the legend) translated into English. Thus, in addition to the various modern adaptations of parts of the total legend of the Trojan war (e.g., Brad Pitt's *Troy*), the ancient versions are still very current.

The Royal House of Atreus

The most famous (or notorious) human family in Western literature is the House of Atreus, the royal family of Mycenae, which suffered from an ancestral crime, variously described. Most commonly Tantalus, son of Zeus and Pluto, stole the food of the gods. In another version he kills his son Pelops and feeds the flesh to the gods (who later, when they discover what they have eaten, bring Pelops back to life). Having eaten the food of the gods, Tantalus is immortal and so cannot be killed. In Homer's *Odyssey*, Tantalus is punished everlastingly in the underworld.

The family curse originates with Pelops, who won his wife Hippodamia in a chariot race by cheating and betraying and killing his co-conspirator (who, as he was drowning, cursed the family of Pelops). The curse blighted the next generation: the brothers Atreus and Thyestes quarrelled. Atreus killed Thyestes's sons and served them to their father at a reconciliation banquet.

To obtain revenge, Thyestes fathered a son on his surviving child, his daughter Pelopia. This child was Aegisthus, whose task it was to avenge the murder of his brothers. When Agamemnon set off for Troy (sacrificing his daughter Iphigeneia so that the fleet could sail from Aulis), Aegisthus seduced Clytaemnestra and established himself as a power in Argos.

When Agamemnon returned, Clytaemnestra and Aegisthus killed him (and his captive Cassandra)--Aegisthus in revenge for his brothers, Clytaemnestra in revenge for the sacrifice of Iphigeneia. Orestes at the time was away, and Electra had been disgraced.

Orestes returned to Argos to avenge his father. With the help of a friend, Pylades, and his sister Electra, he succeeded by killing his mother, Clytaemnestra, and her lover, Aegisthus. After many adventures (depending upon the narrative) he finally received absolution for the matricide, and the curse was over.

Many Greek poets focused on this story. Homer repeatedly mentions the murder of Agamemnon in the *Odyssey* and the revenge of Orestes on Aegisthus (paying no attention to the murder of Clytaemnestra); Aeschylus's great trilogy the *Oresteia* is the most famous classical treatment of the tale; Sophocles and Euripides both wrote plays on Orestes and Electra.

One curious note is the almost exact parallel between the story of Orestes in this family tale and the story of Hamlet. These two stories arose, it seems, absolutely independently of each other, and yet in many crucial respects are extraordinarily similar. This match has puzzled many a comparative literature scholar and invited all sorts of psychological theories about the trans-cultural importance of matricide as a theme.

- Read about the influence of Homer.

Poetry was very important in Ancient Greece. Poets weren't just entertainers; they were also educators. Poetry was taught in schools and held as an example for Greeks to strive for. And there was arguably no greater works of literature in all of Ancient Greece as Homer's two epic poems: the *Iliad* and the *Odyssey*.

Not much is known about Homer aside from these two epic poems he contributed to Greek culture. The *Iliad* tells the story of the Trojan War. The *Odyssey* is sort of the epilogue and tells the adventures of Odysseus as he returns to Ithaca from helping the Greeks in the Trojan War.

These two epic poems set examples for the Greeks that they strived to uphold. The works defined Greek culture and continue to be used in modern schooling. They have stood the test of time as truly great, epic in more than one sense of the word.

Lesson 39

- Read this introduction to *The Odyssey*.

In the tenth and final year of the Trojan War, the Greeks performed a grand deception when they gifted a giant horse to the enemy who brought it inside the walls of the city of Troy. Little did they know that Greek soldiers, commanded by Odysseus, were hidden inside the giant horse. The soldiers came out of the horse inside the city and opened the gates to the rest of the Greek army, who conquered the city, ending the war. We join the story as it is time for Odysseus and the other Greek warriors to return to their kingdoms across the sea.

- Something to keep in mind as you read this: The summaries and some quizzes will refer to characters by the Greek version of their name (for example, *Odysseus*). The reading/book will refer to characters by the Roman version of their name (for example, *Ulysses*). It will be helpful if you make note of these names as you go along. Here are a few of the Greek/Roman names you might come across in *The Odyssey*.

Greek	Roman
Odysseus	Ulysses
Zeus	Jupiter
Hera	Juno
Poseidon	Neptune
Athena	Minerva
Artemis	Diana
Aphrodite	Venus
Hermes	Mercury
Ares	Mars
Hephaestus	Vulcan

- Read Book 1 of *The Odyssey*.
- If you need help understanding this book, there are study guides with summaries linked in the online course.
- You have a study guide in your Language Arts workbook. You'll want to fill it out as you read each day.

The Odyssey
By Homer
Written 800 B.C.E.
Translated by Samuel Butler
Book 1

Tell me, O muse, of that ingenious hero who traveled far and wide after he had sacked the famous town of Troy. Many cities did he visit, and many were the nations with whose manners and customs he was acquainted; moreover he suffered much by sea while trying to save his own life and bring his men safely home; but do what he might he could not save his men, for they perished through their own sheer folly in eating the cattle of the Sun-god Hyperion; so the god prevented them from ever reaching home. Tell me, too, about all these things, O daughter of Jove, from whatsoever source you may know them.

So now all who escaped death in battle or by shipwreck had got safely home except Ulysses, and he, though he was longing to return to his wife and country, was detained by the goddess Calypso, who had got him into a large cave and wanted to marry him. But as years went by, there came a time when the gods settled that he should go back to Ithaca; even then, however, when he was among his own people, his troubles were not yet over; nevertheless all the gods had now begun to pity him except Neptune, who still persecuted him without ceasing and would not let him get home.

Now Neptune had gone off to the Ethiopians, who are at the world's end, and lie in two halves, the one looking West and the other East. He had gone there to accept a hecatomb of sheep and oxen, and was enjoying himself at his festival; but the other gods met in the house of Olympian Jove, and the sire of gods and men spoke first. At that moment he was thinking of Aegisthus, who had been killed by Agamemnon's son Orestes; so he said to the other gods:

"See now, how men lay blame upon us gods for what is after all nothing but their own folly. Look at Aegisthus; he must needs make love to Agamemnon's wife unrighteously and then kill Agamemnon, though he knew it would be the death of him; for I sent Mercury to warn him not to do either of these things, inasmuch as Orestes would be sure to take his revenge when he grew up and wanted to return home. Mercury told him this in all good will but he would not listen, and now he has paid for everything in full."

Then Minerva said, "Father, son of Saturn, King of kings, it served Aegisthus right, and so it would any one else who does as he did; but Aegisthus is neither here nor there; it is for Ulysses that my heart bleeds, when I think of his sufferings in that lonely sea-girt island, far away, poor man, from all his friends. It is an island covered with forest, in the very middle of the sea, and a goddess lives there, daughter of the magician Atlas, who looks after the bottom of the ocean, and carries the great columns that keep heaven and earth asunder. This daughter of Atlas has got hold of poor unhappy Ulysses, and keeps trying by every kind of blandishment to make him forget his home, so that he is tired of life, and thinks of nothing but how he may once more see the smoke of his own chimneys. You, sir, take no heed of this, and yet when Ulysses was before Troy did he not propitiate you with many a burnt sacrifice? Why then should you keep on being so angry with him?"

And Jove said, "My child, what are you talking about? How can I forget Ulysses than whom there is no more capable man on earth, nor more liberal in his offerings to the immortal gods that live in heaven? Bear in mind, however, that Neptune is still furious with Ulysses for having blinded an eye of Polyphemus king of the Cyclopes. Polyphemus is son to Neptune by the nymph Thoosa, daughter to the sea-king Phorcys; therefore though he will not kill Ulysses outright, he torments him by preventing him from getting home. Still, let us lay our heads together and see how we can help him to return; Neptune will then be pacified, for if we are all of a mind he can hardly stand out against us."

And Minerva said, "Father, son of Saturn, King of kings, if, then, the gods now mean that Ulysses should get home, we should first send Mercury to the Ogygian island to tell Calypso that we have made up our minds and that he is to return. In the meantime I will go to Ithaca, to put heart into Ulysses' son Telemachus; I will embolden him to call the Achaeans in assembly, and speak out to the suitors of his mother Penelope, who persist in eating up any number of his sheep and oxen; I will also conduct him to Sparta and to Pylos, to see if he can hear anything about the return of his dear father- for this will make people speak well of him."

So saying she bound on her glittering golden sandals, imperishable, with which she can fly like the wind over land or sea; she grasped the redoubtable bronze-shod spear, so stout and sturdy and strong, wherewith she quells the ranks of heroes who have displeased her, and down she darted from the topmost summits of Olympus, whereon forthwith she was in Ithaca, at the gateway of Ulysses' house, disguised as a visitor, Mentes, chief of the Taphians, and she held a bronze spear in her hand. There she found the lordly suitors seated on hides of the oxen which they had killed and eaten, and playing draughts in front of the house. Men-servants and pages were bustling about to wait upon them, some mixing wine with water in the mixing-bowls, some cleaning down the tables with wet sponges and laying them out again, and some cutting up great quantities of meat.

Telemachus saw her long before any one else did. He was sitting moodily among the suitors thinking about his brave father, and how he would send them flying out of the house, if he were to come to his own again and be honored as in days gone by. Thus brooding as he sat among them, he caught sight of Minerva and went straight to the gate, for he was vexed that a stranger should be kept waiting for admittance. He took her right hand in his own, and bade her give him her spear.

"Welcome," said he, "to our house, and when you have partaken of food you shall tell us what you have come for."

He led the way as he spoke, and Minerva followed him. When they were within he took her spear and set it in the spear-stand against a strong bearing-post along with the many other spears of his unhappy father, and he conducted her to a richly decorated seat under which he threw a cloth of damask. There was a footstool also for her feet, and he set another seat near her for himself, away from the suitors, that she might not be annoyed while eating by their noise and insolence, and that he might ask her more freely about his father.

A maid servant then brought them water in a beautiful golden ewer and poured it into a silver basin for them to wash their hands, and she drew a clean table beside them. An upper servant brought them bread, and offered them many good things of what there was in the house, the carver fetched them plates of all manner of meats and set cups of gold by their side, and a man-servant brought them wine and poured it out for them.

Then the suitors came in and took their places on the benches and seats. Forthwith men servants poured water over their hands, maids went round with the bread-baskets, pages filled the mixing-bowls with wine and water, and they laid their hands upon the good things that were before them. As soon as they had had enough to eat and drink they wanted music and dancing, which are the crowning embellishments of a banquet, so a servant brought a lyre to Phemius, whom they compelled perforce to sing to them. As soon as he touched his lyre and began to sing Telemachus spoke low to Minerva, with his head close to hers that no man might hear.

"I hope, sir," said he, "that you will not be offended with what I am going to say. Singing comes cheap to those who do not pay for it, and all this is done at the cost of one whose bones lie rotting in some wilderness or grinding to powder in the surf. If these men were to see my father come back to Ithaca they would pray for longer legs rather than a longer purse, for money would not serve them; but he, alas, has fallen on an ill fate, and even when people do sometimes say that he is coming, we no longer heed them; we shall never see him again. And now, sir, tell me and tell me true, who you are and where you come from. Tell me of your town and parents, what manner of ship you came in, how your crew brought you to Ithaca, and of what nation they declared themselves to be- for you cannot have come by land. Tell me also truly, for I want to know, are you a stranger to this house, or have you been here in my father's time? In the old days we had many visitors for my father went about much himself."

And Minerva answered, "I will tell you truly and particularly all about it. I am Mentes, son of Anchialus, and I am King of the Taphians. I have come here with my ship and crew, on a voyage to men of a foreign tongue being bound for Temesa with a cargo of iron, and I shall bring back copper. As for my ship, it lies over yonder off the open country away from the town, in the harbor Rheithron under the wooded mountain Neritum. Our fathers were friends before us, as old Laertes will tell you, if you will go and ask him. They say, however, that he never comes to town now, and lives by himself in the country, faring hardly, with an old woman to look after him and get his dinner for him, when he comes in tired from pottering about his vineyard. They told me your father was at home again, and that was why I came, but it seems the gods are still keeping him back, for he is not dead yet not on the mainland. It is more likely he is on some sea-girt island in mid ocean, or a prisoner among savages who are detaining him against his will I am no prophet, and know very little about omens, but I speak as it is borne in upon me from heaven, and assure you that he will not be away much longer; for he is a man of such resource that even though he were in chains of iron he would find some means of getting home again. But tell me, and tell me true, can Ulysses really have such a fine looking fellow for a son? You are indeed wonderfully like him about the head and eyes, for we were close friends before he set sail for Troy where the flower of all the Argives went also. Since that time we have never either of us seen the other."

"My mother," answered Telemachus, "tells me I am son to Ulysses, but it is a wise child that knows his own father. Would that I were son to one who had grown old upon his own estates, for, since you ask me, there is no more ill-starred man under heaven than he who they tell me is my father."

And Minerva said, "There is no fear of your race dying out yet, while Penelope has such a fine son as you are. But tell me, and tell me true, what is the meaning of all this feasting, and who are these people? What is it all about? Have you some banquet, or is there a wedding in the family- for no one seems to be bringing any provisions of his own? And the guests- how atrociously they are behaving; what riot they make over the whole house; it is enough to disgust any respectable person who comes near them."

"Sir," said Telemachus, "as regards your question, so long as my father was here it was well with us and with the house, but the gods in their displeasure have willed it otherwise, and have hidden him away more closely than mortal man was ever yet hidden. I could have borne it better even though he were dead, if he had fallen with his men before Troy, or had died with friends around him when the days of his fighting were done; for then the Achaeans would have built a mound over his ashes, and I should myself have been heir to his renown; but now the storm-winds have spirited him away we know not wither; he is gone without leaving so much as a trace behind him, and I inherit nothing but dismay. Nor does the matter end simply with grief for the loss of my father; heaven has laid sorrows upon me of yet another kind; for the chiefs from all our islands, Dulichium, Same, and the woodland island of Zacynthus, as also all the principal men of Ithaca itself, are eating up my house under the pretext of paying their court to my mother, who will neither point blank say that she will not marry, nor yet bring matters to an end; so they are making havoc of my estate, and before long will do so also with myself."

"Is that so?" exclaimed Minerva, "then you do indeed want Ulysses home again. Give him his helmet, shield, and a couple lances, and if he is the man he was when I first knew him in our house, drinking and making merry, he would soon lay his hands about these rascally suitors, were he to stand once more upon his own threshold. He was then coming from Ephyra, where he had been to beg poison for his arrows from Ilus, son of Mermerus. Ilus feared the ever-living gods and would not give him any, but my father let him have some, for he was very fond of him. If Ulysses is the man he then was these suitors will have a short shrift and a sorry wedding.

"But there! It rests with heaven to determine whether he is to return, and take his revenge in his own house or no; I would, however, urge you to set about trying to get rid of these suitors at once. Take my advice, call the Achaean heroes in assembly to-morrow -lay your case before them, and call heaven to bear you witness. Bid the suitors take themselves off, each to his own place, and if your mother's mind is set on marrying again, let her go back to her father, who will find her a husband and provide her with all the marriage gifts that so dear a daughter may expect. As for yourself, let me prevail upon you to take the best ship you can get, with a crew of twenty men, and go in quest of your father who has so long been missing. Some one may tell you something, or (and people often hear things in this way) some heaven-sent message may direct you. First go to Pylos and ask Nestor; thence go on to Sparta and visit Menelaus, for he got home last of all the Achaeans; if you hear that your father is alive and on his way home, you can put up with the waste these suitors will make for yet another twelve months. If on the other hand you hear of his death, come home at once, celebrate his funeral rites with all due pomp, build a barrow to his memory, and make your mother marry again. Then, having done all this, think it well over in your mind how, by fair means or foul, you may kill these suitors in your own house. You are too old to plead infancy any longer; have you not heard how people are singing Orestes' praises for having killed his father's murderer Aegisthus? You are a fine, smart looking fellow; show your mettle, then, and make yourself a name in story. Now, however, I must go back to my ship and to my crew, who will be impatient if I keep them waiting longer; think the matter over for yourself, and remember what I have said to you."

"Sir," answered Telemachus, "it has been very kind of you to talk to me in this way, as though I were your own son, and I will do all you tell me; I know you want to be getting on with your voyage, but stay a little longer till you have taken a bath and refreshed yourself. I will then give you a present, and you shall go on your way rejoicing; I will give you one of great beauty and value- a keepsake such as only dear friends give to one another."

Minerva answered, "Do not try to keep me, for I would be on my way at once. As for any present you may be disposed to make me, keep it till I come again, and I will take it home with me. You shall give me a very good one, and I will give you one of no less value in return."

With these words she flew away like a bird into the air, but she had given Telemachus courage, and had made him think more than ever about his father. He felt the change, wondered at it, and knew that the stranger had been a god, so he went straight to where the suitors were sitting.

Phemius was still singing, and his hearers sat rapt in silence as he told the sad tale of the return from Troy, and the ills Minerva had laid upon the Achaeans. Penelope, daughter of Icarius, heard his song from her room upstairs, and came down by the great staircase, not alone, but attended by two of her handmaids. When she reached the suitors she stood by one of the bearing posts that supported the roof of the cloisters with a staid maiden on either side of her. She held a veil, moreover, before her face, and was weeping bitterly.

"Phemius," she cried, "you know many another feat of gods and heroes, such as poets love to celebrate. Sing the suitors some one of these, and let them drink their wine in silence, but cease this sad tale, for it breaks my sorrowful heart, and reminds me of my lost husband whom I mourn ever without ceasing, and whose name was great over all Hellas and middle Argos."

"Mother," answered Telemachus, "let the bard sing what he has a mind to; bards do not make the ills they sing of; it is Jove, not they, who makes them, and who sends weal or woe upon mankind according to his own good pleasure. This fellow means no harm by singing the ill-fated return of the Danaans, for people always applaud the latest songs most warmly. Make up your mind to it and bear it; Ulysses is not the only man who never came back from Troy, but many another went down as well as he. Go, then, within the house and busy yourself with your daily duties, your loom, your distaff, and the ordering of your servants; for speech is man's matter, and mine above all others- for it is I who am master here."

She went wondering back into the house, and laid her son's saying in her heart. Then, going upstairs with her handmaids into her room, she mourned her dear husband till Minerva shed sweet sleep over her eyes. But the suitors were clamorous throughout the covered cloisters, and prayed each one that he might be her bed fellow.

Then Telemachus spoke, "Shameless," he cried, "and insolent suitors, let us feast at our pleasure now, and let there be no brawling, for it is a rare thing to hear a man with such a divine voice as Phemius has; but in the morning meet me in full assembly that I may give you formal notice to depart, and feast at one another's houses, turn and turn about, at your own cost. If on the other hand you choose to persist in spunging upon one man, heaven help me, but Jove shall reckon with you in full, and when you fall in my father's house there shall be no man to avenge you."

The suitors bit their lips as they heard him, and marveled at the boldness of his speech. Then, Antinous, son of Eupeithes, said, "The gods seem to have given you lessons in bluster and tall talking; may Jove never grant you to be chief in Ithaca as your father was before you."

Telemachus answered, "Antinous, do not chide with me, but, god willing, I will be chief too if I can. Is this the worst fate you can think of for me? It is no bad thing to be a chief, for it brings both riches and honor. Still, now that Ulysses is dead there are many great men in Ithaca both old and young, and some other may take the lead among them; nevertheless I will be chief in my own house, and will rule those whom Ulysses has won for me."

Then Eurymachus, son of Polybus, answered, "It rests with heaven to decide who shall be chief among us, but you shall be master in your own house and over your own possessions; no one while there is a man in Ithaca shall do you violence nor rob you. And now, my good fellow, I want to know about this stranger. What country does he come from? Of what family is he, and where is his estate? Has he brought you news about the return of your father, or was he on business of his own? He seemed a well-to-do man, but he hurried off so suddenly that he was gone in a moment before we could get to know him."

"My father is dead and gone," answered Telemachus, "and even if some rumor reaches me I put no more faith in it now. My mother does indeed sometimes send for a soothsayer and question him, but I give his prophecyings no heed. As for the stranger, he was Mentes, son of Anchialus, chief of the Taphians, an old friend of my father's." But in his heart he knew that it had been the goddess.

The suitors then returned to their singing and dancing until the evening; but when night fell upon their pleasuring they went home to bed each in his own abode. Telemachus's room was high up in a tower that looked on to the outer court; hither, then, he hied, brooding and full of thought. A good old woman, Euryclea, daughter of Ops, the son of Pisenor, went before him with a couple of blazing torches. Laertes had bought her with his own money when she was quite young; he gave the worth of twenty oxen for her, and shewed as much respect to her in his household as he did to his own wedded wife, but he did not take her to his bed for he feared his wife's resentment. She it was who now lighted Telemachus to his room, and she loved him better than any of the other women in the house did, for she had nursed him when he was a baby. He opened the door of his bed room and sat down upon the bed; as he took off his shirt he gave it to the good old woman, who folded it tidily up, and hung it for him over a peg by his bed side, after which she went out, pulled the door to by a silver catch, and drew the bolt home by means of the strap. But Telemachus as he lay covered with a woolen fleece kept thinking all night through of his intended voyage of the counsel that Minerva had given him.

Lesson 40

- Read Book 2 of *The Odyssey*.

Book 2

Now when the child of morning, rosy-fingered Dawn, appeared, Telemachus rose and dressed himself. He bound his sandals on to his comely feet, girded his sword about his shoulder, and left his room looking like an immortal god. He at once sent the criers round to call the people in assembly, so they called them and the people gathered thereon; then, when they were got together, he went to the place of assembly spear in hand- not alone, for his two hounds went with him. Minerva endowed him with a presence of such divine comeliness that all marveled at him as he went by, and when he took his place' in his father's seat even the oldest councilors made way for him.

Aegyptius, a man bent double with age, and of infinite experience, the first to speak His son Antiphus had gone with Ulysses to Ilius, land of noble steeds, but the savage Cyclops had killed him when they were all shut up in the cave, and had cooked his last dinner for him, He had three sons left, of whom two still worked on their father's land, while the third, Eurynomus, was one of the suitors; nevertheless their father could not get over the loss of Antiphus, and was still weeping for him when he began his speech.

"Men of Ithaca," he said, "hear my words. From the day Ulysses left us there has been no meeting of our councilors until now; who then can it be, whether old or young, that finds it so necessary to convene us? Has he got wind of some host approaching, and does he wish to warn us, or would he speak upon some other matter of public moment? I am sure he is an excellent person, and I hope Jove will grant him his heart's desire."

Telemachus took this speech as of good omen and rose at once, for he was bursting with what he had to say. He stood in the middle of the assembly and the good herald Pisenor brought him his staff. Then, turning to Aegyptius, "Sir," said he, "it is I, as you will shortly learn, who have convened you, for it is I who am the most aggrieved. I have not got wind of any host approaching about which I would warn you, nor is there any matter of public moment on which I would speak. My grievance is purely personal, and turns on two great misfortunes which have fallen upon my house. The first of these is the loss of my excellent father, who was chief among all you here present, and was like a father to every one of you; the second is much more serious, and ere long will be the utter ruin of my estate. The sons of all the chief men among you are pestering my mother to marry them against her will. They are afraid to go to her father Icarius, asking him to choose the one he likes best, and to provide marriage gifts for his daughter, but day by day they keep hanging about my father's house, sacrificing our oxen, sheep, and fat goats for their banquets, and never giving so much as a thought to the quantity of wine they drink. No estate can stand such recklessness; we have now no Ulysses to ward off harm from our doors, and I cannot hold my own against them. I shall never all my days be as good a man as he was, still I would indeed defend myself if I had power to do so, for I cannot stand such treatment any longer; my house is being disgraced and ruined. Have respect, therefore, to your own consciences and to public opinion. Fear, too, the wrath of heaven, lest the gods should be displeased and turn upon you. I pray you by Jove and Themis, who is the beginning and the end of councils, [do not] hold back, my friends, and leave me single-handed – unless it be that my brave father Ulysses did some wrong to the Achaeans which you would now avenge on me, by aiding and abetting these suitors. Moreover, if I am to be eaten out of house and home at all, I had rather you did the eating yourselves, for I could then take action against you to some purpose, and serve you with notices from house to house till I got paid in full, whereas now I have no remedy."

With this Telemachus dashed his staff to the ground and burst into tears. Every one was very sorry for him, but they all sat still and no one ventured to make him an angry answer, save only Antinous, who spoke thus:

"Telemachus, insolent braggart that you are, how dare you try to throw the blame upon us suitors? It is your mother's fault not ours, for she is a very artful woman. This three years past, and close on four, she has been driving us out of our minds, by encouraging each one of us, and sending him messages without meaning one word of what she says. And then there was that other trick she played us. She set up a great tambour frame in her room, and began to work on an enormous piece of fine needlework. 'Sweet hearts,' said she, 'Ulysses is indeed dead, still do not press me to marry again immediately, wait- for I would not have skill in needlework perish unrecorded- till I have completed a pall for the hero Laertes, to be in readiness against the time when death shall take him. He is very rich, and the women of the place will talk if he is laid out without a pall.'

"This was what she said, and we assented; whereon we could see her working on her great web all day long, but at night she would unpick the stitches again by torchlight. She fooled us in this way for three years and we never found her out, but as time wore on and she was now in her fourth year, one of her maids who knew what she was doing told us, and we caught her in the act of undoing her work, so she had to finish it whether she would or no. The suitors, therefore, make you this answer, that both you and the Achaeans may understand-'Send your mother away, and bid her marry the man of her own and of her father's choice'; for I do not know what will happen if she goes on plaguing us much longer with the airs she gives herself on the score of the accomplishments Minerva has taught her, and because she is so clever. We never yet heard of such a woman; we know all about Tyro, Alcmena, Mycene, and the famous women of old, but they were nothing to your mother, any one of them. It was not fair of her to treat us in that way, and as long as she continues in the mind with which heaven has now endowed her, so long shall we go on eating up your estate; and I do not see why she should change, for she gets all the honor and glory, and it is you who pay for it, not she. Understand, then, that we will not go back to our lands, neither here nor elsewhere, till she has made her choice and married some one or other of us."

Telemachus answered, "Antinous, how can I drive the mother who bore me from my father's house? My father is abroad and we do not know whether he is alive or dead. It will be hard on me if I have to pay Icarius the large sum which I must give him if I insist on sending his daughter back to him. Not only will he deal rigorously with me, but heaven will also punish me; for my mother when she leaves the house will calf on the Erinyes to avenge her; besides, it would not be a creditable thing to do, and I will have nothing to say to it. If you choose to take offence at this, leave the house and feast elsewhere at one another's houses at your own cost turn and turn about. If, on the other hand, you elect to persist in spunging upon one man, heaven help me, but Jove shall reckon with you in full, and when you fall in my father's house there shall be no man to avenge you."

As he spoke Jove sent two eagles from the top of the mountain, and they flew on and on with the wind, sailing side by side in their own lordly flight. When they were right over the middle of the assembly they wheeled and circled about, beating the air with their wings and glaring death into the eyes of them that were below; then, fighting fiercely and tearing at one another, they flew off towards the right over the town. The people wondered as they saw them, and asked each other what an this might be; whereon Halitherses, who was the best prophet and reader of omens among them, spoke to them plainly and in all honesty, saying:

"Hear me, men of Ithaca, and I speak more particularly to the suitors, for I see mischief brewing for them. Ulysses is not going to be away much longer; indeed he is close at hand to deal out death and destruction, not on them alone, but on many another of us who live in Ithaca. Let us then be wise in time, and put a stop to this wickedness before he comes. Let the suitors do so of their own accord; it will be better for them, for I am not prophesying without due knowledge; everything has happened to Ulysses as I foretold when the Argives set out for Troy, and he with them. I said that after going through much hardship and losing all his men he should come home again in the twentieth year and that no one would know him; and now all this is coming true."

Eurymachus son of Polybus then said, "Go home, old man, and prophesy to your own children, or it may be worse for them. I can read these omens myself much better than you can; birds are always flying about in the sunshine somewhere or other, but they seldom mean anything. Ulysses has died in a far country, and it is a pity you are not dead along with him, instead of prating here about omens and adding fuel to the anger of Telemachus which is fierce enough as it is. I suppose you think he will give you something for your family, but I tell you- and it shall surely be- when an old man like you, who should know better, talks a young one over till he becomes troublesome, in the first place his young friend will only fare so much the worse- he will take nothing by it, for the suitors will prevent this- and in the next, we will lay a heavier fine, sir, upon yourself than you will at all like paying, for it will bear hardly upon you. As for Telemachus, I warn him in the presence of you all to send his mother back to her father, who will find her a husband and provide her with all the marriage gifts so dear a daughter may expect. Till we shall go on harassing him with our suit; for we fear no man, and care neither for him, with all his fine speeches, nor for any fortune-telling of yours. You may preach as much as you please, but we shall only hate you the more. We shall go back and continue to eat up Telemachus's estate without paying him, till such time as his mother leaves off tormenting us by keeping us day after day on the tiptoe of expectation, each vying with the other in his suit for a prize of such rare perfection. Besides we cannot go after the other women whom we should marry in due course, but for the way in which she treats us."

Then Telemachus said, "Eurymachus, and you other suitors, I shall say no more, and entreat you no further, for the gods and the people of Ithaca now know my story. Give me, then, a ship and a crew of twenty men to take me hither and thither, and I will go to Sparta and to Pylos in quest of my father who has so long been missing. Some one may tell me something, or (and people often hear things in this way) some heaven-sent message may direct me. If I can hear of him as alive and on his way home I will put up with the waste you suitors will make for yet another twelve months. If on the other hand I hear of his death, I will return at once, celebrate his funeral rites with all due pomp, build a barrow to his memory, and make my mother marry again."

With these words he sat down, and Mentor who had been a friend of Ulysses, and had been left in charge of everything with full authority over the servants, rose to speak. He, then, plainly and in all honesty addressed them thus:

"Hear me, men of Ithaca, I hope that you may never have a kind and well-disposed ruler any more, nor one who will govern you equitably; I hope that all your chiefs henceforward may be cruel and unjust, for there is not one of you but has forgotten Ulysses, who ruled you as though he were your father. I am not half so angry with the suitors, for if they choose to do violence in the naughtiness of their hearts, and wager their heads that Ulysses will not return, they can take the high hand and eat up his estate, but as for you others I am shocked at the way in which you all sit still without even trying to stop such scandalous goings on-which you could do if you chose, for you are many and they are few."

Leiocritus, son of Evenor, answered him saying, "Mentor, what folly is all this, that you should set the people to stay us? It is a hard thing for one man to fight with many about his victuals. Even though Ulysses himself were to set upon us while we are feasting in his house, and do his best to oust us, his wife, who wants him back so very badly, would have small cause for rejoicing, and his blood would be upon his own head if he fought against such great odds. There is no sense in what you have been saying. Now, therefore, do you people go about your business, and let his father's old friends, Mentor and Halitherses, speed this boy on his journey, if he goes at all- which I do not think he will, for he is more likely to stay where he is till some one comes and tells him something."

On this he broke up the assembly, and every man went back to his own abode, while the suitors returned to the house of Ulysses.

Then Telemachus went all alone by the sea side, washed his hands in the grey waves, and prayed to Minerva.

"Hear me," he cried, "you god who visited me yesterday, and bade me sail the seas in search of my father who has so long been missing. I would obey you, but the Achaeans, and more particularly the wicked suitors, are hindering me that I cannot do so."

As he thus prayed, Minerva came close up to him in the likeness and with the voice of Mentor. "Telemachus," said she, "if you are made of the same stuff as your father you will be neither fool nor coward henceforward, for Ulysses never broke his word nor left his work half done. If, then, you take after him, your voyage will not be fruitless, but unless you have the blood of Ulysses and of Penelope in your veins I see no likelihood of your succeeding. Sons are seldom as good men as their fathers; they are generally worse, not better; still, as you are not going to be either fool or coward henceforward, and are not entirely without some share of your father's wise discernment, I look with hope upon your undertaking. But mind you never make common cause with any of those foolish suitors, for they have neither sense nor virtue, and give no thought to death and to the doom that will shortly fall on one and all of them, so that they shall perish on the same day. As for your voyage, it shall not be long delayed; your father was such an old friend of mine that I will find you a ship, and will come with you myself. Now, however, return home, and go about among the suitors; begin getting provisions ready for your voyage; see everything well stowed, the wine in jars, and the barley meal, which is the staff of life, in leathern bags, while I go round the town and beat up volunteers at once. There are many ships in Ithaca both old and new; I will run my eye over them for you and will choose the best; we will get her ready and will put out to sea without delay."

Thus spoke Minerva daughter of Jove, and Telemachus lost no time in doing as the goddess told him. He went moodily and found the suitors flaying goats and singeing pigs in the outer court. Antinous came up to him at once and laughed as he took his hand in his own, saying, "Telemachus, my fine fire-eater, bear no more ill blood neither in word nor deed, but eat and drink with us as you used to do. The Achaeans will find you in everything- a ship and a picked crew to boot- so that you can set sail for Pylos at once and get news of your noble father."

"Antinous," answered Telemachus, "I cannot eat in peace, nor take pleasure of any kind with such men as you are. Was it not enough that you should waste so much good property of mine while I was yet a boy? Now that I am older and know more about it, I am also stronger, and whether here among this people, or by going to Pylos, I will do you all the harm I can. I shall go, and my going will not be in vain though, thanks to you suitors, I have neither ship nor crew of my own, and must be passenger not captain."

As he spoke he snatched his hand from that of Antinous. Meanwhile the others went on getting dinner ready about the buildings, jeering at him tauntingly as they did so.

"Telemachus," said one youngster, "means to be the death of us; I suppose he thinks he can bring friends to help him from Pylos, or again from Sparta, where he seems bent on going. Or will he go to Ephyra as well, for poison to put in our wine and kill us?"

Another said, "Perhaps if Telemachus goes on board ship, he will be like his father and perish far from his friends. In this case we should have plenty to do, for we could then divide up his property amongst us: as for the house we can let his mother and the man who marries her have that."

This was how they talked. But Telemachus went down into the lofty and spacious store-room where his father's treasure of gold and bronze lay heaped up upon the floor, and where the linen and spare clothes were kept in open chests. Here, too, there was a store of fragrant olive oil, while casks of old, well-ripened wine, unblended and fit for a god to drink, were ranged against the wall in case Ulysses should come home again after all. The room was closed with well-made doors opening in the middle; moreover the faithful old house-keeper Euryclea, daughter of Ops the son of Pisenor, was in charge of everything both night and day. Telemachus called her to the store-room and said:

"Nurse, draw me off some of the best wine you have, after what you are keeping for my father's own drinking, in case, poor man, he should escape death, and find his way home again after all. Let me have twelve jars, and see that they all have lids; also fill me some well-sewn leathern bags with barley meal- about twenty measures in all. Get these things put together at once, and say nothing about it. I will take everything away this evening as soon as my mother has gone upstairs for the night. I am going to Sparta and to Pylos to see if I can hear anything about the return of my dear father.

When Euryclea heard this she began to cry, and spoke fondly to him, saying, "My dear child, what ever can have put such notion as that into your head? Where in the world do you want to go to- you, who are the one hope of the house? Your poor father is dead and gone in some foreign country nobody knows where, and as soon as your back is turned these wicked ones here will be scheming to get you put out of the way, and will share all your possessions among themselves; stay where you are among your own people, and do not go wandering and worrying your life out on the barren ocean."

"Fear not, nurse," answered Telemachus, "my scheme is not without heaven's sanction; but swear that you will say nothing about all this to my mother, till I have been away some ten or twelve days, unless she hears of my having gone, and asks you; for I do not want her to spoil her beauty by crying."

The old woman swore most solemnly that she would not, and when she had completed her oath, she began drawing off the wine into jars, and getting the barley meal into the bags, while Telemachus went back to the suitors.

Then Minerva bethought her of another matter. She took his shape, and went round the town to each one of the crew, telling them to meet at the ship by sundown. She went also to Noemon son of Phronius, and asked him to let her have a ship- which he was very ready to do. When the sun had set and darkness was over all the land, she got the ship into the water, put all the tackle on board her that ships generally carry, and stationed her at the end of the harbor. Presently the crew came up, and the goddess spoke encouragingly to each of them.

Furthermore she went to the house of Ulysses, and threw the suitors into a deep slumber. She caused their drink to fuddle them, and made them drop their cups from their hands, so that instead of sitting over their wine, they went back into the town to sleep, with their eyes heavy and full of drowsiness. Then she took the form and voice of Mentor, and called Telemachus to come outside.

"Telemachus," said she, "the men are on board and at their oars, waiting for you to give your orders, so make haste and let us be off."

On this she led the way, while Telemachus followed in her steps. When they got to the ship they found the crew waiting by the water side, and Telemachus said, "Now my men, help me to get the stores on board; they are all put together in the cloister, and my mother does not know anything about it, nor any of the maid servants except one."

With these words he led the way and the others followed after. When they had brought the things as he told them, Telemachus went on board, Minerva going before him and taking her seat in the stern of the vessel, while Telemachus sat beside her. Then the men loosed the hawsers and took their places on the benches. Minerva sent them a fair wind from the West, that whistled over the deep blue waves whereon Telemachus told them to catch hold of the ropes and hoist sail, and they did as he told them. They set the mast in its socket in the cross plank, raised it, and made it fast with the forestays; then they hoisted their white sails aloft with ropes of twisted ox hide. As the sail bellied out with the wind, the ship flew through the deep blue water, and the foam hissed against her bows as she sped onward. Then they made all fast throughout the ship, filled the mixing-bowls to the brim, and made drink offerings to the immortal gods that are from everlasting, but more particularly to the grey-eyed daughter of Jove.

Thus, then, the ship sped on her way through the watches of the night from dark till dawn.

Lesson 41

- Read Book 3 of *The Odyssey.*

Book 3

But as the sun was rising from the fair sea into the firmament of heaven to shed light on mortals and immortals, they reached Pylos the city of Neleus. Now the people of Pylos were gathered on the sea shore to offer sacrifice of black bulls to Neptune lord of the Earthquake. There were nine guilds with five hundred men in each, and there were nine bulls to each guild. As they were eating the inward meats and burning the thigh bones [on the embers] in the name of Neptune, Telemachus and his crew arrived, furled their sails, brought their ship to anchor, and went ashore.

Minerva led the way and Telemachus followed her. Presently she said, "Telemachus, you must not be in the least shy or nervous; you have taken this voyage to try and find out where your father is buried and how he came by his end; so go straight up to Nestor that we may see what he has got to tell us. Beg of him to speak the truth, and he will tell no lies, for he is an excellent person."

"But how, Mentor," replied Telemachus, "dare I go up to Nestor, and how am I to address him? I have never yet been used to holding long conversations with people, and am ashamed to begin questioning one who is so much older than myself."

"Some things, Telemachus," answered Minerva, "will be suggested to you by your own instinct, and heaven will prompt you further; for I am assured that the gods have been with you from the time of your birth until now."

She then went quickly on, and Telemachus followed in her steps till they reached the place where the guilds of the Pylian people were assembled. There they found Nestor sitting with his sons, while his company round him were busy getting dinner ready, and putting pieces of meat on to the spits while other pieces were cooking. When they saw the strangers they crowded round them, took them by the hand and bade them take their places. Nestor's son Pisistratus at once offered his hand to each of them, and seated them on some soft sheepskins that were lying on the sands near his father and his brother Thrasymedes. Then he gave them their portions of the inward meats and poured wine for them into a golden cup, handing it to Minerva first, and saluting her at the same time.

"Offer a prayer, sir," said he, "to King Neptune, for it is his feast that you are joining; when you have duly prayed and made your drink-offering, pass the cup to your friend that he may do so also. I doubt not that he too lifts his hands in prayer, for man cannot live without God in the world. Still he is younger than you are, and is much of an age with myself, so I he handed I will give you the precedence."

As he spoke he handed her the cup. Minerva thought it very right and proper of him to have given it to herself first; she accordingly began praying heartily to Neptune. "O thou," she cried, "that encirclest the earth, vouchsafe to grant the prayers of thy servants that call upon thee. More especially we pray thee send down thy grace on Nestor and on his sons; thereafter also make the rest of the Pylian people some handsome return for the goodly hecatomb they are offering you. Lastly, grant Telemachus and myself a happy issue, in respect of the matter that has brought us in our to Pylos."

When she had thus made an end of praying, she handed the cup to Telemachus and he prayed likewise. By and by, when the outer meats were roasted and had been taken off the spits, the carvers gave every man his portion and they all made an excellent dinner. As soon as they had had enough to eat and drink, Nestor, knight of Gerene, began to speak.

"Now," said he, "that our guests have done their dinner, it will be best to ask them who they are. Who, then, sir strangers, are you, and from what port have you sailed? Are you traders? or do you sail the seas as rovers with your hand against every man, and every man's hand against you?"

Telemachus answered boldly, for Minerva had given him courage to ask about his father and get himself a good name.

"Nestor," said he, "son of Neleus, honor to the Achaean name, you ask whence we come, and I will tell you. We come from Ithaca under Neritum, and the matter about which I would speak is of private not public import. I seek news of my unhappy father Ulysses, who is said to have sacked the town of Troy in company with yourself. We know what fate befell each one of the other heroes who fought at Troy, but as regards Ulysses heaven has hidden from us the knowledge even that he is dead at all, for no one can certify us in what place he perished, nor say whether he fell in battle on the mainland, or was lost at sea amid the waves of Amphitrite. Therefore I am suppliant at your knees, if haply you may be pleased to tell me of his melancholy end, whether you saw it with your own eyes, or heard it from some other traveler, for he was a man born to trouble. Do not soften things out of any pity for me, but tell me in all plainness exactly what you saw. If my brave father Ulysses ever did you loyal service, either by word or deed, when you Achaeans were harassed among the Trojans, bear it in mind now as in my favor and tell me truly all."

"My friend," answered Nestor, "you recall a time of much sorrow to my mind, for the brave Achaeans suffered much both at sea, while privateering under Achilles, and when fighting before the great city of King Priam. Our best men all of them fell there- Ajax, Achilles, Patroclus peer of gods in counsel, and my own dear son Antilochus, a man singularly fleet of foot and in fight valiant. But we suffered much more than this; what mortal tongue indeed could tell the whole story? Though you were to stay here and question me for five years, or even six, I could not tell you all that the Achaeans suffered, and you would turn homeward weary of my tale before it ended. Nine long years did we try every kind of stratagem, but the hand of heaven was against us; during all this time there was no one who could compare with your father in subtlety- if indeed you are his son- I can hardly believe my eyes- and you talk just like him too- no one would say that people of such different ages could speak so much alike. He and I never had any kind of difference from first to last neither in camp nor council, but in singleness of heart and purpose we advised the Argives how all might be ordered for the best.

"When however, we had sacked the city of Priam, and were setting sail in our ships as heaven had dispersed us, then Jove saw fit to vex the Argives on their homeward voyage; for they had Not all been either wise or understanding, and hence many came to a bad end through the displeasure of Jove's daughter Minerva, who brought about a quarrel between the two sons of Atreus.

"The sons of Atreus called a meeting which was not as it should be, for it was sunset and the Achaeans were heavy with wine. When they explained why they had called-the people together, it seemed that Menelaus was for sailing homeward at once, and this displeased Agamemnon, who thought that we should wait till we had offered hecatombs to appease the anger of Minerva. Fool that he was, he might have known that he would not prevail with her, for when the gods have made up their minds they do not change them lightly. So the two stood bandying hard words, whereon the Achaeans sprang to their feet with a cry that rent the air, and were of two minds as to what they should do.

"That night we rested and nursed our anger, for Jove was hatching mischief against us. But in the morning some of us drew our ships into the water and put our goods with our women on board, while the rest, about half in number, stayed behind with Agamemnon. We- the other half- embarked and sailed; and the ships went well, for heaven had smoothed the sea. When we reached Tenedos we offered sacrifices to the gods, for we were longing to get home; cruel Jove, however, did not yet mean that we should do so, and raised a second quarrel in the course of which some among us turned their ships back again, and sailed away under Ulysses to make their peace with Agamemnon; but I, and all the ships that were with me pressed forward, for I saw that mischief was brewing. The son of Tydeus went on also with me, and his crews with him. Later on Menelaus joined us at Lesbos, and found us making up our minds about our course- for we did not know whether to go outside Chios by the island of Psyra, keeping this to our left, or inside Chios, over against the stormy headland of Mimas. So we asked heaven for a sign, and were shown one to the effect that we should be soonest out of danger if we headed our ships across the open sea to Euboea. This we therefore did, and a fair wind sprang up which gave us a quick passage during the night to Geraestus, where we offered many sacrifices to Neptune for having helped us so far on our way. Four days later Diomed and his men stationed their ships in Argos, but I held on for Pylos, and the wind never fell light from the day when heaven first made it fair for me.

"Therefore, my dear young friend, I returned without hearing anything about the others. I know neither who got home safely nor who were lost but, as in duty bound,

I will give you without reserve the reports that have reached me since I have been here in my own house. They say the Myrmidons returned home safely under Achilles' son Neoptolemus; so also did the valiant son of Poias, Philoctetes. Idomeneus, again, lost no men at sea, and all his followers who escaped death in the field got safe home with him to Crete. No matter how far out of the world you live, you will have heard of Agamemnon and the bad end he came to at the hands of Aegisthus- and a fearful reckoning did Aegisthus presently pay. See what a good thing it is for a man to leave a son behind him to do as Orestes did, who killed false Aegisthus the murderer of his noble father. You too, then- for you are a tall, smart-looking fellow- show your mettle and make yourself a name in story."

"Nestor son of Neleus," answered Telemachus, "honor to the Achaean name, the Achaeans applaud Orestes and his name will live through all time for he has avenged his father nobly. Would that heaven might grant me to do like vengeance on the insolence of the wicked suitors, who are ill treating me and plotting my ruin; but the gods have no such happiness in store for me and for my father, so we must bear it as best we may."

"My friend," said Nestor, "now that you remind me, I remember to have heard that your mother has many suitors, who are ill disposed towards you and are making havoc of your estate. Do you submit to this tamely, or are public feeling and the voice of heaven against you? Who knows but what Ulysses may come back after all, and pay these scoundrels in full, either single-handed or with a force of Achaeans behind him? If Minerva were to take as great a liking to you as she did to Ulysses when we were fighting before Troy (for I never yet saw the gods so openly fond of any one as Minerva then was of your father), if she would take as good care of you as she did of him, these wooers would soon some of them him, forget their wooing."

Telemachus answered, "I can expect nothing of the kind; it would be far too much to hope for. I dare not let myself think of it. Even though the gods themselves willed it no such good fortune could befall me."

On this Minerva said, "Telemachus, what are you talking about? Heaven has a long arm if it is minded to save a man; and if it were me, I should not care how much I suffered before getting home, provided I could be safe when I was once there. I would rather this, than get home quickly, and then be killed in my own house as

Agamemnon was by the treachery of Aegisthus and his wife. Still, death is certain, and when a man's hour is come, not even the gods can save him, no matter how fond they are of him."

"Mentor," answered Telemachus, "do not let us talk about it any more. There is no chance of my father's ever coming back; the gods have long since counselled his destruction. There is something else, however, about which I should like to ask Nestor, for he knows much more than any one else does. They say he has reigned for three generations so that it is like talking to an immortal. Tell me, therefore, Nestor, and tell me true; how did Agamemnon come to die in that way? What was Menelaus doing? And how came false Aegisthus to kill so far better a man than himself? Was Menelaus away from Achaean Argos, voyaging elsewhither among mankind, that Aegisthus took heart and killed Agamemnon?"

"I will tell you truly," answered Nestor, "and indeed you have yourself divined how it all happened. If Menelaus when he got back from Troy had found Aegisthus still alive in his house, there would have been no barrow heaped up for him, not even when he was dead, but he would have been thrown outside the city to dogs and vultures, and not a woman would have mourned him, for he had done a deed of great wickedness; but we were over there, fighting hard at Troy, and Aegisthus who was taking his ease quietly in the heart of Argos, cajoled Agamemnon's wife Clytemnestra with incessant flattery.

"At first she would have nothing to do with his wicked scheme, for she was of a good natural disposition; moreover there was a bard with her, to whom Agamemnon had given strict orders on setting out for Troy, that he was to keep guard over his wife; but when heaven had counselled her destruction, Aegisthus thus this bard off to a desert island and left him there for crows and seagulls to batten upon- after which she went willingly enough to the house of Aegisthus. Then he offered many burnt sacrifices to the gods, and decorated many temples with tapestries and gilding, for he had succeeded far beyond his expectations.

"Meanwhile Menelaus and I were on our way home from Troy, on good terms with one another. When we got to Sunium, which is the point of Athens, Apollo with his painless shafts killed Phrontis the steersman of Menelaus' ship (and never man knew better how to handle a vessel in rough weather) so that he died then and there with the helm in his hand, and Menelaus, though very anxious to press forward, had to wait in order to bury his comrade and give him his due funeral rites. Presently, when he too could put to sea again, and had sailed on as far as the Malean heads, Jove counselled evil against him and made it it blow hard till the waves ran mountains high. Here he divided his fleet and took the one half towards Crete where the Cydonians dwell round about the waters of the river Iardanus. There is a high headland hereabouts stretching out into the sea from a place called Gortyn, and all along this part of the coast as far as Phaestus the sea runs high when there is a south wind blowing, but after Phaestus the coast is more protected, for a small headland can make a great shelter. Here this part of the fleet was driven on to the rocks and wrecked; but the crews just managed to save themselves. As for the other five ships, they were taken by winds and seas to Egypt, where Menelaus gathered much gold and substance among people of an alien speech. Meanwhile Aegisthus here at home plotted his evil deed. For seven years after he had killed Agamemnon he ruled in Mycene, and the people were obedient under him, but in the eighth year Orestes came back from Athens to be his bane, and killed the murderer of his father. Then he celebrated the funeral rites of his mother and of false Aegisthus by a banquet to the people of Argos, and on that very day Menelaus came home, with as much treasure as his ships could carry.

"Take my advice then, and do not go travelling about for long so far from home, nor leave your property with such dangerous people in your house; they will eat up everything you have among them, and you will have been on a fool's errand. Still, I should advise you by all means to go and visit Menelaus, who has lately come off a voyage among such distant peoples as no man could ever hope to get back from, when the winds had once carried him so far out of his reckoning; even birds cannot fly the distance in a twelvemonth, so vast and terrible are the seas that they must cross. Go to him, therefore, by sea, and take your own men with you; or if you would rather travel by land you can have a chariot, you can have horses, and here are my sons who can escort you to Lacedaemon where Menelaus lives. Beg of him to speak the truth, and he will tell you no lies, for he is an excellent person."

As he spoke the sun set and it came on dark, whereon Minerva said, "Sir, all that you have said is well; now, however, order the tongues of the victims to be cut, and mix wine that we may make drink-offerings to Neptune, and the other immortals, and then go to bed, for it is bed time. People should go away early and not keep late hours at a religious festival."

Thus spoke the daughter of Jove, and they obeyed her saying. Men servants poured water over the hands of the guests, while pages filled the mixing-bowls with wine and water, and handed it round after giving every man his drink-offering; then they threw the tongues of the victims into the fire, and stood up to make their drink-offerings. When they had made their offerings and had drunk each as much as he was minded, Minerva and Telemachus were forgoing on board their ship, but Nestor caught them up at once and stayed them.

"Heaven and the immortal gods," he exclaimed, "forbid that you should leave my house to go on board of a ship. Do you think I am so poor and short of clothes, or that I have so few cloaks and as to be unable to find comfortable beds both for myself and for my guests? Let me tell you I have store both of rugs and cloaks, and shall not permit the son of my old friend Ulysses to camp down on the deck of a ship- not while I live- nor yet will my sons after me, but they will keep open house as have done."

Then Minerva answered, "Sir, you have spoken well, and it will be much better that Telemachus should do as you have said; he, therefore, shall return with you and sleep at your house, but I must go back to give orders to my crew, and keep them in good heart. I am the only older person among them; the rest are all young men of Telemachus' own age, who have taken this voyage out of friendship; so I must return to the ship and sleep there. Moreover to-morrow I must go to the Cauconians where I have a large sum of money long owing to me. As for Telemachus, now that he is your guest, send him to Lacedaemon in a chariot, and let one of your sons go with him. Be pleased also to provide him with your best and fleetest horses."

When she had thus spoken, she flew away in the form of an eagle, and all marveled as they beheld it. Nestor was astonished, and took Telemachus by the hand. "My friend," said he, "I see that you are going to be a great hero some day, since the gods wait upon you thus while you are still so young. This can have been none other of those who dwell in heaven than Jove's redoubtable daughter, the Trito-born, who showed such favor towards your brave father among the Argives. Holy queen," he continued, "vouchsafe to send down thy grace upon myself, my good wife, and my children. In return, I will offer you in sacrifice a broad-browed heifer of a year old, unbroken, and never yet brought by man under the yoke. I will gild her horns, and will offer her up to you in sacrifice."

Thus did he pray, and Minerva heard his prayer. He then led the way to his own house, followed by his sons and sons-in-law. When they had got there and had taken their places on the benches and seats, he mixed them a bowl of sweet wine that was eleven years old when the housekeeper took the lid off the jar that held it. As he mixed the wine, he prayed much and made drink-offerings to Minerva, daughter of Aegis-bearing Jove. Then, when they had made their drink-offerings and had drunk each as much as he was minded, the others went home to bed each in his own abode; but Nestor put Telemachus to sleep in the room that was over the gateway along with Pisistratus, who was the only unmarried son now left him. As for himself, he slept in an inner room of the house, with the queen his wife by his side.

Now when the child of morning, rosy-fingered Dawn, appeared, Nestor left his couch and took his seat on the benches of white and polished marble that stood in front of his house. Here aforetime sat Neleus, peer of gods in counsel, but he was now dead, and had gone to the house of Hades; so Nestor sat in his seat, sceptre in hand, as guardian of the public weal. His sons as they left their rooms gathered round him, Echephron, Stratius, Perseus, Aretus, and Thrasymedes; the sixth son was Pisistratus, and when Telemachus joined them they made him sit with them. Nestor then addressed them.

"My sons," said he, "make haste to do as I shall bid you. I wish first and foremost to propitiate the great goddess Minerva, who manifested herself visibly to me during yesterday's festivities. Go, then, one or other of you to the plain, tell the stockman to look me out a heifer, and come on here with it at once. Another must go to Telemachus's ship, and invite all the crew, leaving two men only in charge of the vessel. Some one else will run and fetch Laerceus the goldsmith to gild the horns of the heifer. The rest, stay all of you where you are; tell the maids in the house to prepare an excellent dinner, and to fetch seats, and logs of wood for a burnt offering. Tell them also- to bring me some clear spring water."

On this they hurried off on their several errands. The heifer was brought in from the plain, and Telemachus's crew came from the ship; the goldsmith brought the anvil, hammer, and tongs, with which he worked his gold, and Minerva herself came to the sacrifice. Nestor gave out the gold, and the smith gilded the horns of the heifer that the goddess might have pleasure in their beauty. Then Stratius and Echephron brought her in by the horns; Aretus fetched water from the house in a ewer that had a flower pattern on it, and in his other hand he held a basket of barley meal; sturdy Thrasymedes stood by with a sharp ax, ready to strike the heifer, while Perseus held a bucket. Then Nestor began with washing his hands and sprinkling the barley meal, and he offered many a prayer to Minerva as he threw a lock from the heifer's head upon the fire.

When they had done praying and sprinkling the barley meal Thrasymedes dealt his blow, and brought the heifer down with a stroke that cut through the tendons at the base of her neck, whereon the daughters and daughters-in-law of Nestor, and his venerable wife Eurydice (she was eldest daughter to Clymenus) screamed with delight. Then they lifted the heifer's head from off the ground, and Pisistratus cut her throat. When she had done bleeding and was quite dead, they cut her up. They cut out the thigh bones all in due course, wrapped them round in two layers of fat, and set some pieces of raw meat on the top of them; then Nestor laid them upon the wood fire and poured wine over them, while the young men stood near him with five-pronged spits in their hands. When the thighs were burned and they had tasted the inward meats, they cut the rest of the meat up small, put the pieces on the spits and toasted them over the fire.

Meanwhile lovely Polycaste, Nestor's youngest daughter, washed Telemachus. When she had washed him and anointed him with oil, she brought him a fair mantle and shirt, and he looked like a god as he came from the bath and took his seat by the side of Nestor. When the outer meats were done they drew them off the spits and sat down to dinner where they were waited upon by some worthy henchmen, who kept pouring them out their wine in cups of gold. As soon as they had had had enough to eat and drink Nestor said, "Sons, put Telemachus's horses to the chariot that he may start at once."

Thus did he speak, and they did even as he had said, and yoked the fleet horses to the chariot. The housekeeper packed them up a provision of bread, wine, and sweetmeats fit for the sons of princes. Then Telemachus got into the chariot, while Pisistratus gathered up the reins and took his seat beside him. He lashed the horses on and they flew forward nothing loth into the open country, leaving the high citadel of Pylos behind them. All that day did they travel, swaying the yoke upon their necks till the sun went down and darkness was over all the land. Then they reached Pherae where Diocles lived, who was son to Ortilochus and grandson to Alpheus. Here they passed the night and Diocles entertained them hospitably.

When the child of morning, rosy-fingered Dawn; appeared, they again yoked their horses and drove out through the gateway under the echoing gatehouse. Pisistratus lashed the horses on and they flew forward nothing loth; presently they came to the corn lands Of the open country, and in the course of time completed their journey, so well did their steeds take them.

Now the sun had set and darkness was over the land.

Lesson 42

- Read Book 4 of *The Odyssey*.

Book 4

They reached the low lying city of Lacedaemon them where they drove straight to the of abode Menelaus [and found him in his own house, feasting with his many clansmen in honor of the wedding of his son, and also of his daughter, whom he was marrying to the son of that valiant warrior Achilles. He had given his consent and promised her to him while he was still at Troy, and now the gods were bringing the marriage about; so he was sending her with chariots and horses to the city of the Myrmidons over whom Achilles' son was reigning. For his only son he had found a bride from Sparta, daughter of Alector. This son, Megapenthes, was born to him of a bondwoman, for heaven vouchsafed Helen no more children after she had borne Hermione, who was fair as golden Venus herself.

So the neighbors and kinsmen of Menelaus were feasting and making merry in his house. There was a bard also to sing to them and play his lyre, while two tumblers went about performing in the midst of them when the man struck up with his tune.]

Telemachus and the son of Nestor stayed their horses at the gate, whereon Eteoneus servant to Menelaus came out, and as soon as he saw them ran hurrying back into the house to tell his Master. He went close up to him and said, "Menelaus, there are some strangers come here, two men, who look like sons of Jove. What are we to do? Shall we take their horses out, or tell them to find friends elsewhere as they best can?"

Menelaus was very angry and said, "Eteoneus, son of Boethous, you never used to be a fool, but now you talk like a simpleton. Take their horses out, of course, and show the strangers in that they may have supper; you and I have stayed often enough at other people's houses before we got back here, where heaven grant that we may rest in peace henceforward."

So Eteoneus bustled back and bade other servants come with him. They took their sweating hands from under the yoke, made them fast to the mangers, and gave them a feed of oats and barley mixed. Then they leaned the chariot against the end wall of the courtyard, and led the way into the house. Telemachus and Pisistratus were astonished when they saw it, for its splendor was as that of the sun and moon; then, when they had admired everything to their heart's content, they went into the bath room and washed themselves.

When the servants had washed them and anointed them with oil, they brought them woolen cloaks and shirts, and the two took their seats by the side of Menelaus. A maidservant brought them water in a beautiful golden ewer, and poured it into a silver basin for them to wash their hands; and she drew a clean table beside them. An upper servant brought them bread, and offered them many good things of what there was in the house, while the carver fetched them plates of all manner of meats and set cups of gold by their side.

Menelaus then greeted them saying, "Fall to, and welcome; when you have done supper I shall ask who you are, for the lineage of such men as you cannot have been lost. You must be descended from a line of scepter-bearing kings, for poor people do not have such sons as you are."

On this he handed them a piece of fat roast loin, which had been set near him as being a prime part, and they laid their hands on the good things that were before them; as soon as they had had enough to eat and drink, Telemachus said to the son of Nestor, with his head so close that no one might hear, "Look, Pisistratus, man after my own heart, see the gleam of bronze and gold- of amber, ivory, and silver. Everything is so splendid that it is like seeing the palace of Olympian Jove. I am lost in admiration."

Menelaus overheard him and said, "No one, my sons, can hold his own with Jove, for his house and everything about him is immortal; but among mortal men- well, there may be another who has as much wealth as I have, or there may not; but at all events I have traveled much and have undergone much hardship, for it was nearly eight years before I could get home with my fleet. I went to Cyprus, Phoenicia and the Egyptians; I went also to the Ethiopians, the Sidonians, and the Erembians, and to Libya where the lambs have horns as soon as they are born, and the sheep lamb down three times a year. Every one in that country, whether master or man, has plenty of cheese, meat, and good milk, for the ewes yield all the year round. But while I was travelling and getting great riches among these people, my brother was secretly and shockingly murdered through the perfidy of his wicked wife, so that I have no pleasure in being lord of all this wealth. Whoever your parents may be they must have told you about all this, and of my heavy loss in the ruin of a stately mansion fully and magnificently furnished. Would that I had only a third of what I now have so that I had stayed at home, and all those were living who perished on the plain of Troy, far from Argos. I of grieve, as I sit here in my house, for one and all of them. At times I cry aloud for sorrow, but presently I leave off again, for crying is cold comfort and one soon tires of it. Yet grieve for these as I may, I do so for one man more than for them all. I cannot even think of him without loathing both food and sleep, so miserable does he make me, for no one of all the Achaeans worked so hard or risked so much as he did. He took nothing by it, and has left a legacy of sorrow to myself, for he has been gone a long time, and we know not whether he is alive or dead. His old father, his long-suffering wife Penelope, and his son Telemachus, whom he left behind him an infant in arms, are plunged in grief on his account."

Thus spoke Menelaus, and the heart of Telemachus yearned as he bethought him of his father. Tears fell from his eyes as he heard him thus mentioned, so that he held his cloak before his face with both hands. When Menelaus saw this he doubted whether to let him choose his own time for speaking, or to ask him at once and find what it was all about.

While he was thus in two minds Helen came down from her high vaulted and perfumed room, looking as lovely as Diana herself. Adraste brought her a seat, Alcippe a soft woolen rug while Phylo fetched her the silver work-box which Alcandra wife of Polybus had given her. Polybus lived in Egyptian Thebes, which is the richest city in the whole world; he gave Menelaus two baths, both of pure silver, two tripods, and ten talents of gold; besides all this, his wife gave Helen some beautiful presents, to wit, a golden distaff, and a silver work-box that ran on wheels, with a gold band round the top of it. Phylo now placed this by her side, full of fine spun yarn, and a distaff charged with violet colored wool was laid upon the top of it. Then Helen took her seat, put her feet upon the footstool, and began to question her husband.

"Do we know, Menelaus," said she, "the names of these strangers who have come to visit us? Shall I guess right or wrong?-but I cannot help saying what I think. Never yet have I seen either man or woman so like somebody else (indeed when I look at him I hardly know what to think) as this young man is like Telemachus, whom Ulysses left as a baby behind him, when you Achaeans went to Troy with battle in your hearts, on account of my most shameless self."

"My dear wife," replied Menelaus, "I see the likeness just as you do. His hands and feet are just like Ulysses'; so is his hair, with the shape of his head and the expression of his eyes. Moreover, when I was talking about Ulysses, and saying how much he had suffered on my account, tears fell from his eyes, and he hid his face in his mantle."

Then Pisistratus said, "Menelaus, son of Atreus, you are right in thinking that this young man is Telemachus, but he is very modest, and is ashamed to come here and begin opening up discourse with one whose conversation is so divinely interesting as your own. My father, Nestor, sent me to escort him hither, for he wanted to know whether you could give him any counsel or suggestion. A son has always trouble at home when his father has gone away leaving him without supporters; and this is how Telemachus is now placed, for his father is absent, and there is no one among his own people to stand by him."

"Bless my heart," replied Menelaus, "then I am receiving a visit from the son of a very dear friend, who suffered much hardship for my sake. I had always hoped to entertain him with most marked distinction when heaven had granted us a safe return from beyond the seas. I should have founded a city for him in Argos, and built him a house. I should have made him leave Ithaca with his goods, his son, and all his people, and should have sacked for them some one of the neighboring cities that are subject to me. We should thus have seen one another continually, and nothing but death could have interrupted so close and happy an intercourse. I suppose, however, that heaven grudged us such great good fortune, for it has prevented the poor fellow from ever getting home at all."

Thus did he speak, and his words set them all a weeping. Helen wept, Telemachus wept, and so did Menelaus, nor could Pisistratus keep his eyes from filling, when he remembered his dear brother Antilochus whom the son of bright Dawn had killed. Thereon he said to Menelaus,

"Sir, my father Nestor, when we used to talk about you at home, told me you were a person of rare and excellent understanding. If, then, it be possible, do as I would urge you. I am not fond of crying while I am getting my supper. Morning will come in due course, and in the forenoon I care not how much I cry for those that are dead and gone. This is all we can do for the poor things. We can only shave our heads for them and wring the tears from our cheeks. I had a brother who died at Troy; he was by no means the worst man there; you are sure to have known him- his name was Antilochus; I never set eyes upon him myself, but they say that he was singularly fleet of foot and in fight valiant."

"Your discretion, my friend," answered Menelaus, "is beyond your years. It is plain you take after your father. One can soon see when a man is son to one whom heaven has blessed both as regards wife and offspring- and it has blessed Nestor from first to last all his days, giving him a green old age in his own house, with sons about him who are both we disposed and valiant. We will put an end therefore to all this weeping, and attend to our supper again. Let water be poured over our hands. Telemachus and I can talk with one another fully in the morning."

On this Asphalion, one of the servants, poured water over their hands and they laid their hands on the good things that were before them.

Then Jove's daughter Helen bethought her of another matter. She drugged the wine with an herb that banishes all care, sorrow, and ill humor. Whoever drinks wine thus drugged cannot shed a single tear all the rest of the day, not even though his father and mother both of them drop down dead, or he sees a brother or a son hewn in pieces before his very eyes. This drug, of such sovereign power and virtue, had been given to Helen by Polydamna wife of Thon, a woman of Egypt, where there grow all sorts of herbs, some good to put into the mixing-bowl and others poisonous. Moreover, every one in the whole country is a skilled physician, for they are of the race of Paeeon. When Helen had put this drug in the bowl, and had told the servants to serve the wine round, she said:

"Menelaus, son of Atreus, and you my good friends, sons of honorable men (which is as Jove wills, for he is the giver both of good and evil, and can do what he chooses), feast here as you will, and listen while I tell you a tale in season. I cannot indeed name every single one of the exploits of Ulysses, but I can say what he did when he was before Troy, and you Achaeans were in all sorts of difficulties. He covered himself with wounds and bruises, dressed himself all in rags, and entered the enemy's city looking like a menial or a beggar. and quite different from what he did when he was among his own people. In this disguise he entered the city of Troy, and no one said anything to him. I alone recognized him and began to question him, but he was too cunning for me. When, however, I had washed and anointed him and had given him clothes, and after I had sworn a solemn oath not to betray him to the Trojans till he had got safely back to his own camp and to the ships, he told me all that the Achaeans meant to do. He killed many Trojans and got much information before he reached the Argive camp, for all which things the Trojan women made lamentation, but for my own part I was glad, for my heart was beginning to roam after my home, and I was unhappy about wrong that Venus had done me in taking me over there, away from my country, my girl, and my lawful wedded husband, who is indeed by no means deficient either in person or understanding."

Then Menelaus said, "All that you have been saying, my dear wife, is true. I have traveled much, and have had much to do with heroes, but I have never seen such another man as Ulysses. What endurance too, and what courage he displayed within the wooden horse, wherein all the bravest of the Argives were lying in wait to bring death and destruction upon the Trojans. At that moment you came up to us; some god who wished well to the Trojans must have set you on to it and you had Deiphobus with you. Three times did you go all round our hiding place and pat it; you called our chiefs each by his own name, and mimicked all our wives -Diomed, Ulysses, and I from our seats inside heard what a noise you made. Diomed and I could not make up our minds whether to spring out then and there, or to answer you from inside, but Ulysses held us all in check, so we sat quite still, all except Anticlus, who was beginning to answer you, when Ulysses clapped his two brawny hands over his mouth, and kept them there. It was this that saved us all, for he muzzled Anticlus till Minerva took you away again."

"How sad," exclaimed Telemachus, "that all this was of no avail to save him, nor yet his own iron courage. But now, sir, be pleased to send us all to bed, that we may lie down and enjoy the blessed boon of sleep."

On this Helen told the maid servants to set beds in the room that was in the gatehouse, and to make them with good red rugs, and spread coverlets on the top of them with woolen cloaks for the guests to wear. So the maids went out, carrying a torch, and made the beds, to which a man-servant presently conducted the strangers. Thus, then, did Telemachus and Pisistratus sleep there in the forecourt, while the son of Atreus lay in an inner room with lovely Helen by his side.

When the child of morning, rosy-fingered Dawn, appeared, Menelaus rose and dressed himself. He bound his sandals on to his comely feet, girded his sword about his shoulders, and left his room looking like an immortal god. Then, taking a seat near Telemachus he said:

"And what, Telemachus, has led you to take this long sea voyage to Lacedaemon? Are you on public or private business? Tell me all about it."

"I have come, sir," replied Telemachus, "to see if you can tell me anything about my father. I am being eaten out of house and home; my fair estate is being wasted, and my house is full of miscreants who keep killing great numbers of my sheep and oxen, on the pretense of paying their addresses to my mother. Therefore, I am suppliant at your knees if haply you may tell me about my father's melancholy end, whether you saw it with your own eyes, or heard it from some other traveler; for he was a man born to trouble. Do not soften things out of any pity for myself, but tell me in all plainness exactly what you saw. If my brave father Ulysses ever did you loyal service either by word or deed, when you Achaeans were harassed by the Trojans, bear it in mind now as in my favor and tell me truly all."

Menelaus on hearing this was very much shocked. "So," he exclaimed, "these cowards would usurp a brave man's bed? A hind might as well lay her new born young in the lair of a lion, and then go off to feed in the forest or in some grassy dell: the lion when he comes back to his lair will make short work with the pair of them- and so will Ulysses with these suitors. By father Jove, Minerva, and Apollo, if Ulysses is still the man that he was when he wrestled with Philomeleides in Lesbos, and threw him so heavily that all the Achaeans cheered him- if he is still such and were to come near these suitors, they would have a short shrift and a sorry wedding. As regards your questions, however, I will not prevaricate nor deceive you, but will tell you without concealment all that the old man of the sea told me.

"I was trying to come on here, but the gods detained me in Egypt, for my hecatombs had not given them full satisfaction, and the gods are very strict about having their dues. Now off Egypt, about as far as a ship can sail in a day with a good stiff breeze behind her, there is an island called Pharos- it has a good harbor from which vessels can get out into open sea when they have taken in water- and the gods becalmed me twenty days without so much as a breath of fair wind to help me forward. We should have run clean out of provisions and my men would have starved, if a goddess had not taken pity upon me and saved me in the person of Idothea, daughter to Proteus, the old man of the sea, for she had taken a great fancy to me.

"She came to me one day when I was by myself, as I often was, for the men used to go with their barbed hooks, all over the island in the hope of catching a fish or two to save them from the pangs of hunger. 'Stranger,' said she, 'it seems to me that you like starving in this way- at any rate it does not greatly trouble you, for you stick here day after day, without even trying to get away though your men are dying by inches.'

"'Let me tell you,' said I, 'whichever of the goddesses you may happen to be, that I am not staying here of my own accord, but must have offended the gods that live in heaven. Tell me, therefore, for the gods know everything. which of the immortals it is that is hindering me in this way, and tell me also how I may sail the sea so as to reach my home.'

"'Stranger,' replied she, 'I will make it all quite clear to you. There is an old immortal who lives under the sea hereabouts and whose name is Proteus. He is an Egyptian, and people say he is my father; he is Neptune's head man and knows every inch of ground all over the bottom of the sea. If you can snare him and hold him tight, he will tell you about your voyage, what courses you are to take, and how you are to sail the sea so as to reach your home. He will also tell you, if you so will, all that has been going on at your house both good and bad, while you have been away on your long and dangerous journey.'

"'Can you show me,' said I, 'some stratagem by means of which I may catch this old god without his suspecting it and finding me out? For a god is not easily caught- not by a mortal man.'

"'Stranger,' said she, 'I will make it all quite clear to you. About the time when the sun shall have reached mid heaven, the old man of the sea comes up from under the waves, heralded by the West wind that furs the water over his head. As soon as he has come up he lies down, and goes to sleep in a great sea cave, where the seals- Halosydne's chickens as they call them- come up also from the grey sea, and go to sleep in shoals all round him; and a very strong and fish-like smell do they bring with them. Early to-morrow morning I will take you to this place and will lay you in ambush. Pick out, therefore, the three best men you have in your fleet, and I will tell you all the tricks that the old man will play you.

"'First he will look over all his seals, and count them; then, when he has seen them and tallied them on his five fingers, he will go to sleep among them, as a shepherd among his sheep. The moment you see that he is asleep seize him; put forth all your strength and hold him fast, for he will do his very utmost to get away from you. He will turn himself into every kind of creature that goes upon the earth, and will become also both fire and water; but you must hold him fast and grip him tighter and tighter, till he begins to talk to you and comes back to what he was when you saw him go to sleep; then you may slacken your hold and let him go; and you can ask him which of the gods it is that is angry with you, and what you must do to reach your home over the seas.'

"Having so said she dived under the waves, whereon I turned back to the place where my ships were ranged upon the shore; and my heart was clouded with care as I went along. When I reached my ship we got supper ready, for night was falling, and camped down upon the beach.

"When the child of morning, rosy-fingered Dawn, appeared, I took the three men on whose prowess of all kinds I could most rely, and went along by the sea-side, praying heartily to heaven. Meanwhile the goddess fetched me up four seal skins from the bottom of the sea, all of them just skinned, for she meant playing a trick upon her father. Then she dug four pits for us to lie in, and sat down to wait till we should come up. When we were close to her, she made us lie down in the pits one after the other, and threw a seal skin over each of us. Our ambuscade would have been intolerable, for the stench of the fishy seals was most distressing- who would go to bed with a sea monster if he could help it?-but here, too, the goddess helped us, and thought of something that gave us great relief, for she put some ambrosia under each man's nostrils, which was so fragrant that it killed the smell of the seals.

"We waited the whole morning and made the best of it, watching the seals come up in hundreds to bask upon the sea shore, till at noon the old man of the sea came up too, and when he had found his fat seals he went over them and counted them. We were among the first he counted, and he never suspected any guile, but laid himself down to sleep as soon as he had done counting. Then we rushed upon him with a shout and seized him; on which he began at once with his old tricks, and changed himself first into a lion with a great mane; then all of a sudden he became a dragon, a leopard, a wild boar; the next moment he was running water, and then again directly he was a tree, but we stuck to him and never lost hold, till at last the cunning old creature became distressed, and said, 'Which of the gods was it, Son of Atreus, that hatched this plot with you for snaring me and seizing me against my will? What do you want?'

"'You know that yourself, old man,' I answered, 'you will gain nothing by trying to put me off. It is because I have been kept so long in this island, and see no sign of my being able to get away. I am losing all heart; tell me, then, for you gods know everything, which of the immortals it is that is hindering me, and tell me also how I may sail the sea so as to reach my home?'

"'Then,' he said, 'if you would finish your voyage and get home quickly, you must offer sacrifices to Jove and to the rest of the gods before embarking; for it is decreed that you shall not get back to your friends, and to your own house, till you have returned to the heaven fed stream of Egypt, and offered holy hecatombs to the immortal gods that reign in heaven. When you have done this they will let you finish your voyage.'

"I was broken-hearted when I heard that I must go back all that long and terrible voyage to Egypt; nevertheless, I answered, 'I will do all, old man, that you have laid upon me; but now tell me, and tell me true, whether all the Achaeans whom

Nestor and I left behind us when we set sail from Troy have got home safely, or whether any one of them came to a bad end either on board his own ship or among his friends when the days of his fighting were done.'

"'Son of Atreus,' he answered, 'why ask me? You had better not know what I can tell you, for your eyes will surely fill when you have heard my story. Many of those about whom you ask are dead and gone, but many still remain, and only two of the chief men among the Achaeans perished during their return home. As for what happened on the field of battle- you were there yourself. A third Achaean leader is still at sea, alive, but hindered from returning. Ajax was wrecked, for Neptune drove him on to the great rocks of Gyrae; nevertheless, he let him get safe out of the water, and in spite of all Minerva's hatred he would have escaped death, if he had not ruined himself by boasting. He said the gods could not drown him even though they had tried to do so, and when Neptune heard this large talk, he seized his trident in his two brawny hands, and split the rock of Gyrae in two pieces. The base remained where it was, but the part on which Ajax was sitting fell headlong into the sea and carried Ajax with it; so he drank salt water and was drowned.

"'Your brother and his ships escaped, for Juno protected him, but when he was just about to reach the high promontory of Malea, he was caught by a heavy gale which carried him out to sea again sorely against his will, and drove him to the foreland where Thyestes used to dwell, but where Aegisthus was then living. By and by, however, it seemed as though he was to return safely after all, for the gods backed the wind into its old quarter and they reached home; whereon Agamemnon kissed his native soil, and shed tears of joy at finding himself in his own country.

"'Now there was a watchman whom Aegisthus kept always on the watch, and to whom he had promised two talents of gold. This man had been looking out for a whole year to make sure that Agamemnon did not give him the slip and prepare war; when, therefore, this man saw Agamemnon go by, he went and told Aegisthus who at once began to lay a plot for him. He picked twenty of his bravest warriors and placed them in ambuscade on one side the cloister, while on the opposite side he prepared a banquet. Then he sent his chariots and horsemen to Agamemnon, and invited him to the feast, but he meant foul play. He got him there, all unsuspicious of the doom that was awaiting him, and killed him when the banquet was over as though he were butchering an ox in the shambles; not one of Agamemnon's followers was left alive, nor yet one of Aegisthus', but they were all killed there in the cloisters.'

"Thus spoke Proteus, and I was broken-hearted as I heard him. I sat down upon the sands and wept; I felt as though I could no longer bear to live nor look upon the light of the sun. Presently, when I had had my fill of weeping and writhing upon the ground, the old man of the sea said, 'Son of Atreus, do not waste any more time in crying so bitterly; it can do no manner of good; find your way home as fast as ever you can, for Aegisthus be still alive, and even though Orestes has beforehand with you in kilting him, you may yet come in for his funeral.'

"On this I took comfort in spite of all my sorrow, and said, 'I know, then, about these two; tell me, therefore, about the third man of whom you spoke; is he still alive, but at sea, and unable to get home? or is he dead? Tell me, no matter how much it may grieve me.'

"'The third man,' he answered, 'is Ulysses who dwells in Ithaca. I can see him in an island sorrowing bitterly in the house of the nymph Calypso, who is keeping him prisoner, and he cannot reach his home for he has no ships nor sailors to take him over the sea. As for your own end, Menelaus, you shall not die in Argos, but the gods will take you to the Elysian plain, which is at the ends of the world. There fair-haired Rhadamanthus reigns, and men lead an easier life than any where else in the world, for in Elysium there falls not rain, nor hail, nor snow, but Oceanus breathes ever with a West wind that sings softly from the sea, and gives fresh life to all men. This will happen to you because you have married Helen, and are Jove's son-in-law.'

"As he spoke he dived under the waves, whereon I turned back to the ships with my companions, and my heart was clouded with care as I went along. When we reached the ships we got supper ready, for night was falling, and camped down upon the beach. When the child of morning, rosy-fingered Dawn appeared, we drew our ships into the water, and put our masts and sails within them; then we went on board ourselves, took our seats on the benches, and smote the grey sea with our oars. I again stationed my ships in the heaven-fed stream of Egypt, and offered hecatombs that were full and sufficient. When I had thus appeased heaven's anger, I raised a barrow to the memory of Agamemnon that his name might live for ever, after which I had a quick passage home, for the gods sent me a fair wind.

"And now for yourself- stay here some ten or twelve days longer, and I will then speed you on your way. I will make you a noble present of a chariot and three horses. I will also give you a beautiful chalice that so long as you live you may think of me whenever you make a drink-offering to the immortal gods."

"Son of Atreus," replied Telemachus, "do not press me to stay longer; I should be contented to remain with you for another twelve months; I find your conversation so delightful that I should never once wish myself at home with my parents; but my crew whom I have left at Pylos are already impatient, and you are detaining me from them. As for any present you may be disposed to make me, I had rather that it should he a piece of plate. I will take no horses back with me to Ithaca, but will leave them to adorn your own stables, for you have much flat ground in your kingdom where lotus thrives, as also meadowsweet and wheat and barley, and oats with their white and spreading ears; whereas in Ithaca we have neither open fields nor racecourses, and the country is more fit for goats than horses, and I like it the better for that. None of our islands have much level ground, suitable for horses, and Ithaca least of all."

Menelaus smiled and took Telemachus's hand within his own. "What you say," said he, "shows that you come of good family. I both can, and will, make this exchange for you, by giving you the finest and most precious piece of plate in all my house. It is a mixing-bowl by Vulcan's own hand, of pure silver, except the rim, which is inlaid with gold. Phaedimus, king of the Sidonians, gave it me in the course of a visit which I paid him when I returned thither on my homeward journey. I will make you a present of it."

Thus did they converse [and guests kept coming to the king's house. They brought sheep and wine, while their wives had put up bread for them to take with them; so they were busy cooking their dinners in the courts].

Meanwhile the suitors were throwing discs or aiming with spears at a mark on the leveled ground in front of Ulysses' house, and were behaving with all their old insolence. Antinous and Eurymachus, who were their ringleaders and much the foremost among them all, were sitting together when Noemon son of Phronius came up and said to Antinous,

"Have we any idea, Antinous, on what day Telemachus returns from Pylos? He has a ship of mine, and I want it, to cross over to Elis: I have twelve brood mares there with yearling mule foals by their side not yet broken in, and I want to bring one of them over here and break him."

They were astounded when they heard this, for they had made sure that Telemachus had not gone to the city of Neleus. They thought he was only away somewhere on the farms, and was with the sheep, or with the swineherd; so Antinous said, "When did he go? Tell me truly, and what young men did he take with him? Were they freemen or his own bondsmen- for he might manage that too? Tell me also, did you let him have the ship of your own free will because he asked you, or did he take it without your leave?"

"I lent it him," answered Noemon, "what else could I do when a man of his position said he was in a difficulty, and asked me to oblige him? I could not possibly refuse. As for those who went with him they were the best young men we have, and I saw Mentor go on board as captain- or some god who was exactly like him. I cannot understand it, for I saw Mentor here myself yesterday morning, and yet he was then setting out for Pylos."

Noemon then went back to his father's house, but Antinous and Eurymachus were very angry. They told the others to leave off playing, and to come and sit down along with themselves. When they came, Antinous son of Eupeithes spoke in anger. His heart was black with rage, and his eyes flashed fire as he said:

"Good heavens, this voyage of Telemachus is a very serious matter; we had made sure that it would come to nothing, but the young fellow has got away in spite of us, and with a picked crew too. He will be giving us trouble presently; may Jove take him before he is full grown. Find me a ship, therefore, with a crew of twenty men, and I will lie in wait for him in the straits between Ithaca and Samos; he will then rue the day that he set out to try and get news of his father."

Thus did he speak, and the others applauded his saying; they then all of them went inside the buildings.

It was not long ere Penelope came to know what the suitors were plotting; for a man servant, Medon, overheard them from outside the outer court as they were laying their schemes within, and went to tell his mistress. As he crossed the threshold of her room Penelope said: "Medon, what have the suitors sent you here for? Is it to tell the maids to leave their master's business and cook dinner for them? I wish they may neither woo nor dine henceforward, neither here nor anywhere else, but let this be the very last time, for the waste you all make of my son's estate. Did not your fathers tell you when you were children how good Ulysses had been to them- never doing anything high-handed, nor speaking harshly to anybody? Kings may say things sometimes, and they may take a fancy to one man and dislike another, but Ulysses never did an unjust thing by anybody- which shows what bad hearts you have, and that there is no such thing as gratitude left in this world."

Then Medon said, "I wish, Madam, that this were all; but they are plotting something much more dreadful now- may heaven frustrate their design. They are going to try and murder Telemachus as he is coming home from Pylos and Lacedaemon, where he has been to get news of his father."

Then Penelope's heart sank within her, and for a long time she was speechless; her eyes filled with tears, and she could find no utterance. At last, however, she said, "Why did my son leave me? What business had he to go sailing off in ships that make long voyages over the ocean like sea-horses? Does he want to die without leaving any one behind him to keep up his name?"

"I do not know," answered Medon, "whether some god set him on to it, or whether he went on his own impulse to see if he could find out if his father was dead, or alive and on his way home."

Then he went downstairs again, leaving Penelope in an agony of grief. There were plenty of seats in the house, but she. had no heart for sitting on any one of them; she could only fling herself on the floor of her own room and cry; whereon all the maids in the house, both old and young, gathered round her and began to cry too, till at last in a transport of sorrow she exclaimed,

"My dears, heaven has been pleased to try me with more affliction than any other woman of my age and country. First I lost my brave and lion-hearted husband, who had every good quality under heaven, and whose name was great over all Hellas and middle Argos, and now my darling son is at the mercy of the winds and waves, without my having heard one word about his leaving home. You hussies, there was not one of you would so much as think of giving me a call out of my bed, though you all of you very well knew when he was starting. If I had known he meant taking this voyage, he would have had to give it up, no matter how much he was bent upon it, or leave me a corpse behind him- one or other. Now, however, go some of you and call old Dolius, who was given me by my father on my marriage, and who is my gardener. Bid him go at once and tell everything to Laertes, who may be able to hit on some plan for enlisting public sympathy on our side, as against those who are trying to exterminate his own race and that of Ulysses."

Then the dear old nurse Euryclea said, "You may kill me, Madam, or let me live on in your house, whichever you please, but I will tell you the real truth. I knew all about it, and gave him everything he wanted in the way of bread and wine, but he made me take my solemn oath that I would not tell you anything for some ten or twelve days, unless you asked or happened to hear of his having gone, for he did not want you to spoil your beauty by crying. And now, Madam, wash your face, change your dress, and go upstairs with your maids to offer prayers to Minerva, daughter of Aegis-bearing Jove, for she can save him even though he be in the jaws of death. Do not trouble Laertes: he has trouble enough already. Besides, I cannot think that the gods hate die race of the race of the son of Arceisius so much, but there will be a son left to come up after him, and inherit both the house and the fair fields that lie far all round it."

With these words she made her mistress leave off crying, and dried the tears from her eyes. Penelope washed her face, changed her dress, and went upstairs with her maids. She then put some bruised barley into a basket and began praying to Minerva.

"Hear me," she cried, "Daughter of Aegis-bearing Jove, unweariable. If ever Ulysses while he was here burned you fat thigh bones of sheep or heifer, bear it in mind now as in my favor, and save my darling son from the villainy of the suitors."

She cried aloud as she spoke, and the goddess heard her prayer; meanwhile the suitors were clamorous throughout the covered cloister, and one of them said:

"The queen is preparing for her marriage with one or other of us. Little does she dream that her son has now been doomed to die."

This was what they said, but they did not know what was going to happen. Then Antinous said, "Comrades, let there be no loud talking, lest some of it get carried inside. Let us be up and do that in silence, about which we are all of a mind."

He then chose twenty men, and they went down to their. ship and to the sea side; they drew the vessel into the water and got her mast and sails inside her; they bound the oars to the thole-pins with twisted thongs of leather, all in due course, and spread the white sails aloft, while their fine servants brought them their armour. Then they made the ship fast a little way out, came on shore again, got their suppers, and waited till night should fall.

But Penelope lay in her own room upstairs unable to eat or drink, and wondering whether her brave son would escape, or be overpowered by the wicked suitors. Like a lioness caught in the toils with huntsmen hemming her in on every side she thought and thought till she sank into a slumber, and lay on her bed bereft of thought and motion.

Then Minerva bethought her of another matter, and made a vision in the likeness of Penelope's sister Iphthime daughter of Icarius who had married Eumelus and lived in Pherae. She told the vision to go to the house of Ulysses, and to make Penelope leave off crying, so it came into her room by the hole through which the thong went for pulling the door to, and hovered over her head, saying,

"You are asleep, Penelope: the gods who live at ease will not suffer you to weep and be so sad. Your son has done them no wrong, so he will yet come back to you."

Penelope, who was sleeping sweetly at the gates of dreamland, answered, "Sister, why have you come here? You do not come very often, but I suppose that is because you live such a long way off. Am I, then, to leave off crying and refrain from all the sad thoughts that torture me? I, who have lost my brave and lion-hearted husband, who had every good quality under heaven, and whose name was great over all Hellas and middle Argos; and now my darling son has gone off on board of a ship- a foolish fellow who has never been used to roughing it, nor to going about among gatherings of men. I am even more anxious about him than about my husband; I am all in a tremble when I think of him, lest something should happen to him, either from the people among whom he has gone, or by sea, for he has many enemies who are plotting against him, and are bent on killing him before he can return home."

Then the vision said, "Take heart, and be not so much dismayed. There is one gone with him whom many a man would be glad enough to have stand by his side, I mean Minerva; it is she who has compassion upon you, and who has sent me to bear you this message."

"Then," said Penelope, "if you are a god or have been sent here by divine commission, tell me also about that other unhappy one- is he still alive, or is he already dead and in the house of Hades?"

And the vision said, "I shall not tell you for certain whether he is alive or dead, and there is no use in idle conversation."

Then it vanished through the thong-hole of the door and was dissipated into thin air; but Penelope rose from her sleep refreshed and comforted, so vivid had been her dream.

Meantime the suitors went on board and sailed their ways over the sea, intent on murdering Telemachus. Now there is a rocky islet called Asteris, of no great size, in mid channel between Ithaca and Samos, and there is a harbor on either side of it where a ship can lie. Here then the Achaeans placed themselves in ambush.

Lesson 43

- Read Book 5 of *The Odyssey*.

Book 5

And now, as Dawn rose from her couch beside Tithonus- harbinger of light alike to mortals and immortals- the gods met in council and with them, Jove the lord of thunder, who is their king. Thereon Minerva began to tell them of the many sufferings of Ulysses, for she pitied him away there in the house of the nymph Calypso.

"Father Jove," said she, "and all you other gods that live in everlasting bliss, I hope there may never be such a thing as a kind and well-disposed ruler any more, nor one who will govern equitably. I hope they will be all henceforth cruel and unjust, for there is not one of his subjects but has forgotten Ulysses, who ruled them as though he were their father. There he is, lying in great pain in an island where dwells the nymph Calypso, who will not let him go; and he cannot get back to his own country, for he can find neither ships nor sailors to take him over the sea. Furthermore, wicked people are now trying to murder his only son Telemachus, who is coming home from Pylos and Lacedaemon, where he has been to see if he can get news of his father."

"What, my dear, are you talking about?" replied her father, "did you not send him there yourself, because you thought it would help Ulysses to get home and punish the suitors? Besides, you are perfectly able to protect Telemachus, and to see him safely home again, while the suitors have to come hurry-skurrying back without having killed him."

When he had thus spoken, he said to his son Mercury, "Mercury, you are our messenger, go therefore and tell Calypso we have decreed that poor Ulysses is to return home. He is to be convoyed neither by gods nor men, but after a perilous voyage of twenty days upon a raft he is to reach fertile Scheria, the land of the Phaeacians, who are near of kin to the gods, and will honor him as though he were one of ourselves. They will send him in a ship to his own country, and will give him more bronze and gold and raiment than he would have brought back from Troy, if he had had had all his prize money and had got home without disaster. This is how we have settled that he shall return to his country and his friends."

Thus he spoke, and Mercury, guide and guardian, slayer of Argus, did as he was told. Forthwith he bound on his glittering golden sandals with which he could fly like the wind over land and sea. He took the wand with which he seals men's eyes in sleep or wakes them just as he pleases, and flew holding it in his hand over Pieria; then he swooped down through the firmament till he reached the level of the sea, whose waves he skimmed like a cormorant that flies fishing every hole and corner of the ocean, and drenching its thick plumage in the spray. He flew and flew over many a weary wave, but when at last he got to the island which was his journey's end, he left the sea and went on by land till he came to the cave where the nymph Calypso lived.

He found her at home. There was a large fire burning on the hearth, and one could smell from far the fragrant reek of burning cedar and sandal wood. As for herself, she was busy at her loom, shooting her golden shuttle through the warp and singing beautifully. Round her cave there was a thick wood of alder, poplar, and sweet smelling cypress trees, wherein all kinds of great birds had built their nests- owls, hawks, and chattering sea-crows that occupy their business in the waters. A vine loaded with grapes was trained and grew luxuriantly about the mouth of the cave; there were also four running rills of water in channels cut pretty close together, and turned hither and thither so as to irrigate the beds of violets and luscious herbage over which they flowed. Even a god could not help being charmed with such a lovely spot, so Mercury stood still and looked at it; but when he had admired it sufficiently he went inside the cave.

Calypso knew him at once- for the gods all know each other, no matter how far they live from one another- but Ulysses was not within; he was on the sea-shore as usual, looking out upon the barren ocean with tears in his eyes, groaning and breaking his heart for sorrow. Calypso gave Mercury a seat and said: "Why have you come to see me, Mercury – honored, and ever welcome – for you do not visit me often? Say what you want; I will do it for be you at once if I can, and if it can be done at all; but come inside, and let me set refreshment before you."

As she spoke she drew a table loaded with ambrosia beside him and mixed him some red nectar, so Mercury ate and drank till he had had enough, and then said:

"We are speaking god and goddess to one another, one another, and you ask me why I have come here, and I will tell you truly as you would have me do. Jove sent me; it was no doing of mine; who could possibly want to come all this way over the sea where there are no cities full of people to offer me sacrifices or choice hecatombs? Nevertheless I had to come, for none of us other gods can cross Jove, nor transgress his orders. He says that you have here the most ill-starred of all those who fought nine years before the city of King Priam and sailed home in the tenth year after having sacked it. On their way home they sinned against Minerva, who raised both wind and waves against them, so that all his brave companions perished, and he alone was carried hither by wind and tide. Jove says that you are to let this by man go at once, for it is decreed that he shall not perish here, far from his own people, but shall return to his house and country and see his friends again."

Calypso trembled with rage when she heard this, "You gods," she exclaimed, "ought to be ashamed of yourselves. You are always jealous and hate seeing a goddess take a fancy to a mortal man, and live with him in open matrimony. So when rosy-fingered Dawn made love to Orion, you precious gods were all of you furious till Diana went and killed him in Ortygia. So again when Ceres fell in love with Iasion, and yielded to him in a thrice plowed fallow field, Jove came to hear of it before so long and killed Iasion with his thunder-bolts. And now you are angry with me too because I have a man here. I found the poor creature sitting all alone astride of a keel, for Jove had struck his ship with lightning and sunk it in mid ocean, so that all his crew were drowned, while he himself was driven by wind and waves on to my island. I got fond of him and cherished him, and had set my heart on making him immortal, so that he should never grow old all his days; still I cannot cross Jove, nor bring his counsels to nothing; therefore, if he insists upon it, let the man go beyond the seas again; but I cannot send him anywhere myself for I have neither ships nor men who can take him. Nevertheless I will readily give him such advice, in all good faith, as will be likely to bring him safely to his own country."

"Then send him away," said Mercury, "or Jove will be angry with you and punish you."

On this he took his leave, and Calypso went out to look for Ulysses, for she had heard Jove's message. She found him sitting upon the beach with his eyes ever filled with tears, and dying of sheer home-sickness; for he had got tired of Calypso, and though he was forced to sleep with her in the cave by night, it was she, not he, that would have it so. As for the day time, he spent it on the rocks and on the sea-shore, weeping, crying aloud for his despair, and always looking out upon the sea. Calypso then went close up to him said:

"My poor fellow, you shall not stay here grieving and fretting your life out any longer. I am going to send you away of my own free will; so go, cut some beams of wood, and make yourself a large raft with an upper deck that it may carry you safely over the sea. I will put bread, wine, and water on board to save you from starving. I will also give you clothes, and will send you a fair wind to take you home, if the gods in heaven so will it- for they know more about these things, and can settle them better than I can."

Ulysses shuddered as he heard her. "Now goddess," he answered, "there is something behind all this; you cannot be really meaning to help me home when you bid me do such a dreadful thing as put to sea on a raft. Not even a well-found ship with a fair wind could venture on such a distant voyage: nothing that you can say or do shall mage me go on board a raft unless you first solemnly swear that you mean me no mischief."

Calypso smiled at this and caressed him with her hand: "You know a great deal," said she, "but you are quite wrong here. May heaven above and earth below be my witnesses, with the waters of the river Styx- and this is the most solemn oath which a blessed god can take- that I mean you no sort of harm, and am only advising you to do exactly what I should do myself in your place. I am dealing with you quite straightforwardly; my heart is not made of iron, and I am very sorry for you."

When she had thus spoken she led the way rapidly before him, and Ulysses followed in her steps; so the pair, goddess and man, went on and on till they came to Calypso's cave, where Ulysses took the seat that Mercury had just left. Calypso set meat and drink before him of the food that mortals eat; but her maids brought ambrosia and nectar for herself, and they laid their hands on the good things that were before them. When they had satisfied themselves with meat and drink, Calypso spoke, saying:

"Ulysses, noble son of Laertes, so you would start home to your own land at once? Good luck go with you, but if you could only know how much suffering is in store for you before you get back to your own country, you would stay where you are, keep house along with me, and let me make you immortal, no matter how anxious you may be to see this wife of yours, of whom you are thinking all the time day after day; yet I flatter myself that at am no whit less tall or well-looking than she is, for it is not to be expected that a mortal woman should compare in beauty with an immortal."

"Goddess," replied Ulysses, "do not be angry with me about this. I am quite aware that my wife Penelope is nothing like so tall or so beautiful as yourself. She is only a woman, whereas you are an immortal. Nevertheless, I want to get home, and can think of nothing else. If some god wrecks me when I am on the sea, I will bear it and make the best of it. I have had infinite trouble both by land and sea already, so let this go with the rest."

Presently the sun set and it became dark, whereon the pair retired into the inner part of the cave and went to bed.

When the child of morning, rosy-fingered Dawn, appeared, Ulysses put on his shirt and cloak, while the goddess wore a dress of a light gossamer fabric, very fine and graceful, with a beautiful golden girdle about her waist and a veil to cover her head. She at once set herself to think how she could speed Ulysses on his way. So she gave him a great bronze axe that suited his hands; it was sharpened on both sides, and had a beautiful olive-wood handle fitted firmly on to it. She also gave him a sharp adze, and then led the way to the far end of the island where the largest trees grew- alder, poplar and pine, that reached the sky- very dry and well seasoned, so as to sail light for him in the water. Then, when she had shown him where the best trees grew, Calypso went home, leaving him to cut them, which he soon finished doing. He cut down twenty trees in all and adzed them smooth, squaring them by rule in good workmanlike fashion. Meanwhile Calypso came back with some augers, so he bored holes with them and fitted the timbers together with bolts and rivets. He made the raft as broad as a skilled shipwright makes the beam of a large vessel, and he filed a deck on top of the ribs, and ran a gunwale all round it. He also made a mast with a yard arm, and a rudder to steer with. He fenced the raft all round with wicker hurdles as a protection against the waves, and then he threw on a quantity of wood. By and by Calypso brought him some linen to make the sails, and he made these too, excellently, making them fast with braces and sheets. Last of all, with the help of levers, he drew the raft down into the water.

In four days he had completed the whole work, and on the fifth Calypso sent him from the island after washing him and giving him some clean clothes. She gave him a goat skin full of black wine, and another larger one of water; she also gave him a wallet full of provisions, and found him in much good meat. Moreover, she made the wind fair and warm for him, and gladly did Ulysses spread his sail before it, while he sat and guided the raft skillfully by means of the rudder. He never closed his eyes, but kept them fixed on the Pleiads, on late-setting Bootes, and on the Bear- which men also call the wain, and which turns round and round where it is, facing

Orion, and alone never dipping into the stream of Oceanus- for Calypso had told him to keep this to his left. Days seven and ten did he sail over the sea, and on the eighteenth the dim outlines of the mountains on the nearest part of the Phaeacian coast appeared, rising like a shield on the horizon.

But King Neptune, who was returning from the Ethiopians, caught sight of Ulysses a long way off, from the mountains of the Solymi. He could see him sailing upon the sea, and it made him very angry, so he wagged his head and muttered to himself, saying, "Goodheavens, so the gods have been changing their minds about Ulysses while I was away in Ethiopia, and now he is close to the land of the Phaeacians, where it is decreed that he shall escape from the calamities that have befallen him. Still, he shall have plenty of hardship yet before he has done with it."

Thereon he gathered his clouds together, grasped his trident, stirred it round in the sea, and roused the rage of every wind that blows till earth, sea, and sky were hidden in cloud, and night sprang forth out of the heavens. Winds from East, South, North, and West fell upon him all at the same time, and a tremendous sea got up, so that Ulysses' heart began to fail him. "Alas," he said to himself in his dismay, "what ever will become of me? I am afraid Calypso was right when she said I should have trouble by sea before I got back home. It is all coming true. How black is Jove making heaven with his clouds, and what a sea the winds are raising from every quarter at once. I am now safe to perish. Blessed and thrice blessed were those Danaans who fell before Troy in the cause of the sons of Atreus. Would that had been killed on the day when the Trojans were pressing me so sorely about the dead body of Achilles, for then I should have had due burial and the Achaeans would have honored my name; but now it seems that I shall come to a most pitiable end."

As he spoke a sea broke over him with such terrific fury that the raft reeled again, and he was carried overboard a long way off. He let go the helm, and the force of the hurricane was so great that it broke the mast half way up, and both sail and yard went over into the sea. For a long time Ulysses was under water, and it was all he could do to rise to the surface again, for the clothes Calypso had given him weighed him down; but at last he got his head above water and spat out the bitter brine that was running down his face in streams. In spite of all this, however, he did not lose sight of his raft, but swam as fast as he could towards it, got hold of it, and climbed on board again so as to escape drowning. The sea took the raft and tossed it about as Autumn winds whirl thistledown round and round upon a road. It was as though the South, North, East, and West winds were all playing battledore and shuttlecock with it at once.

When he was in this plight, Ino daughter of Cadmus, also called Leucothea, saw him. She had formerly been a mere mortal, but had been since raised to the rank of a marine goddess. Seeing in what great distress Ulysses now was, she had compassion upon him, and, rising like a sea-gull from the waves, took her seat upon the raft.

"My poor good man," said she, "why is Neptune so furiously angry with you? He is giving you a great deal of trouble, but for all his bluster he will not kill you. You seem to be a sensible person, do then as I bid you; strip, leave your raft to drive before the wind, and swim to the Phaecian coast where better luck awaits you. And here, take my veil and put it round your chest; it is enchanted, and you can come to no harm so long as you wear it. As soon as you touch land take it off, throw it back as far as you can into the sea, and then go away again." With these words she took off her veil and gave it him. Then she dived down again like a sea-gull and vanished beneath the dark blue waters.

But Ulysses did not know what to think. "Alas," he said to himself in his dismay, "this is only some one or other of the gods who is luring me to ruin by advising me to quit my raft. At any rate I will not do so at present, for the land where she said I should be quit of all troubles seemed to be still a good way off. I know what I will do- I am sure it will be best- no matter what happens I will stick to the raft as long as her timbers hold together, but when the sea breaks her up I will swim for it; I do not see how I can do any better than this."

While he was thus in two minds, Neptune sent a terrible great wave that seemed to rear itself above his head till it broke right over the raft, which then went to pieces as though it were a heap of dry chaff tossed about by a whirlwind. Ulysses got astride of one plank and rode upon it as if he were on horseback; he then took off the clothes Calypso had given him, bound Ino's veil under his arms, and plunged into the sea- meaning to swim on shore. King Neptune watched him as he did so, and wagged his head, muttering to himself and saying, "'There now, swim up and down as you best can till you fall in with well-to-do people. I do not think you will be able to say that I have let you off too lightly." On this he lashed his horses and drove to Aegae where his palace is.

But Minerva resolved to help Ulysses, so she bound the ways of all the winds except one, and made them lie quite still; but she roused a good stiff breeze from the North that should lay the waters till Ulysses reached the land of the Phaeacians where he would be safe.

Thereon he floated about for two nights and two days in the water, with a heavy swell on the sea and death staring him in the face; but when the third day broke, the wind fell and there was a dead calm without so much as a breath of air stirring. As he rose on the swell he looked eagerly ahead, and could see land quite near. Then, as children rejoice when their dear father begins to get better after having for a long time borne sore affliction sent him by some angry spirit, but the gods deliver him from evil, so was Ulysses thankful when he again saw land and trees, and swam on with all his strength that he might once more set foot upon dry ground. When, however, he got within earshot, he began to hear the surf thundering up against the rocks, for the swell still broke against them with a terrific roar. Everything was enveloped in spray; there were no harbors where a ship might ride, nor shelter of any kind, but only headlands, low-lying rocks, and mountain tops.

Ulysses' heart now began to fail him, and he said despairingly to himself, "Alas, Jove has let me see land after swimming so far that I had given up all hope, but I can find no landing place, for the coast is rocky and surf-beaten, the rocks are smooth and rise sheer from the sea, with deep water close under them so that I cannot climb out for want of foothold. I am afraid some great wave will lift me off my legs and dash me against the rocks as I leave the water- which would give me a sorry landing. If, on the other hand, I swim further in search of some shelving beach or harbor, a hurricane may carry me out to sea again sorely against my will, or heaven may send some great monster of the deep to attack me; for Amphitrite breeds many such, and I know that Neptune is very angry with me."

While he was thus in two minds a wave caught him and took him with such force against the rocks that he would have been smashed and torn to pieces if Minerva had not shown him what to do. He caught hold of the rock with both hands and clung to it groaning with pain till the wave retired, so he was saved that time; but presently the wave came on again and carried him back with it far into the sea-tearing his hands as the suckers of a polypus are torn when some one plucks it from its bed, and the stones come up along with it even so did the rocks tear the skin from his strong hands, and then the wave drew him deep down under the water.

Here poor Ulysses would have certainly perished even in spite of his own destiny, if Minerva had not helped him to keep his wits about him. He swam seaward again, beyond reach of the surf that was beating against the land, and at the same time he kept looking towards the shore to see if he could find some haven, or a spit that should take the waves aslant. By and by, as he swam on, he came to the mouth of a river, and here he thought would be the best place, for there were no rocks, and it afforded shelter from the wind. He felt that there was a current, so he prayed inwardly and said:

"Hear me, O King, whoever you may be, and save me from the anger of the sea-god Neptune, for I approach you prayerfully. Any one who has lost his way has at all times a claim even upon the gods, wherefore in my distress I draw near to your stream, and cling to the knees of your riverhood. Have mercy upon me, O king, for I declare myself your suppliant."

Then the god stayed his stream and stilled the waves, making all calm before him, and bringing him safely into the mouth of the river. Here at last Ulysses' knees and strong hands failed him, for the sea had completely broken him. His body was all swollen, and his mouth and nostrils ran down like a river with sea-water, so that he could neither breathe nor speak, and lay swooning from sheer exhaustion; presently, when he had got his breath and came to himself again, he took off the scarf that Ino had given him and threw it back into the salt stream of the river, whereon Ino received it into her hands from the wave that bore it towards her. Then he left the river, laid himself down among the rushes, and kissed the bounteous earth.

"Alas," he cried to himself in his dismay, "what ever will become of me, and how is it all to end? If I stay here upon the river bed through the long watches of the night, I am so exhausted that the bitter cold and damp may make an end of me- for towards sunrise there will be a keen wind blowing from off the river. If, on the other hand, I climb the hill side, find shelter in the woods, and sleep in some thicket, I may escape the cold and have a good night's rest, but some savage beast may take advantage of me and devour me."

In the end he deemed it best to take to the woods, and he found one upon some high ground not far from the water. There he crept beneath two shoots of olive that grew from a single stock- the one an ungrafted sucker, while the other had been grafted. No wind, however squally, could break through the cover they afforded, nor could the sun's rays pierce them, nor the rain get through them, so closely did they grow into one another. Ulysses crept under these and began to make himself a bed to lie on, for there was a great litter of dead leaves lying about- enough to make a covering for two or three men even in hard winter weather. He was glad enough to see this, so he laid himself down and heaped the leaves all round him. Then, as one who lives alone in the country, far from any neighbor, hides a brand as fire-seed in the ashes to save himself from having to get a light elsewhere, even so did Ulysses cover himself up with leaves; and Minerva shed a sweet sleep upon his eyes, closed his eyelids, and made him lose all memories of his sorrows.

Lesson 44

- Read Book 6 of *The Odyssey*.

Book 6

So here Ulysses slept, overcome by sleep and toil; but Minerva went off to the country and city of the Phaecians- a people who used to live in the fair town of Hypereia, near the lawless Cyclopes. Now the Cyclopes were stronger than they and plundered them, so their king Nausithous moved them thence and settled them in Scheria, far from all other people. He surrounded the city with a wall, built houses and temples, and divided the lands among his people; but he was dead and gone to the house of Hades, and King Alcinous, whose counsels were inspired of heaven, was now reigning. To his house, then, did Minerva hie in furtherance of the return of Ulysses.

She went straight to the beautifully decorated bedroom in which there slept a girl who was as lovely as a goddess, Nausicaa, daughter to King Alcinous. Two maid servants were sleeping near her, both very pretty, one on either side of the doorway, which was closed with well-made folding doors. Minerva took the form of the famous sea captain Dymas's daughter, who was a bosom friend of Nausicaa and just her own age; then, coming up to the girl's bedside like a breath of wind, she hovered over her head and said:

"Nausicaa, what can your mother have been about, to have such a lazy daughter? Here are your clothes all lying in disorder, yet you are going to be married almost immediately, and should not only be well dressed yourself, but should find good clothes for those who attend you. This is the way to get yourself a good name, and to make your father and mother proud of you. Suppose, then, that we make tomorrow a washing day, and start at daybreak. I will come and help you so that you may have everything ready as soon as possible, for all the best young men among your own people are courting you, and you are not going to remain a maid much longer. Ask your father, therefore, to have a wagon and mules ready for us at daybreak, to take the rugs, robes, and girdles; and you can ride, too, which will be much pleasanter for you than walking, for the washing-cisterns are some way from the town."

When she had said this Minerva went away to Olympus, which they say is the everlasting home of the gods. Here no wind beats roughly, and neither rain nor snow can fall; but it abides in everlasting sunshine and in a great peacefulness of light, wherein the blessed gods are illumined for ever and ever. This was the place to which the goddess went when she had given instructions to the girl.

By and by morning came and woke Nausicaa, who began wondering about her dream; she therefore went to the other end of the house to tell her father and mother all about it, and found them in their own room. Her mother was sitting by the fireside spinning her purple yarn with her maids around her, and she happened to catch her father just as he was going out to attend a meeting of the town council, which the Phaeacian aldermen had convened. She stopped him and said:

"Papa dear, could you manage to let me have a good big wagon? I want to take all our dirty clothes to the river and wash them. You are the chief man here, so it is only right that you should have a clean shirt when you attend meetings of the council. Moreover, you have five sons at home, two of them married, while the other three are good-looking bachelors; you know they always like to have clean linen when they go to a dance, and I have been thinking about all this."

She did not say a word about her own wedding, for she did not like to, but her father knew and said, "You shall have the mules, my love, and whatever else you have a mind for. Be off with you, and the men shall get you a good strong wagon with a body to it that will hold all your clothes."

On this he gave his orders to the servants, who got the wagon out, harnessed the mules, and put them to, while the girl brought the clothes down from the linen room and placed them on the wagon. Her mother prepared her a basket of provisions with all sorts of good things, and a goat skin full of wine; the girl now got into the wagon, and her mother gave her also a golden cruse of oil, that she and her women might anoint themselves. Then she took the whip and reins and lashed the mules on, whereon they set off, and their hoofs clattered on the road. They pulled without flagging, and carried not only Nausicaa and her wash of clothes, but the maids also who were with her.

When they reached the water side they went to the washing-cisterns, through which there ran at all times enough pure water to wash any quantity of linen, no matter how dirty. Here they unharnessed the mules and turned them out to feed on the sweet juicy herbage that grew by the water side. They took the clothes out of the wagon, put them in the water, and vied with one another in treading them in the pits to get the dirt out. After they had washed them and got them quite clean, they laid them out by the sea side, where the waves had raised a high beach of shingle, and set about washing themselves and anointing themselves with olive oil. Then they got their dinner by the side of the stream, and waited for the sun to finish drying the clothes. When they had done dinner they threw off the veils that covered their heads and began to play at ball, while Nausicaa sang for them. As the huntress Diana goes forth upon the mountains of Taygetus or Erymanthus to hunt wild boars or deer, and the wood-nymphs, daughters of Aegis-bearing Jove, take their sport along with her (then is Leto proud at seeing her daughter stand a full head taller than the others, and eclipse the loveliest amid a whole bevy of beauties), even so did the girl outshine her handmaids.

When it was time for them to start home, and they were folding the clothes and putting them into the wagon, Minerva began to consider how Ulysses should wake up and see the handsome girl who was to conduct him to the city of the Phaeacians. The girl, therefore, threw a ball at one of the maids, which missed her and fell into deep water. On this they all shouted, and the noise they made woke Ulysses, who sat up in his bed of leaves and began to wonder what it might all be.

"Alas," said he to himself, "what kind of people have I come amongst? Are they cruel, savage, and uncivilized, or hospitable and humane? I seem to hear the voices of young women, and they sound like those of the nymphs that haunt mountain tops, or springs of rivers and meadows of green grass. At any rate I am among a race of men and women. Let me try if I cannot manage to get a look at them."

As he said this he crept from under his bush, and broke off a bough covered with thick leaves to hide his nakedness. He looked like some lion of the wilderness that stalks about exulting in his strength and defying both wind and rain; his eyes glare as he prowls in quest of oxen, sheep, or deer, for he is famished, and will dare break even into a well-fenced homestead, trying to get at the sheep- even such did Ulysses seem to the young women, as he drew near to them all naked as he was, for he was in great want. On seeing one so unkempt and so begrimed with salt water, the others scampered off along the spits that jutted out into the sea, but the daughter of Alcinous stood firm, for Minerva put courage into her heart and took away all fear from her. She stood right in front of Ulysses, and he doubted whether he should go up to her, throw himself at her feet, and embrace her knees as a suppliant, or stay where he was and entreat her to give him some clothes and show him the way to the town. In the end he deemed it best to entreat her from a distance in case the girl should take offence at his coming near enough to clasp her knees, so he addressed her in honeyed and persuasive language.

"O queen," he said, "I implore your aid- but tell me, are you a goddess or are you a mortal woman? If you are a goddess and dwell in heaven, I can only conjecture that you are Jove's daughter Diana, for your face and figure resemble none but hers; if on the other hand you are a mortal and live on earth, thrice happy are your father and mother- thrice happy, too, are your brothers and sisters; how proud and delighted they must feel when they see so fair a scion as yourself going out to a dance; most happy, however, of all will he be whose wedding gifts have been the richest, and who takes you to his own home. I never yet saw any one so beautiful, neither man nor woman, and am lost in admiration as I behold you. I can only compare you to a young palm tree which I saw when I was at Delos growing near the altar of Apollo- for I was there, too, with much people after me, when I was on that journey which has been the source of all my troubles. Never yet did such a young plant shoot out of the ground as that was, and I admired and wondered at it exactly as I now admire and wonder at yourself. I dare not clasp your knees, but I am in great distress; yesterday made the twentieth day that I had been tossing about upon the sea. The winds and waves have taken me all the way from the Ogygian island, and now fate has flung me upon this coast that I may endure still further suffering; for I do not think that I have yet come to the end of it, but rather that heaven has still much evil in store for me.

"And now, O queen, have pity upon me, for you are the first person I have met, and I know no one else in this country. Show me the way to your town, and let me have anything that you may have brought hither to wrap your clothes in. May heaven grant you in all things your heart's desire- husband, house, and a happy, peaceful home; for there is nothing better in this world than that man and wife should be of one mind in a house. It discomfits their enemies, makes the hearts of their friends glad, and they themselves know more about it than any one."

To this Nausicaa answered, "Stranger, you appear to be a sensible, well-disposed person. There is no accounting for luck; Jove gives prosperity to rich and poor just as he chooses, so you must take what he has seen fit to send you, and make the best of it. Now, however, that you have come to this our country, you shall not want for clothes nor for anything else that a foreigner in distress may reasonably look for. I will show you the way to the town, and will tell you the name of our people; we are called Phaeacians, and I am daughter to Alcinous, in whom the whole power of the state is vested."

Then she called her maids and said, "Stay where you are, you girls. Can you not see a man without running away from him? Do you take him for a robber or a murderer? Neither he nor any one else can come here to do us Phaeacians any harm, for we are dear to the gods, and live apart on a land's end that juts into the sounding sea, and have nothing to do with any other people. This is only some poor man who has lost his way, and we must be kind to him, for strangers and foreigners in distress are under Jove's protection, and will take what they can get and be thankful; so, girls, give the poor fellow something to eat and drink, and wash him in the stream at some place that is sheltered from the wind."

On this the maids left off running away and began calling one another back. They made Ulysses sit down in the shelter as Nausicaa had told them, and brought him a shirt and cloak. They also brought him the little golden cruse of oil, and told him to go wash in the stream. But Ulysses said, "Young women, please to stand a little on one side that I may wash the brine from my shoulders and anoint myself with oil, for it is long enough since my skin has had a drop of oil upon it. I cannot wash as long as you all keep standing there. I am ashamed to strip before a number of good-looking young women."

Then they stood on one side and went to tell the girl, while Ulysses washed himself in the stream and scrubbed the brine from his back and from his broad shoulders. When he had thoroughly washed himself, and had got the brine out of his hair, he anointed himself with oil, and put on the clothes which the girl had given him; Minerva then made him look taller and stronger than before, she also made the hair grow thick on the top of his head, and flow down in curls like hyacinth blossoms; she glorified him about the head and shoulders as a skillful workman who has studied art of all kinds under Vulcan and Minerva enriches a piece of silver plate by gilding it- and his work is full of beauty. Then he went and sat down a little way off upon the beach, looking quite young and handsome, and the girl gazed on him with admiration; then she said to her maids:

"Hush, my dears, for I want to say something. I believe the gods who live in heaven have sent this man to the Phaeacians. When I first saw him I thought him plain, but now his appearance is like that of the gods who dwell in heaven. I should like my future husband to be just such another as he is, if he would only stay here and not want to go away. However, give him something to eat and drink."

They did as they were told, and set food before Ulysses, who ate and drank ravenously, for it was long since he had had food of any kind. Meanwhile, Nausicaa bethought her of another matter. She got the linen folded and placed in the wagon, she then yoked the mules, and, as she took her seat, she called Ulysses:

"Stranger," said she, "rise and let us be going back to the town; I will introduce you at the house of my excellent father, where I can tell you that you will meet all the best people among the Phaecians. But be sure and do as I bid you, for you seem to be a sensible person. As long as we are going past the fields- and farm lands, follow briskly behind the wagon along with the maids and I will lead the way myself. Presently, however, we shall come to the town, where you will find a high wall running all round it, and a good harbor on either side with a narrow entrance into the city, and the ships will be drawn up by the road side, for every one has a place where his own ship can lie. You will see the market place with a temple of Neptune in the middle of it, and paved with large stones bedded in the earth. Here people deal in ship's gear of all kinds, such as cables and sails, and here, too, are the places where oars are made, for the Phaeacians are not a nation of archers; they know nothing about bows and arrows, but are a sea-faring folk, and pride themselves on their masts, oars, and ships, with which they travel far over the sea.

"I am afraid of the gossip and scandal that may be set on foot against me later on; for the people here are very ill-natured, and some low fellow, if he met us, might say, 'Who is this fine-looking stranger that is going about with Nausicaa? Where did she End him? I suppose she is going to marry him. Perhaps he is a vagabond sailor whom she has taken from some foreign vessel, for we have no neighbors; or some god has at last come down from heaven in answer to her prayers, and she is going to live with him all the rest of her life. It would be a good thing if she would take herself off and find a husband somewhere else, for she will not look at one of the many excellent young Phaeacians who are in with her.' This is the kind of disparaging remark that would be made about me, and I could not complain, for I should myself be scandalized at seeing any other girl do the like, and go about with men in spite of everybody, while her father and mother were still alive, and without having been married in the face of all the world.

"If, therefore, you want my father to give you an escort and to help you home, do as I bid you; you will see a beautiful grove of poplars by the road side dedicated to Minerva; it has a well in it and a meadow all round it. Here my father has a field of rich garden ground, about as far from the town as a man' voice will carry. Sit down there and wait for a while till the rest of us can get into the town and reach my father's house. Then, when you think we must have done this, come into the town and ask the way to the house of my father Alcinous. You will have no difficulty in finding it; any child will point it out to you, for no one else in the whole town has anything like such a fine house as he has. When you have got past the gates and through the outer court, go right across the inner court till you come to my mother. You will find her sitting by the fire and spinning her purple wool by firelight. It is a fine sight to see her as she leans back against one of the bearing-posts with her maids all ranged behind her. Close to her seat stands that of my father, on which he sits and topes like an immortal god. Never mind him, but go up to my mother, and lay your hands upon her knees if you would get home quickly.

If you can gain her over, you may hope to see your own country again, no matter how distant it may be."

So saying she lashed the mules with her whip and they left the river. The mules drew well and their hoofs went up and down upon the road. She was careful not to go too fast for Ulysses and the maids who were following on foot along with the wagon, so she plied her whip with judgement. As the sun was going down they came to the sacred grove of Minerva, and there Ulysses sat down and prayed to the mighty daughter of Jove.

"Hear me," he cried, "daughter of Aegis-bearing Jove, unweariable, hear me now, for you gave no heed to my prayers when Neptune was wrecking me. Now, therefore, have pity upon me and grant that I may find friends and be hospitably received by the Phaecians."

Thus did he pray, and Minerva heard his prayer, but she would not show herself to him openly, for she was afraid of her uncle Neptune, who was still furious in his endeavors to prevent Ulysses from getting home.

Lesson 45

- Read Book 7 of *The Odyssey*.

Book 7

Thus, then, did Ulysses wait and pray; but the girl drove on to the town. When she reached her father's house she drew up at the gateway, and her brothers- comely as the gods- gathered round her, took the mules out of the wagon, and carried the clothes into the house, while she went to her own room, where an old servant, Eurymedusa of Apeira, lit the fire for her. This old woman had been brought by sea from Apeira, and had been chosen as a prize for Alcinous because he was king over the Phaecians, and the people obeyed him as though he were a god. She had been nurse to Nausicaa, and had now lit the fire for her, and brought her supper for her into her own room.

Presently Ulysses got up to go towards the town; and Minerva shed a thick mist all round him to hide him in case any of the proud Phaecians who met him should be rude to him, or ask him who he was. Then, as he was just entering the town, she came towards him in the likeness of a little girl carrying a pitcher. She stood right in front of him, and Ulysses said:

"My dear, will you be so kind as to show me the house of King Alcinous? I am an unfortunate foreigner in distress, and do not know one in your town and country."

Then Minerva said, "Yes, father stranger, I will show you the house you want, for Alcinous lives quite close to my own father. I will go before you and show the way, but say not a word as you go, and do not look at any man, nor ask him questions; for the people here cannot abide strangers, and do not like men who come from some other place. They are a sea-faring folk, and sail the seas by the grace of Neptune in ships that glide along like thought, or as a bird in the air."

On this she led the way, and Ulysses followed in her steps; but not one of the Phaecians could see him as he passed through the city in the midst of them; for the great goddess Minerva in her good will towards him had hidden him in a thick cloud of darkness. He admired their harbors, ships, places of assembly, and the lofty walls of the city, which, with the palisade on top of them, were very striking, and when they reached the king's house Minerva said:

"This is the house, father stranger, which you would have me show you. You will find a number of great people sitting at table, but do not be afraid; go straight in, for the bolder a man is the more likely he is to carry his point, even though he is a stranger. First find the queen. Her name is Arete, and she comes of the same family as her husband Alcinous. They both descend originally from Neptune, who was father to Nausithous by Periboea, a woman of great beauty. Periboea was the youngest daughter of Eurymedon, who at one time reigned over the giants, but he ruined his ill-fated people and lost his own life to boot.

"Neptune, however, lay with his daughter, and she had a son by him, the great Nausithous, who reigned over the Phaecians. Nausithous had two sons Rhexenor and Alcinous; Apollo killed the first of them while he was still a bridegroom and without male issue; but he left a daughter Arete, whom Alcinous married, and honours as no other woman is honored of all those that keep house along with their husbands.

"Thus she both was, and still is, respected beyond measure by her children, by Alcinous himself, and by the whole people, who look upon her as a goddess, and greet her whenever she goes about the city, for she is a thoroughly good woman both in head and heart, and when any women are friends of hers, she will help their husbands also to settle their disputes. If you can gain her good will, you may have every hope of seeing your friends again, and getting safely back to your home and country."

Then Minerva left Scheria and went away over the sea. She went to Marathon and to the spacious streets of Athens, where she entered the abode of Erechtheus; but Ulysses went on to the house of Alcinous, and he pondered much as he paused a while before reaching the threshold of bronze, for the splendor of the palace was like that of the sun or moon. The walls on either side were of bronze from end to end, and the cornice was of blue enamel. The doors were gold, and hung on pillars of silver that rose from a floor of bronze, while the lintel was silver and the hook of the door was of gold.

On either side there stood gold and silver mastiffs which Vulcan, with his consummate skill, had fashioned expressly to keep watch over the palace of King Alcinous; so they were immortal and could never grow old. Seats were ranged all along the wall, here and there from one end to the other, with coverings of fine woven work which the women of the house had made. Here the chief persons of the Phaecians used to sit and eat and drink, for there was abundance at all seasons; and there were golden figures of young men with lighted torches in their hands, raised on pedestals, to give light by night to those who were at table. There are fifty maid servants in the house, some of whom are always grinding rich yellow grain at the mill, while others work at the loom, or sit and spin, and their shuttles go, backwards and forwards like the fluttering of aspen leaves, while the linen is so closely woven that it will turn oil. As the Phaecians are the best sailors in the world, so their women excel all others in weaving, for Minerva has taught them all manner of useful arts, and they are very intelligent.

Outside the gate of the outer court there is a large garden of about four acres with a wall all round it. It is full of beautiful trees- pears, pomegranates, and the most delicious apples. There are luscious figs also, and olives in full growth. The fruits never rot nor fail all the year round, neither winter nor summer, for the air is so soft that a new crop ripens before the old has dropped. Pear grows on pear, apple on apple, and fig on fig, and so also with the grapes, for there is an excellent vineyard: on the level ground of a part of this, the grapes are being made into raisins; in another part they are being gathered; some are being trodden in the wine tubs, others further on have shed their blossom and are beginning to show fruit, others again are just changing color. In the furthest part of the ground there are beautifully arranged beds of flowers that are in bloom all the year round. Two streams go through it, the one turned in ducts throughout the whole garden, while the other is carried under the ground of the outer court to the house itself, and the town's people draw water from it. Such, then, were the splendors with which the gods had endowed the house of King Alcinous.

So here Ulysses stood for a while and looked about him, but when he had looked long enough he crossed the threshold and went within the precincts of the house. There he found all the chief people among the Phaecians making their drink-offerings to Mercury, which they always did the last thing before going away for the night. He went straight through the court, still hidden by the cloak of darkness in which Minerva had enveloped him, till he reached Arete and King Alcinous; then he laid his hands upon the knees of the queen, and at that moment the miraculous darkness fell away from him and he became visible. Every one was speechless with surprise at seeing a man there, but Ulysses began at once with his petition.

"Queen Arete," he exclaimed, "daughter of great Rhexenor, in my distress I humbly pray you, as also your husband and these your guests (whom may heaven prosper with long life and happiness, and may they leave their possessions to their children, and all the honors conferred upon them by the state) to help me home to my own country as soon as possible; for I have been long in trouble and away from my friends."

Then he sat down on the hearth among the ashes and they all held their peace, till presently the old hero Echeneus, who was an excellent speaker and an elder among the Phaeacians, plainly and in all honesty addressed them thus:

"Alcinous," said he, "it is not creditable to you that a stranger should be seen sitting among the ashes of your hearth; every one is waiting to hear what you are about to say; tell him, then, to rise and take a seat on a stool inlaid with silver, and bid your servants mix some wine and water that we may make a drink-offering to Jove the lord of thunder, who takes all well-disposed suppliants under his protection; and let the housekeeper give him some supper, of whatever there may be in the house."

When Alcinous heard this he took Ulysses by the hand, raised him from the hearth, and bade him take the seat of Laodamas, who had been sitting beside him, and was his favorite son. A maid servant then brought him water in a beautiful golden ewer and poured it into a silver basin for him to wash his hands, and she drew a clean table beside him; an upper servant brought him bread and offered him many good things of what there was in the house, and Ulysses ate and drank. Then Alcinous said to one of the servants, "Pontonous, mix a cup of wine and hand it round that we may make drink-offerings to Jove the lord of thunder, who is the protector of all well-disposed suppliants."

Pontonous then mixed wine and water, and handed it round after giving every man his drink-offering. When they had made their offerings, and had drunk each as much as he was minded, Alcinous said:

"Aldermen and town councilors of the Phaeacians, hear my words. You have had your supper, so now go home to bed. To-morrow morning I shall invite a still larger number of aldermen, and will give a sacrificial banquet in honor of our guest; we can then discuss the question of his escort, and consider how we may at once send him back rejoicing to his own country without trouble or inconvenience to himself, no matter how distant it may be. We must see that he comes to no harm while on his homeward journey, but when he is once at home he will have to take the luck he was born with for better or worse like other people. It is possible, however, that the stranger is one of the immortals who has come down from heaven to visit us; but in this case the gods are departing from their usual practice, for hitherto they have made themselves perfectly clear to us when we have been offering them hecatombs. They come and sit at our feasts just like one of our selves, and if any solitary wayfarer happens to stumble upon some one or other of them, they affect no concealment, for we are as near of kin to the gods as the Cyclopes and the savage giants are."

Then Ulysses said: "Pray, Alcinous, do not take any such notion into your head. I have nothing of the immortal about me, neither in body nor mind, and most resemble those among you who are the most afflicted. Indeed, were I to tell you all that heaven has seen fit to lay upon me, you would say that I was still worse off than they are. Nevertheless, let me sup in spite of sorrow, for an empty stomach is a very importunate thing, and thrusts itself on a man's notice no matter how dire is his distress. I am in great trouble, yet it insists that I shall eat and drink, bids me lay aside all memory of my sorrows and dwell only on the due replenishing of itself. As for yourselves, do as you propose, and at break of day set about helping me to get home. I shall be content to die if I may first once more behold my property, my bondsmen, and all the greatness of my house."

Thus did he speak. Every one approved his saying, and agreed that he should have his escort inasmuch as he had spoken reasonably. Then when they had made their drink-offerings, and had drunk each as much as he was minded they went home to bed every man in his own abode, leaving Ulysses in the cloister with Arete and Alcinous while the servants were taking the things away after supper. Arete was the first to speak, for she recognized the shirt, cloak, and good clothes that Ulysses was wearing, as the work of herself and of her maids; so she said, "Stranger, before we go any further, there is a question I should like to ask you. Who, and whence are you, and who gave you those clothes? Did you not say you had come here from beyond the sea?"

And Ulysses answered, "It would be a long story Madam, were I to relate in full the tale of my misfortunes, for the hand of heaven has been laid heavy upon me; but as regards your question, there is an island far away in the sea which is called 'the Ogygian.' Here dwells the cunning and powerful goddess Calypso, daughter of Atlas. She lives by herself far from all neighbors human or divine. Fortune, however, me to her hearth all desolate and alone, for Jove struck my ship with his thunderbolts, and broke it up in mid-ocean. My brave comrades were drowned every man of them, but I stuck to the keel and was carried hither and thither for the space of nine days, till at last during the darkness of the tenth night the gods brought me to the Ogygian island where the great goddess Calypso lives. She took me in and treated me with the utmost kindness; indeed she wanted to make me immortal that I might never grow old, but she could not persuade me to let her do so.

"I stayed with Calypso seven years straight on end, and watered the good clothes she gave me with my tears during the whole time; but at last when the eighth year came round she bade me depart of her own free will, either because Jove had told her she must, or because she had changed her mind. She sent me from her island on a raft, which she provisioned with abundance of bread and wine. Moreover she gave me good stout clothing, and sent me a wind that blew both warm and fair. Days seven and ten did I sail over the sea, and on the eighteenth I caught sight of the first outlines of the mountains upon your coast- and glad indeed was I to set eyes upon them. Nevertheless there was still much trouble in store for me, for at this point Neptune would let me go no further, and raised a great storm against me; the sea was so terribly high that I could no longer keep to my raft, which went to pieces under the fury of the gale, and I had to swim for it, till wind and current brought me to your shores.

"There I tried to land, but could not, for it was a bad place and the waves dashed me against the rocks, so I again took to the sea and swam on till I came to a river that seemed the most likely landing place, for there were no rocks and it was sheltered from the wind. Here, then, I got out of the water and gathered my senses together again. Night was coming on, so I left the river, and went into a thicket, where I covered myself all over with leaves, and presently heaven sent me off into a very deep sleep. Sick and sorry as I was I slept among the leaves all night, and through the next day till afternoon, when I woke as the sun was westering, and saw your daughter's maid servants playing upon the beach, and your daughter among them looking like a goddess. I besought her aid, and she proved to be of an excellent disposition, much more so than could be expected from so young a person- for young people are apt to be thoughtless. She gave me plenty of bread and wine, and when she had had me washed in the river she also gave me the clothes in which you see me. Now, therefore, though it has pained me to do so, I have told you the whole truth."

Then Alcinous said, "Stranger, it was very wrong of my daughter not to bring you on at once to my house along with the maids, seeing that she was the first person whose aid you asked."

"Pray do not scold her," replied Ulysses; "she is not to blame. She did tell me to follow along with the maids, but I was ashamed and afraid, for I thought you might perhaps be displeased if you saw me. Every human being is sometimes a little suspicious and irritable."

"Stranger," replied Alcinous, "I am not the kind of man to get angry about nothing; it is always better to be reasonable; but by Father Jove, Minerva, and Apollo, now that I see what kind of person you are, and how much you think as I do, I wish you would stay here, marry my daughter, and become my son-in-law. If you will stay I will give you a house and an estate, but no one (heaven forbid) shall keep you here against your own wish, and that you may be sure of this I will attend to-morrow to the matter of your escort. You can sleep during the whole voyage if you like, and the men shall sail you over smooth waters either to your own home, or wherever you please, even though it be a long way further off than Euboea, which those of my people who saw it when they took yellow-haired Rhadamanthus to see Tityus the son of Gaia, tell me is the furthest of any place- and yet they did the whole voyage in a single day without distressing themselves, and came back again afterwards. You will thus see how much my ships excel all others, and what magnificent oarsmen my sailors are."

Then was Ulysses glad and prayed aloud saying, "Father Jove, grant that Alcinous may do all as he has said, for so he will win an imperishable name among mankind, and at the same time I shall return to my country."

Thus did they converse. Then Arete told her maids to set a bed in the room that was in the gatehouse, and make it with good red rugs, and to spread coverlets on the top of them with woolen cloaks for Ulysses to wear. The maids thereon went out with torches in their hands, and when they had made the bed they came up to Ulysses and said, "Rise, sir stranger, and come with us for your bed is ready," and glad indeed was he to go to his rest.

So Ulysses slept in a bed placed in a room over the echoing gateway; but Alcinous lay in the inner part of the house, with the queen his wife by his side.

(As a reminder, be sure to check your Language Arts Workbook and your Vocabulary Workbook for the rest of your assignments for the course.)

Lesson 46

- Read Book 8 of *The Odyssey*.

Book 8

Now when the child of morning, rosy-fingered Dawn, appeared, Alcinous and Ulysses both rose, and Alcinous led the way to the Phaecian place of assembly, which was near the ships. When they got there they sat down side by side on a seat of polished stone, while Minerva took the form of one of Alcinous' servants, and went round the town in order to help Ulysses to get home. She went up to the citizens, man by man, and said, "Aldermen and town councilors of the Phaeacians, come to the assembly all of you and listen to the stranger who has just come off a long voyage to the house of King Alcinous; he looks like an immortal god."

With these words she made them all want to come, and they flocked to the assembly till seats and standing room were alike crowded. Every one was struck with the appearance of Ulysses, for Minerva had beautified him about the head and shoulders, making him look taller and stouter than he really was, that he might impress the Phaecians favorably as being a very remarkable man, and might come off well in the many trials of skill to which they would challenge him. Then, when they were got together, Alcinous spoke:

"Hear me," said he, "aldermen and town councilors of the Phaeacians, that I may speak even as I am minded. This stranger, whoever he may be, has found his way to my house from somewhere or other either East or West. He wants an escort and wishes to have the matter settled. Let us then get one ready for him, as we have done for others before him; indeed, no one who ever yet came to my house has been able to complain of me for not speeding on his way soon enough. Let us draw a ship into the sea- one that has never yet made a voyage- and man her with two and fifty of our smartest young sailors. Then when you have made fast your oars each by his own seat, leave the ship and come to my house to prepare a feast. I will find you in everything. I am giving will these instructions to the young men who will form the crew, for as regards you aldermen and town councilors, you will join me in entertaining our guest in the cloisters. I can take no excuses, and we will have Demodocus to sing to us; for there is no bard like him whatever he may choose to sing about."

Alcinous then led the way, and the others followed after, while a servant went to fetch Demodocus. The fifty-two picked oarsmen went to the sea shore as they had been told, and when they got there they drew the ship into the water, got her mast and sails inside her, bound the oars to the thole-pins with twisted thongs of leather, all in due course, and spread the white sails aloft. They moored the vessel a little way out from land, and then came on shore and went to the house of King Alcinous. The outhouses, yards, and all the precincts were filled with crowds of men in great multitudes both old and young; and Alcinous killed them a dozen sheep, eight full grown pigs, and two oxen. These they skinned and dressed so as to provide a magnificent banquet.

A servant presently led in the famous bard Demodocus, whom the muse had dearly loved, but to whom she had given both good and evil, for though she had endowed him with a divine gift of song, she had robbed him of his eyesight. Pontonous set a seat for him among the guests, leaning it up against a bearing-post. He hung the lyre for him on a peg over his head, and showed him where he was to feel for it with his hands. He also set a fair table with a basket of victuals by his side, and a cup of wine from which he might drink whenever he was so disposed.

The company then laid their hands upon the good things that were before them, but as soon as they had had enough to eat and drink, the muse inspired Demodocus to sing the feats of heroes, and more especially a matter that was then in the mouths of all men, to wit, the quarrel between Ulysses and Achilles, and the fierce words that they heaped on one another as they sat together at a banquet. But Agamemnon was glad when he heard his chieftains quarreling with one another, for Apollo had foretold him this at Pytho when he crossed the stone floor to consult the oracle. Here was the beginning of the evil that by the will of Jove fell both Danaans and Trojans.

Thus sang the bard, but Ulysses drew his purple mantle over his head and covered his face, for he was ashamed to let the Phaeacians see that he was weeping. When the bard left off singing he wiped the tears from his eyes, uncovered his face, and, taking his cup, made a drink-offering to the gods; but when the Phaeacians pressed

Demodocus to sing further, for they delighted in his lays, then Ulysses again drew his mantle over his head and wept bitterly. No one noticed his distress except Alcinous, who was sitting near him, and heard the heavy sighs that he was heaving. So he at once said, "Aldermen and town councilors of the Phaeacians, we have had enough now, both of the feast, and of the minstrelsy that is its due accompaniment; let us proceed therefore to the athletic sports, so that our guest on his return home may be able to tell his friends how much we surpass all other nations as boxers, wrestlers, jumpers, and runners."

With these words he led the way, and the others followed after. A servant hung Demodocus's lyre on its peg for him, led him out of the cloister, and set him on the same way as that along which all the chief men of the Phaeacians were going to see the sports; a crowd of several thousands of people followed them, and there were many excellent competitors for all the prizes. Acroneos, Ocyalus, Elatreus, Nauteus, Prymneus, Anchialus, Eretmeus, Ponteus, Proreus, Thoon, Anabesineus, and Amphialus son of Polyneus son of Tecton. There was also Euryalus son of Naubolus, who was like Mars himself, and was the best looking man among the Phaecians except Laodamas. Three sons of Alcinous, Laodamas, Halios, and Clytoneus, competed also.

The foot races came first. The course was set out for them from the starting post, and they raised a dust upon the plain as they all flew forward at the same moment. Clytoneus came in first by a long way; he left every one else behind him by the length of the furrow that a couple of mules can plow in a fallow field. They then turned to the painful art of wrestling, and here Euryalus proved to be the best man. Amphialus excelled all the others in jumping, while at throwing the disc there was no one who could approach Elatreus. Alcinous's son Laodamas was the best boxer, and he it was who presently said, when they had all been diverted with the games, "Let us ask the stranger whether he excels in any of these sports; he seems very powerfully built; his thighs, claves, hands, and neck are of prodigious strength, nor is he at all old, but he has suffered much lately, and there is nothing like the sea for making havoc with a man, no matter how strong he is."

"You are quite right, Laodamas," replied Euryalus, "go up to your guest and speak to him about it yourself."

When Laodamas heard this he made his way into the middle of the crowd and said to Ulysses, "I hope, Sir, that you will enter yourself for some one or other of our competitions if you are skilled in any of them- and you must have gone in for many a one before now. There is nothing that does any one so much credit all his life long as the showing himself a proper man with his hands and feet. Have a try therefore at something, and banish all sorrow from your mind. Your return home will not be long delayed, for the ship is already drawn into the water, and the crew is found."

Ulysses answered, "Laodamas, why do you taunt me in this way? my mind is set rather on cares than contests; I have been through infinite trouble, and am come among you now as a suppliant, praying your king and people to further me on my return home."

Then Euryalus reviled him outright and said, "I gather, then, that you are unskilled in any of the many sports that men generally delight in. I suppose you are one of those grasping traders that go about in ships as captains or merchants, and who think of nothing but of their outward freights and homeward cargoes. There does not seem to be much of the athlete about you."

"For shame, Sir," answered Ulysses, fiercely, "you are an insolent fellow- so true is it that the gods do not grace all men alike in speech, person, and understanding. One man may be of weak presence, but heaven has adorned this with such a good conversation that he charms every one who sees him; his honeyed moderation carries his hearers with him so that he is leader in all assemblies of his fellows, and wherever he goes he is looked up to. Another may be as handsome as a god, but his good looks are not crowned with discretion. This is your case. No god could make a finer looking fellow than you are, but you are a fool. Your ill-judged remarks have made me exceedingly angry, and you are quite mistaken, for I excel in a great many athletic exercises; indeed, so long as I had youth and strength, I was among the first athletes of the age. Now, however, I am worn out by labor and sorrow, for I have gone through much both on the field of battle and by the waves of the weary sea; still, in spite of all this I will compete, for your taunts have stung me to the quick." So he hurried up without even taking his cloak off, and seized a disc, larger, more massive and much heavier than those used by the Phaeacians when disc-throwing among themselves. Then, swinging it back, he threw it from his brawny hand, and it made a humming sound in the air as he did so. The Phaeacians quailed beneath the rushing of its flight as it sped gracefully from his hand, and flew beyond any mark that had been made yet. Minerva, in the form of a man, came and marked the place where it had fallen. "A blind man, Sir," said she, "could easily tell your mark by groping for it- it is so far ahead of any other. You may make your mind easy about this contest, for no Phaeacian can come near to such a throw as yours."

Ulysses was glad when he found he had a friend among the lookers-on, so he began to speak more pleasantly. "Young men," said he, "come up to that throw if you can, and I will throw another disc as heavy or even heavier. If anyone wants to have a bout with me let him come on, for I am exceedingly angry; I will box, wrestle, or run, I do not care what it is, with any man of you all except Laodamas, but not with him because I am his guest, and one cannot compete with one's own personal friend. At least I do not think it a prudent or a sensible thing for a guest to challenge his host's family at any game, especially when he is in a foreign country. He will cut the ground from under his own feet if he does; but I make no exception as regards any one else, for I want to have the matter out and know which is the best man. I am a good hand at every kind of athletic sport known among mankind. I am an excellent archer. In battle I am always the first to bring a man down with my arrow, no matter how many more are taking aim at him alongside of me. Philoctetes was the only man who could shoot better than I could when we Achaeans were before Troy and in practice. I far excel every one else in the whole world, of those who still eat bread upon the face of the earth, but I should not like to shoot against the mighty dead, such as Hercules, or Eurytus the Cechalian-men who could shoot against the gods themselves. This in fact was how Eurytus came prematurely by his end, for Apollo was angry with him and killed him because he challenged him as an archer. I can throw a dart farther than any one else can shoot an arrow. Running is the only point in respect of which I am afraid some of the Phaecians might beat me, for I have been brought down very low at sea; my provisions ran short, and therefore I am still weak."

They all held their peace except King Alcinous, who began, "Sir, we have had much pleasure in hearing all that you have told us, from which I understand that you are willing to show your prowess, as having been displeased with some insolent remarks that have been made to you by one of our athletes, and which could never have been uttered by any one who knows how to talk with propriety. I hope you will apprehend my meaning, and will explain to any be one of your chief men who may be dining with yourself and your family when you get home, that we have an hereditary aptitude for accomplishments of all kinds. We are not particularly remarkable for our boxing, nor yet as wrestlers, but we are singularly fleet of foot and are excellent sailors. We are extremely fond of good dinners, music, and dancing; we also like frequent changes of linen, warm baths, and good beds, so now, please, some of you who are the best dancers set about dancing, that our guest on his return home may be able to tell his friends how much we surpass all other nations as sailors, runners, dancers, minstrels. Demodocus has left his lyre at my house, so run some one or other of you and fetch it for him."

On this a servant hurried off to bring the lyre from the king's house, and the nine men who had been chosen as stewards stood forward. It was their business to manage everything connected with the sports, so they made the ground smooth and marked a wide space for the dancers. Presently the servant came back with Demodocus's lyre, and he took his place in the midst of them, whereon the best young dancers in the town began to foot and trip it so nimbly that Ulysses was delighted with the merry twinkling of their feet.

Meanwhile the bard began to sing the loves of Mars and Venus, and how they first began their intrigue in the house of Vulcan. Mars made Venus many presents, and defiled King Vulcan's marriage bed, so the sun, who saw what they were about, told Vulcan. Vulcan was very angry when he heard such dreadful news, so he went to his smithy brooding mischief, got his great anvil into its place, and began to forge some chains which none could either unloose or break, so that they might stay there in that place. When he had finished his snare he went into his bedroom and festooned the bed-posts all over with chains like cobwebs; he also let many hang down from the great beam of the ceiling. Not even a god could see them, so fine and subtle were they. As soon as he had spread the chains all over the bed, he made as though he were setting out for the fair state of Lemnos, which of all places in the world was the one he was most fond of. But Mars kept no blind look out, and as soon as he saw him start, hurried off to his house, burning with love for Venus.

Now Venus was just come in from a visit to her father Jove, and was about sitting down when Mars came inside the house, an said as he took her hand in his own, "Let us go to the couch of Vulcan: he is not at home, but is gone off to Lemnos among the Sintians, whose speech is barbarous."

She was nothing loth, so they went to the couch to take their rest, whereon they were caught in the toils which cunning Vulcan had spread for them, and could neither get up nor stir hand or foot, but found too late that they were in a trap. Then Vulcan came up to them, for he had turned back before reaching Lemnos, when his scout the sun told him what was going on. He was in a furious passion, and stood in the vestibule making a dreadful noise as he shouted to all the gods.

"Father Jove," he cried, "and all you other blessed gods who live for ever, come here and see the ridiculous and disgraceful sight that I will show you. Jove's daughter Venus is always dishonoring me because I am lame. She is in love with Mars, who is handsome and clean built, whereas I am a cripple- but my parents are to blame for that, not I; they ought never to have begotten me. Come and see the pair together asleep on my bed. It makes me furious to look at them. They are very fond of one another, but I do not think they will lie there longer than they can help, nor do I think that they will sleep much; there, however, they shall stay till her father has repaid me the sum I gave him for his baggage of a daughter, who is fair but not honest."

On this the gods gathered to the house of Vulcan. Earth-encircling Neptune came, and Mercury the bringer of luck, and King Apollo, but the goddesses stayed at home all of them for shame. Then the givers of all good things stood in the doorway, and the blessed gods roared with inextinguishable laughter, as they saw how cunning Vulcan had been, whereon one would turn towards his neighbor saying:

"Ill deeds do not prosper, and the weak confound the strong. See how limping Vulcan, lame as he is, has caught Mars who is the fleetest god in heaven; and now Mars will be cast in heavy damages."

Thus did they converse, but King Apollo said to Mercury, "Messenger Mercury, giver of good things, you would not care how strong the chains were, would you, if you could sleep with Venus?"

"King Apollo," answered Mercury, "I only wish I might get the chance, though there were three times as many chains- and you might look on, all of you, gods and goddesses, but would sleep with her if I could."

The immortal gods burst out laughing as they heard him, but Neptune took it all seriously, and kept on imploring Vulcan to set Mars free again. "Let him go," he cried, "and I will undertake, as you require, that he shall pay you all the damages that are held reasonable among the immortal gods."

"Do not," replied Vulcan, "ask me to do this; a bad man's bond is bad security; what remedy could I enforce against you if Mars should go away and leave his debts behind him along with his chains?"

"Vulcan," said Neptune, "if Mars goes away without paying his damages, I will pay you myself." So Vulcan answered, "In this case I cannot and must not refuse you."

Thereon he loosed the bonds that bound them, and as soon as they were free they scampered off, Mars to Thrace and laughter-loving Venus to Cyprus and to Paphos, where is her grove and her altar fragrant with burnt offerings. Here the Graces hathed her, and anointed her with oil of ambrosia such as the immortal gods make use of, and they clothed her in raiment of the most enchanting beauty.

Thus sang the bard, and both Ulysses and the seafaring Phaeacians were charmed as they heard him.

Then Alcinous told Laodamas and Halius to dance alone, for there was no one to compete with them. So they took a red ball which Polybus had made for them, and one of them bent himself backwards and threw it up towards the clouds, while the other jumped from off the ground and caught it with ease before it came down again. When they had done throwing the ball straight up into the air they began to dance, and at the same time kept on throwing it backwards and forwards to one another, while all the young men in the ring applauded and made a great stamping with their feet. Then Ulysses said:

"King Alcinous, you said your people were the nimblest dancers in the world, and indeed they have proved themselves to be so. I was astonished as I saw them."

The king was delighted at this, and exclaimed to the Phaecians "Aldermen and town councilors, our guest seems to be a person of singular judgement; let us give him such proof of our hospitality as he may reasonably expect. There are twelve chief men among you, and counting myself there are thirteen; contribute, each of you, a clean cloak, a shirt, and a talent of fine gold; let us give him all this in a lump down at once, so that when he gets his supper he may do so with a light heart. As for Euryalus he will have to make a formal apology and a present too, for he has been rude."

Thus did he speak. The others all of them applauded his saying, and sent their servants to fetch the presents. Then Euryalus said, "King Alcinous, I will give the stranger all the satisfaction you require. He shall have sword, which is of bronze, all but the hilt, which is of silver. I will also give him the scabbard of newly sawn ivory into which it fits. It will be worth a great deal to him."

As he spoke he placed the sword in the hands of Ulysses and said, "Good luck to you, father stranger; if anything has been said amiss may the winds blow it away with them, and may heaven grant you a safe return, for I understand you have been long away from home, and have gone through much hardship."

To which Ulysses answered, "Good luck to you too my friend, and may the gods grant you every happiness. I hope you will not miss the sword you have given me along with your apology."

With these words he girded the sword about his shoulders and towards sundown the presents began to make their appearance, as the servants of the donors kept bringing them to the house of King Alcinous; here his sons received them, and placed them under their mother's charge. Then Alcinous led the way to the house and bade his guests take their seats.

"Wife," said he, turning to Queen Arete, "Go, fetch the best chest we have, and put a clean cloak and shirt in it. Also, set a copper on the fire and heat some water; our guest will take a warm bath; see also to the careful packing of the presents that the noble Phaeacians have made him; he will thus better enjoy both his supper and the singing that will follow. I shall myself give him this golden goblet- which is of exquisite workmanship- that he may be reminded of me for the rest of his life whenever he makes a drink-offering to Jove, or to any of the gods."

Then Arete told her maids to set a large tripod upon the fire as fast as they could, whereon they set a tripod full of bath water on to a clear fire; they threw on sticks to make it blaze, and the water became hot as the flame played about the belly of the tripod. Meanwhile Arete brought a magnificent chest her own room, and inside it she packed all the beautiful presents of gold and raiment which the Phaeacians had brought. Lastly she added a cloak and a good shirt from Alcinous, and said to Ulysses:

"See to the lid yourself, and have the whole bound round at once, for fear any one should rob you by the way when you are asleep in your ship."

When Ulysses heard this he put the lid on the chest and made it fast with a bond that Circe had taught him. He had done so before an upper servant told him to come to the bath and wash himself. He was very glad of a warm bath, for he had had no one to wait upon him ever since he left the house of Calypso, who as long as he remained with her had taken as good care of him as though he had been a god. When the servants had done washing and anointing him with oil, and had given him a clean cloak and shirt, he left the bath room and joined the guests who were sitting over their wine. Lovely Nausicaa stood by one of the bearing-posts supporting the roof if the cloister, and admired him as she saw him pass. "Farewell stranger," said she, "do not forget me when you are safe at home again, for it is to me first that you owe a ransom for having saved your life."

And Ulysses said, "Nausicaa, daughter of great Alcinous, may Jove the mighty husband of Juno, grant that I may reach my home; so shall I bless you as my guardian angel all my days, for it was you who saved me."

When he had said this, he seated himself beside Alcinous. Supper was then served, and the wine was mixed for drinking. A servant led in the favorite bard Demodocus, and set him in the midst of the company, near one of the bearing-posts supporting the cloister, that he might lean against it. Then Ulysses cut off a piece of roast pork with plenty of fat (for there was abundance left on the joint) and said to a servant, "Take this piece of pork over to Demodocus and tell him to eat it; for all the pain his lays may cause me I will salute him none the less; bards are honored and respected throughout the world, for the muse teaches them their songs and loves them."

The servant carried the pork in his fingers over to Demodocus, who took it and was very much pleased. They then laid their hands on the good things that were before them, and as soon as they had had to eat and drink, Ulysses said to Demodocus, "Demodocus, there is no one in the world whom I admire more than I do you. You must have studied under the Muse, Jove's daughter, and under Apollo, so accurately do you sing the return of the Achaeans with all their sufferings and adventures. If you were not there yourself, you must have heard it all from some one who was. Now, however, change your song and tell us of the wooden horse which Epeus made with the assistance of Minerva, and which Ulysses got by stratagem into the fort of Troy after freighting it with the men who afterwards sacked the city. If you will sing this tale aright I will tell all the world how magnificently heaven has endowed you."

The bard inspired of heaven took up the story at the point where some of the Argives set fire to their tents and sailed away while others, hidden within the horse, were waiting with Ulysses in the Trojan place of assembly. For the Trojans themselves had drawn the horse into their fortress, and it stood there while they sat in council round it, and were in three minds as to what they should do. Some were for breaking it up then and there; others would have it dragged to the top of the rock on which the fortress stood, and then thrown down the precipice; while yet others were for letting it remain as an offering and propitiation for the gods. And this was how they settled it in the end, for the city was doomed when it took in that horse, within which were all the bravest of the Argives waiting to bring death and destruction on the Trojans. Anon he sang how the sons of the Achaeans issued from the horse, and sacked the town, breaking out from their ambuscade. He sang how they over ran the city hither and thither and ravaged it, and how Ulysses went raging like Mars along with Menelaus to the house of Deiphobus. It was there that the fight raged most furiously, nevertheless by Minerva's help he was victorious.

All this he told, but Ulysses was overcome as he heard him, and his cheeks were wet with tears. He wept as a woman weeps when she throws herself on the body of her husband who has fallen before his own city and people, fighting bravely in defense of his home and children. She screams aloud and flings her arms about him as he lies gasping for breath and dying, but her enemies beat her from behind about the back and shoulders, and carry her off into slavery, to a life of labor and sorrow, and the beauty fades from her cheeks- even so piteously did Ulysses weep, but none of those present perceived his tears except Alcinous, who was sitting near him, and could hear the sobs and sighs that he was heaving. The king, therefore, at once rose and said:

"Aldermen and town councilors of the Phaeacians, let Demodocus cease his song, for there are those present who do not seem to like it. From the moment that we had done supper and Demodocus began to sing, our guest has been all the time groaning and lamenting. He is evidently in great trouble, so let the bard leave off, that we may all enjoy ourselves, hosts and guest alike. This will be much more as it should be, for all these festivities, with the escort and the presents that we are making with so much good will, are wholly in his honor, and any one with even a moderate amount of right feeling knows that he ought to treat a guest and a suppliant as though he were his own brother.

"Therefore, Sir, do you on your part affect no more concealment nor reserve in the matter about which I shall ask you; it will be more polite in you to give me a plain answer; tell me the name by which your father and mother over yonder used to call you, and by which you were known among your neighbors and fellow-citizens. There is no one, neither rich nor poor, who is absolutely without any name whatever, for people's fathers and mothers give them names as soon as they are born. Tell me also your country, nation, and city, that our ships may shape their purpose accordingly and take you there. For the Phaeacians have no pilots; their vessels have no rudders as those of other nations have, but the ships themselves understand what it is that we are thinking about and want; they know all the cities and countries in the whole world, and can traverse the sea just as well even when it is covered with mist and cloud, so that there is no danger of being wrecked or coming to any harm. Still I do remember hearing my father say that Neptune was angry with us for being too easy-going in the matter of giving people escorts. He said that one of these days he should wreck a ship of ours as it was returning from having escorted some one, and bury our city under a high mountain. This is what my used to say, but whether the god will carry out his threat or no is a matter which he will decide for himself.

"And now, tell me and tell me true. Where have you been wandering, and in what countries have you traveled? Tell us of the peoples themselves, and of their cities- who were hostile, savage and uncivilized, and who, on the other hand, hospitable and humane. Tell us also why you are made unhappy on hearing about the return of the Argive Danaans from Troy. The gods arranged all this, and sent them their misfortunes in order that future generations might have something to sing about. Did you lose some brave kinsman of your wife's when you were before Troy? a son-in-law or father-in-law- which are the nearest relations a man has outside his own flesh and blood? or was it some brave and kindly-natured comrade- for a good friend is as dear to a man as his own brother?"

Lesson 47

- Read Book 9 of *The Odyssey*.

Book 9

And Ulysses answered, "King Alcinous, it is a good thing to hear a bard with such a divine voice as this man has. There is nothing better or more delightful than when a whole people make merry together, with the guests sitting orderly to listen, while the table is loaded with bread and meats, and the cup-bearer draws wine and fills his cup for every man. This is indeed as fair a sight as a man can see. Now, however, since you are inclined to ask the story of my sorrows, and rekindle my own sad memories in respect of them, I do not know how to begin, nor yet how to continue and conclude my tale, for the hand of heaven has been laid heavily upon me.

"Firstly, then, I will tell you my name that you too may know it, and one day, if I outlive this time of sorrow, may become my there guests though I live so far away from all of you. I am Ulysses son of Laertes, renowned among mankind for all manner of subtlety, so that my fame ascends to heaven. I live in Ithaca, where there is a high mountain called Neritum, covered with forests; and not far from it there is a group of islands very near to one another- Dulichium, Same, and the wooded island of Zacynthus. It lies squat on the horizon, all highest up in the sea towards the sunset, while the others lie away from it towards dawn. It is a rugged island, but it breeds brave men, and my eyes know none that they better love to look upon. The goddess Calypso kept me with her in her cave, and wanted me to marry her, as did also the cunning Aeaean goddess Circe; but they could neither of them persuade me, for there is nothing dearer to a man than his own country and his parents, and however splendid a home he may have in a foreign country, if it be far from father or mother, he does not care about it. Now, however, I will tell you of the many hazardous adventures which by Jove's will I met with on my return from Troy.

"When I had set sail thence the wind took me first to Ismarus, which is the city of the Cicons. There I sacked the town and put the people to the sword. We took their wives and also much booty, which we divided equitably amongst us, so that none might have reason to complain. I then said that we had better make off at once, but my men very foolishly would not obey me, so they stayed there drinking much wine and killing great numbers of sheep and oxen on the sea shore. Meanwhile the Cicons cried out for help to other Cicons who lived inland. These were more in number, and stronger, and they were more skilled in the art of war, for they could fight, either from chariots or on foot as the occasion served; in the morning, therefore, they came as thick as leaves and bloom in summer, and the hand of heaven was against us, so that we were hard pressed. They set the battle in array near the ships, and the hosts aimed their bronze-shod spears at one another. So long as the day waxed and it was still morning, we held our own against them, though they were more in number than we; but as the sun went down, towards the time when men loose their oxen, the Cicons got the better of us, and we lost half a dozen men from every ship we had; so we got away with those that were left.

"Thence we sailed onward with sorrow in our hearts, but glad to have escaped death though we had lost our comrades, nor did we leave till we had thrice invoked each one of the poor fellows who had perished by the hands of the Cicons. Then Jove raised the North wind against us till it blew a hurricane, so that land and sky were hidden in thick clouds, and night sprang forth out of the heavens. We let the ships run before the gale, but the force of the wind tore our sails to tatters, so we took them down for fear of shipwreck, and rowed our hardest towards the land. There we lay two days and two nights suffering much alike from toil and distress of mind, but on the morning of the third day we again raised our masts, set sail, and took our places, letting the wind and steersmen direct our ship. I should have got home at that time unharmed had not the North wind and the currents been against me as I was doubling Cape Malea, and set me off my course hard by the island of Cythera.

"I was driven thence by foul winds for a space of nine days upon the sea, but on the tenth day we reached the land of the Lotus-eater, who live on a food that comes from a kind of flower. Here we landed to take in fresh water, and our crews got their mid-day meal on the shore near the ships. When they had eaten and drunk I sent two of my company to see what manner of men the people of the place might be, and they had a third man under them. They started at once, and went about among the Lotus-eaters, who did them no hurt, but gave them to eat of the lotus, which was so delicious that those who ate of it left off caring about home, and did not even want to go back and say what had happened to them, but were for staying and munching lotus with the Lotus-eater without thinking further of their return; nevertheless, though they wept bitterly I forced them back to the ships and made them fast under the benches. Then I told the rest to go on board at once, lest any of them should taste of the lotus and leave off wanting to get home, so they took their places and smote the grey sea with their oars.

"We sailed hence, always in much distress, till we came to the land of the lawless and inhuman Cyclopes. Now the Cyclopes neither plant nor plow, but trust in providence, and live on such wheat, barley, and grapes as grow wild without any kind of tillage, and their wild grapes yield them wine as the sun and the rain may grow them. They have no laws nor assemblies of the people, but live in caves on the tops of high mountains; each is lord and master in his family, and they take no account of their neighbors.

"Now off their harbor there lies a wooded and fertile island not quite close to the land of the Cyclopes, but still not far. It is overrun with wild goats, that breed there in great numbers and are never disturbed by foot of man; for sportsmen- who as a rule will suffer so much hardship in forest or among mountain precipices- do not go there, nor yet again is it ever plowed or fed down, but it lies a wilderness untilled and unsown from year to year, and has no living thing upon it but only goats. For the Cyclopes have no ships, nor yet shipwrights who could make ships for them; they cannot therefore go from city to city, or sail over the sea to one another's country as people who have ships can do; if they had had these they would have colonized the island, for it is a very good one, and would yield everything in due season. There are meadows that in some places come right down to the sea shore, well watered and full of luscious grass; grapes would do there excellently; there is level land for plowing, and it would always yield heavily at harvest time, for the soil is deep. There is a good harbor where no cables are wanted, nor yet anchors, nor need a ship be moored, but all one has to do is to beach one's vessel and stay there till the wind becomes fair for putting out to sea again. At the head of the harbor there is a spring of clear water coming out of a cave, and there are poplars growing all round it.

"Here we entered, but so dark was the night that some god must have brought us in, for there was nothing whatever to be seen. A thick mist hung all round our ships; the moon was hidden behind a mass of clouds so that no one could have seen the island if he had looked for it, nor were there any breakers to tell us we were close in shore before we found ourselves upon the land itself; when, however, we had beached the ships, we took down the sails, went ashore and camped upon the beach till daybreak.

"When the child of morning, rosy-fingered Dawn, appeared, we admired the island and wandered all over it, while the nymphs Jove's daughters roused the wild goats that we might get some meat for our dinner. On this we fetched our spears and bows and arrows from the ships, and dividing ourselves into three bands began to shoot the goats. Heaven sent us excellent sport; I had twelve ships with me, and each ship got nine goats, while my own ship had ten; thus through the livelong day to the going down of the sun we ate and drank our fill, and we had plenty of wine left, for each one of us had taken many jars full when we sacked the city of the Cicons, and this had not yet run out. While we were feasting we kept turning our eyes towards the land of the Cyclopes, which was hard by, and saw the smoke of their stubble fires. We could almost fancy we heard their voices and the bleating of their sheep and goats, but when the sun went down and it came on dark, we camped down upon the beach, and next morning I called a council.

"'Stay here, my brave fellows,' said I, 'all the rest of you, while I go with my ship and exploit these people myself: I want to see if they are uncivilized savages, or a hospitable and humane race.'

"I went on board, bidding my men to do so also and loose the hawsers; so they took their places and smote the grey sea with their oars. When we got to the land, which was not far, there, on the face of a cliff near the sea, we saw a great cave overhung with laurels. It was a station for a great many sheep and goats, and outside there was a large yard, with a high wall round it made of stones built into the ground and of trees both pine and oak. This was the abode of a huge monster who was then away from home shepherding his flocks. He would have nothing to do with other people, but led the life of an outlaw. He was a horrid creature, not like a human being at all, but resembling rather some crag that stands out boldly against the sky on the top of a high mountain.

"I told my men to draw the ship ashore, and stay where they were, all but the twelve best among them, who were to go along with myself. I also took a goatskin of sweet black wine which had been given me by Maron, Apollo son of Euanthes, who was priest of Apollo the patron god of Ismarus, and lived within the wooded precincts of the temple. When we were sacking the city we respected him, and spared his life, as also his wife and child; so he made me some presents of great value- seven talents of fine gold, and a bowl of silver, with twelve jars of sweet wine, unblended, and of the most exquisite flavor. Not a man nor maid in the house knew about it, but only himself, his wife, and one housekeeper: when he drank it he mixed twenty parts of water to one of wine, and yet the fragrance from the mixing-bowl was so exquisite that it was impossible to refrain from drinking. I filled a large skin with this wine, and took a wallet full of provisions with me, for my mind misgave me that I might have to deal with some savage who would be of great strength, and would respect neither right nor law.

"We soon reached his cave, but he was out shepherding, so we went inside and took stock of all that we could see. His cheese-racks were loaded with cheeses, and he had more lambs and kids than his pens could hold. They were kept in separate flocks; first there were the hoggets [young sheep], then the oldest of the younger lambs and lastly the very young ones all kept apart from one another; as for his dairy, all the vessels, bowls, and milk pails into which he milked, were swimming with whey. When they saw all this, my men begged me to let them first steal some cheeses, and make off with them to the ship; they would then return, drive down the lambs and kids, put them on board and sail away with them. It would have been indeed better if we had done so but I would not listen to them, for I wanted to see the owner himself, in the hope that he might give me a present. When, however, we saw him my poor men found him ill to deal with.

"We lit a fire, offered some of the cheeses in sacrifice, ate others of them, and then sat waiting till the Cyclops should come in with his sheep. When he came, he brought in with him a huge load of dry firewood to light the fire for his supper, and this he flung with such a noise on to the floor of his cave that we hid ourselves for fear at the far end of the cavern. Meanwhile he drove all the ewes inside, as well as the she-goats that he was going to milk, leaving the males, both rams and he-goats, outside in the yards. Then he rolled a huge stone to the mouth of the cave- so huge that two and twenty strong four-wheeled wagons would not be enough to draw it from its place against the doorway. When he had so done he sat down and milked his ewes and goats, all in due course, and then let each of them have her own young. He curdled half the milk and set it aside in wicker strainers, but the other half he poured into bowls that he might drink it for his supper. When he had got through with all his work, he lit the fire, and then caught sight of us, whereon he said:

"'Strangers, who are you? Where do sail from? Are you traders, or do you sail the as rovers, with your hands against every man, and every man's hand against you?'

"We were frightened out of our senses by his loud voice and monstrous form, but I managed to say, 'We are Achaeans on our way home from Troy, but by the will of Jove, and stress of weather, we have been driven far out of our course. We are the people of Agamemnon, son of Atreus, who has won infinite renown throughout the whole world, by sacking so great a city and killing so many people. We therefore humbly pray you to show us some hospitality, and otherwise make us such presents as visitors may reasonably expect. May your excellency fear the wrath of heaven, for we are your suppliants, and Jove takes all respectable travelers under his protection, for he is the avenger of all suppliants and foreigners in distress.'

"To this he gave me but a pitiless answer, 'Stranger,' said he, 'you are a fool, or else you know nothing of this country. Talk to me, indeed, about fearing the gods or shunning their anger? We Cyclopes do not care about Jove or any of your blessed gods, for we are ever so much stronger than they. I shall not spare either yourself or your companions out of any regard for Jove, unless I am in the humor for doing so. And now tell me where you made your ship fast when you came on shore. Was it round the point, or is she lying straight off the land?'

"He said this to draw me out, but I was too cunning to be caught in that way, so I answered with a lie; 'Neptune,' said I, 'sent my ship on to the rocks at the far end of your country, and wrecked it. We were driven on to them from the open sea, but I and those who are with me escaped the jaws of death.'

"The cruel wretch vouchsafed me not one word of answer, but with a sudden clutch he gripped up two of my men at once and dashed them down upon the ground as though they had been puppies. Their brains were shed upon the ground, and the earth was wet with their blood. Then he tore them limb from limb and supped upon them. He gobbled them up like a lion in the wilderness, flesh, bones, marrow, and entrails, without leaving anything uneaten. As for us, we wept and lifted up our hands to heaven on seeing such a horrid sight, for we did not know what else to do; but when the Cyclops had filled his huge paunch, and had washed down his meal of human flesh with a drink of neat milk, he stretched himself full length upon the ground among his sheep, and went to sleep. I was at first inclined to seize my sword, draw it, and drive it into his vitals, but I reflected that if I did we should all certainly be lost, for we should never be able to shift the stone which the monster had put in front of the door. So we stayed sobbing and sighing where we were till morning came.

"When the child of morning, rosy-fingered Dawn, appeared, he again lit his fire, milked his goats and ewes, all quite rightly, and then let each have her own young one; as soon as he had got through with all his work, he clutched up two more of my men, and began eating them for his morning's meal. Presently, with the utmost ease, he rolled the stone away from the door and drove out his sheep, but he at once put it back again- as easily as though he were merely clapping the lid on to a quiver full of arrows. As soon as he had done so he shouted, and cried 'Shoo, shoo,' after his sheep to drive them on to the mountain; so I was left to scheme some way of taking my revenge and covering myself with glory.

"In the end I deemed it would be the best plan to do as follows. The Cyclops had a great club which was lying near one of the sheep pens; it was of green olive wood, and he had cut it intending to use it for a staff as soon as it should be dry. It was so huge that we could only compare it to the mast of a twenty-oared merchant vessel of large burden, and able to venture out into open sea. I went up to this club and cut off about six feet of it; I then gave this piece to the men and told them to fine it evenly off at one end, which they proceeded to do, and lastly I brought it to a point myself, charring the end in the fire to make it harder. When I had done this I hid it under dung, which was lying about all over the cave, and told the men to cast lots which of them should venture along with myself to lift it and bore it into the monster's eye while he was asleep. The lot fell upon the very four whom I should have chosen, and I myself made five. In the evening the wretch came back from shepherding, and drove his flocks into the cave - this time driving them all inside, and not leaving any in the yards; I suppose some fancy must have taken him, or a god must have prompted him to do so. As soon as he had put the stone back to its place against the door, he sat down, milked his ewes and his goats all quite rightly, and then let each have her own young one; when he had got through with all this work, he gripped up two more of my men, and made his supper off them. So I went up to him with an ivy-wood bowl of black wine in my hands:

"'Look here, Cyclops,' said I, you have been eating a great deal of man's flesh, so take this and drink some wine, that you may see what kind of liquor we had on board my ship. I was bringing it to you as a drink-offering, in the hope that you would take compassion upon me and further me on my way home, whereas all you do is to go on ramping and raving most intolerably. You ought to be ashamed yourself; how can you expect people to come see you any more if you treat them in this way?'

"He then took the cup and drank. He was so delighted with the taste of the wine that he begged me for another bowl full. 'Be so kind,' he said, 'as to give me some more, and tell me your name at once. I want to make you a present that you will be glad to have. We have wine even in this country, for our soil grows grapes and the sun ripens them, but this drinks like nectar and ambrosia all in one.'

"I then gave him some more; three times did I fill the bowl for him, and three times did he drain it without thought or heed; then, when I saw that the wine had got into his head, I said to him as plausibly as I could: 'Cyclops, you ask my name and I will tell it you; give me, therefore, the present you promised me; my name is Noman; this is what my father and mother and my friends have always called me.'

"But the cruel wretch said, 'Then I will eat all Noman's comrades before Noman himself, and will keep Noman for the last. This is the present that I will make him.'

As he spoke he reeled, and fell sprawling face upwards on the ground. His great neck hung heavily backwards and a deep sleep took hold upon him. Presently he turned sick, and threw up both wine and the gobbets of human flesh on which he had been gorging, for he was very drunk. Then I thrust the beam of wood far into the embers to heat it, and encouraged my men lest any of them should turn faint-hearted. When the wood, green though it was, was about to blaze, I drew it out of the fire glowing with heat, and my men gathered round me, for heaven had filled their hearts with courage. We drove the sharp end of the beam into the monster's eye, and bearing upon it with all my weight I kept turning it round and round as though I were boring a hole in a ship's plank with an auger, which two men with a wheel and strap can keep on turning as long as they choose. Even thus did we bore the red hot beam into his eye, till the boiling blood bubbled all over it as we worked it round and round, so that the steam from the burning eyeball scalded his eyelids and eyebrows, and the roots of the eye sputtered in the fire. As a blacksmith plunges an ax or hatchet into cold water to temper it- for it is this that gives strength to the iron- and it makes a great hiss as he does so, even thus did the Cyclops' eye hiss round the beam of olive wood, and his hideous yells made the cave ring again. We ran away in a fright, but he plucked the beam all besmirched with gore from his eye, and hurled it from him in a frenzy of rage and pain, shouting as he did so to the other Cyclopes who lived on the bleak headlands near him; so they gathered from all quarters round his cave when they heard him crying, and asked what was the matter with him.

"'What ails you, Polyphemus,' said they, 'that you make such a noise, breaking the stillness of the night, and preventing us from being able to sleep? Surely no man is carrying off your sheep? Surely no man is trying to kill you either by fraud or by force?'

"But Polyphemus shouted to them from inside the cave, 'Noman is killing me by fraud! Noman is killing me by force!'

"'Then,' said they, 'if no man is attacking you, you must be ill; when Jove makes people ill, there is no help for it, and you had better pray to your father Neptune.'

"Then they went away, and I laughed inwardly at the success of my clever stratagem, but the Cyclops, groaning and in an agony of pain, felt about with his hands till he found the stone and took it from the door; then he sat in the doorway and stretched his hands in front of it to catch anyone going out with the sheep, for he thought I might be foolish enough to attempt this.

"As for myself I kept on puzzling to think how I could best save my own life and those of my companions; I schemed and schemed, as one who knows that his life depends upon it, for the danger was very great. In the end I deemed that this plan would be the best. The male sheep were well grown, and carried a heavy black fleece, so I bound them noiselessly in threes together, with some of the withies [branches] on which the wicked monster used to sleep. There was to be a man under the middle sheep, and the two on either side were to cover him, so that there were three sheep to each man. As for myself there was a ram finer than any of the others, so I caught hold of him by the back, ensconced myself in the thick wool under his belly, and flung on patiently to his fleece, face upwards, keeping a firm hold on it all the time.

"Thus, then, did we wait in great fear of mind till morning came, but when the child of morning, rosy-fingered Dawn, appeared, the male sheep hurried out to feed, while the ewes remained bleating about the pens waiting to be milked, for their udders were full to bursting; but their master in spite of all his pain felt the backs of all the sheep as they stood upright, without being sharp enough to find out that the men were underneath their bellies. As the ram was going out, last of all, heavy with its fleece and with the weight of my crafty self; Polyphemus laid hold of it and said:

"'My good ram, what is it that makes you the last to leave my cave this morning? You are not wont to let the ewes go before you, but lead the mob with a run whether to flowery mead or bubbling fountain, and are the first to come home again at night; but now you lag last of all. Is it because you know your master has lost his eye, and are sorry because that wicked Noman and his horrid crew have got him down in his drink and blinded him? But I will have his life yet. If you could understand and talk, you would tell me where the wretch is hiding, and I would dash his brains upon the ground till they flew all over the cave. I should thus have some satisfaction for the harm a this no-good Noman has done me.'

"As spoke he drove the ram outside, but when we were a little way out from the cave and yards, I first got from under the ram's belly, and then freed my comrades; as for the sheep, which were very fat, by constantly heading them in the right direction we managed to drive them down to the ship. The crew rejoiced greatly at seeing those of us who had escaped death, but wept for the others whom the Cyclops had killed. However, I made signs to them by nodding and frowning that they were to hush their crying, and told them to get all the sheep on board at once and put out to sea; so they went aboard, took their places, and smote the grey sea with their oars. Then, when I had got as far out as my voice would reach, I began to jeer at the Cyclops.

"'Cyclops,' said I, 'you should have taken better measure of your man before eating up his comrades in your cave. You wretch, eat up your visitors in your own house?

You might have known that your sin would find you out, and now Jove and the other gods have punished you.'

"He got more and more furious as he heard me, so he tore the top from off a high mountain, and flung it just in front of my ship so that it was within a little of hitting the end of the rudder. The sea quaked as the rock fell into it, and the wash of the wave it raised carried us back towards the mainland, and forced us towards the shore. But I snatched up a long pole and kept the ship off, making signs to my men by nodding my head, that they must row for their lives, whereon they laid out with a will. When we had got twice as far as we were before, I was for jeering at the Cyclops again, but the men begged and prayed of me to hold my tongue.

"'Do not,' they exclaimed, 'be mad enough to provoke this savage creature further; he has thrown one rock at us already which drove us back again to the mainland, and we made sure it had been the death of us; if he had then heard any further sound of voices he would have pounded our heads and our ship's timbers into a jelly with the rugged rocks he would have heaved at us, for he can throw them a long way.'

"But I would not listen to them, and shouted out to him in my rage, 'Cyclops, if any one asks you who it was that put your eye out and spoiled your beauty, say it was the valiant warrior Ulysses, son of Laertes, who lives in Ithaca.'

"On this he groaned, and cried out, 'Alas, alas, then the old prophecy about me is coming true. There was a prophet here, at one time, a man both brave and of great stature, Telemus son of Eurymus, who was an excellent seer, and did all the prophesying for the Cyclopes till he grew old; he told me that all this would happen to me some day, and said I should lose my sight by the hand of Ulysses. I have been all along expecting some one of imposing presence and superhuman strength, whereas he turns out to be a little insignificant weakling, who has managed to blind my eye by taking advantage of me in my drink; come here, then, Ulysses, that I may make you presents to show my hospitality, and urge Neptune to help you forward on your journey- for Neptune and I are father and son. He, if he so will, shall heal me, which no one else neither god nor man can do.'

"Then I said, 'I wish I could be as sure of killing you outright and sending you down to the house of Hades, as I am that it will take more than Neptune to cure that eye of yours.'

"On this he lifted up his hands to the firmament of heaven and prayed, saying, 'Hear me, great Neptune; if I am indeed your own true-begotten son, grant that Ulysses may never reach his home alive; or if he must get back to his friends at last, let him do so late and in sore plight after losing all his men [let him reach his home in another man's ship and find trouble in his house.']

"Thus did he pray, and Neptune heard his prayer. Then he picked up a rock much larger than the first, swung it aloft and hurled it with prodigious force. It fell just short of the ship, but was within a little of hitting the end of the rudder. The sea quaked as the rock fell into it, and the wash of the wave it raised drove us onwards on our way towards the shore of the island.

"When at last we got to the island where we had left the rest of our ships, we found our comrades lamenting us, and anxiously awaiting our return. We ran our vessel upon the sands and got out of her on to the sea shore; we also landed the Cyclops' sheep, and divided them equitably amongst us so that none might have reason to complain. As for the ram, my companions agreed that I should have it as an extra share; so I sacrificed it on the sea shore, and burned its thigh bones to Jove, who is the lord of all. But he heeded not my sacrifice, and only thought how he might destroy my ships and my comrades.

"Thus through the livelong day to the going down of the sun we feasted our fill on meat and drink, but when the sun went down and it came on dark, we camped upon the beach. When the child of morning, rosy-fingered Dawn, appeared, I bade my men on board and loose the hawsers. Then they took their places and smote the grey sea with their oars; so we sailed on with sorrow in our hearts, but glad to have escaped death though we had lost our comrades.

Lesson 48

- Read Book 10 of *The Odyssey*.

Book 10

"Thence we went on to the Aeoli island where lives Aeolus son of Hippotas, dear to the immortal gods. It is an island that floats (as it were) upon the sea, iron bound with a wall that girds it. Now, Aeolus has six daughters and six lusty sons, so he made the sons marry the daughters, and they all live with their dear father and mother, feasting and enjoying every conceivable kind of luxury. All day long the atmosphere of the house is loaded with the savor of roasting meats till it groans again, yard and all; but by night they sleep on their well-made bedsteads, each with his own wife between the blankets. These were the people among whom we had now come.

"Aeolus entertained me for a whole month asking me questions all the time about Troy, the Argive fleet, and the return of the Achaeans. I told him exactly how everything had happened, and when I said I must go, and asked him to further me on my way, he made no sort of difficulty, but set about doing so at once. Moreover, he flayed me a prime ox-hide to hold the ways of the roaring winds, which he shut up in the hide as in a sack- for Jove had made him captain over the winds, and he could stir or still each one of them according to his own pleasure. He put the sack in the ship and bound the mouth so tightly with a silver thread that not even a breath of a side-wind could blow from any quarter. The West wind which was fair for us did he alone let blow as it chose; but it all came to nothing, for we were lost through our own folly.

"Nine days and nine nights did we sail, and on the tenth day our native land showed on the horizon. We got so close in that we could see the stubble fires burning, and I, being then dead beat, fell into a light sleep, for I had never let the rudder out of my own hands, that we might get home the faster. On this the men fell to talking among themselves, and said I was bringing back gold and silver in the sack that Aeolus had given me. 'Bless my heart,' would one turn to his neighbor, saying, 'how this man gets honored and makes friends to whatever city or country he may go. See what fine prizes he is taking home from Troy, while we, who have traveled just as far as he has, come back with hands as empty as we set out with- and now Aeolus has given him ever so much more. Quick- let us see what it all is, and how much gold and silver there is in the sack he gave him.'

"Thus they talked and evil counsels prevailed. They loosed the sack, whereupon the wind flew howling forth and raised a storm that carried us weeping out to sea and away from our own country. Then I awoke, and knew not whether to throw myself into the sea or to live on and make the best of it; but I bore it, covered myself up, and lay down in the ship, while the men lamented bitterly as the fierce winds bore our fleet back to the Aeolian island.

"When we reached it we went ashore to take in water, and dined hard by the ships. Immediately after dinner I took a herald and one of my men and went straight to the house of Aeolus, where I found him feasting with his wife and family; so we sat down as suppliants on the threshold. They were astounded when they saw us and said, 'Ulysses, what brings you here? What god has been ill-treating you? We took great pains to further you on your way home to Ithaca, or wherever it was that you wanted to go to.'

"Thus did they speak, but I answered sorrowfully, 'My men have undone me; they, and cruel sleep, have ruined me. My friends, mend me this mischief, for you can if you will.'

"I spoke as movingly as I could, but they said nothing, till their father answered, 'Vilest of mankind, get you gone at once out of the island; him whom heaven hates will I in no wise help. Be off, for you come here as one abhorred of heaven." And with these words he sent me sorrowing from his door.

"Thence we sailed sadly on till the men were worn out with long and fruitless rowing, for there was no longer any wind to help them. Six days, night and day did we toil, and on the seventh day we reached the rocky stronghold of Lamus-Telepylus, the city of the Laestrygonians, where the shepherd who is driving in his sheep and goats [to be milked] salutes him who is driving out his flock [to feed] and this last answers the salute. In that country a man who could do without sleep might earn double wages, one as a herdsman of cattle, and another as a shepherd, for they work much the same by night as they do by day.

"When we reached the harbor we found it land-locked under steep cliffs, with a narrow entrance between two headlands. My captains took all their ships inside, and made them fast close to one another, for there was never so much as a breath of wind inside, but it was always dead calm. I kept my own ship outside, and moored it to a rock at the very end of the point; then I climbed a high rock to reconnoiter, but could see no sign neither of man nor cattle, only some smoke rising from the ground. So I sent two of my company with an attendant to find out what sort of people the inhabitants were.

"The men when they got on shore followed a level road by which the people draw their firewood from the mountains into the town, till presently they met a young woman who had come outside to fetch water, and who was daughter to a Laestrygonian named Antiphates. She was going to the fountain Artacia from which the people bring in their water, and when my men had come close up to her, they asked her who the king of that country might be, and over what kind of people he ruled; so she directed them to her father's house, but when they got there they found his wife to be a giantess as huge as a mountain, and they were horrified at the sight of her.

"She at once called her husband Antiphates from the place of assembly, and forthwith he set about killing my men. He snatched up one of them, and began to make his dinner off him then and there, whereon the other two ran back to the ships as fast as ever they could. But Antiphates raised a hue and cry after them, and thousands of sturdy Laestrygonians sprang up from every quarter- ogres, not men. They threw vast rocks at us from the cliffs as though they had been mere stones, and I heard the horrid sound of the ships crunching up against one another, and the death cries of my men, as the Laestrygonians speared them like fishes and took them home to eat them. While they were thus killing my men within the harbor I drew my sword, cut the cable of my own ship, and told my men to row with all their might if they too would not fare like the rest; so they laid out for their lives, and we were thankful enough when we got into open water out of reach of the rocks they hurled at us. As for the others there was not one of them left.

"Thence we sailed sadly on, glad to have escaped death, though we had lost our comrades, and came to the Aeaean island, where Circe lives a great and cunning goddess who is own sister to the magician Aeetes- for they are both children of the sun by Perse, who is daughter to Oceanus. We brought our ship into a safe harbor without a word, for some god guided us thither, and having landed we there for two days and two nights, worn out in body and mind. When the morning of the third day came I took my spear and my sword, and went away from the ship to reconnoiter, and see if I could discover signs of human handiwork, or hear the sound of voices. Climbing to the top of a high look-out I espied the smoke of Circe's house rising upwards amid a dense forest of trees, and when I saw this I doubted whether, having seen the smoke, I would not go on at once and find out more, but in the end I deemed it best to go back to the ship, give the men their dinners, and send some of them instead of going myself.

"When I had nearly got back to the ship some god took pity upon my solitude, and sent a fine antlered stag right into the middle of my path. He was coming down his pasture in the forest to drink of the river, for the heat of the sun drove him, and as he passed I struck him in the middle of the back; the bronze point of the spear went clean through him, and he lay groaning in the dust until the life went out of him. Then I set my foot upon him, drew my spear from the wound, and laid it down; I also gathered rough grass and rushes and twisted them into a fathom or so of good stout rope, with which I bound the four feet of the noble creature together; having so done I hung him round my neck and walked back to the ship leaning upon my spear, for the stag was much too big for me to be able to carry him on my shoulder, steadying him with one hand. As I threw him down in front of the ship, I called the men and spoke cheeringly man by man to each of them. 'Look here my friends,' said I, 'we are not going to die so much before our time after all, and at any rate we will not starve so long as we have got something to eat and drink on board.' On this they uncovered their heads upon the sea shore and admired the stag, for he was indeed a splendid fellow. Then, when they had feasted their eyes upon him sufficiently, they washed their hands and began to cook him for dinner.

"Thus through the livelong day to the going down of the sun we stayed there eating and drinking our fill, but when the sun went down and it came on dark, we camped upon the sea shore. When the child of morning, fingered Dawn, appeared, I called a council and said, 'My friends, we are in very great difficulties; listen therefore to me. We have no idea where the sun either sets or rises, so that we do not even know East from West. I see no way out of it; nevertheless, we must try and find one. We are certainly on an island, for I went as high as I could this morning, and saw the sea reaching all round it to the horizon; it lies low, but towards the middle I saw smoke rising from out of a thick forest of trees.'

"Their hearts sank as they heard me, for they remembered how they had been treated by the Laestrygonian Antiphates, and by the savage ogre Polyphemus. They wept bitterly in their dismay, but there was nothing to be got by crying, so I divided them into two companies and set a captain over each; I gave one company to Eurylochus, while I took command of the other myself. Then we cast lots in a helmet, and the lot fell upon Eurylochus; so he set out with his twenty-two men, and they wept, as also did we who were left behind.

"When they reached Circe's house they found it built of cut stones, on a site that could be seen from far, in the middle of the forest. There were wild mountain wolves and lions prowling all round it- poor bewitched creatures whom she had tamed by her enchantments and drugged into subjection. They did not attack my men, but wagged their great tails, fawned upon them, and rubbed their noses lovingly against them. As hounds crowd round their master when they see him coming from dinner- for they know he will bring them something- even so did these wolves and lions with their great claws fawn upon my men, but the men were terribly frightened at seeing such strange creatures. Presently they reached the gates of the goddess's house, and as they stood there they could hear Circe within, singing most beautifully as she worked at her loom, making a web so fine, so soft, and of such dazzling colors as no one but a goddess could weave. On this Polites, whom I valued and trusted more than any other of my men, said, 'There is some one inside working at a loom and singing most beautifully; the whole place resounds with it, let us call her and see whether she is woman or goddess.'

"They called her and she came down, unfastened the door, and bade them enter. They, thinking no evil, followed her, all except Eurylochus, who suspected mischief and stayed outside. When she had got them into her house, she set them upon benches and seats and mixed them a mess with cheese, honey, meal, and Pramnian but she drugged it with wicked poisons to make them forget their homes, and when they had drunk she turned them into pigs by a stroke of her wand, and shut them up in her pigsties. They were like pigs-head, hair, and all, and they grunted just as pigs do; but their senses were the same as before, and they remembered everything.

"Thus then were they shut up squealing, and Circe threw them some acorns and beech masts such as pigs eat, but Eurylochus hurried back to tell me about the sad fate of our comrades. He was so overcome with dismay that though he tried to speak he could find no words to do so; his eyes filled with tears and he could only sob and sigh, till at last we forced his story out of him, and he told us what had happened to the others.

"'We went,' said he, 'as you told us, through the forest, and in the middle of it there was a fine house built with cut stones in a place that could be seen from far. There we found a woman, or else she was a goddess, working at her loom and singing sweetly; so the men shouted to her and called her, whereon she at once came down, opened the door, and invited us in. The others did not suspect any mischief so they followed her into the house, but I stayed where I was, for I thought there might be some treachery. From that moment I saw them no more, for not one of them ever came out, though I sat a long time watching for them.'

"Then I took my sword of bronze and slung it over my shoulders; I also took my bow, and told Eurylochus to come back with me and show me the way. But he laid hold of me with both his hands and spoke piteously, saying, 'Sir, do not force me to go with you, but let me stay here, for I know you will not bring one of them back with you, nor even return alive yourself; let us rather see if we cannot escape at any rate with the few that are left us, for we may still save our lives.'

"'Stay where you are, then,' answered I, 'eating and drinking at the ship, but I must go, for I am most urgently bound to do so.'

"With this I left the ship and went up inland. When I got through the charmed grove, and was near the great house of the enchantress Circe, I met Mercury with his golden wand, disguised as a young man in the hey-day of his youth and beauty with the down just coming upon his face. He came up to me and took my hand within his own, saying, 'My poor unhappy man, whither are you going over this mountain top, alone and without knowing the way? Your men are shut up in Circe's pigsties, like so many wild boars in their lairs. You surely do not fancy that you can set them free? I can tell you that you will never get back and will have to stay there with the rest of them. But never mind, I will protect you and get you out of your difficulty. Take this herb, which is one of great virtue, and keep it about you when you go to Circe's house, it will be a talisman to you against every kind of mischief.

"'And I will tell you of all the wicked witchcraft that Circe will try to practice upon you. She will mix a mess for you to drink, and she will drug the meal with which she makes it, but she will not be able to charm you, for the virtue of the herb that I shall give you will prevent her spells from working. I will tell you all about it. When Circe strikes you with her wand, draw your sword and spring upon her as though you were goings to kill her. She will then be frightened and will desire you to go to bed with her; on this you must not point blank refuse her, for you want her to set your companions free, and to take good care also of yourself, but you make her swear solemnly by all the blessed that she will plot no further mischief against you, or else when she has got you naked she will unman you and make you fit for nothing.'

"As he spoke he pulled the herb out of the ground and showed me what it was like. The root was black, while the flower was as white as milk; the gods call it Moly, and mortal men cannot uproot it, but the gods can do whatever they like.

"Then Mercury went back to high Olympus passing over the wooded island; but I fared onward to the house of Circe, and my heart was clouded with care as I walked along. When I got to the gates I stood there and called the goddess, and as soon as she heard me she came down, opened the door, and asked me to come in; so I followed her- much troubled in my mind. She set me on a richly decorated seat inlaid with silver, there was a footstool also under my feet, and she mixed a mess in a golden goblet for me to drink; but she drugged it, for she meant me mischief. When she had given it me, and I had drunk it without its charming me, she struck me with her wand. 'There now,' she cried, 'be off to the pigsty, and make your lair with the rest of them.'

"But I rushed at her with my sword drawn as though I would kill her, whereon she fell with a loud scream, clasped my knees, and spoke piteously, saying, 'Who and whence are you? from what place and people have you come? How can it be that my drugs have no power to charm you? Never yet was any man able to stand so much as a taste of the herb I gave you; you must be spell-proof; surely you can be none other than the bold hero Ulysses, who Mercury always said would come here some day with his ship while on his way home form Troy; so be it then; sheathe your sword and let us go to bed, that we may make friends and learn to trust each other.'

"And I answered, 'Circe, how can you expect me to be friendly with you when you have just been turning all my men into pigs? And now that you have got me here myself, you mean me mischief when you ask me to go to bed with you, and will unman me and make me fit for nothing. I shall certainly not consent to go to bed with you unless you will first take your solemn oath to plot no further harm against me.'

"So she swore at once as I had told her, and when she had completed her oath then I went to bed with her.

"Meanwhile her four servants, who are her housemaids, set about their work. They are the children of the groves and fountains, and of the holy waters that run down into the sea. One of them spread a fair purple cloth over a seat, and laid a carpet underneath it. Another brought tables of silver up to the seats, and set them with baskets of gold. A third mixed some sweet wine with water in a silver bowl and put golden cups upon the tables, while the fourth she brought in water and set it to boil in a large cauldron over a good fire which she had lighted. When the water in the cauldron was boiling, she poured cold into it till it was just as I liked it, and then she set me in a bath and began washing me from the cauldron about the head and shoulders, to take the tire and stiffness out of my limbs. As soon as she had done washing me and anointing me with oil, she arrayed me in a good cloak and shirt and led me to a richly decorated seat inlaid with silver; there was a footstool also under my feet. A maid servant then brought me water in a beautiful golden ewer and poured it into a silver basin for me to wash my hands, and she drew a clean table beside me; an upper servant brought me bread and offered me many things of what there was in the house, and then Circe bade me eat, but I would not, and sat without heeding what was before me, still moody and suspicious.

"When Circe saw me sitting there without eating, and in great grief, she came to me and said, 'Ulysses, why do you sit like that as though you were dumb, gnawing at your own heart, and refusing both meat and drink? Is it that you are still suspicious? You ought not to be, for I have already sworn solemnly that I will not hurt you.'

"And I said, 'Circe, no man with any sense of what is right can think of either eating or drinking in your house until you have set his friends free and let him see them. If you want me to eat and drink, you must free my men and bring them to me that I may see them with my own eyes.'

"When I had said this she went straight through the court with her wand in her hand and opened the pigsty doors. My men came out like so many prime hogs and stood looking at her, but she went about among them and anointed each with a second drug, whereon the bristles that the bad drug had given them fell off, and they became men again, younger than they were before, and much taller and better looking. They knew me at once, seized me each of them by the hand, and wept for joy till the whole house was filled with the sound of their hullabalooing, and Circe herself was so sorry for them that she came up to me and said, 'Ulysses, noble son of Laertes, go back at once to the sea where you have left your ship, and first draw it on to the land. Then, hide all your ship's gear and property in some cave, and come back here with your men.'

"I agreed to this, so I went back to the sea shore, and found the men at the ship weeping and wailing most piteously. When they saw me the silly blubbering fellows began frisking round me as calves break out and gambol round their mothers, when they see them coming home to be milked after they have been feeding all day, and the homestead resounds with their lowing. They seemed as glad to see me as though they had got back to their own rugged Ithaca, where they had been born and bred. 'Sir,' said the affectionate creatures, 'we are as glad to see you back as though we had got safe home to Ithaca; but tell us all about the fate of our comrades.'

"I spoke comfortingly to them and said, 'We must draw our ship on to the land, and hide the ship's gear with all our property in some cave; then come with me all of you as fast as you can to Circe's house, where you will find your comrades eating and drinking in the midst of great abundance.'

"On this the men would have come with me at once, but Eurylochus tried to hold them back and said, 'Alas, poor wretches that we are, what will become of us? Rush not on your ruin by going to the house of Circe, who will turn us all into pigs or wolves or lions, and we shall have to keep guard over her house. Remember how the Cyclops treated us when our comrades went inside his cave, and Ulysses with them. It was all through his sheer folly that those men lost their lives.'

"When I heard him I was in two minds whether or no to draw the keen blade that hung by my sturdy thigh and cut his head off in spite of his being a near relation of my own; but the men interceded for him and said, 'Sir, if it may so be, let this fellow stay here and mind the ship, but take the rest of us with you to Circe's housc.'

"On this we all went inland, and Eurylochus was not left behind after all, but came on too, for he was frightened by the severe reprimand that I had given him.

"Meanwhile Circe had been seeing that the men who had been left behind were washed and anointed with olive oil; she had also given them woolen cloaks and shirts, and when we came we found them all comfortably at dinner in her house. As soon as the men saw each other face to face and knew one another, they wept for joy and cried aloud till the whole palace rang again. Thereon Circe came up to me and said, 'Ulysses, noble son of Laertes, tell your men to leave off crying; I know how much you have all of you suffered at sea, and how ill you have fared among cruel savages on the mainland, but that is over now, so stay here, and eat and drink till you are once more as strong and hearty as you were when you left Ithaca; for at present you are weakened both in body and mind; you keep all the time thinking of the hardships- you have suffered during your travels, so that you have no more cheerfulness left in you.'

"Thus did she speak and we assented. We stayed with Circe for a whole twelvemonth feasting upon an untold quantity both of meat and wine. But when the year had passed in the waning of moons and the long days had come round, my men called me apart and said, 'Sir, it is time you began to think about going home, if so be you are to be spared to see your house and native country at all.'

"Thus did they speak and I assented. Thereon through the livelong day to the going down of the sun we feasted our fill on meat and wine, but when the sun went down and it came on dark the men laid themselves down to sleep in the covered cloisters. I, however, after I had got into bed with Circe, besought her by her knees, and the goddess listened to what I had got to say. 'Circe,' said I, 'please to keep the promise you made me about furthering me on my homeward voyage. I want to get back and so do my men, they are always pestering me with their complaints as soon as ever your back is turned.'

"And the goddess answered, 'Ulysses, noble son of Laertes, you shall none of you stay here any longer if you do not want to, but there is another journey which you have got to take before you can sail homewards. You must go to the house of Hades and of dread Proserpine to consult the ghost of the blind Theban prophet Teiresias whose reason is still unshaken. To him alone has Proserpine left his understanding even in death, but the other ghosts flit about aimlessly.'

"I was dismayed when I heard this. I sat up in bed and wept, and would gladly have lived no longer to see the light of the sun, but presently when I was tired of weeping and tossing myself about, I said, 'And who shall guide me upon this voyage- for the house of Hades is a port that no ship can reach.'

"'You will want no guide,' she answered; 'raise you mast, set your white sails, sit quite still, and the North Wind will blow you there of itself. When your ship has traversed the waters of Oceanus, you will reach the fertile shore of Proserpine's country with its groves of tall poplars and willows that shed their fruit untimely; here beach your ship upon the shore of Oceanus, and go straight on to the dark abode of Hades. You will find it near the place where the rivers Pyriphlegethon and Cocytus (which is a branch of the river Styx) flow into Acheron, and you will see a rock near it, just where the two roaring rivers run into one another.

"'When you have reached this spot, as I now tell you, dig a trench a cubit or so in length, breadth, and depth, and pour into it as a drink-offering to all the dead, first, honey mixed with milk, then wine, and in the third place water-sprinkling white barley meal over the whole. Moreover you must offer many prayers to the poor feeble ghosts, and promise them that when you get back to Ithaca you will sacrifice a barren heifer to them, the best you have, and will load the pyre with good things. More particularly you must promise that Teiresias shall have a black sheep all to himself, the finest in all your flocks.

"'When you shall have thus besought the ghosts with your prayers, offer them a ram and a black ewe, bending their heads towards Erebus; but yourself turn away from them as though you would make towards the river. On this, many dead men's ghosts will come to you, and you must tell your men to skin the two sheep that you have just killed, and offer them as a burnt sacrifice with prayers to Hades and to Proserpine. Then draw your sword and sit there, so as to prevent any other poor ghost from coming near the split blood before Teiresias shall have answered your questions. The seer will presently come to you, and will tell you about your voyage- what stages you are to make, and how you are to sail the see so as to reach your home.'

"It was day-break by the time she had done speaking, so she dressed mc in my shirt and cloak. As for herself she threw a beautiful light gossamer fabric over her shoulders, fastening it with a golden girdle round her waist, and she covered her head with a mantle. Then I went about among the men everywhere all over the house, and spoke kindly to each of them man by man: 'You must not lie sleeping here any longer,' said I to them, 'we must be going, for Circe has told me all about it.' And this they did as I bade them.

"Even so, however, I did not get them away without misadventure. We had with us a certain youth named Elpenor, not very remarkable for sense or courage, who had got drunk and was lying on the house-top away from the rest of the men, to sleep off his liquor in the cool. When he heard the noise of the men bustling about, he jumped up on a sudden and forgot all about coming down by the main staircase, so he tumbled right off the roof and broke his neck, and his soul went down to the house of Hades.

"When I had got the men together I said to them, 'You think you are about to start home again, but Circe has explained to me that instead of this, we have got to go to the house of Hades and Proserpine to consult the ghost of the Theban prophet Teiresias.'

"The men were broken-hearted as they heard me, and threw themselves on the ground groaning and tearing their hair, but they did not mend matters by crying. When we reached the sea shore, weeping and lamenting our fate, Circe brought the ram and the ewe, and we made them fast hard by the ship. She passed through the midst of us without our knowing it, for who can see the comings and goings of a god, if the god does not wish to be seen?

Lesson 49

- Read Book 11 of *The Odyssey.*

Book 11

"Then, when we had got down to the sea shore we drew our ship into the water and got her mast and sails into her; we also put the sheep on board and took our places, weeping and in great distress of mind. Circe, that great and cunning goddess, sent us a fair wind that blew dead aft and stayed steadily with us keeping our sails all the time well filled; so we did whatever wanted doing to the ship's gear and let her go as the wind and helmsman headed her. All day long her sails were full as she held her course over the sea, but when the sun went down and darkness was over all the earth, we got into the deep waters of the river Oceanus, where lie the land and city of the Cimmerians who live enshrouded in mist and darkness which the rays of the sun never pierce neither at his rising nor as he goes down again out of the heavens, but the poor wretches live in one long melancholy night. When we got there we beached the ship, took the sheep out of her, and went along by the waters of Oceanus till we came to the place of which Circe had told us.

"Here Perimedes and Eurylochus held the victims, while I drew my sword and dug the trench a cubit each way. I made a drink-offering to all the dead, first with honey and milk, then with wine, and thirdly with water, and I sprinkled white barley meal over the whole, praying earnestly to the poor feckless ghosts, and promising them that when I got back to Ithaca I would sacrifice a barren heifer for them, the best I had, and would load the pyre with good things. I also particularly promised that Teiresias should have a black sheep to himself, the best in all my flocks. When I had prayed sufficiently to the dead, I cut the throats of the two sheep and let the blood run into the trench, whereon the ghosts came trooping up from Erebus-brides, young bachelors, old men worn out with toil, maids who had been crossed in love, and brave men who had been killed in battle, with their armor still smirched with blood; they came from every quarter and flitted round the trench with a strange kind of screaming sound that made me turn pale with fear. When I saw them coming I told the men to be quick and flay the carcasses of the two dead sheep and make burnt offerings of them, and at the same time to repeat prayers to Hades and to Proserpine; but I sat where I was with my sword drawn and would not let the poor feckless ghosts come near the blood till Teiresias should have answered my questions.

"The first ghost that came was that of my comrade Elpenor, for he had not yet been laid beneath the earth. We had left his body unwaked and unburied in Circe's house, for we had had too much else to do. I was very sorry for him, and cried when I saw him: 'Elpenor,' said I, 'how did you come down here into this gloom and darkness? You have got here on foot quicker than I have with my ship.'

"'Sir,' he answered with a groan, 'it was all bad luck, and my own unspeakable drunkenness. I was lying asleep on the top of Circe's house, and never thought of coming down again by the great staircase but fell right off the roof and broke my neck, so my soul came down to the house of Hades. And now I beseech you by all those whom you have left behind you, though they are not here, by your wife, by the father who brought you up when you were a child, and by Telemachus who is the one hope of your house, do what I shall now ask you. I know that when you leave this limbo you will again hold your ship for the Aeaean island. Do not go thence leaving me unwaked and unburied behind you, or I may bring heaven's anger upon you; but burn me with whatever armor I have, build a barrow for me on the sea shore, that may tell people in days to come what a poor unlucky fellow I was, and plant over my grave the oar I used to row with when I was yet alive and with my messmates.' And I said, 'My poor fellow, I will do all that you have asked of me.'

"Thus, then, did we sit and hold sad talk with one another, I on the one side of the trench with my sword held over the blood, and the ghost of my comrade saying all this to me from the other side. Then came the ghost of my dead mother Anticlea, daughter to Autolycus. I had left her alive when I set out for Troy and was moved to tears when I saw her, but even so, for all my sorrow I would not let her come near the blood till I had asked my questions of Teiresias.

"Then came also the ghost of Theban Teiresias, with his golden scepter in his hand. He knew me and said, 'Ulysses, noble son of Laertes, why, poor man, have you left the light of day and come down to visit the dead in this sad place? Stand back from the trench and withdraw your sword that I may drink of the blood and answer your questions truly.'

"So I drew back, and sheathed my sword, whereon when he had drank of the blood he began with his prophecy.

"You want to know,' said he, 'about your return home, but heaven will make this hard for you. I do not think that you will escape the eye of Neptune, who still nurses his bitter grudge against you for having blinded his son. Still, after much suffering you may get home if you can restrain yourself and your companions when your ship reaches the Thrinacian island, where you will find the sheep and cattle belonging to the sun, who sees and gives ear to everything. If you leave these flocks unharmed and think of nothing but of getting home, you may yet after much hardship reach Ithaca; but if you harm them, then I forewarn you of the destruction both of your ship and of your men. Even though you may yourself escape, you will return in bad plight after losing all your men, [in another man's ship, and you will find trouble in your house, which will be overrun by high-handed people, who are devouring your substance under the pretext of paying court and making presents to your wife.

"'When you get home you will take your revenge on these suitors; and after you have killed them by force or fraud in your own house, you must take a well-made oar and carry it on and on, till you come to a country where the people have never heard of the sea and do not even mix salt with their food, nor do they know anything about ships, and oars that are as the wings of a ship. I will give you this certain token which cannot escape your notice. A wayfarer will meet you and will say it must be a winnowing shovel that you have got upon your shoulder; on this you must fix the oar in the ground and sacrifice a ram, a bull, and a boar to Neptune. Then go home and offer hecatombs to an the gods in heaven one after the other. As for yourself, death shall come to you from the sea, and your life shall ebb away very gently when you are full of years and peace of mind, and your people shall bless you. All that I have said will come true].'

"'This,' I answered, 'must be as it may please heaven, but tell me and tell me and tell me true, I see my poor mother's ghost close by us; she is sitting by the blood without saying a word, and though I am her own son she does not remember me and speak to me; tell me, Sir, how I can make her know me.'

"'That,' said he, 'I can soon do. Any ghost that you let taste of the blood will talk with you like a reasonable being, but if you do not let them have any blood they will go away again.'

"On this the ghost of Teiresias went back to the house of Hades, for his prophecyings had now been spoken, but I sat still where I was until my mother came up and tasted the blood. Then she knew me at once and spoke fondly to me, saying, 'My son, how did you come down to this abode of darkness while you are still alive? It is a hard thing for the living to see these places, for between us and them there are great and terrible waters, and there is Oceanus, which no man can cross on foot, but he must have a good ship to take him. Are you all this time trying to find your way home from Troy, and have you never yet got back to Ithaca nor seen your wife in your own house?'

"'Mother,' said I, 'I was forced to come here to consult the ghost of the Theban prophet Teiresias. I have never yet been near the Achaean land nor set foot on my native country, and I have had nothing but one long series of misfortunes from the very first day that I set out with Agamemnon for Ilius, the land of noble steeds, to fight the Trojans. But tell me, and tell me true, in what way did you die? Did you have a long illness, or did heaven vouchsafe you a gentle easy passage to eternity? Tell me also about my father, and the son whom I left behind me; is my property still in their hands, or has some one else got hold of it, who thinks that I shall not return to claim it? Tell me again what my wife intends doing, and in what mind she is; does she live with my son and guard my estate securely, or has she made the best match she could and married again?'

"My mother answered, 'Your wife still remains in your house, but she is in great distress of mind and spends her whole time in tears both night and day. No one as yet has got possession of your fine property, and Telemachus still holds your lands undisturbed. He has to entertain largely, as of course he must, considering his position as a magistrate, and how every one invites him; your father remains at his old place in the country and never goes near the town. He has no comfortable bed nor bedding; in the winter he sleeps on the floor in front of the fire with the men and goes about all in rags, but in summer, when the warm weather comes on again, he lies out in the vineyard on a bed of vine leaves thrown anyhow upon the ground. He grieves continually about your never having come home, and suffers more and more as he grows older. As for my own end it was in this wise: heaven did not take me swiftly and painlessly in my own house, nor was I attacked by any illness such as those that generally wear people out and kill them, but my longing to know what you were doing and the force of my affection for you- this it was that was the death of me.'

"Then I tried to find some way of embracing my mother's ghost. Thrice I sprang towards her and tried to clasp her in my arms, but each time she flitted from my embrace as it were a dream or phantom, and being touched to the quick I said to her, 'Mother, why do you not stay still when I would embrace you? If we could throw our arms around one another we might find sad comfort in the sharing of our sorrows even in the house of Hades; does Proserpine want to lay a still further load of grief upon me by mocking me with a phantom only?'

"'My son,' she answered, 'most ill-fated of all mankind, it is not Proserpine that is beguiling you, but all people are like this when they are dead. The sinews no longer hold the flesh and bones together; these perish in the fierceness of consuming fire as soon as life has left the body, and the soul flits away as though it were a dream. Now, however, go back to the light of day as soon as you can, and note all these things that you may tell them to your wife hereafter.'

"Thus did we converse, and anon Proserpine sent up the ghosts of the wives and daughters of all the most famous men. They gathered in crowds about the blood, and I considered how I might question them severally. In the end I deemed that it would be best to draw the keen blade that hung by my sturdy thigh, and keep them from all drinking the blood at once. So they came up one after the other, and each one as I questioned her told me her race and lineage.

"The first I saw was Tyro. She was daughter of Salmoneus and wife of Cretheus the son of Aeolus. She fell in love with the river Enipeus who is much the most beautiful river in the whole world. Once when she was taking a walk by his side as usual, Neptune, disguised as her lover, lay with her at the mouth of the river, and a huge blue wave arched itself like a mountain over them to hide both woman and god, whereon he loosed her virgin girdle and laid her in a deep slumber. When the god had accomplished the deed of love, he took her hand in his own and said, 'Tyro, rejoice in all good will; the embraces of the gods are not fruitless, and you will have fine twins about this time twelve months. Take great care of them. I am Neptune, so now go home, but hold your tongue and do not tell any one.'

"Then he dived under the sea, and she in due course bore Pelias and Neleus, who both of them served Jove with all their might. Pelias was a great breeder of sheep and lived in Iolcus, but the other lived in Pylos. The rest of her children were by Cretheus, namely, Aeson, Pheres, and Amythaon, who was a mighty warrior and charioteer.

"Next to her I saw Antiope, daughter to Asopus, who could boast of having slept in the arms of even Jove himself, and who bore him two sons Amphion and Zethus. These founded Thebes with its seven gates, and built a wall all round it; for strong though they were they could not hold Thebes till they had walled it.

"Then I saw Alcmena, the wife of Amphitryon, who also bore to Jove indomitable Hercules; and Megara who was daughter to great King Creon, and married the redoubtable son of Amphitryon.

"I also saw fair Epicaste mother of King Œdipodes whose awful lot it was to marry her own son without suspecting it. He married her after having killed his father, but the gods proclaimed the whole story to the world; whereon he remained king of Thebes, in great grief for the spite the gods had borne him; but Epicaste went to the house of the mighty jailer Hades, having hanged herself for grief, and the avenging spirits haunted him as for an outraged mother- to his ruing bitterly thereafter.

"Then I saw Chloris, whom Neleus married for her beauty, having given priceless presents for her. She was youngest daughter to Amphion son of Iasus and king of Minyan Orchomenus, and was Queen in Pylos. She bore Nestor, Chromius, and Periclymenus, and she also bore that marvellously lovely woman Pero, who was wooed by all the country round; but Neleus would only give her to him who should raid the cattle of Iphicles from the grazing grounds of Phylace, and this was a hard task. The only man who would undertake to raid them was a certain excellent seer, but the will of heaven was against him, for the rangers of the cattle caught him and put him in prison; nevertheless when a full year had passed and the same season came round again, Iphicles set him at liberty, after he had expounded all the oracles of heaven. Thus, then, was the will of Jove accomplished.

"And I saw Leda the wife of Tyndarus, who bore him two famous sons, Castor breaker of horses, and Pollux the mighty boxer. Both these heroes are lying under the earth, though they are still alive, for by a special dispensation of Jove, they die and come to life again, each one of them every other day throughout all time, and they have the rank of gods.

"After her I saw Iphimedeia wife of Aloeus who boasted the embrace of Neptune. She bore two sons Otus and Ephialtes, but both were short lived. They were the finest children that were ever born in this world, and the best looking, Orion only excepted; for at nine years old they were nine fathoms high, and measured nine cubits round the chest. They threatened to make war with the gods in Olympus, and tried to set Mount Ossa on the top of Mount Olympus, and Mount Pelion on the top of Ossa, that they might scale heaven itself, and they would have done it too if they had been grown up, but Apollo, son of Leto, killed both of them, before they had got so much as a sign of hair upon their cheeks or chin.

"Then I saw Phaedra, and Procris, and fair Ariadne daughter of the magician Minos, whom Theseus was carrying off from Crete to Athens, but he did not enjoy her, for before he could do so Diana killed her in the island of Dia on account of what Bacchus had said against her.

"I also saw Maera and Clymene and hateful Eriphyle, who sold her own husband for gold. But it would take me all night if I were to name every single one of the wives and daughters of heroes whom I saw, and it is time for me to go to bed, either on board ship with my crew, or here. As for my escort, heaven and yourselves will see to it."

Here he ended, and the guests sat all of them enthralled and speechless throughout the covered cloister. Then Arete said to them:

"What do you think of this man, O Phaecians? Is he not tall and good looking, and is he not Clever? True, he is my own guest, but all of you share in the distinction. Do not he a hurry to send him away, nor niggardly in the presents you make to one who is in such great need, for heaven has blessed all of you with great abundance."

Then spoke the aged hero Echeneus who was one of the oldest men among them, "My friends," said he, "what our august queen has just said to us is both reasonable and to the purpose, therefore be persuaded by it; but the decision whether in word or deed rests ultimately with King Alcinous."

"The thing shall be done," exclaimed Alcinous, "as surely as I still live and reign over the Phaeacians. Our guest is indeed very anxious to get home, still we must persuade him to remain with us until to-morrow, by which time I shall be able to get together the whole sum that I mean to give him. As regards- his escort it will be a matter for you all, and mine above all others as the chief person among you."

And Ulysses answered, “King Alcinous, if you were to bid me to stay here for a whole twelve months, and then speed me on my way, loaded with your noble gifts, I should obey you gladly and it would redound greatly to my advantage, for I should return fuller-handed to my own people, and should thus be more respected and beloved by all who see me when I get back to Ithaca.”

“Ulysses,” replied Alcinous, “not one of us who sees you has any idea that you are a charlatan or a swindler. I know there are many people going about who tell such plausible stories that it is very hard to see through them, but there is a style about your language which assures me of your good disposition. Moreover you have told the story of your own misfortunes, and those of the Argives, as though you were a practiced bard; but tell me, and tell me true, whether you saw any of the mighty heroes who went to Troy at the same time with yourself, and perished there. The evenings are still at their longest, and it is not yet bed time- go on, therefore, with your divine story, for I could stay here listening till to-morrow morning, so long as you will continue to tell us of your adventures.”

“Alcinous,” answered Ulysses, “there is a time for making speeches, and a time for going to bed; nevertheless, since you so desire, I will not refrain from telling you the still sadder tale of those of my comrades who did not fall fighting with the Trojans, but perished on their return, through the treachery of a wicked woman.

“When Proserpine had dismissed the female ghosts in all directions, the ghost of Agamemnon son of Atreus came sadly up tome, surrounded by those who had perished with him in the house of Aegisthus. As soon as he had tasted the blood he knew me, and weeping bitterly stretched out his arms towards me to embrace me; but he had no strength nor substance any more, and I too wept and pitied him as I beheld him. ‘How did you come by your death,’ said I, ‘King Agamemnon? Did Neptune raise his winds and waves against you when you were at sea, or did your enemies make an end of you on the mainland when you were cattle-lifting or sheep-stealing, or while they were fighting in defense of their wives and city?’

“‘Ulysses,’ he answered, ‘noble son of Laertes, was not lost at sea in any storm of Neptune’s raising, nor did my foes dispatch me upon the mainland, but Aegisthus and my wicked wife were the death of me between them. He asked me to his house, feasted me, and then butchered me most miserably as though I were a fat beast in a slaughter house, while all around me my comrades were slain like sheep or pigs for the wedding breakfast, or picnic, or gorgeous banquet of some great nobleman. You must have seen numbers of men killed either in a general engagement, or in single combat, but you never saw anything so truly pitiable as the way in which we fell in that cloister, with the mixing-bowl and the loaded tables lying all about, and the ground reeking with our-blood. I heard Priam's daughter Cassandra scream as Clytemnestra killed her close beside me. I lay dying upon the earth with the sword in my body, and raised my hands to kill the slut of a murderess, but she slipped away from me; she would not even close my lips nor my eyes when I was dying, for there is nothing in this world so cruel and so shameless as a woman when she has fallen into such guilt as hers was. Fancy murdering her own husband! I thought I was going to be welcomed home by my children and my servants, but her abominable crime has brought disgrace on herself and all women who shall come after- even on the good ones.'

"And I said, 'In truth Jove has hated the house of Atreus from first to last in the matter of their women's counsels. See how many of us fell for Helen's sake, and now it seems that Clytemnestra hatched mischief against too during your absence.'

"'Be sure, therefore,' continued Agamemnon, 'and not be too friendly even with your own wife. Do not tell her all that you know perfectly well yourself. Tell her a part only, and keep your own counsel about the rest. Not that your wife, Ulysses, is likely to murder you, for Penelope is a very admirable woman, and has an excellent nature. We left her a young bride with an infant at her breast when we set out for Troy. This child no doubt is now grown up happily to man's estate, and he and his father will have a joyful meeting and embrace one another as it is right they should do, whereas my wicked wife did not even allow me the happiness of looking upon my son, but killed me ere I could do so. Furthermore I say- and lay my saying to your heart- do not tell people when you are bringing your ship to Ithaca, but steal a march upon them, for after all this there is no trusting women. But now tell me, and tell me true, can you give me any news of my son Orestes? Is he in Orchomenus, or at Pylos, or is he at Sparta with Menelaus- for I presume that he is still living.'

"And I said, 'Agamemnon, why do you ask me? I do not know whether your son is alive or dead, and it is not right to talk when one does not know.'

"As we two sat weeping and talking thus sadly with one another the ghost of Achilles came up to us with Patroclus, Antilochus, and Ajax who was the finest and goodliest man of all the Danaans after the son of Peleus. The fleet descendant of Aeacus knew me and spoke piteously, saying, 'Ulysses, noble son of Laertes, what deed of daring will you undertake next, that you venture down to the house of Hades among us silly dead, who are but the ghosts of them that can labor no more?'

"And I said, 'Achilles, son of Peleus, foremost champion of the Achaeans, I came to consult Teiresias, and see if he could advise me about my return home to Ithaca, for I have never yet been able to get near the Achaean land, nor to set foot in my own country, but have been in trouble all the time. As for you, Achilles, no one was ever yet so fortunate as you have been, nor ever will be, for you were adored by all us Argives as long as you were alive, and now that you are here you are a great prince among the dead. Do not, therefore, take it so much to heart even if you are dead.'

"'Say not a word,' he answered, 'in death's favor; I would rather be a paid servant in a poor man's house and be above ground than king of kings among the dead. But give me news about son; is he gone to the wars and will he be a great soldier, or is this not so? Tell me also if you have heard anything about my father Peleus- does he still rule among the Myrmidons, or do they show him no respect throughout Hellas and Phthia now that he is old and his limbs fail him? Could I but stand by his side, in the light of day, with the same strength that I had when I killed the bravest of our foes upon the plain of Troy- could I but be as I then was and go even for a short time to my father's house, any one who tried to do him violence or supersede him would soon me it.'

"'I have heard nothing,' I answered, 'of Peleus, but I can tell you all about your son Neoptolemus, for I took him in my own ship from Scyros with the Achaeans. In our councils of war before Troy he was always first to speak, and his judgement was unerring. Nestor and I were the only two who could surpass him; and when it came to fighting on the plain of Troy, he would never remain with the body of his men, but would dash on far in front, foremost of them all in valor. Many a man did he kill in battle- I cannot name every single one of those whom he slew while fighting on the side of the Argives, but will only say how he killed that valiant hero Eurypylus son of Telephus, who was the handsomest man I ever saw except Memnon; many others also of the Ceteians fell around him by reason of a woman's bribes. Moreover, when all the bravest of the Argives went inside the horse that Epeus had made, and it was left to me to settle when we should either open the door of our ambuscade, or close it, though all the other leaders and chief men among the Danaans were drying their eyes and quaking in every limb, I never once saw him turn pale nor wipe a tear from his cheek; he was all the time urging me to break out from the horse- grasping the handle of his sword and his bronze-shod spear, and breathing fury against the foe. Yet when we had sacked the city of Priam he got his handsome share of the prize money and went on board (such is the fortune of war) without a wound upon him, neither from a thrown spear nor in close combat, for the rage of Mars is a matter of great chance.'

"When I had told him this, the ghost of Achilles strode off across a meadow full of asphodel, exulting over what I had said concerning the prowess of his son.

"The ghosts of other dead men stood near me and told me each his own melancholy tale; but that of Ajax son of Telamon alone held aloof- still angry with me for having won the cause in our dispute about the armor of Achilles. Thetis had offered it as a prize, but the Trojan prisoners and Minerva were the judges. Would that I had never gained the day in such a contest, for it cost the life of Ajax, who was foremost of all the Danaans after the son of Peleus, alike in stature and prowess.

"When I saw him I tried to pacify him and said, 'Ajax, will you not forget and forgive even in death, but must the judgement about that hateful armor still rankle with you? It cost us Argives dear enough to lose such a tower of strength as you were to us. We mourned you as much as we mourned Achilles son of Peleus himself, nor can the blame be laid on anything but on the spite which Jove bore against the Danaans, for it was this that made him counsel your destruction- come hither, therefore, bring your proud spirit into subjection, and hear what I can tell you.'

"He would not answer, but turned away to Erebus and to the other ghosts; nevertheless, I should have made him talk to me in spite of his being so angry, or I should have gone talking to him, only that there were still others among the dead whom I desired to see.

"Then I saw Minos son of Jove with his golden scepter in his hand sitting in judgement on the dead, and the ghosts were gathered sitting and standing round him in the spacious house of Hades, to learn his sentences upon them.

"After him I saw huge Orion in a meadow full of asphodel driving the ghosts of the wild beasts that he had killed upon the mountains, and he had a great bronze club in his hand, unbreakable for ever and ever.

"And I saw Tityus son of Gaia stretched upon the plain and covering some nine acres of ground. Two vultures on either side of him were digging their beaks into his liver, and he kept on trying to beat them off with his hands, but could not; for he had violated Jove's mistress Leto as she was going through Panopeus on her way to Pytho.

"I saw also the dreadful fate of Tantalus, who stood in a lake that reached his chin; he was dying to quench his thirst, but could never reach the water, for whenever the poor creature stooped to drink, it dried up and vanished, so that there was nothing but dry ground- parched by the spite of heaven. There were tall trees, moreover, that shed their fruit over his head- pears, pomegranates, apples, sweet figs and juicy olives, but whenever the poor creature stretched out his hand to take some, the wind tossed the branches back again to the clouds.

"And I saw Sisyphus at his endless task raising his prodigious stone with both his hands. With hands and feet he tried to roll it up to the top of the hill, but always, just before he could roll it over on to the other side, its weight would be too much for him, and the pitiless stone would come thundering down again on to the plain. Then he would begin trying to push it up hill again, and the sweat ran off him and the steam rose after him.

"After him I saw mighty Hercules, but it was his phantom only, for he is feasting ever with the immortal gods, and has lovely Hebe to wife, who is daughter of Jove and Juno. The ghosts were screaming round him like scared birds flying all whithers. He looked black as night with his bare bow in his hands and his arrow on the string, glaring around as though ever on the point of taking aim. About his breast there was a wondrous golden belt adorned in the most marvellous fashion with bears, wild boars, and lions with gleaming eyes; there was also war, battle, and death. The man who made that belt, do what he might, would never be able to make another like it. Hercules knew me at once when he saw me, and spoke piteously, saying, my poor Ulysses, noble son of Laertes, are you too leading the same sorry kind of life that I did when I was above ground? I was son of Jove, but I went through an infinity of suffering, for I became bondsman to one who was far beneath me- a low fellow who set me all manner of labors. He once sent me here to fetch the hell-hound- for he did not think he could find anything harder for me than this, but I got the hound out of Hades and brought him to him, for Mercury and Minerva helped me.'

"On this Hercules went down again into the house of Hades, but I stayed where I was in case some other of the mighty dead should come to me. And I should have seen still other of them that are gone before, whom I would fain have seen- Theseus and Pirithous glorious children of the gods, but so many thousands of ghosts came round me and uttered such appalling cries, that I was panic stricken lest Proserpine should send up from the house of Hades the head of that awful monster Gorgon. On this I hastened back to my ship and ordered my men to go on board at once and loose the hawsers; so they embarked and took their places, whereon the ship went down the stream of the river Oceanus. We had to row at first, but presently a fair wind sprang up.

Lesson 50

- Read Book 12 of *The Odyssey.*

Book 12

"After we were clear of the river Oceanus, and had got out into the open sea, we went on till we reached the Aeaean island where there is dawn and sunrise as in other places. We then drew our ship on to the sands and got out of her on to the shore, where we went to sleep and waited till day should break.

"Then, when the child of morning, rosy-fingered Dawn, appeared, I sent some men to Circe's house to fetch the body of Elpenor. We cut firewood from a wood where the headland jutted out into the sea, and after we had wept over him and lamented him we performed his funeral rites. When his body and armor had been burned to ashes, we raised a cairn, set a stone over it, and at the top of the cairn we fixed the oar that he had been used to row with.

“While we were doing all this, Circe, who knew that we had got back from the house of Hades, dressed herself and came to us as fast as she could; and her maid servants came with her bringing us bread, meat, and wine. Then she stood in the midst of us and said, ‘You have done a bold thing in going down alive to the house of Hades, and you will have died twice, to other people’s once; now, then, stay here for the rest of the day, feast your fill, and go on with your voyage at daybreak tomorrow morning. In the meantime I will tell Ulysses about your course, and will explain everything to him so as to prevent your suffering from misadventure either by land or sea.’

“We agreed to do as she had said, and feasted through the livelong day to the going down of the sun, but when the sun had set and it came on dark, the men laid themselves down to sleep by the stern cables of the ship. Then Circe took me by the hand and bade me be seated away from the others, while she reclined by my side and asked me all about our adventures.

“‘So far so good,’ said she, when I had ended my story, ‘and now pay attention to what I am about to tell you- heaven itself, indeed, will recall it to your recollection. First you will come to the Sirens who enchant all who come near them. If any one unwarily draws in too close and hears the singing of the Sirens, his wife and children will never welcome him home again, for they sit in a green field and warble him to death with the sweetness of their song. There is a great heap of dead men’s bones lying all around, with the flesh still rotting off them. Therefore pass these Sirens by, and stop your men’s ears with wax that none of them may hear; but if you like you can listen yourself, for you may get the men to bind you as you stand upright on a cross-piece half way up the mast, and they must lash the rope’s ends to the mast itself, that you may have the pleasure of listening. If you beg and pray the men to unloose you, then they must bind you faster.

“‘When your crew have taken you past these Sirens, I cannot give you coherent directions as to which of two courses you are to take; I will lay the two alternatives before you, and you must consider them for yourself. On the one hand there are some overhanging rocks against which the deep blue waves of Amphitrite beat with terrific fury; the blessed gods call these rocks the Wanderers. Here not even a bird may pass, no, not even the timid doves that bring ambrosia to Father Jove, but the sheer rock always carries off one of them, and Father Jove has to send another to make up their number; no ship that ever yet came to these rocks has got away again, but the waves and whirlwinds of fire are freighted with wreckage and with the bodies of dead men. The only vessel that ever sailed and got through, was the famous Argo on her way from the house of Aetes, and she too would have gone against these great rocks, only that Juno piloted her past them for the love she bore to Jason.

"'Of these two rocks the one reaches heaven and its peak is lost in a dark cloud. This never leaves it, so that the top is never clear not even in summer and early autumn. No man though he had twenty hands and twenty feet could get a foothold on it and climb it, for it runs sheer up, as smooth as though it had been polished. In the middle of it there is a large cavern, looking West and turned towards Erebus; you must take your ship this way, but the cave is so high up that not even the stoutest archer could send an arrow into it. Inside it Scylla sits and yelps with a voice that you might take to be that of a young hound, but in truth she is a dreadful monster and no one- not even a god- could face her without being terror-struck. She has twelve misshapen feet, and six necks of the most prodigious length; and at the end of each neck she has a frightful head with three rows of teeth in each, all set very close together, so that they would crunch any one to death in a moment, and she sits deep within her shady cell thrusting out her heads and peering all round the rock, fishing for dolphins or dogfish or any larger monster that she can catch, of the thousands with which Amphitrite teems. No ship ever yet got past her without losing some men, for she shoots out all her heads at once, and carries off a man in each mouth.

"'You will find the other rocks lie lower, but they are so close together that there is not more than a bowshot between them. [A large fig tree in full leaf grows upon it], and under it lies the sucking whirlpool of Charybdis. Three times in the day does she vomit forth her waters, and three times she sucks them down again; see that you be not there when she is sucking, for if you are, Neptune himself could not save you; you must hug the Scylla side and drive ship by as fast as you can, for you had better lose six men than your whole crew.'

"'Is there no way,' said I, 'of escaping Charybdis, and at the same time keeping Scylla off when she is trying to harm my men?'

"'You dare-devil,' replied the goddess, 'you are always wanting to fight somebody or something; you will not let yourself be beaten even by the immortals. For Scylla is not mortal; moreover she is savage, extreme, rude, cruel and invincible. There is no help for it; your best chance will be to get by her as fast as ever you can, for if you dawdle about her rock while you are putting on your armor, she may catch you with a second cast of her six heads, and snap up another half dozen of your men; so drive your ship past her at full speed, and roar out lustily to Crataiis who is Scylla's dam, bad luck to her; she will then stop her from making a second raid upon you.

"'You will now come to the Thrinacian island, and here you will see many herds of cattle and flocks of sheep belonging to the sun-god- seven herds of cattle and seven flocks of sheep, with fifty head in each flock. They do not breed, nor do they become fewer in number, and they are tended by the goddesses Phaethusa and Lampetie, who are children of the sun-god Hyperion by Neaera. Their mother when she had borne them and had done suckling them sent them to the Thrinacian island, which was a long way off, to live there and look after their father's flocks and herds. If you leave these flocks unharmed, and think of nothing but getting home, you may yet after much hardship reach Ithaca; but if you harm them, then I forewarn you of the destruction both of your ship and of your comrades; and even though you may yourself escape, you will return late, in bad plight, after losing all your men.'

"Here she ended, and dawn enthroned in gold began to show in heaven, whereon she returned inland. I then went on board and told my men to loose the ship from her moorings; so they at once got into her, took their places, and began to smite the grey sea with their oars. Presently the great and cunning goddess Circe befriended us with a fair wind that blew dead aft, and stayed steadily with us, keeping our sails well filled, so we did whatever wanted doing to the ship's gear, and let her go as wind and helmsman headed her.

"Then, being much troubled in mind, I said to my men, 'My friends, it is not right that one or two of us alone should know the prophecies that Circe has made me, I will therefore tell you about them, so that whether we live or die we may do so with our eyes open. First she said we were to keep clear of the Sirens, who sit and sing most beautifully in a field of flowers; but she said I might hear them myself so long as no one else did. Therefore, take me and bind me to the crosspiece half way up the mast; bind me as I stand upright, with a bond so fast that I cannot possibly break away, and lash the rope's ends to the mast itself. If I beg and pray you to set me free, then bind me more tightly still.'

"I had hardly finished telling everything to the men before we reached the island of the two Sirens, for the wind had been very favorable. Then all of a sudden it fell dead calm; there was not a breath of wind nor a ripple upon the water, so the men furled the sails and stowed them; then taking to their oars they whitened the water with the foam they raised in rowing. Meanwhile I look a large wheel of wax and cut it up small with my sword. Then I kneaded the wax in my strong hands till it became soft, which it soon did between the kneading and the rays of the sun-god son of Hyperion. Then I stopped the ears of all my men, and they bound me hands and feet to the mast as I stood upright on the crosspiece; but they went on rowing themselves. When we had got within earshot of the land, and the ship was going at a good rate, the Sirens saw that we were getting in shore and began with their singing.

"'Come here,' they sang, 'renowned Ulysses, honor to the Achaean name, and listen to our two voices. No one ever sailed past us without staying to hear the enchanting sweetness of our song- and he who listens will go on his way not only charmed, but wiser, for we know all the ills that the gods laid upon the Argives and Trojans before Troy, and can tell you everything that is going to happen over the whole world.'

"They sang these words most musically, and as I longed to hear them further I made by frowning to my men that they should set me free; but they quickened their stroke, and Eurylochus and Perimedes bound me with still stronger bonds till we had got out of hearing of the Sirens' voices. Then my men took the wax from their ears and unbound me.

"Immediately after we had got past the island I saw a great wave from which spray was rising, and I heard a loud roaring sound. The men were so frightened that they loosed hold of their oars, for the whole sea resounded with the rushing of the waters, but the ship stayed where it was, for the men had left off rowing. I went round, therefore, and exhorted them man by man not to lose heart.

"'My friends,' said I, 'this is not the first time that we have been in danger, and we are in nothing like so bad a case as when the Cyclops shut us up in his cave;

nevertheless, my courage and wise counsel saved us then, and we shall live to look back on all this as well. Now, therefore, let us all do as I say, trust in Jove and row on with might and main. As for you, coxswain, these are your orders; attend to them, for the ship is in your hands; turn her head away from these steaming rapids and hug the rock, or she will give you the slip and be over yonder before you know where you are, and you will be the death of us.'

"So they did as I told them; but I said nothing about the awful monster Scylla, for I knew the men would not go on rowing if I did, but would huddle together in the hold. In one thing only did I disobey Circe's strict instructions- I put on my armor. Then seizing two strong spears I took my stand on the ship's bows, for it was there that I expected first to see the monster of the rock, who was to do my men so much harm; but I could not make her out anywhere, though I strained my eyes with looking the gloomy rock all over and over.

"Then we entered the Straits in great fear of mind, for on the one hand was Scylla, and on the other dread Charybdis kept sucking up the salt water. As she vomited it up, it was like the water in a cauldron when it is boiling over upon a great fire, and the spray reached the top of the rocks on either side. When she began to suck again, we could see the water all inside whirling round and round, and it made a deafening sound as it broke against the rocks. We could see the bottom of the whirlpool all black with sand and mud, and the men were at their wit's ends for fear. While we were taken up with this, and were expecting each moment to be our last, Scylla pounced down suddenly upon us and snatched up my six best men. I was looking at once after both ship and men, and in a moment I saw their hands and feet ever so high above me, struggling in the air as Scylla was carrying them off, and I heard them call out my name in one last despairing cry. As a fisherman, seated, spear in hand, upon some jutting rock throws bait into the water to deceive the poor little fishes, and spears them with the ox's horn with which his spear is shod, throwing them gasping on to the land as he catches them one by one- even so did Scylla land these panting creatures on her rock and munch them up at the mouth of her den, while they screamed and stretched out their hands to me in their mortal agony. This was the most sickening sight that I saw throughout all my voyages.

"When we had passed the [Wandering] rocks, with Scylla and terrible Charybdis, we reached the noble island of the sun-god, where were the goodly cattle and sheep belonging to the sun Hyperion. While still at sea in my ship I could bear the cattle lowing as they came home to the yards, and the sheep bleating. Then I remembered what the blind Theban prophet Teiresias had told me, and how carefully Aeaean Circe had warned me to shun the island of the blessed sun-god. So being much troubled I said to the men, 'My men, I know you are hard pressed, but listen while I tell you the prophecy that Teiresias made me, and how carefully Aeaean Circe warned me to shun the island of the blessed sun-god, for it was here, she said, that our worst danger would lie. Head the ship, therefore, away from the island.'

"The men were in despair at this, and Eurylochus at once gave me an insolent answer. 'Ulysses,' said he, 'you are cruel; you are very strong yourself and never get worn out; you seem to be made of iron, and now, though your men are exhausted with toil and want of sleep, you will not let them land and cook themselves a good supper upon this island, but bid them put out to sea and go faring fruitlessly on through the watches of the flying night. It is by night that the winds blow hardest and do so much damage; how can we escape should one of those sudden squalls spring up from South West or West, which so often wreck a vessel when our lords the gods are unpropitious? Now, therefore, let us obey the of night and prepare our supper here hard by the ship; to-morrow morning we will go on board again and put out to sea.'

"Thus spoke Eurylochus, and the men approved his words. I saw that heaven meant us a mischief and said, 'You force me to yield, for you are many against one, but at any rate each one of you must take his solemn oath that if he meet with a herd of cattle or a large flock of sheep, he will not be so mad as to kill a single head of either, but will be satisfied with the food that Circe has given us.'

"They all swore as I bade them, and when they had completed their oath we made the ship fast in a harbor that was near a stream of fresh water, and the men went ashore and cooked their suppers. As soon as they had had enough to eat and drink, they began talking about their poor comrades whom Scylla had snatched up and eaten; this set them weeping and they went on crying till they fell off into a sound sleep.

"In the third watch of the night when the stars had shifted their places, Jove raised a great gale of wind that flew a hurricane so that land and sea were covered with thick clouds, and night sprang forth out of the heavens. When the child of morning, rosy-fingered Dawn, appeared, we brought the ship to land and drew her into a cave wherein the sea-nymphs hold their courts and dances, and I called the men together in council.

"'My friends,' said I, 'we have meat and drink in the ship, let us mind, therefore, and not touch the cattle, or we shall suffer for it; for these cattle and sheep belong to the mighty sun, who sees and gives ear to everything.' And again they promised that they would obey.

"For a whole month the wind blew steadily from the South, and there was no other wind, but only South and East. As long as corn and wine held out the men did not touch the cattle when they were hungry; when, however, they had eaten all there was in the ship, they were forced to go further afield, with hook and line, catching birds, and taking whatever they could lay their hands on; for they were starving. One day, therefore, I went up inland that I might pray heaven to show me some means of getting away. When I had gone far enough to be clear of all my men, and had found a place that was well sheltered from the wind, I washed my hands and prayed to all the gods in Olympus till by and by they sent me off into a sweet sleep.

"Meanwhile Eurylochus had been giving evil counsel to the men, 'Listen to me,' said he, 'my poor comrades. All deaths are bad enough but there is none so bad as famine. Why should not we drive in the best of these cows and offer them in sacrifice to the immortal Rods? If we ever get back to Ithaca, we can build a fine temple to the sun-god and enrich it with every kind of ornament; if, however, he is determined to sink our ship out of revenge for these homed cattle, and the other gods are of the same mind, I for one would rather drink salt water once for all and have done with it, than be starved to death by inches in such a desert island as this is.'

"Thus spoke Eurylochus, and the men approved his words. Now the cattle, so fair and goodly, were feeding not far from the ship; the men, therefore drove in the best of them, and they all stood round them saying their prayers, and using young oak-shoots instead of barley-meal, for there was no barley left. When they had done praying they killed the cows and dressed their carcasses; they cut out the thigh bones, wrapped them round in two layers of fat, and set some pieces of raw meat on top of them. They had no wine with which to make drink-offerings over the sacrifice while it was cooking, so they kept pouring on a little water from time to time while the inward meats were being grilled; then, when the thigh bones were burned and they had tasted the inward meats, they cut the rest up small and put the pieces upon the spits.

"By this time my deep sleep had left me, and I turned back to the ship and to the sea shore. As I drew near I began to smell hot roast meat, so I groaned out a prayer to the immortal gods. 'Father Jove,' I exclaimed, 'and all you other gods who live in everlasting bliss, you have done me a cruel mischief by the sleep into which you have sent me; see what fine work these men of mine have been making in my absence.'

"Meanwhile Lampetie went straight off to the sun and told him we had been killing his cows, whereon he flew into a great rage, and said to the immortals, 'Father Jove, and all you other gods who live in everlasting bliss, I must have vengeance on the crew of Ulysses' ship: they have had the insolence to kill my cows, which were the one thing I loved to look upon, whether I was going up heaven or down again. If they do not square accounts with me about my cows, I will go down to Hades and shine there among the dead.'

"'Sun,' said Jove, 'go on shining upon us gods and upon mankind over the fruitful earth. I will shiver their ship into little pieces with a bolt of white lightning as soon as they get out to sea.'

"I was told all this by Calypso, who said she had heard it from the mouth of Mercury.

"As soon as I got down to my ship and to the sea shore I rebuked each one of the men separately, but we could see no way out of it, for the cows were dead already. And indeed the gods began at once to show signs and wonders among us, for the hides of the cattle crawled about, and the joints upon the spits began to low like cows, and the meat, whether cooked or raw, kept on making a noise just as cows do.

"For six days my men kept driving in the best cows and feasting upon them, but when Jove the son of Saturn had added a seventh day, the fury of the gale abated; we therefore went on board, raised our masts, spread sail, and put out to sea. As soon as we were well away from the island, and could see nothing but sky and sea, the son of Saturn raised a black cloud over our ship, and the sea grew dark beneath it. We not get on much further, for in another moment we were caught by a terrific squall from the West that snapped the forestays of the mast so that it fell aft, while all the ship's gear tumbled about at the bottom of the vessel. The mast fell upon the head of the helmsman in the ship's stern, so that the bones of his head were crushed to pieces, and he fell overboard as though he were diving, with no more life left in him.

"Then Jove let fly with his thunderbolts, and the ship went round and round, and was filled with fire and brimstone as the lightning struck it. The men all fell into the sea; they were carried about in the water round the ship, looking like so many sea-gulls, but the god presently deprived them of all chance of getting home again.

"I stuck to the ship till the sea knocked her sides from her keel (which drifted about by itself) and struck the mast out of her in the direction of the keel; but there was a backstay of stout ox-thong still hanging about it, and with this I lashed the mast and keel together, and getting astride of them was carried wherever the winds chose to take me.

"[The gale from the West had now spent its force, and the wind got into the South again, which frightened me lest I should be taken back to the terrible whirlpool of Charybdis. This indeed was what actually happened, for I was borne along by the waves all night, and by sunrise had reacfied the rock of Scylla, and the whirlpool. She was then sucking down the salt sea water, but I was carried aloft toward the fig tree, which I caught hold of and clung on to like a bat. I could not plant my feet anywhere so as to stand securely, for the roots were a long way off and the boughs that overshadowed the whole pool were too high, too vast, and too far apart for me to reach them; so I hung patiently on, waiting till the pool should discharge my mast and raft again- and a very long while it seemed. A juryman is not more glad to get home to supper, after having been long detained in court by troublesome cases, than I was to see my raft beginning to work its way out of the whirlpool again. At last I let go with my hands and feet, and fell heavily into the sea, bard by my raft on to which I then got, and began to row with my hands. As for Scylla, the father of gods and men would not let her get further sight of me- otherwise I should have certainly been lost.]

"Hence I was carried along for nine days till on the tenth night the gods stranded me on the Ogygian island, where dwells the great and powerful goddess Calypso.

She took me in and was kind to me, but I need say no more about this, for I told you and your noble wife all about it yesterday, and I hate saying the same thing over and over again."

Lesson 51

- Read Book 13 of *The Odyssey*.

Book 13

Thus did he speak, and they all held their peace throughout the covered cloister, enthralled by the charm of his story, till presently Alcinous began to speak.

"Ulysses," said he, "now that you have reached my house I doubt not you will get home without further misadventure no matter how much you have suffered in the past. To you others, however, who come here night after night to drink my choicest wine and listen to my bard, I would insist as follows. Our guest has already packed up the clothes, wrought gold, and other valuables which you have brought for his acceptance; let us now, therefore, present him further, each one of us, with a large tripod and a cauldron. We will recoup ourselves by the levy of a general rate; for private individuals cannot be expected to bear the burden of such a handsome present."

Every one approved of this, and then they went home to bed each in his own abode. When the child of morning, rosy-fingered Dawn, appeared, they hurried down to the ship and brought their cauldrons with them. Alcinous went on board and saw everything so securely stowed under the ship's benches that nothing could break adrift and injure the rowers. Then they went to the house of Alcinous to get dinner, and he sacrificed a bull for them in honor of Jove who is the lord of all. They set the steaks to grill and made an excellent dinner, after which the inspired bard, Demodocus, who was a favorite with every one, sang to them; but Ulysses kept on turning his eyes towards the sun, as though to hasten his setting, for he was longing to be on his way. As one who has been all day plowing a fallow field with a couple of oxen keeps thinking about his supper and is glad when night comes that he may go and get it, for it is all his legs can do to carry him, even so did Ulysses rejoice when the sun went down, and he at once said to the Phaecians, addressing himself more particularly to King Alcinous:

“Sir, and all of you, farewell. Make your drink-offerings and send me on my way rejoicing, for you have fulfilled my heart’s desire by giving me an escort, and making me presents, which heaven grant that I may turn to good account; may I find my admirable wife living in peace among friends, and may you whom I leave behind me give satisfaction to your wives and children; may heaven vouchsafe you every good grace, and may no evil thing come among your people.”

Thus did he speak. His hearers all of them approved his saying and agreed that he should have his escort inasmuch as he had spoken reasonably. Alcinous therefore said to his servant, “Pontonous, mix some wine and hand it round to everybody, that we may offer a prayer to father Jove, and speed our guest upon his way.”

Pontonous mixed the wine and handed it to every one in turn; the others each from his own seat made a drink-offering to the blessed gods that live in heaven, but Ulysses rose and placed the double cup in the hands of queen Arete.

“Farewell, queen,” said he, “henceforward and for ever, till age and death, the common lot of mankind, lay their hands upon you. I now take my leave; be happy in this house with your children, your people, and with King Alcinous.”

As he spoke he crossed the threshold, and Alcinous sent a man to conduct him to his ship and to the sea shore. Arete also sent some maid servants with him- one with a clean shirt and cloak, another to carry his strong-box, and a third with corn and wine. When they got to the water side the crew took these things and put them on board, with all the meat and drink; but for Ulysses they spread a rug and a linen sheet on deck that he might sleep soundly in the stern of the ship. Then he too went on board and lay down without a word, but the crew took every man his place and loosed the hawser from the pierced stone to which it had been bound. Thereon, when they began rowing out to sea, Ulysses fell into a deep, sweet, and almost deathlike slumber.

The ship bounded forward on her way as a four in hand chariot flies over the course when the horses feel the whip. Her prow curved as it were the neck of a stallion, and a great wave of dark blue water seethed in her wake. She held steadily on her course, and even a falcon, swiftest of all birds, could not have kept pace with her. Thus, then, she cut her way through the water. carrying one who was as cunning as the gods, but who was now sleeping peacefully, forgetful of all that he had suffered both on the field of battle and by the waves of the weary sea.

When the bright star that heralds the approach of dawn began to show, the ship drew near to land. Now there is in Ithaca a haven of the old merman Phorcys, which lies between two points that break the line of the sea and shut the harbor in. These shelter it from the storms of wind and sea that rage outside, so that, when once within it, a ship may lie without being even moored. At the head of this harbor there is a large olive tree, and at no distance a fine overarching cavern sacred to the nymphs who are called Naiads. There are mixing-bowls within it and wine-jars of stone, and the bees hive there. Moreover, there are great looms of stone on which the nymphs weave their robes of sea purple- very curious to see- and at all times there is water within it. It has two entrances, one facing North by which mortals can go down into the cave, while the other comes from the South and is more mysterious; mortals cannot possibly get in by it, it is the way taken by the gods.

Into this harbor, then, they took their ship, for they knew the place, She had so much way upon her that she ran half her own length on to the shore; when, however, they had landed, the first thing they did was to lift Ulysses with his rug and linen sheet out of the ship, and lay him down upon the sand still fast asleep. Then they took out the presents which Minerva had persuaded the Phaeacians to give him when he was setting out on his voyage homewards. They put these all together by the root of the olive tree, away from the road, for fear some passer by might come and steal them before Ulysses awoke; and then they made the best of their way home again.

But Neptune did not forget the threats with which he had already threatened Ulysses, so he took counsel with Jove. "Father Jove," said he, "I shall no longer be held in any sort of respect among you gods, if mortals like the Phaeacians, who are my own flesh and blood, show such small regard for me. I said I would Ulysses get home when he had suffered sufficiently. I did not say that he should never get home at all, for I knew you had already nodded your head about it, and promised that he should do so; but now they have brought him in a ship fast asleep and have landed him in Ithaca after loading him with more magnificent presents of bronze, gold, and raiment than he would ever have brought back from Troy, if he had had his share of the spoil and got home without misadventure."

And Jove answered, "What, O Lord of the Earthquake, are you talking about? The gods are by no means wanting in respect for you. It would be monstrous were they to insult one so old and honored as you are. As regards mortals, however, if any of them is indulging in insolence and treating you disrespectfully, it will always rest with yourself to deal with him as you may think proper, so do just as you please."

"I should have done so at once," replied Neptune, "if I were not anxious to avoid anything that might displease you; now, therefore, I should like to wreck the Phaecian ship as it is returning from its escort. This will stop them from escorting people in future; and I should also like to bury their city under a huge mountain."

"My good friend," answered Jove, "I should recommend you at the very moment when the people from the city are watching the ship on her way, to turn it into a rock near the land and looking like a ship. This will astonish everybody, and you can then bury their city under the mountain."

When earth-encircling Neptune heard this he went to Scheria where the Phaecians live, and stayed there till the ship, which was making rapid way, had got close-in. Then he went up to it, turned it into stone, and drove it down with the flat of his hand so as to root it in the ground. After this he went away.

The Phaeacians then began talking among themselves, and one would turn towards his neighbor, saying, "Bless my heart, who is it that can have rooted the ship in the sea just as she was getting into port? We could see the whole of her only moment ago."

This was how they talked, but they knew nothing about it; and Alcinous said, "I remember now the old prophecy of my father. He said that Neptune would be angry with us for taking every one so safely over the sea, and would one day wreck a Phaeacian ship as it was returning from an escort, and bury our city under a high mountain. This was what my old father used to say, and now it is all coming true. Now therefore let us all do as I say; in the first place we must leave off giving people escorts when they come here, and in the next let us sacrifice twelve picked bulls to Neptune that he may have mercy upon us, and not bury our city under the high mountain." When the people heard this they were afraid and got ready the bulls.

Thus did the chiefs and rulers of the Phaecians to King Neptune, standing round his altar; and at the same time Ulysses woke up once more upon his own soil. He had been so long away that he did not know it again; moreover, Jove's daughter Minerva had made it a foggy day, so that people might not know of his having come, and that she might tell him everything without either his wife or his fellow citizens and friends recognizing him until he had taken his revenge upon the wicked suitors. Everything, therefore, seemed quite different to him- the long straight tracks, the harbors, the precipices, and the goodly trees, appeared all changed as he started up and looked upon his native land. So he smote his thighs with the flat of his hands and cried aloud despairingly.

"Alas," he exclaimed, "among what manner of people am I fallen? Are they savage and uncivilized or hospitable and humane? Where shall I put all this treasure, and which way shall I go? I wish I had stayed over there with the Phaeacians; or I could have gone to some other great chief who would have been good to me and given me an escort. As it is I do not know where to put my treasure, and I cannot leave it here for fear somebody else should get hold of it. In good truth the chiefs and rulers of the Phaeacians have not been dealing fairly by me, and have left me in the wrong country; they said they would take me back to Ithaca and they have not done so: may Jove the protector of suppliants chastise them, for he watches over everybody and punishes those who do wrong. Still, I suppose I must count my goods and see if the crew have gone off with any of them."

He counted his goodly coppers and cauldrons, his gold and all his clothes, but there was nothing missing; still he kept grieving about not being in his own country, and wandered up and down by the shore of the sounding sea bewailing his hard fate. Then Minerva came up to him disguised as a young shepherd of delicate and princely mien, with a good cloak folded double about her shoulders; she had sandals on her comely feet and held a javelin in her hand. Ulysses was glad when he saw her, and went straight up to her.

"My friend," said he, "you are the first person whom I have met with in this country; I salute you, therefore, and beg you to be will disposed towards me. Protect these my goods, and myself too, for I embrace your knees and pray to you as though you were a god. Tell me, then, and tell me truly, what land and country is this? Who are its inhabitants? Am I on an island, or is this the sea board of some continent?"

Minerva answered, "Stranger, you must be very simple, or must have come from somewhere a long way off, not to know what country this is. It is a very celebrated place, and everybody knows it East and West. It is rugged and not a good driving country, but it is by no means a bid island for what there is of it. It grows any quantity of corn and also wine, for it is watered both by rain and dew; it breeds cattle also and goats; all kinds of timber grow here, and there are watering places where the water never runs dry; so, sir, the name of Ithaca is known even as far as Troy, which I understand to be a long way off from this Achaean country."

Ulysses was glad at finding himself, as Minerva told him, in his own country, and he began to answer, but he did not speak the truth, and made up a lying story in the instinctive wiliness of his heart.

"I heard of Ithaca," said he, "when I was in Crete beyond the seas, and now it seems I have reached it with all these treasures. I have left as much more behind me for my children, but am flying because I killed Orsilochus son of Idomeneus, the fleetest runner in Crete. I killed him because he wanted to rob me of the spoils I had got from Troy with so much trouble and danger both on the field of battle and by the waves of the weary sea; he said I had not served his father loyally at Troy as vassal, but had set myself up as an independent ruler, so I lay in wait for him and with one of my followers by the road side, and speared him as he was coming into town from the country. It was a very dark night and nobody saw us; it was not known, therefore, that I had killed him, but as soon as I had done so I went to a ship and besought the owners, who were Phoenicians, to take me on board and set me in Pylos or in Elis where the Epeans rule, giving them as much spoil as satisfied them. They meant no guile, but the wind drove them off their course, and we sailed on till we came hither by night. It was all we could do to get inside the harbor, and none of us said a word about supper though we wanted it badly, but we all went on shore and lay down just as we were. I was very tired and fell asleep directly, so they took my goods out of the ship, and placed them beside me where I was lying upon the sand. Then they sailed away to Sidonia, and I was left here in great distress of mind."

Such was his story, but Minerva smiled and caressed him with her hand. Then she took the form of a woman, fair, stately, and wise, "He must be indeed a shifty lying fellow," said she, "who could surpass you in all manner of craft even though you had a god for your antagonist. Dare-devil that you are, full of guile, unwearying in deceit, can you not drop your tricks and your instinctive falsehood, even now that you are in your own country again? We will say no more, however, about this, for we can both of us deceive upon occasion- you are the most accomplished counselor and orator among all mankind, while I for diplomacy and subtlety have no equal among the gods. Did you not know Jove's daughter Minerva- me, who have been ever with you, who kept watch over you in all your troubles, and who made the Phaeacians take so great a liking to you? And now, again, I am come here to talk things over with you, and help you to hide the treasure I made the Phaeacians give you; I want to tell you about the troubles that await you in your own house; you have got to face them, but tell no one, neither man nor woman, that you have come home again. Bear everything, and put up with every man's insolence, without a word."

And Ulysses answered, "A man, goddess, may know a great deal, but you are so constantly changing your appearance that when he meets you it is a hard matter for him to know whether it is you or not. This much, however, I know exceedingly well; you were very kind to me as long as we Achaeans were fighting before Troy, but from the day on which we went on board ship after having sacked the city of Priam, and heaven dispersed us- from that day, Minerva, I saw no more of you, and cannot ever remember your coming to my ship to help me in a difficulty; I had to wander on sick and sorry till the gods delivered me from evil and I reached the city of the Phaeacians, where you encouraged me and took me into the town. And now, I beseech you in your father's name, tell me the truth, for I do not believe I am really back in Ithaca. I am in some other country and you are mocking me and deceiving me in all you have been saying. Tell me then truly, have I really got back to my own country?"

"You are always taking something of that sort into your head," replied Minerva, "and that is why I cannot desert you in your afflictions; you are so plausible, shrewd and shifty. Any one but yourself on returning from so long a voyage would at once have gone home to see his wife and children, but you do not seem to care about asking after them or hearing any news about them till you have exploited your wife, who remains at home vainly grieving for you, and having no peace night or day for the tears she sheds on your behalf. As for my not coming near you, I was never uneasy about you, for I was certain you would get back safely though you would lose all your men, and I did not wish to quarrel with my uncle Neptune, who never forgave you for having blinded his son. I will now, however, point out to you the lie of the land, and you will then perhaps believe me. This is the haven of the old merman Phorcys, and here is the olive tree that grows at the head of it; [near it is the cave sacred to the Naiads;] here too is the overarching cavern in which you have offered many an acceptable hecatomb to the nymphs, and this is the wooded mountain Neritum."

As she spoke the goddess dispersed the mist and the land appeared. Then Ulysses rejoiced at finding himself again in his own land, and kissed the bounteous soil; he lifted up his hands and prayed to the nymphs, saying, "Naiad nymphs, daughters of Jove, I made sure that I was never again to see you, now therefore I greet you with all loving salutations, and I will bring you offerings as in the old days, if Jove's redoubtable daughter will grant me life, and bring my son to manhood."

"Take heart, and do not trouble yourself about that," rejoined Minerva, "let us rather set about stowing your things at once in the cave, where they will be quite safe. Let us see how we can best manage it all."

Therewith she went down into the cave to look for the safest hiding places, while Ulysses brought up all the treasure of gold, bronze, and good clothing which the Phaecians had given him. They stowed everything carefully away, and Minerva set a stone against the door of the cave. Then the two sat down by the root of the great olive, and consulted how to compass the destruction of the wicked suitors.

"Ulysses," said Minerva, "noble son of Laertes, think how you can lay hands on these disreputable people who have been lording it in your house these three years, courting your wife and making wedding presents to her, while she does nothing but lament your absence, giving hope and sending your encouraging messages to every one of them, but meaning the very opposite of all she says."

And Ulysses answered, "In good truth, goddess, it seems I should have come to much the same bad end in my own house as Agamemnon did, if you had not given me such timely information. Advise me how I shall best avenge myself. Stand by my side and put your courage into my heart as on the day when we loosed Troy's fair diadem from her brow. Help me now as you did then, and I will fight three hundred men, if you, goddess, will be with me."

"Trust me for that," said she, "I will not lose sight of you when once we set about it, and I would imagine that some of those who are devouring your substance will then bespatter the pavement with their blood and brains. I will begin by disguising you so that no human being shall know you; I will cover your body with wrinkles; you shall lose all your yellow hair; I will clothe you in a garment that shall fill all who see it with loathing; I will blear your fine eyes for you, and make you an unseemly object in the sight of the suitors, of your wife, and of the son whom you left behind you. Then go at once to the swineherd who is in charge of your pigs; he has been always well affected towards you, and is devoted to Penelope and your son; you will find him feeding his pigs near the rock that is called Raven by the fountain Arethusa, where they are fattening on beechmast and spring water after their manner. Stay with him and find out how things are going, while I proceed to Sparta and see your son, who is with Menelaus at Lacedaemon, where he has gone to try and find out whether you are still alive."

"But why," said Ulysses, "did you not tell him, for you knew all about it? Did you want him too to go sailing about amid all kinds of hardship while others are eating up his estate?"

Minerva answered, "Never mind about him, I sent him that he might be well spoken of for having gone. He is in no sort of difficulty, but is staying quite comfortably with Menelaus, and is surrounded with abundance of every kind. The suitors have put out to sea and are lying in wait for him, for they mean to kill him before he can get home. I do not much think they will succeed, but rather that some of those who are now eating up your estate will first find a grave themselves."

As she spoke Minerva touched him with her wand and covered him with wrinkles, took away all his yellow hair, and withered the flesh over his whole body; she bleared his eyes, which were naturally very fine ones; she changed his clothes and threw an old rag of a wrap about him, and a tunic, tattered, filthy, and begrimed with smoke; she also gave him an undressed deer skin as an outer garment, and furnished him with a staff and a wallet all in holes, with a twisted thong for him to sling it over his shoulder.

When the pair had thus laid their plans they parted, and the goddess went straight to Lacedaemon to fetch Telemachus.

Lesson 52

- Read Book 14 of *The Odyssey*.

Book 14

Ulysses now left the haven, and took the rough track up through the wooded country and over the crest of the mountain till he reached the place where Minerva had said that he would find the swineherd, who was the most thrifty servant he had. He found him sitting in front of his hut, which was by the yards that he had built on a site which could be seen from far. He had made them spacious and fair to see, with a free run for the pigs all round them; he had built them during his master's absence, of stones which he had gathered out of the ground, without saying anything to Penelope or Laertes, and he had fenced them on top with thorn bushes. Outside the yard he had run a strong fence of oaken posts, split, and set pretty close together, while inside he had built twelve sties near one another for the sows to lie in. There were fifty pigs wallowing in each sty, all of them breeding sows; but the boars slept outside and were much fewer in number, for the suitors kept on eating them, and the swineherd had to send them the best he had continually. There were three hundred and sixty boar pigs, and the herdsman's four hounds, which were as fierce as wolves, slept always with them. The swineherd was at that moment cutting out a pair of sandals from a good stout ox hide. Three of his men were out herding the pigs in one place or another, and he had sent the fourth to town with a boar that he had been forced to send the suitors that they might sacrifice it and have their fill of meat.

When the hounds saw Ulysses they set up a furious barking and flew at him, but Ulysses was cunning enough to sit down and loose his hold of the stick that he had in his hand: still, he would have been torn by them in his own homestead had not the swineherd dropped his ox hide, rushed full speed through the gate of the yard and driven the dogs off by shouting and throwing stones at them. Then he said to Ulysses, "Old man, the dogs were likely to have made short work of you, and then you would have got me into trouble. The gods have given me quite enough worries without that, for I have lost the best of masters, and am in continual grief on his account. I have to attend swine for other people to eat, while he, if he yet lives to see the light of day, is starving in some distant land. But come inside, and when you have had your fill of bread and wine, tell me where you come from, and all about your misfortunes."

On this the swineherd led the way into the hut and bade him sit down. He strewed a good thick bed of rushes upon the floor, and on the top of this he threw the shaggy chamois skin- a great thick one- on which he used to sleep by night. Ulysses was pleased at being made thus welcome, and said "May Jove, sir, and the rest of the gods grant you your heart's desire in return for the kind way in which you have received me."

To this you answered, O swineherd Eumaeus, "Stranger, though a still poorer man should come here, it would not be right for me to insult him, for all strangers and beggars are from Jove. You must take what you can get and be thankful, for servants live in fear when they have young lords for their masters; and this is my misfortune now, for heaven has hindered the return of him who would have been always good to me and given me something of my own- a house, a piece of land, a good looking wife, and all else that a liberal master allows a servant who has worked hard for him, and whose labour the gods have prospered as they have mine in the situation which I hold. If my master had grown old here he would have done great things by me, but he is gone, and I wish that Helen's whole race were utterly destroyed, for she has been the death of many a good man. It was this matter that took my master to Ilius, the land of noble steeds, to fight the Trojans in the cause of kin Agamemnon."

As he spoke he bound his girdle round him and went to the sties where the young sucking pigs were penned. He picked out two which he brought back with him and sacrificed. He singed them, cut them up, and spitted them; when the meat was cooked he brought it all in and set it before Ulysses, hot and still on the spit, whereon Ulysses sprinkled it over with white barley meal. The swineherd then mixed wine in a bowl of ivy-wood, and taking a seat opposite Ulysses told him to begin.

"Fall to, stranger," said he, "on a dish of servant's pork. The fat pigs have to go to the suitors, who eat them up without shame or scruple; but the blessed gods love not such shameful doings, and respect those who do what is lawful and right. Even the fierce free-booters who go raiding on other people's land, and Jove gives them their spoil- even they, when they have filled their ships and got home again live conscience-stricken, and look fearfully for judgement; but some god seems to have told these people that Ulysses is dead and gone; they will not, therefore, go back to their own homes and make their offers of marriage in the usual way, but waste his estate by force, without fear or stint. Not a day or night comes out of heaven, but they sacrifice not one victim nor two only, and they take the run of his wine, for he was exceedingly rich. No other great man either in Ithaca or on the mainland is as rich as he was; he had as much as twenty men put together. I will tell you what he had. There are twelve herds of cattle upon the mainland, and as many flocks of sheep, there are also twelve droves of pigs, while his own men and hired strangers feed him twelve widely spreading herds of goats. Here in Ithaca he runs even large flocks of goats on the far end of the island, and they are in the charge of excellent goatherds. Each one of these sends the suitors the best goat in the flock every day. As for myself, I am in charge of the pigs that you see here, and I have to keep picking out the best I have and sending it to them."

This was his story, but Ulysses went on eating and drinking ravenously without a word, brooding his revenge. When he had eaten enough and was satisfied, the swineherd took the bowl from which he usually drank, filled it with wine, and gave it to Ulysses, who was pleased, and said as he took it in his hands, "My friend, who was this master of yours that bought you and paid for you, so rich and so powerful as you tell me? You say he perished in the cause of King Agamemnon; tell me who he was, in case I may have met with such a person. Jove and the other gods know, but I may be able to give you news of him, for I have traveled much."

Eumaeus answered, "Old man, no traveler who comes here with news will get Ulysses' wife and son to believe his story. Nevertheless, tramps in want of a lodging keep coming with their mouths full of lies, and not a word of truth; every one who finds his way to Ithaca goes to my mistress and tells her falsehoods, whereon she takes them in, makes much of them, and asks them all manner of questions, crying all the time as women will when they have lost their husbands. And you too, old man, for a shirt and a cloak would doubtless make up a very pretty story. But the wolves and birds of prey have long since torn Ulysses to pieces, or the fishes of the sea have eaten him, and his bones are lying buried deep in sand upon some foreign shore; he is dead and gone, and a bad business it is for all his friends- for me especially; go where I may I shall never find so good a master, not even if I were to go home to my mother and father where I was bred and born. I do not so much care, however, about my parents now, though I should dearly like to see them again in my own country; it is the loss of Ulysses that grieves me most; I cannot speak of him without reverence though he is here no longer, for he was very fond of me, and took such care of me that wherever he may be I shall always honour his memory."

"My friend," replied Ulysses, "you are very positive, and very hard of belief about your master's coming home again, nevertheless I will not merely say, but will swear, that he is coming. Do not give me anything for my news till he has actually come, you may then give me a shirt and cloak of good wear if you will. I am in great want, but I will not take anything at all till then, for I hate a man, even as I hate hell fire, who lets his poverty tempt him into lying. I swear by King Jove, by the rites of hospitality, and by that hearth of Ulysses to which I have now come, that all will surely happen as I have said it will. Ulysses will return in this self same year; with the end of this moon and the beginning of the next he will be here to do vengeance on all those who are ill treating his wife and son."

To this you answered, O swineherd Eumaeus, "Old man, you will neither get paid for bringing good news, nor will Ulysses ever come home; drink you wine in peace, and let us talk about something else. Do not keep on reminding me of all this; it always pains me when any one speaks about my honored master. As for your oath we will let it alone, but I only wish he may come, as do Penelope, his old father Laertes, and his son Telemachus. I am terribly unhappy too about this same boy of his; he was running up fast into manhood, and bade fare to be no worse man, face and figure, than his father, but some one, either god or man, has been unsettling his mind, so he has gone off to Pylos to try and get news of his father, and the suitors are lying in wait for him as he is coming home, in the hope of leaving the house of Arceisius without a name in Ithaca. But let us say no more about him, and leave him to be taken, or else to escape if the son of Saturn holds his hand over him to protect him. And now, old man, tell me your own story; tell me also, for I want to know, who you are and where you come from. Tell me of your town and parents, what manner of ship you came in, how crew brought you to Ithaca, and from what country they professed to come- for you cannot have come by land."

And Ulysses answered, "I will tell you all about it. If there were meat and wine enough, and we could stay here in the hut with nothing to do but to eat and drink while the others go to their work, I could easily talk on for a whole twelve months without ever finishing the story of the sorrows with which it has pleased heaven to visit me.

"I am by birth a Cretan; my father was a well-to-do man, who had many sons born in marriage, whereas I was the son of a slave whom he had purchased for a concubine; nevertheless, my father Castor son of Hylax (whose lineage I claim, and who was held in the highest honor among the Cretans for his wealth, prosperity, and the valour of his sons) put me on the same level with my brothers who had been born in wedlock. When, however, death took him to the house of Hades, his sons divided his estate and cast lots for their shares, but to me they gave a holding and little else; nevertheless, my valor enabled me to marry into a rich family, for I was not given to bragging, or shirking on the field of battle. It is all over now; still, if you look at the straw you can see what the ear was, for I have had trouble enough and to spare. Mars and Minerva made me doughty in war; when I had picked my men to surprise the enemy with an ambuscade I never gave death so much as a thought, but was the first to leap forward and spear all whom I could overtake. Such was I in battle, but I did not care about farm work, nor the frugal home life of those who would bring up children. My delight was in ships, fighting, javelins, and arrows- things that most men shudder to think of; but one man likes one thing and another another, and this was what I was most naturally inclined to. Before the Achaeans went to Troy, nine times was I in command of men and ships on foreign service, and I amassed much wealth. I had my pick of the spoil in the first instance, and much more was allotted to me later on.

"My house grew apace and I became a great man among the Cretans, but when Jove counselled that terrible expedition, in which so many perished, the people required me and Idomeneus to lead their ships to Troy, and there was no way out of it, for they insisted on our doing so. There we fought for nine whole years, but in the tenth we sacked the city of Priam and sailed home again as heaven dispersed us. Then it was that Jove devised evil against me. I spent but one month happily with my children, wife, and property, and then I conceived the idea of making a descent on

Egypt, so I fitted out a fine fleet and manned it. I had nine ships, and the people flocked to fill them. For six days I and my men made feast, and I found them many victims both for sacrifice to the gods and for themselves, but on the seventh day we went on board and set sail from Crete with a fair North wind behind us though we were going down a river. Nothing went ill with any of our ships, and we had no sickness on board, but sat where we were and let the ships go as the wind and steersmen took them. On the fifth day we reached the river Aegyptus; there I stationed my ships in the river, bidding my men stay by them and keep guard over them while I sent out scouts to reconnoiter from every point of vantage.

"But the men disobeyed my orders, took to their own devices, and ravaged the land of the Egyptians, killing the men, and taking their wives and children captive. The alarm was soon carried to the city, and when they heard the war cry, the people came out at daybreak till the plain was filled with horsemen and foot soldiers and with the gleam of armor. Then Jove spread panic among my men, and they would no longer face the enemy, for they found themselves surrounded. The Egyptians killed many of us, and took the rest alive to do forced labor for them. Jove, however, put it in my mind to do thus- and I wish I had died then and there in Egypt instead, for there was much sorrow in store for me- I took off my helmet and shield and dropped my spear from my hand; then I went straight up to the king's chariot, clasped his knees and kissed them, whereon he spared my life, bade me get into his chariot, and took me weeping to his own home. Many made at me with their ashen spears and tried to kill me in their fury, but the king protected me, for he feared the wrath of Jove the protector of strangers, who punishes those who do evil.

"I stayed there for seven years and got together much money among the Egyptians, for they all gave me something; but when it was now going on for eight years there came a certain Phoenician, a cunning rascal, who had already committed all sorts of villainy, and this man talked me over into going with him to Phoenicia, where his house and his possessions lay. I stayed there for a whole twelve months, but at the end of that time when months and days had gone by till the same season had come round again, he set me on board a ship bound for Libya, on a pretense that I was to take a cargo along with him to that place, but really that he might sell me as a slave and take the money I fetched. I suspected his intention, but went on board with him, for I could not help it.

"The ship ran before a fresh North wind till we had reached the sea that lies between Crete and Libya; there, however, Jove counselled their destruction, for as soon as we were well out from Crete and could see nothing but sea and sky, he raised a black cloud over our ship and the sea grew dark beneath it. Then Jove let fly with his thunderbolts and the ship went round and round and was filled with fire and brimstone as the lightning struck it. The men fell all into the sea; they were carried about in the water round the ship looking like so many sea-gulls, but the god presently deprived them of all chance of getting home again. I was all dismayed; Jove, however, sent the ship's mast within my reach, which saved my life, for I clung to it, and drifted before the fury of the gale. Nine days did I drift but in the darkness of the tenth night a great wave bore me on to the Thesprotian coast. There Pheidon king of the Thesprotians entertained me hospitably without charging me anything at all for his son found me when I was nearly dead with cold and fatigue, whereon he raised me by the hand, took me to his father's house and gave me clothes to wear.

"There it was that I heard news of Ulysses, for the king told me he had entertained him, and shown him much hospitality while he was on his homeward journey. He showed me also the treasure of gold, and wrought iron that Ulysses had got together. There was enough to keep his family for ten generations, so much had he left in the house of King Pheidon. But the king said Ulysses had gone to Dodona that he might learn Jove's mind from the god's high oak tree, and know whether after so long an absence he should return to Ithaca openly, or in secret. Moreover the king swore in my presence, making drink-offerings in his own house as he did so, that the ship was by the water side, and the crew found, that should take him to his own country. He sent me off however before Ulysses returned, for there happened to be a Thesprotian ship sailing for the wheat-growing island of Dulichium, and he told those in charge of her to be sure and take me safely to King Acastus.

"These men hatched a plot against me that would have reduced me to the very extreme of misery, for when the ship had got some way out from land they resolved on selling me as a slave. They stripped me of the shirt and cloak that I was wearing, and gave me instead the tattered old clouts in which you now see me; then, towards nightfall, they reached the tilled lands of Ithaca, and there they bound me with a strong rope fast in the ship, while they went on shore to get supper by the sea side. But the gods soon undid my bonds for me, and having drawn my rags over my head

I slid down the rudder into the sea, where I struck out and swam till I was well clear of them, and came ashore near a thick wood in which I lay concealed. They were very angry at my having escaped and went searching about for me, till at last they thought it was no further use and went back to their ship. The gods, having hidden me thus easily, then took me to a good man's door- for it seems that I am not to die yet awhile."

To this you answered, O swineherd Eumaeus, "Poor unhappy stranger, I have found the story of your misfortunes extremely interesting, but that part about Ulysses is not right; and you will never get me to believe it. Why should a man like you go about telling lies in this way? I know all about the return of my master. The gods one and all of them detest him, or they would have taken him before Troy, or let him die with friends around him when the days of his fighting were done; for then the Achaeans would have built a mound over his ashes and his son would have been heir to his renown, but now the storm winds have spirited him away we know not whither.

"As for me I live out of the way here with the pigs, and never go to the town unless when Penelope sends for me on the arrival of some news about Ulysses. Then they all sit round and ask questions, both those who grieve over the king's absence, and those who rejoice at it because they can eat up his property without paying for it. For my own part I have never cared about asking anyone else since the time when I was taken in by an Aetolian, who had killed a man and come a long way till at last he reached my station, and I was very kind to him. He said he had seen Ulysses with Idomeneus among the Cretans, refitting his ships which had been damaged in a gale. He said Ulysses would return in the following summer or autumn with his men, and that he would bring back much wealth. And now you, you unfortunate old man, since fate has brought you to my door, do not try to flatter me in this way with vain hopes. It is not for any such reason that I shall treat you kindly, but only out of respect for Jove the god of hospitality, as fearing him and pitying you."

Ulysses answered, "I see that you are of an unbelieving mind; I have given you my oath, and yet you will not credit me; let us then make a bargain, and call all the gods in heaven to witness it. If your master comes home, give me a cloak and shirt of good wear, and send me to Dulichium where I want to go; but if he does not come as I say he will, set your men on to me, and tell them to throw me from yonder precipice, as a warning to tramps not to go about the country telling lies."

"And a pretty figure I should cut then," replied Eumaeus, "both now and hereafter, if I were to kill you after receiving you into my hut and showing you hospitality. I should have to say my prayers in good earnest if I did; but it is just supper time and I hope my men will come in directly, that we may cook something savory for supper."

Thus did they converse, and presently the swineherds came up with the pigs, which were then shut up for the night in their sties, and a tremendous squealing they made as they were being driven into them. But Eumaeus called to his men and said, "Bring in the best pig you have, that I may sacrifice for this stranger, and we will take toll of him ourselves. We have had trouble enough this long time feeding pigs, while others reap the fruit of our labor."

On this he began chopping firewood, while the others brought in a fine fat five year old boar pig, and set it at the altar. Eumaeus did not forget the gods, for he was a man of good principles, so the first thing he did was to cut bristles from the pig's face and throw them into the fire, praying to all the gods as he did so that Ulysses might return home again. Then he clubbed the pig with a billet of oak which he had kept back when he was chopping the firewood, and stunned it, while the others slaughtered and singed it. Then they cut it up, and Eumaeus began by putting raw pieces from each joint on to some of the fat; these he sprinkled with barley meal, and laid upon the embers; they cut the rest of the meat up small, put the pieces upon the spits and roasted them till they were done; when they had taken them off the spits they threw them on to the dresser in a heap. The swineherd, who was a most equitable man, then stood up to give every one his share. He made seven portions; one of these he set apart for Mercury the son of Maia and the nymphs, praying to them as he did so; the others he dealt out to the men man by man. He gave Ulysses some slices cut lengthwise down the loin as a mark of especial honour, and Ulysses was much pleased. "I hope, Eumaeus," said he, "that Jove will be as well disposed towards you as I am, for the respect you are showing to an outcast like myself."

To this you answered, O swineherd Eumaeus, "Eat, my good fellow, and enjoy your supper, such as it is. God grants this, and withholds that, just as he thinks right, for he can do whatever he chooses."

As he spoke he cut off the first piece and offered it as a burnt sacrifice to the immortal gods; then he made them a drink-offering, put the cup in the hands of Ulysses, and sat down to his own portion. Mesaulius brought them their bread; the swineherd had bought this man on his own account from among the Taphians during his master's absence, and had paid for him with his own money without saying anything either to his mistress or Laertes. They then laid their hands upon the good things that were before them, and when they had had enough to eat and drink, Mesaulius took away what was left of the bread, and they all went to bed after having made a hearty supper.

Now the night came on stormy and very dark, for there was no moon. It poured without ceasing, and the wind blew strong from the West, which is a wet quarter, so Ulysses thought he would see whether Eumaeus, in the excellent care he took of him, would take off his own cloak and give it him, or make one of his men give him one. "Listen to me," said he, "Eumaeus and the rest of you; when I have said a prayer I will tell you something. It is the wine that makes me talk in this way; wine will make even a wise man fall to singing; it will make him chuckle and dance and say many a word that he had better leave unspoken; still, as I have begun, I will go on. Would that I were still young and strong as when we got up an ambuscade before Troy. Menelaus and Ulysses were the leaders, but I was in command also, for the other two would have it so. When we had come up to the wall of the city we crouched down beneath our armor and lay there under cover of the reeds and thick brush-wood that grew about the swamp. It came on to freeze with a North wind blowing; the snow fell small and fine like hoarfrost, and our shields were coated thick with rime. The others had all got cloaks and shirts, and slept comfortably enough with their shields about their shoulders, but I had carelessly left my cloak behind me, not thinking that I should be too cold, and had gone off in nothing but my shirt and shield. When the night was two-thirds through and the stars had shifted their their places, I nudged Ulysses who was close to me with my elbow, and he at once gave me his ear.

"'Ulysses,' said I, 'this cold will be the death of me, for I have no cloak; some god fooled me into setting off with nothing on but my shirt, and I do not know what to do.'

"Ulysses, who was as crafty as he was valiant, hit upon the following plan:

"'Keep still,' said he in a low voice, 'or the others will hear you.' Then he raised his head on his elbow.

"'My friends,' said he, 'I have had a dream from heaven in my sleep. We are a long way from the ships; I wish some one would go down and tell Agamemnon to send us up more men at once.'

"On this Thoas son of Andraemon threw off his cloak and set out running to the ships, whereon I took the cloak and lay in it comfortably enough till morning. Would that I were still young and strong as I was in those days, for then some one of you swineherds would give me a cloak both out of good will and for the respect due to a brave soldier; but now people look down upon me because my clothes are shabby."

And Eumaeus answered, "Old man, you have told us an excellent story, and have said nothing so far but what is quite satisfactory; for the present, therefore, you shall want neither clothing nor anything else that a stranger in distress may reasonably expect, but to-morrow morning you have to shake your own old rags about your body again, for we have not many spare cloaks nor shirts up here, but every man has only one. When Ulysses' son comes home again he will give you both cloak and shirt, and send you wherever you may want to go."

With this he got up and made a bed for Ulysses by throwing some goatskins and sheepskins on the ground in front of the fire. Here Ulysses lay down, and Eumaeus covered him over with a great heavy cloak that he kept for a change in case of extraordinarily bad weather.

Thus did Ulysses sleep, and the young men slept beside him. But the swineherd did not like sleeping away from his pigs, so he got ready to go and Ulysses was glad to see that he looked after his property during his master's absence. First he slung his sword over his brawny shoulders and put on a thick cloak to keep out the wind. He also took the skin of a large and well fed goat, and a javelin in case of attack from men or dogs. Thus equipped he went to his rest where the pigs were camping under an overhanging rock that gave them shelter from the North wind.

Lesson 53

- Read Book 15 of *The Odyssey.*

Book 15

But Minerva went to the fair city of Lacedaemon to tell Ulysses' son that he was to return at once. She found him and Pisistratus sleeping in the forecourt of Menelaus's house; Pisistratus was fast asleep, but Telemachus could get no rest all night for thinking of his unhappy father, so Minerva went close up to him and said:

"Telemachus, you should not remain so far away from home any longer, nor leave your property with such dangerous people in your house; they will eat up everything you have among them, and you will have been on a fool's errand. Ask Menelaus to send you home at once if you wish to find your excellent mother still there when you get back. Her father and brothers are already urging her to marry Eurymachus, who has given her more than any of the others, and has been greatly increasing his wedding presents. I hope nothing valuable may have been taken from the house in spite of you, but you know what women are- they always want to do the best they can for the man who marries them, and never give another thought to the children of their first husband, nor to their father either when he is dead and done with. Go home, therefore, and put everything in charge of the most respectable woman servant that you have, until it shall please heaven to send you a wife of your own. Let me tell you also of another matter which you had better attend to. The chief men among the suitors are lying in wait for you in the Strait between Ithaca and Samos, and they mean to kill you before you can reach home. I do not much think they will succeed; it is more likely that some of those who are now eating up your property will find a grave themselves. Sail night and day, and keep your ship well away from the islands; the god who watches over you and protects you will send you a fair wind. As soon as you get to Ithaca send your ship and men on to the town, but yourself go straight to the swineherd who has charge your pigs; he is well disposed towards you, stay with him, therefore, for the night, and then send him to Penelope to tell her that you have got back safe from Pylos."

Then she went back to Olympus; but Telemachus stirred Pisistratus with his heel to rouse him, and said, "Wake up Pisistratus, and yoke the horses to the chariot, for we must set off home."

But Pisistratus said, "No matter what hurry we are in we cannot drive in the dark. It will be morning soon; wait till Menelaus has brought his presents and put them in the chariot for us; and let him say good-bye to us in the usual way. So long as he lives a guest should never forget a host who has shown him kindness."

As he spoke day began to break, and Menelaus, who had already risen, leaving Helen in bed, came towards them. When Telemachus saw him he put on his shirt as fast as he could, threw a great cloak over his shoulders, and went out to meet him. "Menelaus," said he, "let me go back now to my own country, for I want to get home."

And Menelaus answered, "Telemachus, if you insist on going I will not detain you. I do not like to see a host either too fond of his guest or too rude to him. Moderation is best in all things, and not letting a man go when he wants to do so is as bad as telling him to go if he would like to stay. One should treat a guest well as long as he is in the house and speed him when he wants to leave it. Wait, then, till I can get your beautiful presents into your chariot, and till you have yourself seen them. I will tell the women to prepare a sufficient dinner for you of what there may be in the house; it will be at once more proper and cheaper for you to get your dinner before setting out on such a long journey. If, moreover, you have a fancy for making a tour in Hellas or in the Peloponnese, I will yoke my horses, and will conduct you myself through all our principal cities. No one will send us away empty handed; every one will give us something- a bronze tripod, a couple of mules, or a gold cup."

"Menelaus," replied Telemachus, "I want to go home at once, for when I came away I left my property without protection, and fear that while looking for my father I shall come to ruin myself, or find that something valuable has been stolen during my absence."

When Menelaus heard this he immediately told his wife and servants to prepare a sufficient dinner from what there might be in the house. At this moment Eteoneus joined him, for he lived close by and had just got up; so Menelaus told him to light the fire and cook some meat, which he at once did. Then Menelaus went down into his fragrant store room, not alone, but Helen went too, with Megapenthes. When he reached the place where the treasures of his house were kept, he selected a double cup, and told his son Megapenthes to bring also a silver mixing-bowl. Meanwhile Helen went to the chest where she kept the lovely dresses which she had made with her own hands, and took out one that was largest and most beautifully enriched with embroidery; it glittered like a star, and lay at the very bottom of the chest. Then they all came back through the house again till they got to Telemachus, and Menelaus said, "Telemachus, may Jove, the mighty husband of Juno, bring you safely home according to your desire. I will now present you with the finest and most precious piece of plate in all my house. It is a mixing-bowl of pure silver, except the rim, which is inlaid with gold, and it is the work of Vulcan. Phaedimus king of the Sidonians made me a present of it in the course of a visit that I paid him while I was on my return home. I should like to give it to you."

With these words he placed the double cup in the hands of Telemachus, while Megapenthes brought the beautiful mixing-bowl and set it before him. Hard by stood lovely Helen with the robe ready in her hand.

"I too, my son," said she, "have something for you as a keepsake from the hand of Helen; it is for your bride to wear upon her wedding day. Till then, get your dear mother to keep it for you; thus may you go back rejoicing to your own country and to your home."

So saying she gave the robe over to him and he received it gladly. Then Pisistratus put the presents into the chariot, and admired them all as he did so. Presently Menelaus took Telemachus and Pisistratus into the house, and they both of them sat down to table. A maid servant brought them water in a beautiful golden ewer, and poured it into a silver basin for them to wash their hands, and she drew a clean table beside them; an upper servant brought them bread and offered them many good things of what there was in the house. Eteoneus carved the meat and gave them each their portions, while Megapenthes poured out the wine. Then they laid their hands upon the good things that were before them, but as soon as they had had had enough to eat and drink Telemachus and Pisistratus yoked the horses, and took their places in the chariot. They drove out through the inner gateway and under the echoing gatehouse of the outer court, and Menelaus came after them with a golden goblet of wine in his right hand that they might make a drink-offering before they set out. He stood in front of the horses and pledged them, saying, “Farewell to both of you; see that you tell Nestor how I have treated you, for he was as kind to me as any father could be while we Achaeans were fighting before Troy.”

“We will be sure, sir,” answered Telemachus, “to tell him everything as soon as we see him. I wish I were as certain of finding Ulysses returned when I get back to Ithaca, that I might tell him of the very great kindness you have shown me and of the many beautiful presents I am taking with me.”

As he was thus speaking a bird flew on his right hand- an eagle with a great white goose in its talons which it had carried off from the farm yard- and all the men and women were running after it and shouting. It came quite close up to them and flew away on their right hands in front of the horses. When they saw it they were glad, and their hearts took comfort within them, whereon Pisistratus said, “Tell me, Menelaus, has heaven sent this omen for us or for you?”

Menelaus was thinking what would be the most proper answer for him to make, but Helen was too quick for him and said, “I will read this matter as heaven has put it in my heart, and as I doubt not that it will come to pass. The eagle came from the mountain where it was bred and has its nest, and in like manner Ulysses, after having traveled far and suffered much, will return to take his revenge- if indeed he is not back already and hatching mischief for the suitors.”

“May Jove so grant it,” replied Telemachus; “if it should prove to be so, I will make vows to you as though you were a god, even when I am at home.”

As he spoke he lashed his horses and they started off at full speed through the town towards the open country. They swayed the yoke upon their necks and traveled the whole day long till the sun set and darkness was over all the land. Then they reached Pherae, where Diocles lived who was son of Ortilochus, the son of Alpheus. There they passed the night and were treated hospitably. When the child of morning, rosy-fingered Dawn, appeared, they again yoked their horses and their places in the chariot. They drove out through the inner gateway and under the echoing gatehouse of the outer court. Then Pisistratus lashed his horses on and they flew forward nothing loath; ere long they came to Pylos, and then Telemachus said:

"Pisistratus, I hope you will promise to do what I am going to ask you. You know our fathers were old friends before us; moreover, we are both of an age, and this journey has brought us together still more closely; do not, therefore, take me past my ship, but leave me there, for if I go to your father's house he will try to keep me in the warmth of his good will towards me, and I must go home at once."

Pisistratus thought how he should do as he was asked, and in the end he deemed it best to turn his horses towards the ship, and put Menelaus's beautiful presents of gold and raiment in the stern of the vessel. Then he said, "Go on board at once and tell your men to do so also before I can reach home to tell my father. I know how obstinate he is, and am sure he will not let you go; he will come down here to fetch you, and he will not go back without you. But he will be very angry."

With this he drove his goodly steeds back to the city of the Pylians and soon reached his home, but Telemachus called the men together and gave his orders. "Now, my men," said he, "get everything in order on board the ship, and let us set out home."

Thus did he speak, and they went on board even as he had said. But as Telemachus was thus busied, praying also and sacrificing to Minerva in the ship's stern, there came to him a man from a distant country, a seer, who was flying from Argos because he had killed a man. He was descended from Melampus, who used to live in Pylos, the land of sheep; he was rich and owned a great house, but he was driven into exile by the great and powerful King Neleus. Neleus seized his goods and held them for a whole year, during which he was a close prisoner in the house of King Phylacus, and in much distress of mind both on account of the daughter of Neleus and because he was haunted by a great sorrow that dread Erinyes had laid upon him. In the end, however, he escaped with his life, drove the cattle from Phylace to Pylos, avenged the wrong that had been done him, and gave the daughter of Neleus to his brother. Then he left the country and went to Argos, where it was ordained that he should reign over much people. There he married, established himself, and had two famous sons Antiphates and Mantius. Antiphates became father of Oicleus, and Oicleus of Amphiaraus, who was dearly loved both by Jove and by Apollo, but he did not live to old age, for he was killed in Thebes by reason of a woman's gifts. His sons were Alcmaeon and Amphilochus. Mantius, the other son of Melampus, was father to Polypheides and Cleitus. Aurora, throned in gold, carried off Cleitus for his beauty's sake, that he might dwell among the immortals, but Apollo made Polypheides the greatest seer in the whole world now that Amphiaraus was dead. He quarreled with his father and went to live in Hyperesia, where he remained and prophesied for all men.

His son, Theoclymenus, it was who now came up to Telemachus as he was making drink-offerings and praying in his ship. "Friend'" said he, "now that I find you sacrificing in this place, I beseech you by your sacrifices themselves, and by the god to whom you make them, I pray you also by your own head and by those of your followers, tell me the truth and nothing but the truth. Who and whence are you? Tell me also of your town and parents."

Telemachus said, "I will answer you quite truly. I am from Ithaca, and my father is Ulysses, as surely as that he ever lived. But he has come to some miserable end. Therefore I have taken this ship and got my crew together to see if I can hear any news of him, for he has been away a long time."

"I too," answered Theoclymenus, "am an exile, for I have killed a man of my own race. He has many brothers and kinsmen in Argos, and they have great power among the Argives. I am flying to escape death at their hands, and am thus doomed to be a wanderer on the face of the earth. I am your suppliant; take me, therefore, on board your ship that they may not kill me, for I know they are in pursuit."

"I will not refuse you," replied Telemachus, "if you wish to join us. Come, therefore, and in Ithaca we will treat you hospitably according to what we have."

On this he received Theoclymenus' spear and laid it down on the deck of the ship. He went on board and sat in the stern, bidding Theoclymenus sit beside him; then the men let go the hawsers. Telemachus told them to catch hold of the ropes, and they made all haste to do so. They set the mast in its socket in the cross plank, raised it and made it fast with the forestays, and they hoisted their white sails with sheets of twisted ox hide. Minerva sent them a fair wind that blew fresh and strong to take the ship on her course as fast as possible. Thus then they passed by Crouni and Chalcis.

Presently the sun set and darkness was over all the land. The vessel made a quick passage to Pheae and thence on to Elis, where the Epeans rule. Telemachus then headed her for the flying islands, wondering within himself whether he should escape death or should be taken prisoner.

Meanwhile Ulysses and the swineherd were eating their supper in the hut, and the men supped with them. As soon as they had had to eat and drink, Ulysses began trying to prove the swineherd and see whether he would continue to treat him kindly, and ask him to stay on at the station or pack him off to the city; so he said:

"Eumaeus, and all of you, to-morrow I want to go away and begin begging about the town, so as to be no more trouble to you or to your men. Give me your advice therefore, and let me have a good guide to go with me and show me the way. I will go the round of the city begging as I needs must, to see if any one will give me a drink and a piece of bread. I should like also to go to the house of Ulysses and bring news of her husband to queen Penelope. I could then go about among the suitors and see if out of all their abundance they will give me a dinner. I should soon make them an excellent servant in all sorts of ways. Listen and believe when I tell you that by the blessing of Mercury who gives grace and good name to the works of all men, there is no one living who would make a more handy servant than I should-to put fresh wood on the fire, chop fuel, carve, cook, pour out wine, and do all those services that poor men have to do for their betters."

The swineherd was very much disturbed when he heard this. "Heaven help me," he exclaimed, "what ever can have put such a notion as that into your head? If you go near the suitors you will be undone to a certainty, for their pride and insolence reach the very heavens. They would never think of taking a man like you for a servant. Their servants are all young men, well dressed, wearing good cloaks and shirts, with well looking faces and their hair always tidy, the tables are kept quite clean and are loaded with bread, meat, and wine. Stay where you are, then; you are not in anybody's way; I do not mind your being here, no more do any of the others, and when Telemachus comes home he will give you a shirt and cloak and will send you wherever you want to go."

Ulysses answered, "I hope you may be as dear to the gods as you are to me, for having saved me from going about and getting into trouble; there is nothing worse than being always ways on the tramp; still, when men have once got low down in the world they will go through a great deal on behalf of their miserable bellies. Since however you press me to stay here and await the return of Telemachus, tell about Ulysses' mother, and his father whom he left on the threshold of old age when he set out for Troy. Are they still living or are they already dead and in the house of Hades?"

"I will tell you all about them," replied Eumaeus, "Laertes is still living and prays heaven to let him depart peacefully his own house, for he is terribly distressed about the absence of his son, and also about the death of his wife, which grieved him greatly and aged him more than anything else did. She came to an unhappy end through sorrow for her son: may no friend or neighbor who has dealt kindly by me come to such an end as she did. As long as she was still living, though she was always grieving, I used to like seeing her and asking her how she did, for she brought me up along with her daughter Ctimene, the youngest of her children; we were boy and girl together, and she made little difference between us. When, however, we both grew up, they sent Ctimene to Same and received a splendid dowry for her. As for me, my mistress gave me a good shirt and cloak with a pair of sandals for my feet, and sent me off into the country, but she was just as fond of me as ever. This is all over now. Still it has pleased heaven to prosper my work in the situation which I now hold. I have enough to eat and drink, and can find something for any respectable stranger who comes here; but there is no getting a kind word or deed out of my mistress, for the house has fallen into the hands of wicked people. Servants want sometimes to see their mistress and have a talk with her; they like to have something to eat and drink at the house, and something too to take back with them into the country. This is what will keep servants in a good humor."

Ulysses answered, "Then you must have been a very little fellow, Eumaeus, when you were taken so far away from your home and parents. Tell me, and tell me true, was the city in which your father and mother lived sacked and pillaged, or did some enemies carry you off when you were alone tending sheep or cattle, ship you off here, and sell you for whatever your master gave them?"

"Stranger," replied Eumaeus, "as regards your question: sit still, make yourself comfortable, drink your wine, and listen to me. The nights are now at their longest; there is plenty of time both for sleeping and sitting up talking together; you ought not to go to bed till bed time, too much sleep is as bad as too little; if any one of the others wishes to go to bed let him leave us and do so; he can then take my master's pigs out when he has done breakfast in the morning. We two will sit here eating and drinking in the hut, and telling one another stories about our misfortunes; for when a man has suffered much, and been buffeted about in the world, he takes pleasure in recalling the memory of sorrows that have long gone by. As regards your question, then, my tale is as follows:

"You may have heard of an island called Syra that lies over above Ortygia, where the land begins to turn round and look in another direction. It is not very thickly peopled, but the soil is good, with much pasture fit for cattle and sheep, and it abounds with wine and wheat. Dearth never comes there, nor are the people plagued by any sickness, but when they grow old Apollo comes with Diana and kills them with his painless shafts. It contains two communities, and the whole country is divided between these two. My father Ctesius son of Ormenus, a man comparable to the gods, reigned over both.

"Now to this place there came some cunning traders from Phoenicia (for the Phoenicians are great mariners) in a ship which they had freighted with gewgaws of all kinds. There happened to be a Phoenician woman in my father's house, very tall and comely, and an excellent servant; these scoundrels got hold of her one day when she was washing near their ship, seduced her, and cajoled her in ways that no woman can resist, no matter how good she may be by nature. The man who had seduced her asked her who she was and where she came from, and on this she told him her father's name. 'I come from Sidon,' said she, 'and am daughter to Arybas, a man rolling in wealth. One day as I was coming into the town from the country some Taphian pirates seized me and took me here over the sea, where they sold me to the man who owns this house, and he gave them their price for me.'

"The man who had seduced her then said, 'Would you like to come along with us to see the house of your parents and your parents themselves? They are both alive and are said to be well off.'

"'I will do so gladly,' answered she, 'if you men will first swear me a solemn oath that you will do me no harm by the way.'

"They all swore as she told them, and when they had completed their oath the woman said, 'Hush; and if any of your men meets me in the street or at the well, do not let him speak to me, for fear some one should go and tell my master, in which case he would suspect something. He would put me in prison, and would have all of you murdered; keep your own counsel therefore; buy your merchandise as fast as you can, and send me word when you have done loading. I will bring as much gold as I can lay my hands on, and there is something else also that I can do towards paying my fare. I am nurse to the son of the good man of the house, a funny little fellow just able to run about. I will carry him off in your ship, and you will get a great deal of money for him if you take him and sell him in foreign parts.'

"On this she went back to the house. The Phoenicians stayed a whole year till they had loaded their ship with much precious merchandise, and then, when they had got freight enough, they sent to tell the woman. Their messenger, a very cunning fellow, came to my father's house bringing a necklace of gold with amber beads strung among it; and while my mother and the servants had it in their hands admiring it and bargaining about it, he made a sign quietly to the woman and then went back to the ship, whereon she took me by the hand and led me out of the house. In the fore part of the house she saw the tables set with the cups of guests who had been feasting with my father, as being in attendance on him; these were now all gone to a meeting of the public assembly, so she snatched up three cups and carried them off in the bosom of her dress, while I followed her, for I knew no better. The sun was now set, and darkness was over all the land, so we hurried on as fast as we could till we reached the harbor, where the Phoenician ship was lying. When they had got on board they sailed their ways over the sea, taking us with them, and Jove sent then a fair wind; six days did we sail both night and day, but on the seventh day Diana struck the woman and she fell heavily down into the ship's hold as though she were a sea gull alighting on the water; so they threw her overboard to the seals and fishes, and I was left all sorrowful and alone. Presently the winds and waves took the ship to Ithaca, where Laertes gave sundry of his chattels for me, and thus it was that ever I came to set eyes upon this country."

Ulysses answered, "Eumaeus, I have heard the story of your misfortunes with the most lively interest and pity, but Jove has given you good as well as evil, for in spite of everything you have a good master, who sees that you always have enough to eat and drink; and you lead a good life, whereas I am still going about begging my way from city to city."

Thus did they converse, and they had only a very little time left for sleep, for it was soon daybreak. In the meantime Telemachus and his crew were nearing land, so they loosed the sails, took down the mast, and rowed the ship into the harbor. They cast out their mooring stones and made fast the hawsers; they then got out upon the sea shore, mixed their wine, and got dinner ready. As soon as they had had enough to eat and drink Telemachus said, "Take the ship on to the town, but leave me here, for I want to look after the herdsmen on one of my farms. In the evening, when I have seen all I want, I will come down to the city, and to-morrow morning in return for your trouble I will give you all a good dinner with meat and wine."

Then Theoclymenus said, "And what, my dear young friend, is to become of me? To whose house, among all your chief men, am I to repair? or shall I go straight to your own house and to your mother?"

"At any other time," replied Telemachus, "I should have bidden you go to my own house, for you would find no want of hospitality; at the present moment, however, you would not be comfortable there, for I shall be away, and my mother will not see you; she does not often show herself even to the suitors, but sits at her loom weaving in an upper chamber, out of their way; but I can tell you a man whose house you can go to- I mean Eurymachus the son of Polybus, who is held in the highest estimation by every one in Ithaca. He is much the best man and the most persistent wooer, of all those who are paying court to my mother and trying to take Ulysses' place. Jove, however, in heaven alone knows whether or no they will come to a bad end before the marriage takes place."

As he was speaking a bird flew by upon his right hand- a hawk, Apollo's messenger. It held a dove in its talons, and the feathers, as it tore them off, fell to the ground midway between Telemachus and the ship. On this Theoclymenus called him apart and caught him by the hand. "Telemachus," said he, "that bird did not fly on your right hand without having been sent there by some god. As soon as I saw it I knew it was an omen; it means that you will remain powerful and that there will be no house in Ithaca more royal than your own."

"I wish it may prove so," answered Telemachus. "If it does, I will show you so much good will and give you so many presents that all who meet you will congratulate you."

Then he said to his friend Piraeus, "Piraeus, son of Clytius, you have throughout shown yourself the most willing to serve me of all those who have accompanied me to Pylos; I wish you would take this stranger to your own house and entertain him hospitably till I can come for him."

And Piraeus answered, "Telemachus, you may stay away as long as you please, but I will look after him for you, and he shall find no lack of hospitality."

As he spoke he went on board, and bade the others do so also and loose the hawsers, so they took their places in the ship. But Telemachus bound on his sandals, and took a long and doughty spear with a head of sharpened bronze from the deck of the ship. Then they loosed the hawsers, thrust the ship off from land, and made on towards the city as they had been told to do, while Telemachus strode on as fast as he could, till he reached the homestead where his countless herds of swine were feeding, and where dwelt the excellent swineherd, who was so devoted a servant to his master.

Lesson 54

- Read Book 16 of *The Odyssey*.

Book 16

Meanwhile Ulysses and the swineherd had lit a fire in the hut and were were getting breakfast ready at daybreak for they had sent the men out with the pigs. When Telemachus came up, the dogs did not bark, but fawned upon him, so Ulysses, hearing the sound of feet and noticing that the dogs did not bark, said to Eumaeus:

"Eumaeus, I hear footsteps; I suppose one of your men or some one of your acquaintance is coming here, for the dogs are fawning upon him and not barking."

The words were hardly out of his mouth before his son stood at the door. Eumaeus sprang to his feet, and the bowls in which he was mixing wine fell from his hands, as he made towards his master. He kissed his head and both his beautiful eyes, and wept for joy. A father could not be more delighted at the return of an only son, the child of his old age, after ten years' absence in a foreign country and after having gone through much hardship. He embraced him, kissed him all over as though he had come back from the dead, and spoke fondly to him saying:

"So you are come, Telemachus, light of my eyes that you are. When I heard you had gone to Pylos I made sure I was never going to see you any more. Come in, my dear child, and sit down, that I may have a good look at you now you are home again; it is not very often you come into the country to see us herdsmen; you stick pretty close to the town generally. I suppose you think it better to keep an eye on what the suitors are doing."

"So be it, old friend," answered Telemachus, "but I am come now because I want to see you, and to learn whether my mother is still at her old home or whether some one else has married her, so that the bed of Ulysses is without bedding and covered with cobwebs."

"She is still at the house," replied Eumaeus, "grieving and breaking her heart, and doing nothing but weep, both night and day continually."

As spoke he took Telemachus' spear, whereon he crossed the stone threshold and came inside. Ulysses rose from his seat to give him place as he entered, but Telemachus checked him; "Sit down, stranger." said he, "I can easily find another seat, and there is one here who will lay it for me."

Ulysses went back to his own place, and Eumaeus strewed some green brushwood on the floor and threw a sheepskin on top of it for Telemachus to sit upon. Then the swineherd brought them platters of cold meat, the remains from what they had eaten the day before, and he filled the bread baskets with bread as fast as he could. He mixed wine also in bowls of ivy-wood, and took his seat facing Ulysses. Then they laid their hands on the good things that were before them, and as soon as they had had enough to eat and drink Telemachus said to Eumaeus, "Old friend, where does this stranger come from? How did his crew bring him to Ithaca, and who were they?-for assuredly he did not come here by land"

To this you answered, O swineherd Eumaeus, "My son, I will tell you the real truth. He says he is a Cretan, and that he has been a great traveler. At this moment he is running away from a Thesprotian ship, and has refuge at my station, so I will put him into your hands. Do whatever you like with him, only remember that he is your suppliant."

"I am very much distressed," said Telemachus, "by what you have just told me. How can I take this stranger into my house? I am as yet young, and am not strong enough to hold my own if any man attacks me. My mother cannot make up her mind whether to stay where she is and look after the house out of respect for public opinion and the memory of her husband, or whether the time is now come for her to take the best man of those who are wooing her, and the one who will make her the most advantageous offer; still, as the stranger has come to your station I will find him a cloak and shirt of good wear, with a sword and sandals, and will send him wherever he wants to go. Or if you like you can keep him here at the station, and I will send him clothes and food that he may be no burden on you and on your men; but I will not have him go near the suitors, for they are very insolent, and are sure to ill-treat him in a way that would greatly grieve me; no matter how valiant a man may be he can do nothing against numbers, for they will be too strong for him."

Then Ulysses said, "Sir, it is right that I should say something myself. I am much shocked about what you have said about the insolent way in which the suitors are behaving in despite of such a man as you are. Tell me, do you submit to such treatment tamely, or has some god set your people against you? May you not complain of your brothers- for it is to these that a man may look for support, however great his quarrel may be? I wish I were as young as you are and in my present mind; if I were son to Ulysses, or, indeed, Ulysses himself, I would rather some one came and cut my head off, but I would go to the house and be the bane of every one of these men. If they were too many for me- I being single-handed- I would rather die fighting in my own house than see such disgraceful sights day after day, strangers grossly maltreated, and men dragging the women servants about the house in an unseemly way, wine drawn recklessly, and bread wasted all to no purpose for an end that shall never be accomplished."

And Telemachus answered, "I will tell you truly everything. There is no enmity between me and my people, nor can I complain of brothers, to whom a man may look for support however great his quarrel may be. Jove has made us a race of only sons. Laertes was the only son of Arceisius, and Ulysses only son of Laertes. I am myself the only son of Ulysses who left me behind him when he went away, so that

I have never been of any use to him. Hence it comes that my house is in the hands of numberless marauders; for the chiefs from all the neighboring islands, Dulichium, Same, Zacynthus, as also all the principal men of Ithaca itself, are eating up my house under the pretext of paying court to my mother, who will neither say point blank that she will not marry, nor yet bring matters to an end, so they are making havoc of my estate, and before long will do so with myself into the bargain. The issue, however, rests with heaven. But do you, old friend Eumaeus, go at once and tell Penelope that I am safe and have returned from Pylos. Tell it to herself alone, and then come back here without letting any one else know, for there are many who are plotting mischief against me."

"I understand and heed you," replied Eumaeus; "you need instruct me no further, only I am going that way say whether I had not better let poor Laertes know that you are returned. He used to superintend the work on his farm in spite of his bitter sorrow about Ulysses, and he would eat and drink at will along with his servants; but they tell me that from the day on which you set out for Pylos he has neither eaten nor drunk as he ought to do, nor does he look after his farm, but sits weeping and wasting the flesh from off his bones."

"More's the pity," answered Telemachus, "I am sorry for him, but we must leave him to himself just now. If people could have everything their own way, the first thing I should choose would be the return of my father; but go, and give your message; then make haste back again, and do not turn out of your way to tell Laertes. Tell my mother to send one of her women secretly with the news at once, and let him hear it from her."

Thus did he urge the swineherd; Eumaeus, therefore, took his sandals, bound them to his feet, and started for the town. Minerva watched him well off the station, and then came up to it in the form of a woman- fair, stately, and wise. She stood against the side of the entry, and revealed herself to Ulysses, but Telemachus could not see her, and knew not that she was there, for the gods do not let themselves be seen by everybody. Ulysses saw her, and so did the dogs, for they did not bark, but went scared and whining off to the other side of the yards. She nodded her head and motioned to Ulysses with her eyebrows; whereon he left the hut and stood before her outside the main wall of the yards. Then she said to him:

"Ulysses, noble son of Laertes, it is now time for you to tell your son: do not keep him in the dark any longer, but lay your plans for the destruction of the suitors, and then make for the town. I will not be long in joining you, for I too am eager for the fray."

As she spoke she touched him with her golden wand. First she threw a fair clean shirt and cloak about his shoulders; then she made him younger and of more imposing presence; she gave him back his color, filled out his cheeks, and let his beard become dark again. Then she went away and Ulysses came back inside the hut. His son was astounded when he saw him, and turned his eyes away for fear he might be looking upon a god.

"Stranger," said he, "how suddenly you have changed from what you were a moment or two ago. You are dressed differently and your color is not the same. Are you some one or other of the gods that live in heaven? If so, be propitious to me till I can make you due sacrifice and offerings of wrought gold. Have mercy upon me."

And Ulysses said, "I am no god, why should you take me for one? I am your father, on whose account you grieve and suffer so much at the hands of lawless men."

As he spoke he kissed his son, and a tear fell from his cheek on to the ground, for he had restrained all tears till now. But Telemachus could not yet believe that it was his father, and said:

"You are not my father, but some god is flattering me with vain hopes that I may grieve the more hereafter; no mortal man could of himself contrive to do as you have been doing, and make yourself old and young at a moment's notice, unless a god were with him. A second ago you were old and all in rags, and now you are like some god come down from heaven."

Ulysses answered, "Telemachus, you ought not to be so immeasurably astonished at my being really here. There is no other Ulysses who will come hereafter. Such as I am, it is I, who after long wandering and much hardship have got home in the twentieth year to my own country. What you wonder at is the work of the redoubtable goddess Minerva, who does with me whatever she will, for she can do what she pleases. At one moment she makes me like a beggar, and the next I am a young man with good clothes on my back; it is an easy matter for the gods who live in heaven to make any man look either rich or poor."

As he spoke he sat down, and Telemachus threw his arms about his father and wept. They were both so much moved that they cried aloud like eagles or vultures with crooked talons that have been robbed of their half fledged young by peasants. Thus piteously did they weep, and the sun would have gone down upon their mourning if Telemachus had not suddenly said, "In what ship, my dear father, did your crew bring you to Ithaca? Of what nation did they declare themselves to be- for you cannot have come by land?"

"I will tell you the truth, my son," replied Ulysses. "It was the Phaeacians who brought me here. They are great sailors, and are in the habit of giving escorts to any one who reaches their coasts. They took me over the sea while I was fast asleep, and landed me in Ithaca, after giving me many presents in bronze, gold, and raiment. These things by heaven's mercy are lying concealed in a cave, and I am now come here on the suggestion of Minerva that we may consult about killing our enemies. First, therefore, give me a list of the suitors, with their number, that I may learn who, and how many, they are. I can then turn the matter over in my mind, and see whether we two can fight the whole body of them ourselves, or whether we must find others to help us."

To this Telemachus answered, "Father, I have always heard of your renown both in the field and in council, but the task you talk of is a very great one: I am awed at the mere thought of it; two men cannot stand against many and brave ones. There are not ten suitors only, nor twice ten, but ten many times over; you shall learn their number at once. There are fifty-two chosen youths from Dulichium, and they have six servants; from Same there are twenty-four; twenty young Achaeans from Zacynthus, and twelve from Ithaca itself, all of them well born. They have with them a servant Medon, a bard, and two men who can carve at table. If we face such numbers as this, you may have bitter cause to rue your coming, and your revenge. See whether you cannot think of some one who would be willing to come and help us."

"Listen to me," replied Ulysses, "and think whether Minerva and her father Jove may seem sufficient, or whether I am to try and find some one else as well."

“Those whom you have named,” answered Telemachus, “are a couple of good allies, for though they dwell high up among the clouds they have power over both gods and men.”

“These two,” continued Ulysses, “will not keep long out of the fray, when the suitors and we join fight in my house. Now, therefore, return home early to-morrow morning, and go about among the suitors as before. Later on the swineherd will bring me to the city disguised as a miserable old beggar. If you see them ill-treating me, steel your heart against my sufferings; even though they drag me feet foremost out of the house, or throw things at me, look on and do nothing beyond gently trying to make them behave more reasonably; but they will not listen to you, for the day of their reckoning is at hand. Furthermore I say, and lay my saying to your heart, when Minerva shall put it in my mind, I will nod my head to you, and on seeing me do this you must collect all the armour that is in the house and hide it in the strong store room. Make some excuse when the suitors ask you why you are removing it; say that you have taken it to be out of the way of the smoke, inasmuch as it is no longer what it was when Ulysses went away, but has become soiled and begrimed with soot. Add to this more particularly that you are afraid Jove may set them on to quarrel over their wine, and that they may do each other some harm which may disgrace both banquet and wooing, for the sight of arms sometimes tempts people to use them. But leave a sword and a spear apiece for yourself and me, and a couple oxhide shields so that we can snatch them up at any moment; Jove and Minerva will then soon quiet these people. There is also another matter; if you are indeed my son and my blood runs in your veins, let no one know that Ulysses is within the house- neither Laertes, nor yet the swineherd, nor any of the servants, nor even Penelope herself. Let you and me exploit the women alone, and let us also make trial of some other of the men servants, to see who is on our side and whose hand is against us.”

“Father,” replied Telemachus, “you will come to know me by and by, and when you do you will find that I can keep your counsel. I do not think, however, the plan you propose will turn out well for either of us. Think it over. It will take us a long time to go the round of the farms and exploit the men, and all the time the suitors will be wasting your estate with impunity and without compunction. Prove the women by all means, to see who are disloyal and who guiltless, but I am not in favor of going round and trying the men. We can attend to that later on, if you really have some sign from Jove that he will support you.”

Thus did they converse, and meanwhile the ship which had brought Telemachus and his crew from Pylos had reached the town of Ithaca. When they had come inside the harbor they drew the ship on to the land; their servants came and took their armor from them, and they left all the presents at the house of Clytius. Then they sent a servant to tell Penelope that Telemachus had gone into the country, but had sent the ship to the town to prevent her from being alarmed and made unhappy. This servant and Eumaeus happened to meet when they were both on the same errand of going to tell Penelope. When they reached the House, the servant stood up and said to the queen in the presence of the waiting women, "Your son, Madam, is now returned from Pylos"; but Eumaeus went close up to Penelope, and said privately that her son had given bidden him tell her. When he had given his message he left the house with its outbuildings and went back to his pigs again.

The suitors were surprised and angry at what had happened, so they went outside the great wall that ran round the outer court, and held a council near the main entrance. Eurymachus, son of Polybus, was the first to speak.

"My friends," said he, "this voyage of Telemachus's is a very serious matter; we had made sure that it would come to nothing. Now, however, let us draw a ship into the water, and get a crew together to send after the others and tell them to come back as fast as they can."

He had hardly done speaking when Amphinomus turned in his place and saw the ship inside the harbor, with the crew lowering her sails, and putting by their oars; so he laughed, and said to the others, "We need not send them any message, for they are here. Some god must have told them, or else they saw the ship go by, and could not overtake her.

On this they rose and went to the water side. The crew then drew the ship on shore; their servants took their armor from them, and they went up in a body to the place of assembly, but they would not let any one old or young sit along with them, and Antinous, son of Eupeithes, spoke first.

"Good heavens," said he, "see how the gods have saved this man from destruction. We kept a succession of scouts upon the headlands all day long, and when the sun was down we never went on shore to sleep, but waited in the ship all night till morning in the hope of capturing and killing him; but some god has conveyed him home in spite of us. Let us consider how we can make an end of him. He must not escape us; our affair is never likely to come off while is alive, for he is very shrewd, and public feeling is by no means all on our side. We must make haste before he can call the Achaeans in assembly; he will lose no time in doing so, for he will be furious with us, and will tell all the world how we plotted to kill him, but failed to take him. The people will not like this when they come to know of it; we must see that they do us no hurt, nor drive us from our own country into exile. Let us try and lay hold of him either on his farm away from the town, or on the road hither. Then we can divide up his property amongst us, and let his mother and the man who marries her have the house. If this does not please you, and you wish Telemachus to live on and hold his father's property, then we must not gather here and eat up his goods in this way, but must make our offers to Penelope each from his own house, and she can marry the man who will give the most for her, and whose lot it is to win her."

They all held their peace until Amphinomus rose to speak. He was the son of Nisus, who was son to King Aretias, and he was foremost among all the suitors from the wheat-growing and well grassed island of Dulichium; his conversation, moreover, was more agreeable to Penelope than that of any of the other for he was a man of good natural disposition. "My friends," said he, speaking to them plainly and in all honestly, "I am not in favor of killing Telemachus. It is a heinous thing to kill one who is of noble blood. Let us first take counsel of the gods, and if the oracles of Jove advise it, I will both help to kill him myself, and will urge everyone else to do so; but if they dissuade us, I would have you hold your hands."

Thus did he speak, and his words pleased them well, so they rose forthwith and went to the house of Ulysses where they took their accustomed seats.

Then Penelope resolved that she would show herself to the suitors. She knew of the plot against Telemachus, for the servant Medon had overheard their counsels and had told her; she went down therefore to the court attended by her maidens, and when she reached the suitors she stood by one of the bearing-posts supporting the roof of the cloister holding a veil before her face, and rebuked Antinous saying:

"Antinous, insolent and wicked schemer, they say you are the best speaker and counselor of any man your own age in Ithaca, but you are nothing of the kind.

Madman, why should you try to compass the death of Telemachus, and take no heed of suppliants, whose witness is Jove himself? It is not right for you to plot thus against one another. Do you not remember how your father fled to this house in fear of the people, who were enraged against him for having gone with some Taphian pirates and plundered the Thesprotians who were at peace with us? They wanted to tear him in pieces and eat up everything he had, but Ulysses stayed their hands although they were infuriated, and now you devour his property without paying for it, and break my heart by his wooing his wife and trying to kill his son. Leave off doing so, and stop the others also."

To this Eurymachus son of Polybus answered, "Take heart, Queen Penelope daughter of Icarius, and do not trouble yourself about these matters. The man is not yet born, nor never will be, who shall lay hands upon your son Telemachus, while I yet live to look upon the face of the earth. I say- and it shall surely be- that my spear shall be reddened with his blood; for many a time has Ulysses taken me on his knees, held wine up to my lips to drink, and put pieces of meat into my hands. Therefore Telemachus is much the dearest friend I have, and has nothing to fear from the hands of us suitors. Of course, if death comes to him from the gods, he cannot escape it." He said this to quiet her, but in reality he was plotting against Telemachus.

Then Penelope went upstairs again and mourned her husband till Minerva shed sleep over her eyes. In the evening Eumaeus got back to Ulysses and his son, who had just sacrificed a young pig of a year old and were ready; helping one another to get supper ready; Minerva therefore came up to Ulysses, turned him into an old man with a stroke of her wand, and clad him in his old clothes again, for fear that the swineherd might recognize him and not keep the secret, but go and tell Penelope.

Telemachus was the first to speak. "So you have got back, Eumaeus," said he. "What is the news of the town? Have the suitors returned, or are they still waiting over yonder, to take me on my way home?"

"I did not think of asking about that," replied Eumaeus, "when I was in the town. I thought I would give my message and come back as soon as I could. I met a man sent by those who had gone with you to Pylos, and he was the first to tell the new your mother, but I can say what I saw with my own eyes; I had just got on to the crest of the hill of Mercury above the town when I saw a ship coming into harbor with a number of men in her. They had many shields and spears, and I thought it was the suitors, but I cannot be sure."

On hearing this Telemachus smiled to his father, but so that Eumaeus could not see him.

Then, when they had finished their work and the meal was ready, they ate it, and every man had his full share so that all were satisfied. As soon as they had had enough to eat and drink, they laid down to rest and enjoyed the boon of sleep.

Lesson 55

- Read Book 17 of *The Odyssey.*

Book 17

When the child of morning, rosy-fingered Dawn, appeared, Telemachus bound on his sandals and took a strong spear that suited his hands, for he wanted to go into the city. "Old friend," said he to the swineherd, "I will now go to the town and show myself to my mother, for she will never leave off grieving till she has seen me. As for this unfortunate stranger, take him to the town and let him beg there of any one who will give him a drink and a piece of bread. I have trouble enough of my own, and cannot be burdened with other people. If this makes him angry so much the worse for him, but I like to say what I mean."

Then Ulysses said, "Sir, I do not want to stay here; a beggar can always do better in town than country, for any one who likes can give him something. I am too old to care about remaining here at the beck and call of a master. Therefore let this man do as you have just told him, and take me to the town as soon as I have had a warm by the fire, and the day has got a little heat in it. My clothes are wretchedly thin, and this frosty morning I shall be perished with cold, for you say the city is some way off."

On this Telemachus strode off through the yards, brooding his revenge upon the suitors. When he reached home he stood his spear against a bearing-post of the cloister, crossed the stone floor of the cloister itself, and went inside.

Nurse Euryclea saw him long before any one else did. She was putting the fleeces on to the seats, and she burst out crying as she ran up to him; all the other maids came up too, and covered his head and shoulders with their kisses. Penelope came out of her room looking like Diana or Venus, and wept as she flung her arms about her son. She kissed his forehead and both his beautiful eyes, "Light of my eyes," she cried as she spoke fondly to him, "so you are come home again; I made sure I was never going to see you any more. To think of your having gone off to Pylos without saying anything about it or obtaining my consent. But come, tell me what you saw."

"Do not scold me, mother,' answered Telemachus, "nor vex me, seeing what a narrow escape I have had, but wash your face, change your dress, go upstairs with your maids, and promise full and sufficient hecatombs to all the gods if Jove will only grant us our revenge upon the suitors. I must now go to the place of assembly to invite a stranger who has come back with me from Pylos. I sent him on with my crew, and told Piraeus to take him home and look after him till I could come for him myself."

She heeded her son's words, washed her face, changed her dress, and vowed full and sufficient hecatombs to all the gods if they would only vouchsafe her revenge upon the suitors.

Telemachus went through, and out of, the cloisters spear in hand- not alone, for his two fleet dogs went with him. Minerva endowed him with a presence of such divine comeliness that all marveled at him as he went by, and the suitors gathered round him with fair words in their mouths and malice in their hearts; but he avoided them, and went to sit with Mentor, Antiphus, and Halitherses, old friends of his father's house, and they made him tell them all that had happened to him. Then Piraeus came up with Theoclymenus, whom he had escorted through the town to the place of assembly, whereon Telemachus at once joined them. Piraeus was first to speak: "Telemachus," said he, "I wish you would send some of your women to my house to take away the presents Menelaus gave you."

"We do not know, Piraeus," answered Telemachus, "what may happen. If the suitors kill me in my own house and divide my property among them, I would rather you had the presents than that any of those people should get hold of them. If on the other hand I manage to kill them, I shall be much obliged if you will kindly bring me my presents."

With these words he took Theoclymenus to his own house. When they got there they laid their cloaks on the benches and seats, went into the baths, and washed themselves. When the maids had washed and anointed them, and had given them cloaks and shirts, they took their seats at table. A maid servant then brought them water in a beautiful golden ewer, and poured it into a silver basin for them to wash their hands; and she drew a clean table beside them. An upper servant brought them bread and offered them many good things of what there was in the house. Opposite them sat Penelope, reclining on a couch by one of the bearing-posts of the cloister, and spinning. Then they laid their hands on the good things that were before them, and as soon as they had had enough to eat and drink Penelope said:

"Telemachus, I shall go upstairs and lie down on that sad couch, which I have not ceased to water with my tears, from the day Ulysses set out for Troy with the sons of Atreus. You failed, however, to make it clear to me before the suitors came back to the house, whether or no you had been able to hear anything about the return of your father."

"I will tell you then truth," replied her son. "We went to Pylos and saw Nestor, who took me to his house and treated me as hospitably as though I were a son of his own who had just returned after a long absence; so also did his sons; but he said he had not heard a word from any human being about Ulysses, whether he was alive or dead. He sent me, therefore, with a chariot and horses to Menelaus. There I saw Helen, for whose sake so many, both Argives and Trojans, were in heaven's wisdom doomed to suffer. Menelaus asked me what it was that had brought me to Lacedaemon, and I told him the whole truth, whereon he said, 'So, then, these cowards would usurp a brave man's bed? A hind might as well lay her new-born young in the lair of a lion, and then go off to feed in the forest or in some grassy dell. The lion, when he comes back to his lair, will make short work with the pair of them, and so will Ulysses with these suitors. By father Jove, Minerva, and Apollo, if Ulysses is still the man that he was when he wrestled with Philomeleides in

Lesbos, and threw him so heavily that all the Greeks cheered him- if he is still such, and were to come near these suitors, they would have a short shrift and a sorry wedding. As regards your question, however, I will not prevaricate nor deceive you, but what the old man of the sea told me, so much will I tell you in full. He said he could see Ulysses on an island sorrowing bitterly in the house of the nymph Calypso, who was keeping him prisoner, and he could not reach his home, for he had no ships nor sailors to take him over the sea.' This was what Menelaus told me, and when I had heard his story I came away; the gods then gave me a fair wind and soon brought me safe home again."

With these words he moved the heart of Penelope. Then Theoclymenus said to her:

"Madam, wife of Ulysses, Telemachus does not understand these things; listen therefore to me, for I can divine them surely, and will hide nothing from you. May Jove the king of heaven be my witness, and the rites of hospitality, with that hearth of Ulysses to which I now come, that Ulysses himself is even now in Ithaca, and, either going about the country or staying in one place, is inquiring into all these evil deeds and preparing a day of reckoning for the suitors. I saw an omen when I was on the ship which meant this, and I told Telemachus about it."

"May it be even so," answered Penelope; "if your words come true, you shall have such gifts and such good will from me that all who see you shall congratulate you."

Thus did they converse. Meanwhile the suitors were throwing discs, or aiming with spears at a mark on the leveled ground in front of the house, and behaving with all their old insolence. But when it was now time for dinner, and the flock of sheep and goats had come into the town from all the country round, with their shepherds as usual, then Medon, who was their favorite servant, and who waited upon them at table, said, "Now then, my young masters, you have had enough sport, so come inside that we may get dinner ready. Dinner is not a bad thing, at dinner time."

They left their sports as he told them, and when they were within the house, they laid their cloaks on the benches and seats inside, and then sacrificed some sheep, goats, pigs, and a heifer, all of them fat and well grown. Thus they made ready for their meal. In the meantime Ulysses and the swineherd were about starting for the town, and the swineherd said, "Stranger, I suppose you still want to go to town to-day, as my master said you were to do; for my own part I should have liked you to stay here as a station hand, but I must do as my master tells me, or he will scold me later on, and a scolding from one's master is a very serious thing. Let us then be off, for it is now broad day; it will be night again directly and then you will find it colder."

"I know, and understand you," replied Ulysses; "you need say no more. Let us be going, but if you have a stick ready cut, let me have it to walk with, for you say the road is a very rough one."

As he spoke he threw his shabby old tattered wallet over his shoulders, by the cord from which it hung, and Eumaeus gave him a stick to his liking. The two then started, leaving the station in charge of the dogs and herdsmen who remained behind; the swineherd led the way and his master followed after, looking like some broken-down old tramp as he leaned upon his staff, and his clothes were all in rags. When they had got over the rough steep ground and were nearing the city, they reached the fountain from which the citizens drew their water. This had been made by Ithacus, Neritus, and Polyctor. There was a grove of water-loving poplars planted in a circle all round it, and the clear cold water came down to it from a rock high up, while above the fountain there was an altar to the nymphs, at which all wayfarers used to sacrifice. Here Melanthius son of Dolius overtook them as he was driving down some goats, the best in his flock, for the suitors' dinner, and there were two shepherds with him. When he saw Eumaeus and Ulysses he reviled them with outrageous and unseemly language, which made Ulysses very angry.

"There you go," cried he, "and a precious pair you are. See how heaven brings birds of the same feather to one another. Where, pray, master swineherd, are you taking this poor miserable object? It would make any one sick to see such a creature at table. A fellow like this never won a prize for anything in his life, but will go about rubbing his shoulders against every man's door post, and begging, not for swords and cauldrons like a man, but only for a few scraps not worth begging for. If you would give him to me for a hand on my station, he might do to clean out the folds, or bring a bit of sweet feed to the kids, and he could fatten his thighs as much as he pleased on whey; but he has taken to bad ways and will not go about any kind of work; he will do nothing but beg victuals all the town over, to feed his insatiable belly. I say, therefore and it shall surely be- if he goes near Ulysses' house he will get his head broken by the stools they will fling at him, till they turn him out."

On this, as he passed, he gave Ulysses a kick on the hip out of pure wantonness, but Ulysses stood firm, and did not budge from the path. For a moment he doubted whether or no to fly at Melanthius and kill him with his staff, or fling him to the ground and beat his brains out; he resolved, however, to endure it and keep himself in check, but the swineherd looked straight at Melanthius and rebuked him, lifting up his hands and praying to heaven as he did so.

"Fountain nymphs," he cried, "children of Jove, if ever Ulysses burned you thigh bones covered with fat whether of lambs or kids, grant my prayer that heaven may send him home. He would soon put an end to the swaggering threats with which such men as you go about insulting people-gadding all over the town while your flocks are going to ruin through bad shepherding."

Then Melanthius the goatherd answered, "You ill-conditioned cur, what are you talking about? Some day or other I will put you on board ship and take you to a foreign country, where I can sell you and pocket the money you will fetch. I wish I were as sure that Apollo would strike Telemachus dead this very day, or that the suitors would kill him, as I am that Ulysses will never come home again."

With this he left them to come on at their leisure, while he went quickly forward and soon reached the house of his master. When he got there he went in and took his seat among the suitors opposite Eurymachus, who liked him better than any of the others. The servants brought him a portion of meat, and an upper woman servant set bread before him that he might eat. Presently Ulysses and the swineherd came up to the house and stood by it, amid a sound of music, for Phemius was just beginning to sing to the suitors. Then Ulysses took hold of the swineherd's hand, and said:

"Eumaeus, this house of Ulysses is a very fine place. No matter how far you go you will find few like it. One building keeps following on after another. The outer court has a wall with battlements all round it; the doors are double folding, and of good workmanship; it would be a hard matter to take it by force of arms. I perceive, too, that there are many people banqueting within it, for there is a smell of roast meat, and I hear a sound of music, which the gods have made to go along with feasting."

Then Eumaeus said, "You have perceived aright, as indeed you generally do; but let us think what will be our best course. Will you go inside first and join the suitors, leaving me here behind you, or will you wait here and let me go in first? But do not wait long, or some one may see you loitering about outside, and throw something at you. Consider this matter I pray you."

And Ulysses answered, "I understand and heed. Go in first and leave me here where I am. I am quite used to being beaten and having things thrown at me. I have been so much buffeted about in war and by sea that I am case-hardened, and this too may go with the rest. But a man cannot hide away the cravings of a hungry belly; this is an enemy which gives much trouble to all men; it is because of this that ships are fitted out to sail the seas, and to make war upon other people."

As they were thus talking, a dog that had been lying asleep raised his head and pricked up his ears. This was Argos, whom Ulysses had bred before setting out for Troy, but he had never had any work out of him. In the old days he used to be taken out by the young men when they went hunting wild goats, or deer, or hares, but now that his master was gone he was lying neglected on the heaps of mule and cow dung that lay in front of the stable doors till the men should come and draw it away to manure the great close; and he was full of fleas. As soon as he saw Ulysses standing there, he dropped his ears and wagged his tail, but he could not get close up to his master. When Ulysses saw the dog on the other side of the yard, dashed a tear from his eyes without Eumaeus seeing it, and said:

"Eumaeus, what a noble hound that is over yonder on the manure heap: his build is splendid; is he as fine a fellow as he looks, or is he only one of those dogs that come begging about a table, and are kept merely for show?"

"This hound," answered Eumaeus, "belonged to him who has died in a far country. If he were what he was when Ulysses left for Troy, he would soon show you what he could do. There was not a wild beast in the forest that could get away from him when he was once on its tracks. But now he has fallen on evil times, for his master is dead and gone, and the women take no care of him. Servants never do their work when their master's hand is no longer over them, for Jove takes half the goodness out of a man when he makes a slave of him."

As he spoke he went inside the buildings to the cloister where the suitors were, but Argos died as soon as he had recognized his master.

Telemachus saw Eumaeus long before any one else did, and beckoned him to come and sit beside him; so he looked about and saw a seat lying near where the carver sat serving out their portions to the suitors; he picked it up, brought it to Telemachus's table, and sat down opposite him. Then the servant brought him his portion, and gave him bread from the bread-basket.

Immediately afterwards Ulysses came inside, looking like a poor miserable old beggar, leaning on his staff and with his clothes all in rags. He sat down upon the threshold of ash-wood just inside the doors leading from the outer to the inner court, and against a bearing-post of cypress-wood which the carpenter had skillfully planed, and had made to join truly with rule and line. Telemachus took a whole loaf from the bread-basket, with as much meat as he could hold in his two hands, and said to Eumaeus, "Take this to the stranger, and tell him to go the round of the suitors, and beg from them; a beggar must not be shamefaced."

So Eumaeus went up to him and said, "Stranger, Telemachus sends you this, and says you are to go the round of the suitors begging, for beggars must not be shamefaced."

Ulysses answered, "May King Jove grant all happiness to Telemachus, and fulfill the desire of his heart."

Then with both hands he took what Telemachus had sent him, and laid it on the dirty old wallet at his feet. He went on eating it while the bard was singing, and had just finished his dinner as he left off. The suitors applauded the bard, whereon Minerva went up to Ulysses and prompted him to beg pieces of bread from each one of the suitors, that he might see what kind of people they were, and tell the good from the bad; but come what might she was not going to save a single one of them. Ulysses, therefore, went on his round, going from left to right, and stretched out his hands to beg as though he were a real beggar. Some of them pitied him, and were curious about him, asking one another who he was and where he came from; whereon the goatherd Melanthius said, "Suitors of my noble mistress, I can tell you something about him, for I have seen him before. The swineherd brought him here, but I know nothing about the man himself, nor where he comes from."

On this Antinous began to abuse the swineherd. "You precious idiot," he cried, "what have you brought this man to town for? Have we not tramps and beggars enough already to pester us as we sit at meat? Do you think it a small thing that such people gather here to waste your master's property and must you needs bring this man as well?"

And Eumaeus answered, "Antinous, your birth is good but your words evil. It was no doing of mine that he came here. Who is likely to invite a stranger from a foreign country, unless it be one of those who can do public service as a seer, a healer of hurts, a carpenter, or a bard who can charm us with his singing. Such men are welcome all the world over, but no one is likely to ask a beggar who will only worry him. You are always harder on Ulysses' servants than any of the other suitors are, and above all on me, but I do not care so long as Telemachus and Penelope are alive and here."

But Telemachus said, "Hush, do not answer him; Antinous has the bitterest tongue of all the suitors, and he makes the others worse."

Then turning to Antinous he said, "Antinous, you take as much care of my interests as though I were your son. Why should you want to see this stranger turned out of the house? Heaven forbid; take something and give it him yourself; I do not grudge it; I bid you take it. Never mind my mother, nor any of the other servants in the house; but I know you will not do what I say, for you are more fond of eating things yourself than of giving them to other people."

"What do you mean, Telemachus," replied Antinous, "by this swaggering talk? If all the suitors were to give him as much as I will, he would not come here again for another three months."

As he spoke he drew the stool on which he rested his dainty feet from under the table, and made as though he would throw it at Ulysses, but the other suitors all gave him something, and filled his wallet with bread and meat; he was about, therefore, to go back to the threshold and eat what the suitors had given him, but he first went up to Antinous and said:

"Sir, give me something; you are not, surely, the poorest man here; you seem to be a chief, foremost among them all; therefore you should be the better giver, and I will tell far and wide of your bounty. I too was a rich man once, and had a fine house of my own; in those days I gave to many a tramp such as I now am, no matter who he might be nor what he wanted. I had any number of servants, and all the other things which people have who live well and are accounted wealthy, but it pleased Jove to take all away from me. He sent me with a band of roving robbers to Egypt; it was a long voyage and I was undone by it. I stationed my ships in the river Aegyptus, and bade my men stay by them and keep guard over them, while I sent out scouts to reconnoiter from every point of vantage.

"But the men disobeyed my orders, took to their own devices, and ravaged the land of the Egyptians, killing the men, and taking their wives and children captives. The alarm was soon carried to the city, and when they heard the war-cry, the people came out at daybreak till the plain was filled with soldiers horse and foot, and with the gleam of armor. Then Jove spread panic among my men, and they would no longer face the enemy, for they found themselves surrounded. The Egyptians killed many of us, and took the rest alive to do forced labor for them; as for myself, they gave me to a friend who met them, to take to Cyprus, Dmetor by name, son of Iasus, who was a great man in Cyprus. Thence I am come hither in a state of great misery."

Then Antinous said, "What god can have sent such a pestilence to plague us during our dinner? Get out, into the open part of the court, or I will give you Egypt and Cyprus over again for your insolence and importunity; you have begged of all the others, and they have given you lavishly, for they have abundance round them, and it is easy to be free with other people's property when there is plenty of it."

On this Ulysses began to move off, and said, "Your looks, my fine sir, are better than your breeding; if you were in your own house you would not spare a poor man so much as a pinch of salt, for though you are in another man's, and surrounded with abundance, you cannot find it in you to give him even a piece of bread."

This made Antinous very angry, and he scowled at him saying, "You shall pay for this before you get clear of the court." With these words he threw a footstool at him, and hit him on the right shoulder-blade near the top of his back. Ulysses stood firm as a rock and the blow did not even stagger him, but he shook his head in silence as he brooded on his revenge. Then he went back to the threshold and sat down there, laying his well-filled wallet at his feet.

"Listen to me," he cried, "you suitors of Queen Penelope, that I may speak even as I am minded. A man knows neither ache nor pain if he gets hit while fighting for his money, or for his sheep or his cattle; and even so Antinous has hit me while in the service of my miserable belly, which is always getting people into trouble. Still, if the poor have gods and avenging deities at all, I pray them that Antinous may come to a bad end before his marriage."

"Sit where you are, and eat your victuals in silence, or be off elsewhere," shouted Antinous. "If you say more I will have you dragged hand and foot through the courts, and the servants shall flay you alive."

The other suitors were much displeased at this, and one of the young men said, "Antinous, you did ill in striking that poor wretch of a tramp: it will be worse for you if he should turn out to be some god- and we know the gods go about disguised in all sorts of ways as people from foreign countries, and travel about the world to see who do amiss and who righteously."

Thus said the suitors, but Antinous paid them no heed. Meanwhile Telemachus was furious about the blow that had been given to his father, and though no tear fell from him, he shook his head in silence and brooded on his revenge.

Now when Penelope heard that the beggar had been struck in the banqueting-cloister, she said before her maids, "Would that Apollo would so strike you, Antinous," and her waiting woman Eurynome answered, "If our prayers were answered not one of the suitors would ever again see the sun rise." Then Penelope said, "Nurse, I hate every single one of them, for they mean nothing but mischief, but I hate Antinous like the darkness of death itself. A poor unfortunate tramp has come begging about the house for sheer want. Every one else has given him something to put in his wallet, but Antinous has hit him on the right shoulder-blade with a footstool."

Thus did she talk with her maids as she sat in her own room, and in the meantime Ulysses was getting his dinner. Then she called for the swineherd and said, "Eumaeus, go and tell the stranger to come here, I want to see him and ask him some questions. He seems to have traveled much, and he may have seen or heard something of my unhappy husband."

To this you answered, O swineherd Eumaeus, "If these Achaeans, Madam, would only keep quiet, you would be charmed with the history of his adventures. I had him three days and three nights with me in my hut, which was the first place he reached after running away from his ship, and he has not yet completed the story of his misfortunes. If he had been the most heaven-taught minstrel in the whole world, on whose lips all hearers hang entranced, I could not have been more charmed as I sat in my hut and listened to him. He says there is an old friendship between his house and that of Ulysses, and that he comes from Crete where the descendants of Minos live, after having been driven hither and thither by every kind of misfortune; he also declares that he has heard of Ulysses as being alive and near at hand among the Thesprotians, and that he is bringing great wealth home with him."

"Call him here, then," said Penelope, "that I too may hear his story. As for the suitors, let them take their pleasure indoors or out as they will, for they have nothing to fret about. Their corn and wine remain unwasted in their houses with none but servants to consume them, while they keep hanging about our house day after day sacrificing our oxen, sheep, and fat goats for their banquets, and never giving so much as a thought to the quantity of wine they drink. No estate can stand such recklessness, for we have now no Ulysses to protect us. If he were to come again, he and his son would soon have their revenge."

As she spoke Telemachus sneezed so loudly that the whole house resounded with it. Penelope laughed when she heard this, and said to Eumaeus, "Go and call the stranger; did you not hear how my son sneezed just as I was speaking? This can only mean that all the suitors are going to be killed, and that not one of them shall escape. Furthermore I say, and lay my saying to your heart: if I am satisfied that the stranger is speaking the truth I shall give him a shirt and cloak of good wear."

When Eumaeus heard this he went straight to Ulysses and said, "Father stranger, my mistress Penelope, mother of Telemachus, has sent for you; she is in great grief, but she wishes to hear anything you can tell her about her husband, and if she is satisfied that you are speaking the truth, she will give you a shirt and cloak, which are the very things that you are most in want of. As for bread, you can get enough of that to fill your belly, by begging about the town, and letting those give that will."

"I will tell Penelope," answered Ulysses, "nothing but what is strictly true. I know all about her husband, and have been partner with him in affliction, but I am afraid of passing through this crowd of cruel suitors, for their pride and insolence reach heaven. Just now, moreover, as I was going about the house without doing any harm, a man gave me a blow that hurt me very much, but neither Telemachus nor any one else defended me. Tell Penelope, therefore, to be patient and wait till sundown. Let her give me a seat close up to the fire, for my clothes are worn very thin- you know they are, for you have seen them ever since I first asked you to help me- she can then ask me about the return of her husband."

The swineherd went back when he heard this, and Penelope said as she saw him cross the threshold, "Why do you not bring him here, Eumaeus? Is he afraid that some one will ill-treat him, or is he shy of coming inside the house at all? Beggars should not be shamefaced."

To this you answered, O swineherd Eumaeus, "The stranger is quite reasonable. He is avoiding the suitors, and is only doing what any one else would do. He asks you to wait till sundown, and it will be much better, madam, that you should have him all to yourself, when you can hear him and talk to him as you will."

"The man is no fool," answered Penelope, "it would very likely be as he says, for there are no such abominable people in the whole world as these men are."

When she had done speaking Eumaeus went back to the suitors, for he had explained everything. Then he went up to Telemachus and said in his ear so that none could overhear him, "My dear sir, I will now go back to the pigs, to see after your property and my own business. You will look to what is going on here, but above all be careful to keep out of danger, for there are many who bear you ill will. May Jove bring them to a bad end before they do us a mischief."

"Very well," replied Telemachus, "go home when you have had your dinner, and in the morning come here with the victims we are to sacrifice for the day. Leave the rest to heaven and me."

On this Eumaeus took his seat again, and when he had finished his dinner he left the courts and the cloister with the men at table, and went back to his pigs. As for the suitors, they presently began to amuse themselves with singing and dancing, for it was now getting on towards evening.

Lesson 56

- Read Book 18 of *The Odyssey*.

Book 18

Now there came a certain common tramp who used to go begging all over the city of Ithaca, and was notorious as an incorrigible glutton and drunkard. This man had no strength nor stay in him, but he was a great hulking fellow to look at; his real name, the one his mother gave him, was Arnaeus, but the young men of the place called him Irus, because he used to run errands for any one who would send him. As soon as he came he began to insult Ulysses, and to try and drive him out of his own house.

"Be off, old man," he cried, "from the doorway, or you shall be dragged out neck and heels. Do you not see that they are all giving me the wink, and wanting me to turn you out by force, only I do not like to do so? Get up then, and go of yourself, or we shall come to blows."

Ulysses frowned on him and said, "My friend, I do you no manner of harm; people give you a great deal, but I am not jealous. There is room enough in this doorway for the pair of us, and you need not grudge me things that are not yours to give. You seem to be just such another tramp as myself, but perhaps the gods will give us better luck by and by. Do not, however, talk too much about fighting or you will incense me, and old though I am, I shall cover your mouth and chest with blood. I shall have more peace to-morrow if I do, for you will not come to the house of Ulysses any more."

Irus was very angry and answered, “You filthy glutton, you run on trippingly like an old fish-fag [a woman who sells fish]. I have a good mind to lay both hands about you, and knock your teeth out of your head like so many boar’s tusks. Get ready, therefore, and let these people here stand by and look on. You will never be able to fight one who is so much younger than yourself.”

Thus roundly did they rate one another on the smooth pavement in front of the doorway, and when Antinous saw what was going on he laughed heartily and said to the others, “This is the finest sport that you ever saw; heaven never yet sent anything like it into this house. The stranger and Irus have quarreled and are going to fight, let us set them on to do so at once.”

The suitors all came up laughing, and gathered round the two ragged tramps. “Listen to me,” said Antinous, “there are some goats’ paunches down at the fire, which we have filled with blood and fat, and set aside for supper; he who is victorious and proves himself to be the better man shall have his pick of the lot; he shall be free of our table and we will not allow any other beggar about the house at all.”

The others all agreed, but Ulysses, to throw them off the scent, said, “Sirs, an old man like myself, worn out with suffering, cannot hold his own against a young one; but my irrepressible belly urges me on, though I know it can only end in my getting a drubbing. You must swear, however that none of you will give me a foul blow to favor Irus and secure him the victory.”

They swore as he told them, and when they had completed their oath Telemachus put in a word and said, “Stranger, if you have a mind to settle with this fellow, you need not be afraid of any one here. Whoever strikes you will have to fight more than one. I am host, and the other chiefs, Antinous and Eurymachus, both of them men of understanding, are of the same mind as I am.”

Every one assented, and Ulysses girded his old rags about his loins, thus baring his stalwart thighs, his broad chest and shoulders, and his mighty arms; but Minerva came up to him and made his limbs even stronger still. The suitors were beyond measure astonished, and one would turn towards his neighbor saying, “The stranger has brought such a thigh out of his old rags that there will soon be nothing left of Irus.”

Irus began to be very uneasy as he heard them, but the servants girded him by force, and brought him [into the open part of the court] in such a fright that his limbs were all of a tremble. Antinous scolded him and said, "You swaggering bully, you ought never to have been born at all if you are afraid of such an old broken-down creature as this tramp is. I say, therefore- and it shall surely be- if he beats you and proves himself the better man, I shall pack you off on board ship to the mainland and send you to King Echetus, who kills every one that comes near him. He will cut off your nose and ears, and draw out your entrails for the dogs to eat."

This frightened Irus still more, but they brought him into the middle of the court, and the two men raised their hands to fight. Then Ulysses considered whether he should let drive so hard at him as to make an end of him then and there, or whether he should give him a lighter blow that should only knock him down; in the end he deemed it best to give the lighter blow for fear the Achaeans should begin to suspect who he was. Then they began to fight, and Irus hit Ulysses on the right shoulder; but Ulysses gave Irus a blow on the neck under the ear that broke in the bones of his skull, and the blood came gushing out of his mouth; he fell groaning in the dust, gnashing his teeth and kicking on the ground, but the suitors threw up their hands and nearly died of laughter, as Ulysses caught hold of him by the foot and dragged him into the outer court as far as the gate-house. There he propped him up against the wall and put his staff in his hands. "Sit here," said he, "and keep the dogs and pigs off; you are a pitiful creature, and if you try to make yourself king of the beggars any more you shall fare still worse."

Then he threw his dirty old wallet, all tattered and torn, over his shoulder with the cord by which it hung, and went back to sit down upon the threshold; but the suitors went within the cloisters, laughing and saluting him, "May Jove, and all the other gods," said they, "grant you whatever you want for having put an end to the importunity of this insatiable tramp. We will take him over to the mainland presently, to king Echetus, who kills every one that comes near him."

Ulysses hailed this as of good omen, and Antinous set a great goat's paunch before him filled with blood and fat. Amphinomus took two loaves out of the bread-basket and brought them to him, pledging him as he did so in a golden goblet of wine. "Good luck to you," he said, "father stranger, you are very badly off at present, but I hope you will have better times by and by."

To this Ulysses answered, "Amphinomus, you seem to be a man of good understanding, as indeed you may well be, seeing whose son you are. I have heard your father well spoken of; he is Nisus of Dulichium, a man both brave and wealthy. They tell me you are his son, and you appear to be a considerable person; listen, therefore, and take heed to what I am saying. Man is the vainest of all creatures that have their being upon earth. As long as heaven vouchsafes him health and strength, he thinks that he shall come to no harm hereafter, and even when the blessed gods bring sorrow upon him, he bears it as he needs must, and makes the best of it; for God Almighty gives men their daily minds day by day. I know all about it, for I was a rich man once, and did much wrong in the stubbornness of my pride, and in the confidence that my father and my brothers would support me; therefore let a man fear God in all things always, and take the good that heaven may see fit to send him without vainglory. Consider the infamy of what these suitors are doing; see how they are wasting the estate, and doing dishonor to the wife, of one who is certain to return some day, and that, too, not long hence. Nay, he will be here soon; may heaven send you home quietly first that you may not meet with him in the day of his coming, for once he is here the suitors and he will not part bloodlessly."

With these words he made a drink-offering, and when he had drunk he put the gold cup again into the hands of Amphinomus, who walked away serious and bowing his head, for he foreboded evil. But even so he did not escape destruction, for Minerva had doomed him fall by the hand of Telemachus. So he took his seat again at the place from which he had come.

Then Minerva put it into the mind of Penelope to show herself to the suitors, that she might make them still more enamored of her, and win still further honor from her son and husband. So she feigned a mocking laugh and said, "Eurynome, I have changed my mind and have a fancy to show myself to the suitors although I detest them. I should like also to give my son a hint that he had better not have anything more to do with them. They speak fairly enough but they mean mischief."

"My dear child," answered Eurynome, "all that you have said is true, go and tell your son about it, but first wash yourself and anoint your face. Do not go about with your cheeks all covered with tears; it is not right that you should grieve so incessantly; for Telemachus, whom you always prayed that you might live to see with a beard, is already grown up."

"I know, Eurynome," replied Penelope, "that you mean well, but do not try and persuade me to wash and to anoint myself, for heaven robbed me of all my beauty on the day my husband sailed; nevertheless, tell Autonoe and Hippodamia that I want them. They must be with me when I am in the cloister; I am not going among the men alone; it would not be proper for me to do so."

On this the old woman went out of the room to bid the maids go to their mistress. In the meantime Minerva bethought her of another matter, and sent Penelope off into a sweet slumber; so she lay down on her couch and her limbs became heavy with sleep. Then the goddess shed grace and beauty over her that all the Achaeans might admire her. She washed her face with the ambrosial loveliness that Venus wears when she goes dancing with the Graces; she made her taller and of a more commanding figure, while as for her complexion it was whiter than sawn ivory. When Minerva had done all this she went away, whereon the maids came in from the women's room and woke Penelope with the sound of their talking.

"What an exquisitely delicious sleep I have been having," said she, as she passed her hands over her face, "in spite of all my misery. I wish Diana would let me die so sweetly now at this very moment, that I might no longer waste in despair for the loss of my dear husband, who possessed every kind of good quality and was the most distinguished man among the Achaeans."

With these words she came down from her upper room, not alone but attended by two of her maidens, and when she reached the suitors she stood by one of the bearing-posts supporting the roof of the cloister, holding a veil before her face, and with a staid maid servant on either side of her. As they beheld her the suitors were so overpowered and became so desperately enamored of her, that each one prayed he might win her for his own bed fellow.

"Telemachus," said she, addressing her son, "I fear you are no longer so discreet and well conducted as you used to be. When you were younger you had a greater sense of propriety; now, however, that you are grown up, though a stranger to look at you would take you for the son of a well-to-do father as far as size and good looks go, your conduct is by no means what it should be. What is all this disturbance that has been going on, and how came you to allow a stranger to be so disgracefully ill-treated? What would have happened if he had suffered serious injury while a suppliant in our house? Surely this would have been very discreditable to you."

"I am not surprised, my dear mother, at your displeasure," replied Telemachus, "I understand all about it and know when things are not as they should be, which I could not do when I was younger; I cannot, however, behave with perfect propriety at all times. First one and then another of these wicked people here keeps driving me out of my mind, and I have no one to stand by me. After all, however, this fight between Irus and the stranger did not turn out as the suitors meant it to do, for the stranger got the best of it. I wish Father Jove, Minerva, and Apollo would break the neck of every one of these wooers of yours, some inside the house and some out; and I wish they might all be as limp as Irus is over yonder in the gate of the outer court. See how he nods his head like a drunken man; he has had such a thrashing that he cannot stand on his feet nor get back to his home, wherever that may be, for has no strength left in him."

Thus did they converse. Eurymachus then came up and said, "Queen Penelope, daughter of Icarius, if all the Achaeans in Iasian Argos could see you at this moment, you would have still more suitors in your house by tomorrow morning, for you are the most admirable woman in the whole world both as regards personal beauty and strength of understanding."

To this Penelope replied, "Eurymachus, heaven robbed me of all my beauty whether of face or figure when the Argives set sail for Troy and my dear husband with them. If he were to return and look after my affairs, I should both be more respected and show a better presence to the world. As it is, I am oppressed with care, and with the afflictions which heaven has seen fit to heap upon me. My husband foresaw it all, and when he was leaving home he took my right wrist in his hand- 'Wife, 'he said, 'we shall not all of us come safe home from Troy, for the Trojans fight well both with bow and spear. They are excellent also at fighting from chariots, and nothing decides the issue of a fight sooner than this. I know not, therefore, whether heaven will send me back to you, or whether I may not fall over there at Troy. In the meantime do you look after things here. Take care of my father and mother as at present, and even more so during my absence, but when you see our son growing a beard, then marry whom you will, and leave this your present home. This is what he said and now it is all coming true. A night will come when I shall have to yield myself to a marriage which I detest, for Jove has taken from me all hope of happiness. This further grief, moreover, cuts me to the very heart. You suitors are not wooing me after the custom of my country. When men are courting a woman who they think will be a good wife to them and who is of noble birth, and when they are each trying to win her for himself, they usually bring oxen and sheep to feast the friends of the lady, and they make her magnificent presents, instead of eating up other people's property without paying for it."

This was what she said, and Ulysses was glad when he heard her trying to get presents out of the suitors, and flattering them with fair words which he knew she did not mean.

Then Antinous said, "Queen Penelope, daughter of Icarius, take as many presents as you please from any one who will give them to you; it is not well to refuse a present; but we will not go about our business nor stir from where we are, till you have married the best man among us whoever he may be."

The others applauded what Antinous had said, and each one sent his servant to bring his present. Antinous's man returned with a large and lovely dress most exquisitely embroidered. It had twelve beautifully made brooch pins of pure gold with which to fasten it. Eurymachus immediately brought her a magnificent chain of gold and amber beads that gleamed like sunlight. Eurydamas's two men returned with some earrings fashioned into three brilliant pendants which glistened most beautifully; while King Pisander son of Polyctor gave her a necklace of the rarest workmanship, and every one else brought her a beautiful present of some kind.

Then the queen went back to her room upstairs, and her maids brought the presents after her. Meanwhile the suitors took to singing and dancing, and stayed till evening came. They danced and sang till it grew dark; they then brought in three braziers to give light, and piled them up with chopped firewood very and dry, and they lit torches from them, which the maids held up turn and turn about. Then Ulysses said:

"Maids, servants of Ulysses who has so long been absent, go to the queen inside the house; sit with her and amuse her, or spin, and pick wool. I will hold the light for all these people. They may stay till morning, but shall not beat me, for I can stand a great deal."

The maids looked at one another and laughed, while pretty Melantho began to gibe at him contemptuously. She was daughter to Dolius, but had been brought up by Penelope, who used to give her toys to play with, and looked after her when she was a child; but in spite of all this she showed no consideration for the sorrows of her mistress, and used to misconduct herself with Eurymachus, with whom she was in love.

"Poor wretch," said she, "are you gone clean out of your mind? Go and sleep in some smithy, or place of public gossips, instead of chattering here. Are you not ashamed of opening your mouth before your betters- so many of them too? Has the wine been getting into your head, or do you always babble in this way? You seem to have lost your wits because you beat the tramp Irus; take care that a better man than he does not come and cudgel you about the head till he pack you bleeding out of the house."

"Vixen," replied Ulysses, scowling at her, "I will go and tell Telemachus what you have been saying, and he will have you torn limb from limb."

With these words he scared the women, and they went off into the body of the house. They trembled all aver, for they thought he would do as he said. But Ulysses took his stand near the burning braziers, holding up torches and looking at the people- brooding the while on things that should surely come to pass.

But Minerva would not let the suitors for one moment cease their insolence, for she wanted Ulysses to become even more bitter against them; she therefore set Eurymachus son of Polybus on to gibe at him, which made the others laugh. "Listen to me," said he, "you suitors of Queen Penelope, that I may speak even as I am minded. It is not for nothing that this man has come to the house of Ulysses; I believe the light has not been coming from the torches, but from his own head- for his hair is all gone, every bit of it."

Then turning to Ulysses he said, "Stranger, will you work as a servant, if I send you to the wolds and see that you are well paid? Can you build a stone fence, or plant trees? I will have you fed all the year round, and will find you in shoes and clothing. Will you go, then? Not you; for you have got into bad ways, and do not want to work; you had rather fill your belly by going round the country begging."

"Eurymachus," answered Ulysses, "if you and I were to work one against the other in early summer when the days are at their longest- give me a good scythe, and take another yourself, and let us see which will fast the longer or mow the stronger, from dawn till dark when the mowing grass is about. Or if you will plough against me, let us each take a yoke of tawny oxen, well-mated and of great strength and endurance: turn me into a four acre field, and see whether you or I can drive the straighter furrow. If, again, war were to break out this day, give me a shield, a couple of spears and a helmet fitting well upon my temples- you would find me foremost in the fray, and would cease your gibes about my belly. You are insolent and cruel, and think yourself a great man because you live in a little world, and that a bad one. If Ulysses comes to his own again, the doors of his house are wide, but you will find them narrow when you try to fly through them."

Eurymachus was furious at all this. He scowled at him and cried, "You wretch, I will soon pay you out for daring to say such things to me, and in public too. Has the wine been getting into your head or do you always babble in this way? You seem to have lost your wits because you beat the tramp Irus." With this he caught hold of a footstool, but Ulysses sought protection at the knees of Amphinomus of Dulichium, for he was afraid. The stool hit the cupbearer on his right hand and knocked him down: the man fell with a cry flat on his back, and his wine-jug fell ringing to the ground. The suitors in the covered cloister were now in an uproar, and one would turn towards his neighbor, saying, "I wish the stranger had gone somewhere else, bad luck to hide, for all the trouble he gives us. We cannot permit such disturbance about a beggar; if such ill counsels are to prevail we shall have no more pleasure at our banquet."

On this Telemachus came forward and said, "Sirs, are you mad? Can you not carry your meat and your liquor decently? Some evil spirit has possessed you. I do not wish to drive any of you away, but you have had your suppers, and the sooner you all go home to bed the better."

The suitors bit their lips and marveled at the boldness of his speech; but Amphinomus the son of Nisus, who was son to Aretias, said, "Do not let us take offence; it is reasonable, so let us make no answer. Neither let us do violence to the stranger nor to any of Ulysses' servants. Let the cupbearer go round with the drink-offerings, that we may make them and go home to our rest. As for the stranger, let us leave Telemachus to deal with him, for it is to his house that he has come."

Thus did he speak, and his saying pleased them well, so Mulius of Dulichium, servant to Amphinomus, mixed them a bowl of wine and water and handed it round to each of them man by man, whereon they made their drink-offerings to the blessed gods: Then, when they had made their drink-offerings and had drunk each one as he was minded, they took their several ways each of them to his own abode.

Lesson 57

- Read Book 19 of *The Odyssey*.

Book 19

Ulysses was left in the cloister, pondering on the means whereby with Minerva's help he might be able to kill the suitors. Presently he said to Telemachus, "Telemachus, we must get the armor together and take it down inside. Make some excuse when the suitors ask you why you have removed it. Say that you have taken it to be out of the way of the smoke, inasmuch as it is no longer what it was when Ulysses went away, but has become soiled and begrimed with soot. Add to this more particularly that you are afraid Jove may set them on to quarrel over their wine, and that they may do each other some harm which may disgrace both banquet and wooing, for the sight of arms sometimes tempts people to use them."

Telemachus approved of what his father had said, so he called nurse Euryclea and said, "Nurse, shut the women up in their room, while I take the armor that my father left behind him down into the store room. No one looks after it now my father is gone, and it has got all smirched with soot during my own boyhood. I want to take it down where the smoke cannot reach it."

"I wish, child," answered Euryclea, "that you would take the management of the house into your own hands altogether, and look after all the property yourself. But who is to go with you and light you to the store room? The maids would have so, but you would not let them.

"The stranger," said Telemachus, "shall show me a light; when people eat my bread they must earn it, no matter where they come from."

Euryclea did as she was told, and bolted the women inside their room. Then Ulysses and his son made all haste to take the helmets, shields, and spears inside; and Minerva went before them with a gold lamp in her hand that shed a soft and brilliant radiance, whereon Telemachus said, "Father, my eyes behold a great marvel: the walls, with the rafters, crossbeams, and the supports on which they rest are all aglow as with a flaming fire. Surely there is some god here who has come down from heaven."

"Hush," answered Ulysses, "hold your peace and ask no questions, for this is the manner of the gods. Get you to your bed, and leave me here to talk with your mother and the maids. Your mother in her grief will ask me all sorts of questions."

On this Telemachus went by torch-light to the other side of the inner court, to the room in which he always slept. There he lay in his bed till morning, while Ulysses was left in the cloister pondering on the means whereby with Minerva's help he might be able to kill the suitors.

Then Penelope came down from her room looking like Venus or Diana, and they set her a seat inlaid with scrolls of silver and ivory near the fire in her accustomed place. It had been made by Icmalius and had a footstool all in one piece with the seat itself; and it was covered with a thick fleece: on this she now sat, and the maids came from the women's room to join her. They set about removing the tables at which the wicked suitors had been dining, and took away the bread that was left, with the cups from which they had drunk. They emptied the embers out of the braziers, and heaped much wood upon them to give both light and heat; but Melantho began to rail at Ulysses a second time and said, "Stranger, do you mean to plague us by hanging about the house all night and spying upon the women? Be off, you wretch, outside, and eat your supper there, or you shall be driven out with a firebrand."

Ulysses scowled at her and answered, "My good woman, why should you be so angry with me? Is it because I am not clean, and my clothes are all in rags, and because I am obliged to go begging about after the manner of tramps and beggars general? I too was a rich man once, and had a fine house of my own; in those days I gave to many a tramp such as I now am, no matter who he might be nor what he wanted. I had any number of servants, and all the other things which people have who live well and are accounted wealthy, but it pleased Jove to take all away from me; therefore, woman, beware lest you too come to lose that pride and place in which you now wanton above your fellows; have a care lest you get out of favor with your mistress, and lest Ulysses should come home, for there is still a chance that he may do so. Moreover, though he be dead as you think he is, yet by Apollo's will he has left a son behind him, Telemachus, who will note anything done amiss by the maids in the house, for he is now no longer in his boyhood."

Penelope heard what he was saying and scolded the maid, "Impudent baggage," said she, "I see how abominably you are behaving, and you shall smart for it. You knew perfectly well, for I told you myself, that I was going to see the stranger and ask him about my husband, for whose sake I am in such continual sorrow."

Then she said to her head waiting woman Eurynome, "Bring a seat with a fleece upon it, for the stranger to sit upon while he tells his story, and listens to what I have to say. I wish to ask him some questions."

Eurynome brought the seat at once and set a fleece upon it, and as soon as Ulysses had sat down Penelope began by saying, "Stranger, I shall first ask you who and whence are you? Tell me of your town and parents."

"Madam;" answered Ulysses, "who on the face of the whole earth can dare to chide with you? Your fame reaches the firmament of heaven itself; you are like some blameless king, who upholds righteousness, as the monarch over a great and valiant nation: the earth yields its wheat and barley, the trees are loaded with fruit, the ewes bring forth lambs, and the sea abounds with fish by reason of his virtues, and his people do good deeds under him. Nevertheless, as I sit here in your house, ask me some other question and do not seek to know my race and family, or you will recall memories that will yet more increase my sorrow. I am full of heaviness, but I ought not to sit weeping and wailing in another person's house, nor is it well to be thus grieving continually. I shall have one of the servants or even yourself complaining of me, and saying that my eyes swim with tears because I am heavy with wine."

Then Penelope answered, "Stranger, heaven robbed me of all beauty, whether of face or figure, when the Argives set sail for Troy and my dear husband with them. If he were to return and look after my affairs I should be both more respected and should show a better presence to the world. As it is, I am oppressed with care, and with the afflictions which heaven has seen fit to heap upon me. The chiefs from all our islands- Dulichium, Same, and Zacynthus, as also from Ithaca itself, are wooing me against my will and are wasting my estate. I can therefore show no attention to strangers, nor suppliants, nor to people who say that they are skilled artisans, but am all the time brokenhearted about Ulysses. They want me to marry again at once, and I have to invent stratagems in order to deceive them. In the first place heaven put it in my mind to set up a great tambour-frame in my room, and to begin working upon an enormous piece of fine needlework. Then I said to them, 'Sweethearts, Ulysses is indeed dead, still, do not press me to marry again immediately; wait- for I would not have my skill in needlework perish unrecorded- till I have finished making a pall for the hero Laertes, to be ready against the time when death shall take him. He is very rich, and the women of the place will talk if he is laid out without a pall.' This was what I said, and they assented; whereon I used to keep working at my great web all day long, but at night I would unpick the stitches again by torch light. I fooled them in this way for three years without their finding it out, but as time wore on and I was now in my fourth year, in the waning of moons, and many days had been accomplished, those good-for-nothing hussies my maids betrayed me to the suitors, who broke in upon me and caught me; they were very angry with me, so I was forced to finish my work whether I would or no. And now I do not see how I can find any further shift for getting out of this marriage. My parents are putting great pressure upon me, and my son chafes at the ravages the suitors are making upon his estate, for he is now old enough to understand all about it and is perfectly able to look after his own affairs, for heaven has blessed him with an excellent disposition. Still, notwithstanding all this, tell me who you are and where you come from- for you must have had father and mother of some sort; you cannot be the son of an oak or of a rock."

Then Ulysses answered, "Madam, wife of Ulysses, since you persist in asking me about my family, I will answer, no matter what it costs me: people must expect to be pained when they have been exiles as long as I have, and suffered as much among as many peoples. Nevertheless, as regards your question I will tell you all you ask. There is a fair and fruitful island in mid-ocean called Crete; it is thickly peopled and there are nine cities in it: the people speak many different languages which overlap one another, for there are Achaeans, brave Eteocretans, Dorians of three-fold race, and noble Pelasgi. There is a great town there, Cnossus, where Minos reigned who every nine years had a conference with Jove himself. Minos was father to Deucalion, whose son I am, for Deucalion had two sons Idomeneus and myself. Idomeneus sailed for Troy, and I, who am the younger, am called Aethon; my brother, however, was at once the older and the more valiant of the two; hence it was in Crete that I saw Ulysses and showed him hospitality, for the winds took him there as he was on his way to Troy, carrying him out of his course from cape Malea and leaving him in Amnisus off the cave of Ilithuia, where the harbors are difficult to enter and he could hardly find shelter from the winds that were then raging. As soon as he got there he went into the town and asked for Idomeneus, claiming to be his old and valued friend, but Idomeneus had already set sail for Troy some ten or twelve days earlier, so I took him to my own house and showed him every kind of hospitality, for I had abundance of everything. Moreover, I fed the men who were with him with barley meal from the public store, and got subscriptions of wine and oxen for them to sacrifice to their heart's content. They stayed with me twelve days, for there was a gale blowing from the North so strong that one could hardly keep one's feet on land. I suppose some unfriendly god had raised it for them, but on the thirteenth day the wind dropped, and they got away."

Many a plausible tale did Ulysses further tell her, and Penelope wept as she listened, for her heart was melted. As the snow wastes upon the mountain tops when the winds from South East and West have breathed upon it and thawed it till the rivers run bank full with water, even so did her cheeks overflow with tears for the husband who was all the time sitting by her side. Ulysses felt for her and was sorry for her, but he kept his eyes as hard as or iron without letting them so much as quiver, so cunningly did he restrain his tears. Then, when she had relieved herself by weeping, she turned to him again and said: "Now, stranger, I shall put you to the test and see whether or no you really did entertain my husband and his men, as you say you did. Tell me, then, how he was dressed, what kind of a man he was to look at, and so also with his companions."

"Madam," answered Ulysses, "it is such a long time ago that I can hardly say. Twenty years are come and gone since he left my home, and went elsewhither; but I will tell you as well as I can recollect. Ulysses wore a mantle of purple wool, double lined, and it was fastened by a gold brooch with two catches for the pin. On the face of this there was a device that showed a dog holding a spotted fawn between his fore paws, and watching it as it lay panting upon the ground. Every one marveled at the way in which these things had been done in gold, the dog looking at the fawn, and strangling it, while the fawn was struggling convulsively to escape. As for the shirt that he wore next his skin, it was so soft that it fitted him like the skin of an onion, and glistened in the sunlight to the admiration of all the women who beheld it. Furthermore I say, and lay my saying to your heart, that I do not know whether Ulysses wore these clothes when he left home, or whether one of his companions had given them to him while he was on his voyage; or possibly some one at whose house he was staying made him a present of them, for he was a man of many friends and had few equals among the Achaeans. I myself gave him a sword of bronze and a beautiful purple mantle, double lined, with a shirt that went down to his feet, and I sent him on board his ship with every mark of honor. He had a servant with him, a little older than himself, and I can tell you what he was like; his shoulders were hunched, he was dark, and he had thick curly hair. His name was Eurybates, and Ulysses treated him with greater familiarity than he did any of the others, as being the most like-minded with himself."

Penelope was moved still more deeply as she heard the indisputable proofs that Ulysses laid before her; and when she had again found relief in tears she said to him, "Stranger, I was already disposed to pity you, but henceforth you shall be honored and made welcome in my house. It was I who gave Ulysses the clothes you speak of. I took them out of the store room and folded them up myself, and I gave him also the gold brooch to wear as an ornament. Alas! I shall never welcome him home again. It was by an ill fate that he ever set out for that detested city whose very name I cannot bring myself even to mention."

Then Ulysses answered, "Madam, wife of Ulysses, do not disfigure yourself further by grieving thus bitterly for your loss, though I can hardly blame you for doing so. A woman who has loved her husband and borne him children, would naturally be grieved at losing him, even though he were a worse man than Ulysses, who they say was like a god. Still, cease your tears and listen to what I can tell. I will hide nothing from you, and can say with perfect truth that I have lately heard of Ulysses as being alive and on his way home; he is among the Thesprotians, and is bringing back much valuable treasure that he has begged from one and another of them; but his ship and all his crew were lost as they were leaving the Thrinacian island, for Jove and the sun-god were angry with him because his men had slaughtered the sun-god's cattle, and they were all drowned to a man. But Ulysses stuck to the keel of the ship and was drifted on to the land of the Phaecians, who are near of kin to the immortals, and who treated him as though he had been a god, giving him many presents, and wishing to escort him home safe and sound. In fact Ulysses would have been here long ago, had he not thought better to go from land to land gathering wealth; for there is no man living who is so wily as he is; there is no one can compare with him. Pheidon king of the Thesprotians told me all this, and he swore to me- making drink-offerings in his house as he did so- that the ship was by the water side and the crew found who would take Ulysses to his own country. He sent me off first, for there happened to be a Thesprotian ship sailing for the wheat-growing island of Dulichium, but he showed me all treasure Ulysses had got together, and he had enough lying in the house of King Pheidon to keep his family for ten generations; but the king said Ulysses had gone to Dodona that he might learn Jove's mind from the high oak tree, and know whether after so long an absence he should return to Ithaca openly or in secret. So you may know he is safe and will be here shortly; he is close at hand and cannot remain away from home much longer; nevertheless I will confirm my words with an oath, and call Jove who is the first and mightiest of all gods to witness, as also that hearth of Ulysses to which I have now come, that all I have spoken shall surely come to pass. Ulysses will return in this self same year; with the end of this moon and the beginning of the next he will be here."

"May it be even so," answered Penelope; "if your words come true you shall have such gifts and such good will from me that all who see you shall congratulate you; but I know very well how it will be. Ulysses will not return, neither will you get your escort hence, for so surely as that Ulysses ever was, there are now no longer any such masters in the house as he was, to receive honorable strangers or to further them on their way home. And now, you maids, wash his feet for him, and make him a bed on a couch with rugs and blankets, that he may be warm and quiet till morning. Then, at day break wash him and anoint him again, that he may sit in the cloister and take his meals with Telemachus. It shall be the worse for any one of these hateful people who is uncivil to him; like it or not, he shall have no more to do in this house. For how, sir, shall you be able to learn whether or no I am superior to others of my sex both in goodness of heart and understanding, if I let you dine in my cloisters squalid and ill clad? Men live but for a little season; if they are hard, and deal hardly, people wish them ill so long as they are alive, and speak contemptuously of them when they are dead, but he that is righteous and deals righteously, the people tell of his praise among all lands, and many shall call him blessed."

Ulysses answered, "Madam, I have foresworn rugs and blankets from the day that I left the snowy ranges of Crete to go on shipboard. I will lie as I have lain on many a sleepless night hitherto. Night after night have I passed in any rough sleeping place, and waited for morning. Nor, again, do I like having my feet washed; I shall not let any of the young hussies about your house touch my feet; but, if you have any old and respectable woman who has gone through as much trouble as I have, I will allow her to wash them."

To this Penelope said, "My dear sir, of all the guests who ever yet came to my house there never was one who spoke in all things with such admirable propriety as you do. There happens to be in the house a most respectable old woman- the same who received my poor dear husband in her arms the night he was born, and nursed him in infancy. She is very feeble now, but she shall wash your feet." "Come here," said she, "Euryclea, and wash your master's age-mate; I suppose Ulysses' hands and feet are very much the same now as his are, for trouble ages all of us dreadfully fast."

On these words the old woman covered her face with her hands; she began to weep and made lamentation saying, "My dear child, I cannot think whatever I am to do with you. I am certain no one was ever more god-fearing than yourself, and yet Jove hates you. No one in the whole world ever burned him more thigh bones, nor gave him finer hecatombs when you prayed you might come to a green old age yourself and see your son grow up to take after you; yet see how he has prevented you alone from ever getting back to your own home. I have no doubt the women in some foreign palace which Ulysses has got to are gibing at him as all these sluts here have been gibing you. I do not wonder at your not choosing to let them wash you after the manner in which they have insulted you; I will wash your feet myself gladly enough, as Penelope has said that I am to do so; I will wash them both for Penelope's sake and for your own, for you have raised the most lively feelings of compassion in my mind; and let me say this moreover, which pray attend to; we have had all kinds of strangers in distress come here before now, but I make bold to say that no one ever yet came who was so like Ulysses in figure, voice, and feet as you are."

"Those who have seen us both," answered Ulysses, "have always said we were wonderfully like each other, and now you have noticed it too."

Then the old woman took the cauldron in which she was going to wash his feet, and poured plenty of cold water into it, adding hot till the bath was warm enough. Ulysses sat by the fire, but ere long he turned away from the light, for it occurred to him that when the old woman had hold of his leg she would recognize a certain scar which it bore, whereon the whole truth would come out. And indeed as soon as she began washing her master, she at once knew the scar as one that had been given him by a wild boar when he was hunting on Mount Parnassus with his excellent grandfather Autolycus- who was the most accomplished thief and perjurer in the whole world- and with the sons of Autolycus. Mercury himself had endowed him with this gift, for he used to burn the thigh bones of goats and kids to him, so he took pleasure in his companionship. It happened once that Autolycus had gone to Ithaca and had found the child of his daughter just born. As soon as he had done supper Euryclea set the infant upon his knees and said, "You must find a name for your grandson; you greatly wished that you might have one."

"Son-in-law and daughter," replied Autolycus, "call the child thus: I am highly displeased with a large number of people in one place and another, both men and women; so name the child 'Ulysses,' or the child of anger. When he grows up and comes to visit his mother's family on Mount Parnassus, where my possessions lie, I will make him a present and will send him on his way rejoicing."

Ulysses, therefore, went to Parnassus to get the presents from Autolycus, who with his sons shook hands with him and gave him welcome. His grandmother Amphithea threw her arms about him, and kissed his head, and both his beautiful eyes, while Autolycus desired his sons to get dinner ready, and they did as he told them. They brought in a five year old bull, flayed it, made it ready and divided it into joints; these they then cut carefully up into smaller pieces and spitted them; they roasted them sufficiently and served the portions round. Thus through the livelong day to the going down of the sun they feasted, and every man had his full share so that all were satisfied; but when the sun set and it came on dark, they went to bed and enjoyed the boon of sleep.

When the child of morning, rosy-fingered Dawn, appeared, the sons of Autolycus went out with their hounds hunting, and Ulysses went too. They climbed the wooded slopes of Parnassus and soon reached its breezy upland valleys; but as the sun was beginning to beat upon the fields, fresh-risen from the slow still currents of Oceanus, they came to a mountain dell. The dogs were in front searching for the tracks of the beast they were chasing, and after them came the sons of Autolycus, among whom was Ulysses, close behind the dogs, and he had a long spear in his hand. Here was the lair of a huge boar among some thick brushwood, so dense that the wind and rain could not get through it, nor could the sun's rays pierce it, and the ground underneath lay thick with fallen leaves. The boar heard the noise of the men's feet, and the hounds baying on every side as the huntsmen came up to him, so rushed from his lair, raised the bristles on his neck, and stood at bay with fire flashing from his eyes. Ulysses was the first to raise his spear and try to drive it into the brute, but the boar was too quick for him, and charged him sideways, ripping him above the knee with a gash that tore deep though it did not reach the bone. As for the boar, Ulysses hit him on the right shoulder, and the point of the spear went right through him, so that he fell groaning in the dust until the life went out of him. The sons of Autolycus busied themselves with the carcass of the boar, and bound Ulysses' wound; then, after saying a spell to stop the bleeding, they went home as fast as they could. But when Autolycus and his sons had thoroughly healed Ulysses, they made him some splendid presents, and sent him back to Ithaca with much mutual good will. When he got back, his father and mother were rejoiced to see him, and asked him all about it, and how he had hurt himself to get the scar; so he told them how the boar had ripped him when he was out hunting with Autolycus and his sons on Mount Parnassus.

As soon as Euryclea had got the scarred limb in her hands and had well hold of it, she recognized it and dropped the foot at once. The leg fell into the bath, which rang out and was overturned, so that all the water was spilled on the ground; Euryclea's eyes between her joy and her grief filled with tears, and she could not speak, but she caught Ulysses by the beard and said, "My dear child, I am sure you must be Ulysses himself, only I did not know you till I had actually touched and handled you."

As she spoke she looked towards Penelope, as though wanting to tell her that her dear husband was in the house, but Penelope was unable to look in that direction and observe what was going on, for Minerva had diverted her attention; so Ulysses caught Euryclea by the throat with his right hand and with his left drew her close to him, and said, "Nurse, do you wish to be the ruin of me, you who nursed me at your own breast, now that after twenty years of wandering I am at last come to my own home again? Since it has been borne in upon you by heaven to recognize me, hold your tongue, and do not say a word about it any one else in the house, for if you do I tell you- and it shall surely be- that if heaven grants me to take the lives of these suitors, I will not spare you, though you are my own nurse, when I am killing the other women."

"My child," answered Euryclea, "what are you talking about? You know very well that nothing can either bend or break me. I will hold my tongue like a stone or a piece of iron; furthermore let me say, and lay my saying to your heart, when heaven has delivered the suitors into your hand, I will give you a list of the women in the house who have been ill-behaved, and of those who are guiltless."

And Ulysses answered, "Nurse, you ought not to speak in that way; I am well able to form my own opinion about one and all of them; hold your tongue and leave everything to heaven."

As he said this Euryclea left the cloister to fetch some more water, for the first had been all spilled; and when she had washed him and anointed him with oil, Ulysses drew his seat nearer to the fire to warm himself, and hid the scar under his rags. Then Penelope began talking to him and said:

"Stranger, I should like to speak with you briefly about another matter. It is indeed nearly bed time- for those, at least, who can sleep in spite of sorrow. As for myself, heaven has given me a life of such unmeasurable woe, that even by day when I am attending to my duties and looking after the servants, I am still weeping and lamenting during the whole time; then, when night comes, and we all of us go to bed, I lie awake thinking, and my heart comes a prey to the most incessant and cruel tortures. As the dun nightingale, daughter of Pandareus, sings in the early spring from her seat in shadiest covert hid, and with many a plaintive trill pours out the tale how by mishap she killed her own child Itylus, son of King Zethus, even so does my mind toss and turn in its uncertainty whether I ought to stay with my son here, and safeguard my substance, my bondsmen, and the greatness of my house, out of regard to public opinion and the memory of my late husband, or whether it is not now time for me to go with the best of these suitors who are wooing me and making me such magnificent presents. As long as my son was still young, and unable to understand, he would not hear of my leaving my husband's house, but now that he is full grown he begs and prays me to do so, being incensed at the way in which the suitors are eating up his property. Listen, then, to a dream that I have had and interpret it for me if you can. I have twenty geese about the house that eat mash out of a trough, and of which I am exceedingly fond. I dreamed that a great eagle came swooping down from a mountain, and dug his curved beak into the neck of each of them till he had killed them all. Presently he soared off into the sky, and left them lying dead about the yard; whereon I wept in my room till all my maids gathered round me, so piteously was I grieving because the eagle had killed my geese. Then he came back again, and perching on a projecting rafter spoke to me with human voice, and told me to leave off crying. 'Be of good courage,' he said, 'daughter of Icarius; this is no dream, but a vision of good omen that shall surely come to pass. The geese are the suitors, and I am no longer an eagle, but your own husband, who am come back to you, and who will bring these suitors to a disgraceful end.' On this I woke, and when I looked out I saw my geese at the trough eating their mash as usual."

"This dream, Madam," replied Ulysses, "can admit but of one interpretation, for had not Ulysses himself told you how it shall be fulfilled? The death of the suitors is portended, and not one single one of them will escape."

And Penelope answered, "Stranger, dreams are very curious and unaccountable things, and they do not by any means invariably come true. There are two gates through which these unsubstantial fancies proceed; the one is of horn, and the other ivory. Those that come through the gate of ivory are fatuous, but those from the gate of horn mean something to those that see them. I do not think, however, that my own dream came through the gate of horn, though I and my son should be most thankful if it proves to have done so. Furthermore I say- and lay my saying to your heart- the coming dawn will usher in the ill-omened day that is to sever me from the house of Ulysses, for I am about to hold a tournament of axes. My husband used to set up twelve axes in the court, one in front of the other, like the stays upon which a ship is built; he would then go back from them and shoot an arrow through the whole twelve. I shall make the suitors try to do the same thing, and whichever of them can string the bow most easily, and send his arrow through all the twelve axes, him will I follow, and quit this house of my lawful husband, so goodly and so abounding in wealth. But even so, I doubt not that I shall remember it in my dreams."

Then Ulysses answered, "Madam wife of Ulysses, you need not defer your tournament, for Ulysses will return ere ever they can string the bow, handle it how they will, and send their arrows through the iron."

To this Penelope said, "As long, sir, as you will sit here and talk to me, I can have no desire to go to bed. Still, people cannot do permanently without sleep, and heaven has appointed us dwellers on earth a time for all things. I will therefore go upstairs and recline upon that couch which I have never ceased to flood with my tears from the day Ulysses set out for the city with a hateful name."

She then went upstairs to her own room, not alone, but attended by her maidens, and when there, she lamented her dear husband till Minerva shed sweet sleep over her eyelids.

Lesson 58

- Read Book 20 of *The Odyssey*.

Book 20

Ulysses slept in the cloister upon an undressed bullock's hide, on the top of which he threw several skins of the sheep the suitors had eaten, and Eurynome threw a cloak over him after he had laid himself down. There, then, Ulysses lay wakefully brooding upon the way in which he should kill the suitors; and by and by, the women who had been in the habit of misconducting themselves with them, left the house giggling and laughing with one another. This made Ulysses very angry, and he doubted whether to get up and kill every single one of them then and there, or to let them sleep one more and last time with the suitors. His heart growled within him, and as a bitch with puppies growls and shows her teeth when she sees a stranger, so did his heart growl with anger at the evil deeds that were being done: but he beat his breast and said, "Heart, be still, you had worse than this to bear on the day when the terrible Cyclops ate your brave companions; yet you bore it in silence till your cunning got you safe out of the cave, though you made sure of being killed."

Thus he chided with his heart, and checked it into endurance, but he tossed about as one who turns a paunch full of blood and fat in front of a hot fire, doing it first on one side and then on the other, that he may get it cooked as soon as possible, even so did he turn himself about from side to side, thinking all the time how, single handed as he was, he should contrive to kill so large a body of men as the wicked suitors. But by and by Minerva came down from heaven in the likeness of a woman, and hovered over his head saying, "My poor unhappy man, why do you lie awake in this way? This is your house: your wife is safe inside it, and so is your son who is just such a young man as any father may be proud of."

"Goddess," answered Ulysses, "all that you have said is true, but I am in some doubt as to how I shall be able to kill these wicked suitors single handed, seeing what a number of them there always are. And there is this further difficulty, which is still more considerable. Supposing that with Jove's and your assistance I succeed in killing them, I must ask you to consider where I am to escape to from their avengers when it is all over."

"For shame," replied Minerva, "why, any one else would trust a worse ally than myself, even though that ally were only a mortal and less wise than I am. Am I not a goddess, and have I not protected you throughout in all your troubles? I tell you plainly that even though there were fifty bands of men surrounding us and eager to kill us, you should take all their sheep and cattle, and drive them away with you. But go to sleep; it is a very bad thing to lie awake all night, and you shall be out of your troubles before long."

As she spoke she shed sleep over his eyes, and then went back to Olympus.

While Ulysses was thus yielding himself to a very deep slumber that eased the burden of his sorrows, his admirable wife awoke, and sitting up in her bed began to cry. When she had relieved herself by weeping she prayed to Diana saying, "Great Goddess Diana, daughter of Jove, drive an arrow into my heart and slay me; or let some whirlwind snatch me up and bear me through paths of darkness till it drop me into the mouths of overflowing Oceanus, as it did the daughters of Pandareus. The daughters of Pandareus lost their father and mother, for the gods killed them, so they were left orphans. But Venus took care of them, and fed them on cheese, honey, and sweet wine. Juno taught them to excel all women in beauty of form and understanding; Diana gave them an imposing presence, and Minerva endowed them with every kind of accomplishment; but one day when Venus had gone up to Olympus to see Jove about getting them married (for well does he know both what shall happen and what not happen to every one) the storm winds came and spirited them away to become handmaids to the dread Erinyes. Even so I wish that the gods who live in heaven would hide me from mortal sight, or that fair Diana might strike me, for I would fain go even beneath the sad earth if I might do so still looking towards Ulysses only, and without having to yield myself to a worse man than he was. Besides, no matter how much people may grieve by day, they can put up with it so long as they can sleep at night, for when the eyes are closed in slumber people forget good and ill alike; whereas my misery haunts me even in my dreams. This very night methought there was one lying by my side who was like Ulysses as he was when he went away with his host, and I rejoiced, for I believed that it was no dream, but the very truth itself."

On this the day broke, but Ulysses heard the sound of her weeping, and it puzzled him, for it seemed as though she already knew him and was by his side. Then he gathered up the cloak and the fleeces on which he had lain, and set them on a seat in the cloister, but he took the bullock's hide out into the open. He lifted up his hands to heaven, and prayed, saying "Father Jove, since you have seen fit to bring me over land and sea to my own home after all the afflictions you have laid upon me, give me a sign out of the mouth of some one or other of those who are now waking within the house, and let me have another sign of some kind from outside."

Thus did he pray. Jove heard his prayer and forthwith thundered high up among the from the splendor of Olympus, and Ulysses was glad when he heard it. At the same time within the house, a miller-woman from hard by in the mill room lifted up her voice and gave him another sign. There were twelve miller-women whose business it was to grind wheat and barley which are the staff of life. The others had ground their task and had gone to take their rest, but this one had not yet finished, for she was not so strong as they were, and when she heard the thunder she stopped grinding and gave the sign to her master. "Father Jove," said she, "you who rule over heaven and earth, you have thundered from a clear sky without so much as a cloud in it, and this means something for somebody; grant the prayer, then, of me your poor servant who calls upon you, and let this be the very last day that the suitors dine in the house of Ulysses. They have worn me out with the labor of grinding meal for them, and I hope they may never have another dinner anywhere at all."

Ulysses was glad when he heard the omens conveyed to him by the woman's speech, and by the thunder, for he knew they meant that he should avenge himself on the suitors.

Then the other maids in the house rose and lit the fire on the hearth; Telemachus also rose and put on his clothes. He girded his sword about his shoulder, bound his sandals on his comely feet, and took a doughty spear with a point of sharpened bronze; then he went to the threshold of the cloister and said to Euryclea, "Nurse, did you make the stranger comfortable both as regards bed and board, or did you let him shift for himself?- for my mother, good woman though she is, has a way of paying great attention to second-rate people, and of neglecting others who are in reality much better men."

"Do not find fault child," said Euryclea, "when there is no one to find fault with. The stranger sat and drank his wine as long as he liked: your mother did ask him if he would take any more bread and he said he would not. When he wanted to go to bed she told the servants to make one for him, but he said he was such wretched outcast that he would not sleep on a bed and under blankets; he insisted on having an undressed bullock's hide and some sheepskins put for him in the cloister and I threw a cloak over him myself."

Then Telemachus went out of the court to the place where the Achaeans were meeting in assembly; he had his spear in his hand, and he was not alone, for his two dogs went with him. But Euryclea called the maids and said, "Come, wake up; set about sweeping the cloisters and sprinkling them with water to lay the dust; put the covers on the seats; wipe down the tables, some of you, with a wet sponge; clean out the mixing-jugs and the cups, and go for water from the fountain at once; the suitors will be here directly; they will be here early, for it is a feast day."

Thus did she speak, and they did even as she had said: twenty of them went to the fountain for water, and the others set themselves busily to work about the house. The men who were in attendance on the suitors also came up and began chopping firewood. By and by the women returned from the fountain, and the swineherd came after them with the three best pigs he could pick out. These he let feed about the premises, and then he said good-humoredly to Ulysses, "Stranger, are the suitors treating you any better now, or are they as insolent as ever?"

"May heaven," answered Ulysses, "requite to them the wickedness with which they deal high-handedly in another man's house without any sense of shame."

Thus did they converse; meanwhile Melanthius the goatherd came up, for he too was bringing in his best goats for the suitors' dinner; and he had two shepherds with him. They tied the goats up under the gatehouse, and then Melanthius began gibing at Ulysses. "Are you still here, stranger," said he, "to pester people by begging about the house? Why can you not go elsewhere? You and I shall not come to an understanding before we have given each other a taste of our fists. You beg without any sense of decency: are there not feasts elsewhere among the Achaeans, as well as here?"

Ulysses made no answer, but bowed his head and brooded. Then a third man, Philoetius, joined them, who was bringing in a barren heifer and some goats. These were brought over by the boatmen who are there to take people over when any one comes to them. So Philoetius made his heifer and his goats secure under the gatehouse, and then went up to the swineherd. "Who, Swineherd," said he, "is this stranger that is lately come here? Is he one of your men? What is his family? Where does he come from? Poor fellow, he looks as if he had been some great man, but the gods give sorrow to whom they will- even to kings if it so pleases them

As he spoke he went up to Ulysses and saluted him with his right hand; "Good day to you, father stranger," said he, "you seem to be very poorly off now, but I hope you will have better times by and by. Father Jove, of all gods you are the most malicious. We are your own children, yet you show us no mercy in all our misery and afflictions. A sweat came over me when I saw this man, and my eyes filled with tears, for he reminds me of Ulysses, who I fear is going about in just such rags as this man's are, if indeed he is still among the living. If he is already dead and in the house of Hades, then, alas! for my good master, who made me his stockman when I was quite young among the Cephallenians, and now his cattle are countless; no one could have done better with them than I have, for they have bred like ears of corn; nevertheless I have to keep bringing them in for others to eat, who take no heed of his son though he is in the house, and fear not the wrath of heaven, but are already eager to divide Ulysses' property among them because he has been away so long. I have often thought- only it would not be right while his son is living- of going off with the cattle to some foreign country; bad as this would be, it is still harder to stay here and be ill-treated about other people's herds. My position is intolerable, and I should long since have run away and put myself under the protection of some other chief, only that I believe my poor master will yet return, and send all these suitors flying out of the house."

"Stockman," answered Ulysses, "you seem to be a very well-disposed person, and I can see that you are a man of sense. Therefore I will tell you, and will confirm my words with an oath: by Jove, the chief of all gods, and by that hearth of Ulysses to which I am now come, Ulysses shall return before you leave this place, and if you are so minded you shall see him killing the suitors who are now masters here."

"If Jove were to bring this to pass," replied the stockman, "you should see how I would do my very utmost to help him."

And in like manner Eumaeus prayed that Ulysses might return home. Thus did they converse. Meanwhile the suitors were hatching a plot to murder Telemachus: but a bird flew near them on their left hand- an eagle with a dove in its talons. On this Amphinomus said, "My friends, this plot of ours to murder Telemachus will not succeed; let us go to dinner instead."

The others assented, so they went inside and laid their cloaks on the benches and seats. They sacrificed the sheep, goats, pigs, and the heifer, and when the inward meats were cooked they served them round. They mixed the wine in the mixing-bowls, and the swineherd gave every man his cup, while Philoetius handed round the bread in the breadbaskets, and Melanthius poured them out their wine. Then they laid their hands upon the good things that were before them.

Telemachus purposely made Ulysses sit in the part of the cloister that was paved with stone; he gave him a shabby-looking seat at a little table to himself, and had his portion of the inward meats brought to him, with his wine in a gold cup. "Sit there," said he, "and drink your wine among the great people. I will put a stop to the gibes and blows of the suitors, for this is no public house, but belongs to Ulysses, and has passed from him to me. Therefore, suitors, keep your hands and your tongues to yourselves, or there will be mischief."

The suitors bit their lips, and marveled at the boldness of his speech; then Antinous said, "We do not like such language but we will put up with it, for Telemachus is threatening us in good earnest. If Jove had let us we should have put a stop to his brave talk ere now."

Thus spoke Antinous, but Telemachus heeded him not. Meanwhile the heralds were bringing the holy hecatomb through the city, and the Achaeans gathered under the shady grove of Apollo.

Then they roasted the outer meat, drew it off the spits, gave every man his portion, and feasted to their hearts' content; those who waited at table gave Ulysses exactly the same portion as the others had, for Telemachus had told them to do so.

But Minerva would not let the suitors for one moment drop their insolence, for she wanted Ulysses to become still more bitter against them. Now there happened to be among them a ribald fellow, whose name was Ctesippus, and who came from Same. This man, confident in his great wealth, was paying court to the wife of Ulysses, and said to the suitors, "Hear what I have to say. The stranger has already had as large a portion as any one else; this is well, for it is not right nor reasonable to ill-treat any guest of Telemachus who comes here. I will, however, make him a present on my own account, that he may have something to give to the bath-woman, or to some other of Ulysses' servants."

As he spoke he picked up a heifer's foot from the meat-basket in which it lay, and threw it at Ulysses, but Ulysses turned his head a little aside, and avoided it, smiling grimly Sardinian fashion as he did so, and it hit the wall, not him. On this Telemachus spoke fiercely to Ctesippus, "It is a good thing for you," said he, "that the stranger turned his head so that you missed him. If you had hit him I should have run you through with my spear, and your father would have had to see about getting you buried rather than married in this house. So let me have no more unseemly behavior from any of you, for I am grown up now to the knowledge of good and evil and understand what is going on, instead of being the child that I have been heretofore. I have long seen you killing my sheep and making free with my corn and wine: I have put up with this, for one man is no match for many, but do me no further violence. Still, if you wish to kill me, kill me; I would far rather die than see such disgraceful scenes day after day- guests insulted, and men dragging the women servants about the house in an unseemly way."

They all held their peace till at last Agelaus son of Damastor said, "No one should take offence at what has just been said, nor gainsay it, for it is quite reasonable. Leave off, therefore, ill-treating the stranger, or any one else of the servants who are about the house; I would say, however, a friendly word to Telemachus and his mother, which I trust may commend itself to both. 'As long,' I would say, 'as you had ground for hoping that Ulysses would one day come home, no one could complain of your waiting and suffering the suitors to be in your house. It would have been better that he should have returned, but it is now sufficiently clear that he will never do so; therefore talk all this quietly over with your mother, and tell her to marry the best man, and the one who makes her the most advantageous offer. Thus you will yourself be able to manage your own inheritance, and to eat and drink in peace, while your mother will look after some other man's house, not yours."

To this Telemachus answered, "By Jove, Agelaus, and by the sorrows of my unhappy father, who has either perished far from Ithaca, or is wandering in some distant land, I throw no obstacles in the way of my mother's marriage; on the contrary I urge her to choose whomsoever she will, and I will give her numberless gifts into the bargain, but I dare not insist point blank that she shall leave the house against her own wishes. Heaven forbid that I should do this."

Minerva now made the suitors fall to laughing immoderately, and set their wits wandering; but they were laughing with a forced laughter. Their meat became smeared with blood; their eyes filled with tears, and their hearts were heavy with forebodings. Theoclymenus saw this and said, "Unhappy men, what is it that ails you? There is a shroud of darkness drawn over you from head to foot, your cheeks are wet with tears; the air is alive with wailing voices; the walls and roof-beams drip blood; the gate of the cloisters and the court beyond them are full of ghosts trooping down into the night of hell; the sun is blotted out of heaven, and a blighting gloom is over all the land."

Thus did he speak, and they all of them laughed heartily. Eurymachus then said, "This stranger who has lately come here has lost his senses. Servants, turn him out into the streets, since he finds it so dark here."

But Theoclymenus said, "Eurymachus, you need not send any one with me. I have eyes, ears, and a pair of feet of my own, to say nothing of an understanding mind. I will take these out of the house with me, for I see mischief overhanging you, from which not one of you men who are insulting people and plotting ill deeds in the house of Ulysses will be able to escape."

He left the house as he spoke, and went back to Piraeus who gave him welcome, but the suitors kept looking at one another and provoking Telemachus fly laughing at the strangers. One insolent fellow said to him, "Telemachus, you are not happy in your guests; first you have this importunate tramp, who comes begging bread and wine and has no skill for work or for hard fighting, but is perfectly useless, and now here is another fellow who is setting himself up as a prophet. Let me persuade you, for it will be much better, to put them on board ship and send them off to the Sicels to sell for what they will bring."

Telemachus gave him no heed, but sat silently watching his father, expecting every moment that he would begin his attack upon the suitors.

Meanwhile the daughter of Icarius, wise Penelope, had had had a rich seat placed for her facing the court and cloisters, so that she could hear what every one was saying. The dinner indeed had been prepared amid merriment; it had been both good and abundant, for they had sacrificed many victims; but the supper was yet to come, and nothing can be conceived more gruesome than the meal which a goddess and a brave man were soon to lay before them- for they had brought their doom upon themselves.

Lesson 59

- Read Book 21 of *The Odyssey*.

Book 21

Minerva now put it in Penelope's mind to make the suitors try their skill with the bow and with the iron axes, in contest among themselves, as a means of bringing about their destruction. She went upstairs and got the store room key, which was made of bronze and had a handle of ivory; she then went with her maidens into the store room at the end of the house, where her husband's treasures of gold, bronze, and wrought iron were kept, and where was also his bow, and the quiver full of deadly arrows that had been given him by a friend whom he had met in Lacedaemon-Iphitus the son of Eurytus. The two fell in with one another in Messene at the house of Ortilochus, where Ulysses was staying in order to recover a debt that was owing from the whole people; for the Messenians had carried off three hundred sheep from Ithaca, and had sailed away with them and with their shepherds. In quest of these Ulysses took a long journey while still quite young, for his father and the other chieftains sent him on a mission to recover them. Iphitus had gone there also to try and get back twelve brood mares that he had lost, and the mule foals that were running with them. These mares were the death of him in the end, for when he went to the house of Jove's son, mighty Hercules, who performed such prodigies of valor, Hercules to his shame killed him, though he was his guest, for he feared not heaven's vengeance, nor yet respected his own table which he had set before Iphitus, but killed him in spite of everything, and kept the mares himself. It was when claiming these that Iphitus met Ulysses, and gave him the bow which mighty Eurytus had been used to carry, and which on his death had been left by him to his son. Ulysses gave him in return a sword and a spear, and this was the beginning of a fast friendship, although they never visited at one another's houses, for Jove's son Hercules killed Iphitus ere they could do so. This bow, then, given him by Iphitus, had not been taken with him by Ulysses when he sailed for Troy; he had used it so long as he had been at home, but had left it behind as having been a keepsake from a valued friend.

Penelope presently reached the oak threshold of the store room; the carpenter had planed this duly, and had drawn a line on it so as to get it quite straight; he had then set the door posts into it and hung the doors. She loosed the strap from the handle of the door, put in the key, and drove it straight home to shoot back the bolts that held the doors; these flew open with a noise like a bull bellowing in a meadow, and Penelope stepped upon the raised platform, where the chests stood in which the fair linen and clothes were laid by along with fragrant herbs: reaching thence, she took down the bow with its bow case from the peg on which it hung. She sat down with it on her knees, weeping bitterly as she took the bow out of its case, and when her tears had relieved her, she went to the cloister where the suitors were, carrying the bow and the quiver, with the many deadly arrows that were inside it. Along with her came her maidens, bearing a chest that contained much iron and bronze which her husband had won as prizes. When she reached the suitors, she stood by one of the bearing-posts supporting the roof of the cloister, holding a veil before her face, and with a maid on either side of her. Then she said:

"Listen to me you suitors, who persist in abusing the hospitality of this house because its owner has been long absent, and without other pretext than that you want to marry me; this, then, being the prize that you are contending for, I will bring out the mighty bow of Ulysses, and whomsoever of you shall string it most easily and send his arrow through each one of twelve axes, him will I follow and quit this house of my lawful husband, so goodly, and so abounding in wealth. But even so I doubt not that I shall remember it in my dreams."

As she spoke, she told Eumaeus to set the bow and the pieces of iron before the suitors, and Eumaeus wept as he took them to do as she had bidden him. Hard by, the stockman wept also when he saw his master's bow, but Antinous scolded them. "You country louts," said he, "silly simpletons; why should you add to the sorrows of your mistress by crying in this way? She has enough to grieve her in the loss of her husband; sit still, therefore, and eat your dinners in silence, or go outside if you want to cry, and leave the bow behind you. We suitors shall have to contend for it with might and main, for we shall find it no light matter to string such a bow as this is. There is not a man of us all who is such another as Ulysses; for I have seen him and remember him, though I was then only a child."

This was what he said, but all the time he was expecting to be able to string the bow and shoot through the iron, whereas in fact he was to be the first that should taste of the arrows from the hands of Ulysses, whom he was dishonoring in his own house- egging the others on to do so also.

Then Telemachus spoke. "Great heavens!" he exclaimed, "Jove must have robbed me of my senses. Here is my dear and excellent mother saying she will quit this house and marry again, yet I am laughing and enjoying myself as though there were nothing happening. But, suitors, as the contest has been agreed upon, let it go forward. It is for a woman whose peer is not to be found in Pylos, Argos, or Mycene, nor yet in Ithaca nor on the mainland. You know this as well as I do; what need have I to speak in praise of my mother? Come on, then, make no excuses for delay, but let us see whether you can string the bow or no. I too will make trial of it, for if I can string it and shoot through the iron, I shall not suffer my mother to quit this house with a stranger, not if I can win the prizes which my father won before me."

As he spoke he sprang from his seat, threw his crimson cloak from him, and took his sword from his shoulder. First he set the axes in a row, in a long groove which he had dug for them, and had made straight by line. Then he stamped the earth tight round them, and everyone was surprised when they saw him set up so orderly, though he had never seen anything of the kind before. This done, he went on to the pavement to make trial of the bow; thrice did he tug at it, trying with all his might to draw the string, and thrice he had to leave off, though he had hoped to string the bow and shoot through the iron. He was trying for the fourth time, and would have strung it had not Ulysses made a sign to check him in spite of all his eagerness. So he said:

"Alas! I shall either be always feeble and of no prowess, or I am too young, and have not yet reached my full strength so as to be able to hold my own if any one attacks me. You others, therefore, who are stronger than I, make trial of the bow and get this contest settled."

On this he put the bow down, letting it lean against the door [that led into the house] with the arrow standing against the top of the bow. Then he sat down on the seat from which he had risen, and Antinous said:

"Come on each of you in his turn, going towards the right from the place at which the cupbearer begins when he is handing round the wine."

The rest agreed, and Leiodes son of OEnops was the first to rise. He was sacrificial priest to the suitors, and sat in the corner near the mixing-bowl. He was the only man who hated their evil deeds and was indignant with the others. He was now the first to take the bow and arrow, so he went on to the pavement to make his trial, but he could not string the bow, for his hands were weak and unused to hard work, they therefore soon grew tired, and he said to the suitors, "My friends, I cannot string it; let another have it; this bow shall take the life and soul out of many a chief among us, for it is better to die than to live after having missed the prize that we have so long striven for, and which has brought us so long together. Some one of us is even now hoping and praying that he may marry Penelope, but when he has seen this bow and tried it, let him woo and make bridal offerings to some other woman, and let Penelope marry whoever makes her the best offer and whose lot it is to win her."

On this he put the bow down, letting it lean against the door, with the arrow standing against the tip of the bow. Then he took his seat again on the seat from which he had risen; and Antinous rebuked him saying:

"Leiodes, what are you talking about? Your words are monstrous and intolerable; it makes me angry to listen to you. Shall, then, this bow take the life of many a chief among us, merely because you cannot bend it yourself? True, you were not born to be an archer, but there are others who will soon string it."

Then he said to Melanthius the goatherd, "Look sharp, light a fire in the court, and set a seat hard by with a sheep skin on it; bring us also a large ball of lard, from what they have in the house. Let us warm the bow and grease it we will then make trial of it again, and bring the contest to an end."

Melanthius lit the fire, and set a seat covered with sheep skins beside it. He also brought a great ball of lard from what they had in the house, and the suitors warmed the bow and again made trial of it, but they were none of them nearly strong enough to string it. Nevertheless there still remained Antinous and Eurymachus, who were the ringleaders among the suitors and much the foremost among them all.

Then the swineherd and the stockman left the cloisters together, and Ulysses followed them. When they had got outside the gates and the outer yard, Ulysses said to them quietly:

"Stockman, and you swineherd, I have something in my mind which I am in doubt whether to say or no; but I think I will say it. What manner of men would you be to stand by Ulysses, if some god should bring him back here all of a sudden? Say which you are disposed to do- to side with the suitors, or with Ulysses?"

"Father Jove," answered the stockman, "would indeed that you might so ordain it. If some god were but to bring Ulysses back, you should see with what might and main I would fight for him."

In like words Eumaeus prayed to all the gods that Ulysses might return; when, therefore, he saw for certain what mind they were of, Ulysses said, "It is I, Ulysses, who am here. I have suffered much, but at last, in the twentieth year, I am come back to my own country. I find that you two alone of all my servants are glad that I should do so, for I have not heard any of the others praying for my return. To you two, therefore, will I unfold the truth as it shall be. If heaven shall deliver the suitors into my hands, I will find wives for both of you, will give you house and holding close to my own, and you shall be to me as though you were brothers and friends of Telemachus. I will now give you convincing proofs that you may know me and be assured. See, here is the scar from the boar's tooth that ripped me when I was out hunting on Mount Parnassus with the sons of Autolycus."

As he spoke he drew his rags aside from the great scar, and when they had examined it thoroughly, they both of them wept about Ulysses, threw their arms round him and kissed his head and shoulders, while Ulysses kissed their hands and faces in return. The sun would have gone down upon their mourning if Ulysses had not checked them and said:

"Cease your weeping, lest some one should come outside and see us, and tell those who are within. When you go in, do so separately, not both together; I will go first, and do you follow afterwards; Let this moreover be the token between us; the suitors will all of them try to prevent me from getting hold of the bow and quiver; do you, therefore, Eumaeus, place it in my hands when you are carrying it about, and tell the women to close the doors of their apartment. If they hear any groaning or uproar as of men fighting about the house, they must not come out; they must keep quiet, and stay where they are at their work. And I charge you, Philoetius, to make fast the doors of the outer court, and to bind them securely at once."

When he had thus spoken, he went back to the house and took the seat that he had left. Presently, his two servants followed him inside.

At this moment the bow was in the hands of Eurymachus, who was warming it by the fire, but even so he could not string it, and he was greatly grieved. He heaved a deep sigh and said, “I grieve for myself and for us all; I grieve that I shall have to forgo the marriage, but I do not care nearly so much about this, for there are plenty of other women in Ithaca and elsewhere; what I feel most is the fact of our being so inferior to Ulysses in strength that we cannot string his bow. This will disgrace us in the eyes of those who are yet unborn.”

“It shall not be so, Eurymachus,” said Antinous, “and you know it yourself. To-day is the feast of Apollo throughout all the land; who can string a bow on such a day as this? Put it on one side--as for the axes they can stay where they are, for no one is likely to come to the house and take them away: let the cupbearer go round with his cups, that we may make our drink-offerings and drop this matter of the bow; we will tell Melanthius to bring us in some goats to-morrow- the best he has; we can then offer thigh bones to Apollo the mighty archer, and again make trial of the bow, so as to bring the contest to an end.”

The rest approved his words, and thereon men servants poured water over the hands of the guests, while pages filled the mixing-bowls with wine and water and handed it round after giving every man his drink-offering. Then, when they had made their offerings and had drunk each as much as he desired, Ulysses craftily said:

“Suitors of the illustrious queen, listen that I may speak even as I am minded. I appeal more especially to Eurymachus, and to Antinous who has just spoken with so much reason. Cease shooting for the present and leave the matter to the gods, but in the morning let heaven give victory to whom it will. For the moment, however, give me the bow that I may prove the power of my hands among you all, and see whether I still have as much strength as I used to have, or whether travel and neglect have made an end of it.”

This made them all very angry, for they feared he might string the bow; Antinous therefore rebuked him fiercely saying, “Wretched creature, you have not so much as a grain of sense in your whole body; you ought to think yourself lucky in being allowed to dine unharmed among your betters, without having any smaller portion served you than we others have had, and in being allowed to hear our conversation. No other beggar or stranger has been allowed to hear what we say among ourselves; the wine must have been doing you a mischief, as it does with all those drink immoderately. It was wine that inflamed the Centaur Eurytion when he was staying with Peirithous among the Lapithae. When the wine had got into his head he went mad and did ill deeds about the house of Peirithous; this angered the heroes who were there assembled, so they rushed at him and cut off his ears and nostrils; then they dragged him through the doorway out of the house, so he went away crazed, and bore the burden of his crime, bereft of understanding. Henceforth, therefore, there was war between mankind and the centaurs, but he brought it upon himself through his own drunkenness. In like manner I can tell you that it will go hardly with you if you string the bow: you will find no mercy from any one here, for we shall at once ship you off to King Echetus, who kills every one that comes near him: you will never get away alive, so drink and keep quiet without getting into a quarrel with men younger than yourself."

Penelope then spoke to him. "Antinous," said she, "it is not right that you should ill-treat any guest of Telemachus who comes to this house. If the stranger should prove strong enough to string the mighty bow of Ulysses, can you suppose that he would take me home with him and make me his wife? Even the man himself can have no such idea in his mind: none of you need let that disturb his feasting; it would be out of all reason."

"Queen Penelope," answered Eurymachus, "we do not suppose that this man will take you away with him; it is impossible; but we are afraid lest some of the baser sort, men or women among the Achaeans, should go gossiping about and say, 'These suitors are a feeble folk; they are paying court to the wife of a brave man whose bow not one of them was able to string, and yet a beggarly tramp who came to the house strung it at once and sent an arrow through the iron.' This is what will be said, and it will be a scandal against us."

"Eurymachus," Penelope answered, "people who persist in eating up the estate of a great chieftain and dishonoring his house must not expect others to think well of them. Why then should you mind if men talk as you think they will? This stranger is strong and well-built, he says moreover that he is of noble birth. Give him the bow, and let us see whether he can string it or no. I say- and it shall surely be- that if Apollo vouchsafes him the glory of stringing it, I will give him a cloak and shirt of good wear, with a javelin to keep off dogs and robbers, and a sharp sword. I will also give him sandals, and will see him sent safely wherever he wants to go."

Then Telemachus said, "Mother, I am the only man either in Ithaca or in the islands that are over against Elis who has the right to let any one have the bow or to refuse it. No one shall force me one way or the other, not even though I choose to make the stranger a present of the bow outright, and let him take it away with him. Go, then, within the house and busy yourself with your daily duties, your loom, your distaff, and the ordering of your servants. This bow is a man's matter, and mine above all others, for it is I who am master here."

She went wondering back into the house, and laid her son's saying in her heart. Then going upstairs with her handmaids into her room, she mourned her dear husband till Minerva sent sweet sleep over her eyelids.

The swineherd now took up the bow and was for taking it to Ulysses, but the suitors clamored at him from all parts of the cloisters, and one of them said, "You idiot, where are you taking the bow to? Are you out of your wits? If Apollo and the other gods will grant our prayer, your own boarhounds shall get you into some quiet little place, and worry you to death."

Eumaeus was frightened at the outcry they all raised, so he put the bow down then and there, but Telemachus shouted out at him from the other side of the cloisters, and threatened him saying, "Father Eumaeus, bring the bow on in spite of them, or young as I am I will pelt you with stones back to the country, for I am the better man of the two. I wish I was as much stronger than all the other suitors in the house as I am than you, I would soon send some of them off sick and sorry, for they mean mischief."

Thus did he speak, and they all of them laughed heartily, which put them in a better humor with Telemachus; so Eumaeus brought the bow on and placed it in the hands of Ulysses. When he had done this, he called Euryclea apart and said to her, "Euryclea, Telemachus says you are to close the doors of the women's apartments. If they hear any groaning or uproar as of men fighting about the house, they are not to come out, but are to keep quiet and stay where they are at their work."

Euryclea did as she was told and closed the doors of the women's apartments.

Meanwhile Philoetius slipped quietly out and made fast the gates of the outer court. There was a ship's cable of byblus fiber lying in the gatehouse, so he made the gates fast with it and then came in again, resuming the seat that he had left, and keeping an eye on Ulysses, who had now got the bow in his hands, and was turning it every way about, and proving it all over to see whether the worms had been eating into its two horns during his absence. Then would one turn towards his neighbor saying, "This is some tricky old bow-fancier; either he has got one like it at home, or he wants to make one, in such workmanlike style does the old vagabond handle it."

Another said, "I hope he may be no more successful in other things than he is likely to be in stringing this bow."

But Ulysses, when he had taken it up and examined it all over, strung it as easily as a skilled bard strings a new peg of his lyre and makes the twisted gut fast at both ends. Then he took it in his right hand to prove the string, and it sang sweetly under his touch like the twittering of a swallow. The suitors were dismayed, and turned color as they heard it; at that moment, moreover, Jove thundered loudly as a sign, and the heart of Ulysses rejoiced as he heard the omen that the son of scheming Saturn had sent him.

He took an arrow that was lying upon the table- for those which the Achaeans were so shortly about to taste were all inside the quiver- he laid it on the center-piece of the bow, and drew the notch of the arrow and the string toward him, still seated on his seat. When he had taken aim he let fly, and his arrow pierced every one of the handle-holes of the axes from the first onwards till it had gone right through them, and into the outer courtyard. Then he said to Telemachus:

"Your guest has not disgraced you, Telemachus. I did not miss what I aimed at, and I was not long in stringing my bow. I am still strong, and not as the suitors twit me with being. Now, however, it is time for the Achaeans to prepare supper while there is still daylight, and then otherwise to disport themselves with song and dance which are the crowning ornaments of a banquet."

As he spoke he made a sign with his eyebrows, and Telemachus girded on his sword, grasped his spear, and stood armed beside his father's seat.

Lesson 60

- Read Book 22 of *The Odyssey.*

Book 22

Then Ulysses tore off his rags, and sprang on to the broad pavement with his bow and his quiver full of arrows. He shed the arrows on to the ground at his feet and said, "The mighty contest is at an end. I will now see whether Apollo will vouchsafe it to me to hit another mark which no man has yet hit."

On this he aimed a deadly arrow at Antinous, who was about to take up a two-handled gold cup to drink his wine and already had it in his hands. He had no thought of death- who amongst all the revelers would think that one man, however brave, would stand alone among so many and kill him? The arrow struck Antinous in the throat, and the point went clean through his neck, so that he fell over and the cup dropped from his hand, while a thick stream of blood gushed from his nostrils. He kicked the table from him and upset the things on it, so that the bread and roasted meats were all soiled as they fell over on to the ground. The suitors were in an uproar when they saw that a man had been hit; they sprang in dismay one and all of them from their seats and looked everywhere towards the walls, but there was neither shield nor spear, and they rebuked Ulysses very angrily. "Stranger," said they, "you shall pay for shooting people in this way: you shall see no other contest; you are a doomed man; he whom you have slain was the foremost youth in Ithaca, and the vultures shall devour you for having killed him."

Thus they spoke, for they thought that he had killed Antinous by mistake, and did not perceive that death was hanging over the head of every one of them. But Ulysses glared at them and said:

"Dogs, did you think that I should not come back from Troy? You have wasted my substance, have forced my women servants to lie with you, and have wooed my wife while I was still living. You have feared neither God nor man, and now you shall die."

They turned pale with fear as he spoke, and every man looked round about to see whither he might fly for safety, but Eurymachus alone spoke.

"If you are Ulysses," said he, "then what you have said is just. We have done much wrong on your lands and in your house. But Antinous who was the head and front of the offending lies low already. It was all his doing. It was not that he wanted to marry Penelope; he did not so much care about that; what he wanted was something quite different, and Jove has not vouchsafed it to him; he wanted to kill your son and to be chief man in Ithaca. Now, therefore, that he has met the death which was his due, spare the lives of your people. We will make everything good among ourselves, and pay you in full for all that we have eaten and drunk. Each one of us shall pay you a fine worth twenty oxen, and we will keep on giving you gold and bronze till your heart is softened. Until we have done this no one can complain of your being enraged against us."

Ulysses again glared at him and said, "Though you should give me all that you have in the world both now and all that you ever shall have, I will not stay my hand till I have paid all of you in full. You must fight, or fly for your lives; and fly, not a man of you shall."

Their hearts sank as they heard him, but Eurymachus again spoke saying:

"My friends, this man will give us no quarter. He will stand where he is and shoot us down till he has killed every man among us. Let us then show fight; draw your swords, and hold up the tables to shield you from his arrows. Let us have at him with a rush, to drive him from the pavement and doorway: we can then get through into the town, and raise such an alarm as shall soon stay his shooting."

As he spoke he drew his keen blade of bronze, sharpened on both sides, and with a loud cry sprang towards Ulysses, but Ulysses instantly shot an arrow into his breast that caught him by the nipple and fixed itself in his liver. He dropped his sword and fell doubled up over his table. The cup and all the meats went over on to the ground as he smote the earth with his forehead in the agonies of death, and he kicked the stool with his feet until his eyes were closed in darkness.

Then Amphinomus drew his sword and made straight at Ulysses to try and get him away from the door; but Telemachus was too quick for him, and struck him from behind; the spear caught him between the shoulders and went right through his chest, so that he fell heavily to the ground and struck the earth with his forehead. Then Telemachus sprang away from him, leaving his spear still in the body, for he feared that if he stayed to draw it out, some one of the Achaeans might come up and hack at him with his sword, or knock him down, so he set off at a run, and immediately was at his father's side. Then he said:

"Father, let me bring you a shield, two spears, and a brass helmet for your temples. I will arm myself as well, and will bring other armor for the swineherd and the stockman, for we had better be armed."

"Run and fetch them," answered Ulysses, "while my arrows hold out, or when I am alone they may get me away from the door."

Telemachus did as his father said, and went off to the store room where the armor was kept. He chose four shields, eight spears, and four brass helmets with horse-hair plumes. He brought them with all speed to his father, and armed himself first, while the stockman and the swineherd also put on their armor, and took their places near Ulysses. Meanwhile Ulysses, as long as his arrows lasted, had been shooting the suitors one by one, and they fell thick on one another: when his arrows gave out, he set the bow to stand against the end wall of the house by the door post, and hung a shield four hides thick about his shoulders; on his comely head he set his helmet, well wrought with a crest of horse-hair that nodded menacingly above it, and he grasped two redoubtable bronze-shod spears.

Now there was a trap door on the wall, while at one end of the pavement there was an exit leading to a narrow passage, and this exit was closed by a well-made door. Ulysses told Philoetius to stand by this door and guard it, for only one person could attack it at a time. But Agelaus shouted out, "Cannot some one go up to the trap door and tell the people what is going on? Help would come at once, and we should soon make an end of this man and his shooting."

"This may not be, Agelaus," answered Melanthius, "the mouth of the narrow passage is dangerously near the entrance to the outer court. One brave man could prevent any number from getting in. But I know what I will do, I will bring you arms from the store room, for I am sure it is there that Ulysses and his son have put them."

On this the goatherd Melanthius went by back passages to the store room of Ulysses' house. There he chose twelve shields, with as many helmets and spears, and brought them back as fast as he could to give them to the suitors. Ulysses' heart began to fail him when he saw the suitors putting on their armor and brandishing their spears. He saw the greatness of the danger, and said to Telemachus, "Some one of the women inside is helping the suitors against us, or it may be Melanthius." Telemachus answered, "The fault, father, is mine, and mine only; I left the store room door open, and they have kept a sharper look out than I have. Go, Eumaeus, put the door to, and see whether it is one of the women who is doing this, or whether, as I suspect, it is Melanthius the son of Dolius."

Thus did they converse. Meanwhile Melanthius was again going to the store room to fetch more armor, but the swineherd saw him and said to Ulysses who was beside him, "Ulysses, noble son of Laertes, it is that scoundrel Melanthius, just as we suspected, who is going to the store room. Say, shall I kill him, if I can get the better of him, or shall I bring him here that you may take your own revenge for all the many wrongs that he has done in your house?"

Ulysses answered, "Telemachus and I will hold these suitors in check, no matter what they do; go back both of you and bind Melanthius' hands and feet behind him. Throw him into the store room and make the door fast behind you; then fasten a noose about his body, and string him close up to the rafters from a high bearing-post, that he may linger on in an agony."

Thus did he speak, and they did even as he had said; they went to the store room, which they entered before Melanthius saw them, for he was busy searching for arms in the innermost part of the room, so the two took their stand on either side of the door and waited. By and by Melanthius came out with a helmet in one hand, and an old dry-rotted shield in the other, which had been borne by Laertes when he was young, but which had been long since thrown aside, and the straps had become unsewn; on this the two seized him, dragged him back by the hair, and threw him struggling to the ground. They bent his hands and feet well behind his back, and bound them tight with a painful bond as Ulysses had told them; then they fastened a noose about his body and strung him up from a high pillar till he was close up to the rafters, and over him did you then vaunt, O swineherd Eumaeus, saying, "Melanthius, you will pass the night on a soft bed as you deserve. You will know very well when morning comes from the streams of Oceanus, and it is time for you to be driving in your goats for the suitors to feast on."

There, then, they left him in very cruel bondage, and having put on their armor they closed the door behind them and went back to take their places by the side of Ulysses; whereon the four men stood in the cloister, fierce and full of fury; nevertheless, those who were in the body of the court were still both brave and many. Then Jove's daughter Minerva came up to them, having assumed the voice and form of Mentor. Ulysses was glad when he saw her and said, "Mentor, lend me your help, and forget not your old comrade, nor the many good turns he has done you. Besides, you are my age-mate."

But all the time he felt sure it was Minerva, and the suitors from the other side raised an uproar when they saw her. Agelaus was the first to reproach her. "Mentor," he cried, "do not let Ulysses beguile you into siding with him and fighting the suitors. This is what we will do: when we have killed these people, father and son, we will kill you too. You shall pay for it with your head, and when we have killed you, we will take all you have, in doors or out, and bring it into hotch-pot [combining properties in order to divide them equally] with Ulysses' property; we will not let your sons live in your house, nor your daughters, nor shall your widow continue to live in the city of Ithaca."

This made Minerva still more furious, so she scolded Ulysses very angrily. "Ulysses," said she, "your strength and prowess are no longer what they were when you fought for nine long years among the Trojans about the noble lady Helen. You killed many a man in those days, and it was through your stratagem that Priam's city was taken. How comes it that you are so lamentably less valiant now that you are on your own ground, face to face with the suitors in your own house? Come on, my good fellow, stand by my side and see how Mentor, son of Alcinous shall fight your foes and requite your kindnesses conferred upon him."

But she would not give him full victory as yet, for she wished still further to prove his own prowess and that of his brave son, so she flew up to one of the rafters in the roof of the cloister and sat upon it in the form of a swallow.

Meanwhile Agelaus son of Damastor, Eurynomus, Amphimedon, Demoptolemus, Pisander, and Polybus son of Polyctor bore the brunt of the fight upon the suitors' side; of all those who were still fighting for their lives they were by far the most valiant, for the others had already fallen under the arrows of Ulysses. Agelaus shouted to them and said, “My friends, he will soon have to leave off, for Mentor has gone away after having done nothing for him but brag. They are standing at the doors unsupported. Do not aim at him all at once, but six of you throw your spears first, and see if you cannot cover yourselves with glory by killing him. When he has fallen we need not be uneasy about the others.”

They threw their spears as he bade them, but Minerva made them all of no effect. One hit the door post; another went against the door; the pointed shaft of another struck the wall; and as soon as they had avoided all the spears of the suitors Ulysses said to his own men, “My friends, I should say we too had better let drive into the middle of them, or they will crown all the harm they have done us by us outright.”

They therefore aimed straight in front of them and threw their spears. Ulysses killed Demoptolemus, Telemachus Euryades, Eumaeus Elatus, while the stockman killed Pisander. These all bit the dust, and as the others drew back into a corner Ulysses and his men rushed forward and regained their spears by drawing them from the bodies of the dead.

The suitors now aimed a second time, but again Minerva made their weapons for the most part without effect. One hit a bearing-post of the cloister; another went against the door; while the pointed shaft of another struck the wall. Still, Amphimedon just took a piece of the top skin from off Telemachus’s wrist, and Ctesippus managed to graze Eumaeus’s shoulder above his shield; but the spear went on and fell to the ground. Then Ulysses and his men let drive into the crowd of suitors. Ulysses hit Eurydamas, Telemachus Amphimedon, and Eumaeus Polybus. After this the stockman hit Ctesippus in the breast, and taunted him saying, “Foul-mouthed son of Polytherses, do not be so foolish as to talk wickedly another time, but let heaven direct your speech, for the gods are far stronger than men. I make you a present of this advice to repay you for the foot which you gave Ulysses when he was begging about in his own house.”

Thus spoke the stockman, and Ulysses struck the son of Damastor with a spear in close fight, while Telemachus hit Leocritus son of Evenor in the belly, and the dart went clean through him, so that he fell forward full on his face upon the ground. Then Minerva from her seat on the rafter held up her deadly aegis, and the hearts of the suitors quailed. They fled to the other end of the court like a herd of cattle maddened by the gadfly in early summer when the days are at their longest. As eagle-beaked, crook-taloned vultures from the mountains swoop down on the smaller birds that cower in flocks upon the ground, and kill them, for they cannot either fight or fly, and lookers on enjoy the sport- even so did Ulysses and his men fall upon the suitors and smite them on every side. They made a horrible groaning as their brains were being battered in, and the ground seethed with their blood.

Leiodes then caught the knees of Ulysses and said, "Ulysses I beseech you have mercy upon me and spare me. I never wronged any of the women in your house either in word or deed, and I tried to stop the others. I saw them, but they would not listen, and now they are paying for their folly. I was their sacrificing priest; if you kill me, I shall die without having done anything to deserve it, and shall have got no thanks for all the good that I did."

Ulysses looked sternly at him and answered, "If you were their sacrificing priest, you must have prayed many a time that it might be long before I got home again, and that you might marry my wife and have children by her. Therefore you shall die."

With these words he picked up the sword that Agelaus had dropped when he was being killed, and which was lying upon the ground. Then he struck Leiodes on the back of his neck, so that his head fell rolling in the dust while he was yet speaking.

The minstrel Phemius son of Terpes- he who had been forced by the suitors to sing to them- now tried to save his life. He was standing near towards the trap door, and held his lyre in his hand. He did not know whether to fly out of the cloister and sit down by the altar of Jove that was in the outer court, and on which both Laertes and Ulysses had offered up the thigh bones of many an ox, or whether to go straight up to Ulysses and embrace his knees, but in the end he deemed it best to embrace Ulysses' knees. So he laid his lyre on the ground the ground between the mixing-bowl and the silver-studded seat; then going up to Ulysses he caught hold of his knees and said, "Ulysses, I beseech you have mercy on me and spare me. You will be sorry for it afterwards if you kill a bard who can sing both for gods and men as I can. I make all my lays myself, and heaven visits me with every kind of inspiration. I would sing to you as though you were a god, do not therefore be in such a hurry to cut my head off. Your own son Telemachus will tell you that I did not want to frequent your house and sing to the suitors after their meals, but they were too many and too strong for me, so they made me."

Telemachus heard him, and at once went up to his father. "Hold!" he cried, "the man is guiltless, do him no hurt; and we will Medon too, who was always good to me when I was a boy, unless Philoetius or Eumaeus has already killed him, or he has fallen in your way when you were raging about the court."

Medon caught these words of Telemachus, for he was crouching under a seat beneath which he had hidden by covering himself up with a freshly flayed heifer's hide, so he threw off the hide, went up to Telemachus, and laid hold of his knees.

"Here I am, my dear sir," said he, "stay your hand therefore, and tell your father, or he will kill me in his rage against the suitors for having wasted his substance and been so foolishly disrespectful to yourself."

Ulysses smiled at him and answered, "Fear not; Telemachus has saved your life, that you may know in future, and tell other people, how greatly better good deeds prosper than evil ones. Go, therefore, outside the cloisters into the outer court, and be out of the way of the slaughter- you and the bard- while I finish my work here inside."

The pair went into the outer court as fast as they could, and sat down by Jove's great altar, looking fearfully round, and still expecting that they would be killed. Then Ulysses searched the whole court carefully over, to see if anyone had managed to hide himself and was still living, but he found them all lying in the dust and weltering in their blood. They were like fishes which fishermen have netted out of the sea, and thrown upon the beach to lie gasping for water till the heat of the sun makes an end of them. Even so were the suitors lying all huddled up one against the other.

Then Ulysses said to Telemachus, "Call nurse Euryclea; I have something to say to her."

Telemachus went and knocked at the door of the women's room. "Make haste," said he, "you old woman who have been set over all the other women in the house. Come outside; my father wishes to speak to you."

When Euryclea heard this she unfastened the door of the women's room and came out, following Telemachus. She found Ulysses among the corpses bespattered with blood and filth like a lion that has just been devouring an ox, and his breast and both his cheeks are all bloody, so that he is a fearful sight; even so was Ulysses besmirched from head to foot with gore. When she saw all the corpses and such a quantity of blood, she was beginning to cry out for joy, for she saw that a great deed had been done; but Ulysses checked her, "Old woman," said he, "rejoice in silence; restrain yourself, and do not make any noise about it; it is an unholy thing to vaunt over dead men. Heaven's doom and their own evil deeds have brought these men to destruction, for they respected no man in the whole world, neither rich nor poor, who came near them, and they have come to a bad end as a punishment for their wickedness and folly. Now, however, tell me which of the women in the house have misconducted themselves, and who are innocent."

"I will tell you the truth, my son," answered Euryclea. "There are fifty women in the house whom we teach to do things, such as carding wool, and all kinds of household work. Of these, twelve in all have misbehaved, and have been wanting in respect to me, and also to Penelope. They showed no disrespect to Telemachus, for he has only lately grown and his mother never permitted him to give orders to the female servants; but let me go upstairs and tell your wife all that has happened, for some god has been sending her to sleep."

"Do not wake her yet," answered Ulysses, "but tell the women who have misconducted themselves to come to me."

Euryclea left the cloister to tell the women, and make them come to Ulysses; in the meantime he called Telemachus, the stockman, and the swineherd. "Begin," said he, "to remove the dead, and make the women help you. Then, get sponges and clean water to swill down the tables and seats. When you have thoroughly cleansed the whole cloisters, take the women into the space between the domed room and the wall of the outer court, and run them through with your swords till they are quite dead, and have forgotten all about love and the way in which they used to lie in secret with the suitors."

On this the women came down in a body, weeping and wailing bitterly. First they carried the dead bodies out, and propped them up against one another in the gatehouse. Ulysses ordered them about and made them do their work quickly, so they had to carry the bodies out. When they had done this, they cleaned all the tables and seats with sponges and water, while Telemachus and the two others shoveled up the blood and dirt from the ground, and the women carried it all away and put it out of doors. Then when they had made the whole place quite clean and orderly, they took the women out and hemmed them in the narrow space between the wall of the domed room and that of the yard, so that they could not get away: and Telemachus said to the other two, "I shall not let these women die a clean death, for they were insolent to me and my mother, and used to sleep with the suitors."

So saying he made a ship's cable fast to one of the bearing-posts that supported the roof of the domed room, and secured it all around the building, at a good height, lest any of the women's feet should touch the ground; and as thrushes or doves beat against a net that has been set for them in a thicket just as they were getting to their nest, and a terrible fate awaits them, even so did the women have to put their heads in nooses one after the other and die most miserably. Their feet moved convulsively for a while, but not for very long.

As for Melanthius, they took him through the cloister into the inner court. There they cut off his nose and his ears; they drew out his vitals and gave them to the dogs raw, and then in their fury they cut off his hands and his feet.

When they had done this they washed their hands and feet and went back into the house, for all was now over; and Ulysses said to the dear old nurse Euryclea, "Bring me sulfur, which cleanses all pollution, and fetch fire also that I may burn it, and purify the cloisters. Go, moreover, and tell Penelope to come here with her attendants, and also all the maid servants that are in the house."

"All that you have said is true," answered Euryclea, "but let me bring you some clean clothes- a shirt and cloak. Do not keep these rags on your back any longer. It is not right."

"First light me a fire," replied Ulysses.

She brought the fire and sulfur, as he had bidden her, and Ulysses thoroughly purified the cloisters and both the inner and outer courts. Then she went inside to call the women and tell them what had happened; whereon they came from their apartment with torches in their hands, and pressed round Ulysses to embrace him, kissing his head and shoulders and taking hold of his hands. It made him feel as if he should like to weep, for he remembered every one of them.

Lesson 61

- Read Book 23 of *The Odyssey.*

Book 23

Euryclea now went upstairs laughing to tell her mistress that her dear husband had come home. Her aged knees became young again and her feet were nimble for joy as she went up to her mistress and bent over her head to speak to her. "Wake up Penelope, my dear child," she exclaimed, "and see with your own eyes something that you have been wanting this long time past. Ulysses has at last indeed come home again, and has killed the suitors who were giving so much trouble in his house, eating up his estate and ill-treating his son."

"My good nurse," answered Penelope, "you must be mad. The gods sometimes send some very sensible people out of their minds, and make foolish people become sensible. This is what they must have been doing to you; for you always used to be a reasonable person. Why should you thus mock me when I have trouble enough already- talking such nonsense, and waking me up out of a sweet sleep that had taken possession of my eyes and closed them? I have never slept so soundly from the day my poor husband went to that city with the ill-omened name. Go back again into the women's room; if it had been any one else, who had woke me up to bring me such absurd news I should have sent her away with a severe scolding. As it is, your age shall protect you."

"My dear child," answered Euryclea, "I am not mocking you. It is quite true as I tell you that Ulysses is come home again. He was the stranger whom they all kept on treating so badly in the cloister. Telemachus knew all the time that he was come back, but kept his father's secret that he might have his revenge on all these wicked people.

Then Penelope sprang up from her couch, threw her arms round Euryclea, and wept for joy. "But my dear nurse," said she, "explain this to me; if he has really come home as you say, how did he manage to overcome the wicked suitors single handed, seeing what a number of them there always were?"

"I was not there," answered Euryclea, "and do not know; I only heard them groaning while they were being killed. We sat crouching and huddled up in a corner of the women's room with the doors closed, till your son came to fetch me because his father sent him. Then I found Ulysses standing over the corpses that were lying on the ground all round him, one on top of the other. You would have enjoyed it if you could have seen him standing there all bespattered with blood and filth, and looking just like a lion. But the corpses are now all piled up in the gatehouse that is in the outer court, and Ulysses has lit a great fire to purify the house with sulfur. He has sent me to call you, so come with me that you may both be happy together after all; for now at last the desire of your heart has been fulfilled; your husband is come home to find both wife and son alive and well, and to take his revenge in his own house on the suitors who behaved so badly to him."

"My dear nurse," said Penelope, "do not exult too confidently over all this. You know how delighted every one would be to see Ulysses come home- more particularly myself, and the son who has been born to both of us; but what you tell me cannot be really true. It is some god who is angry with the suitors for their great wickedness, and has made an end of them; for they respected no man in the whole world, neither rich nor poor, who came near them, who came near them, and they have come to a bad end in consequence of their iniquity. Ulysses is dead far away from the Achaean land; he will never return home again."

Then nurse Euryclea said, "My child, what are you talking about? but you were all hard of belief and have made up your mind that your husband is never coming, although he is in the house and by his own fire side at this very moment. Besides I can give you another proof; when I was washing him I perceived the scar which the wild boar gave him, and I wanted to tell you about it, but in his wisdom he would not let me, and clapped his hands over my mouth; so come with me and I will make this bargain with you- if I am deceiving you, you may have me killed by the most cruel death you can think of."

"My dear nurse," said Penelope, "however wise you may be you can hardly fathom the counsels of the gods. Nevertheless, we will go in search of my son, that I may see the corpses of the suitors, and the man who has killed them."

On this she came down from her upper room, and while doing so she considered whether she should keep at a distance from her husband and question him, or whether she should at once go up to him and embrace him. When, however, she had crossed the stone floor of the cloister, she sat down opposite Ulysses by the fire, against the wall at right angles [to that by which she had entered], while Ulysses sat near one of the bearing-posts, looking upon the ground, and waiting to see what his wife would say to him when she saw him. For a long time she sat silent and as one lost in amazement. At one moment she looked him full in the face, but then again directly, she was misled by his shabby clothes and failed to recognize him, till Telemachus began to reproach her and said:

"Mother- but you are so hard that I cannot call you by such a name- why do you keep away from my father in this way? Why do you not sit by his side and begin talking to him and asking him questions? No other woman could bear to keep away from her husband when he had come back to her after twenty years of absence, and after having gone through so much; but your heart always was as hard as a stone."

Penelope answered, "My son, I am so lost in astonishment that I can find no words in which either to ask questions or to answer them. I cannot even look him straight in the face. Still, if he really is Ulysses come back to his own home again, we shall get to understand one another better by and by, for there are tokens with which we two are alone acquainted, and which are hidden from all others."

Ulysses smiled at this, and said to Telemachus, "Let your mother put me to any proof she likes; she will make up her mind about it presently. She rejects me for the moment and believes me to be somebody else, because I am covered with dirt and have such bad clothes on; let us, however, consider what we had better do next. When one man has killed another, even though he was not one who would leave many friends to take up his quarrel, the man who has killed him must still say good bye to his friends and fly the country; whereas we have been killing the stay of a whole town, and all the picked youth of Ithaca. I would have you consider this matter."

"Look to it yourself, father," answered Telemachus, "for they say you are the wisest counselor in the world, and that there is no other mortal man who can compare with you. We will follow you with right good will, nor shall you find us fail you in so far as our strength holds out."

"I will say what I think will be best," answered Ulysses. "First wash and put your shirts on; tell the maids also to go to their own room and dress; Phemius shall then strike up a dance tune on his lyre, so that if people outside hear, or any of the neighbors, or some one going along the street happens to notice it, they may think there is a wedding in the house, and no rumors about the death of the suitors will get about in the town, before we can escape to the woods upon my own land. Once there, we will settle which of the courses heaven vouchsafes us shall seem wisest."

Thus did he speak, and they did even as he had said. First they washed and put their shirts on, while the women got ready. Then Phemius took his lyre and set them all longing for sweet song and stately dance. The house re-echoed with the sound of men and women dancing, and the people outside said, "I suppose the queen has been getting married at last. She ought to be ashamed of herself for not continuing to protect her husband's property until he comes home."

This was what they said, but they did not know what it was that had been happening. The upper servant Eurynome washed and anointed Ulysses in his own house and gave him a shirt and cloak, while Minerva made him look taller and stronger than before; she also made the hair grow thick on the top of his head, and flow down in curls like hyacinth blossoms; she glorified him about the head and shoulders just as a skillful workman who has studied art of all kinds under Vulcan or Minerva- and his work is full of beauty- enriches a piece of silver plate by gilding it. He came from the bath looking like one of the immortals, and sat down opposite his wife on the seat he had left. "My dear," said he, "heaven has endowed you with a heart more unyielding than woman ever yet had. No other woman could bear to keep away from her husband when he had come back to her after twenty years of absence, and after having gone through so much. But come, nurse, get a bed ready for me; I will sleep alone, for this woman has a heart as hard as iron."

"My dear," answered Penelope, "I have no wish to set myself up, nor to depreciate you; but I am not struck by your appearance, for I very well remember what kind of a man you were when you set sail from Ithaca. Nevertheless, Euryclea, take his bed outside the bed chamber that he himself built. Bring the bed outside this room, and put bedding upon it with fleeces, good coverlets, and blankets."

She said this to try him, but Ulysses was very angry and said, "Wife, I am much displeased at what you have just been saying. Who has been taking my bed from the place in which I left it? He must have found it a hard task, no matter how skilled a workman he was, unless some god came and helped him to shift it. There is no man living, however strong and in his prime, who could move it from its place, for it is a marvelous curiosity which I made with my very own hands. There was a young olive growing within the precincts of the house, in full vigor, and about as thick as a bearing-post. I built my room round this with strong walls of stone and a roof to cover them, and I made the doors strong and well-fitting. Then I cut off the top boughs of the olive tree and left the stump standing. This I dressed roughly from the root upwards and then worked with carpenter's tools well and skillfully, straightening my work by drawing a line on the wood, and making it into a bed-prop. I then bored a hole down the middle, and made it the center-post of my bed, at which I worked till I had finished it, inlaying it with gold and silver; after this I stretched a hide of crimson leather from one side of it to the other. So you see I know all about it, and I desire to learn whether it is still there, or whether any one has been removing it by cutting down the olive tree at its roots."

When she heard the sure proofs Ulysses now gave her, she fairly broke down. She flew weeping to his side, flung her arms about his neck, and kissed him. "Do not be angry with me Ulysses," she cried, "you, who are the wisest of mankind. We have suffered, both of us. Heaven has denied us the happiness of spending our youth, and of growing old, together; do not then be aggrieved or take it amiss that I did not embrace you thus as soon as I saw you. I have been shuddering all the time through fear that someone might come here and deceive me with a lying story; for there are many very wicked people going about. Jove's daughter Helen would never have yielded herself to a man from a foreign country, if she had known that the sons of Achaeans would come after her and bring her back. Heaven put it in her heart to do wrong, and she gave no thought to that sin, which has been the source of all our sorrows. Now, however, that you have convinced me by showing that you know all about our bed (which no human being has ever seen but you and I and a single maid servant, the daughter of Actor, who was given me by my father on my marriage, and who keeps the doors of our room) hard of belief though I have been I can mistrust no longer."

Then Ulysses in his turn melted, and wept as he clasped his dear and faithful wife to his bosom. As the sight of land is welcome to men who are swimming towards the shore, when Neptune has wrecked their ship with the fury of his winds and waves- a few alone reach the land, and these, covered with brine, are thankful when they find themselves on firm ground and out of danger- even so was her husband welcome to her as she looked upon him, and she could not tear her two fair arms from about his neck. Indeed they would have gone on indulging their sorrow till rosy-fingered morn appeared, had not Minerva determined otherwise, and held night back in the far west, while she would not suffer Dawn to leave Oceanus, nor to yoke the two steeds Lampus and Phaethon that bear her onward to break the day upon mankind.

At last, however, Ulysses said, "Wife, we have not yet reached the end of our troubles. I have an unknown amount of toil still to undergo. It is long and difficult, but I must go through with it, for thus the shade of Teiresias prophesied concerning me, on the day when I went down into Hades to ask about my return and that of my companions. But now let us go to bed, that we may lie down and enjoy the blessed boon of sleep."

"You shall go to bed as soon as you please," replied Penelope, "now that the gods have sent you home to your own good house and to your country. But as heaven has put it in your mind to speak of it, tell me about the task that lies before you. I shall have to hear about it later, so it is better that I should be told at once."

"My dear," answered Ulysses, "why should you press me to tell you? Still, I will not conceal it from you, though you will not like it. I do not like it myself, for Teiresias bade me travel far and wide, carrying an oar, till I came to a country where the people have never heard of the sea, and do not even mix salt with their food. They know nothing about ships, nor oars that are as the wings of a ship. He gave me this certain token which I will not hide from you. He said that a wayfarer should meet me and ask me whether it was a winnowing shovel that I had on my shoulder. On this, I was to fix my oar in the ground and sacrifice a ram, a bull, and a boar to

Neptune; after which I was to go home and offer hecatombs to all the gods in heaven, one after the other. As for myself, he said that death should come to me from the sea, and that my life should ebb away very gently when I was full of years and peace of mind, and my people should bless me. All this, he said, should surely come to pass."

And Penelope said, "If the gods are going to vouchsafe you a happier time in your old age, you may hope then to have some respite from misfortune."

Thus did they converse. Meanwhile Eurynome and the nurse took torches and made the bed ready with soft coverlets; as soon as they had laid them, the nurse went back into the house to go to her rest, leaving the bed chamber woman Eurynome to show Ulysses and Penelope to bed by torch light. When she had conducted them to their room she went back, and they then came joyfully to the rites of their own old bed. Telemachus, Philoetius, and the swineherd now left off dancing, and made the women leave off also. They then laid themselves down to sleep in the cloisters.

When Ulysses and Penelope had had their fill of love they fell talking with one another. She told him how much she had had to bear in seeing the house filled with a crowd of wicked suitors who had killed so many sheep and oxen on her account, and had drunk so many casks of wine. Ulysses in his turn told her what he had suffered, and how much trouble he had himself given to other people. He told her everything, and she was so delighted to listen that she never went to sleep till he had ended his whole story.

He began with his victory over the Cicons, and how he thence reached the fertile land of the Lotus-eaters. He told her all about the Cyclops and how he had punished him for having so ruthlessly eaten his brave comrades; how he then went on to Aeolus, who received him hospitably and furthered him on his way, but even so he was not to reach home, for to his great grief a hurricane carried him out to sea again; how he went on to the Laestrygonian city Telepylos, where the people destroyed all his ships with their crews, save himself and his own ship only. Then he told of cunning Circe and her craft, and how he sailed to the chill house of Hades, to consult the ghost of the Theban prophet Teiresias, and how he saw his old comrades in arms, and his mother who bore him and brought him up when he was a child; how he then heard the wondrous singing of the Sirens, and went on to the wandering rocks and terrible Charybdis and to Scylla, whom no man had ever yet passed in safety; how his men then ate the cattle of the sun-god, and how Jove therefore struck the ship with his thunderbolts, so that all his men perished together, himself alone being left alive; how at last he reached the Ogygian island and the nymph Calypso, who kept him there in a cave, and fed him, and wanted him to marry her, in which case she intended making him immortal so that he should never grow old, but she could not persuade him to let her do so; and how after much suffering he had found his way to the Phaeacians, who had treated him as though he had been a god, and sent him back in a ship to his own country after having given him gold, bronze, and raiment in great abundance. This was the last thing about which he told her, for here a deep sleep took hold upon him and eased the burden of his sorrows.

Then Minerva bethought her of another matter. When she deemed that Ulysses had had both of his wife and of repose, she bade gold-enthroned Dawn rise out of Oceanus that she might shed light upon mankind. On this, Ulysses rose from his comfortable bed and said to Penelope, "Wife, we have both of us had our full share of troubles, you, here, in lamenting my absence, and I in being prevented from getting home though I was longing all the time to do so. Now, however, that we have at last come together, take care of the property that is in the house. As for the sheep and goats which the wicked suitors have eaten, I will take many myself by force from other people, and will compel the Achaeans to make good the rest till they shall have filled all my yards. I am now going to the wooded lands out in the country to see my father who has so long been grieved on my account, and to yourself I will give these instructions, though you have little need of them. At sunrise it will at once get abroad that I have been killing the suitors; go upstairs, therefore, and stay there with your women. See nobody and ask no questions."

As he spoke he girded on his armor. Then he roused Telemachus, Philoetius, and Eumaeus, and told them all to put on their armor also. This they did, and armed themselves. When they had done so, they opened the gates and sallied forth, Ulysses leading the way. It was now daylight, but Minerva nevertheless concealed them in darkness and led them quickly out of the town.

Lesson 62

- Read Book 24 of *The Odyssey*.

Book 24

Then Mercury of Cyllene summoned the ghosts of the suitors, and in his hand he held the fair golden wand with which he seals men's eyes in sleep or wakes them just as he pleases; with this he roused the ghosts and led them, while they followed whining and gibbering behind him. As bats fly squealing in the hollow of some great cave, when one of them has fallen out of the cluster in which they hang, even so did the ghosts whine and squeal as Mercury the healer of sorrow led them down into the dark abode of death. When they had passed the waters of Oceanus and the rock Leucas, they came to the gates of the sun and the land of dreams, whereon they reached the meadow of asphodel where dwell the souls and shadows of them that can labor no more.

Here they found the ghost of Achilles son of Peleus, with those of Patroclus, Antilochus, and Ajax, who was the finest and handsomest man of all the Danaans after the son of Peleus himself.

They gathered round the ghost of the son of Peleus, and the ghost of Agamemnon joined them, sorrowing bitterly. Round him were gathered also the ghosts of those who had perished with him in the house of Aeisthus; and the ghost of Achilles spoke first.

"Son of Atreus," it said, "we used to say that Jove had loved you better from first to last than any other hero, for you were captain over many and brave men, when we were all fighting together before Troy; yet the hand of death, which no mortal can escape, was laid upon you all too early. Better for you had you fallen at Troy in the hey-day of your renown, for the Achaeans would have built a mound over your ashes, and your son would have been heir to your good name, whereas it has now been your lot to come to a most miserable end."

"Happy son of Peleus," answered the ghost of Agamemnon, "for having died at Troy far from Argos, while the bravest of the Trojans and the Achaeans fell round you fighting for your body. There you lay in the whirling clouds of dust, all huge and hugely, heedless now of your chivalry. We fought the whole of the livelong day, nor should we ever have left off if Jove had not sent a hurricane to stay us. Then, when we had borne you to the ships out of the fray, we laid you on your bed and cleansed your fair skin with warm water and with ointments. The Danaans tore their hair and wept bitterly round about you. Your mother, when she heard, came with her immortal nymphs from out of the sea, and the sound of a great wailing went forth over the waters so that the Achaeans quaked for fear. They would have fled panic-stricken to their ships had not wise old Nestor whose counsel was ever truest checked them saying, 'Hold, Argives, fly not sons of the Achaeans, this is his mother coming from the sea with her immortal nymphs to view the body of her son.'

"Thus he spoke, and the Achaeans feared no more. The daughters of the old man of the sea stood round you weeping bitterly, and clothed you in immortal raiment. The nine muses also came and lifted up their sweet voices in lament- calling and answering one another; there was not an Argive but wept for pity of the dirge they chanted. Days and nights seven and ten we mourned you, mortals and immortals, but on the eighteenth day we gave you to the flames, and many a fat sheep with many an ox did we slay in sacrifice around you. You were burnt in raiment of the gods, with rich resins and with honey, while heroes, horse and foot, clashed their armor round the pile as you were burning, with the tramp as of a great multitude. But when the flames of heaven had done their work, we gathered your white bones at daybreak and laid them in ointments and in pure wine. Your mother brought us a golden vase to hold them- gift of Bacchus, and work of Vulcan himself; in this we mingled your bleached bones with those of Patroclus who had gone before you, and separate we enclosed also those of Antilochus, who had been closer to you than any other of your comrades now that Patroclus was no more.

"Over these the host of the Argives built a noble tomb, on a point jutting out over the open Hellespont, that it might be seen from far out upon the sea by those now living and by them that shall be born hereafter. Your mother begged prizes from the gods, and offered them to be contended for by the noblest of the Achaeans. You must have been present at the funeral of many a hero, when the young men gird themselves and make ready to contend for prizes on the death of some great chieftain, but you never saw such prizes as silver-footed Thetis offered in your honor; for the gods loved you well. Thus even in death your fame, Achilles, has not been lost, and your name lives evermore among all mankind. But as for me, what solace had I when the days of my fighting were done? For Jove willed my destruction on my return, by the hands of Aegisthus and those of my wicked wife."

Thus did they converse, and presently Mercury came up to them with the ghosts of the suitors who had been killed by Ulysses. The ghosts of Agamemnon and Achilles were astonished at seeing them, and went up to them at once. The ghost of Agamemnon recognized Amphimedon son of Melaneus, who lived in Ithaca and had been his host, so it began to talk to him.

"Amphimedon," it said, "what has happened to all you fine young men- all of an age too- that you are come down here under the ground? One could pick no finer body of men from any city. Did Neptune raise his winds and waves against you when you were at sea, or did your enemies make an end of you on the mainland when you were cattle-lifting or sheep-stealing, or while fighting in defense of their wives and city? Answer my question, for I have been your guest. Do you not remember how I came to your house with Menelaus, to persuade Ulysses to join us with his ships against Troy? It was a whole month ere we could resume our voyage, for we had hard work to persuade Ulysses to come with us."

And the ghost of Amphimedon answered, "Agamemnon, son of Atreus, king of men, I remember everything that you have said, and will tell you fully and accurately about the way in which our end was brought about. Ulysses had been long gone, and we were courting his wife, who did not say point blank that she would not marry, nor yet bring matters to an end, for she meant to compass our destruction: this, then, was the trick she played us. She set up a great tambour frame in her room and began to work on an enormous piece of fine needlework. 'Sweethearts,' said she, 'Ulysses is indeed dead, still, do not press me to marry again immediately; wait- for I would not have my skill in needlework perish unrecorded- till I have completed a pall for the hero Laertes, against the time when death shall take him. He is very rich, and the women of the place will talk if he is laid out without a pall.' This is what she said, and we assented; whereupon we could see her working upon her great web all day long, but at night she would unpick the stitches again by torchlight. She fooled us in this way for three years without our finding it out, but as time wore on and she was now in her fourth year, in the waning of moons and many days had been accomplished, one of her maids who knew what she was doing told us, and we caught her in the act of undoing her work, so she had to finish it whether she would or no; and when she showed us the robe she had made, after she had had it washed, its splendor was as that of the sun or moon.

"Then some malicious god conveyed Ulysses to the upland farm where his swineherd lives. Thither presently came also his son, returning from a voyage to Pylos, and the two came to the town when they had hatched their plot for our destruction. Telemachus came first, and then after him, accompanied by the swineherd, came Ulysses, clad in rags and leaning on a staff as though he were some miserable old beggar. He came so unexpectedly that none of us knew him, not even the older ones among us, and we reviled him and threw things at him. He endured both being struck and insulted without a word, though he was in his own house; but when the will of Aegis-bearing Jove inspired him, he and Telemachus took the armor and hid it in an inner chamber, bolting the doors behind them. Then he cunningly made his wife offer his bow and a quantity of iron to be contended for by us ill-fated suitors; and this was the beginning of our end, for not one of us could string the bow- nor nearly do so. When it was about to reach the hands of Ulysses, we all of us shouted out that it should not be given him, no matter what he might say, but Telemachus insisted on his having it. When he had got it in his hands he strung it with ease and sent his arrow through the iron. Then he stood on the floor of the cloister and poured his arrows on the ground, glaring fiercely about him. First he killed Antinous, and then, aiming straight before him, he let fly his deadly darts and they fell thick on one another. It was plain that some one of the gods was helping them, for they fell upon us with might and main throughout the cloisters, and there was a hideous sound of groaning as our brains were being battered in, and the ground seethed with our blood. This, Agamemnon, is how we came by our end, and our bodies are lying still un-cared for in the house of Ulysses, for our friends at home do not yet know what has happened, so that they cannot lay us out and wash the black blood from our wounds, making moan over us according to the offices due to the departed."

"Happy Ulysses, son of Laertes," replied the ghost of Agamemnon, "you are indeed blessed in the possession of a wife endowed with such rare excellence of understanding, and so faithful to her wedded lord as Penelope the daughter of Icarius. The fame, therefore, of her virtue shall never die, and the immortals shall compose a song that shall be welcome to all mankind in honor of the constancy of Penelope. How far otherwise was the wickedness of the daughter of Tyndareus who killed her lawful husband; her song shall be hateful among men, for she has brought disgrace on all womankind even on the good ones."

Thus did they converse in the house of Hades deep down within the bowels of the earth. Meanwhile Ulysses and the others passed out of the town and soon reached the fair and well-tilled farm of Laertes, which he had reclaimed with infinite labor. Here was his house, with a lean-to running all round it, where the slaves who worked for him slept and sat and ate, while inside the house there was an old Sicel woman, who looked after him in this his country-farm. When Ulysses got there, he said to his son and to the other two:

"Go to the house, and kill the best pig that you can find for dinner. Meanwhile I want to see whether my father will know me, or fail to recognize me after so long an absence."

He then took off his armor and gave it to Eumaeus and Philoetius, who went straight on to the house, while he turned off into the vineyard to make trial of his father. As he went down into the great orchard, he did not see Dolius, nor any of his sons nor of the other bondsmen, for they were all gathering thorns to make a fence for the vineyard, at the place where the old man had told them; he therefore found his father alone, hoeing a vine. He had on a dirty old shirt, patched and very shabby; his legs were bound round with thongs of oxhide to save him from the brambles, and he also wore sleeves of leather; he had a goat skin cap on his head, and was looking very woe-begone. When Ulysses saw him so worn, so old and full of sorrow, he stood still under a tall pear tree and began to weep. He doubted whether to embrace him, kiss him, and tell him all about his having come home, or whether he should first question him and see what he would say. In the end he deemed it best to be crafty with him, so in this mind he went up to his father, who was bending down and digging about a plant.

"I see, sir," said Ulysses, "that you are an excellent gardener- what pains you take with it, to be sure. There is not a single plant, not a fig tree, vine, olive, pear, nor flower bed, but bears the trace of your attention. I trust, however, that you will not be offended if I say that you take better care of your garden than of yourself. You are old, unsavory, and very meanly clad. It cannot be because you are idle that your master takes such poor care of you, indeed your face and figure have nothing of the slave about them, and proclaim you of noble birth. I should have said that you were one of those who should wash well, eat well, and lie soft at night as old men have a right to do; but tell me, and tell me true, whose bondman are you, and in whose garden are you working? Tell me also about another matter. Is this place that I have come to really Ithaca? I met a man just now who said so, but he was a dull fellow, and had not the patience to hear my story out when I was asking him about an old friend of mine, whether he was still living, or was already dead and in the house of Hades. Believe me when I tell you that this man came to my house once when I was in my own country and never yet did any stranger come to me whom I liked better. He said that his family came from Ithaca and that his father was Laertes, son of Arceisius. I received him hospitably, making him welcome to all the abundance of my house, and when he went away I gave him all customary presents. I gave him seven talents of fine gold, and a cup of solid silver with flowers chased upon it. I gave him twelve light cloaks, and as many pieces of tapestry; I also gave him twelve cloaks of single fold, twelve rugs, twelve fair mantles, and an equal number of shirts. To all this I added four good looking women skilled in all useful arts, and I let him take his choice."

His father shed tears and answered, "Sir, you have indeed come to the country that you have named, but it is fallen into the hands of wicked people. All this wealth of presents has been given to no purpose. If you could have found your friend here alive in Ithaca, he would have entertained you hospitably and would have required your presents amply when you left him- as would have been only right considering what you have already given him. But tell me, and tell me true, how many years is it since you entertained this guest- my unhappy son, as ever was? Alas! He has perished far from his own country; the fishes of the sea have eaten him, or he has fallen a prey to the birds and wild beasts of some continent. Neither his mother, nor I his father, who were his parents, could throw our arms about him and wrap him in his shroud, nor could his excellent and richly dowered wife Penelope bewail her husband as was natural upon his death bed, and close his eyes according to the offices due to the departed. But now, tell me truly for I want to know. Who and whence are you- tell me of your town and parents? Where is the ship lying that has brought you and your men to Ithaca? Or were you a passenger on some other man's ship, and those who brought you here have gone on their way and left you?"

"I will tell you everything," answered Ulysses, "quite truly. I come from Alybas, where I have a fine house. I am son of King Apheidas, who is the son of Polypemon. My own name is Eperitus; heaven drove me off my course as I was leaving Sicania, and I have been carried here against my will. As for my ship it is lying over yonder, off the open country outside the town, and this is the fifth year since Ulysses left my country. Poor fellow, yet the omens were good for him when he left me. The birds all flew on our right hands, and both he and I rejoiced to see them as we parted, for we had every hope that we should have another friendly meeting and exchange presents."

A dark cloud of sorrow fell upon Laertes as he listened. He filled both hands with the dust from off the ground and poured it over his grey head, groaning heavily as he did so. The heart of Ulysses was touched, and his nostrils quivered as he looked upon his father; then he sprang towards him, flung his arms about him and kissed him, saying, "I am he, father, about whom you are asking- I have returned after having been away for twenty years. But cease your sighing and lamentation- we have no time to lose, for I should tell you that I have been killing the suitors in my house, to punish them for their insolence and crimes."

"If you really are my son Ulysses," replied Laertes, "and have come back again, you must give me such manifest proof of your identity as shall convince me."

"First observe this scar," answered Ulysses, "which I got from a boar's tusk when I was hunting on Mount Parnassus. You and my mother had sent me to Autolycus, my mother's father, to receive the presents which when he was over here he had promised to give me. Furthermore I will point out to you the trees in the vineyard which you gave me, and I asked you all about them as I followed you round the garden. We went over them all, and you told me their names and what they all were. You gave me thirteen pear trees, ten apple trees, and forty fig trees; you also said you would give me fifty rows of vines; there was corn planted between each row, and they yield grapes of every kind when the heat of heaven has been laid heavy upon them."

Laertes' strength failed him when he heard the convincing proofs which his son had given him. He threw his arms about him, and Ulysses had to support him, or he would have gone off into a swoon; but as soon as he came to, and was beginning to recover his senses, he said, "O father Jove, then you gods are still in Olympus after all, if the suitors have really been punished for their insolence and folly. Nevertheless, I am much afraid that I shall have all the townspeople of Ithaca up here directly, and they will be sending messengers everywhere throughout the cities of the Cephallenians."

Ulysses answered, "Take heart and do not trouble yourself about that, but let us go into the house hard by your garden. I have already told Telemachus, Philoetius, and Eumaeus to go on there and get dinner ready as soon as possible."

Thus conversing the two made their way towards the house. When they got there they found Telemachus with the stockman and the swineherd cutting up meat and mixing wine with water. Then the old Sicel woman took Laertes inside and washed him and anointed him with oil. She put him on a good cloak, and Minerva came up to him and gave him a more imposing presence, making him taller and stouter than before. When he came back his son was surprised to see him looking so like an immortal, and said to him, "My dear father, some one of the gods has been making you much taller and better-looking."

Laertes answered, "Would, by Father Jove, Minerva, and Apollo, that I were the man I was when I ruled among the Cephallenians, and took Nericum, that strong fortress on the foreland. If I were still what I then was and had been in our house yesterday with my armor on, I should have been able to stand by you and help you against the suitors. I should have killed a great many of them, and you would have rejoiced to see it."

Thus did they converse; but the others, when they had finished their work and the feast was ready, left off working, and took each his proper place on the benches and seats. Then they began eating; by and by old Dolius and his sons left their work and came up, for their mother, the Sicel woman who looked after Laertes now that he was growing old, had been to fetch them. When they saw Ulysses and were certain it was he, they stood there lost in astonishment; but Ulysses scolded them good-naturedly and said, "Sit down to your dinner, old man, and never mind about your surprise; we have been wanting to begin for some time and have been waiting for you."

Then Dolius put out both his hands and went up to Ulysses. "Sir," said he, seizing his master's hand and kissing it at the wrist, "we have long been wishing you home: and now heaven has restored you to us after we had given up hoping. All hail, therefore, and may the gods prosper you. But tell me, does Penelope already know of your return, or shall we send some one to tell her?"

"Old man," answered Ulysses, "she knows already, so you need not trouble about that." On this he took his seat, and the sons of Dolius gathered round Ulysses to give him greeting and embrace him one after the other; then they took their seats in due order near Dolius their father.

While they were thus busy getting their dinner ready, Rumor went round the town, and noised abroad the terrible fate that had befallen the suitors; as soon, therefore, as the people heard of it they gathered from every quarter, groaning and hooting before the house of Ulysses. They took the dead away, buried every man his own, and put the bodies of those who came from elsewhere on board the fishing vessels, for the fishermen to take each of them to his own place. They then met angrily in the place of assembly, and when they were got together Eupeithes rose to speak. He was overwhelmed with grief for the death of his son Antinous, who had been the first man killed by Ulysses, so he said, weeping bitterly, "My friend, this man has done the Achaeans great wrong. He took many of our best men away with him in his fleet, and he has lost both ships and men; now, moreover, on his return he has been killing all the foremost men among the Cephallenians. Let us be up and doing before he can get away to Pylos or to Elis where the Epeans rule, or we shall be ashamed of ourselves for ever afterwards. It will be an everlasting disgrace to us if we do not avenge the murder of our sons and brothers. For my own part I should have no more pleasure in life, but had rather die at once. Let us be up, then, and after them, before they can cross over to the mainland."

He wept as he spoke and every one pitied him. But Medon and the bard Phemius had now woke up, and came to them from the house of Ulysses. Every one was astonished at seeing them, but they stood in the middle of the assembly, and Medon said, "Hear me, men of Ithaca. Ulysses did not do these things against the will of heaven. I myself saw an immortal god take the form of Mentor and stand beside him. This god appeared, now in front of him encouraging him, and now going furiously about the court and attacking the suitors whereon they fell thick on one another."

On this pale fear laid hold of them, and old Halitherses, son of Mastor, rose to speak, for he was the only man among them who knew both past and future; so he spoke to them plainly and in all honesty, saying,

"Men of Ithaca, it is all your own fault that things have turned out as they have; you would not listen to me, nor yet to Mentor, when we bade you check the folly of your sons who were doing much wrong in the wantonness of their hearts- wasting the substance and dishonoring the wife of a chieftain who they thought would not return. Now, however, let it be as I say, and do as I tell you. Do not go out against Ulysses, or you may find that you have been drawing down evil on your own heads."

This was what he said, and more than half raised a loud shout, and at once left the assembly. But the rest stayed where they were, for the speech of Halitherses displeased them, and they sided with Eupeithes; they therefore hurried off for their armor, and when they had armed themselves, they met together in front of the city, and Eupeithes led them on in their folly. He thought he was going to avenge the murder of his son, whereas in truth he was never to return, but was himself to perish in his attempt.

Then Minerva said to Jove, "Father, son of Saturn, king of kings, answer me this question--What do you propose to do? Will you set them fighting still further, or will you make peace between them?"

And Jove answered, "My child, why should you ask me? Was it not by your own arrangement that Ulysses came home and took his revenge upon the suitors? Do whatever you like, but I will tell you what I think will be most reasonable arrangement. Now that Ulysses is revenged, let them swear to a solemn covenant, in virtue of which he shall continue to rule, while we cause the others to forgive and forget the massacre of their sons and brothers. Let them then all become friends as heretofore, and let peace and plenty reign."

This was what Minerva was already eager to bring about, so down she darted from off the topmost summits of Olympus.

Now when Laertes and the others had done dinner, Ulysses began by saying, "Some of you go out and see if they are not getting close up to us." So one of Dolius's sons went as he was bid. Standing on the threshold he could see them all quite near, and said to Ulysses, "Here they are, let us put on our armor at once."

They put on their armor as fast as they could- that is to say Ulysses, his three men, and the six sons of Dolius. Laertes also and Dolius did the same- warriors by necessity in spite of their grey hair. When they had all put on their armor, they opened the gate and sallied forth, Ulysses leading the way.

Then Jove's daughter Minerva came up to them, having assumed the form and voice of Mentor. Ulysses was glad when he saw her, and said to his son Telemachus, "Telemachus, now that are about to fight in an engagement, which will show every man's mettle, be sure not to disgrace your ancestors, who were eminent for their strength and courage all the world over."

"You say truly, my dear father," answered Telemachus, "and you shall see, if you will, that I am in no mind to disgrace your family."

Laertes was delighted when he heard this. "Good heavens, he exclaimed, "what a day I am enjoying: I do indeed rejoice at it. My son and grandson are vying with one another in the matter of valor."

On this Minerva came close up to him and said, "Son of Arceisius- best friend I have in the world- pray to the blue-eyed damsel, and to Jove her father; then poise your spear and hurl it."

As she spoke she infused fresh vigor into him, and when he had prayed to her he poised his spear and hurled it. He hit Eupeithes' helmet, and the spear went right through it, for the helmet stayed it not, and his armor rang rattling round him as he fell heavily to the ground. Meantime Ulysses and his son fell the front line of the foe and smote them with their swords and spears; indeed, they would have killed every one of them, and prevented them from ever getting home again, only Minerva raised her voice aloud, and made every one pause. "Men of Ithaca," she cried, cease this dreadful war, and settle the matter at once without further bloodshed."

On this pale fear seized every one; they were so frightened that their arms dropped from their hands and fell upon the ground at the sound of the goddess's voice, and they fled back to the city for their lives. But Ulysses gave a great cry, and gathering himself together swooped down like a soaring eagle. Then the son of Saturn sent a thunderbolt of fire that fell just in front of Minerva, so she said to Ulysses, "Ulysses, noble son of Laertes, stop this warful strife, or Jove will be angry with you."

Thus spoke Minerva, and Ulysses obeyed her gladly. Then Minerva assumed the form and voice of Mentor, and presently made a covenant of peace between the two contending parties.

THE END

Lesson 67 (no reading for Lessons 63-66)

- Read the newspaper for 15-20 minutes. (If you don't have access to a newspaper, there are plenty of online newspapers you can choose from. The New York Times (www.nytimes.com/pages/todayspaper/index.html), and Alter Net (www.alternet.org) are two used in the online course.

Lesson 68

- Read the newspaper for 15-20 minutes.

Lesson 69

- Read the newspaper for 15-20 minutes.

Lesson 70

- Read the newspaper for 15-20 minutes.

Lesson 71

- Read the newspaper for 15-20 minutes.

Lesson 72

- Read the following terms and definitions.

barbarian: a member of an uncivilized people
chivalry: the medieval principles (including bravery, skill, honor, etc.) governing knighthood and knightly conduct
imperious: having or showing arrogant superiority
legitimize: justify or make legal
motif: a central theme or dominant idea
scoundrel: a disreputable person
succor: aid or help
knight: a person of noble birth trained to arms and chivalry

Lesson 73

- Read about feudalism, knights, and King Arthur.

Feudalism

Feudalism was the governing law of the Middle Ages. Kings owned land that was passed down through generations. In order to maintain control over their vast lands, the kings had to delegate to barons. The barons received large portions of the king's land (known as fiefs or manors). In return, the baron gave the king unwavering support, governed the land he was given, and provided troops to fight on the king's behalf if needed. Barons often divided their fiefs and gave tracts to others to govern in exchange for loyalty, just like the king did. This pattern continued down the line until the king's land was subdivided into a sort of pyramid system with the king at the top and a trickle down system of lords under him.

Over time, as this land passed from generation to generation, a class of "lords" developed who felt superior to the "common" people: peasants, or serfs, as they were called. The lords demanded much from the peasants. The church began to follow a similar role, having control over large areas and dividing into dioceses under the "rule" of a bishop. The church became a great influencer of the peasants. They believed that the more they gave to and served the church, the better the after-life would be for them.

A system like this naturally led to vastly wealthy kings, lords, and churches, while the common people were starving to death. About 90% of the people in the Middle Ages were considered peasants. Peasants were under the absolute rule of the lord of the manor. He decided what they could do or not do and not do and the punishments for any disobedience. If he sold his land, rule and authority over the peasant transferred with the sale.

The feudal system began as a system of security. In order for the nobles to maintain control over distant parts of their kingdoms, the natural response was to delegate power to local control. Peasants wanting security from raiders or invading armies devoted their lives to serve the lord who could in turn protect them. It came at a great cost to the vast majority of the population.

Knights

At the center of feudalism was the medieval knight. As lords began to protect the land granted to them, they would gather around them fighting-age men to help defend against dominant neighbors or unruly vassals (feudal tenants, serfs, peasants). As this practice went on, these men would begin to outfit themselves for fighting, amassing weapons and armor to help them be successful. Eventually, a formal training system was born.

Training began at a very early age. A prospective knight would be sent to live with someone who could train them in the weaponry and horsemanship required to be a successful knight. Often, this young knight-to-be would serve as the assistant (known as a squire) for a full-fledged knight, helping him put on his armor, preparing his horse, and other tasks.

Once he completed his training and reached fighting age, usually around 16-20 years old, a knighting ceremony would take place and he would become an established knight. A knight's duties included guarding the castle, being part of the lord's bodyguard, and of course, fighting in battles. Tournaments were also big for knights with jousting as a popular event.

The knight's code of conduct was known as the code of chivalry. Chief among the rules was the knight's duty to protect the poor, women and children, and the church. However, most knights killed and stole often, despite what romanticized literature may tell us about them and their strict adherence to chivalry.

King Arthur

The most famous of these romanticized stories are the stories of King Arthur and his Knights of the Round Table. King Arthur as we know him today is a compilation of several different legends, coming to us from different authors and different time periods. Historians cannot find any record of an actual King Arthur. Some of the authors who wrote of him were so skilled at blending myth and fact, their writing appealed to mass audiences who latched onto the legend. Bards, or troubadours, wrote songs or ballads to help them remember aspects of the Arthur story, further romanticizing and popularizing it.

More than likely, you've heard bits and pieces of Arthur's legend. Most have heard of Camelot, stories of Merlin, the name "Sir Lancelot," the quest for the Holy Grail, or of King Arthur's famous sword, Excalibur. In the following lessons you're going to read a few different stories about King Arthur and his knights.

Lesson 74

- Read *The Sword in the Stone.*[3]

The Sword in the Stone
(The Legend of Arthur and Excalibur)

The King was worse, was like to die.

The ominous news ran over the castle, and from the castle over the country, like the black brew from a pot that over-boils. At every street-corner women babbled it, men talked it over grave-faced and with surprise.

True, King Uther had ailed now for many weary months, and of a fatal malady. That the ardour of his illness should have increased surprised no one; it was the strange twist the malady had taken that awakened astonishment and dismay. For it was known that the King was dumb.

But a few days since, he had been borne, prone like a stricken lion, to the field of battle, that his presence might bring victory to his men. It had brought victory, victory for which the valiant monarch had paid dearly. He lay now facing death, and with dumb lips.

In the castle, in grey corners, the knights chattered. "All evil thing indeed is this that hath befallen the King, and the realm," murmured one, harping on the one note of complaint. "Since the King must die, the King must die – it is the lot of all men, and feared little by the valiant, rebut that King Uther should die having named no successor – there one has a grievance indeed!"

---

[3] From GAVL, creative commons 3.0 [https://creativecommons.org/licenses/by/3.0/], http://cms. gavirtualschool.org/Shared/Language%20Arts/10thLitComp/06_TheArthurianLegends/Sword_in_the_Stone_Text.pdf

"With so many barons eager to snatch at the crown of this fair realm, it had been a good thing had the King left a son to succeed him," said another.

"Ay, but since he hath not left a son," retorted the first, "it had been well had Providence left him the use of his tongue to declare his successor!"

Thus they brawled among them, till a sudden footstep made their glances turn, whereupon they became immediately silent.

Yet the footstep was not that of any mighty baron. Merlin the Enchanter it was who passed through the entrance-hall, his dark cloak drawn high around him, shadowing his face.

There was silence till he had passed.

"Merlin goes to the King's chamber," observed one of the gossips, his eye following the dark form.

"'Tis a sad day for Merlin, for he was a good friend of King Uther's," said another. "I have ever heard that by his charms he aided the King much in the matter of his marriage."

"He will aid him little now," muttered a third speaker. "Death is stronger than Merlin's arts, and he hath laid a finger upon the King."

At this moment appeared another loiterer, coming upon the group with eye agleam and a lip curled with the scorn of one who has knowledge of great events and would enlighten his neighbours' ignorance to the tune of his own rising importance.

"Saw ye Merlin pass?" asked he, with chin cocked and with an arrogant air.

"Ay, we saw him," was the response, "and right somber was his step. He goes to visit the King, who may well expire before he reaches him."

"May the Saints forbid" ejaculated the new-comer. "That would be an ill thing for Merlin. Hath he not promised that today, in the witness of the Queen and barons, he, by his witchcraft, and with the aid of Heaven, will make the King speak?"

At this choice news all mouths fell agape; and eyes were rounded at the speaker, the while the gossips drew close.

The newsmonger, relishing the effect he had produced, proceeded with his tale, pouring out particulars with the air of one who dispenses a choice wine. And, as if it were a choice wine, his listeners drank in the story.

Meanwhile Merlin the Enchanter had found the King's chamber.

The door being closed behind him, he drew down his cloak from his face, surveying the assembled barons and the weeping Queen.

"The King still lives?" queried he harshly.

"He still lives, but that is all," one answered in a lamentable voice.

"And hath not spoken?"

"He hath spoken not one word," murmured a baron. "Remember, Merlin, thy promise, given to us yester-eve: 'Gather ye in the King's chamber to-morrow at this hour, and by the grace of God and the aid of my charms King Uther shall name his successor to this realm'."

"It is a true remembrance," said the Enchanter indifferently. "Such indeed were the words I uttered."

He drew near to the King's bed, and a cloud gathered in his eyes as one may gather in the heavens before rain.

"It is the will of all," he spake, turning, "that I make the King speak, thus disturbing his drowsing spirit? Shall he name his successor to ye?"

"It is our will," said the barons; and the Queen answered also: "It is our will."

Merlin covered his eyes for a moment, then, turning toward the bed, "Sire," said he to the King, "tell us thy will concerning the welfare of thy kingdom. Is it thy will that thy son Arthur succeed thee, becoming ruler of this fair realm?"

These words were scarcely uttered when the King replied, in his own voice, and without halt in the speech: "It is my earnest wish and desire that my son Arthur wear my crown. I bid him therefore that he claim it, when the right time comes, in a righteous and just spirit, knowing that to rule this realm is his duty and his responsibility. If he do not this thing, then shall he forfeit the blessing I bestow upon him now."

The King had hardly uttered these words, when, with a sigh, his breath went from him, and he died.

Then the barons, in despair and anger, began to accuse Merlin among themselves, calling him impostor, and other like names. "This is a trick of Merlin's," said they, "which he hath worked through the mouth of the King; for well does he know that King Uther hath no son! It were better had he made the King name one of us to succeed him; then had the matter been a plain one, and the land not turned to confusion!"

Whispering thus among themselves, they cast angry glances at the Enchanter. But he, shrouding his face from them, turned, and without a word went away.

Thus died King Uther, having named as his successor a son, of whom the barons knew nothing; and for many years that fair realm which he had governed was torn by strife, by battle, and by bitter feud. For there was many a powerful baron who cast eyes upon the crown, and who would raise up a tempest of battle with a better grace than he would utter a prayer.

Thus the barons strove, quarrelled, and made warfare, the while the years passed, and the glory of the realm waxed dim. But there dawned a day when the barons were as weary of themselves, and their claims, as the country was, and were not unwilling that from among them one should be chosen to be king.

Then was Merlin the Enchanter seen again, passing in and out among the people, his dark cloak wrapping him round. It was known that he sought audience of the Archbishop of Canterbury. When he was come before the Archbishop, Merlin said:

"Is not this a grievous thing that the fair realm of England should be so torn, through the hopes of ambitious men? Yet dawns another day, and to thee may be a portion of its glory. Call together, I pray of thee, all the lords of this realm, and gentlemen of arms, that they may make prayer to God that by some sign He shall reveal the rightful king of the realm."

The Archbishop pondered these words, and when he had examined well this advice of Merlin's, it seemed good to him, and well worthy a Christian people. Therefore he said: "I will call them together."

Merlin rested his eyes upon the ground, hiding his thoughts. After a while he said: "Call them together at Christmas-time, for since at that time God gave us the great gift of His Son, His heart may be inclined to give us other gifts."

When he had said this he went away. Where he went I know not; but for many a day men saw naught Of Merlin the Enchanter.

The Archbishop called together the lords and gentlemen of arms; and none knew that he had followed any thought but his own.

To London came they, in response to the call, and many a knight had fasted first, and others had otherwise mortified themselves, that their prayers might be the better heard in Heaven.

On Christmas Day they gathered together, and with them the common People, a goodly company, either in St. Paul's, or some other great church; and all men prayed with a marvellous earnestness that the sign should be vouchsafed to them which they craved.

One knight was there who, as he prayed, felt before his closed eyes a sudden flash, as it were of some great light. Whether he prayed more earnestly than his fellows, that a great matter should first be revealed to him, we know not, for to judge of such things is beyond human wit. But it is known that, on uncovering his eyes and glancing about him, this knight beheld, through the open door of the church, something that shone with a great fury, and reminded him of the light he had seen. The which, when he had observed it for some time, he made out to be a great white stone, and in the stone an anvil, and, struck through the anvil and the stone, a golden sword.

When the youth was certain of these things, trembling seized him, for he perceived that they were not of earth. Whereupon he whispered to his neighbour of this strange happening, and his neighbour to another, and that other to whoso sat next; till at length the matter reached the ear of the Archbishop where he stood.

But he, setting first the glory of God, advised that the service should be finished before any should enquire into the thing.

Thereupon, when the service was over, all men passed out of church, agape to see the miracle; and found the matter even as the knight had declared.

The white stone lay in the churchyard, and in the stone was the anvil, and through anvil and stone was a golden sword. And about the sword were words written that shone like flames.

The Archbishop read them, stooping, his hands upon his knees.

"Whoso shall lift this sword from the stone and the anvil" – so read he, for so it was written "the same is rightly born King of England."

At these words the lords and gentlemen looked one at another; and the commons shot out their lips and looked at the Archbishop. And he, having bent his head some minutes longer, as hearing some voice in the words which others heard not, said: "The sign is given, are ye content to abide by it?"

And they replied, with one voice: "We are content."

Then said the Archbishop: "God having vouchsafed us this sign of the sword in the stone and the anvil, at Twelfth Day it shall be given to any man to try his skill at withdrawing the sword. Until that day let all be patient, and until then shall certain knights of pure fame be set to guard the stone."

Having arranged these things, the Archbishop went his way, bearing a joyful heart within him; and he contrived that on New Year's Day there should be jousts and a tournament, and other fine doings, that the lords and commons should be kept together till the king should be revealed.

On New Year's Day the roads were gay with the bravery of the lords and commons who were on their way to the fields, the lords to show their skill, the commons to behold it and make holiday.

With the throng rode Sir Ector, a noble knight and one who had loved King Uther well, and in his company his son Sir Kay (who had received his knighthood but last Hallowmas), and young Arthur his adopted son, who was but a stripling.

Young Arthur rode a pace or two behind, but that was his own doing. In his eye was the glamour of the road, in his heart quaked a happy wonder at the gay world and its happenings. These emotions so held him that he perceived not the confusion of his brother, whose face grew suddenly red and halfshamed.

At length Sir Kay brought his horse up with so sudden a jerk that Arthur had almost been upon him.

"Why, brother," cried he, amazed, "what ails thee? My head was in the clouds, in truth, but thou hadst almost brought it to the earth in thy hurry!"

Sir Kay's visage was like a harvest moon, but held nothing of jollity: "I have forgotten my sword; a fool's trick!" mumbled he, sputtering over the words. "Now it falls upon me to wind back the length of the road and fetch it."

"Nay," said the boy quickly, "that were an unnecessary to do. Haste thee on with our father, I will return to the town at a great speed, and will fetch thy sword."

With that he turned about, right glad to have excuse to time his horse's pace nearer to that of his blood. Youth rose high in his heart, touched his pulse, quickened his eye. With a clatter he flew along the road upon which he alone turned his face to the city; and heedless of any glance, grave or tender, made his way to his lodging.

Having reached the house, he reined in his horse, and battered hard upon the door. The blows rang out finely, but they brought never a response. Young Arthur twitched his brows, brought out another volley of blows, listened. There was a quiet in the street like that of the tomb.

The boy clapped his hand upon his side so that his horse started. "The tournament, the tournament! – it hath sucked them in, every one of them!"

And so indeed it had.

Meanwhile Sir Ector and Sir Kay went plodding on, Sir Kay enlarging upon his plight, and young Arthur's tardiness. Ever and anon he would cast an anxious glance behind him, pitching a new lament to his father's ears as the glance found naught. At length he perceived a cloud of dust. It came nearer and nearer, thickened, rose high. Arthur rode from the midst of it, his hair blowing in the breeze he made.

"See, brother, a sword to thy hand!" cried he. "Say not that I failed thee, though thine own sword lay behind barred doors!"

Sir Kay grasped the sword, well satisfied. His eye ran down it, and as the glance grew, his cheek paled. He trembled, then rode on.

But young Arthur, perceiving nothing, fell again behind, taking up his thoughts.

Sir Kay hastened to rejoin his father, full of tidings.

"Sir," cried he in a tremulous tone, "surely I, and none other, am chosen to be King of England, since in my hand I bear the sword of the stone!"

At this speech Sir Ector turned, and, having beheld the sword which his son carried, he saw that it was indeed the sword of the stone.

"Tell me, didst thou pluck it from the stone" asked he.

Sir Kay's face fell, but he answered stoutly: "Nay, I plucked it not from the stone. My brother Arthur, who returned to seek what I had forgotten, he brought me the sword."

Then said Sir Ector to Arthur: "Tell me, didst thou pluck the sword from the stone?"

Thus was the boy awakened from his dreams of sweet wit, and he confessed how, having found all doors barred upon his brother's sword, he made all haste to the churchyard and plucked the sword from the stone that rested there.

"Were none there," asked Sir Ector, "to forbid the act?"

"Nay," said the boy, "they had gone, every one, to the tournament."

This was true, for the knights had gone to try their skill.

Then was Sir Ector thoughtful, and he would have it that they turned about, all three, and rode back to the churchyard, that lay some distance behind them. This being done, young Arthur replaced the sword in the anvil and the stone.

"My son, draw out the sword," said Sir Ector to Sir Kay.

And Sir Kay essayed, bending down, the better to use his strength. Once he strove, and twice, his muscles cracking and his face aflame; but he could not withdraw the sword.

"Yield place to me," said Sir Ector, and, laying his hands upon the sword, he, too, strove to wrest it from the anvil and stone, but he could not move it one hair-breadth from its place.

But when Arthur laid his hand upon the sword, it slid from the stone as a sunbeam across a wall. And when he had replaced it, it stuck as fast as before.

Then said Sir Ector to the boy: "By King Uther's desire wert thou entrusted to me, whilst yet a babe, and of thy parentage would the King reveal nothing. Now I begin to think that thou art of a higher destiny than I thought of. Let us travel to the Archbishop, and tell him of these events."

And straightway they went to the Archbishop, who was struck with a great wonder on hearing their story; but he advised that nothing should be said of the matter, since Twelfth Day was near at hand, when it would be given to every man to try his skill.

Now when Twelfth Day was come all the world was agog, since there were few who did not wish to see the judgment of the sword. Like twining ribbons were the roads of the city, being gay with the costumes of those that thronged to the churchyard. Barons and gay gentlemen, young and old, rich and poor, lords and commons, these encountered at street corners, and jostled as they passed by. To the churchyard stretched the hopes of all; and in the churchyard were bright hopes to be shattered. For there the game went merrily, yet with a sharp echo to its music; many a fine fellow trying his skill with a cheerful heart, and having striven till he was like to break in two, going on his way with puckered chin, not having moved the sword the breadth of a hair. Ever the crowd of champions grew; but as it grew fat on one side it waxed thin on another, as one strong fellow after another grasped the sword with hope and left it with despair.

"'Tis as if some massive chain bound sword and stone," said one disappointed gentleman.

"'Tis as if great nails fastened it," said another, flourishing a white handkerchief about his brow.

"Here comes a fine fellow!" cried a spectator of a lower order. He nudged his neighbour. "'Tis a fine knight; surely if any can move the sword 'twill be this same."

"It is Sir Kay, son of Sir Ector; may he have joy of his task!" quoth the other, scowling. "He begins well. Ah, he means to have the sword!"

It was well said that Sir Kay meant to have the golden sword. Many a bold knight had striven hard, but he strove hardest of all. Evening was now come, and but few remained to try their skill. Everywhere were to be seen crowds of scowling or bantering faces – it is as disappointment affects a man, – the faces of those who had grasped the Sword, only to loose the grasp and leave it. Sir Kay's brows bent fiercely; had not the sword rested in his hand before to-day? If he did not gain it 'twould be because it was not to be gained. If he could not wrest it from the anvil, 'twould be because the task was beyond any man. His face grew livid, his teeth closed tight as he tugged, and pulled, bent himself over the sword, reared above it, knelt, doubled, twisted. That was a sight – to see him! Of all gay knights he laid longest and bravest siege to the sword in the stone.

"What now, hath he gained the sword?" asked a rosycheeked lad at last of his elders. He reared upon his toes, kicking the heels of his neighbours.

"Nay, he turns away in bitter confusion. Pale is his cheek, and cold his eye. But the sword remains in the stone."

"It is like to remain there!" said the boy. "Who comes now?"

"Young Arthur, Sir Ector's adopted son. 'Tis said he is one of Merlin's changelings, foisted upon Sir Ector when a babe. Nay, thou mayest turn thine eyes away; he is but a stripling, scarce of greater height than thou art. He cannot withdraw the sword."

"I would fain see him," said the lad. "I have fear of Merlin; his eyes are like the water that lies behind the mill. Show me this changeling." He craned, and craned again, stretching out his thin young neck. "Is he fine-looking, neighbour? – I can see nothing of him. What a hub-bub! Speak, neighbour, what is the meaning of it?"

A thousand voices answered the question. "He hath worked the miracle, the sword is withdrawn! The stripling holds it! Didst thou notice? – it sprang to his hand as if it but waited for the touch!"

"Lift me up," said Master Rosy-Cheeks, his eyes shining. "I would see him." Someone raised him: he caught a glimpse of a fair young figure, of bright tost hair, of eyes that seemed to flash into his soul.

He saw in the hand of the valiant figure a sword that glittered as it were shrouded in fire. About it were words written that shone with the brilliance of stars.

The boy dropt to his heels, covering his face.

"How now?" queried his benefactor.

"I have seen the sun," muttered the boy, blinking, and dashing water from his eyes.

Still the clatter of tongues uprose, angry voices that merged into dispute.

Master Rosy-Cheeks came back to earth.

"The barons complain," his neighbour told him. "They say he is but a boy – in faith it is a true word! They say the realm cannot be rightly governed by an unbearded stripling. They complain that none knows whence he came; perchance, who knows, he may be some beggar's brat! See, he hath replaced the sword, and it sticks fast as before. The Archbishop hath yielded to the barons. At Candlemas men shall strive again to withdraw the sword."

It was a true word, the Archbishop had given way. At Candlemas there would be a new trial. The crowd, chattering over this, and, disputing, began to break.

At Candlemas young Arthur again withdrew the sword, and no other could move it from its place.

Wherefore again the barons disputed, casting waspish glances at the youth; and they demanded at Easter a new reckoning.

And at Easter the same matters befell, whereupon the matter was delayed till Pentecost.

And at Pentecost the sword leapt again to greet the stripling, and would yield itself to none other.

Then rose the commons, crying with one voice: "Arthur shall be our King! Hath not the sword revealed him to us, and the voice of God? We will have no other than he, and no further delay in the matter. And our prayer is that he will pardon us for what delay hath been!" So they cried, bending their knees.

Whereupon many a gallant gentleman fell, too, to crying: "Arthur shall be our King!" and so great a noise was there, and clamour, that no other cry could be heard. And such as would have piped to a different tune had to swallow their grievance, with as good a grace as they could muster, and bend the knee with their fellows.

After this fashion was young Arthur acclaimed King of the realm of England, as revealed by God in answer to earnest prayer. The sword of the stone he laid straightway upon the altar, and he was made knight of the best man there.

Ere the year was old, Merlin the Enchanter was again seen among men, walking in ways few understood. Then, having come upon a concourse of barons who would have harboured still their discontent, he thus spake, throwing out at them the fire of his eyes.

"Know ye," said he, "that this beardless youth, whom ye have welcomed so tardily, is none other than the rightfully born son of King Uther, now rightfully reigning in his father's stead? Merlin the Enchanter it was who demanded the babe from the King as a price for service done to King Uther in the matter of his marriage, but privily for the babe's own weal. For the child was feeble, and the King near death and unable to protect him, and I knew the hearts of ye, that ye were bodeful men and would work the child ill. Wherefore I, Merlin, claimed this price from King Uther, bargaining that Sir Ector, that just knight, should rear the babe.

"Answer me now; ask ye from Heaven a truer King than this King is?"

Then were they all silent, hanging low their heads.

Lesson 75

- For the next few lessons we'll read excerpts from *Idylls of the King*. If you need summaries to help you understand what you are reading, they are linked in the online course.

Idylls of the King
Lord Alfred Tennyson
Dedication

These to His Memory–since he held them dear,
Perchance as finding there unconsciously
Some image of himself–I dedicate,
I dedicate, I consecrate with tears–
These Idylls.
And indeed He seems to me
Scarce other than my king's ideal knight,
"Who reverenced his conscience as his king;
Whose glory was, redressing human wrong;
Who spake no slander, no, nor listened to it;
Who loved one only and who clave to her–"
Her–over all whose realms to their last isle,
Commingled with the gloom of imminent war,
The shadow of His loss drew like eclipse,
Darkening the world. We have lost him: he is gone:
We know him now: all narrow jealousies
Are silent; and we see him as he moved,
How modest, kindly, all-accomplished, wise,
With what sublime repression of himself,
And in what limits, and how tenderly;
Not swaying to this faction or to that;
Not making his high place the lawless perch
Of winged ambitions, nor a vantage-ground
For pleasure; but through all this tract of years
Wearing the white flower of a blameless life,
Before a thousand peering littlenesses,
In that fierce light which beats upon a throne,
And blackens every blot: for where is he,
Who dares foreshadow for an only son
A lovelier life, a more unstained, than his?
Or how should England dreaming of his sons
Hope more for these than some inheritance
Of such a life, a heart, a mind as thine,

Thou noble Father of her Kings to be,
Laborious for her people and her poor–
Voice in the rich dawn of an ampler day–
Far-sighted summoner of War and Waste
To fruitful strifes and rivalries of peace–
Sweet nature gilded by the gracious gleam
Of letters, dear to Science, dear to Art,
Dear to thy land and ours, a Prince indeed,
Beyond all titles, and a household name,
Hereafter, through all times, Albert the Good.
Break not, O woman's-heart, but still endure;
Break not, for thou art Royal, but endure,
Remembering all the beauty of that star
Which shone so close beside Thee that ye made
One light together, but has past and leaves
The Crown a lonely splendour.
May all love,
His love, unseen but felt, o'ershadow Thee,
The love of all Thy sons encompass Thee,
The love of all Thy daughters cherish Thee,
The love of all Thy people comfort Thee,
Till God's love set Thee at his side again!

The Coming of Arthur

Leodogran, the King of Cameliard,
Had one fair daughter, and none other child;
And she was fairest of all flesh on earth,
Guinevere, and in her his one delight.
For many a petty king ere Arthur came
Ruled in this isle, and ever waging war
Each upon other, wasted all the land;
And still from time to time the heathen host
Swarmed overseas, and harried what was left.
And so there grew great tracts of wilderness,
Wherein the beast was ever more and more,

But man was less and less, till Arthur came.
For first Aurelius lived and fought and died,
And after him King Uther fought and died,
But either failed to make the kingdom one.
And after these King Arthur for a space,
And through the puissance of his Table Round,
Drew all their petty princedoms under him,
Their king and head, and made a realm, and reigned.
And thus the land of Cameliard was waste,
Thick with wet woods, and many a beast therein,
And none or few to scare or chase the beast;
So that wild dog, and wolf and boar and bear
Came night and day, and rooted in the fields,
And wallowed in the gardens of the King.
And ever and anon the wolf would steal
The children and devour, but now and then,
Her own brood lost or dead, lent her fierce teat
To human sucklings; and the children, housed
In her foul den, there at their meat would growl,
And mock their foster-mother on four feet,
Till, straightened, they grew up to wolf-like men,
Worse than the wolves. And King Leodogran
Groaned for the Roman legions here again,
And Caesar's eagle: then his brother king,
Urien, assailed him: last a heathen horde,
Reddening the sun with smoke and earth with blood,
And on the spike that split the mother's heart
Spitting the child, brake on him, till, amazed,
He knew not whither he should turn for aid.
But–for he heard of Arthur newly crowned,
Though not without an uproar made by those
Who cried, "He is not Uther's son"–the King
Sent to him, saying, "Arise, and help us thou!
For here between the man and beast we die."
And Arthur yet had done no deed of arms,
But heard the call, and came: and Guinevere
Stood by the castle walls to watch him pass;

But since he neither wore on helm or shield
The golden symbol of his kinglihood,
But rode a simple knight among his knights,
And many of these in richer arms than he,
She saw him not, or marked not, if she saw,
One among many, though his face was bare.
But Arthur, looking downward as he past,
Felt the light of her eyes into his life
Smite on the sudden, yet rode on, and pitched
His tents beside the forest. Then he drave
The heathen; after, slew the beast, and felled
The forest, letting in the sun, and made
Broad pathways for the hunter and the knight
And so returned.
For while he lingered there,
A doubt that ever smouldered in the hearts
Of those great Lords and Barons of his realm
Flashed forth and into war: for most of these,
Colleaguing with a score of petty kings,
Made head against him, crying, "Who is he
That he should rule us? who hath proven him
King Uther's son? for lo! we look at him,
And find nor face nor bearing, limbs nor voice,
Are like to those of Uther whom we knew.
This is the son of Gorloïs, not the King;
This is the son of Anton, not the King."
And Arthur, passing thence to battle, felt
Travail, and throes and agonies of the life,
Desiring to be joined with Guinevere;
And thinking as he rode, "Her father said
That there between the man and beast they die.
Shall I not lift her from this land of beasts
Up to my throne, and side by side with me?
What happiness to reign a lonely king,
Vext–O ye stars that shudder over me,
O earth that soundest hollow under me,
Vext with waste dreams? for saving I be joined

To her that is the fairest under heaven,
I seem as nothing in the mighty world,
And cannot will my will, nor work my work
Wholly, nor make myself in mine own realm
Victor and lord. But were I joined with her,
Then might we live together as one life,
And reigning with one will in everything
Have power on this dark land to lighten it,
And power on this dead world to make it live."
Thereafter–as he speaks who tells the tale–
When Arthur reached a field-of-battle bright
With pitched pavilions of his foe, the world
Was all so clear about him, that he saw
The smallest rock far on the faintest hill,
And even in high day the morning star.
So when the King had set his banner broad,
At once from either side, with trumpet-blast,
And shouts, and clarions shrilling unto blood,
The long-lanced battle let their horses run.
And now the Barons and the kings prevailed,
And now the King, as here and there that war
Went swaying; but the Powers who walk the world
Made lightnings and great thunders over him,
And dazed all eyes, till Arthur by main might,
And mightier of his hands with every blow,
And leading all his knighthood threw the kings
Carados, Urien, Cradlemont of Wales,
Claudias, and Clariance of Northumberland,
The King Brandagoras of Latangor,
With Anguisant of Erin, Morganore,
And Lot of Orkney. Then, before a voice
As dreadful as the shout of one who sees
To one who sins, and deems himself alone
And all the world asleep, they swerved and brake
Flying, and Arthur called to stay the brands
That hacked among the flyers, "Ho! they yield!"
So like a painted battle the war stood

Silenced, the living quiet as the dead,
And in the heart of Arthur joy was lord.
He laughed upon his warrior whom he loved
And honoured most. "Thou dost not doubt me King,
So well thine arm hath wrought for me today."
"Sir and my liege," he cried, "the fire of God
Descends upon thee in the battle-field:
I know thee for my King!" Whereat the two,
For each had warded either in the fight,
Sware on the field of death a deathless love.
And Arthur said, "Man's word is God in man:
Let chance what will, I trust thee to the death."
Then quickly from the foughten field he sent
Ulfius, and Brastias, and Bedivere,
His new-made knights, to King Leodogran,
Saying, "If I in aught have served thee well,
Give me thy daughter Guinevere to wife."
Whom when he heard, Leodogran in heart
Debating– "How should I that am a king,
However much he holp me at my need,
Give my one daughter saving to a king,
And a king's son?"–lifted his voice, and called
A hoary man, his chamberlain, to whom
He trusted all things, and of him required
His counsel: "Knowest thou aught of Arthur's birth?"
Then spake the hoary chamberlain and said,
"Sir King, there be but two old men that know:
And each is twice as old as I; and one
Is Merlin, the wise man that ever served
King Uther through his magic art; and one
Is Merlin's master (so they call him) Bleys,
Who taught him magic; but the scholar ran
Before the master, and so far, that Bleys
Laid magic by, and sat him down, and wrote
All things and whatsoever Merlin did
In one great annal-book, where after-years
Will learn the secret of our Arthur's birth."

To whom the King Leodogran replied,
"O friend, had I been holpen half as well
By this King Arthur as by thee today,
Then beast and man had had their share of me:
But summon here before us yet once more
Ulfius, and Brastias, and Bedivere."
Then, when they came before him, the King said,
"I have seen the cuckoo chased by lesser fowl,
And reason in the chase: but wherefore now
Do these your lords stir up the heat of war,
Some calling Arthur born of Gorloïs,
Others of Anton? Tell me, ye yourselves,
Hold ye this Arthur for King Uther's son?"
And Ulfius and Brastias answered, "Ay."
Then Bedivere, the first of all his knights
Knighted by Arthur at his crowning, spake–
For bold in heart and act and word was he,
Whenever slander breathed against the King–
"Sir, there be many rumours on this head:
For there be those who hate him in their hearts,
Call him baseborn, and since his ways are sweet,
And theirs are bestial, hold him less than man:
And there be those who deem him more than man,
And dream he dropt from heaven: but my belief
In all this matter–so ye care to learn–
Sir, for ye know that in King Uther's time
The prince and warrior Gorlois, he that held
Tintagil castle by the Cornish sea,
Was wedded with a winsome wife, Ygerne:
And daughters had she borne him,–one whereof,
Lot's wife, the Queen of Orkney, Bellicent,
Hath ever like a loyal sister cleaved
To Arthur,–but a son she had not borne.
And Uther cast upon her eyes of love:
But she, a stainless wife to Gorloïs,
So loathed the bright dishonour of his love,
That Gorloïs and King Uther went to war:

And overthrown was Gorloïs and slain.
Then Uther in his wrath and heat besieged
Ygerne within Tintagil, where her men,
Seeing the mighty swarm about their walls,
Left her and fled, and Uther entered in,
And there was none to call to but himself.
So, compassed by the power of the King,
Enforced she was to wed him in her tears,
And with a shameful swiftness: afterward,
Not many moons, King Uther died himself,
Moaning and wailing for an heir to rule
After him, lest the realm should go to wrack.
And that same night, the night of the new year,
By reason of the bitterness and grief
That vext his mother, all before his time
Was Arthur born, and all as soon as born
Delivered at a secret postern-gate
To Merlin, to be holden far apart
Until his hour should come; because the lords
Of that fierce day were as the lords of this,
Wild beasts, and surely would have torn the child
Piecemeal among them, had they known; for each
But sought to rule for his own self and hand,
And many hated Uther for the sake
Of Gorloïs. Wherefore Merlin took the child,
And gave him to Sir Anton, an old knight
And ancient friend of Uther; and his wife
Nursed the young prince, and reared him with her own;
And no man knew. And ever since the lords
Have foughten like wild beasts among themselves,
So that the realm has gone to wrack: but now,
This year, when Merlin (for his hour had come)
Brought Arthur forth, and set him in the hall,
Proclaiming, "Here is Uther's heir, your king,"
A hundred voices cried, "Away with him!
No king of ours! a son of Gorloïs he,
Or else the child of Anton, and no king,

Or else baseborn." Yet Merlin through his craft,
And while the people clamoured for a king,
Had Arthur crowned; but after, the great lords
Banded, and so brake out in open war.
Then while the King debated with himself
If Arthur were the child of shamefulness,
Or born the son of Gorloïs, after death,
Or Uther's son, and born before his time,
Or whether there were truth in anything
Said by these three, there came to Cameliard,
With Gawain and young Modred, her two sons,
Lot's wife, the Queen of Orkney, Bellicent;
Whom as he could, not as he would, the King
Made feast for, saying, as they sat at meat,
"A doubtful throne is ice on summer seas.
Ye come from Arthur's court. Victor his men
Report him! Yea, but ye–think ye this king–
So many those that hate him, and so strong,
So few his knights, however brave they be–
Hath body enow to hold his foemen down?"
"O King," she cried, "and I will tell thee: few,
Few, but all brave, all of one mind with him;
For I was near him when the savage yells
Of Uther's peerage died, and Arthur sat
Crowned on the daïs, and his warriors cried,
'Be thou the king, and we will work thy will
Who love thee.' Then the King in low deep tones,
And simple words of great authority,
Bound them by so strait vows to his own self,
That when they rose, knighted from kneeling, some
Were pale as at the passing of a ghost,
Some flushed, and others dazed, as one who wakes
Half-blinded at the coming of a light.
"But when he spake and cheered his Table Round
With large, divine, and comfortable words,
Beyond my tongue to tell thee–I beheld
From eye to eye through all their Order flash

A momentary likeness of the King:
And ere it left their faces, through the cross
And those around it and the Crucified,
Down from the casement over Arthur, smote
Flame-colour, vert and azure, in three rays,
One falling upon each of three fair queens,
Who stood in silence near his throne, the friends
Of Arthur, gazing on him, tall, with bright
Sweet faces, who will help him at his need.
"And there I saw mage Merlin, whose vast wit
And hundred winters are but as the hands
Of loyal vassals toiling for their liege.
"And near him stood the Lady of the Lake,
Who knows a subtler magic than his own–
Clothed in white samite, mystic, wonderful.
She gave the King his huge cross-hilted sword,
Whereby to drive the heathen out: a mist
Of incense curled about her, and her face
Wellnigh was hidden in the minster gloom;
But there was heard among the holy hymns
A voice as of the waters, for she dwells
Down in a deep; calm, whatsoever storms
May shake the world, and when the surface rolls,
Hath power to walk the waters like our Lord.
"There likewise I beheld Excalibur
Before him at his crowning borne, the sword
That rose from out the bosom of the lake,
And Arthur rowed across and took it–rich
With jewels, elfin Urim, on the hilt,
Bewildering heart and eye–the blade so bright
That men are blinded by it–on one side,
Graven in the oldest tongue of all this world,
'Take me,' but turn the blade and ye shall see,
And written in the speech ye speak yourself,
'Cast me away!' And sad was Arthur's face
Taking it, but old Merlin counselled him,
'Take thou and strike! the time to cast away

Is yet far-off.' So this great brand the king
Took, and by this will beat his foemen down."
Thereat Leodogran rejoiced, but thought
To sift his doubtings to the last, and asked,
Fixing full eyes of question on her face,
"The swallow and the swift are near akin,
But thou art closer to this noble prince,
Being his own dear sister;" and she said,
"Daughter of Gorloïs and Ygerne am I;"
"And therefore Arthur's sister?" asked the King.
She answered, "These be secret things," and signed
To those two sons to pass, and let them be.
And Gawain went, and breaking into song
Sprang out, and followed by his flying hair
Ran like a colt, and leapt at all he saw:
But Modred laid his ear beside the doors,
And there half-heard; the same that afterward
Struck for the throne, and striking found his doom.
And then the Queen made answer, "What know I?
For dark my mother was in eyes and hair,
And dark in hair and eyes am I; and dark
Was Gorloïs, yea and dark was Uther too,
Wellnigh to blackness; but this King is fair
Beyond the race of Britons and of men.
Moreover, always in my mind I hear
A cry from out the dawning of my life,
A mother weeping, and I hear her say,
'O that ye had some brother, pretty one,
To guard thee on the rough ways of the world.'"
"Ay," said the King, "and hear ye such a cry?
But when did Arthur chance upon thee first?"
"O King!" she cried, "and I will tell thee true:
He found me first when yet a little maid:
Beaten I had been for a little fault
Whereof I was not guilty; and out I ran
And flung myself down on a bank of heath,
And hated this fair world and all therein,

And wept, and wished that I were dead; and he–
I know not whether of himself he came,
Or brought by Merlin, who, they say, can walk
Unseen at pleasure–he was at my side,
And spake sweet words, and comforted my heart,
And dried my tears, being a child with me.
And many a time he came, and evermore
As I grew greater grew with me; and sad
At times he seemed, and sad with him was I,
Stern too at times, and then I loved him not,
But sweet again, and then I loved him well.
And now of late I see him less and less,
But those first days had golden hours for me,
For then I surely thought he would be king.
"But let me tell thee now another tale:
For Bleys, our Merlin's master, as they say,
Died but of late, and sent his cry to me,
To hear him speak before he left his life.
Shrunk like a fairy changeling lay the mage;
And when I entered told me that himself
And Merlin ever served about the King,
Uther, before he died; and on the night
When Uther in Tintagil past away
Moaning and wailing for an heir, the two
Left the still King, and passing forth to breathe,
Then from the castle gateway by the chasm
Descending through the dismal night–a night
In which the bounds of heaven and earth were lost–
Beheld, so high upon the dreary deeps
It seemed in heaven, a ship, the shape thereof
A dragon winged, and all from stem to stern
Bright with a shining people on the decks,
And gone as soon as seen. And then the two
Dropt to the cove, and watched the great sea fall,
Wave after wave, each mightier than the last,
Till last, a ninth one, gathering half the deep
And full of voices, slowly rose and plunged

Roaring, and all the wave was in a flame:
And down the wave and in the flame was borne
A naked babe, and rode to Merlin's feet,
Who stoopt and caught the babe, and cried, 'The King!
Here is an heir for Uther!' And the fringe
Of that great breaker, sweeping up the strand,
Lashed at the wizard as he spake the word,
And all at once all round him rose in fire,
So that the child and he were clothed in fire.
And presently thereafter followed calm,
Free sky and stars: 'And this same child,' he said,
'Is he who reigns; nor could I part in peace
Till this were told.' And saying this the seer
Went through the strait and dreadful pass of death,
Not ever to be questioned any more
Save on the further side; but when I met
Merlin, and asked him if these things were truth–
The shining dragon and the naked child
Descending in the glory of the seas–
He laughed as is his wont, and answered me
In riddling triplets of old time, and said:
"'Rain, rain, and sun! a rainbow in the sky!
A young man will be wiser by and by;
An old man's wit may wander ere he die.
Rain, rain, and sun! a rainbow on the lea!
And truth is this to me, and that to thee;
And truth or clothed or naked let it be.
Rain, sun, and rain! and the free blossom blows:
Sun, rain, and sun! and where is he who knows?
From the great deep to the great deep he goes.'
"So Merlin riddling angered me; but thou
Fear not to give this King thine only child,
Guinevere: so great bards of him will sing
Hereafter; and dark sayings from of old
Ranging and ringing through the minds of men,
And echoed by old folk beside their fires
For comfort after their wage-work is done,

Speak of the King; and Merlin in our time
Hath spoken also, not in jest, and sworn
Though men may wound him that he will not die,
But pass, again to come; and then or now
Utterly smite the heathen underfoot,
Till these and all men hail him for their king."
She spake and King Leodogran rejoiced,
But musing "Shall I answer yea or nay?"
Doubted, and drowsed, nodded and slept, and saw,
Dreaming, a slope of land that ever grew,
Field after field, up to a height, the peak
Haze-hidden, and thereon a phantom king,
Now looming, and now lost; and on the slope
The sword rose, the hind fell, the herd was driven,
Fire glimpsed; and all the land from roof and rick,
In drifts of smoke before a rolling wind,
Streamed to the peak, and mingled with the haze
And made it thicker; while the phantom king
Sent out at times a voice; and here or there
Stood one who pointed toward the voice, the rest
Slew on and burnt, crying, "No king of ours,
No son of Uther, and no king of ours;"
Till with a wink his dream was changed, the haze
Descended, and the solid earth became
As nothing, but the King stood out in heaven,
Crowned. And Leodogran awoke, and sent
Ulfius, and Brastias and Bedivere,
Back to the court of Arthur answering yea.
Then Arthur charged his warrior whom he loved
And honoured most, Sir Lancelot, to ride forth
And bring the Queen;–and watched him from the gates:
And Lancelot past away among the flowers,
(For then was latter April) and returned
Among the flowers, in May, with Guinevere.
To whom arrived, by Dubric the high saint,
Chief of the church in Britain, and before
The stateliest of her altar-shrines, the King

That morn was married, while in stainless white,
The fair beginners of a nobler time,
And glorying in their vows and him, his knights
Stood round him, and rejoicing in his joy.
Far shone the fields of May through open door,
The sacred altar blossomed white with May,
The Sun of May descended on their King,
They gazed on all earth's beauty in their Queen,
Rolled incense, and there past along the hymns
A voice as of the waters, while the two
Sware at the shrine of Christ a deathless love:
And Arthur said, "Behold, thy doom is mine.
Let chance what will, I love thee to the death!"
To whom the Queen replied with drooping eyes,
"King and my lord, I love thee to the death!"
And holy Dubric spread his hands and spake,
"Reign ye, and live and love, and make the world
Other, and may thy Queen be one with thee,
And all this Order of thy Table Round
Fulfil the boundless purpose of their king!"
So Dubric said; but when they left the shrine
Great Lords from Rome before the portal stood,
In scornful stillness gazing as they past;
Then while they paced a city all on fire
With sun and cloth of gold, the trumpets blew,
And Arthur's knighthood sang before the King:–
"Blow trumpet, for the world is white with May;
Blow trumpet, the long night hath rolled away!
Blow through the living world-'Let the King reign.'
"Shall Rome or Heathen rule in Arthur's realm?
Flash brand and lance, fall battleaxe upon helm,
Fall battleaxe, and flash brand! Let the King reign.
"Strike for the King and live! his knights have heard
That God hath told the King a secret word.
Fall battleaxe, and flash brand! Let the King reign.
"Blow trumpet! he will lift us from the dust.
Blow trumpet! live the strength and die the lust!

Clang battleaxe, and clash brand! Let the King reign.
"Strike for the King and die! and if thou diest,
The King is King, and ever wills the highest.
Clang battleaxe, and clash brand! Let the King reign.
"Blow, for our Sun is mighty in his May!
Blow, for our Sun is mightier day by day!
Clang battleaxe, and clash brand! Let the King reign.
"The King will follow Christ, and we the King
In whom high God hath breathed a secret thing.
Fall battleaxe, and flash brand! Let the King reign."
So sang the knighthood, moving to their hall.
There at the banquet those great Lords from Rome,
The slowly-fading mistress of the world,
Strode in, and claimed their tribute as of yore.
But Arthur spake, "Behold, for these have sworn
To wage my wars, and worship me their King;
The old order changeth, yielding place to new;
And we that fight for our fair father Christ,
Seeing that ye be grown too weak and old
To drive the heathen from your Roman wall,
No tribute will we pay:" so those great lords
Drew back in wrath, and Arthur strove with Rome.
And Arthur and his knighthood for a space
Were all one will, and through that strength the King
Drew in the petty princedoms under him,
Fought, and in twelve great battles overcame
The heathen hordes, and made a realm and reigned.

Lesson 76

- Read "Guinevere" from *Idylls of the King*.

Guinevere

Queen Guinevere had fled the court, and sat
There in the holy house at Almesbury
Weeping, none with her save a little maid,
A novice: one low light betwixt them burned
Blurred by the creeping mist, for all abroad,
Beneath a moon unseen albeit at full,
The white mist, like a face-cloth to the face,
Clung to the dead earth, and the land was still.

For hither had she fled, her cause of flight
Sir Modred; he that like a subtle beast
Lay couchant with his eyes upon the throne,
Ready to spring, waiting a chance: for this
He chilled the popular praises of the King
With silent smiles of slow disparagement;
And tampered with the Lords of the White Horse,
Heathen, the brood by Hengist left; and sought
To make disruption in the Table Round
Of Arthur, and to splinter it into feuds
Serving his traitorous end; and all his aims
Were sharpened by strong hate for Lancelot.

For thus it chanced one morn when all the court,
Green-suited, but with plumes that mocked the may,
Had been, their wont, a-maying and returned,
That Modred still in green, all ear and eye,
Climbed to the high top of the garden-wall
To spy some secret scandal if he might,
And saw the Queen who sat betwixt her best
Enid, and lissome Vivien, of her court
The wiliest and the worst; and more than this
He saw not, for Sir Lancelot passing by
Spied where he couched, and as the gardener's hand
Picks from the colewort a green caterpillar,
So from the high wall and the flowering grove

Of grasses Lancelot plucked him by the heel,
And cast him as a worm upon the way;
But when he knew the Prince though marred with dust,
He, reverencing king's blood in a bad man,
Made such excuses as he might, and these
Full knightly without scorn; for in those days
No knight of Arthur's noblest dealt in scorn;
But, if a man were halt or hunched, in him
By those whom God had made full-limbed and tall,
Scorn was allowed as part of his defect,
And he was answered softly by the King
And all his Table. So Sir Lancelot holp
To raise the Prince, who rising twice or thrice
Full sharply smote his knees, and smiled, and went:
But, ever after, the small violence done
Rankled in him and ruffled all his heart,
As the sharp wind that ruffles all day long
A little bitter pool about a stone
On the bare coast.

But when Sir Lancelot told
This matter to the Queen, at first she laughed
Lightly, to think of Modred's dusty fall,
Then shuddered, as the village wife who cries
'I shudder, some one steps across my grave;'
Then laughed again, but faintlier, for indeed
She half-foresaw that he, the subtle beast,
Would track her guilt until he found, and hers
Would be for evermore a name of scorn.
Henceforward rarely could she front in hall,
Or elsewhere, Modred's narrow foxy face,
Heart-hiding smile, and gray persistent eye:
Henceforward too, the Powers that tend the soul,
To help it from the death that cannot die,
And save it even in extremes, began
To vex and plague her. Many a time for hours,
Beside the placid breathings of the King,

In the dead night, grim faces came and went
Before her, or a vague spiritual fear--
Like to some doubtful noise of creaking doors,
Heard by the watcher in a haunted house,
That keeps the rust of murder on the walls--
Held her awake: or if she slept, she dreamed
An awful dream; for then she seemed to stand
On some vast plain before a setting sun,
And from the sun there swiftly made at her
A ghastly something, and its shadow flew
Before it, till it touched her, and she turned--
When lo! her own, that broadening from her feet,
And blackening, swallowed all the land, and in it
Far cities burnt, and with a cry she woke.
And all this trouble did not pass but grew;
Till even the clear face of the guileless King,
And trustful courtesies of household life,
Became her bane; and at the last she said,
'O Lancelot, get thee hence to thine own land,
For if thou tarry we shall meet again,
And if we meet again, some evil chance
Will make the smouldering scandal break and blaze
Before the people, and our lord the King.'
And Lancelot ever promised, but remained,
And still they met and met. Again she said,
'O Lancelot, if thou love me get thee hence.'
And then they were agreed upon a night
(When the good King should not be there) to meet
And part for ever. Vivien, lurking, heard.
She told Sir Modred. Passion-pale they met
And greeted. Hands in hands, and eye to eye,
Low on the border of her couch they sat
Stammering and staring. It was their last hour,
A madness of farewells. And Modred brought
His creatures to the basement of the tower
For testimony; and crying with full voice
'Traitor, come out, ye are trapt at last,' aroused

Lancelot, who rushing outward lionlike
Leapt on him, and hurled him headlong, and he fell
Stunned, and his creatures took and bare him off,
And all was still: then she, 'The end is come,
And I am shamed for ever;' and he said,
'Mine be the shame; mine was the sin: but rise,
And fly to my strong castle overseas:
There will I hide thee, till my life shall end,
There hold thee with my life against the world.'
She answered, 'Lancelot, wilt thou hold me so?
Nay, friend, for we have taken our farewells.
Would God that thou couldst hide me from myself!
Mine is the shame, for I was wife, and thou
Unwedded: yet rise now, and let us fly,
For I will draw me into sanctuary,
And bide my doom.' So Lancelot got her horse,
Set her thereon, and mounted on his own,
And then they rode to the divided way,
There kissed, and parted weeping: for he past,
Love-loyal to the least wish of the Queen,
Back to his land; but she to Almesbury
Fled all night long by glimmering waste and weald,
And heard the Spirits of the waste and weald
Moan as she fled, or thought she heard them moan:
And in herself she moaned 'Too late, too late!'
Till in the cold wind that foreruns the morn,
A blot in heaven, the Raven, flying high,
Croaked, and she thought, 'He spies a field of death;
For now the Heathen of the Northern Sea,
Lured by the crimes and frailties of the court,
Begin to slay the folk, and spoil the land.'

And when she came to Almesbury she spake
There to the nuns, and said, 'Mine enemies
Pursue me, but, O peaceful Sisterhood,
Receive, and yield me sanctuary, nor ask
Her name to whom ye yield it, till her time

To tell you:' and her beauty, grace and power,
Wrought as a charm upon them, and they spared
To ask it.

So the stately Queen abode
For many a week, unknown, among the nuns;
Nor with them mixed, nor told her name, nor sought,
Wrapt in her grief, for housel or for shrift,
But communed only with the little maid,
Who pleased her with a babbling heedlessness
Which often lured her from herself; but now,
This night, a rumour wildly blown about
Came, that Sir Modred had usurped the realm,
And leagued him with the heathen, while the King
Was waging war on Lancelot: then she thought,
'With what a hate the people and the King
Must hate me,' and bowed down upon her hands
Silent, until the little maid, who brooked
No silence, brake it, uttering, 'Late! so late!
What hour, I wonder, now?' and when she drew
No answer, by and by began to hum
An air the nuns had taught her; 'Late, so late!'
Which when she heard, the Queen looked up, and said,
'O maiden, if indeed ye list to sing,
Sing, and unbind my heart that I may weep.'
Whereat full willingly sang the little maid.

'Late, late, so late! and dark the night and chill!
Late, late, so late! but we can enter still.
Too late, too late! ye cannot enter now.

'No light had we: for that we do repent;
And learning this, the bridegroom will relent.
Too late, too late! ye cannot enter now.

'No light: so late! and dark and chill the night!
O let us in, that we may find the light!

Too late, too late: ye cannot enter now.

'Have we not heard the bridegroom is so sweet?
O let us in, though late, to kiss his feet!
No, no, too late! ye cannot enter now.'

So sang the novice, while full passionately,
Her head upon her hands, remembering
Her thought when first she came, wept the sad Queen.
Then said the little novice prattling to her,

'O pray you, noble lady, weep no more;
But let my words, the words of one so small,
Who knowing nothing knows but to obey,
And if I do not there is penance given--
Comfort your sorrows; for they do not flow
From evil done; right sure am I of that,
Who see your tender grace and stateliness.
But weigh your sorrows with our lord the King's,
And weighing find them less; for gone is he
To wage grim war against Sir Lancelot there,
Round that strong castle where he holds the Queen;
And Modred whom he left in charge of all,
The traitor--Ah sweet lady, the King's grief
For his own self, and his own Queen, and realm,
Must needs be thrice as great as any of ours.
For me, I thank the saints, I am not great.
For if there ever come a grief to me
I cry my cry in silence, and have done.
None knows it, and my tears have brought me good:
But even were the griefs of little ones
As great as those of great ones, yet this grief
Is added to the griefs the great must bear,
That howsoever much they may desire
Silence, they cannot weep behind a cloud:
As even here they talk at Almesbury
About the good King and his wicked Queen,

And were I such a King with such a Queen,
Well might I wish to veil her wickedness,
But were I such a King, it could not be.'

Then to her own sad heart muttered the Queen,
'Will the child kill me with her innocent talk?'
But openly she answered, 'Must not I,
If this false traitor have displaced his lord,
Grieve with the common grief of all the realm?'

'Yea,' said the maid, 'this is all woman's grief,
That she is woman, whose disloyal life
Hath wrought confusion in the Table Round
Which good King Arthur founded, years ago,
With signs and miracles and wonders, there
At Camelot, ere the coming of the Queen.'

Then thought the Queen within herself again,
'Will the child kill me with her foolish prate?'
But openly she spake and said to her,
'O little maid, shut in by nunnery walls,
What canst thou know of Kings and Tables Round,
Or what of signs and wonders, but the signs
And simple miracles of thy nunnery?'

To whom the little novice garrulously,
'Yea, but I know: the land was full of signs
And wonders ere the coming of the Queen.
So said my father, and himself was knight
Of the great Table--at the founding of it;
And rode thereto from Lyonnesse, and he said
That as he rode, an hour or maybe twain
After the sunset, down the coast, he heard
Strange music, and he paused, and turning--there,
All down the lonely coast of Lyonnesse,
Each with a beacon-star upon his head,
And with a wild sea-light about his feet,

He saw them--headland after headland flame
Far on into the rich heart of the west:
And in the light the white mermaiden swam,
And strong man-breasted things stood from the sea,
And sent a deep sea-voice through all the land,
To which the little elves of chasm and cleft
Made answer, sounding like a distant horn.
So said my father--yea, and furthermore,
Next morning, while he past the dim-lit woods,
Himself beheld three spirits mad with joy
Come dashing down on a tall wayside flower,
That shook beneath them, as the thistle shakes
When three gray linnets wrangle for the seed:
And still at evenings on before his horse
The flickering fairy-circle wheeled and broke
Flying, and linked again, and wheeled and broke
Flying, for all the land was full of life.
And when at last he came to Camelot,
A wreath of airy dancers hand-in-hand
Swung round the lighted lantern of the hall;
And in the hall itself was such a feast
As never man had dreamed; for every knight
Had whatsoever meat he longed for served
By hands unseen; and even as he said
Down in the cellars merry bloated things
Shouldered the spigot, straddling on the butts
While the wine ran: so glad were spirits and men
Before the coming of the sinful Queen.'

Then spake the Queen and somewhat bitterly,
'Were they so glad? ill prophets were they all,
Spirits and men: could none of them foresee,
Not even thy wise father with his signs
And wonders, what has fallen upon the realm?'

To whom the novice garrulously again,
'Yea, one, a bard; of whom my father said,

Full many a noble war-song had he sung,
Even in the presence of an enemy's fleet,
Between the steep cliff and the coming wave;
And many a mystic lay of life and death
Had chanted on the smoky mountain-tops,
When round him bent the spirits of the hills
With all their dewy hair blown back like flame:
So said my father--and that night the bard
Sang Arthur's glorious wars, and sang the King
As wellnigh more than man, and railed at those
Who called him the false son of Gorlois:
For there was no man knew from whence he came;
But after tempest, when the long wave broke
All down the thundering shores of Bude and Bos,
There came a day as still as heaven, and then
They found a naked child upon the sands
Of dark Tintagil by the Cornish sea;
And that was Arthur; and they fostered him
Till he by miracle was approven King:
And that his grave should be a mystery
From all men, like his birth; and could he find
A woman in her womanhood as great
As he was in his manhood, then, he sang,
The twain together well might change the world.
But even in the middle of his song
He faltered, and his hand fell from the harp,
And pale he turned, and reeled, and would have fallen,
But that they stayed him up; nor would he tell
His vision; but what doubt that he foresaw
This evil work of Lancelot and the Queen?'

Then thought the Queen, 'Lo! they have set her on,
Our simple-seeming Abbess and her nuns,
To play upon me,' and bowed her head nor spake.
Whereat the novice crying, with clasped hands,
Shame on her own garrulity garrulously,
Said the good nuns would check her gadding tongue

Full often, 'and, sweet lady, if I seem
To vex an ear too sad to listen to me,
Unmannerly, with prattling and the tales
Which my good father told me, check me too
Nor let me shame my father's memory, one
Of noblest manners, though himself would say
Sir Lancelot had the noblest; and he died,
Killed in a tilt, come next, five summers back,
And left me; but of others who remain,
And of the two first-famed for courtesy--
And pray you check me if I ask amiss-
But pray you, which had noblest, while you moved
Among them, Lancelot or our lord the King?'

Then the pale Queen looked up and answered her,
'Sir Lancelot, as became a noble knight,
Was gracious to all ladies, and the same
In open battle or the tilting-field
Forbore his own advantage, and the King
In open battle or the tilting-field
Forbore his own advantage, and these two
Were the most nobly-mannered men of all;
For manners are not idle, but the fruit
Of loyal nature, and of noble mind.'

'Yea,' said the maid, 'be manners such fair fruit?'
Then Lancelot's needs must be a thousand-fold
Less noble, being, as all rumour runs,
The most disloyal friend in all the world.'

To which a mournful answer made the Queen:
'O closed about by narrowing nunnery-walls,
What knowest thou of the world, and all its lights
And shadows, all the wealth and all the woe?
If ever Lancelot, that most noble knight,
Were for one hour less noble than himself,
Pray for him that he scape the doom of fire,

And weep for her that drew him to his doom.'

'Yea,' said the little novice, 'I pray for both;
But I should all as soon believe that his,
Sir Lancelot's, were as noble as the King's,
As I could think, sweet lady, yours would be
Such as they are, were you the sinful Queen.'

So she, like many another babbler, hurt
Whom she would soothe, and harmed where she would heal;
For here a sudden flush of wrathful heat
Fired all the pale face of the Queen, who cried,
'Such as thou art be never maiden more
For ever! thou their tool, set on to plague
And play upon, and harry me, petty spy
And traitress.' When that storm of anger brake
From Guinevere, aghast the maiden rose,
White as her veil, and stood before the Queen
As tremulously as foam upon the beach
Stands in a wind, ready to break and fly,
And when the Queen had added 'Get thee hence,'
Fled frighted. Then that other left alone
Sighed, and began to gather heart again,
Saying in herself, 'The simple, fearful child
Meant nothing, but my own too-fearful guilt,
Simpler than any child, betrays itself.
But help me, heaven, for surely I repent.
For what is true repentance but in thought--
Not even in inmost thought to think again
The sins that made the past so pleasant to us:
And I have sworn never to see him more,
To see him more.'

And even in saying this,
Her memory from old habit of the mind
Went slipping back upon the golden days
In which she saw him first, when Lancelot came,

Reputed the best knight and goodliest man,
Ambassador, to lead her to his lord
Arthur, and led her forth, and far ahead
Of his and her retinue moving, they,
Rapt in sweet talk or lively, all on love
And sport and tilts and pleasure, (for the time
Was maytime, and as yet no sin was dreamed,)
Rode under groves that looked a paradise
Of blossom, over sheets of hyacinth
That seemed the heavens upbreaking through the earth,
And on from hill to hill, and every day
Beheld at noon in some delicious dale
The silk pavilions of King Arthur raised
For brief repast or afternoon repose
By couriers gone before; and on again,
Till yet once more ere set of sun they saw
The Dragon of the great Pendragonship,
That crowned the state pavilion of the King,
Blaze by the rushing brook or silent well.

But when the Queen immersed in such a trance,
And moving through the past unconsciously,
Came to that point where first she saw the King
Ride toward her from the city, sighed to find
Her journey done, glanced at him, thought him cold,
High, self-contained, and passionless, not like him,
'Not like my Lancelot'--while she brooded thus
And grew half-guilty in her thoughts again,
There rode an armed warrior to the doors.
A murmuring whisper through the nunnery ran,
Then on a sudden a cry, 'The King.' She sat
Stiff-stricken, listening; but when armed feet
Through the long gallery from the outer doors
Rang coming, prone from off her seat she fell,
And grovelled with her face against the floor:
There with her milkwhite arms and shadowy hair
She made her face a darkness from the King:

And in the darkness heard his armed feet
Pause by her; then came silence, then a voice,
Monotonous and hollow like a Ghost's
Denouncing judgment, but though changed, the King's:

'Liest thou here so low, the child of one
I honoured, happy, dead before thy shame?
Well is it that no child is born of thee.
The children born of thee are sword and fire,
Red ruin, and the breaking up of laws,
The craft of kindred and the Godless hosts
Of heathen swarming o'er the Northern Sea;
Whom I, while yet Sir Lancelot, my right arm,
The mightiest of my knights, abode with me,
Have everywhere about this land of Christ
In twelve great battles ruining overthrown.
And knowest thou now from whence I come--from him
From waging bitter war with him: and he,
That did not shun to smite me in worse way,
Had yet that grace of courtesy in him left,
He spared to lift his hand against the King
Who made him knight: but many a knight was slain;
And many more, and all his kith and kin
Clave to him, and abode in his own land.
And many more when Modred raised revolt,
Forgetful of their troth and fealty, clave
To Modred, and a remnant stays with me.
And of this remnant will I leave a part,
True men who love me still, for whom I live,
To guard thee in the wild hour coming on,
Lest but a hair of this low head be harmed.
Fear not: thou shalt be guarded till my death.
Howbeit I know, if ancient prophecies
Have erred not, that I march to meet my doom.
Thou hast not made my life so sweet to me,
That I the King should greatly care to live;
For thou hast spoilt the purpose of my life.

Bear with me for the last time while I show,
Even for thy sake, the sin which thou hast sinned.
For when the Roman left us, and their law
Relaxed its hold upon us, and the ways
Were filled with rapine, here and there a deed
Of prowess done redressed a random wrong.
But I was first of all the kings who drew
The knighthood-errant of this realm and all
The realms together under me, their Head,
In that fair Order of my Table Round,
A glorious company, the flower of men,
To serve as model for the mighty world,
And be the fair beginning of a time.
I made them lay their hands in mine and swear
To reverence the King, as if he were
Their conscience, and their conscience as their King,
To break the heathen and uphold the Christ,
To ride abroad redressing human wrongs,
To speak no slander, no, nor listen to it,
To honour his own word as if his God's,
To lead sweet lives in purest chastity,
To love one maiden only, cleave to her,
And worship her by years of noble deeds,
Until they won her; for indeed I knew
Of no more subtle master under heaven
Than is the maiden passion for a maid,
Not only to keep down the base in man,
But teach high thought, and amiable words
And courtliness, and the desire of fame,
And love of truth, and all that makes a man.
And all this throve before I wedded thee,
Believing, "lo mine helpmate, one to feel
My purpose and rejoicing in my joy."
Then came thy shameful sin with Lancelot;
Then came the sin of Tristram and Isolt;
Then others, following these my mightiest knights,
And drawing foul ensample from fair names,

Sinned also, till the loathsome opposite
Of all my heart had destined did obtain,
And all through thee! so that this life of mine
I guard as God's high gift from scathe and wrong,
Not greatly care to lose; but rather think
How sad it were for Arthur, should he live,
To sit once more within his lonely hall,
And miss the wonted number of my knights,
And miss to hear high talk of noble deeds
As in the golden days before thy sin.
For which of us, who might be left, could speak
Of the pure heart, nor seem to glance at thee?
And in thy bowers of Camelot or of Usk
Thy shadow still would glide from room to room,
And I should evermore be vext with thee
In hanging robe or vacant ornament,
Or ghostly footfall echoing on the stair.
For think not, though thou wouldst not love thy lord,
Thy lord hast wholly lost his love for thee.
I am not made of so slight elements.
Yet must I leave thee, woman, to thy shame.
I hold that man the worst of public foes
Who either for his own or children's sake,
To save his blood from scandal, lets the wife
Whom he knows false, abide and rule the house:
For being through his cowardice allowed
Her station, taken everywhere for pure,
She like a new disease, unknown to men,
Creeps, no precaution used, among the crowd,
Makes wicked lightnings of her eyes, and saps
The fealty of our friends, and stirs the pulse
With devil's leaps, and poisons half the young.
Worst of the worst were that man he that reigns!
Better the King's waste hearth and aching heart
Than thou reseated in thy place of light,
The mockery of my people, and their bane.'

He paused, and in the pause she crept an inch
Nearer, and laid her hands about his feet.
Far off a solitary trumpet blew.
Then waiting by the doors the warhorse neighed
At a friend's voice, and he spake again:

'Yet think not that I come to urge thy crimes,
I did not come to curse thee, Guinevere,
I, whose vast pity almost makes me die
To see thee, laying there thy golden head,
My pride in happier summers, at my feet.
The wrath which forced my thoughts on that fierce law,
The doom of treason and the flaming death,
(When first I learnt thee hidden here) is past.
The pang--which while I weighed thy heart with one
Too wholly true to dream untruth in thee,
Made my tears burn--is also past--in part.
And all is past, the sin is sinned, and I,
Lo! I forgive thee, as Eternal God
Forgives: do thou for thine own soul the rest.
But how to take last leave of all I loved?
O golden hair, with which I used to play
Not knowing! O imperial-moulded form,
And beauty such as never woman wore,
Until it became a kingdom's curse with thee--
I cannot touch thy lips, they are not mine,
But Lancelot's: nay, they never were the King's.
I cannot take thy hand: that too is flesh,
And in the flesh thou hast sinned; and mine own flesh,
Here looking down on thine polluted, cries
"I loathe thee:" yet not less, O Guinevere,
For I was ever virgin save for thee,
My love through flesh hath wrought into my life
So far, that my doom is, I love thee still.
Let no man dream but that I love thee still.
Perchance, and so thou purify thy soul,
And so thou lean on our fair father Christ,

Hereafter in that world where all are pure
We two may meet before high God, and thou
Wilt spring to me, and claim me thine, and know
I am thine husband--not a smaller soul,
Nor Lancelot, nor another. Leave me that,
I charge thee, my last hope. Now must I hence.
Through the thick night I hear the trumpet blow:
They summon me their King to lead mine hosts
Far down to that great battle in the west,
Where I must strike against the man they call
My sister's son--no kin of mine, who leagues
With Lords of the White Horse, heathen, and knights,
Traitors--and strike him dead, and meet myself
Death, or I know not what mysterious doom.
And thou remaining here wilt learn the event;
But hither shall I never come again,
Never lie by thy side; see thee no more--
Farewell!'

And while she grovelled at his feet,
She felt the King's breath wander o'er her neck,
And in the darkness o'er her fallen head,
Perceived the waving of his hands that blest.

Then, listening till those armed steps were gone,
Rose the pale Queen, and in her anguish found
The casement: 'peradventure,' so she thought,
'If I might see his face, and not be seen.'
And lo, he sat on horseback at the door!
And near him the sad nuns with each a light
Stood, and he gave them charge about the Queen,
To guard and foster her for evermore.
And while he spake to these his helm was lowered,
To which for crest the golden dragon clung
Of Britain; so she did not see the face,
Which then was as an angel's, but she saw,
Wet with the mists and smitten by the lights,

The Dragon of the great Pendragonship
Blaze, making all the night a steam of fire.
And even then he turned; and more and more
The moony vapour rolling round the King,
Who seemed the phantom of a Giant in it,
Enwound him fold by fold, and made him gray
And grayer, till himself became as mist
Before her, moving ghostlike to his doom.

Then she stretched out her arms and cried aloud
'Oh Arthur!' there her voice brake suddenly,
Then--as a stream that spouting from a cliff
Fails in mid air, but gathering at the base
Re-makes itself, and flashes down the vale--
Went on in passionate utterance:

'Gone--my lord!
Gone through my sin to slay and to be slain!
And he forgave me, and I could not speak.
Farewell? I should have answered his farewell.
His mercy choked me. Gone, my lord the King,
My own true lord! how dare I call him mine?
The shadow of another cleaves to me,
And makes me one pollution: he, the King,
Called me polluted: shall I kill myself?
What help in that? I cannot kill my sin,
If soul be soul; nor can I kill my shame;
No, nor by living can I live it down.
The days will grow to weeks, the weeks to months
The months will add themselves and make the years,
The years will roll into the centuries,
And mine will ever be a name of scorn.
I must not dwell on that defeat of fame.
Let the world be; that is but of the world.
What else? what hope? I think there was a hope,
Except he mocked me when he spake of hope;
His hope he called it; but he never mocks,

For mockery is the fume of little hearts.
And blessed be the King, who hath forgiven
My wickedness to him, and left me hope
That in mine own heart I can live down sin
And be his mate hereafter in the heavens
Before high God. Ah great and gentle lord,
Who wast, as is the conscience of a saint
Among his warring senses, to thy knights--
To whom my false voluptuous pride, that took
Full easily all impressions from below,
Would not look up, or half-despised the height
To which I would not or I could not climb--
I thought I could not breathe in that fine air
That pure severity of perfect light--
I yearned for warmth and colour which I found
In Lancelot--now I see thee what thou art,
Thou art the highest and most human too,
Not Lancelot, nor another. Is there none
Will tell the King I love him though so late?
Now--ere he goes to the great Battle? none:
Myself must tell him in that purer life,
But now it were too daring. Ah my God,
What might I not have made of thy fair world,
Had I but loved thy highest creature here?
It was my duty to have loved the highest:
It surely was my profit had I known:
It would have been my pleasure had I seen.
We needs must love the highest when we see it,
Not Lancelot, nor another.'

Here her hand
Grasped, made her vail her eyes: she looked and saw
The novice, weeping, suppliant, and said to her,
'Yea, little maid, for am I not forgiven?'
Then glancing up beheld the holy nuns
All round her, weeping; and her heart was loosed
Within her, and she wept with these and said,

‘Ye know me then, that wicked one, who broke
The vast design and purpose of the King.
O shut me round with narrowing nunnery-walls,
Meek maidens, from the voices crying "shame."
I must not scorn myself: he loves me still.
Let no one dream but that he loves me still.
So let me, if you do not shudder at me,
Nor shun to call me sister, dwell with you;
Wear black and white, and be a nun like you,
Fast with your fasts, not feasting with your feasts;
Grieve with your griefs, not grieving at your joys,
But not rejoicing; mingle with your rites;
Pray and be prayed for; lie before your shrines;
Do each low office of your holy house;
Walk your dim cloister, and distribute dole
To poor sick people, richer in His eyes
Who ransomed us, and haler too than I;
And treat their loathsome hurts and heal mine own;
And so wear out in almsdeed and in prayer
The sombre close of that voluptuous day,
Which wrought the ruin of my lord the King.’

She said: they took her to themselves; and she
Still hoping, fearing ‘is it yet too late?’
Dwelt with them, till in time their Abbess died.
Then she, for her good deeds and her pure life,
And for the power of ministration in her,
And likewise for the high rank she had borne,
Was chosen Abbess, there, an Abbess, lived
For three brief years, and there, an Abbess, past
To where beyond these voices there is peace.

Lesson 77

- Read "The Passing of Arthur" from *Idylls of the King.*

The Passing of Arthur

That story which the bold Sir Bedivere,
First made and latest left of all the knights,
Told, when the man was no more than a voice
In the white winter of his age, to those
With whom he dwelt, new faces, other minds.

For on their march to westward, Bedivere,
Who slowly paced among the slumbering host,
Heard in his tent the moanings of the King:

'I found Him in the shining of the stars,
I marked Him in the flowering of His fields,
But in His ways with men I find Him not.
I waged His wars, and now I pass and die.
O me! for why is all around us here
As if some lesser god had made the world,
But had not force to shape it as he would,
Till the High God behold it from beyond,
And enter it, and make it beautiful?
Or else as if the world were wholly fair,
But that these eyes of men are dense and dim,
And have not power to see it as it is:
Perchance, because we see not to the close;--
For I, being simple, thought to work His will,
And have but stricken with the sword in vain;
And all whereon I leaned in wife and friend
Is traitor to my peace, and all my realm
Reels back into the beast, and is no more.
My God, thou hast forgotten me in my death;

Nay--God my Christ--I pass but shall not die.'

Then, ere that last weird battle in the west,
There came on Arthur sleeping, Gawain killed
In Lancelot's war, the ghost of Gawain blown
Along a wandering wind, and past his ear
Went shrilling, 'Hollow, hollow all delight!
Hail, King! tomorrow thou shalt pass away.
Farewell! there is an isle of rest for thee.
And I am blown along a wandering wind,
And hollow, hollow, hollow all delight.'
And fainter onward, like wild birds that change
Their season in the night and wail their way
From cloud to cloud, down the long wind the dream
Shrilled; but in going mingled with dim cries
Far in the moonlit haze among the hills,
As of some lonely city sacked by night,
When all is lost, and wife and child with wail
Pass to new lords; and Arthur woke and called,
'Who spake? A dream. O light upon the wind,
Thine, Gawain, was the voice--are these dim cries
Thine? or doth all that haunts the waste and wild
Mourn, knowing it will go along with me?'

This heard the bold Sir Bedivere and spake:
'O me, my King, let pass whatever will,
Elves, and the harmless glamour of the field;
But in their stead thy name and glory cling
To all high places like a golden cloud
For ever: but as yet thou shalt not pass.
Light was Gawain in life, and light in death
Is Gawain, for the ghost is as the man;
And care not thou for dreams from him, but rise--
I hear the steps of Modred in the west,
And with him many of thy people, and knights
Once thine, whom thou hast loved, but grosser grown
Than heathen, spitting at their vows and thee.

Right well in heart they know thee for the King.
Arise, go forth and conquer as of old.'

Then spake King Arthur to Sir Bedivere:
'Far other is this battle in the west
Whereto we move, than when we strove in youth,
And brake the petty kings, and fought with Rome,
Or thrust the heathen from the Roman wall,
And shook him through the north. Ill doom is mine
To war against my people and my knights.
The king who fights his people fights himself.
And they my knights, who loved me once, the stroke
That strikes them dead is as my death to me.
Yet let us hence, and find or feel a way
Through this blind haze, which ever since I saw
One lying in the dust at Almesbury,
Hath folded in the passes of the world.'

Then rose the King and moved his host by night,
And ever pushed Sir Modred, league by league,
Back to the sunset bound of Lyonnesse--
A land of old upheaven from the abyss
By fire, to sink into the abyss again;
Where fragments of forgotten peoples dwelt,
And the long mountains ended in a coast
Of ever-shifting sand, and far away
The phantom circle of a moaning sea.
There the pursuer could pursue no more,
And he that fled no further fly the King;
And there, that day when the great light of heaven
Burned at his lowest in the rolling year,
On the waste sand by the waste sea they closed.
Nor ever yet had Arthur fought a fight
Like this last, dim, weird battle of the west.
A deathwhite mist slept over sand and sea:
Whereof the chill, to him who breathed it, drew
Down with his blood, till all his heart was cold

With formless fear; and even on Arthur fell
Confusion, since he saw not whom he fought.
For friend and foe were shadows in the mist,
And friend slew friend not knowing whom he slew;
And some had visions out of golden youth,
And some beheld the faces of old ghosts
Look in upon the battle; and in the mist
Was many a noble deed, many a base,
And chance and craft and strength in single fights,
And ever and anon with host to host
Shocks, and the splintering spear, the hard mail hewn,
Shield-breakings, and the clash of brands, the crash
Of battleaxes on shattered helms, and shrieks
After the Christ, of those who falling down
Looked up for heaven, and only saw the mist;
And shouts of heathen and the traitor knights,
Oaths, insults, filth, and monstrous blasphemies,
Sweat, writhings, anguish, labouring of the lungs
In that close mist, and cryings for the light,
Moans of the dying, and voices of the dead.

Last, as by some one deathbed after wail
Of suffering, silence follows, or through death
Or deathlike swoon, thus over all that shore,
Save for some whisper of the seething seas,
A dead hush fell; but when the dolorous day
Grew drearier toward twilight falling, came
A bitter wind, clear from the North, and blew
The mist aside, and with that wind the tide
Rose, and the pale King glanced across the field
Of battle: but no man was moving there;
Nor any cry of Christian heard thereon,
Nor yet of heathen; only the wan wave
Brake in among dead faces, to and fro
Swaying the helpless hands, and up and down
Tumbling the hollow helmets of the fallen,
And shivered brands that once had fought with Rome,

And rolling far along the gloomy shores
The voice of days of old and days to be.

Then spake King Arthur to Sir Bedivere,
And whiter than the mist that all day long
Had held the field of battle was the King:

'Hearest thou this great voice that shakes the world,
And wastes the narrow realm whereon we move,
And beats upon the faces of the dead,
My dead, as though they had not died for me?--
O Bedivere, for on my heart hath fallen
Confusion, till I know not what I am,
Nor whence I am, nor whether I be King.
Behold, I seem but King among the dead.'

Then spake the bold Sir Bedivere: 'My King,
King everywhere! and so the dead have kings,
There also will I worship thee as King.
Yet still thy life is whole, and still I live
Who love thee; but who hates thee, he that brought
The heathen back among us, yonder stands,
Modred, unharmed, the traitor of thine house.'

Then spake the King: 'My house hath been my doom.
But call not thou this traitor of my house
Who hath but dwelt beneath one roof with me.
My house are rather they who sware my vows,
Yea, even while they brake them, owned me King.
And well for thee, saying in my dark hour,
When all the purport of my throne hath failed,
That quick or dead thou holdest me for King.
King am I, whatsoever be their cry;
And one last act of kinghood shalt thou see
Yet, ere I pass.' And uttering this the King
Made at the man: then Modred smote his liege
Hard on that helm which many a heathen sword

Had beaten thin; while Arthur at one blow,
Striking the last stroke with Excalibur,
Slew him, and all but slain himself, he fell.

So all day long the noise of battle rolled
Among the mountains by the winter sea;
Until King Arthur's Table, man by man,
Had fallen in Lyonnesse about their lord,
King Arthur. Then, because his wound was deep,
The bold Sir Bedivere uplifted him,
And bore him to a chapel nigh the field,
A broken chancel with a broken cross,
That stood on a dark strait of barren land:
On one side lay the Ocean, and on one
Lay a great water, and the moon was full.

Then spake King Arthur to Sir Bedivere:
'The sequel of today unsolders all
The goodliest fellowship of famous knights
Whereof this world holds record. Such a sleep
They sleep--the men I loved. I think that we
Shall never more, at any future time,
Delight our souls with talk of knightly deeds,
Walking about the gardens and the halls
Of Camelot, as in the days that were.
I perish by this people which I made,--
Though Merlin sware that I should come again
To rule once more; but, let what will be, be,
I am so deeply smitten through the helm
That without help I cannot last till morn.
Thou therefore take my brand Excalibur,
Which was my pride: for thou rememberest how
In those old days, one summer noon, an arm
Rose up from out the bosom of the lake,
Clothed in white samite, mystic, wonderful,
Holding the sword--and how I rowed across
And took it, and have worn it, like a king;

And, wheresoever I am sung or told
In aftertime, this also shall be known:
But now delay not: take Excalibur,
And fling him far into the middle mere:
Watch what thou seest, and lightly bring me word.'

To him replied the bold Sir Bedivere:
'It is not meet, Sir King, to leave thee thus,
Aidless, alone, and smitten through the helm--
A little thing may harm a wounded man;
Yet I thy hest will all perform at full,
Watch what I see, and lightly bring thee word.'

So saying, from the ruined shrine he stept,
And in the moon athwart the place of tombs,
Where lay the mighty bones of ancient men,
Old knights, and over them the sea-wind sang
Shrill, chill, with flakes of foam. He, stepping down
By zigzag paths, and juts of pointed rock,
Came on the shining levels of the lake.

There drew he forth the brand Excalibur,
And o'er him, drawing it, the winter moon,
Brightening the skirts of a long cloud, ran forth
And sparkled keen with frost against the hilt:
For all the haft twinkled with diamond sparks,
Myriads of topaz-lights, and jacinth-work
Of subtlest jewellery. He gazed so long
That both his eyes were dazzled as he stood,
This way and that dividing the swift mind,
In act to throw: but at the last it seemed
Better to leave Excalibur concealed
There in the many-knotted waterflags,
That whistled stiff and dry about the marge.
So strode he back slow to the wounded King.

Then spake King Arthur to Sir Bedivere:

'Hast thou performed my mission which I gave?
What is it thou hast seen? or what hast heard?'

And answer made the bold Sir Bedivere:
'I heard the ripple washing in the reeds,
And the wild water lapping on the crag.'

To whom replied King Arthur, faint and pale:
'Thou hast betrayed thy nature and thy name,
Not rendering true answer, as beseemed
Thy fealty, nor like a noble knight:
For surer sign had followed, either hand,
Or voice, or else a motion of the mere.
This is a shameful thing for men to lie.
Yet now, I charge thee, quickly go again,
As thou art lief and dear, and do the thing
I bade thee, watch, and lightly bring me word.'

Then went Sir Bedivere the second time
Across the ridge, and paced beside the mere,
Counting the dewy pebbles, fixed in thought;
But when he saw the wonder of the hilt,
How curiously and strangely chased, he smote
His palms together, and he cried aloud:

'And if indeed I cast the brand away,
Surely a precious thing, one worthy note,
Should thus be lost for ever from the earth,
Which might have pleased the eyes of many men.
What good should follow this, if this were done?
What harm, undone? Deep harm to disobey,
Seeing obedience is the bond of rule.
Were it well to obey then, if a king demand
An act unprofitable, against himself?
The King is sick, and knows not what he does.
What record, or what relic of my lord
Should be to aftertime, but empty breath

And rumours of a doubt? But were this kept,
Stored in some treasure-house of mighty kings,
Some one might show it at a joust of arms,
Saying, "King Arthur's sword, Excalibur,
Wrought by the lonely maiden of the Lake.
Nine years she wrought it, sitting in the deeps
Upon the hidden bases of the hills."
So might some old man speak in the aftertime
To all the people, winning reverence.
But now much honour and much fame were lost.'

So spake he, clouded with his own conceit,
And hid Excalibur the second time,
And so strode back slow to the wounded King.

Then spoke King Arthur, breathing heavily:
'What is it thou hast seen? or what hast heard?'

And answer made the bold Sir Bedivere:
'I heard the water lapping on the crag,
And the long ripple washing in the reeds.'

To whom replied King Arthur, much in wrath:
'Ah, miserable and unkind, untrue,
Unknightly, traitor-hearted! Woe is me!
Authority forgets a dying king,
Laid widowed of the power in his eye
That bowed the will. I see thee what thou art,
For thou, the latest-left of all my knights,
In whom should meet the offices of all,
Thou wouldst betray me for the precious hilt;
Either from lust of gold, or like a girl
Valuing the giddy pleasure of the eyes.
Yet, for a man may fail in duty twice,
And the third time may prosper, get thee hence:
But, if thou spare to fling Excalibur,
I will arise and slay thee with my hands.'

Then quickly rose Sir Bedivere, and ran,
And, leaping down the ridges lightly, plunged
Among the bulrush beds, and clutched the sword,
And strongly wheeled and threw it. The great brand
Made lightnings in the splendour of the moon,
And flashing round and round, and whirled in an arch,
Shot like a streamer of the northern morn,
Seen where the moving isles of winter shock
By night, with noises of the Northern Sea.
So flashed and fell the brand Excalibur:
But ere he dipt the surface, rose an arm
Clothed in white samite, mystic, wonderful,
And caught him by the hilt, and brandished him
Three times, and drew him under in the mere.
And lightly went the other to the King.

Then spoke King Arthur, drawing thicker breath:
'Now see I by thine eyes that this is done.
Speak out: what is it thou hast heard, or seen?'

And answer made the bold Sir Bedivere:
'Sir King, I closed mine eyelids, lest the gems
Should blind my purpose, for I never saw,
Nor shall see, here or elsewhere, till I die,
Not though I live three lives of mortal men,
So great a miracle as yonder hilt.
Then with both hands I flung him, wheeling him;
But when I looked again, behold an arm,
Clothed in white samite, mystic, wonderful,
That caught him by the hilt, and brandished him
Three times, and drew him under in the mere.'

And answer made King Arthur, breathing hard:
'My end draws nigh; 'tis time that I were gone.
Make broad thy shoulders to receive my weight,
And bear me to the margin; yet I fear

My wound hath taken cold, and I shall die.'

So saying, from the pavement he half rose,
Slowly, with pain, reclining on his arm,
And looking wistfully with wide blue eyes
As in a picture. Him Sir Bedivere
Remorsefully regarded through his tears,
And would have spoken, but he found not words;
Then took with care, and kneeling on one knee,
O'er both his shoulders drew the languid hands,
And rising bore him through the place of tombs.

But, as he walked, King Arthur panted hard,
Like one that feels a nightmare on his bed
When all the house is mute. So sighed the King,
Muttering and murmuring at his ear, 'Quick, quick!
I fear it is too late, and I shall die.'

But the other swiftly strode from ridge to ridge,
Clothed with his breath, and looking, as he walked,
Larger than human on the frozen hills.
He heard the deep behind him, and a cry
Before. His own thought drove him like a goad.
Dry clashed his harness in the icy caves
And barren chasms, and all to left and right
The bare black cliff clanged round him, as he based
His feet on juts of slippery crag that rang
Sharp-smitten with the dint of armed heels--
And on a sudden, lo! the level lake,
And the long glories of the winter moon.

Then saw they how there hove a dusky barge,
Dark as a funeral scarf from stem to stern,
Beneath them; and descending they were ware
That all the decks were dense with stately forms,
Black-stoled, black-hooded, like a dream--by these
Three Queens with crowns of gold: and from them rose

A cry that shivered to the tingling stars,
And, as it were one voice, an agony
Of lamentation, like a wind that shrills
All night in a waste land, where no one comes,
Or hath come, since the making of the world.

Then murmured Arthur, 'Place me in the barge.'
So to the barge they came. There those three Queens
Put forth their hands, and took the King, and wept.
But she, that rose the tallest of them all
And fairest, laid his head upon her lap,
And loosed the shattered casque, and chafed his hands,
And called him by his name, complaining loud,
And dropping bitter tears against a brow
Striped with dark blood: for all his face was white
And colourless, and like the withered moon
Smote by the fresh beam of the springing east;
And all his greaves and cuisses dashed with drops
Of onset; and the light and lustrous curls--
That made his forehead like a rising sun
High from the dais-throne--were parched with dust;
Or, clotted into points and hanging loose,
Mixed with the knightly growth that fringed his lips.
So like a shattered column lay the King;
Not like that Arthur who, with lance in rest,
From spur to plume a star of tournament,
Shot through the lists at Camelot, and charged
Before the eyes of ladies and of kings.

Then loudly cried the bold Sir Bedivere:
'Ah! my Lord Arthur, whither shall I go?
Where shall I hide my forehead and my eyes?
For now I see the true old times are dead,
When every morning brought a noble chance,
And every chance brought out a noble knight.
Such times have been not since the light that led
The holy Elders with the gift of myrrh.

But now the whole Round Table is dissolved
Which was an image of the mighty world,
And I, the last, go forth companionless,
And the days darken round me, and the years,
Among new men, strange faces, other minds.'

And slowly answered Arthur from the barge:
'The old order changeth, yielding place to new,
And God fulfils himself in many ways,
Lest one good custom should corrupt the world.
Comfort thyself: what comfort is in me?
I have lived my life, and that which I have done
May He within himself make pure! but thou,
If thou shouldst never see my face again,
Pray for my soul. More things are wrought by prayer
Than this world dreams of. Wherefore, let thy voice
Rise like a fountain for me night and day.
For what are men better than sheep or goats
That nourish a blind life within the brain,
If, knowing God, they lift not hands of prayer
Both for themselves and those who call them friend?
For so the whole round earth is every way
Bound by gold chains about the feet of God.
But now farewell. I am going a long way
With these thou seest--if indeed I go
(For all my mind is clouded with a doubt)--
To the island-valley of Avilion;
Where falls not hail, or rain, or any snow,
Nor ever wind blows loudly; but it lies
Deep-meadowed, happy, fair with orchard lawns
And bowery hollows crowned with summer sea,
Where I will heal me of my grievous wound.'

So said he, and the barge with oar and sail
Moved from the brink, like some full-breasted swan
That, fluting a wild carol ere her death,
Ruffles her pure cold plume, and takes the flood

With swarthy webs. Long stood Sir Bedivere
Revolving many memories, till the hull
Looked one black dot against the verge of dawn,
And on the mere the wailing died away.

But when that moan had past for evermore,
The stillness of the dead world's winter dawn
Amazed him, and he groaned, 'The King is gone.'
And therewithal came on him the weird rhyme,
'From the great deep to the great deep he goes.'

Whereat he slowly turned and slowly clomb
The last hard footstep of that iron crag;
Thence marked the black hull moving yet, and cried,
'He passes to be King among the dead,
And after healing of his grievous wound
He comes again; but--if he come no more--
O me, be yon dark Queens in yon black boat,
Who shrieked and wailed, the three whereat we gazed
On that high day, when, clothed with living light,
They stood before his throne in silence, friends
Of Arthur, who should help him at his need?'

Then from the dawn it seemed there came, but faint
As from beyond the limit of the world,
Like the last echo born of a great cry,
Sounds, as if some fair city were one voice
Around a king returning from his wars.

Thereat once more he moved about, and clomb
Even to the highest he could climb, and saw,
Straining his eyes beneath an arch of hand,
Or thought he saw, the speck that bare the King,
Down that long water opening on the deep
Somewhere far off, pass on and on, and go
From less to less and vanish into light.
And the new sun rose bringing the new year.

Lesson 78

- Now we're going to read *Le Morte D'Arthur*. That translates from the French to "The Death of Arthur." Read a bit about the book.

Le Morte D'Arthur was written in the 15th century (1400s) and was the first major work of English prose fiction. It is a myth of the rise and fall of Arthur's kingdom, but it also mirrored the real English kingdom of the day which also seemed doomed by corruption. The work tells the tale of how kingdoms begin and what makes them end. While the book applied to a fictional English kingom, it can really apply to any nation or civilization.

- Read chapter 1.

Le Morte D'Arthur
By Sir Thomas Malory
Chapter 1
How Uther Pendragon sent for the duke of Cornwall and Igraine his wife, and of their departing suddenly again.

It befell in the days of Uther Pendragon, when he was king of all England, and so reigned, that there was a mighty duke in Cornwall that held war against him long time. And the duke was called the Duke of Tintagil. And so by means King Uther sent for this duke, charging him to bring his wife with him, for she was called a fair lady, and a passing wise, and her name was called Igraine.

So when the duke and his wife were come unto the king, by the means of great lords they were accorded both. The king liked and loved this lady well, and he made them great cheer out of measure, and desired to have lain by her. But she was a passing good woman, and would not assent unto the king. And then she told the duke her husband, and said, I suppose that we were sent for that I should be dishonoured; wherefore, husband, I counsel you, that we depart from hence suddenly, that we may ride all night unto our own castle. And in like wise as she said so they departed, that neither the king nor none of his council were ware of their departing. All so soon as King Uther knew of their departing so suddenly, he was wonderly wroth. Then he called to him his privy council, and told them of the sudden departing of the duke and his wife.

Then they advised the king to send for the duke and his wife by a great charge; and if he will not come at your summons, then may ye do your best, then have ye cause to make mighty war upon him. So that was done, and the messengers had their answers; and that was this shortly, that neither he nor his wife would not come at him.

Then was the king wonderly wroth. And then the king sent him plain word again, and bade him be ready and stuff him and garnish him, for within forty days he would fetch him out of the biggest castle that he hath.

When the duke had this warning, anon he went and furnished and garnished two strong castles of his, of the which the one hight Tintagil, and the other castle hight Terrabil. So his wife Dame Igraine he put in the castle of Tintagil, and himself he put in the castle of Terrabil, the which had many issues and posterns out. Then in all haste came Uther with a great host, and laid a siege about the castle of Terrabil. And there he pight many pavilions, and there was great war made on both parties, and much people slain. Then for pure anger and for great love of fair Igraine the king Uther fell sick. So came to the king Uther Sir Ulfius, a noble knight, and asked the king why he was sick. I shall tell thee, said the king, I am sick for anger and for love of fair Igraine, that I may not be whole. Well, my lord, said Sir Ulfius, I shall seek Merlin, and he shall do you remedy, that your heart shall be pleased. So Ulfius departed, and by adventure he met Merlin in a beggar's array, and there Merlin asked Ulfius whom he sought. And he said he had little ado to tell him. Well, said Merlin, I know whom thou seekest, for thou seekest Merlin; therefore seek no farther, for I am he; and if King Uther will well reward me, and be sworn unto me to fulfil my desire, that shall be his honour and profit more than mine; for I shall cause him to have all his desire. All this will I undertake, said Ulfius, that there shall be nothing reasonable but thou shalt have thy desire. Well, said Merlin, he shall have his intent and desire. And therefore, said Merlin, ride on your way, for I will not be long behind.

Lesson 79

- Read chapters 2-6 of *Le Morte D'Arthur.*

Chapter 2
How Uther Pendragon made war on the duke of Cornwall, and how by the mean of Merlin he lay by the duchess and gat Arthur.

Then Ulfius was glad, and rode on more than a pace till that he came to King Uther Pendragon, and told him he had met with Merlin. Where is he? said the king. Sir, said Ulfius, he will not dwell long. Therewithal Ulfius was ware where Merlin stood at the porch of the pavilion's door. And then Merlin was bound to come to the king. When King Uther saw him, he said he was welcome. Sir, said Merlin, I know all your heart every deal; so ye will be sworn unto me as ye be a true king anointed, to fulfil my desire, ye shall have your desire. Then the king was sworn upon the Four Evangelists. Sir, said Merlin, this is my desire: the first night that ye shall lie by Igraine ye shall get a child on her, and when that is born, that it shall be delivered to me for to nourish there as I will have it; for it shall be your worship, and the child's avail, as mickle as the child is worth. I will well, said the king, as thou wilt have it. Now make you ready, said Merlin, this night ye shall lie with Igraine in the castle of Tintagil; and ye shall be like the duke her husband, Ulfius shall be like Sir Brastias, a knight of the duke's, and I will be like a knight that hight Sir Jordanus, a knight of the duke's. But wait ye make not many questions with her nor her men, but say ye are diseased, and so hie you to bed, and rise not on the morn till I come to you, for the castle of Tintagil is but ten miles hence; so this was done as they devised. But the duke of Tintagil espied how the king rode from the siege of Terrabil, and therefore that night he issued out of the castle at a postern for to have distressed the king's host. And so, through his own issue, the duke himself was slain or ever the king came at the castle of Tintagil.

So after the death of the duke, King Uther lay with Igraine more than three hours after his death, and begat on her that night Arthur, and on day came Merlin to the king, and bade him make him ready, and so he kissed the lady Igraine and departed in all haste. But when the lady heard tell of the duke her husband, and by all record he was dead or ever King Uther came to her, then she marvelled who that might be that lay with her in likeness of her lord; so she mourned privily and held her peace. Then all the barons by one assent prayed the king of accord betwixt the lady Igraine and him; the king gave them leave, for fain would he have been accorded with her. So the king put all the trust in Ulfius to entreat between them, so by the entreaty at the last the king and she met together. Now will we do well, said Ulfius, our king is a lusty knight and wifeless, and my lady Igraine is a passing fair lady; it were great joy unto us all, an it might please the king to make her his queen. Unto that they all well accorded and moved it to the king. And anon, like a lusty knight, he assented thereto with good will, and so in all haste they were married in a morning with great mirth and joy.

And King Lot of Lothian and of Orkney then wedded Margawse that was Gawaine's mother, and King Nentres of the land of Garlot wedded Elaine. All this was done at the request of King Uther. And the third sister Morgan le Fay was put to school in a nunnery, and there she learned so much that she was a great clerk of necromancy. And after she was wedded to King Uriens of the land of Gore, that was Sir Ewain's le Blanchemain's father.

Chapter 3
Of the birth of King Arthur and of his nurture.

Then Queen Igraine waxed daily greater and greater, so it befell after within half a year, as King Uther lay by his queen, he asked her, by the faith she owed to him, whose was the child within her body; then she sore abashed to give answer. Dismay you not, said the king, but tell me the truth, and I shall love you the better, by the faith of my body. Sir, said she, I shall tell you the truth. The same night that my lord was dead, the hour of his death, as his knights record, there came into my castle of Tintagil a man like my lord in speech and in countenance, and two knights with him in likeness of his two knights Brastias and Jordanus, and so I went unto bed with him as I ought to do with my lord, and the same night, as I shall answer unto God, this child was begotten upon me. That is truth, said the king, as ye say; for it was I myself that came in the likeness, and therefore dismay you not, for I am father of the child; and there he told her all the cause, how it was by Merlin's counsel. Then the queen made great joy when she knew who was the father of her child.

Soon came Merlin unto the king, and said, Sir, ye must purvey you for the nourishing of your child. As thou wilt, said the king, be it. Well, said Merlin, I know a lord of yours in this land, that is a passing true man and a faithful, and he shall have the nourishing of your child, and his name is Sir Ector, and he is a lord of fair livelihood in many parts in England and Wales; and this lord, Sir Ector, let him be sent for, for to come and speak with you, and desire him yourself, as he loveth you, that he will put his own child to nourishing to another woman, and that his wife nourish yours. And when the child is born let it be delivered to me at yonder privy postern unchristened. So like as Merlin devised it was done. And when Sir Ector was come he made fiaunce to the king for to nourish the child like as the king desired; and there the king granted Sir Ector great rewards. Then when the lady was delivered, the king commanded two knights and two ladies to take the child, bound in a cloth of gold, and that ye deliver him to what poor man ye meet at the postern gate of the castle. So the child was delivered unto Merlin, and so he bare it forth unto Sir Ector, and made an holy man to christen him, and named him Arthur; and so Sir Ector's wife nourished him with her own pap.

Chapter 4
Of the death of King Uther Pendragon.

Then within two years King Uther fell sick of a great malady. And in the meanwhile his enemies usurped upon him, and did a great battle upon his men, and slew many of his people. Sir, said Merlin, ye may not lie so as ye do, for ye must to the field though ye ride on an horse-litter: for ye shall never have the better of your enemies but if your person be there, and then shall ye have the victory. So it was done as Merlin had devised, and they carried the king forth in an horse-litter with a great host towards his enemies. And at St. Albans there met with the king a great host of the North. And that day Sir Ulfius and Sir Brastias did great deeds of arms, and King Uther's men overcame the Northern battle and slew many people, and put the remnant to flight. And then the king returned unto London, and made great joy of his victory. And then he fell passing sore sick, so that three days and three nights he was speechless: wherefore all the barons made great sorrow, and asked Merlin what counsel were best. There is none other remedy, said Merlin, but God will have his will. But look ye all barons be before King Uther to-morn, and God and I shall make him to speak. So on the morn all the barons with Merlin came to-fore the king; then Merlin said aloud unto King Uther, Sir, shall your son Arthur be king after your days, of this realm with all the appurtenance? Then Uther Pendragon turned him, and said in hearing of them all, I give him God's blessing and mine, and bid him pray for my soul, and righteously and worshipfully that he claim the crown, upon forfeiture of my blessing; and therewith he yielded up the ghost, and then was he interred as longed to a king. Wherefore the queen, fair Igraine, made great sorrow, and all the barons.

Chapter 5
How Arthur was chosen king, and of wonders and marvels of a sword taken out of a stone by the said Arthur.

Then stood the realm in great jeopardy long while, for every lord that was mighty of men made him strong, and many weened to have been king. Then Merlin went to the Archbishop of Canterbury, and counselled him for to send for all the lords of the realm, and all the gentlemen of arms, that they should to London come by Christmas, upon pain of cursing; and for this cause, that Jesus, that was born on that night, that he would of his great mercy show some miracle, as he was come to be king of mankind, for to show some miracle who should be rightwise king of this realm. So the Archbishop, by the advice of Merlin, sent for all the lords and gentlemen of arms that they should come by Christmas even unto London. And many of them made them clean of their life, that their prayer might be the more acceptable unto God. So in the greatest church of London, whether it were Paul's or not the French book maketh no mention, all the estates were long or day in the church for to pray. And when matins and the first mass was done, there was seen in the churchyard, against the high altar, a great stone four square, like unto a marble stone; and in midst thereof was like an anvil of steel a foot on high, and therein stuck a fair sword naked by the point, and letters there were written in gold about the sword that said thus:--Whoso pulleth out this sword of this stone and anvil, is rightwise king born of all England. Then the people marvelled, and told it to the Archbishop. I command, said the Archbishop, that ye keep you within your church and pray unto God still, that no man touch the sword till the high mass be all done. So when all masses were done all the lords went to behold the stone and the sword. And when they saw the scripture some assayed, such as would have been king. But none might stir the sword nor move it. He is not here, said the Archbishop, that shall achieve the sword, but doubt not God will make him known. But this is my counsel, said the Archbishop, that we let purvey ten knights, men of good fame, and they to keep this sword. So it was ordained, and then there was made a cry, that every man should assay that would, for to win the sword. And upon New Year's Day the barons let make a jousts and a tournament, that all knights that would joust or tourney there might play, and all this was ordained for to keep the lords together and the commons, for the Archbishop trusted that God would make him known that should win the sword.

So upon New Year's Day, when the service was done, the barons rode unto the field, some to joust and some to tourney, and so it happened that Sir Ector, that had great livelihood about London, rode unto the jousts, and with him rode Sir Kay his son, and young Arthur that was his nourished brother; and Sir Kay was made knight at All Hallowmass afore. So as they rode to the joustsward, Sir Kay lost his sword, for he had left it at his father's lodging, and so he prayed young Arthur for to ride for his sword. I will well, said Arthur, and rode fast after the sword, and when he came home, the lady and all were out to see the jousting. Then was Arthur wroth, and said to himself, I will ride to the churchyard, and take the sword with me that sticketh in the stone, for my brother Sir Kay shall not be without a sword this day. So when he came to the churchyard, Sir Arthur alighted and tied his horse to the stile, and so he went to the tent, and found no knights there, for they were at the jousting. And so he handled the sword by the handles, and lightly and fiercely pulled it out of the stone, and took his horse and rode his way until he came to his brother Sir Kay, and delivered him the sword. And as soon as Sir Kay saw the sword, he wist well it was the sword of the stone, and so he rode to his father Sir Ector, and said: Sir, lo here is the sword of the stone, wherefore I must be king of this land. When Sir Ector beheld the sword, he returned again and came to the church, and there they alighted all three, and went into the church. And anon he made Sir Kay swear upon a book how he came to that sword. Sir, said Sir Kay, by my brother Arthur, for he brought it to me. How gat ye this sword? said Sir Ector to Arthur. Sir, I willtell you. When I came home for my brother's sword, I found nobody at home to deliver me his sword; and so I thought my brother Sir Kay should not be swordless, and so I came hither eagerly and pulled it out of the stone without any pain. Found ye any knights about this sword? said Sir Ector. Nay, said Arthur. Now, said Sir Ector to Arthur, I understand ye must be king of this land. Wherefore I, said Arthur, and for what cause? Sir, said Ector, for God will have it so; for there should never man have drawn out this sword, but he that shall be rightwise king of this land. Now let me see whether ye can put the sword there as it was, and pull it out again. That is no mastery, said Arthur, and so he put it in the stone; wherewithal Sir Ector assayed to pull out the sword and failed.

Chapter 6
How King Arthur pulled out the sword divers times.

Now assay, said Sir Ector unto Sir Kay. And anon he pulled at the sword with all his might; but it would not be. Now shall ye assay, said Sir Ector to Arthur. I will well, said Arthur, and pulled it out easily. And therewithal Sir Ector knelt down to the earth, and Sir Kay. Alas, said Arthur, my own dear father and brother, why kneel ye to me? Nay, nay, my lord Arthur, it is not so; I was never your father nor of your blood, but I wot well ye are of an higher blood than I weened ye were. And then Sir Ector told him all, how he was betaken him for to nourish him, and by whose commandment, and by Merlin's deliverance.

Then Arthur made great dole when he understood that Sir Ector was not his father. Sir, said Ector unto Arthur, will ye be my good and gracious lord when ye are king? Else were I to blame, said Arthur, for ye are the man in the world that I am most beholden to, and my good lady and mother your wife, that as well as her own hath fostered me and kept. And if ever it be God's will that I be king as ye say, ye shall desire of me what I may do, and I shall not fail you; God forbid I should fail you Sir, said Sir Ector, I will ask no more of you, but that ye will make my son, your foster brother, Sir Kay, seneschal of all your lands. That shall be done, said Arthur, and more, by the faith of my body, that never man shall have that office but he, while he and I live Therewithal they went unto the Archbishop, and told him how the sword was achieved, and by whom; and on Twelfth-day all the barons came thither, and to assay to take the sword, who that would assay. But there afore them all, there might none take it out but Arthur; wherefore there were many lords wroth, and said it was great shame unto them all and the realm, to be overgoverned with a boy of no high blood born. And so they fell out at that time that it was put off till Candlemas and then all the barons should meet there again; but always the ten knights were ordained to watch the sword day and night, and so they set a pavilion over the stone and the sword, and five always watched. So at Candlemas many more great lords came thither for to have won the sword, but there might none prevail. And right as Arthur did at Christmas, he did at Candlemas, and pulled out the sword easily, whereof the barons were sore aggrieved and put it off in delay till the high feast of Easter. And as Arthur sped before, so did he at Easter; yet there were some of the great lords had indignation that Arthur should be king, and put it off in a delay till the feast of Pentecost.

Then the Archbishop of Canterbury by Merlin's providence let purvey then of the best knights that they might get, and such knights as Uther Pendragon loved best and most trusted in his days. And such knights were put about Arthur as Sir Baudwin of Britain, Sir Kay, Sir Ulfius, Sir Brastias. All these, with many other, were always about Arthur, day and night, till the feast of Pentecost.

Lesson 80

- Read chapters 7-11 of *Le Morte D'Arthur*.

Chapter 7
How King Arthur was crowned, and how he made officers.

And at the feast of Pentecost all manner of men assayed to pull at the sword that would assay; but none might prevail but Arthur, and pulled it out afore all the lords and commons that were there, wherefore all the commons cried at once, We will have Arthur unto our king, we will put him no more in delay, for we all see that it is God's will that he shall be our king, and who that holdeth against it, we will slay him. And therewithal they kneeled at once, both rich and poor, and cried Arthur mercy because they had delayed him so long, and Arthur forgave them, and took the sword between both his hands, and offered it upon the altar where the Archbishop was, and so was he made knight of the best man that was there. And so anon was the coronation made. And there was he sworn unto his lords and the commons for to be a true king, to stand with true justice from thenceforth the days of this life. Also then he made all lords that held of the crown to come in, and to do service as they ought to do. And many complaints were made unto Sir Arthur of great wrongs that were done since the death of King Uther, of many lands that were bereaved lords, knights, ladies, and gentlemen. Wherefore King Arthur made the lands to be given again unto them that owned them.

When this was done, that the king had stablished all the countries about London, then he let make Sir Kay seneschal of England; and Sir Baudwin of Britain was made constable; and Sir Ulfius was made chamberlain; and Sir Brastias was made warden to wait upon the north from Trent forwards, for it was that time the most party the king's enemies. But within few years after Arthur won all the north, Scotland, and all that were under their obeissance. Also Wales, a part of it, held against Arthur, but he overcame them all, as he did the remnant, through the noble prowess of himself and his knights of the Round Table.

Chapter 8
How King Arthur held in Wales, at a Pentecost, a great feast, and what kings and lords came to his feast.

Then the king removed into Wales, and let cry a great feast that it should be holden at Pentecost after the incoronation of him at the city of Carlion. Unto the feast came King Lot of Lothian and of Orkney, with five hundred knights with him. Also there came to the feast King Uriens of Gore with four hundred knights with him. Also there came to that feast King Nentres of Garlot, with seven hundred knights with him. Also there came to the feast the king of Scotland with six hundred knights with him, and he was but a young man. Also there came to the feast a king that was called the King with the Hundred Knights, but he and his men were passing well beseen at all points. Also there came the king of Carados with five hundred knights. And King Arthur was glad of their coming, for he weened that all the kings and knights had come for great love, and to have done him worship at his feast; wherefore the king made great joy, and sent the kings and knights great presents. But the kings would none receive, but rebuked the messengers shamefully, and said they had no joy to receive no gifts of a beardless boy that was come of low blood, and sent him word they would none of his gifts, but that they were come to give him gifts with hard swords betwixt the neck and the shoulders: and therefore they came thither, so they told to the messengers plainly, for it was great shame to all them to see such a boy to have a rule of so noble a realm as this land was. With this answer the messengers departed and told to King Arthur this answer. Wherefore, by the advice of his barons, he took him to a strong tower with five hundred good men with him. And all the kings aforesaid in a manner laid a siege to-fore him, but King Arthur was well victualed. And within fifteen days there came Merlin among them into the city of Carlion. Then all the kings were passing glad of Merlin, and asked him, For what cause is that boy Arthur made your king? Sirs, said Merlin, I shall tell you the cause, for he is King Uther Pendragon's son, born in wedlock, gotten on Igraine, the duke's wife of Tintagil. Then is he a bastard, they said all. Nay, said Merlin, after the death of the duke, more than three hours, was Arthur begotten, and thirteen days after King Uther wedded Igraine; and therefore I prove him he is no bastard. And who saith nay, he shall be king and overcome all his enemies; and, or he die, he shall be long king of all England, and have under his obeissance Wales, Ireland, and Scotland, and more realms than I will now rehearse. Some of the kings had marvel of Merlin's words, and deemed well that it should be as he said; and some of them laughed him to scorn, as King Lot; and more other called him a witch. But then were they accorded with Merlin, that King Arthur should come out and speak with the kings, and to come safe and to go safe, such surance there was made. So Merlin went unto King Arthur, and told him how he had done, and bade him fear not, but come out boldly and speak with them, and spare them not, but answer them as their king and chieftain; for ye shall overcome them all, whether they will or nill.

Chapter 9
Of the first war that King Arthur had, and how he won the field.

Then King Arthur came out of his tower, and had under his gown a jesseraunt of double mail, and there went with him the Archbishop of Canterbury, and Sir Baudwin of Britain, and Sir Kay, and Sir Brastias: these were the men of most worship that were with him. And when they were met there was no meekness, but stout words on both sides; but always King Arthur answered them, and said he would make them to bow an he lived. Wherefore they departed with wrath, and King Arthur bade keep them well, and they bade the king keep him well. So the king returned him to the tower again and armed him and all his knights. What will ye do? said Merlin to the kings; ye were better for to stint, for ye shall not here prevail though ye were ten times so many. Be we well advised to be afeared of a dream-reader? said King Lot. With that Merlin vanished away, and came to King Arthur, and bade him set on them fiercely; and in the meanwhile there were three hundred good men, of the best that were with the kings, that went straight unto King Arthur, and that comforted him greatly. Sir, said Merlin to Arthur, fight not with the sword that ye had by miracle, till that ye see ye go unto the worse, then draw it out and do your best. So forthwithal King Arthur set upon them in their lodging. And Sir Baudwin, Sir Kay, and Sir Brastias slew on the right hand and on the left hand that it was marvel; and always King Arthur on horseback laid on with a sword, and did marvellous deeds of arms, that many of the kings had great joy of his deeds and hardiness.

Then King Lot brake out on the back side, and the King with the Hundred Knights, and King Carados, and set on Arthur fiercely behind him. With that Sir Arthur turned with his knights, and smote behind and before, and ever Sir Arthur was in the foremost press till his horse was slain underneath him. And therewith King Lot smote down King Arthur. With that his four knights received him and set him on horseback. Then he drew his sword Excalibur, but it was so bright in his enemies' eyes, that it gave light like thirty torches. And therewith he put them a-back, and slew much people. And then the commons of Carlion arose with clubs and staves and slew many knights; but all the kings held them together with their knights that were left alive, and so fled and departed. And Merlin came unto Arthur, and counselled him to follow them no further.

Chapter 10
How Merlin counselled King Arthur to send for King Ban and King Bors, and of their counsel taken for the war.

So after the feast and journey, King Arthur drew him unto London, and so by the counsel of Merlin, the king let call his barons to council, for Merlin had told the king that the six kings that made war upon him would in all haste be awroke on him and on his lands. Wherefore the king asked counsel at them all. They could no counsel give, but said they were big enough. Ye say well, said Arthur; I thank you for your good courage, but will ye all that loveth me speak with Merlin? ye know well that he hath done much for me, and he knoweth many things, and when he is afore you, I would that ye prayed him heartily of his best advice. All the barons said they would pray him and desire him. So Merlin was sent for, and fair desired of all the barons to give them best counsel. I shall say you, said Merlin, I warn you all, your enemies are passing strong for you, and they are good men of arms as be alive, and by this time they have gotten to them four kings more, and a mighty duke; and unless that our king have more chivalry with him than he may make within the bounds of his own realm, an he fight with them in battle, he shall be overcome and slain. What were best to do in this cause? said all the barons. I shall tell you, said Merlin, mine advice; there are two brethren beyond the sea, and they be kings both, and marvelous good men of their hands; and that one hight King Ban of Benwick, and that other hight King Bors of Gaul, that is France. And on these two kings warreth a mighty man of men, the King Claudas, and striveth with them for a castle, and great war is betwixt them. But this Claudas is so mighty of goods whereof he getteth good knights, that he putteth these two kings most part to the worse; wherefore this is my counsel, that our king and sovereign lord send unto the kings Ban and Bors by two trusty knights with letters well devised, that an they will come and see King Arthur and his court, and so help him in his wars, that he will be sworn unto them to help them in their wars against King Claudas. Now, what say ye unto this counsel? said Merlin. This is well counselled, said the king and all the barons.

Right so in all haste there were ordained to go two knights on the message unto the two kings. So were there made letters in the pleasant wise according unto King Arthur's desire. Ulfius and Brastias were made the messengers, and so rode forth well horsed and well armed and as the guise was that time, and so passed the sea and rode toward the city of Benwick. And there besides were eight knights that espied them, and at a strait passage they met with Ulfius and Brastias, and would have taken them prisoners; so they prayed them that they might pass, for they were messengers unto King Ban and Bors sent from King Arthur. Therefore, said the eight knights, ye shall die or be prisoners, for we be knights of King Claudas. And therewith two of them dressed their spears, and Ulfius and Brastias dressed their spears, and ran together with great raundom. And Claudas' knights brake their spears, and theirs to-held and bare the two knights out of their saddles to the earth, and so left them lying, and rode their ways. And the other six knights rode afore to a passage to meet with them again, and so Ulfius and Brastias smote other two down, and so passed on their ways. And at the fourth passage there met two for two, and both were laid unto the earth; so there was none of the eight knights but he was sore hurt or bruised. And when they come to Benwick it fortuned there were both kings, Ban and Bors.

And when it was told the kings that there were come messengers, there were sent unto them two knights of worship, the one hight Lionses, lord of the country of Payarne, and Sir Phariance a worshipful knight. Anon they asked from whence they came, and they said from King Arthur, king of England; so they took them in their arms and made great joy each of other. But anon, as the two kings wist they were messengers of Arthur's, there was made no tarrying, but forthwith they spake with the knights, and welcomed them in the faithfullest wise, and said they were most welcome unto them before all the kings living; and therewith they kissed the letters and delivered them. And when Ban and Bors understood the letters, then they were more welcome than they were before. And after the haste of the letters they gave them this answer, that they would fulfil the desire of King Arthur's writing, and Ulfius and Brastias, tarry there as long as they would, they should have such cheer as might be made them in those marches. Then Ulfius and Brastias told the kings of the adventure at their passages of the eight knights. Ha! ah! said Ban and Bors, they were my good friends. I would I had wist of them; they should not have escaped so. So Ulfius and Brastias had good cheer and great gifts, as much as they might bear away; and had their answer by mouth and by writing, that those two kings would come unto Arthur in all the haste that they might. So the two knights rode on afore, and passed the sea, and came to their lord, and told him how they had sped, whereof King Arthur was passing glad. At what time suppose ye the two kings will be here? Sir, said they, afore All Hallowmass. Then the king let purvey for a great feast, and let cry a great jousts. And by All Hallowmass the two kings were come over the sea with three hundred knights well arrayed both for the peace and for the war. And King Arthur met with them ten mile out of London, and there was great joy as could be thought or made. And on All Hallowmass at the great feast, sat in the hall the three kings, and Sir Kay seneschal served in the hall, and Sir Lucas the butler, that was Duke Corneus' son, and Sir Griflet, that was the son of Cardol, these three knights had the rule of all the service that served the kings. And anon, as they had washen and risen, all knights that would joust made them ready; by then they were ready on horseback there were seven hundred knights. And Arthur, Ban, and Bors, with the Archbishop of Canterbury, and Sir Ector, Kay's father, they were in a place covered with cloth of gold like an hall, with ladies and gentlewomen, for to behold who did best, and thereon to give judgment.

Chapter 11
Of a great tourney made by King Arthur and the two kings Ban and Bors, and how they went over the sea.

And King Arthur and the two kings let depart the seven hundred knights in two parties. And there were three hundred knights of the realm of Benwick and of Gaul turned on the other side. Then they dressed their shields, and began to couch their spears many good knights. So Griflet was the first that met with a knight, one Ladinas, and they met so eagerly that all men had wonder; and they so fought that their shields fell to pieces, and horse and man fell to the earth; and both the French knight and the English knight lay so long that all men weened they had been dead. When Lucas the butler saw Griflet so lie, he horsed him again anon, and they two did marvellous deeds of arms with many bachelors. Also Sir Kay came out of an ambushment with five knights with him, and they six smote other six down. But Sir Kay did that day marvellous deeds of arms, that there was none did so well as he that day. Then there came Ladinas and Gracian, two knights of France, and did passing well, that all men praised them.

Then came there Sir Placidas, a good knight, and met with Sir Kay, and smote him down horse and man, where fore Sir Griflet was wroth, and met with Sir Placidas so hard, that horse and man fell to the earth. But when the five knights wist that Sir Kay had a fall, they were wroth out of wit, and therewith each of them five bare down a knight. When King Arthur and the two kings saw them begin to wax wroth on both parties, they leapt on small hackneys, and let cry that all men should depart unto their lodging. And so they went home and unarmed them, and so to evensong and supper. And after, the three kings went into a garden, and gave the prize unto Sir Kay, and to Lucas the butler, and unto Sir Griflet. And then they went unto council, and with them Gwenbaus, the brother unto Sir Ban and Bors, a wise clerk, and thither went Ulfius and Brastias, and Merlin. And after they had been in council, they went unto bed. And on the morn they heard mass, and to dinner, and so to their council, and made many arguments what were best to do. At the last they were concluded, that Merlin should go with a token of King Ban, and that was a ring, unto his men and King Bors'; and Gracian and Placidas should go again and keep their castles and their countries, as for [dread of King Claudas] King Ban of Benwick, and King Bors of Gaul had ordained them, and so passed the sea and came to Benwick. And when the people saw King Ban's ring, and Gracian and Placidas, they were glad, and asked how the kings fared, and made great joy of their welfare and cording, and according unto the sovereign lords desire, the men of war made them ready in all haste possible, so that they were fifteen thousand on horse and foot, and they had great plenty of victual with them, by Merlin's provision. But Gracian and Placidas were left to furnish and garnish the castles, for dread of King Claudas. Right so Merlin passed the sea, well victualled both by water and by land. And when he came to the sea he sent home the footmen again, and took no more with him but ten thousand men on horseback, the most part men of arms, and so shipped and passed the sea into England, and landed at Dover; and through the wit of Merlin, he had the host northward, the priviest way that could be thought, unto the forest of Bedegraine, and there in a valley he lodged them secretly.

Then rode Merlin unto Arthur and the two kings, and told them how he had sped; whereof they had great marvel, that man on earth might speed so soon, and go and come. So Merlin told them ten thousand were in the forest of Bedegraine, well armed at all points. Then was there no more to say, but to horseback went all the host as Arthur had afore purveyed. So with twenty thousand he passed by night and day, but there was made such an ordinance afore by Merlin, that there should no man of war ride nor go in no country on this side Trent water, but if he had a token from King Arthur, where through the king's enemies durst not ride as they did to-fore to espy.

Lesson 81

- Read chapters 12-16 of *Le Morte D'Arthur*.

Chapter 12
How eleven kings gathered a great host against King Arthur.

And so within a little space the three kings came unto the castle of Bedegraine, and found there a passing fair fellowship, and well beseen, whereof they had great joy, and victual they wanted one. This was the cause of the northern host: that they were reared for the despite and rebuke the six kings had at Carlion. And those six kings by their means, gat unto them five other kings; and thus they began to gather their people.

And now they sware that for weal nor woe, they should not leave other, till they had destroyed Arthur. And then they made an oath. The first that began the oath was the Duke of Cambenet, that he would bring with him five thousand men of arms, the which were ready on horseback. Then sware King Brandegoris of

Stranggore that he would bring five thousand men of arms on horseback. Then sware King Clariance of Northumberland he would bring three thousand men of arms. Then sware the King of the Hundred Knights, that was a passing good man and a young, that he would bring four thousand men of arms on horseback. Then there swore King Lot, a passing good knight, and Sir Gawain's father, that he would bring five thousand men of arms on horseback. Also there swore King Urience, that was Sir Uwain's father, of the land of Gore, and he would bring six thousand men of arms on horseback. Also there swore King Idres of Cornwall, that he would bring five thousand men of arms on horseback. Also there swore King Cradelmas to bring fivethousand men on horseback. Also there swore King Agwisance of Ireland to bring five thousand men of arms on horseback. Also there swore King Nentres to bring five thousand men of arms on horseback. Also there swore King Carados to bring five thousand men of arms on horseback. So their whole host was of clean men of arms on horseback fifty thousand, and a-foot ten thousand of good men's bodies. Then were they soon ready, and mounted upon horse and sent forth their fore-riders, for these eleven kings in their ways laid a siege unto the castle of Bedegraine; and so they departed and drew toward Arthur, and left few to abide at the siege, for the castle of Bedegraine was holden of King Arthur, and the men that were therein were Arthur's.

Chapter 13
Of a dream of the King with the Hundred Knights.

So by Merlin's advice there were sent fore-riders to skim the country, and they met with the fore-riders of the north, and made them to tell which way the host came, and then they told it to Arthur, and by King Ban and Bors' council they let burn and destroy all the country afore them, there they should ride.

The King with the Hundred Knights met a wonder dream two nights afore the battle, that there blew a great wind, and blew down their castles and their towns, and after that came a water and bare it all away. All that heard of the sweven said it was a token of great battle. Then by counsel of Merlin, when they wist which way the eleven kings would ride and lodge that night, at midnight they set upon them, as they were in their pavilions. But the scout-watch by their host cried, Lords! at arms! for here be your enemies at your hand!

Chapter 14
How the eleven kings with their host fought against Arthur and his host, and many great feats of the war.

Then King Arthur and King Ban and King Bors, with their good and trusty knights, set on them so fiercely that they made them overthrow their pavilions on their heads, but the eleven kings, by manly prowess of arms, took a fair champaign, but there was slain that morrowtide ten thousand good men's bodies. And so they had afore them a strong passage, yet were they fifty thousand of hardy men. Then it drew toward day. Now shall ye do by mine advice, said Merlin unto the three kings: I would that King Ban and King Bors, with their fellowship of ten thousand men, were put in a wood here beside, in an ambushment, and keep them privy, and that they be laid or the light of the day come, and that they stir not till ye and your knights have fought with them long. And when it is daylight, dress your battle even afore them and the passage, that they may see all your host, for then will they be the more hardy, when they see you but about twenty thousand men, and cause them to be the gladder to suffer you and your host to come over the passage. All the three kings and the whole barons said that Merlin said passingly well, and it was done anon as Merlin had devised. So on the morn, when either host saw other, the host of the north was well comforted. Then to Ulfius and Brastias were delivered three thousand men of arms, and they set on them fiercely in the passage, and slew on the right hand and on the left hand that it was wonder to tell.

When that the eleven kings saw that there was so few a fellowship did such deeds of arms, they were ashamed and set on them again fiercely; and there was Sir Ulfius's horse slain under him, but he did marvellously well on foot. But the Duke Eustace of Cambenet and King Clariance of Northumberland, were always grievous on Ulfius. Then Brastias saw his fellow fared so withal he smote the duke with a spear, that horse and man fell down. That saw King Clariance and returned unto Brastias, and either smote other so that horse and man went to the earth, and so they lay long astonied, and their horses' knees brast to the hard bone. Then came Sir Kay the seneschal with six fellows with him, and did passing well. With that came the eleven kings, and there was Griflet put to the earth, horse and man, and Lucas the butler, horse and man, by King Brandegoris, and King Idres, and King Agwisance. Then waxed the medley passing hard on both parties. When Sir Kay saw Griflet on foot, he rode on King Nentres and smote him down, and led his horse unto Sir Griflet, and horsed him again. Also Sir Kay with the same spear smote down King Lot, and hurt him passing sore. That saw the King with the Hundred Knights, and ran unto Sir Kay and smote him down, and took his horse, and gave him King Lot, whereof he said gramercy. When Sir Griflet saw Sir Kay and Lucas the butler on foot, he took a sharp spear, great and square, and rode to Pinel, a good man of arms, and smote horse and man down, and then he took his horse, and gave him unto Sir Kay. Then King Lot saw King Nentres on foot, he ran unto Melot de la Roche, and smote him down, horse and man, and gave King Nentres the horse, and horsed him again. Also the King of the Hundred Knights saw King Idres on foot; then he ran unto Gwiniart de Bloi, and smote him down, horse and man, and gave King Idres the horse, and horsed him again; and King Lot smote down Clariance de la Forest Savage, and gave the horse unto Duke Eustace. And so when they had horsed the kings again they drew them, all eleven kings, together, and said they would be revenged of the damage that they had taken that day. The meanwhile came in Sir Ector with an eager countenance, and found Ulfius and Brastias on foot, in great peril of death, that were foul defoiled under horse-feet.

Then Arthur as a lion, ran unto King Cradelment of North Wales, and smote him through the left side, that the horse and the king fell down; and then he took the horse by the rein, and led him unto Ulfius, and said, Have this horse, mine old friend, for great need hast thou of horse. Gramercy, said Ulfius. Then Sir Arthur did so marvellously in arms, that all men had wonder. When the King with the Hundred Knights saw King Cradelment on foot, he ran unto Sir Ector, that was well horsed, Sir Kay's father, and smote horse and man down, and gave the horse unto the king, and horsed him again. And when King Arthur saw the king ride on Sir Ector's horse, he was wroth and with his sword he smote the king on the helm, that a quarter of the helm and shield fell down, and so the sword carved down unto the horse's neck, and so the king and the horse fell down to the ground. Then Sir Kay came unto Sir Morganore, seneschal with the King of the Hundred Knights, and smote him down, horse and man, and led the horse unto his father, Sir Ector; then Sir Ector ran unto a knight, hight Lardans, and smote horse and man down, and led the horse unto Sir Brastias, that great need had of an horse, and was greatly defoiled. When Brastias beheld Lucas the butler, that lay like a dead man under the horses' feet, and ever Sir Griflet did marvellously for to rescue him, and there were always fourteen knights on Sir Lucas; then Brastias smote one of them on the helm, that it went to the teeth, and he rode to another and smote him, that the arm flew into the field. Then he went to the third and smote him on the shoulder, that shoulder and arm flew in the field. And when Griflet saw rescues, he smote a knight on the temples, that head and helm went to the earth, and Griflet took the horse of that knight, and led him unto Sir Lucas, and bade him mount upon the horse and revenge his hurts. For Brastias had slain a knight to-fore and horsed Griflet.

Chapter 15
Yet of the same battle.

Then Lucas saw King Agwisance, that late had slain Moris de la Roche, and Lucas ran to him with a short spear that was great, that he gave him such a fall, that the horse fell down to the earth. Also Lucas found there on foot, Bloias de La Flandres, and Sir Gwinas, two hardy knights, and in that woodness that Lucas was in, he slew two bachelors and horsed them again. Then waxed the battle passing hard on both parties, but Arthur was glad that his knights were horsed again, and then they fought together, that the noise and sound rang by the water and the wood. Wherefore King Ban and King Bors made them ready, and dressed their shields and harness, and they were so courageous that many knights shook and bevered for eagerness. All this while Lucas, and Gwinas, and Briant, and Bellias of Flanders, held strong medley against six kings, that was King Lot, King Nentres, King Brandegoris, King Idres, King Uriens, and King Agwisance. So with the help of Sir Kay and of Sir Griflet they held these six kings hard, that unnethe they had any power to defend them. But when Sir Arthur saw the battle would not be ended by no manner, he fared wood as a lion, and steered his horse here and there, on the right hand, and on the left hand, that he stinted not till he had slain twenty knights. Also he wounded King Lot sore on the shoulder, and made him to leave that ground, for Sir Kay and Griflet did with King Arthur there great deeds of arms. Then Ulfius, and Brastias, and Sir Ector encountered against the Duke Eustace, and King Cradelment, and King Clariance of Northumberland, and King Carados, and against the King with the Hundred Knights. So these knights encountered with these kings, that they made them to avoid the ground. Then King Lot made great dole for his damages and his fellows, and said unto the ten kings, But if ye will do as I devise we shall be slain and destroyed; let me have the King with the Hundred Knights, and King Agwisance, and King Idres, and the Duke of Cambenet, and we five kings will have fifteen thousand men of arms with us, and we will go apart while ye six kings hold medley with twelve thousand; an we see that ye have foughten with them long, then will we come on fiercely, and else shall we never match them, said King Lot, but by this mean. So they departed as they here devised, and six kings made their party strong against Arthur, and made great war long.

In the meanwhile brake the ambushment of King Ban and King Bors, and Lionses and Phariance had the vanguard, and they two knights met with King Idres and his fellowship, and there began a great medley of breaking of spears, and smiting of swords, with slaying of men and horses, and King Idres was near at discomforture.

That saw Agwisance the king, and put Lionses and Phariance in point of death; for the Duke of Cambenet came on withal with a great fellowship. So these two knights were in great danger of their lives that they were fain to return, but always they rescued themselves and their fellowship marvellously When King Bors saw those knights put aback, it grieved him sore; then he came on so fast that his fellowship seemed as black as Inde. When King Lot had espied King Bors, he knew him well, then he said, O Jesu, defend us from death and horrible maims! for I see well we be in great peril of death; for I see yonder a king, one of the most worshipfullest men and one of the best knights of the world, is inclined unto his fellowship. What is he? said the King with the Hundred Knights. It is, said King Lot, King Bors of Gaul; I marvel how they came into this country without witting of us all. It was by Merlin's advice, said the knight. As for him, said King Carados, I will encounter with King Bors, an ye will rescue me when myster is. Go on, said they all, we will do all that we may. Then King Carados and his host rode on a soft pace, till that they came as nigh King Bors as bow-draught; then either battle let their horse run as fast as they might. And Bleoberis, that was godson unto King Bors, he bare his chief standard, that was a passing good knight. Now shall we see, said King Bors, how these northern Britons can bear the arms: and King Bors encountered with a knight, and smote him throughout with a spear that he fell dead unto the earth; and after drew his sword and did marvellous deeds of arms, that all parties had great wonder thereof; and his knights failed not, but did their part, and King Carados was smitten to the earth. With that came the King with the Hundred Knights and rescued King Carados mightily by force of arms, for he was a passing good knight of a king, and but a young man.

Chapter 16
Yet more of the same battle.

By then came into the field King Ban as fierce as a lion, with bands of green and thereupon gold. Ha! a! said King Lot, we must be discomfited, for yonder I see the most valiant knight of the world, and the man of the most renown, for such two brethren as is King Ban and King Bors are not living, wherefore we must needs void or die; and but if we avoid manly and wisely there is but death. When King Ban came into the battle, he came in so fiercely that the strokes redounded again from the wood and the water; wherefore King Lot wept for pity and dole that he saw so many good knights take their end. But through the great force of King Ban they made both the northern battles that were departed hurtled together for great dread; and the three kings and their knights slew on ever, that it was pity on to behold that multitude of the people that fled. But King Lot, and King of the Hundred Knights, and King Morganore gathered the people together passing knightly, and did great prowess of arms, and held the battle all that day, like hard.

When the King of the Hundred Knights beheld the great damage that King Ban did, he thrust unto him with his horse, and smote him on high upon the helm, a great stroke, and astonied him sore. Then King Ban was wroth with him, and followed on him fiercely; the other saw that, and cast up his shield, and spurred his horse forward, but the stroke of King Ban fell down and carved a cantel off the shield, and the sword slid down by the hauberk behind his back, and cut through the trapping of steel and the horse even in two pieces, that the sword felt the earth. Then the King of the Hundred Knights voided the horse lightly, and with his sword he broached the horse of King Ban through and through. With that King Ban voided lightly from the dead horse, and then King Ban smote at the other so eagerly, and smote him on the helm that he fell to the earth. Also in that ire he felled King Morganore, and there was great slaughter of good knights and much people. By then came into the press King Arthur, and found King Ban standing among dead men and dead horses, fighting on foot as a wood lion, that there came none nigh him, as far as he might reach with his sword, but he caught a grievous buffet; whereof King Arthur had great pity. And Arthur was so bloody, that by his shield there might no man know him, for all was blood and brains on his sword. And as Arthur looked by him he saw a knight that was passingly well horsed, and therewith Sir Arthur ran to him, and smote him on the helm, that his sword went unto his teeth, and the knight sank down to the earth dead, and anon Arthur took the horse by the rein, and led him unto King Ban, and said, Fair brother, have this horse, for he have great myster thereof, and me repenteth sore of your great damage. It shall be soon revenged, said King Ban, for I trust in God mine ure is not such but some of them may sore repent this. I will well, said Arthur, for I see your deeds full actual; nevertheless, I might not come at you at that time.

But when King Ban was mounted on horseback, then there began new battle, the which was sore and hard, and passing great slaughter. And so through great force King Arthur, King Ban, and King Bors made their knights a little to withdraw them. But alway the eleven kings with their chivalry never turned back; and so withdrew them to a little wood, and so over a little river, and there they rested them, for on the night they might have no rest on the field. And then the eleven kings and knights put them on a heap all together, as men adread and out of all comfort. But there was no man might pass them, they held them so hard together both behind and before, that King Arthur had marvel of their deeds of arms, and was passing wroth. Ah, Sir Arthur, said King Ban and King Bors, blame them not, for they do as good men ought to do. For by my faith, said King Ban, they are the best fighting men, and knights of most prowess, that ever I saw or heard speak of, and those eleven kings are men of great worship; and if they were longing unto you there were no king under the heaven had such eleven knights, and of such worship. I may not love them, said Arthur, they would destroy me. That wot we well, said King Ban and King Bors, for they are your mortal enemies, and that hath been proved aforehand; and this day they have done their part, and that is great pity of their wilfulness.

Then all the eleven kings drew them together, and then said King Lot, Lords, ye must other ways than ye do, or else the great loss is behind; ye may see what people we have lost, and what good men we lose, because we wait always on these foot-men, and ever in saving of one of the foot-men we lose ten horsemen for him; therefore this is mine advice, let us put our foot-men from us, for it is near night, for the noble Arthur will not tarry on the footmen, for they may save themselves, the wood is near hand. And when we horsemen be together, look every each of you kings let make such ordinance that none break upon pain of death. And who that seeth any man dress him to flee, lightly that he be slain, for it is better that we slay a coward, than through a coward all we to be slain. How say ye? said King Lot, answer me all ye kings. It is well said, quoth King Nentres; so said the King of the Hundred Knights; the same said the King Carados, and King Uriens; so did King Idres and King Brandegoris; and so did King Cradelment, and the Duke of

Cambenet; the same said King Clariance and King Agwisance, and sware they would never fail other, neither for life nor for death. And whoso that fled, but did as they did, should be slain. Then they amended their harness, and righted their shields, and took new spears and set them on their thighs, and stood still as it had been a plump of wood.

Lesson 82

- Read chapters 17-21 of *Le Morte D'Arthur.*

Chapter 17
Yet more of the same battle, and how it was ended by Merlin.

When Sir Arthur and King Ban and Bors beheld them and all their knights, they praised them much for their noble cheer of chivalry, for the hardiest fighters that ever they heard or saw. With that, there dressed them a forty noble knights, and saidunto the three kings, they would break their battle; these were their names: Lionses, Phariance, Ulfius, Brastias, Ector, Kay, Lucas the butler, Griflet le Fise de Dieu, Mariet de la Roche, Guinas de Bloi, Briant de la Forest Savage, Bellaus, Morians of the Castle [of] Maidens, Flannedrius of the Castle of Ladies, Annecians that was King Bors' godson, a noble knight, Ladinas de la Rouse, Emerause, Caulas, Graciens le Castlein, one Blois de la Case, and Sir Colgrevaunce de Gorre; all these knights rode on afore with spears on their thighs, and spurred their horses mightily as the horses might run. And the eleven kings with part of their knights rushed with their horses as fast as they might with their spears, and there they did on both parties marvelous deeds of arms. So came into the thick of the press, Arthur, Ban, and Bors, and slew down right on both hands, that their horses went in blood up to the fetlocks. But ever the eleven kings and their host was ever in the visage of Arthur. Wherefore Ban and Bors had great marvel, considering the great slaughter that there was, but at the last they were driven aback over a little river. With that came Merlin on a great black horse, and said unto Arthur, Thou hast never done! Hast thou not done enough? of three score thousand this day hast thou left alive but fifteen thousand, and it is time to say Ho! For God is wroth with thee, that thou wilt never have done; for yonder eleven kings at this time will not be overthrown, but an thou tarry on them any longer, thy fortune will turn and they shall increase. And therefore withdraw you unto your lodging, and rest you as soon as ye may, and reward your good knights with gold and with silver, for they have well deserved it; there may no riches be too dear for them, for of so few men as ye have, there were never men did more of prowess than they have done today, for ye have matched this day with the best fighters of the world. That is truth, said King Ban and Bors. Also said Merlin, withdraw you where ye list, for this three year I dare undertake they shall not dere you; and by then ye shall hear new tidings. And then Merlin said unto Arthur, These eleven kings have more on hand than they are ware of, for the Saracens are landed in their countries, more than forty thousand, that burn and slay, and have laid siege at the castle Wandesborow, and make great destruction; therefore dread you not this three year. Also, sir, all the goods that be gotten at this battle, let it be searched, and when ye have it in your hands, let it be given freely unto these two kings, Ban and Bors, that they may reward their knights withal; and that shall cause strangers to be of better will to do you service at need. Also you be able to reward your own knights of your own goods whensomever it liketh you. It is well said, quoth Arthur, and as thou hast devised, so shall it be done. When it was delivered to Ban and Bors, they gave the goods as freely to their knights as freely as it was given to them. Then Merlin took his leave of Arthur and of the two kings, for to go and see his master Bleise, that dwelt in Northumberland; and so he departed and came to his master, that was passing glad of his coming; and there he told how Arthur and the two kings had sped at the great battle, and how it was ended, and told the names of every king and knight of worship that was there. And so Bleise wrote the battle word by word, as Merlin told him, how it began, and by whom, and in likewise how it was ended, and who had the worse. All the battles that were done in Arthur's days Merlin did his master Bleise do write; also he did do write all the battles that every worthy knight did of Arthur's court.

After this Merlin departed from his master and came to King Arthur, that was in the castle of Bedegraine, that was one of the castles that stand in the forest of Sherwood. And Merlin was so disguised that King Arthur knew him not, for he was all befurred in black sheep-skins, and a great pair of boots, and a bow and arrows, in a russet gown, and brought wild geese in his hand, and it was on the morn after Candlemas day; but King Arthur knew him not. Sir, said Merlin unto the king, will ye give me a gift? Wherefore, said King Arthur, should I give thee a gift, churl?

Sir, said Merlin, ye were better to give me a gift that is not in your hand than to lose great riches, for here in the same place where the great battle was, is great treasure hid in the earth. Who told thee so, churl? said Arthur. Merlin told me so, said he. Then Ulfius and Brastias knew him well enough, and smiled. Sir, said these two knights, it is Merlin that so speaketh unto you. Then King Arthur was greatly abashed, and had marvel of Merlin, and so had King Ban and King Bors, and so they had great disport at him. So in the meanwhile there came a damosel that was an earl's daughter: his name was Sanam, and her name was Lionors, a passing fair damosel; and so she came thither for to do homage, as other lords did after the great battle. And King Arthur set his love greatly upon her, and so did she upon him, and the king had ado with her, and gat on her a child: his name was Borre, that was after a good knight, and of the Table Round. Then there came word that the King Rience of North Wales made great war on King Leodegrance of Cameliard, for the which thing Arthur was wroth, for he loved him well, and hated King Rience, for he was alway against him. So by ordinance of the three kings that were sent home unto Benwick, all they would depart for dread of King Claudas; and Phariance, and Antemes, and Gratian, and Lionses [of] Payarne, with the leaders of those that should keep the kings' lands.

Chapter 18
How King Arthur, King Ban, and King Bors rescued King Leodegrance, and other incidents.

And then King Arthur, and King Ban, and King Bors departed with their fellowship, a twenty thousand, and came within six days into the country of Cameliard, and there rescued King Leodegrance, and slew there much people of King Rience, unto the number of ten thousand men, and put him to flight. And then had these three kings great cheer of King Leodegrance, that thanked them of their great goodness, that they would revenge him of his enemies; and there had Arthur the first sight of Guenever, the king's daughter of Cameliard, and ever after he loved her. After they were wedded, as it telleth in the book. So, briefly to make an end, they took their leave to go into their own countries, for King Claudas did great destruction on their lands. Then said Arthur, I will go with you. Nay, said the kings, ye shall not at this time, for ye have much to do yet in these lands, therefore we will depart, and with the great goods that we have gotten in these lands by your gifts, we shall wage good knights and withstand the King Claudas' malice, for by the grace of God, an we have need we will send to you for your succour; and if ye have need, send for us, and we will not tarry, by the faith of our bodies. It shall not, said Merlin, need that these two kings come again in the way of war, but I know well King Arthur may not be long from you, for within a year or two ye shall have great need, and then shall he revenge you on your enemies, as ye have done on his. For these eleven kings shall die all in a day, by the great might and prowess of arms of two valiant knights (as it telleth after); their names be Balin le Savage, and Balan, his brother, that be marvellous good knights as be any living.

Now turn we to the eleven kings that returned unto a city that hight Sorhaute, the which city was within King Uriens ‘, and there they refreshed them as well as they might, and made leeches search their wounds, and sorrowed greatly for the death of their people. With that there came a messenger and told how there was come into their lands people that were lawless as well as Saracens, a forty thousand, and have burnt and slain all the people that they may come by, without mercy, and have laid siege on the castle of Wandesborow. Alas, said the eleven kings, here is sorrow upon sorrow, and if we had not warred against Arthur as we have done, he would soon revenge us. As for King Leodegrance, he loveth Arthur better than us, and as for King Rience, he hath enough to do with Leodegrance, for he hath laid siege unto him. So they consented together to keep all the marches of Cornwall, of Wales, and of the North. So first, they put King Idres in the City of Nauntes in Britain, with four thousand men of arms, to watch both the water and the land. Also they put in the city of Windesan, King Nentres of Garlot, with four thousand knights to watch both on water and on land. Also they had of other men of war more than eight thousand, for to fortify all the fortresses in the marches of Cornwall. Also they put more knights in all the marches of Wales and Scotland, with many good men of arms, and so they kept them together the space of three year, and ever allied them with mighty kings and dukes and lords. And to them fell King Rience of North Wales, the which and Nero that was a mighty man of men. And all this while they furnished them and garnished them of good men of arms, and victual, and of all manner of habiliment that pretendeth to the war, to avenge them for the battle of Bedegraine, as it telleth in the book of adventures following.

Chapter 19
How King Arthur rode to Carlion, and of his dream, and how he saw the questing beast.

Then after the departing of King Ban and of King Bors, King Arthur rode into Carlion. And thither came to him, King Lot's wife, of Orkney, in manner of a message, but she was sent thither to espy the court of King Arthur; and she came richly beseen, with her four sons, Gawaine, Gaheris, Agravine, and Gareth, with many other knights and ladies. For she was a passing fair lady, therefore the king cast great love unto her, and desired to lie by her; so they were agreed, and he begat upon her Mordred, and she was his sister, on his mother's side, Igraine. So there she rested her a month, and at the last departed. Then the king dreamed a marvellous dream whereof he was sore adread. But all this time King Arthur knew not that King Lot's wife was his sister. Thus was the dream of Arthur: Him thought there was come into this land griffins and serpents, and him thought they burnt and slew all the people in the land, and then him thought he fought with them, and they did him passing great harm, and wounded him full sore, but at the last he slew them. When the king awaked, he was passing heavy of his dream, and so to put it out of thoughts, he made him ready with many knights to ride a-hunting. As soon as he was in the forest the king saw a great hart afore him. This hart will I chase, said King Arthur, and so he spurred the horse, and rode after long, and so by fine force oft he was like to have smitten the hart; whereas the king had chased the hart so long, that his horse lost his breath, and fell down dead. Then a yeoman fetched the king another horse.

So the king saw the hart enbushed, and his horse dead, he set him down by a fountain, and there he fell in great thoughts. And as he sat so, him thought he heard a noise of hounds, to the sum of thirty. And with that the king saw coming toward him the strangest beast that ever he saw or heard of; so the beast went to the well and drank, and the noise was in the beast's belly like unto the questing of thirty couple hounds; but all the while the beast drank there was no noise in the beast's belly: and there.with the beast departed with a great noise, whereof the king had great marvel. And so he was in a great thought, and therewith he fell asleep. Right so there came a knight afoot unto Arthur and said, Knight full of thought and sleepy, tell me if thou sawest a strange beast pass this way. Such one saw I, said King Arthur, that is past two mile; what would ye with the beast? said Arthur. Sir, I have followed that beast long time, and killed mine horse, so would God I had another to follow my quest. Right so came one with the king's horse, and when the knight saw the horse, he prayed the king to give him the horse: for I have followed this quest this twelvemonth, and either I shall achieve him, or bleed of the best blood of my body. Pellinore, that time king, followed the Questing Beast, and after his death Sir Palamides followed it.

Chapter 20
How King Pellinore took Arthur's horse and followed the Questing Beast, and how Merlin met with Arthur.

Sir knight, said the king, leave that quest, and suffer me to have it, and I will follow it another twelvemonth. Ah, fool, said the knight unto Arthur, it is in vain thy desire, for it shall never be achieved but by me, or my next kin. Therewith he started unto the king's horse and mounted into the saddle, and said, Gramercy, this horse is my own. Well, said the king, thou mayst take my horse by force, but an I might prove thee whether thou were better on horseback or I.--Well, said the knight, seek me here when thou wilt, and here nigh this well thou shalt find me, and so passed on his way. Then the king sat in a study, and bade his men fetch his horse as fast as ever they might. Right so came by him Merlin like a child of fourteen year of age, and saluted the king, and asked him why he was so pensive. I may well be pensive, said the king, for I have seen the marvellest sight that ever I saw. That know I well, said Merlin, as well as thyself, and of all thy thoughts, but thou art but a fool to take thought, for it will not amend thee. Also I know what thou art, and who was thy father, and of whom thou wert begotten; King Uther Pendragon was thy father, and begat thee on Igraine. That is false, said King Arthur, how shouldest thou know it, for thou art not so old of years to know my father? Yes, said Merlin, I know it better than ye or any man living. I will not believe thee, said Arthur, and was wroth with the child. So departed Merlin, and came again in the likeness of an old man of fourscore year of age, whereof the king was right glad, for he seemed to be right wise.

Then said the old man, Why are ye so sad? I may well be heavy, said Arthur, for many things. Also here was a child, and told me many things that meseemeth he should not know, for he was not of age to know my father. Yes, said the old man, the child told you truth, and more would he have told you an ye would have suffered him. But ye have done a thing late that God is displeased with you, for ye have lain by your sister, and on her ye have gotten a child that shall destroy you and all the knights of your realm. What are ye, said Arthur, that tell me these tidings? I am Merlin, and I was he in the child's likeness. Ah, said King Arthur, ye are a marvellous man, but I marvel much of thy words that I must die in battle. Marvel not, said Merlin, for it is God's will your body to be punished for your foul deeds; but I may well be sorry, said Merlin, for I shall die a shameful death, to be put in the earth quick, and ye shall die a worshipful death. And as they talked this, came one with the king's horse, and so the king mounted on his horse, and Merlin on another, and so rode unto Carlion. And anon the king asked Ector and Ulfius how he was begotten, and they told him Uther Pendragon was his father and Queen Igraine his mother. Then he said to Merlin, I will that my mother be sent for that I may speak with her; and if she say so herself then will I believe it. In all haste, the queen was sent for, and she came and brought with her Morgan le Fay, her daughter, that was as fair a lady as any might be, and the king welcomed Igraine in the best manner.

Chapter 21
How Ulfius impeached Queen Igraine, Arthur's mother, of treason; and how a knight came and desired to have the death of his master revenged.

Right so came Ulfius, and said openly, that the king and all might hear that were feasted that day, Ye are the falsest lady of the world, and the most traitress unto the king's person. Beware, said Arthur, what thou sayest; thou speakest a great word. I am well ware, said Ulfius, what I speak, and here is my glove to prove it upon any man that will say the contrary, that this Queen Igraine is causer of your great damage, and of your great war. For, an she would have uttered it in the life of King Uther Pendragon, of the birth of you, and how ye were begotten ye had never had the mortal wars that ye have had; for the most part of your barons of your realm knew never whose son ye were, nor of whom ye were begotten; and she that bare you of her body should have made it known openly in excusing of her worship and yours, and in like wise to all the realm, wherefore I prove her false to God and to you and to all your realm, and who will say the contrary I will prove it on his body.

Then spake Igraine and said, I am a woman and I may not fight, but rather than I should be dishonoured, there would some good man take my quarrel. More, she said, Merlin knoweth well, and ye Sir Ulfius, how King Uther came to me in the

Castle of Tintagil in the likeness of my lord, that was dead three hours to-fore, and thereby gat a child that night upon me. And after the thirteenth day King Uther wedded me, and by his commandment when the child was born it was delivered unto Merlin and nourished by him, and so I saw the child never after, nor wot not what is his name, for I knew him never yet. And there, Ulfius said to the queen, Merlin is more to blame than ye. Well I wot, said the queen, I bare a child by my lord King Uther, but I wot not where he is become. Then Merlin took the king by the hand, saying, This is your mother. And therewith Sir Ector bare witness how he nourished him by Uther's commandment. And therewith King Arthur took his mother, Queen Igraine, in his arms and kissed her, and either wept upon other. And then the king let make a feast that lasted eight days.

Then on a day there came in the court a squire on horseback, leading a knight before him wounded to the death, and told him how there was a knight in the forest had reared up a pavilion by a well, and hath slain my master, a good knight, his name was Miles; wherefore I beseech you that my master may be buried, and that some knight may revenge my master's death. Then the noise was great of that knight's death in the court, and every man said his advice. Then came Griflet that was but a squire, and he was but young, of the age of the king Arthur, so he besought the king for all his service that he had done him to give the order of knighthood.

Lesson 83

- Read chapters 22-27 of *Le Morte D'Arthur*.

Chapter 22
How Griflet was made knight, and jousted with a knight

Thou art full young and tender of age, said Arthur, for to take so high an order on thee. Sir, said Griflet, I beseech you make me knight. Sir, said Merlin, it were great pity to lose Griflet, for he will be a passing good man when he is of age, abiding with you the term of his life. And if he adventure his body with yonder knight at the fountain, it is in great peril if ever he come again, for he is one of the best knights of the world, and the strongest man of arms. Well, said Arthur. So at the desire of Griflet the king made him knight. Now, said Arthur unto Sir Griflet, sith I have made you knight thou must give me a gift. What ye will, said Griflet. Thou shalt promise me by the faith of thy body, when thou hast jousted with the knight at the fountain, whether it fall ye be on foot or on horseback, that right so ye shall come again unto me without making any more debate. I will promise you, said Griflet, as you desire. Then took Griflet his horse in great haste, and dressed his shield and took a spear in his hand, and so he rode a great wallop till he came to the fountain, and thereby he saw a rich pavilion, and thereby under a cloth stood a fair horse well saddled and bridled, and on a tree a shield of divers colours and a great spear. Then Griflet smote on the shield with the butt of his spear, that the shield fell down to the ground. With that the knight came out of the pavilion, and said, Fair knight, why smote ye down my shield? For I will joust with you, said Griflet. It is better ye do not, said the knight, for ye are but young, and late made knight, and your might is nothing to mine. As for that, said Griflet, I will joust with you. That is me loath, said the knight, but sith I must needs, I will dress me thereto. Of whence be ye? said the knight. Sir, I am of Arthur's court. So the two knights ran together that Griflet's spear all to-shivered; and there withal he smote Griflet through the shield and the left side, and brake the spear that the truncheon stuck in his body, that horse and knight fell down.

Chapter 23
How twelve knights came from Rome and asked truage for this land of Arthur, and how Arthur fought with a knight.

When the knight saw him lie so on the ground, he alighted, and was passing heavy, for he weened he had slain him, and then he unlaced his helm and gat him wind, and so with the truncheon he set him on his horse, and so betook him to God, and said he had a mighty heart, and if he might live he would prove a passing good knight. And so Sir Griflet rode to the court, where great dole was made for him. But through good leeches he was healed and saved. Right so came into the court twelve knights, and were aged men, and they came from the Emperor of Rome, and they asked of Arthur truage for this realm, other else the emperor would destroy him and his land. Well, said King Arthur, ye are messengers, therefore ye may say what ye will, other else ye should die therefore. But this is mine answer: I owe the emperor no truage, nor none will I hold him, but on a fair field I shall give him my truage that shall be with a sharp spear, or else with a sharp sword, and that shall not be long, by my father's soul, Uther Pendragon. And therewith the messengers departed passingly wroth, and King Arthur as wroth, for in evil time came they then; for the king was passingly wroth for the hurt of Sir Griflet. And so he commanded a privy man of his chamber that or it be day his best horse and armour, with all that longeth unto his person, be without the city or to-morrow day. Right so or to-morrow day he met with his man and his horse, and so mounted up and dressed his shield and took his spear, and bade his chamberlain tarry there till he came again. And so Arthur rode a soft pace till it was day, and then was he ware of three churls chasing Merlin, and would have slain him. Then the king rode unto them, and bade them: Flee, churls! then were they afeard when they saw a knight, and fled. O Merlin, said Arthur, here hadst thou been slain for all thy crafts had I not been. Nay, said Merlin, not so, for I could save myself an I would; and thou art more near thy death than I am, for thou goest to the deathward, an God be not thy friend.

So as they went thus talking they came to the fountain, and the rich pavilion there by it. Then King Arthur was ware where sat a knight armed in a chair. Sir knight, said Arthur, for what cause abidest thou here, that there may no knight ride this way but if he joust with thee? said the king. I rede thee leave that custom, said Arthur. This custom, said the knight, have I used and will use maugre who saith nay, and who is grieved with my custom let him amend it that will. I will amend it, said Arthur. I shall defend thee, said the knight. Anon he took his horse and dressed his shield and took a spear, and they met so hard either in other's shields, that all to-shivered their spears. Therewith anon Arthur pulled out his sword. Nay, not so, said the knight; it is fairer, said the knight, that we twain run more together with sharp spears. I will well, said Arthur, an I had any more spears. I have enow, said the knight; so there came a squire and brought two good spears, and Arthur chose one and he another; so they spurred their horses and came together with all their mights, that either brake their spears to their hands. Then Arthur set hand on his sword. Nay, said the knight, ye shall do better, ye are a passing good jouster as ever I met withal, and once for the love of the high order of knighthood let us joust once again. I assent me, said Arthur. Anon there were brought two great spears, and every knight gat a spear, and therewith they ran together that Arthur's spear all to-shivered. But the other knight hit him so hard in midst of the shield, that horse and man fell to the earth, and therewith Arthur was eager, and pulled out his sword, and said, I will assay thee, sir knight, on foot, for I have lost the honour on horseback.

I will be on horseback, said the knight. Then was Arthur wroth, and dressed his shield toward him with his sword drawn. When the knight saw that, he alighted, for him thought no worship to have a knight at such avail, he to be on horseback and he on foot, and so he alighted and dressed his shield unto Arthur. And there began a strong battle with many great strokes, and so hewed with their swords that the cantels flew in the fields, and much blood they bled both, that all the place there as they fought was overbled with blood, and thus they fought long and rested them, and then they went to the battle again, and so hurtled together like two rams that either fell to the earth. So at the last they smote together that both their swords met even together. But the sword of the knight smote King Arthur's sword in two pieces, wherefore he was heavy. Then said the knight unto Arthur, Thou art in my daunger whether me list to save thee or slay thee, and but thou yield thee as overcome and recreant, thou shalt die. As for death, said King Arthur, welcome be it when it cometh, but to yield me unto thee as recreant I had liefer die than to be so shamed. And therewithal the king leapt unto Pellinore, and took him by the middle and threw him down, and raced off his helm. When the knight felt that he was adread, for he was a passing big man of might, and anon he brought Arthur under him, and raced off his helm and would have smitten off his head.

Chapter 24
How Merlin saved Arthur's life, and threw an enchantment on King Pellinore and made him to sleep.

Therewithal came Merlin and said, Knight, hold thy hand, for an thou slay that knight thou puttest this realm in the greatest damage that ever was realm: for this knight is a man of more worship than thou wotest of. Why, who is he? said the knight. It is King Arthur. Then would he have slain him for dread of his wrath, and heaved up his sword, and therewith Merlin cast an enchantment to the knight, that he fell to the earth in a great sleep. Then Merlin took up King Arthur, and rode forth on the knight's horse. Alas! said Arthur, what hast thou done, Merlin? hast thou slain this good knight by thy crafts? There liveth not so worshipful a knight as he was; I had liefer than the stint of my land a year that he were alive. Care ye not, said Merlin, for he is wholer than ye; for he is but asleep, and will awake within three hours. I told you, said Merlin, what a knight he was; here had ye been slain had I not been. Also there liveth not a bigger knight than he is one, and he shall hereafter do you right good service; and his name is Pellinore, and he shall have two sons that shall be passing good men; save one they shall have no fellow of prowess and of good living, and their names shall be Percivale of Wales and Lamerake of Wales, and he shall tell you the name of your own son, begotten of your sister, that shall be the destruction of all this realm.

Chapter 25
How Arthur by the mean of Merlin gat Excalibur his sword of the Lady of the Lake.

Right so the king and he departed, and went unto an hermit that was a good man and a great leech. So the hermit searched all his wounds and gave him good salves; so the king was there three days, and then were his wounds well amended that he might ride and go, and so departed. And as they rode, Arthur said, I have no sword. No force, said Merlin, hereby is a sword that shall be yours, an I may. So they rode till they came to a lake, the which was a fair water and broad, and in the midst of the lake Arthur was ware of an arm clothed in white samite, that held a fair sword in that hand. Lo! said Merlin, yonder is that sword that I spake of. With that they saw a damosel going upon the lake. What damosel is that? said Arthur. That is the Lady of the Lake, said Merlin; and within that lake is a rock, and therein is as fair a place as any on earth, and richly beseen; and this damosel will come to you anon, and then speak ye fair to her that she will give you that sword. Anon withal came the damosel unto Arthur, and saluted him, and he her again. Damosel, said Arthur, what sword is that, that yonder the arm holdeth above the water? I would it were mine, for I have no sword. Sir Arthur, king, said the damosel, that sword is mine, and if ye will give me a gift when I ask it you, ye shall have it. By my faith, said Arthur, I will give you what gift ye will ask. Well! said the damosel, go ye into yonder barge, and row yourself to the sword, and take it and the scabbard with you, and I will ask my gift when I see my time. So Sir Arthur and Merlin alighted and tied their horses to two trees, and so they went into the ship, and when they came to the sword that the hand held, Sir Arthur took it up by the handles, and took it with him, and the arm and the hand went under the water. And so [they] came unto the land and rode forth, and then Sir Arthur saw a rich pavilion. What signifieth yonder pavilion? It is the knight's pavilion, said Merlin, that ye fought with last, Sir Pellinore; but he is out, he is not there. He hath ado with a knight of yours that hight Egglame, and they have foughten together, but at the last Egglame fled, and else he had been dead, and he hath chased him even to Carlion, and we shall meet with him anon in the highway. That is well said, said Arthur, now have I a sword, now will I wage battle with him, and be avenged on him. Sir, you shall not so, said Merlin, for the knight is weary of fighting and chasing, so that ye shall have no worship to have ado with him; also he will not be lightly matched of one knight living, and therefore it is my counsel, let him pass, for he shall do you good service in short time, and his sons after his days. Also ye shall see that day in short space, you shall be right glad to give him your sister to wed. When I see him, I will do as ye advise, said Arthur.

Then Sir Arthur looked on the sword, and liked it passing well. Whether liketh you better, said Merlin, the sword or the scabbard? Me liketh better the sword, said Arthur. Ye are more unwise, said Merlin, for the scabbard is worth ten of the swords, for whiles ye have the scabbard upon you, ye shall never lose no blood, be ye never so sore wounded; therefore keep well the scabbard always with you. So they rode unto Carlion, and by the way they met with Sir Pellinore; but Merlin had done such a craft, that Pellinore saw not Arthur, and he passed by without any words. I marvel, said Arthur, that the knight would not speak. Sir, said Merlin, he saw you not, for an he had seen you, ye had not lightly departed. So they came unto Carlion, whereof his knights were passing glad. And when they heard of his adventures, they marvelled that he would jeopard his person so, alone. But all men of worship said it was merry to be under such a chieftain, that would put his person in adventure as other poor knights did.

Chapter 26
How tidings came to Arthur that King Rience had overcome eleven kings, and how he desired Arthur's beard to trim his mantle.

This meanwhile came a messenger from King Rience of North Wales, and king he was of all Ireland, and of many isles. And this was his message, greeting well King Arthur in this manner wise, saying that King Rience had discomfited and overcome eleven kings, and everych of them did him homage, and that was this, they gave him their beards clean flayed off, as much as there was; wherefore the messenger came for King Arthur's beard. For King Rience had purfled a mantle with kings' beards, and there lacked one place of the mantle; wherefore he sent for his beard, or else he would enter into his lands, and burn and slay, and never leave till he have the head and the beard. Well, said Arthur, thou hast said thy message, the which is the most villainous and lewdest message that ever man heard sent unto a king; also thou mayest see my beard is full young yet to make a purfle of it. But tell thou thy king this: I owe him none homage, nor none of mine elders; but or it be long to, he shall do me homage on both his knees, or else he shall lose his head, by the faith of my body, for this is the most shamefulest message that ever I heard speak of. I have espied thy king met never yet with worshipful man, but tell him, I will have his head without he do me homage. Then the messenger departed.

Now is there any here, said Arthur, that knoweth King Rience? Then answered a knight that hight Naram, Sir, I know the king well; he is a passing good man of his body, as few be living, and a passing proud man, and Sir, doubt ye not he will make war on you with a mighty puissance. Well, said Arthur, I shall ordain for him in short time.

Chapter 27
How all the children were sent for that were born on May-day, and how Mordred was saved.

Then King Arthur let send for all the children born on May-day, begotten of lords and born of ladies; for Merlin told King Arthur that he that should destroy him should be born on May-day, wherefore he sent for them all, upon pain of death; and so there were found many lords' sons, and all were sent unto the king, and so was Mordred sent by King Lot's wife, and all were put in a ship to the sea, and some were four weeks old, and some less. And so by fortune the ship drave unto a castle, and was all to-riven, and destroyed the most part, save that Mordred was cast up, and a good man found him, and nourished him till he was fourteen year old, and then he brought him to the court, as it rehearseth afterward, toward the end of the Death of Arthur. So many lords and barons of this realm were displeased, for their children were so lost, and many put the wite on Merlin more than on Arthur; so what for dread and for love, they held their peace. But when the messenger came to King Rience, then was he wood out of measure, and purveyed him for a great host, as it rehearseth after in the book of Balin le Savage, that followeth next after, how by adventure Balin gat the sword.

Lesson 84

- Read chapters 1-5 of Book 2 of *Le Morte D'Arthur.*

Chapter 1
Of a damosel which came girt with a sword for to find a man of such virtue to draw it out of the scabbard.

After the death of Uther Pendragon reigned Arthur his son, the which had great war in his days for to get all England into his hand. For there were many kings within the realm of England, and in Wales, Scotland, and Cornwall. So it befell on a time when King Arthur was at London, there came a knight and told the king tidings how that the King Rience of North Wales had reared a great number of people, and were entered into the land, and burnt and slew the king's true liege people. If this be true, said Arthur, it were great shame unto mine estate but that he were mightily withstood. It is truth, said the knight, for I saw the host myself. Well, said the king, let make a cry, that all the lords, knights, and gentlemen of arms, should draw unto a castle called Camelot in those days, and there the king would let make a council-general and a great jousts.

So when the king was come thither with all his baronage, and lodged as they seemed best, there was come a damosel the which was sent on message from the great lady Lile of Avelion. And when she came before King Arthur, she told from whom she came, and how she was sent on message unto him for these causes. Then she let her mantle fall that was richly furred; and then was she girt with a noble sword whereof the king had marvel, and said, Damosel, for what cause are ye girt with that sword? it beseemeth you not. Now shall I tell you, said the damosel; this sword that I am girt withal doth me great sorrow and cumbrance, for I may not be delivered of this sword but by a knight, but he must be a passing good man of his hands and of his deeds, and without villainy or treachery, and without treason. And if I may find such a knight that hath all these virtues, he may draw out this sword out of the sheath, for I have been at King Rience's it was told me there were passing good knights, and he and all his knights have assayed it and none can speed. This is a great marvel, said Arthur, if this be sooth; I will myself assay to draw out the sword, not presuming upon myself that I am the best knight, but that I will begin to draw at your sword in giving example to all the barons that they shall assay everych one after other when I have assayed it. Then Arthur took the sword by the sheath and by the girdle and pulled at it eagerly, but the sword would not out.

Sir, said the damosel, you need not to pull half so hard, for he that shall pull it out shall do it with little might. Ye say well, said Arthur; now assay ye all my barons; but beware ye be not defiled with shame, treachery, nor guile. Then it will not avail, said the damosel, for he must be a clean knight without villainy, and of a gentle strain of father side and mother side. Most of all the barons of the Round Table that were there at that time assayed all by row, but there might none speed; wherefore the damosel made great sorrow out of measure, and said, Alas! I weened in this court had been the best knights without treachery or treason. By my faith, said Arthur, here are good knights, as I deem, as any be in the world, but their grace is not to help you, wherefore I am displeased.

Chapter 2
How Balin, arrayed like a poor knight, pulled out the sword, which afterward was the cause of his death.

Then fell it so that time there was a poor knight with King Arthur, that had been prisoner with him half a year and more for slaying of a knight, the which was cousin unto King Arthur. The name of this knight was called Balin, and by good means of the barons he was delivered out of prison, for he was a good man named of his body, and he was born in Northumberland. And so he went privily into the court, and saw this adventure, whereof it raised his heart, and he would assay it as other knights did, but for he was poor and poorly arrayed he put him not far in press. But in his heart he was fully assured to do as well, if his grace happed him, as any knight that there was. And as the damosel took her leave of Arthur and of all the barons, so departing, this knight Balin called unto her, and said, Damosel, I pray you of your courtesy, suffer me as well to assay as these lords; though that I be so poorly clothed, in my heart meseemeth I am fully assured as some of these others, and meseemeth in my heart to speed right well. The damosel beheld the poor knight, and saw he was a likely man, but for his poor arrayment she thought he should be of no worship without villainy or treachery. And then she said unto the knight, Sir, it needeth not to put me to more pain or labour, for it seemeth not you to speed there as other have failed. Ah! fair damosel, said Balin, worthiness, and good tatches, and good deeds, are not only in arrayment, but manhood and worship is hid within man's person, and many a worshipful knight is not known unto all people, and therefore worship and hardiness is not in arrayment. By God, said the damosel, ye say sooth; therefore ye shall assay to do what ye may. Then Balin took the sword by the girdle and sheath, and drew it out easily; and when he looked on the sword it pleased him much. Then had the king and all the barons great marvel that Balin had done that adventure, and many knights had great despite of Balin. Certes, said the damosel, this is a passing good knight, and the best that ever I found, and most of worship without treason, treachery, or villainy, and many marvels shall he do. Now, gentle and courteous knight, give me the sword again. Nay, said Balin, for this sword will I keep, but it be taken from me with force. Well, said the damosel, ye are not wise to keep the sword from me, for ye shall slay with the sword the best friend that ye have, and the man that ye most love in the world, and the sword shall be your destruction. I shall take the adventure, said Balin, that God will ordain me, but the sword ye shall not have at this time, by the faith of my body. Ye shall repent it within short time, said the damosel, for I would have the sword more for your avail than for mine, for I am passing heavy for your sake; for ye will not believe that sword shall be your destruction, and that is great pity. With that the damosel departed, making great sorrow.

Anon after, Balin sent for his horse and armour, and so would depart from the court, and took his leave of King Arthur. Nay, said the king, I suppose ye will not depart so lightly from this fellowship, I suppose ye are displeased that I have shewed you unkindness; blame me the less, for I was misinformed against you, but I weened ye had not been such a knight as ye are, of worship and prowess, and if ye will abide in this court among my fellowship, I shall so advance you as ye shall be pleased. God thank your highness, said Balin, your bounty and highness may no man praise half to the value; but at this time I must needs depart, beseeching you alway of your good grace. Truly, said the king, I am right wroth for your departing; I pray you, fair knight, that ye tarry not long, and ye shall be right welcome to me, and to my barons, and I shall amend all miss that I have done against you; God thank your great lordship, said Balin, and therewith made him ready to depart. Then the most part of the knights of the Round Table said that Balin did not this adventure all only by might, but by witchcraft.

Chapter 3
How the Lady of the Lake demanded the knight's head that had won the sword, or the maiden's head.

The meanwhile, that this knight was making him ready to depart, there came into the court a lady that hight the Lady of the Lake. And she came on horseback, richly beseen, and saluted King Arthur, and there asked him a gift that he promised her when she gave him the sword. That is sooth, said Arthur, a gift I promised you, but I have forgotten the name of my sword that ye gave me. The name of it, said the lady, is Excalibur, that is as much to say as Cut-steel. Ye say well, said the king; ask what ye will and ye shall have it, an it lie in my power to give it. Well, said the lady, I ask the head of the knight that hath won the sword, or else the damosel's head that brought it; I take no force though I have both their heads, for he slew my brother, a good knight and a true, and that gentlewoman was causer of my father's death. Truly, said King Arthur, I may not grant neither of their heads with my worship, therefore ask what ye will else, and I shall fulfil your desire. I will ask none other thing, said the lady. When Balin was ready to depart, he saw the Lady of the Lake, that by her means had slain Balin's mother, and he had sought her three years; and when it was told him that she asked his head of King Arthur, he went to her straight and said, Evil be you found; ye would have my head, and therefore ye shall lose yours, and with his sword lightly he smote off her head before King Arthur. Alas, for shame! said Arthur, why have ye done so? ye have shamed me and all my court, for this was a lady that I was beholden to, and hither she came under my safe-conduct; I shall never forgive you that trespass. Sir, said Balin, me forthinketh of your displeasure, for this same lady was the untruest lady living, and by enchantment and sorcery she hath been the destroyer of many good knights, and she was causer that my mother was burnt, through her falsehood and treachery. What cause soever ye had, said Arthur, ye should have forborne her in my presence; therefore, think not the contrary, ye shall repent it, for such another despite had I never in my court; therefore withdraw you out of my court in all haste ye may.

Then Balin took up the head of the lady, and bare it with him to his hostelry, and there he met with his squire, that was sorry he had displeased King Arthur and so they rode forth out of the town. Now, said Balin, we must depart, take thou this head and bear it to my friends, and tell them how I have sped, and tell my friends in Northumberland that my most foe is dead. Also tell them how I am out of prison, and what adventure befell me at the getting of this sword. Alas! said the squire, ye are greatly to blame for to displease King Arthur. As for that, said Balin, I will hie me, in all the haste that I may, to meet with King Rience and destroy him, either else to die therefore; and if it may hap me to win him, then will King Arthur be my good and gracious lord. Where shall I meet with you? said the squire. In King Arthur's court, said Balin. So his squire and he departed at that time. Then King Arthur and all the court made great dole and had shame of the death of the Lady of the Lake. Then the king buried her richly.

Chapter 4
How Merlin told the adventure of this damosel.

AT that time there was a knight, the which was the king's son of Ireland, and his name was Lanceor, the which was an orgulous knight, and counted himself one of the best of the court; and he had great despite at Balin for the achieving of the sword, that any should be accounted more hardy, or more of prowess; and he asked King Arthur if he would give him leave to ride after Balin and to revenge the despite that he had done. Do your best, said Arthur, I am right wroth with Balin; I would he were quit of the despite that he hath done to me and to my court. Then this Lanceor went to his hostelry to make him ready. In the meanwhile came Merlin unto the court of King Arthur, and there was told him the adventure of the sword, and the death of the Lady of the Lake. Now shall I say you, said Merlin; this same damosel that here standeth, that brought the sword unto your court, I shall tell you the cause of her coming: she was the falsest damosel that liveth. Say not so, said they. She hath a brother, a passing good knight of prowess and a full true man; and this damosel loved another knight that held her to paramour, and this good knight her brother met with the knight that held her to paramour, and slew him by force of his hands. When this false damosel understood this, she went to the Lady Lile of Avelion, and besought her of help, to be avenged on her own brother.

Chapter 5
How Balin was pursued by Sir Lanceor, knight of Ireland, and how he jousted and slew him.

And so this Lady Lile of Avelion took her this sword that she brought with her, and told there should no man pull it out of the sheath but if he be one of the best knights of this realm, and he should be hard and full of prowess, and with that sword he should slay her brother. This was the cause that the damosel came into this court. I know it as well as ye. Would God she had not come into this court, but she came never in fellowship of worship to do good, but always great harm; and that knight that hath achieved the sword shall be destroyed by that sword, for the which will be great damage, for there liveth not a knight of more prowess than he is, and he shall do unto you, my Lord Arthur, great honour and kindness; and it is great pity he shall not endure but a while, for of his strength and hardiness I know not his match living.

So the knight of Ireland armed him at all points, and dressed his shield on his shoulder, and mounted upon horseback, and took his spear in his hand, and rode after a great pace, as much as his horse might go; and within a little space on a mountain he had a sight of Balin, and with a loud voice he cried, Abide, knight, for ye shall abide whether ye will or nill, and the shield that is to-fore you shall not help. When Balin heard the noise, he turned his horse fiercely, and said, Fair knight, what will ye with me, will ye joust with me? Yea, said the Irish knight, therefore come I after you. Peradventure, said Balin, it had been better to have holden you at home, for many a man weeneth to put his enemy to a rebuke, and oft it falleth to himself. Of what court be ye sent from? said Balin. I am come from the court of King Arthur, said the knight of Ireland, that come hither for to revenge the despite ye did this day to King Arthur and to his court. Well, said Balin, I see well I must have ado with you, that me forthinketh for to grieve King Arthur, or any of his court; and your quarrel is full simple, said Balin, unto me, for the lady that is dead, did me great damage, and else would I have been loath as any knight that liveth for to slay a lady. Make you ready, said the knight Lanceor, and dress you unto me, for that one shall abide in the field. Then they took their spears, and came together as much as their horses might drive, and the Irish knight smote Balin on the shield, that all went shivers off his spear, and Balin hit him through the shield, and the hauberk perished, and so pierced through his body and the horse's croup, and anon turned his horse fiercely, and drew out his sword, and wist not that he had slain him; and then he saw him lie as a dead corpse.

Lesson 85

- Read chapters 6-10 of Book 2 of *Le Morte D'Arthur*.

Chapter 6
How a damosel, which was love to Lanceor, slew herself for love, and how Balin met with his brother Balan.

Then he looked by him, and was ware of a damosel that came riding full fast as the horse might ride, on a fair palfrey. And when she espied that Lanceor was slain, she made sorrow out of measure, and said, O Balin, two bodies thou hast slain and one heart, and two hearts in one body, and two souls thou hast lost. And therewith she took the sword from her love that lay dead, and fell to the ground in a swoon. And when she arose she made great dole out of measure, the which sorrow grieved Balin passingly sore, and he went unto her for to have taken the sword out of her hand, but she held it so fast he might not take it out of her hand unless he should have hurt her, and suddenly she set the pommel to the ground, and rove herself through the body. When Balin espied her deeds, he was passing heavy in his heart, and ashamed that so fair a damosel had destroyed herself for the love of his death. Alas, said Balin, me repenteth sore the death of this knight, for the love of this damosel, for there was much true love betwixt them both, and for sorrow might not longer behold him, but turned his horse and looked toward a great forest, and there he was ware, by the arms, of his brother Balan. And when they were met they put off their helms and kissed together, and wept for joy and pity. Then Balan said, I little weened to have met with you at this sudden adventure; I am right glad of your deliverance out of your dolorous prisonment, for a man told me, in the castle of Four Stones, that ye were delivered, and that man had seen you in the court of King Arthur, and therefore I came hither into this country, for here I supposed to find you. Anon the knight Balin told his brother of his adventure of the sword, and of the death of the Lady of the Lake, and how King Arthur was displeased with him.

Wherefore he sent this knight after me, that lieth here dead, and the death of this damosel grieveth me sore. So doth it me, said Balan, but ye must take the adventure that God will ordain you. Truly, said Balin, I am right heavy that my Lord Arthur is displeased with me, for he is the most worshipful knight that reigneth now on earth, and his love will I get or else will I put my life in adventure. For the King Rience lieth at a siege at the Castle Terrabil, and thither will we draw in all haste, to prove our worship and prowess upon him. I will well, said Balan, that we do, and we will help each other as brethren ought to do.

Chapter 7
How a dwarf reproved Balin for the death of Lanceor, and how King Mark of Cornwall found them, and made a tomb over them.

Now go we hence, said Balin, and well be we met. The meanwhile as they talked, there came a dwarf from the city of Camelot on horseback, as much as he might; and found the dead bodies, wherefore he made great dole, and pulled out his hair for sorrow, and said, Which of you knights have done this deed? Whereby askest thou it? said Balan. For I would wit it, said the dwarf. It was I, said Balin, that slew this knight in my defence, for hither he came to chase me, and either I must slay him or he me; and this damosel slew herself for his love, which repenteth me, and for her sake I shall owe all women the better love. Alas, said the dwarf, thou hast done great damage unto thyself, for this knight that is here dead was one of the most valiantest men that lived, and trust well, Balin, the kin of this knight will chase you through the world till they have slain you. As for that, said Balin, I fear not greatly, but I am right heavy that I have displeased my lord King Arthur, for the death of this knight. So as they talked together, there came a king of Cornwall riding, the which hight King Mark. And when he saw these two bodies dead, and understood how they were dead, by the two knights above said, then made the king great sorrow for the true love that was betwixt them, and said, I will not depart till I have on this earth made a tomb, and there he pight his pavilions and sought through all the country to find a tomb, and in a church they found one was fair and rich, and then the king let put them both in the earth, and put the tomb upon them, and wrote the names of them both on the tomb. How here lieth Lanceor the king's son of Ireland, that at his own request was slain by the hands of Balin; and how his lady, Colombe, and paramour, slew herself with her love's sword for dole and sorrow.

Chapter 8
How Merlin prophesied that two the best knights of the world should fight there, which were Sir Lancelot and Sir Tristram.

The meanwhile as this was a-doing, in came Merlin to King Mark, and seeing all his doing, said, Here shall be in this same place the greatest battle betwixt two knights that was or ever shall be, and the truest lovers, and yet none of them shall slay other. And there Merlin wrote their names upon the tomb with letters of gold that should fight in that place, whose names were Launcelot de Lake, and Tristram. Thou art a marvellous man, said King Mark unto Merlin, that speakest of such marvels, thou art a boistous man and an unlikely to tell of such deeds. What is thy name? said King Mark. At this time, said Merlin, I will not tell, but at that time when Sir Tristram is taken with his sovereign lady, then ye shall hear and know my name, and at that time ye shall hear tidings that shall not please you. Then said Merlin to Balin, Thou hast done thyself great hurt, because that thou savest not this lady that slew herself, that might have saved her an thou wouldest. By the faith of my body, said Balin, I might not save her, for she slew herself suddenly. Me repenteth, said Merlin; because of the death of that lady thou shalt strike a stroke most dolorous that ever man struck, except the stroke of our Lord, for thou shalt hurt the truest knight and the man of most worship that now liveth, and through that stroke three kingdoms shall be in great poverty, misery and wretchedness twelve years, and the knight shall not be whole of that wound for many years. Then Merlin took his leave of Balin. And Balin said, If I wist it were sooth that ye say I should do such a perilous deed as that, I would slay myself to make thee a liar. Therewith Merlin vanished away suddenly. And then Balan and his brother took their leave of King Mark. First, said the king, tell me your name. Sir, said Balan, ye may see he beareth two swords, thereby ye may call him the Knight with the Two Swords. And so departed King Mark unto Camelot to King Arthur, and Balin took the way toward King Rience; and as they rode together they met with Merlin disguised, but they knew him not. Whither ride you? said Merlin. We have little to do, said the two knights, to tell thee. But what is thy name? said Balin. At this time, said Merlin, I will not tell it thee. It is evil seen, said the knights, that thou art a true man that thou wilt not tell thy name. As for that, said Merlin, be it as it be may, I can tell you wherefore ye ride this way, for to meet King Rience; but it will not avail you without ye have my counsel. Ah! said Balin, ye are Merlin; we will be ruled by your counsel. Come on, said Merlin, ye shall have great worship, and look that ye do knightly, for ye shall have great need. As for that, said Balin, dread you not, we will do what we may.

Chapter 9
How Balin and his brother, by the counsel of Merlin, took King Rience and brought him to King Arthur.

Then Merlin lodged them in a wood among leaves beside the highway, and took off the bridles of their horses and put them to grass and laid them down to rest them till it was nigh midnight. Then Merlin bade them rise, and make them ready, for the king was nigh them, that was stolen away from his host with a three score horses of his best knights, and twenty of them rode to-fore to warn the Lady de Vance that the king was coming; for that night King Rience should have lain with her. Which is the king? said Balin. Abide, said Merlin, here in a strait way ye shall meet with him; and therewith he showed Balin and his brother where he rode.

Anon Balin and his brother met with the king, and smote him down, and wounded him fiercely, and laid him to the ground; and there they slew on the right hand and the left hand, and slew more than forty of his men, and the remnant fled. Then went they again to King Rience and would have slain him had he not yielded him unto their grace. Then said he thus: Knights full of prowess, slay me not, for by my life ye may win, and by my death ye shall win nothing. Then said these two knights, Ye say sooth and truth, and so laid him on a horse-litter. With that Merlin was vanished, and came to King Arthur aforehand, and told him how his most enemy was taken and discomfited. By whom? said King Arthur. By two knights, said Merlin, that would please your lordship, and to-morrow ye shall know what knights they are. Anon after came the Knight with the Two Swords and Balan his brother, and brought with them King Rience of North Wales, and there delivered him to the porters, and charged them with him; and so they two returned again in the dawning of the day. King Arthur came then to King Rience, and said, Sir king, ye are welcome: by what adventure come ye hither? Sir, said King Rience, I came hither by an hard adventure. Who won you? said King Arthur. Sir, said the king, the Knight with the Two Swords and his brother, which are two marvellous knights of prowess. I know them not, said Arthur, but much I am beholden to them. Ah, said Merlin, I shall tell you: it is Balin that achieved the sword, and his brother Balan, a good knight, there liveth not a better of prowess and of worthiness, and it shall be the greatest dole of him that ever I knew of knight, for he shall not long endure. Alas, said King Arthur, that is great pity; for I am much beholden unto him, and I have ill deserved it unto him for his kindness. Nay, said Merlin, he shall do much more for you, and that shall ye know in haste. But, sir, are ye purveyed, said Merlin, for to-morn the host of Nero, King Rience's brother, will set on you or noon with a great host, and therefore make you ready, for I will depart from you.

Chapter 10
How King Arthur had a battle against Nero and King Lot of Orkney, and how King Lot was deceived by Merlin, and how twelve kings were slain.

Then King Arthur made ready his host in ten battles and Nero was ready in the field afore the Castle Terrabil with a great host, and he had ten battles, with many more people than Arthur had. Then Nero had the vanguard with the most part of his people, and Merlin came to King Lot of the Isle of Orkney, and held him with a tale of prophecy, till Nero and his people were destroyed. And there Sir Kay the seneschal did passingly well, that the days of his life the worship went never from him; and Sir Hervis de Revel did marvellous deeds with King Arthur, and King Arthur slew that day twenty knights and maimed forty. At that time came in the Knight with the Two Swords and his brother Balan, but they two did so marvellously that the king and all the knights marvelled of them, and all they that beheld them said they were sent from heaven as angels, or devils from hell; and King Arthur said himself they were the best knights that ever he saw, for they gave such strokes that all men had wonder of them.

In the meanwhile came one to King Lot, and told him while he tarried there Nero was destroyed and slain with all his people. Alas, said King Lot, I am ashamed, for by my default there is many a worshipful man slain, for an we had been together there had been none host under the heaven that had been able for to have matched with us; this faiter with his prophecy hath mocked me. All that did Merlin, for he knew well that an King Lot had been with his body there at the first battle, King Arthur had been slain, and all his people destroyed; and well Merlin knew that one of the kings should be dead that day, and loath was Merlin that any of them both should be slain; but of the twain, he had liefer King Lot had been slain than King Arthur. Now what is best to do? said King Lot of Orkney; whether is me better to treat with King Arthur or to fight, for the greater part of our people are slain and destroyed? Sir, said a knight, set on Arthur for they are weary and forfoughten and we be fresh. As for me, said King Lot, I would every knight would do his part as I would do mine. And then they advanced banners and smote together and all to-shivered their spears; and Arthur's knights, with the help of the Knight with the Two Swords and his brother Balan put King Lot and his host to the worse. But always King Lot held him in the foremost front, and did marvellous deeds of arms, for all his host was borne up by his hands, for he abode all knights. Alas he might not endure, the which was great pity, that so worthy a knight as he was one should be overmatched, that of late time afore had been a knight of King Arthur's, and wedded the sister of King Arthur; and for King Arthur lay by King Lot's wife, the which was Arthur's sister, and gat on her Mordred, therefore King Lot held against Arthur. So there was a knight that was called the Knight with the Strange Beast, and at that time his right name was called Pellinore, the which was a good man of prowess, and he smote a mighty stroke at King Lot as he fought with all his enemies, and he failed of his stroke, and smote the horse's neck, that he fell to the ground with King Lot. And therewith anon Pellinore smote him a great stroke through the helm and head unto the brows. And then all the host of Orkney fled for the death of King Lot, and there were slain many mothers' sons. But King Pellinore bare the wite of the death of King Lot, wherefore Sir Gawaine revenged the death of his father the tenth year after he was made knight, and slew King Pellinore with his own hands. Also there were slain at that battle twelve kings on the side of King Lot with Nero, and all were buried in the Church of Saint Stephen's in Camelot, and the remnant of knights and of others were buried in a great rock.

Lesson 86

- Read chapters 11-14 of Book 2 of *Le Morte D'Arthur*.

Chapter 11
Of the interment of twelve kings, and of the prophecy of Merlin, and how Balin should give the dolorous stroke.

So at the interment came King Lot's wife Margawse with her four sons, Gawaine, Agravaine, Gaheris, and Gareth. Also there came thither King Uriens, Sir Ewaine's father, and Morgan le Fay his wife that was King Arthur's sister. All these came to the interment. But of all these twelve kings King Arthur let make the tomb of King Lot passing richly, and made his tomb by his own; and then Arthur let make twelve images of latten and copper, and over-gilt it with gold, in the sign of twelve kings, and each one of them held a taper of wax that burnt day and night; and King Arthur was made in sign of a figure standing above them with a sword drawn in his hand, and all the twelve figures had countenance like unto men that were overcome. All this made Merlin by his subtle craft, and there he told the king, When I am dead these tapers shall burn no longer, and soon after the adventures of the Sangreal shall come among you and be achieved. Also he told Arthur how Balin the worshipful knight shall give the dolorous stroke, whereof shall fall great vengeance. Oh, where is Balin and Balan and Pellinore? said King Arthur. As for Pellinore, said Merlin, he will meet with you soon; and as for Balin he will not be long from you; but the other brother will depart, ye shall see him no more. By my faith, said Arthur, they are two marvellous knights, and namely Balin passeth of prowess of any knight that ever I found, for much beholden am I unto him; would God he would abide with me. Sir, said Merlin, look ye keep well the scabbard of Excalibur, for ye shall lose no blood while ye have the scabbard upon you, though ye have as many wounds upon you as ye may have. So after, for great trust, Arthur betook the scabbard to Morgan le Fay his sister, and she loved another knight better than her husband King Uriens or King Arthur, and she would have had Arthur her brother slain, and therefore she let make another scabbard like it by enchantment, and gave the scabbard Excalibur to her love; and the knight's name was called Accolon, that after had near slain King Arthur. After this Merlin told unto King Arthur of the prophecy that there should be a great battle beside Salisbury, and Mordred his own son should be against him. Also he told him that Bagdemegus was his cousin, and germain unto King Uriens.

Chapter 12
How a sorrowful knight came before Arthur, and how Balin fetched him, and how that knight was slain by a knight invisible.

Within a day or two King Arthur was somewhat sick, and he let pitch his pavilion in a meadow, and there he laid him down on a pallet to sleep, but he might have no rest. Right so he heard a great noise of an horse, and therewith the king looked out at the porch of the pavilion, and saw a knight coming even by him, making great dole. Abide, fair sir, said Arthur, and tell me wherefore thou makest this sorrow. Ye may little amend me, said the knight, and so passed forth to the castle of Meliot. Anon after there came Balin, and when he saw King Arthur he alighted off his horse, and came to the King on foot, and saluted him. By my head, said Arthur, ye be welcome. Sir, right now came riding this way a knight making great mourn, for what cause I cannot tell; wherefore I would desire of you of your courtesy and of your. gentleness to fetch again that knight either by force or else by his good will. I will do more for your lordship than that, said Balin; and so he rode more than a pace, and found the knight with a damosel in a forest, and said, Sir knight, ye must come with me unto King Arthur, for to tell him of your sorrow. That will I not, said the knight, for it will scathe me greatly, and do you none avail. Sir, said Balin, I pray you make you ready, for ye must go with me, or else I must fight with you and bring you by force, and that were me loath to do. Will ye be my warrant, said the knight, an I go with you? Yea, said Balin, or else I will die therefore. And so he made him ready to go with Balin, and left the damosel still. And as they were even afore King Arthur's pavilion, there came one invisible, and smote this knight that went with Balin throughout the body with a spear. Alas, said the knight, I am slain under your conduct with a knight called Garlon; therefore take my horse that is better than yours, and ride to the damosel, and follow the quest that I was in as she will lead you, and revenge my death when ye may. That shall I do, said Balin, and that I make vow unto knighthood; and so he departed from this knight with great sorrow. So King Arthur let bury this knight richly, and made a mention on his tomb, how there was slain Herlews le Berbeus, and by whom the treachery was done, the knight Garlon. But ever the damosel bare the truncheon of the spear with her that Sir Herlews was slain withal.

Chapter 13
How Balin and the damosel met with a knight which was in likewise slain, and how the damosel bled for the custom of a castle.

So Balin and the damosel rode into a forest, and there met with a knight that had been a-hunting, and that knight asked Balin for what cause he made so great sorrow. Me list not to tell you, said Balin. Now, said the knight, an I were armed as ye be I would fight with you. That should little need, said Balin, I am not afeard to tell you, and told him all the cause how it was. Ah, said the knight, is this all? here I ensure you by the faith of my body never to depart from you while my life lasteth. And so they went to the hostelry and armed them, and so rode forth with Balin. And as they came by an hermitage even by a churchyard, there came the knight Garlon invisible, and smote this knight, Perin de Mountbeliard, through the body with a spear. Alas, said the knight, I am slain by this traitor knight that rideth invisible. Alas, said Balin, it is not the first despite he hath done me; and there the hermit and Balin buried the knight under a rich stone and a tomb royal. And on the morn they found letters of gold written, how Sir Gawaine shall revenge his father's death, King Lot, on the King Pellinore. Anon after this Balin and the damosel rode till they came to a castle, and there Balin alighted, and he and the damosel went to go into the castle, and anon as Balin came within the castle's gate the portcullis fell down at his back, and there fell many men about the damosel, and would have slain her. When Balin saw that, he was sore aggrieved, for he might not help the damosel. Then he went up into the tower, and leapt over walls into the ditch, and hurt him not; and anon he pulled out his sword and would have foughten with them. And they all said nay, they would not fight with him, for they did nothing but the old custom of the castle; and told him how their lady was sick, and had lain many years, and she might not be whole but if she had a dish of silver full of blood of a clean maid and a king's daughter; and therefore the custom of this castle is, there shall no damosel pass this way but she shall bleed of her blood in a silver dish full. Well, said Balin, she shall bleed as much as she may bleed, but I will not lose the life of her whiles my life lasteth. And so Balin made her to bleed by her good will, but her blood helped not the lady. And so he and she rested there all night, and had there right good cheer, and on the morn they passed on their ways. And as it telleth after in the Sangreal, that Sir Percivale's sister helped that lady with her blood, whereof she was dead.

Chapter 14
How Balin met with that knight named Garlon at a feast, and there he slew him, to have his blood to heal therewith the son of his host.

Then they rode three or four days and never met with adventure, and by hap they were lodged with a gentle man that was a rich man and well at ease. And as they sat at their supper Balin overheard one complain grievously by him in a chair. What is this noise? said Balin. Forsooth, said his host, I will tell you. I was but late at a jousting, and there I jousted with a knight that is brother unto King Pellam, and twice smote I him down, and then he promised to quit me on my best friend; and so he wounded my son, that cannot be whole till I have of that knight's blood, and he rideth alway invisible; but I know not his name. Ah! said Balin, I know that knight, his name is Garlon, he hath slain two knights of mine in the same manner, therefore I had liefer meet with that knight than all the gold in this realm, for the despite he hath done me. Well, said his host, I shall tell you, King Pellam of Listeneise hath made do cry in all this country a great feast that shall be within these twenty days, and no knight may come there but if he bring his wife with him, or his paramour; and that knight, your enemy and mine, ye shall see that day. Then I behote you, said Balin, part of his blood to heal your son withal. We will be forward to-morn, said his host. So on the morn they rode all three toward Pellam, and they had fifteen days' journey or they came thither; and that same day began the great feast. And so they alighted and stabled their horses, and went into the castle; but Balin's host might not be let in because he had no lady. Then Balin was well received and brought unto a chamber and unarmed him; and there were brought him robes to his pleasure, and would have had Balin leave his sword behind him. Nay, said Balin, that do I not, for it is the custom of my country a knight always to keep his weapon with him, and that custom will I keep, or else I will depart as I came. Then they gave him leave to wear his sword, and so he went unto the castle, and was set among knights of worship, and his lady afore him.

Soon Balin asked a knight, Is there not a knight in this court whose name is Garlon? Yonder he goeth, said a knight, he with the black face; he is the marvellest knight that is now living, for he destroyeth many good knights, for he goeth invisible. Ah well, said Balin, is that he? Then Balin advised him long: If I slay him here I shall not escape, and if I leave him now, peradventure I shall never meet with him again at such a steven, and much harm he will do an he live. Therewith this Garlon espied that this Balin beheld him, and then he came and smote Balin on the face with the back of his hand, and said, Knight, why beholdest me so? for shame therefore, eat thy meat and do that thou came for. Thou sayest sooth, said Balin, this is not the first despite that thou hast done me, and therefore I will do what I came for, and rose up fiercely and clave his head to the shoulders. Give me the truncheon, said Balin to his lady, wherewith he slew your knight. Anon she gave it him, for always she bare the truncheon with her. And therewith Balin smote him through the body, and said openly, With that truncheon thou hast slain a good knight, and now it sticketh in thy body. And then Balin called unto him his host, saying, Now may ye fetch blood enough to heal your son withal.

Lesson 87

- Read chapters 1-4 of book 21 of *Le Morte D'Arthur*.

Chapter 1
How Sir Mordred presumed and took on him to be king of England, and would have married the queen, his uncle's wife.

As Sir Mordred was ruler of all England, he did do make letters as though that they came from beyond the sea, and the letters specified that king Arthur was slain in battle with Sir Launcelot. Wherefore Sir Mordred made a Parliament, and called the lords together, and there he made them to choose him king, and so was he crowned at Canterbury, and held a feast there fifteen days, and afterward he drew him unto Winchester, and there he took the queen Guenever, and said plainly, that he would wed her which was his uncle's wife, and his father's wife. And so he made ready for the feast, and a day prefixed that they should be wedded; wherefore queen Guenever was passing heavy. But she durst not discover her heart, but spake fair, and agreed to Sir Mordred's will. Then she desired of Sir Mordred for to go to London, to buy all manner of things that longed unto the wedding. And because of her fair speech Sir Mordred trusted her well enough, and gave her leave to go. And so when she came to London, she took the tower of London, and suddenly, in all haste possible, she stuffed it with all manner of victual, and well garnished it with men, and so kept it. Then when Sir Mordred wist and understood how he was beguiled, he was passing wroth out of measure. And a short tale for to make, he went and laid a mighty siege about the tower of London, and made many great assaults thereat, and threw many great engines unto them, and shot great guns. But all might not prevail Sir Mordred, for queen Guenever would never, for fair speech nor for foul, would never trust to come in his hands again. And then came the bishop of Canterbury, the which was a noble clerk and an holy man, and thus he said to Sir Mordred: Sir, what will ye do, will ye first displease God, and sithen shame yourself and all knighthood? Is not king Arthur your uncle, no further but your mother's brother, and are ye not his son, therefore how may ye wed your father's wife? Sir, said the noble clerk, leave this opinion, or else I shall curse you with book, and bell, and candle. Do thou thy worst, said Sir Mordred, wit thou well I shall defy thee. Sir, said the bishop, and wit you well I shall not fear me to do that me ought to do. Also where ye noise where my lord Arthur is slain, and that is not so, and therefore ye will make a foul work in this land. Peace, thou false priest, said Sir Mordred, for, and thou chafe me any more, I shall make strike off thy head. So the bishop departed, and did the curse in the most orgulous wise that might be done. And then Sir Mordred sought the bishop of Canterbury for to have slain him. Then the bishop fled, and took part of his goods with him, and went nigh unto Glastonbury, and there he was as priest hermit in a chapel, and lived in poverty and in holy prayers: for well he understood that mischievous war was at hand. Then Sir Mordred sought on queen Guenever by letters and sondes, and by fair means and foul means, for to have her to come out of the tower of London, but all this availed not, for she answered him shortly, openly and privily, that she had lever slay herself than to be married with him. Then came word to Sir Mordred that king Arthur had raised the siege from Sir Launcelot, and he was coming homeward with a great host, to be avenged upon Sir Mordred. Wherefore Sir Mordred made write writs to all the barony of this land, and much people drew to him. For then was the common voice among them, that with Arthur was none other life but war and strife, and with Sir Mordred was great joy and bliss. Thus was Sir Arthur depraved and evil said of. And many there were that king Arthur had made up of nought, and given them lands, might not then say of him a good word.

Lo ye, all Englishmen, see ye not what a mischief here was, for he that was the most king and knight of the world, and most loved the fellowship of noble knights, and by him they were all upholden. Now might not these Englishmen hold us content with him. Lo, thus was the old custom and usage of this land. And also men say, that we of this land have not yet lost nor forgotten that custom and usage. Alas, this is a great default of all Englishmen, for there may no thing please us no term. And so fared the people at that time; they were better pleased with Sir Mordred than they were with king Arthur, and much people drew unto Sir Mordred, and said they would abide with him for better and for worse. And so Sir Mordred drew with a great host to Dover, for there he heard say that Sir Arthur would arrive, and so he thought to beat his own father from his lands. And the most party of all England held with Sir Mordred, the people were so new fangle.

Chapter 2
How after that king Arthur had tidings he returned and came to Dover, where Sir Mordred met him to let his landing, and of the death of Sir Gawaine.

And so as Sir Mordred was at Dover with his host, there came king Arthur with a great navy of ships, galleys, and carracks. And there was Sir Mordred ready awaiting upon his landage, to let his own father to land upon the land that he was king over. Then there was launching of great boats and small, and full of noble men of arms, and there was much slaughter of gentle knights, and many a full bold baron was laid full low on both parties. But king Arthur was so courageous, that there might no manner of knights let him to land, and his knights fiercely followed him. And so they landed, maugre Sir Mordred and all his power, and put Sir Mordred aback, that he fled and all his people. So when this battle was done, king Arthur let bury his people that were dead, and then was the noble knight Sir Gawaine found in a great boat lying more than half dead. When Sir Arthur wist that Sir Gawaine was laid so low, he went unto him, and there the king made sorrow out of measure, and took Sir Gawaine in his arms, and thrice he there swooned. And when he awaked he said, Alas, Sir Gawaine, my sister's son, here now thou liest, the man in the world that I loved most, and now is my joy gone: for now, my nephew Sir Gawaine, I will discover me unto your person; in Sir Launcelot and you I most had my joy, and mine affiance, and now have I lost my joy of you both, wherefore all mine earthly joy is gone from me. Mine uncle king Arthur, said Sir Gawaine, wit you well, my death day is come, and all is through mine own hastiness and wilfulness, for I am smitten upon the old wound the which Sir Launcelot gave me, on the which I feel well I must die, and had Sir Launcelot been with you as he was, this unhappy war had never begun, and of all this am I causer, for Sir Launcelot and his blood through their prowess held all your cankered enemies in subjection and danger: and now, said Sir Gawaine, ye shall miss Sir Launcelot. But, alas, I would not accord with him, and therefore, said Sir Gawaine, I pray you, fair uncle, that I may have paper, pen, and ink, that I may write to Sir Launcelot a schedule with mine own hands. And then when paper and ink was brought, then Gawaine was set up weakly by king Arthur, for he was shriven a little tofore, and then he wrote thus, as the French book maketh mention,—Unto Sir Launcelot, flower of all noble knights that ever I heard of, or saw by my days, I Sir Gawaine, king Lot's son, of Orkney, sister's son unto the noble king Arthur, send thee greeting, and let thee have knowledge, that the tenth day of May I was smitten upon the old wound that thou gavest me afore the city of Benwick, and through the same wound that thou gavest me I am come to my death-day. And I will that all the world wit that I, Sir Gawaine, knight of the Table Round, sought my death, and not through thy deserving, but it was mine own seeking, wherefore I beseech thee, Sir Launcelot, to return again unto this realm, and see my tomb, and pray some prayer, more or less, for my soul. And this same day that I wrote this schedule, I was hurt to the death in the same wound, the which I had of thy hand, Sir Launcelot. For of a more nobler man might I not be slain. Also, Sir Launcelot, for all the love that ever was betwixt us, make no tarrying, but come over the sea in all haste, that thou mayest with thy noble knights rescue that noble king that made thee knight, that is my lord Arthur, for he is full straitly bestad with a false traitor, that is my half brother Sir Mordred, and he hath let crown him king, and would have wedded my lady queen Guenever, and so had he done, had she not put herself in the tower of London. And so the tenth day of May last past, my lord Arthur and we all landed upon them at Dover, and there we put that false traitor Sir Mordred to flight, and there it misfortuned me to be stricken upon thy stroke, and at the date of this letter was written but two hours and an half afore my death, written with mine own hand, and so subscribed with part of my heart's blood. And I require thee, most famous knight of the world, that thou wilt see my tomb.—And then Sir Gawaine wept, and king Arthur wept, and then they swooned both. And when they awaked both, the king made Sir Gawaine to receive his Saviour. And then Sir Gawaine prayed the king to send for Sir Launcelot, and to cherish him above all other knights. And so at the hour of noon, Sir Gawaine yielded up the spirit. And then the king let inter him in a chapel within Dover castle; and there yet all men may see the skull of him, and the same wound is seen that Sir Launcelot gave him in battle. Then was it told king Arthur that Sir Mordred had pitched a new field upon Barham Down. And upon the morn the king rode thither to him, and there was a great battle betwixt them, and much people were slain on both parties. But at the last Sir Arthur's party stood best, and Sir Mordred and his party fled unto Canterbury.

Chapter 3
How after Sir Gawaine's ghost appeared to king Arthur, and warned him that he should not fight that day.

And then the king let search all the towns for his knights that were slain, and interred them; and salved them with soft salves that so sore were wounded. Then much people drew unto king Arthur. And then they said that Sir Mordred warred upon king Arthur with wrong. And then king Arthur drew him with his host down by the sea side, westward toward Salisbury, and there was a day assigned between king Arthur and Sir Mordred, and they should meet upon a down beside Salisbury, and not far from the sea side, and this day was assigned on a Monday after Trinity Sunday, whereof king Arthur was passing glad, that he might be avenged upon Sir Mordred. Then Sir Mordred araised much people about London, for they of Kent, Southsex, and Surrey, Estsex, and Southfolk, and of Northfolk, held the most party with Sir Mordred, and many a full noble knight drew unto Sir Mordred and to the king; but they that loved Sir Launcelot drew unto Sir Mordred. So upon Trinity Sunday at night king Arthur dreamed a wonderful dream, and that was this, that him seemed he sat upon a chaflet in a chair, and the chair was fast to a wheel, and thereupon sat king Arthur in the richest cloth of gold that might be made: and the king thought there was under him, far from him, an hideous deep black water, and therein were all manner of serpents, and worms, and wild beasts, fowl and horrible: and suddenly the king thought the wheel turned up so down, and he fell among the serpents, and every beast took him by a limb. And then the king cried as he lay in his bed and slept, Help! And then knights, squires, and yeomen awaked the king; and then he was so amazed that he wist not where he was. And then he fell on slumbering again, not sleeping nor thoroughly waking. So the king seemed verily that there came Sir Gawaine unto him with a number of fair ladies with him. And when king Arthur saw him, then he said, Welcome, my sister's son, I wend thou hadst been dead, and now I see thee on live, much am I beholding unto Almighty Jesu. Oh, fair nephew, and my sister's son, what be these ladies that hither be come with you? Sir, said Sir Gawaine, all these be ladies for whom I have foughten when I was man living: and all these are those that I did battle for in righteous quarrel. And God hath given them that grace at their great prayer, because I did battle for them, that they should bring me hither unto you, thus much had God given me leave, for to warn you of your death; for and ye fight as to-morn with Sir Mordred, as ye both have assigned, doubt ye not ye must be slain, and the most part of your people on both parties. And for the great grace and goodness that Almighty Jesu hath unto you, and for pity of you and many more other good men there shall be slain, God hath sent me to you, of his special grace, to give you warning, that in no wise ye do battle as to-morn, but that ye take a treaty for a month day; and proffer you largely, so as to-morn to be put in a delay. For within a month shall come Sir Launcelot, with all his noble knights, and rescue you worshipfully, and slay Sir Mordred and all that ever will hold with him. Then Sir Gawaine and all the ladies vanished. And anon the king called upon his knights, squires, and yeomen, and charged them wightly to fetch his noble lords and wise bishops unto him. And when they were come, the king told them his vision, what Sir Gawaine had told him, and warned him that if he fought on the morn he should be slain. Then the king commanded Sir Lucan de butlere, and his brother Sir Bedivere, with two bishops with them, and charged them in any wise and they might take a treaty for a month day with Sir Mordred;—And spare not, proffer him lands and goods, as much as ye think best. So then they departed, and came to Sir Mordred, where he had a grim host of an hundred thousand men. And there they intreated Sir Mordred long time, and at the last Sir Mordred was agreed for to have Cornwall and Kent, by king Arthur's days:—after, all England, after the days of king Arthur.

Chapter 4
How by misadventure of an adder the battle began, where Mordred was slain, and Arthur hurt to the death.

Then were they condescended that king Arthur and Sir Mordred should meet betwixt both their hosts, and every each of them should bring fourteen persons. And they came with this word unto king Arthur. Then said he, I am glad that this is done. And so he went into the field. And when Arthur should depart, he warned all his host that and they see any sword drawn, Look ye come on fiercely, and slay that traitor Sir Mordred, for I in no wise trust him. In like wise Sir Mordred warned his host that,—And ye see any sword drawn, look that ye come on fiercely, and so slay all that ever before you standeth: for in no wise I will not trust for this treaty: for I know well my father will be avenged upon me. And so they met as their pointment was, and so they were agreed and accorded thoroughly: and wine was fetched, and they drank. Right so came an adder out of a little heath bush, and it stung a knight on the foot. And when the knight felt him stungen, he looked down and saw the adder, and then he drew his sword to slay the adder, and thought of none other harm. And when the host on both parties saw that sword drawn, then they blew beames, trumpets, and horns, and shouted grimly. And so both hosts dressed them together. And king Arthur took his horse, and said, Alas this unhappy day, and so rode to his party: and Sir Mordred in likewise. And never was there seen a more dolefuller battle in no christian land. For there was but rushing and riding, foining and striking, and many a grim word was there spoken either to other, and many a deadly stroke. But ever king Arthur rode throughout the battle of Sir Mordred many times, and did full nobly as a noble king should; and at all times he fainted never. And Sir Mordred that day put him in devoir, and in great peril. And thus they fought all the long day, and never stinted, till the noble knights were laid to the cold ground, and ever they fought still, till it was near night, and by that time was there an hundred thousand laid dead upon the down. Then was Arthur wroth out of measure, when he saw his people so slain from him. Then the king looked about him, and then was he ware of all his host, and of all his good knights, were left no more on live but two knights, that was Sir Lucan de butlere, and his brother Sir Bedivere: and they full were sore wounded. Jesu mercy, said the king, where are all my noble knights becomen. Alas that ever I should see this doleful day. For now, said Arthur, I am come to mine end. But would to God that I wist where were that traitor Sir Mordred, that hath caused all this mischief. Then was king Arthur ware where Sir Mordred leaned upon his sword among a great heap of dead men. Now give me my spear, said Arthur unto Sir Lucan, for yonder I have espied the traitor that all this woe hath wrought. Sir, let him be, said Sir Lucan, for he is unhappy: and if ye pass this unhappy day, ye shall be right well revenged upon him. Good lord, remember ye of your night's dream, and what the spirit of Sir Gawaine told you this night, yet God of his great goodness hath preserved you hitherto. Therefore, for God's sake, my lord, leave off by this. For blessed be God ye have won the field: for here we be three on live, and with Sir Mordred is none on live. And if ye leave off now, this wicked day of destiny is past. Tide me death, betide me life, saith the king, now I see him yonder alone, he shall never escape mine hands, for at a better avail shall I never have him. God speed you well, said Sir Bedivere. Then the king gat his spear in both his hands, and ran toward Sir Mordred, crying, Traitor, now is thy death day come. And when Sir Mordred heard Sir Arthur, he ran until him with his sword drawn in his hand. And then king Arthur smote Sir Mordred under the shield, with a foin of his spear throughout the body more than a fathom. And when Sir Mordred felt that he had his death's wound, he thrust himself, with the might that he had, up to the bur of king Arthur's spear. And right so he smote his father Arthur with his sword holden in both his hands, on the side of the head, that the sword pierced the helmet and the brain-pan, and therewithal Sir Mordred fell stark dead to the earth. And the noble Arthur fell in a swoon to the earth, and there he swooned oft-times. And Sir Lucan de butlere and Sir Bedivere oft-times heaved him up, and so weakly they led him betwixt them both to a little chapel not far from the sea side. And when the king was there, he thought him well eased. Then heard they people cry in the field. Now go thou, Sir Lucan, said the king, and do me to wit what betokens that noise in the field. So Sir Lucan departed, for he was grievously wounded in many places. And so as he went, he saw and hearkened by the moon-light, how the pillers and robbers were come into the field to pill and to rob many a full noble knight of broaches and beads, of many a good ring, and of many a rich jewel; and who that were not dead all out, there they slew them for their harness and their riches. When Sir Lucan understood this work, he came to the king as soon as he might, and told him all what he had heard and seen. Therefore by mine advice, said Sir Lucan, it is best that we bring you to some town. I would it were so, said the king,—

Lesson 88

- Read chapters 5-8 of Book 21 of *Le Morte D'Arthur*.

Chapter 5
How king Arthur commanded to cast his sword Excalibur into the water, and how he was delivered to ladies in a barge.

But I may not stand, my head works so. Ah, Sir Launcelot, said king Arthur, this day have I sore missed thee. Alas, that ever I was against thee, for now have I my death, whereof Sir Gawaine me warned in my dream. Then Sir Lucan took up the king the one part, and Sir Bedivere the other part, and in the lifting, the king swooned, and Sir Lucan fell in a swoon with the lift, that the part of his bowels fell out of his body, and therewith the noble knight's heart brast. And when king Arthur came to himself again, he beheld Sir Lucan how he lay foaming at the mouth, and part of his bowels lay at his feet. Alas, said the king, this is unto me a full heavy sight to see this noble duke so die for my sake, for he would have holpen me that had more need of help than I. Alas, he would not complain him, his heart was so set to help me. Now Jesu have mercy upon his soul. Then Sir Bedivere wept for the death of his brother. Leave this mourning and weeping, said the king, for all this will not avail me: for, wit thou well, and I might live myself the death of Sir Lucan would grieve me evermore; but my time hieth fast, said the king. Therefore, said Arthur, take thou Excalibur, my good sword, and go with it to yonder water side, and when thou comest there, I charge thee throw my sword in that water, and come again, and tell me what thou there seest. My lord, said Bedivere, your commandment shall be done, and lightly bring you word again. So Sir Bedivere departed, and by the way he beheld that noble sword, that the pommel and haft were all of precious stones, and then he said to himself, If I throw this rich sword in the water, thereof shall never come good, but harm and loss. And then Sir Bedivere hid Excalibur under a tree. And as soon as he might he came again unto the king, and said he had been at the water, and had thrown the sword into the water. What sawest thou there? said the king. Sir, he said, I saw nothing but waves and winds. That is untruly said of thee, said the king; therefore go thou lightly again, and do my command as thou art to me lief and dear, spare not, but throw it in. Then Sir Bedivere returned again, and took the sword in his hand; and then him thought sin and shame to throw away that noble sword; and so eft he hid the sword, and returned again, and told to the king that he had been at the water, and done his commandment. What saw thou there? said the king. Sir, he said, I saw nothing but the waters wap and the waves wan. Ah traitor, untrue, said king Arthur, now hast thou betrayed me twice. Who would have wend that thou that hast been to me so lief and dear, and thou art named a noble knight, and would betray me for the riches of the sword. But now go again lightly, for thy long tarrying putteth me in great jeopardy of my life, for I have taken cold. And but if thou do now as I bid thee, if ever I may see thee, I shall slay thee with mine own hands, for thou wouldest for my rich sword see me dead. Then Sir Bedivere departed, and went to the sword, and lightly took it up, and went to the water side, and there he bound the girdle about the hilts, and then he threw the sword as far into the water as he might, and there came an arm and an hand above the water, and met it, and caught it, and so shook it thrice and brandished, and then vanished away the hand with the sword in the water. So Sir Bedivere came again to the king, and told him what he saw. Alas, said the king, help me hence, for I dread me I have tarried over long. Then Sir

Bedivere took the king upon his back, and so went with him to that water side. And when they were at the water side, even fast by the bank hoved a little barge, with many fair ladies in it, and among them all was a queen, and all they had black hoods, and all they wept and shrieked when they saw king Arthur. Now put me into the barge, said the king: and so he did softly. And there received him three queens with great mourning, and so they set him down, and in one of their laps king Arthur laid his head, and then that queen said, Ah, dear brother, why have ye tarried so long from me? Alas, this wound on your head hath caught over much cold. And so then they rowed from the land; and Sir Bedivere beheld all those ladies go from him. Then Sir Bedivere cried, Ah, my lord Arthur, what shall become of me now ye go from me, and leave me here alone among mine enemies. Comfort thyself, said the king, and do as well as thou mayest, for in me is no trust for to trust in. For I will into the vale of Avilion, to heal me of my grievous wound. And if thou hear never more of me, pray for my soul. But ever the queens and the ladies wept and shrieked, that it was pity to hear. And as soon as Sir Bedivere had lost the sight of the barge, he wept and wailed, and so took the forest, and so he went all that night, and in the morning he was ware betwixt two holts hoar of a chapel and an hermitage.

Chapter 6
How Sir Bedivere found him on the morrow dead in an hermitage, and how he abode there with the hermit.

Then was Sir Bedivere glad, and thither he went; and when he came into the chapel, he saw where lay an hermit groveling on all four, there fast by a tomb was new graven. When the hermit saw Sir Bedivere, he knew him well, for he was but a little before bishop of Canterbury, that Sir Mordred banished. Sir, said Sir Bedivere, what man is there interred that ye pray so fast for? Fair son, said the hermit, I wot not verily, but by deeming. But this night, at midnight, here came a number of ladies, and brought hither a dead corpse, and prayed me to bury him; and here they offered an hundred tapers, and gave me an hundred besants. Alas, said Sir Bedivere, that was my lord king Arthur, that here lieth buried in this chapel! Then Sir Bedivere swooned, and when he awoke he prayed the hermit he might abide with him still there, to live with fasting and prayers. For from hence will I never go, said Sir Bedivere, by my will, but all the days of my life here to pray for my lord Arthur. Ye are welcome to me, said the hermit, for I know you better than ye ween that I do. Ye are the bold Bedivere, and the full noble duke Sir Lucan de butlere was your brother. Then Sir Bedivere told the hermit all as ye have heard tofore. So there bode Sir Bedivere with the hermit, that was tofore bishop of Canterbury, and there Sir Bedivere put upon him poor clothes, and served the hermit full lowly in fasting and in prayers.

Thus of Arthur I find never more written in books that be authorized, nor more of the certainty of his death heard I never tell, but thus was he led away in a ship wherein were three queens; that one was king Arthur's sister queen Morgan le Fay; the other was the queen of Northgalis; the third was the queen of the Waste Lands. Also there was Nimue, the chief Lady of the lake, that had wedded Pelleas the good knight; and this lady had done much for king Arthur; for she would never suffer Sir Pelleas to be in no place where he should be in danger of his life, and so he lived to the uttermost of his days with her in great rest. More of the death of king Arthur could I never find, but that ladies brought him to his burials; and such one was buried there, that the hermit bare witness that some time was bishop of Canterbury, but yet the hermit knew not in certain that he was verily the body of king Arthur;—for this tale Sir Bedivere, knight of the Round Table, made it to be written.

Chapter 7
Of the opinion of some men of the death of king Arthur; and how queen Guenever made her a nun in Almesbury.

Yet some men yet say in many parts of England that king Arthur is not dead, but had by the will of our Lord Jesu in another place. And men say that he shall come again, and he shall win the holy cross. I will not say it shall be so, but rather I will say, here in this world he changed his life. But many men say that there is written upon his tomb this verse,

Hic iacet Arthurus Rex quondam Rex que futurus.

Thus leave I here Sir Bedivere with the hermit, that dwelled that time in a chapel beside Glastonbury, and there was his hermitage. And so they lived in their prayers and fastings and great abstinence. And when queen Guenever understood that king Arthur was slain, and all the noble knights, Sir Mordred and all the remnant, then the queen stole away, and five ladies with her, and so she went to Almesbury, and there she let make herself a nun, and wore white clothes and black, and great penance she took, as ever did sinful lady in this land, and never creature could make her merry, but lived in fasting, prayers, and alms-deeds, that all manner of people marvelled how virtuously she was changed. Now leave we queen Guenever in Almesbury a nun in white clothes and black, and there she was abbess and ruler, as reason would; and turn we from her, and speak we of Sir Launcelot du Lake.

Chapter 8
How when Sir Launcelot heard of the death of king Arthur, and of Sir Gawaine, and other matters, he came into England.

And when he heard in his country that Sir Mordred was crowned king in England, and made war against king Arthur his own father, and would let him to land in his own land; also it was told Sir Launcelot how that Sir Mordred had laid siege about the tower of London, because the queen would not wed him; then was Sir Launcelot wroth out of measure, and said to his kinsmen, Alas, that double traitor Sir Mordred, now me repenteth that ever he escaped my hands, for much shame hath he done unto my lord Arthur. For all I feel by the doleful letter that my lord Gawaine sent me, on whose soul Jesu have mercy, that my lord Arthur is right hard bested. Alas, said Sir Launcelot, that ever I should live to hear that most noble king, that made me knight, thus to be overset with his subject in his own realm. And this doleful letter that my lord Sir Gawaine hath sent me afore his death, praying me to see his tomb, wit you well his doleful words shall never go from mine heart. For he was a full noble knight as ever was born, and in an unhappy hour was I born, that ever I should have that unhap to slay first Sir Gawaine, Sir Gaheris the good knight, and mine own friend Sir Gareth, that full noble knight. Alas, I may say I am unhappy, said Sir Launcelot, that ever I should do thus unhappily; and, alas, yet might I never have hap to slay that traitor Sir Mordred. Leave your complaints, said Sir Bors, and first revenge you of the death of Sir Gawaine, and it will be well done that ye see Sir Gawaine's tomb, and secondly that ye revenge my lord Arthur and my lady queen Guenever. I thank you, said Sir Launcelot, for ever ye will my worship. Then they made them ready in all the haste that might be, with ships and galleys with Sir Launcelot and his host, to pass into England. And so he passed over the sea till he came to Dover: and there he landed with seven kings, and the number was hideous to behold. Then Sir Launcelot enquired of men of Dover where was king Arthur become? Then the people told him how that he was slain, and Sir Mordred and an hundred thousand died on a day, and how Sir Mordred gave king Arthur there the first battle at his landing, and there was good Sir Gawaine slain, and on the morn Sir Mordred fought with the king upon Barham Down, and there the king put Sir Mordred to the worse. Alas, said Sir Launcelot, this is the heaviest tidings that ever came to me. Now, fair sirs, said Sir Launcelot, shew me the tomb of Sir Gawaine. And then certain people of the town brought him into the castle of Dover, and showed him the tomb. Then Sir Launcelot kneeled down and wept and prayed heartily for his soul. And that night he made a dole, and all they that would come had as much flesh, fish, wine, and ale, and every man and woman had twelve pence, come who would. Thus with his own hand dealt he his money in a mourning gown; and ever he wept, and prayed them to pray for the soul of Sir Gawaine. And on the morn all the priests and clerks that might be gotten in the country were there, and sung mass of Requiem. And there offered first Sir Launcelot and he offered an hundred pound, and then the seven kings offered forty pound a piece, and also there was a thousand knights, and each of them offered a pound, and the offering dured from morn till night. And Sir Launcelot lay two nights on his tomb in prayers and in weeping. Then on the third day Sir Launcelot called the kings, dukes, earls, barons and knights, and said thus: My fair lords, I thank you all of your coming into this country with me; but we come too late, and that shall repent me while I live, but against death may no man rebel. But sithen it is so, said Sir Launcelot, I will myself ride and seek my lady queen Guenever, for as I hear say, she hath great pain and much disease, and I heard say that she is fled into the west country, therefore ye all that abide me here, and but if I come again within fifteen days, then take your ships, and your fellowship, and depart into your country. For I will do as I say to you.

Lesson 89

- Read the rest of *Le Morte D'Arthur*.

Chapter 9
How Sir Launcelot departed to seek the queen Guenever, and how he found her at Almesbury.

Then came Sir Bors de Ganis, and said, My lord Sir Launcelot, what think ye for to do, now to ride in this realm? wit thou well ye shall find few friends. Be as be may, said Sir Launcelot, keep you still here, for I will forth on my journey, and no man nor child shall go with me. So it was no boot to strive, but he departed and rode westerly, and there he sought a seven or eight days, and at the last he came to a nunnery, and then was queen Guenever ware of Sir Launcelot as he walked in the cloister, and when she saw him there she swooned thrice, that all the ladies and gentlewomen had work enough to hold the queen up. So when she might speak, she called ladies and gentlewomen to her, and said, Ye marvel, fair ladies, why I make this fare. Truly, she said, it is for the sight of yonder knight that yonder standeth: wherefore, I pray you all, call him to me. When Sir Launcelot was brought to her, then she said to all the ladies, Through this man and me hath all this war been wrought, and the death of the most noblest knights of the world; for through our love that we have loved together is my most noble lord slain. Therefore, Sir Launcelot, wit thou well I am set in such a plight to get my soul's health; and yet I trust, through God's grace, that after my death to have a sight of the blessed face of Christ, and at doomsday to sit on his right side, for as sinful as ever I was are saints in heaven. Therefore, Sir Launcelot, I require thee and beseech thee heartily, for all the love that ever was betwixt us, that thou never see me more in the visage; and I command thee on God's behalf, that thou forsake my company, and to thy kingdom thou turn again and keep well thy realm from war and wrack. For as well as I have loved thee, mine heart will not serve me to see thee; for through thee and me is the flower of kings and knights destroyed. Therefore, Sir Launcelot, go to thy realm, and there take thee a wife, and live with her with joy and bliss, and I pray thee heartily pray for me to our Lord, that I may amend my mis-living. Now, sweet madam, said Sir Launcelot, would ye that I should return again unto my country, and there to wed a lady? Nay, madam, wit you well that shall I never do: for I shall never be so false to you of that I have promised, but the same destiny that ye have taken you to, I will take me unto, for to please Jesu, and ever for you I cast me specially to pray. If thou wilt do so, said the queen, hold thy promise; but I may never believe but that thou wilt turn to the world again. Well, madam, said he, ye say as pleaseth you, yet wist you me never false of my promise, and God defend but I should forsake the world as ye have done. For in the quest of the Sancgreal I had forsaken the vanities of the world, had not your lord been. And if I had done so at that time with my heart, will, and thought, I had passed all the knights that were in the Sancgreal, except Sir Galahad my son. And therefore, lady, sithen ye have taken you to perfection, I must needs take me to perfection of right. For I take record of God, in you I have had mine earthly joy. And if I had found you now so disposed, I had cast me to have had you into mine own realm.

Chapter 10
How Sir Launcelot came to the hermitage where the archbishop of Canterbury was, and how he took the habit on him.

But sithen I find you thus disposed, I insure you faithfully I will ever take me to penance, and pray while my life lasteth, if that I may find any hermit either grey or white that will receive me. Wherefore, madam, I pray you kiss me, and never no more. Nay, said the queen, that shall I never do, but abstain you from such works. And they departed. But there was never so hard an hearted man, but he would have wept to see the dolour that they made. For there was lamentation as they had been stung with spears, and many times they swooned. And the ladies bare the queen to her chamber, and Sir Launcelot awoke, and went and took his horse, and rode all that day and all that night in a forest, weeping. And at the last he was ware of an hermitage and a chapel stood betwixt two cliffs, and then he heard a little bell ring to mass, and thither he rode and alight, and tied his horse to the gate, and heard mass. And he that sang mass was the bishop of Canterbury. Both the bishop and Sir Bedivere knew Sir Launcelot, and they spake together after mass. But when Sir Bedivere had told his tale all whole, Sir Launcelot's heart almost brast for sorrow, and Sir Launcelot threw his arms abroad, and said, Alas, who may trust this world! And then he kneeled down on his knees, and prayed the Bishop to shrive him and assoil him. And then he besought the bishop that he might be his brother. Then the bishop said, I will gladly: and there he put an habit upon Sir Launcelot, and there he served God day and night with prayers and fastings.

Thus the great host abode at Dover. And then Sir Lionel took fifteen lords with him, and rode to London to seek Sir Launcelot. And there Sir Lionel was slain and many of his lords. Then Sir Bors de Ganis made the great host for to go home again. And Sir Bors, Sir Ector de Maris, Sir Blamor, Sir Bleoberis, with more other of Sir Launcelot's kin, look on them to ride all England overthwart and endlong, to seek

Sir Launcelot. So Sir Bors by fortune rode so long till he came to the same chapel where Sir Launcelot was. And so Sir Bors heard a little bell knell that rang to mass, and there he alight, and heard mass. And when mass was done, the bishop, Sir Launcelot, and Sir Bedivere came to Sir Bors. And when Sir Bors saw Sir Launcelot in that manner clothing, then he prayed the bishop that he might be in the same suit. And so there was an habit put upon him, and there he lived in prayers and fasting. And within half a year there was come Sir Galihud, Sir Galihodin, Sir Blamor, Sir Bleoberis, Sir Williars, Sir Clarrus, and Sir Gahalantine. So all these seven noble knights there abode still. And when they saw Sir Launcelot had taken him unto such perfection, they had no list to depart, but took such an habit as he had. Thus they endured in great penance six year, and then Sir Launcelot took the habit of priesthood, and a twelvemonth he sang mass. And there was none of these other knights but they read in books, and holp to sing mass, and rang bells, and did bodily all manner of service. And so their horses went where they would, for they took no regard of no worldly riches. For when they saw Sir Launcelot endure such penance, in prayers and fasting, they took no force what pain they endured, for to see the noblest knight of the world take such abstinence, that he waxed full lean. And thus upon a night there came a vision to Sir Launcelot, and charged him, in remission of his sins, to haste him unto Almesbury,—And by then thou come there, thou shalt find queen Guenever dead: and therefore take thy fellows with thee, and purvey them of an horse bier, and fetch thou the corpse of her, and bury her by her husband the noble king Arthur. So this vision came to Launcelot thrice in one night.

Chapter 11
How Sir Launcelot went with his seven fellows to Almesbury, and found there queen Guenever dead, whom they brought to Glastonbury.

Then Sir Launcelot rose up or day, and told the hermit. It were well done, said the hermit, that ye made you ready, and that ye disobey not the vision. Then Sir Launcelot took his seven fellows with him, and on foot they went from Glastonbury to Almesbury, the which is little more than thirty miles. And thither they came within two days, for they were weak and feeble to go. And when Sir Launcelot was come to Almesbury, within the nunnery, queen Guenever died but half an hour before. And the ladies told Sir Launcelot that queen Guenever told them all, or she passed, that Sir Launcelot had been priest near a twelvemonth,—And hither he cometh as fast as he may to fetch my corpse: and beside my lord king Arthur he shall bury me. Wherefore the queen said in hearing of them all, I beseech Almighty God that I may never have power to see Sir Launcelot with my worldly eyes. And thus, said all the ladies, was ever her prayer these two days, till she was dead. Then Sir Launcelot saw her visage, but he wept not greatly, but sighed. And so he did all the observance of the service himself, both the Dirige, and on the morn he sang mass. And there was ordained an horse bier; and so with an hundred torches ever burning about the corpse of the queen, and ever Sir Launcelot with his eight fellows went about the horse bier singing and reading many an holy orison, and frankincense upon the corpse incensed. Thus Sir Launcelot and his eight fellows went on foot from Almesbury unto Glastonbury; and when they were come to the chapel and the hermitage, there she had a Dirige with great devotion. And on the morn the hermit, that sometime was bishop of Canterbury, sang the mass of Requiem with great devotion: and Sir Launcelot was the first that offered, and then all his eight fellows. And then she was wrapped in cered cloth of Raines, from the top to the toe in thirty fold, and after she was put in a web of lead, and then in a coffin of marble. And when she was put in the earth, Sir Launcelot swooned, and lay long still, while the hermit came out and awaked him, and said, Ye be to blame, for ye displease God with such manner of sorrow making. Truly, said Sir Launcelot, I trust I do not displease God, for He knoweth mine intent, for my sorrow was not, nor is not, for any rejoicing of sin, but my sorrow may never have end. For when I remember of her beauty, and of her noblesse, that was both with her king and with her; so when I saw his corpse and her corpse so lie together, truly mine heart would not serve to sustain my careful body. Also when I remember me, how by my default, mine orgule, and my pride, that they were both laid full low, that were peerless that ever was living of Christian people, wit you well, said Sir Launcelot, this remembered, of their kindness and mine unkindness, sank so to my heart, that I might not sustain myself. So the French book maketh mention.

Chapter 12
How Sir Launcelot began to sicken, and after died, whose body was borne to Joyous Gard for to be buried.

Then Sir Launcelot never after eat but little meat, nor drank, till he was dead; for then he sickened more and more, and dried and dwined away; for the bishop nor none of his fellows might not make him to eat, and little he drank, that he was waxen by a cubit shorter than he was, that the people could not know him; for evermore day and night he prayed, but sometime he slumbered a broken sleep, and ever he was lying groveling on the tomb of king Arthur and queen Guenever. And there was no comfort that the bishop, nor Sir Bors, nor none of his fellows could make him, it availed not. So within six weeks after, Sir Launcelot fell sick, and lay in his bed; and then he sent for the bishop that there was hermit, and all his true fellows. Then Sir Launcelot said with dreary voice, Sir bishop, I pray you give to me all my rights that longeth to a Christian man. It shall not need you, said the hermit and all his fellows, it is but heaviness of your blood: ye shall be well amended by the grace of God to-morn. My fair lords, said Sir Launcelot, wit you well, my careful body will into the earth. I have warning more then now I will say, therefore give me my rights. So when he was houseled and eneled, and had all that a Christian man ought to have, he prayed the bishop that his fellows might bear his body to Joyous Gard. Some men say it was Anwick, and some men say it was Bamborow. Howbeit, said Sir Launcelot, me repenteth sore, but I made mine avow sometime that in Joyous Gard I would be buried, and because of breaking of mine avow, I pray you all lead me thither. Then there was weeping and wringing of hands among his fellows. So at a season of the night they went all to their beds, for they all lay in one chamber. And so after midnight, against day, the bishop that was hermit, as he lay in his bed asleep, he fell upon a great laughter: and therewith all the fellowship awoke, and came unto the bishop, and asked him what he ailed. Alas, said the bishop, why did ye awake me, I was never in all my life so merry and so well at ease. Wherefore? said Sir Bors. Truly, said the bishop, here was Sir Launcelot with me, with more angels than ever I saw men upon one day; and I saw the angels heave Sir Launcelot unto heaven, and the gates of heaven opened against him. It is but the vexing of dreams, said Sir Bors, for I doubt not Sir Launcelot aileth nothing but good. It may well be, said the bishop, go ye to his bed, and then shall ye prove the sooth. So when Sir Bors and his fellows came to his bed they found him stark dead, and he lay as he had smiled, and the sweetest savour about him that ever they felt. Then was there weeping and wringing of hands, and the greatest dole they made that ever made men. And on the morn the bishop did his mass of Requiem; and after the bishop and all the nine knights put Sir Launcelot in the same horse bier that queen Guenever was laid in tofore that she was buried: and so the bishop and they altogether went with the corpse of Sir Launcelot daily, till they came to Joyous Gard, and ever they had an hundred torches burning about him; and so within fifteen days they came to Joyous Gard. And there they laid his corpse in the body of the quire, and sang and read many psalters and prayers over him and about him; and ever his visage was laid open and naked, that all folk might behold him; for such was the custom in those days, that all men of worship should so lie with open visage till that they were buried. And right thus as they were at their service, there came Sir Ector de Maris, that had seven year sought all England, Scotland, and Wales, seeking his brother Sir Launcelot.

Chapter 13
How Sir Ector found Sir Launcelot his brother dead. And how Constantine reigned next after Arthur, and of the end of this book.

And when Sir Ector heard such noise and light in the quire of Joyous Gard, he alight and put his horse from him, and came into the quire, and there he saw men sing and weep. And all they knew Sir Ector, but he knew not them. Then went Sir Bors unto Sir Ector, and told him how there lay his brother Sir Launcelot dead. And then Sir Ector threw his shield, sword, and helm from him; and when he beheld Sir Launcelot's visage he fell down in a swoon. And when he awaked it were hard any tongue to tell the doleful complaints that he made for his brother. Ah, Launcelot, he said, thou were head of all Christian knights; and now I dare say, said Sir Ector, thou Sir Launcelot, there thou liest, that thou were never matched of earthly knight's hand; and thou were the courtiest knight that ever bare shield; and thou were the truest friend to thy lover that ever bestrode horse; and thou were the truest lover of a sinful man that ever loved woman; and thou were the kindest man that ever strake with sword; and thou were the goodliest person ever came among press of knights; and thou was the meekest man and the gentlest that ever ate in hall among ladies; and thou were the sternest knight to thy mortal foe that ever put spear in the rest.

Then there was weeping and dolour out of measure. Thus they kept Sir Launcelot's corpse on loft fifteen days, and then they buried it with great devotion. And then at leisure they went all with the bishop of Canterbury to his hermitage, and there they were together more than a month. Then Sir Constantine, that was Sir Cador's son, of Cornwall, was chosen king of England; and he was a full noble knight, and worshipfully he ruled this realm. And then this king Constantine sent for the bishop of Canterbury, for he heard say where he was; and so he was restored unto his bishopric, and left that hermitage; and Sir Bedivere was there ever still hermit to his life's end. Then Sir Bors de Ganis, Sir Ector de Maris, Sir Gahalantine, Sir Galihud, Sir Galihodin, Sir Blamor, Sir Bleoberis, Sir Williars le Valiant, Sir

Clarrus of Cleremont; all these knights drew them to their countries. Howbeit king Constantine would have had them with him, but they would not abide in this realm; and there they lived in their countries as holy men. And some English books make mention that they went never out of England after the death of Sir Launcelot, but that was but favour of makers. For the French book maketh mention, and is authorised, that Sir Bors, Sir Ector, Sir Blamor, and Sir Bleoberis, went into the holy land, there as Jesu Christ was quick and dead, and anon as they had stablished their lands; for the book saith so Sir Launcelot commanded them for to do, or ever he passed out of this world. And these four knights did many battles upon the miscreants or Turks. And there they died upon a Good Friday, for God's sake.

Here is the end of the whole book of king Arthur, and of his noble knights of the Round Table, that when they were whole together there was ever an hundred and forty. And here is the end of the Death of Arthur. I pray you all gentlemen and gentlewomen that read this book of Arthur and his knights from the beginning to the ending, pray for me while I am on live that God send me good deliverance, and when I am dead, I pray you all pray for my soul; for this book was ended the ninth year of the reign of king Edward the Fourth by Sir Thomas Maleore, knight, as Jesu help him for his great might, as he is the servant of Jesu both day and night.

(No reading for Lesson 90.) Congratulations! You're halfway through Literature and Composition II! Your reading lessons will continue in the Literature & Composition II Reader: Lessons 91-180.

Made in the USA
Columbia, SC
28 August 2023

22207030R00357